# Evidence Discovery and Assessment in Social Work Practice

Margaret Pack
*Australian Catholic University, Australia*

Justin Cargill
*Victoria University of Wellington, New Zealand*

A volume in the Advances in Human Services and
Public Health (AHSPH) Book Series

**Information Science**
**REFERENCE**
An Imprint of IGI Global

| Managing Director: | Lindsay Johnston |
| Acquisitions Editor: | Kayla Wolfe |
| Production Editor: | Christina Henning |
| Development Editor: | Allison McGinniss |
| Typesetter: | Lisandro Gonzalez |
| Cover Design: | Jason Mull |

Published in the United States of America by
Information Science Reference (an imprint of IGI Global)
701 E. Chocolate Avenue
Hershey PA, USA 17033
Tel: 717-533-8845
Fax: 717-533-8661
E-mail: cust@igi-global.com
Web site: http://www.igi-global.com

Library of Congress Cataloging-in-Publication Data

Evidence discovery and assessment in social work practice / Margaret Pack and Justin Cargill, editors.
    pages cm
 Includes bibliographical references and index.
 ISBN 978-1-4666-6563-7 (hardcover) -- ISBN 978-1-4666-6564-4 (ebook) -- ISBN 978-1-4666-6566-8 (print & perpetual access) 1. Social service--Practice. 2. Social case work. 3. Evidence-based social work. I. Pack, Margaret, 1961- II. Cargill, Justin, date-
 HV10.5.E95 2015
 361.3'2--dc23
                                            2014032310

This book is published in the IGI Global book series Advances in Human Services and Public Health (AHSPH) (ISSN: pending; eISSN: pending)

British Cataloguing in Publication Data
A Cataloguing in Publication record for this book is available from the British Library.

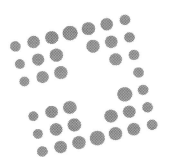

# Advances in Human Services and Public Health (AHSPH) Book Series

ISSN: pending
EISSN: pending

## MISSION

The well-being of the general public should be a primary concern for any modern civilization. Ongoing research in the field of human services and public healthcare is necessary to evaluate, manage, and respond to the health and social needs of the global population.

The **Advances in Human Services and Public Health (AHSPH)** book series aims to publish high-quality reference publications focused on the latest methodologies, tools, issues, and strategies for managing the health and social welfare of the public. The AHSPH book series will be especially relevant for healthcare professionals, policy makers, government officials, and students seeking the latest research in this field.

## COVERAGE

- Access to Healthcare Services
- Poverty
- Health Policy
- Medicare and Medicaid
- Public Welfare
- Assistance Programs
- Social Welfare Policy
- Youth Development
- Domestic Violence
- Social Work

IGI Global is currently accepting manuscripts for publication within this series. To submit a proposal for a volume in this series, please contact our Acquisition Editors at Acquisitions@igi-global.com or visit: http://www.igi-global.com/publish/.

# Titles in this Series

*For a list of additional titles in this series, please visit: www.igi-global.com*

*Handbook of Research on Adult and Community Health Education Tools, Trends, and Methodologies*
Victor C. X. Wang (Florida Atlantic University, USA)
Medical Information Science Reference • copyright 2014 • 485pp • H/C (ISBN: 9781466662605) • US $325.00 (our price)

www.igi-global.com

701 E. Chocolate Ave., Hershey, PA 17033
Order online at www.igi-global.com or call 717-533-8845 x100
To place a standing order for titles released in this series, contact: cust@igi-global.com
Mon-Fri 8:00 am - 5:00 pm (est) or fax 24 hours a day 717-533-8661

*To social workers everywhere.*

# Quotes and Testimonials

*This innovative volume promises to advance discerning debates along with the strategic infusion of evidence-based practices into social work....Cutting edge chapters on practice with diverse populations along with a unique section on self-care for social workers makes this book a most valuable 21st century resource.*

*Professor Katharine Briar-Lawson, MSW, PhD*
*Dean, School of Social Welfare, State University of New York, USA*

*This book brings together an erudite panoply of excellent chapters from academia and practice.*

*Professor Jonathan Parker, PhD, AcSS, FRSA, FHEA*
*Director, Centre for Social Work, Sociology and Social Policy, Bournemouth University, UK*

*This is an ambitious and wide-ranging book which revisits the perennial question for social work practice of what counts as evidence and how do we assess its value and meaning.*

*Professor Roger Smith, MA, MPhil, PhD*
*School of Applied Social Sciences, Durham University, UK*

*A most welcome addition to the growing literature on the applications of the model of evidence-based practice to social work. A particular strength are the chapters describing how practitioners can track down the best available evidence dealing with important practice decisions, such as becoming informed as to the evidentiary status of particular psychosocial interventions. This book was a pleasure to read and contains chapters by a really excellent set of contributing authors....It is heartening to see such a well-crafted work....This is a mature and sophisticated treatment of how the evidence-based practice model for clinical decision-making can inform social work assessment and treatment.*

*Professor Bruce A. Thyer, Ph.D., LCSW, BCBA-D*
*College of Social Work, Florida State University, USA*

*This book is a ground-breaking overview of the nature of evidence-based interventions and their application to social work practice. The editors have done an outstanding job in enlisting the expertise of top academics and practitioners from disparate fields. The book has a number of excellent general chapters on evidence-based practice, and also describes specific applications of this approach to different client groups.*

*Professor Tony Ward, MA(Hons), PhD, DipClinPsyc*
*School of Psychology, Victoria University of Wellington, New Zealand*

*This excellent contribution, edited by Margaret Pack and Justin Cargill, to social work research and practice brings together leading scholars in the field to evaluate the debates and contributions of evidence related approaches. The book is cutting edge in its range and depth of applications and will make a much needed and valuable contribution to social work.*

*Professor Stephen A. Webb, PhD*
*Department of Health and Community Sciences, Glasgow Caledonian University, Scotland, UK*

# Table of Contents

**Quotes and Testimonials** ................................................................................................. vi

**Foreword** ............................................................................................................................. xix

**Preface** ............................................................................................................................... xxii

**Acknowledgment** ............................................................................................................... xxx

## Section 1
## Framing the Search for Evidence

**Chapter 1**
Why Search for Evidence for Practice in Social Work? ........................................................1
*Justin Cargill, Victoria University of Wellington, New Zealand*

**Chapter 2**
Finding the Evidence for Practice in Social Work ...............................................................36
*Justin Cargill, Victoria University of Wellington, New Zealand*

**Chapter 3**
Applying Evidence in Practice: Isn't that Straight-Forward? ..............................................65
*Ian Dore, University of Brighton, UK*

**Chapter 4**
Navigating Practice-Informed Evidence and Evidence-Based Practice: Balancing Multiple
Discourses and Competing Claims to Knowledge ...............................................................82
*Margaret Pack, Australian Catholic University, Australia*

## Section 2
## Social Work Fields of Practice

**Chapter 5**
Refugee Women: Resilient and Reluctant Users of Social Work Services...........................97
*Mary Nash, Massey University, New Zealand*
*Antoinette Umugwaneza, New Zealand Red Cross Refugee Services – Palmerston North, New
    Zealand*

**Chapter 6**
More than Pills and Beds: Contemporary Challenges in Social Work Practice and Mental
Healthcare .................................................................................................................................113
    *Sebastian Rosenberg, University of Sydney, Australia*
    *Fiona McDermott, Monash University, Australia*

**Chapter 7**
Child Protection, "Dirty Work," and Interagency Collaboration .................................................130
    *Annette Flaherty, Centre for Remote Health, Flinders University, Australia*

**Chapter 8**
Social Work and Youth Justice in a Global Context: Practising in Shifting and Conflicting
Paradigms ..................................................................................................................................149
    *Bill Whyte, University of Edinburgh, UK*

**Chapter 9**
Social Work Practice Outcomes: Making a Measurable Difference ............................................166
    *Colin Pritchard, Bournemouth University, UK*
    *Richard Williams, Bournemouth University, UK*

**Chapter 10**
Picking up the Pieces: Working with Adult Women Sexual Abuse Survivors ...............................186
    *Margaret Pack, Australian Catholic University, Australia*

**Chapter 11**
A Social Work Approach in High-Tech Neurosurgery and Social Work Research Approaches in
Health Care ...............................................................................................................................212
    *Colin Pritchard, Bournemouth University, UK*

**Chapter 12**
Recruiting and Engaging Men as Fathers in Social Work Practice .............................................235
    *Joseph Fleming, Deakin University, Australia*
    *Andrew King, Groupwork Solutions, Australia*
    *Tara Hunt, Groupwork Solutions, Australia*

**Chapter 13**
Art Therapy: A Social Work Perspective ....................................................................................261
    *Shiri Hergass, Clinical Social Worker, Australia*

**Section 3**
**Self-Care for Social Workers**

**Chapter 14**
Towards an Evidence-Informed Approach to Clinical Social Work Supervision..............................289
    *Kieran O'Donoghue, Massey University, New Zealand*

**Chapter 15**
Best Practice in Responding to Critical Incidents and Potentially Traumatic Experience within an
Organisational Setting..................................................................................................................302
    *Carole Adamson, University of Auckland, New Zealand*

**Chapter 16**
Post-Qualifying Practice: Implications for Social Workers with a Spiritual Approach to Practice....324
    *Mary Nash, Massey University, New Zealand*

**Chapter 17**
Conclusion: Beyond Binary Oppositions in Evidence-Based Practice in Social Work......................339
    *Margaret Pack, Australian Catholic University, Australia*


**Compilation of References** ............................................................................................................351

**About the Contributors** ..................................................................................................................396

**Index** ..............................................................................................................................................400

# Detailed Table of Contents

**Quotes and Testimonials** ................................................................................................................ vi

**Foreword** ................................................................................................................................... xix

**Preface** ..................................................................................................................................... xxii

**Acknowledgment** ...................................................................................................................... xxx

### Section 1
### Framing the Search for Evidence

*How social workers search for and apply evidence to and for practice.*

**Chapter 1**

Why Search for Evidence for Practice in Social Work? ........................................................................1
*Justin Cargill, Victoria University of Wellington, New Zealand*

How is evidence integrated into the practice relationship between social worker and client? Studies suggest that at the practice level research is not consistently utilised. Evidence-Based Practice (EBP) has been hailed as a means of bringing practice and research together in a way that strengthens the empirical base of social work. Although EBP has had strong endorsement, it has also come under heavy criticism. This chapter explores these concerns in the hope of further clarifying the model. The need for an inclusive definition of evidence is emphasised giving rightful place to empirical research and also to other forms of evidence. The need for a synthesis of evidence-based practice and critical reflection is also explored. Evidence must be used in a critically reflective way if it is to be used effectively. Finally, the language of "evidence-informed" is shown to more clearly articulate the components of the EBP process.

**Chapter 2**
Finding the Evidence for Practice in Social Work ...............................................................................36
    *Justin Cargill, Victoria University of Wellington, New Zealand*

The revolution in information technologies, in particular the growth of the Internet and greater access to computers, has given social workers unprecedented access to information resources. Researching such resources is crucial and it needs to be done efficiently. Planning an efficient search requires knowing which databases and other resources to use, knowing how to formulate an answerable question, identifying terms that inform the question, selecting the appropriate methodological filters, and being able to critically appraise evidence for its quality and relevance. This chapter, therefore, outlines some of the research sources available to social workers, it looks at some principles for finding information for practice in social work, and it outlines some criteria for evaluating the quality of that information.

**Chapter 3**
Applying Evidence in Practice: Isn't that Straight-Forward? ...............................................................65
    *Ian Dore, University of Brighton, UK*

Judgement and decision-making lie at the heart of practice and are feats that practitioners perform under conditions that are complex and uncertain, the attainment of positive outcomes for service-users dependent upon the aptitude of those charged with the task and the scaffolding provided by their employing organisations. Faced with such a challenge, social workers somehow avoid paralysis and take action to support and protect those with whom they work, drawing on experience, skill, information, and intervention evidence. The way they negotiate, orientate, interpret, and apply this knowledge is often through unconscious thought processes that require illumination and balance. This chapter considers how practitioners make sense of the situations that they come into contact with and discusses the intuitive-analytical reasoning continuum integral to this. Attention is given to the role of value as an influence upon perception and subsequent interpretation, together with the role played by cognitive processes.

**Chapter 4**
Navigating Practice-Informed Evidence and Evidence-Based Practice: Balancing Multiple
Discourses and Competing Claims to Knowledge ...............................................................................82
    *Margaret Pack, Australian Catholic University, Australia*

This chapter explores social workers' application of practice evidence in their everyday work in team and agency contexts. Practice evidence concerns the practitioner seeking the best available knowledge, accessed, adapted, and applied to guide practice with clients. How social workers decide which sources to draw from and which are appropriate sources of evidence for practice is based on many considerations. These include the social worker's values and ethics for practice, legislative and policy requirements, professional standards of practice, and the range of theories applied to any case or situation encountered in practice. Practice wisdom, or the experience gained in the repetition of seeing the same kind of client presentations across time, produces a further source which is drawn upon within the social worker's repertoire of knowledge. In this sense, there are multiple knowledge frameworks within which social workers operate, balancing contradictory and competing discourses about "what works" in any practice situation.

## Section 2
## Social Work Fields of Practice

*Evidence-informed practice is explored in relation to differing fields and contexts of social work practice. These fields of practice include refugee resettlement, mental health, youth justice, neurosurgery, social workers in schools, sexual abuse recovery, fathering, and art therapy.*

### Chapter 5

Refugee Women: Resilient and Reluctant Users of Social Work Services...........................................97
    *Mary Nash, Massey University, New Zealand*
    *Antoinette Umugwaneza, New Zealand Red Cross Refugee Services – Palmerston North, New Zealand*

This chapter approaches the topic of resettlement social work with women refugees portrayed as resilient yet reluctant users of social work services. While the field of social work with refugees has already been widely introduced and discussed, less attention has been paid to resettlement work with women refugees. In order to contextualise this discussion, key terms are briefly defined, and relevant legislation together with demographic features are covered. The chapter includes a case study presented by one of the authors, an expert by experience. Research relating to this field of practice is presented and ethical issues discussed. Practical applications and cultural concerns derived from the research suggest how practitioners and refugee women may work together, drawing on the strengths and experience of the refugee women to achieve goals that are consistent with those set out by the United Nations High Commissioner for Refugees (UNHCR).

### Chapter 6

More than Pills and Beds: Contemporary Challenges in Social Work Practice and Mental
Healthcare .................................................................................................................................113
    *Sebastian Rosenberg, University of Sydney, Australia*
    *Fiona McDermott, Monash University, Australia*

Contemporary models of mental healthcare emphasise the importance of multi-disciplinary approaches in supporting recovery for consumers. There is growing evidence of the key role to be played by social workers derived from both the principles of recovery and those underpinning social work theory and practice, particularly a focus on person-in-environment. However, pressures on the way mental healthcare is provided in Australia are threatening this confluence. These pressures are much more concerned with the needs of funders than professionals, consumers, and their families. The aim of this chapter is to explore the evidence to support social work as an integral element in mental health recovery and to better understand these emerging challenges. The role of social work in good mental healthcare is too important to become marginalized; yet this prospect is real. Better understanding of the contemporary landscape of social work can help ensure this does not occur.

**Chapter 7**
Child Protection, "Dirty Work," and Interagency Collaboration ........................................................130
    *Annette Flaherty, Centre for Remote Health, Flinders University, Australia*

Working in partnership is considered a key mechanism for effective delivery of services to children and families. However, child protection system inquiries in Australia and internationally repeatedly highlight strained relationships and poor collaboration within the child protection service system. Despite organisational, technological, legislative, and procedural changes to enhance and facilitate interagency working, these interventions have generally failed to realise this goal. Trust and shared values are considered integral to effective interagency working. Developing trust and thus effective working relationships is fraught when one group of workers in the service system is perceived to be "dirty workers." This chapter explores the concept of "dirty work." It suggests that the way in which failure to attend to belief systems at the organisational, professional, and community level, particularly as they relate to the professional stigma which attaches to the practice of child protection work, inhibits the ability of agencies to work successfully together.

**Chapter 8**
Social Work and Youth Justice in a Global Context: Practising in Shifting and Conflicting Paradigms ......................................................................................................................................149
    *Bill Whyte, University of Edinburgh, UK*

Social work in youth justice is directed by international standards based on an implied socio-educative paradigm that conflicts with the dominant criminal justice paradigm in operation in most jurisdictions. This creates global challenges in establishing "child-centred" policy and practice for dealing with young people under the age of 18 years in conflict with the law. Social work practitioners, directed by international imperatives and professional ethics, operate between shifting and often conflicting paradigms. It is essential they are familiar with international obligations and operate as "culture carriers" providing an ongoing challenge to systems of youth justice. This chapter examines these issues and, in the absence of consensus or of a shared paradigm for social work practice across jurisdictions, considers what a socio-educative paradigm for practice might look like.

**Chapter 9**
Social Work Practice Outcomes: Making a Measurable Difference ................................................166
    *Colin Pritchard, Bournemouth University, UK*
    *Richard Williams, Bournemouth University, UK*

The key issue in all human services is outcome. The authors report on a series of four mixed methods research studies to conclude that good social work can bring about positive measurable differences to inform policy and practice. The first focuses on how effective Western nations have been in reducing Child Abuse Related Deaths (CARD); the second explores a three-year controlled study of a school-based social work service to reduce truancy, delinquency, and school exclusion; the third examines outcomes of "Looked After Children" (LAC); the forth re-evaluates a decade of child homicide assailants to provide evidence of the importance of the child protection-psychiatric interface in benefiting mentally ill parents and improving the psychosocial development and protection of their children. These studies show that social work has a measurable beneficial impact upon the lives of those who had been served and that social work can be cost-effective, that is, self-funding, over time.

**Chapter 10**

Picking up the Pieces: Working with Adult Women Sexual Abuse Survivors ...................................186
*Margaret Pack, Australian Catholic University, Australia*

This chapter reports the findings from a review of contemporary assessment and treatment approaches with adult women who have experienced Child Sexual Abuse (CSA). The social worker who engages with women recovering from CSA in adulthood needs to address issues of trust, relationship, and safety. Services that provide culturally sensitive and appropriate models of intervention are likely to impact positively on client rapport and engagement with the social worker and, therefore, greater therapeutic gains are possible when a relationship of trust is established. The implications for social work practice are discussed in relation to a multi-systems and multi-theoretical approach involving the client and her social networks from within strengths-based and ecological systems perspectives. Future research is recommended on the impact of the availability of culturally appropriate services for CSA survivors and cultural safety supervision for social workers, as these variables influence the therapeutic outcomes for women survivors of CSA.

**Chapter 11**

A Social Work Approach in High-Tech Neurosurgery and Social Work Research Approaches in Health Care ...........................................................................................................................................212
*Colin Pritchard, Bournemouth University, UK*

Psychiatric social work is inherently inter-disciplinary with an interactive bio-psycho-social model of behaviour. This chapter mainly focuses upon an innovative study in neurosurgery. Sub-arachnoid haemorrhage (SAH) is a life-threatening condition and survivors are often left with serious cognitive impairment. Patients and their carers led the design of a two-year controlled prospective study of a patient and family support service, using the Specialist Neurovascular Nurse (SNVN) to speed rehabilitation and family readjustment. Cost-effective measures found the SNVN group gained significant psychosocial and fiscal benefits when compared to the control group, thus highlighting the effectiveness of a social work approach in neurosurgery. Other studies in healthcare, including surgical patient safety, effectiveness in reducing mortality, cultural influence on suicide rates and implications for prevention, and the implications of the changing patterns of neurological mortality in Western nations, are briefly described.

**Chapter 12**

Recruiting and Engaging Men as Fathers in Social Work Practice ....................................................235
*Joseph Fleming, Deakin University, Australia*
*Andrew King, Groupwork Solutions, Australia*
*Tara Hunt, Groupwork Solutions, Australia*

Evidence in the research literature suggests that men are usually not engaged by social workers, particularly in child welfare and child protection settings. Mothers also tend to become the focus of intervention, even when there is growing evidence that men can take an active and important role in a child's development in addition to providing support to the mother and family. Whilst there have been some promising developments in including men in social work practice internationally, there remains a gap in the research regarding the engagement of men as fathers in Australia. Given the growing relevance of the topic of fathers, the purpose of this chapter is to add to the current knowledge base, to support social work students and practitioners to engage with men in their role as fathers, and to offer an evidence-based practice model that may assist social workers in their work with men as fathers.

## Chapter 13
Art Therapy: A Social Work Perspective.............................................................................................261
*Shiri Hergass, Clinical Social Worker, Australia*

Art therapy is universally practiced and has proven to be a successful intervention for trauma. This chapter focuses on how art therapy can be used to heal transgenerational trauma in Aboriginal Australians with a particular focus on children. The effects of trauma in general and transgenerational trauma more specifically on one's brain, physiology, and physical, emotional, and behavioural health are discussed. Promising practices of why art therapy works are outlined, challenges and cultural considerations for working with Aboriginal populations are identified, and solutions and future research are recommended.

## Section 3
## Self-Care for Social Workers

*Areas promoting the self-care of social workers are discussed, including responses to critical incident stress management, the use of clinical supervision, and the importance of spirituality in practice.*

## Chapter 14
Towards an Evidence-Informed Approach to Clinical Social Work Supervision..............................289
*Kieran O'Donoghue, Massey University, New Zealand*

This chapter discusses how research evidence may be used to inform clinical social work supervision and explores how an evidence-informed approach may be applied in practice in a scenario. The chapter concludes by encouraging supervisors to be mindful about the evidence that informs their supervisory practice and to ask their supervisees about the evidence that relates to the issues they are presenting in supervision.

## Chapter 15
Best Practice in Responding to Critical Incidents and Potentially Traumatic Experience within an Organisational Setting...........................................................................................................................302
*Carole Adamson, University of Auckland, New Zealand*

This chapter addresses best practice for organisational support after critical incidents and traumatic events within social work. Critical incidents are situations and incidents within workplace settings or roles, which, whilst able to be anticipated and planned for, have the potential to create a sense of emergency, crisis, and extreme stress, or have a traumatic impact on those directly or indirectly affected. Alongside the notion of critical incidents are concepts of debriefing, psychological debriefing, critical incident stress debriefing (CISD), and critical incident stress management (CISM). Debate about debriefing models has concerned their effectiveness and safety; the terms being loaded with meaning and tensions between scientific and holistic paradigms and between academic and practitioner perspectives. The chapter suggests areas of research and exploration for agency managers and senior practitioners wishing to make sense of the debates and enables the reader to consider best practice for critical incident response within organisational settings.

## Chapter 16

Post-Qualifying Practice: Implications for Social Workers with a Spiritual Approach to Practice....324
    *Mary Nash, Massey University, New Zealand*

A spiritual approach to social work practice is gaining recognition. This chapter considers the implications for practitioners who draw on spirituality in their work and the requirements for post-qualifying practice or Continuous Professional Development (CPD). Key terms are defined drawing on research and publications relating to CPD, and spiritual worldviews and their influence on social work are discussed. A case study illustrates how practitioners may choose to reflect on their own spiritual worldview in order to be better equipped when working with clients for whom the spiritual or religious dimension is important. It is suggested that this helps the practitioner to establish good working relationships across cultures and beliefs, and it consequently increases the chances of successful interventions. A second case study provides an example of how the social work practitioner, through involvement in a creative project, drew on spirituality in order to promote her own self-care.

## Chapter 17

Conclusion: Beyond Binary Oppositions in Evidence-Based Practice in Social Work......................339
    *Margaret Pack, Australian Catholic University, Australia*

This chapter gathers together and synthesises the concepts used and developed throughout this book. These themes include the challenges posed for social work as a profession in relation to notions of rationality and scientific research methods when considering what constitutes "evidence" for social work practice. This critique challenges the definition and application of evidence to complex scenarios where there are no easy answers, yet the agency and systems seem to demand them from social workers. In response to these challenges, social work has developed expertise in the use of case study and action research methods, drawing from interpretive and participative epistemologies. Such research studies aim to give resonance to voices hitherto missed, marginalised, or ignored. To redress this marginalisation and to provide much needed balance in what constitutes "evidence," narratives of service-users and their caregivers have become primary sources of evidence, which are used to guide social work practice.

**Compilation of References** ............................................................................................. 351

**About the Contributors** ................................................................................................ 396

**Index** ......................................................................................................................... 400

# Foreword

## ASSESSMENT AND EVIDENCE IN SOCIAL WORK

This book aims to guide practitioners in the complex endeavour to use assessment and evidence effectively in their practice. It achieves this by demonstrating how to explore evidence critically. Its authors directly examine evidence and its contribution to assessment in specific areas of social work practice. By doing this, they show how connecting research with practice requires social workers to infuse assessment and evidence into all of their practice. Assessment and evidence as a beginning or base are false friends, but as this book illustrates, assessment and evidence integrated with skill into every social work process are a rich resource.

Although assessment and evidence may promise a practice based in certainty and clarity, enabling social work to harvest benefits for its clients and agencies, it has been hard to realise these advantages in practice. This book explores assessment and using evidence in social work practice, both in general and in a number of specialised areas, and social workers might read it to find useful techniques and knowledge that will achieve successful outcomes. But any expectation of certainty in practice is illusory. There is a difference between knowing about something and knowing how to do something about it; the problem is connecting knowing about and knowing how in practice. The message of the book is that validated assessment methods and evidence always require a professional practitioner to make complex judgements in the process of finding knowledge and understanding and to use skill in taking action in multifaceted social situations and multi-professional services to achieve worthwhile outcomes. Using judgement and skill in social work involves professional education and personal development to hone their practice talents. But it is through detailed application of experience and repeated practice that talent for practice becomes an ability to intervene beneficially in social situations.

Just thinking about the general meaning of assessment and evidence, it is easy to see both why they should be important in a profession and also why they present a practitioner with complex difficulties. Assessment is the act of evaluating someone or something; evaluation implies giving a value to or making a judgement about them. Assessments are then taken forward as the basis for designing social work and service interventions. Evidence is information that has been demonstrated to be true. A profession professes; that is, it makes a claim that it has exceptional capacity to understand knowledge within its area of expertise; that understanding is then taken on to join with the assessment as part of the process of designing the intervention.

A professional practitioner in social work, therefore, claims expertise in understanding the social and an ability to intervene to produce benefits. If they are to understand the social, they will have to assess the circumstances that they deal with using information that is true and then act to generate beneficial outcomes.

It is easy enough to say this, but in looking behind the obvious importance of assessment and using evidence, some uncertainties emerge. Whose values and judgements are social workers applying when in making an assessment they evaluate or judge? Do they consider only the values that come from their professional expertise or do they apply values drawn from the society and culture in which they do the assessment? Perhaps they apply values that come from the client, or the client's family, or community, or the social agency that the practitioner works in, or the policy requirements of the funder of that agency. All of these will have some relevance, so the practitioner will be balancing the values applied but in that case, how? Or does one set of values have priority; in which case, which set and why?

Knowledge from some of these sources may be only partially expressed or unspoken, and it may be in conflict with other understandings; for example, individual service-users, their carers, their families, and their communities may all have different understandings of what is needed in a particular aspect of professional social work that affects them. Different sources of knowledge may conflict; for example, an organisation's aims and policies may not reflect all the opportunities available from the policy community or the guidance available to practitioners from systematic research.

Somehow, these different sources of knowledge must be brought together, and assessment is one of the most important sites of the reconciliation of social work's complex sources of knowledge. Assessment has a long history in social work, although it has been known by other words, for example: study, diagnosis, problem specification, critical appraisal (Payne, 2009b, p. 172). There have been social work agencies with assessment as their primary role, such as assessment centres for children being admitted to residential care. More recently, a number of models of social care assessment have been proposed, such as individual programme planning for people with learning disabilities, financial assessment, or person-centred planning for older people and people with long-term disabilities (Payne, 2009a). Almost every theoretical system prescribing social work practice establishes an assessment process at the outset and then requires constant or recurring re-assessment throughout the interaction between clients and practitioners.

I have argued that social work research and scholarship increasingly question the role and methods of absorbing assessment and evidence in social work practice. Social workers, then, should not expect assessment and evidence to give them all the answers in a simple way. Nevertheless, careful, grounded assessment and assiduously analysed evidence questioned with critical acuity will enable them to apply their experience and skill in exploring the lives and social environments that they are working in, and this, in turn, will enable them to ask the right questions. In doing so, they can help their clients and the people around them and their colleagues in other agencies to explore and understand the issues that they are working on together and to make a better job of their shared practice. Assessment and evidence, combined with critical thought and thorough practice, as demonstrated by this book's authors, gives professional practitioners the opportunity to fulfil the potential of their knowledge base.

*Malcolm Payne*
*Manchester Metropolitan University, UK*

**Malcolm Payne** *was Professor and Head of Applied Community Studies at Manchester Metropolitan University from 1987 to 2002 where he is now emeritus professor. From 2008 to 2012, he was Director of Psychosocial and Spiritual Care and Policy and Development Adviser, St Christopher's Hospice, London. He was also Visiting Professor at Opole University, Poland, from 2008-2012 and at the Comenius University, Bratislava, Slovak Republic from 2011-2013. He is currently an Honorary Professor in the School of Social Care Sciences, Kingston University/St George's University of London, England, and he has an honorary appointment at the Department of Social Policy, Helsinki University. His current research interests include end-of-life care.*

## REFERENCES

Payne, M. (2009a). *Social care practice in context*. Basingstoke, UK: Palgrave Macmillan.

Payne, M. (2009b). Understanding social work process. In R. Adams, L. Dominelli, & M. Payne (Eds.), *Social work: Themes, issues and critical debates* (3rd ed., pp. 159–174). Basingstoke, UK: Palgrave Macmillan.

# Preface

## BACKGROUND

This book is written for the beginning and experienced social worker alike in the hope that they will find new ideas and approaches relevant to their practice. The term "advanced practice" is used to refer to social workers who attend to the systems that surround their own practice, including the team and organisational setting. The term is used to acknowledge the way in which social workers develop across the life span with matured insights influencing their practice over time. The literature notes a tendency for beginning social workers to focus predominantly on the interpersonal dynamics in the therapeutic relationship with service-users and their families that is enriched by a socio-political critique later in their career (Pack, 2010b).

The approaches to evidence-based practice in social work have been undergoing widespread debate and controversy in recent years with critiques in the professional journals of social work evident from the 1990s and continuing today. The evidence-based models derived from medicine, which were developed from the early 1990s onwards, have been criticised by some social work theorists for their acceptance of a "top down," expert-knows-best approach. Whether this characterisation of evidence-based practice, at least as it was originally understood, is correctly construed, certainly any top-down model is inappropriate to social work's central ethos, ethics, and key tasks, which emphasise a collaborative supportive relationship with clients and an underlying social justice and human rights focus. Attending to the individual, family systems, and wider social communities of which the client is a core requirement of what social workers do. This systemic approach, deriving from the person-in-environment perspective, involves an imperative for a continuing political as well as social critique of the structures that surround the individual client and the social work profession itself. The evidence-based debate forms a wider part of this ongoing critique of the power inherent in social work roles. This critique suggests that as social workers we need to critically reflect with our colleagues, peers, and clinical supervisors about how we exercise power and authority as social workers within our professional roles and agencies in relation to service-users and their families. Therefore, to work in collaboration with service-users and their families and the social structures that surround them, social work theorists, such as Gambrill (2006, 2008, 2010, 2011, 2013) and Thyer (2004, 2008) have developed models that contextualise the use of evidence-based research to social work to effectively adapt, and in some cases refocus, more traditionally medically based models of evidence-based practice.

The book's title, *Evidence Discovery and Assessment*, may lead the reader to conclude that searching for practice evidence and assessing the relevance and quality of the research found are two discrete and distinct processes and activities when in reality they are interrelated. Ethical social work practitioners aim for assessment to be a collaborative endeavour in which the approaches and goals of contact are formulated in relationship with clients and their teams. Assessment also has a therapeutic value and in critical reflective paradigms is conceptualised as ongoing, with the service-user, caregiver, or family evaluating with the social worker whether, and to what extent, the chosen approach is working to meet the service-user's defined goals. In addition to this, assessment protocols in an agency context are seen as needing to be consistent with the organisational policy and the professional ethics and values held by the social worker. In this sense, assessment is a dynamic and reflexive process in which the social worker and client and supervisor form a triad, their work together involving reflection, action, and evaluation in a continuous cycle. Assessment encompasses the social worker's theoretical framework for practice, so all these elements together guide the nature of the practice modality and intervention to adapt to the unfolding needs of the client whether the "client" is an individual, group, or whole community.

## THE STORY OF HOW THE BOOK CAME TO BE

The initial idea for this book came from an earlier collaboration I had with the allied health staff of the Joanna Briggs Institute (JBI). In 2007, Professor Karen Grimmer-Somers, a physiotherapy academic, was compiling a reader on searching for and applying evidence-based literature in the allied health professions. Professor Grimmer-Somers asked if I would like to contribute to a book she was editing, involving a range of contributors with differing professional training and backgrounds, including phys-iotherapy, speech therapy, and occupational therapy. Titled *Practical Tips to Finding the Evidence: An Allied Health Reader* (Grimmer-Somers, 2009), this edited reader was aimed at assisting new allied health practitioners and those more experienced to develop their research skills for practice. The intention was to equip allied health professionals to find research literature that could be applied continuously to improve practice in such fields as speech pathology, occupational therapy, and physiotherapy. The emphasis of practice in these allied health professions, derived from models prevalent in medicine, involves evidence-based searching techniques grounded in the ranking of research studies methodologically, with randomised controlled trials being seen as the "gold standard." The reviewed research studies located through electronic database searches are then seen as constituting a body of evidence to be applied to a specific case. The aim of the book was, therefore, to teach busy allied health professionals how to find evidence, assess its quality, and then apply the findings in terms of relevance to solving a specific case issue or dilemma. The quality of research studies was considered in relation to sample size and whether the study could be replicated with the same results, so was very much tied to rigour in methodology.

In the context of *Practical Tips to Finding the Evidence*, I was invited to compose a chapter about the key tasks for social work in mental health issues from my practice experience (Pack, 2009) and advised that the technical team at JBI would then run an electronic database search and from this search find evidence to guide practice in relation to a complex case study. The direction from the editor was to formulate a number of practice questions that could be answered by the evidence-based research literature on the topic. As many complex cases have no concrete answers but are usefully informed by the research literature, I remained very curious about what the search would reveal regarding my case study.

In assessing the evidence for *Practical Tips to Finding the Evidence*, I found the technical team supporting the writing of our chapters at JBI approached their search in a very different way from the one I would have adopted. The technical team at JBI preferred to focus the searches for the book on large-scale quantitative research and systematic reviews, in a ranked hierarchy of evidence in relation to the efficacy of interventions for particular diagnoses. I realised this to be the prevailing scientific method for assessing quality of evidence, determining which studies were worthy of inclusion. I also understood this to be the model preferred when assessing the efficacy of medical interventions and approaches, but I wondered how social work as a profession might run this search, assess quality, and use the "evidence" to guide practice.

A question I pondered was whether the concept of what constitutes "evidence" has the same definition and meaning across different professions in allied health. The experience of writing this chapter suggested that social work and other relational therapies, such as counselling and psychotherapy, approach the evaluation of the effectiveness of different interventions differently. Social work uses a broader definition both of what constitutes "evidence" and of what kinds of research findings are considered relevant to practice. I noted that social workers referred to techniques and new literature used in practice across a range of practice environments from a wider range of sources, including small-scale qualitative studies that dealt with a very broad range of issues influencing the practice environment. Practice research in social work focuses on the legal context, work place, and team, all of which influence the practitioner and his or her framework for practice. This framework for practice is actively constructed from years of experience within a particular field and is tailored to the individual service-user, family, and group. Practice wisdom, theory, personal and professional values, and the social worker's ethics and moral judgement are woven together. This fabric constructed over time is then available for the social worker to use and so form part of the "evidence" drawn upon for directions within contact with clients.

Other concerns of the social work research literature related to what was "relevant" theory to particular client problems, the values the social worker brings to practice, personal as well as professional ethics, the nature of the client's presentation, and the practice wisdom of the individual practitioner which develops from seeing many clients across time. The organisational setting, policies, and practices, the prevailing socio-economic and political contexts, and the influence of culture are other variables social workers attend to in their practice. Clinical supervision from within a critical reflective paradigm and the service-users' or consumers' and their caregivers' goals, narratives, and resources also feature prominently in social work literature which ultimately shape one's practice.

As a consequence of these reflections upon the nature of social work practice, its anti-oppressive, holistic orientation, and the use of self of the practitioner, I realised that there were underpinning values to conducting any literature-based search. Considerations about what constitutes "evidence" were less clear-cut in social work and so needed to be defined at the outset and at every stage of the search process from question formulation through to application and evaluation. Therefore, the idea of a book devoted to the information needs of social work practitioners who approach the search for and application of "evidence" to inform practice was born. Out of these deliberations, a number of fellow academics and practice collaborators were approached to contribute to the debate. In their chapters, it is possible to see the influences and roles of ethics, values, and the holistic and anti-oppressive practices, which shape evidence-informed practice for social work.

The second major driver to the writing of this book came from my collaborator in teaching a national post-graduate programme to allied health students at Victoria University of Wellington in New Zealand. Justin Cargill, a reference and subject librarian, and I had collaborated together to teach students the value of researching for their practice assignments. During orientation week our allied health post-graduate students, who were working in hospitals around New Zealand, would study on campus during a five-day intensive (Pack, 2010a). During these five days, the broad approaches taught in the year long programme were outlined and illustrated with practice examples. As part of this orientation, the library session covered the literature searching process, including the use of key terms, creating effective search strategies, the importance of systematically recording search strategies, and assessing the records from each search. This half-day workshop provided students with the tools for approaching research needed for essay writing and problem-based learning. In the problem-based learning which was delivered online I posed various clinical dilemmas common to the experience of working in the mental health services. As a consequence of using this approach to skill-building in searching for evidence to apply to practice, we noted that students not only began to undertake research on their assignment topics but were doing so more systematically when they had attended this workshop (Pack, 2010a). For example, the allied health post-graduates we were teaching began to demonstrate their confidence in critiquing the prevailing theories about DSM diagnoses from a cultural and service-user standpoint (Pack, 2013). During the library orientation, we showed students how to locate the practice research related to clients, caregivers, and families, along with more traditional sources.

The third impetus for writing this book is the ever-changing nature of social work theory and its relationship to the use of professional self in practice. As social workers are eclectic in their use of theory, these theoretical foundations are an important foundation for practice and are themselves adapted through social workers' intuition, decision-making, and experience. Theory for practice in social work provides a lens for viewing all research for relevance and applicability, as well as revealing gaps where there is not yet any theory or if the theory is only partly formulated. The social work theories most often drawn upon by social workers include ecological systems, narrative, and strengths-based, anti-oppressive/ emancipatory, and critical theory. Each of these theories has a role to contribute in structuring the evidence-informed practice discourses as the chapters of this book illustrate. As social work adopts a broad, integrative approach to practice as a profession, social work practitioners select parts of each theory to construct for themselves a coherent framework in working with clients. Evidence in this sense can be considered to inform and refine this framework for practice, representing not one theory or approach but a bricolage of many.

## THE STRUCTURE OF THE BOOK

### Section 1: Framing the Search for Evidence

To demonstrate practically how the research evidence can inform practice, Section 1 of this book is comprised of four foundational chapters. These chapters offer a framework for guiding practitioners wanting to systematically search, find, assess, and apply literature from research to guide their practice. Chapter 1, "Why Search for Evidence for Practice in Social Work?" provides a framework to assess what is "evidence." It deals with the controversy surrounding what constitutes "evidence" for social work practice and its practitioners. Building on this understanding, Chapter 2 outlines step-by-step how to locate and evaluate research evidence. Chapter 3 describes some of the considerations regarding how to apply evidence across different practice settings, domains, and jurisdictions as a social worker. The social worker's understanding and use of professional self and intuition is included in this process. Chapter 4, "Navigating Practice-Informed Evidence and Evidence-Based Practice," distinguishes between the two terms on the basis of there being competing claims to knowledge based in an analysis of the underlying power dynamics underlying these discourses. These discourses position the relationship between social worker and service-user differently and are themselves informed by the multi-theoretical perspectives that social workers work from. These theories of practice drawn upon by social workers in their practice include ecological systems, critical-reflective, strengths-based, cultural, and service-user theories of recovery. Therefore, in Section 1 of the book, the notion of what constitutes "evidence" is assessed in interaction with social work theory, service-user, cultural perspectives, and multi-disciplinary practice.

## Section 2: Social Work Fields of Practice

With this understanding of the spiralling nature of the assessment-practice nexus, Section 2 of the book addresses specific fields of practice and the application of practice-evidence within those fields. Chapters 5 to 13 address many of the major contexts of practice in which social workers operate. The aim of these chapters is to illustrate through description of a practice issue or dilemma how evidence may guide and advance practice in that field.

These contexts of practice include refugee and resettlement issues for women in Chapter 5 and mental health and the impact of multi-disciplinary and cross-sector collaboration in client service provision and well-being in Chapter 6. Chapter 7 is written by a social work academic familiar with the many challenges of child protection social work in remote rural and Aboriginal communities in Alice Springs, Australia. This chapter outlines sociologist Everett Hughes' (1951, 1962) foundational notion of "dirty work" and applies this concept to the child protection social work role. Chapter 8 deals with young men and the rehabilitation of young offenders in the United Kingdom's criminal justice system.

Chapter 9 describes an outcome evaluation of social work services across health and child protection domains to conclude that improved outcomes are obtained when social workers are offering services within a multi-disciplinary team. Chapter 10 explores the assessment and treatment considerations when approaching therapy with adult sexual abuse survivors. Guided by evidence-based literature, the author attends to the stages of recovery from trauma with women who have experiences of childhood sexual abuse. Chapter 11 focuses on a mixed methods quantitative and qualitative evaluation of the services offered within neurosurgical wards and post-discharge in the community. The services provided by social workers to address the wider psychosocial needs of service-users and their families and caregivers demonstrate how social work services integrated into any multi-disciplinary team effort enhance satisfaction and outcomes for service-users and their families. Chapter 12, guided by the research literature, builds a model for social workers who work with men and explores the emphasis on mothering in the research literature. This review and the authors' own research emphasises the need to update the knowledge base to include the role of fathers, thus reconceptualising our understanding of what constitutes parenting within families in the 21st century. Chapter 13 outlines the author's work as an art therapist in remote Aboriginal communities, working in partnership with the local elders and Aboriginal artists. In this context, the author deconstructs Western concepts in art and trauma-informed therapy using Smith's (1999) groundbreaking "decolonising methodologies" to address her own practices as an art therapist to facilitate cultural regeneration in Aboriginal communities where children and their families are experiencing intergenerational trauma.

## Section 3: Self-Care for Social Workers

Section 3 of this book (Chapters 14-17) addresses fields of self-care for social workers from within the research literature. Chapter 14 deals with the use and theories attached to clinical supervision. Clinical supervision was developed within the founding work of Kadushin (1957, 1968) and has been shaped since by a variety of social work theorists. Chapter 15 explores the organisational responses to social workers who face critical incidents, developing a model that aims to prevent and ameliorate compassion fatigue and vicarious traumatisation from critical events in the workplace. The theories underpinning critical incident stress management programmes are explored and extrapolated into a model for social workers working in the NGO and statutory sectors. Finally, Chapter 16 deals with spirituality as an advanced competency in social work practice. Drawing on the evidence-informed literature and personal experiences in community, the author discusses how spirituality in the social worker's everyday life can be used to enhance professional and personal effectiveness and wellbeing. Secondly, spirituality is discussed as a means of ensuring that social workers attend to their clients' sense of spirituality and its role in their healing. The conclusion, Chapter 17, brings the various sections together to pose the question, "What have we learned?"

## CONCLUSION: HOW THE BOOK IMPACTS THE FIELD

In each chapter, the authors bring a wealth of experience as social work practitioners working in the fields they describe alongside their research backgrounds. As researcher-practitioners, they bring a depth of understanding of the ways in which the research literature can assist in guiding our practice with clients on multiple levels: including the families, support networks, groups, and institutions that surround individual clients in their local communities.

In order to illustrate especially important aspects of assessment and intervention in each field of practice, cases encountered in the authors' practice are presented within each chapter relating to a field of social work practice. In all instances, client identity has been rigorously protected by altering some combination of details involving adjustments to age, ethnicity, and circumstances. This process of assembling composite case studies is achieved by summarising and then adjusting the reported circumstances of a range of clients with differing histories but with the same presenting issues. These details are then discussed in terms of the personal narratives gathered from several individual clients, elements of which are condensed into a single narrative. Every effort has, therefore, been made by the authors to de-identify actual cases from their practice.

The "cases" used to illustrate are not always related to client presentations but rather to programmes, an analysis of organisational policies, practices, and the law to reveal gaps in service provision and ethical dilemmas. This broader view of practice in which the worker looks systemically at the institutions and their policies is often associated with social workers who are working in areas where there are conflicting policies and ambiguities in the legal frameworks for practice.

This book is also offered for social work educators and their students to teach the basics of how to find and apply evidence-based practice in their day-to-day work. The reader, whether an advanced practitioner or a beginning social worker, is invited to engage with the authors in their search to answer key dilemmas in their practice. I hope that students, their educators, and new, as well as seasoned, practitioners are encouraged to approach and use the research literature more confidently, to assess quality of evidence, and to learn how to apply and theorise about the practice dilemmas raised. These chapters are offered as critical-reflections on practice and as such represent a "snap shot" of major themes discovered in the empirical and conceptual research literature. Just as Kadushin (1999) reminds us, social work is a dynamic, ever-changing profession as it responds and interacts with its environment. In this sense, this book and each book chapter is of necessity a work in progress.

*Margaret Pack*
*Australian Catholic University, Australia*

## REFERENCES

Gambrill, E. (2006). Evidence-based practice and policy: Choices ahead. *Research on Social Work Practice, 16*(3), 338–357. doi:10.1177/1049731505284205

Gambrill, E. (2008). Evidence-based (informed) macro practice: Process and philosophy. *Journal of Evidence-Based Social Work, 5*(3-4), 423–452. doi:10.1080/15433710802083971 PMID:19042875

Gambrill, E. (2010). Evidence-informed practice: Antidote to propaganda in the helping professions? *Research on Social Work Practice, 20*(3), 302–320. doi:10.1177/1049731509347879

Gambrill, E. (2011). Evidence-based practice and the ethics of discretion. *Journal of Social Work, 11*(1), 26–48. doi:10.1177/1468017310381306

Gambrill, E. (2013). Evidence-informed practice. In B. A. Thyer, C. N. Dulmus, & K. M. Sowers (Eds.), *Developing evidence-based generalist practice skills* (pp. 1–24). Hoboken, NJ: John Wiley.

Grimmer-Somers, K. (Ed.). (2009). *Practical tips in finding the evidence: An allied health primer. España.* Manila: UST.

Hughes, E. (1951). Work and the self. In J. Roher & M. Sherif (Eds.), *Social psychology at the crossroads* (pp. 313–323). New York: Harper and Brothers.

Hughes, E. C. (1962). Good people and dirty work. *Social Problems, 10*(1), 3–11. doi:10.2307/799402

Kadushin, A. (1957). The effect on the client of interview observation at intake. *The Social Service Review, 31*(1), 22–38. doi:10.1086/640166

Kadushin, A. (1968). Games people play in supervision. *Social Work, 3*(3), 23–32. doi:10.1093/sw/13.3.23

Kadushin, A. (1999). The past, the present, and the future of professional social work. *Arete, 23*(3), 76–84.

Pack, M. (2009). Social work (adult). In K. Grimmer-Somers & G. Nehrenz (Eds.), *Practical tips in finding the evidence: An allied health primer* (pp. 176–199). Manila, Philippines: UST.

Pack, M. (2010a). Allies in learning: Critical-reflective practice on-line with allied mental health practitioners. *Social Work Education, 29*(1), 67–79. doi:10.1080/02615470902810876

Pack, M. (2010b). Career themes in the lives of sexual abuse counsellors. *New Zealand Journal of Counselling, 30*(2), 75–92. Retrieved from http://www.nzac.org.nz/new_zealand_journal_of_counselling.cfm

Pack, M. J. (2013). An evaluation of critical-reflection on service-users and their families' narratives as a teaching resource in a post-graduate allied mental health program: An integrative approach. *Social Work in Mental Health, 11*(2), 154–166. doi:10.1080/15332985.2012.748003

Smith, L. T. (1999). *Decolonising methodologies: Research and Indigenous peoples.* London: Zed Books.

Thyer, B. A. (2004). What is evidence-based practice? *Brief Treatment and Crisis Intervention, 4*(2), 167–176. doi:10.1093/brief-treatment/mhh013

Thyer, B. A. (2008). The quest for evidence-based practice?: We are all positivists! *Research on Social Work Practice, 18*(4), 339–345. doi:10.1177/1049731507313998

# Acknowledgment

This book would not have been possible without the collaboration and critical gaze of the editorial board who generously gave of their time and expertise in assisting me in peer reviewing the chapter proposals and full chapters.

I wish to acknowledge the effort and expertise of the individual authors who also peer reviewed one another's work in a double-blind process in the final peer review. I thank you all for joining me on this search for evidence.

On a more personal note, I would like to thank my colleague and friend of the past eight years, Justin Cargill, for his tireless efforts in providing support to the authors of this book. I also wish to thank my mother for supporting me during the highs and lows of this project and my sister, Robyn Pack, Librarian, National Library of New Zealand, for peer review on early chapter drafts. From such faithful and loyal support, all things seem possible.

*Margaret Pack*
*Australian Catholic University, Australia*

Most importantly, I would like to thank Margaret Pack for inviting me to join her as co-editor. It is, of course, impossible to embark on a project of this nature without incurring significant indebtedness! I must certainly thank Allison McGinniss at IGI Global for her guidance and advice throughout the process. I would also like to thank my librarian colleague, Rohini Biradavolu, who as a trained English teacher was readily available to discuss thorny grammatical issues. I also wish to acknowledge my colleagues, Tony Quinn and Pete Nichols, who helpfully provided second opinions over various matters, Simon Chamberlain for his advice in interpreting legal references, and Dr. Deborah Laurs. I would like to thank Medwenna Buckland, Librarian at Australian Catholic University, for double checking the reference lists. She was worth her weight in gold. I also wish to recognise Jeff Hume-Pratuch, Editorial Supervisor, APA Journals, and Charles Rhoades, Manuscript Editor, APA Journals, who in particular answered far more questions than anyone should ever be reasonably expected to address especially in regard to interpreting *The Bluebook* for citation of legal and United Nations materials. In addition, I would like to acknowledge my mother's patience; her frequent question, "When will it end?" was met with the equally frequent but, no doubt, infuriating refrain, "When it is finished." Finally, of course, I would like to thank the contributors to this book who willingly cooperated as the project unfolded. It's been a pleasure.

*Justin Cargill*
*Victoria University of Wellington, New Zealand*

# Section 1
# Framing the Search for Evidence

*How social workers search for and apply evidence to and for practice.*

# Chapter 1
# Why Search for Evidence for Practice in Social Work?

**Justin Cargill**
*Victoria University of Wellington, New Zealand*

## ABSTRACT

*How is evidence integrated into the practice relationship between social worker and client? Studies suggest that at the practice level research is not consistently utilised. Evidence-Based Practice (EBP) has been hailed as a means of bringing practice and research together in a way that strengthens the empirical base of social work. Although EBP has had strong endorsement, it has also come under heavy criticism. This chapter explores these concerns in the hope of further clarifying the model. The need for an inclusive definition of evidence is emphasised giving rightful place to empirical research and also to other forms of evidence. The need for a synthesis of evidence-based practice and critical reflection is also explored. Evidence must be used in a critically reflective way if it is to be used effectively. Finally, the language of "evidence-informed" is shown to more clearly articulate the components of the EBP process.*

## INTRODUCTION

*Experienced social work educators have come to understand that the reason why there are no textbook answers is because the problems practitioners confront are far too complex for simple solutions. The fact is that social work is an exceedingly difficult occupation....This does not mean that there is nothing that can be done to prepare aspiring social workers for the rigors ahead. It is just that there are no simple recipes to present to them. What can be done is to train*

*them in ways of finding and applying the best available evidence when unfamiliar situations arise. (Barber, 2012, p. 192)*

Social work is a very dynamic and demanding activity, and social workers become very practiced at what they do. The problems they address are widely varied and complex. In their daily work, they draw upon a vast array of resources, including personal strengths, formal education, and practice experience. But the question naturally arises as to what role evidence itself plays in social work

DOI: 10.4018/978-1-4666-6563-7.ch001

practice? For our purposes, evidence simply means data upon which practice decisions can be made. What, then, constitutes good evidence, and how is it integrated or incorporated into the practice relationship between social worker and client?

In this chapter we will explore these questions.

## LOW USE OF EMPIRICAL RESEARCH EVIDENCE

Perhaps rather surprisingly, a frequently recurring theme in the social work literature has been the low uptake of empirical evidence by social work practitioners. Osmond and O'Connor (2006) have surveyed a range of studies throughout the twentieth century which demonstrate that social workers rarely use research findings in their practice and conclude "there has been a growing body of research that suggests that theory and research are not routinely guiding social work practice" (p. 7). In their own small-scale investigation, social workers also "did not refer, consider, read or appraise any research during the observed data-collection period (18 months)" (p. 14).

Other writers have similarly pointed to studies which have consistently shown little use of empirical research by social work practitioners to inform their practice (Gray, Plath, & Webb, 2009, p. 2; Mullen, Bledsoe, & Bellamy, 2008, p. 325; Rosen, 2003, p. 201; Rubin & Parrish, 2012, pp. 203-204; Trinder, 2000b, p. 144). D'Cruz and Jones (2014) refer to a "general aversion to social work research" and state their aim to address some of the "fears and misconceptions" that exist among many social workers (p. 2).

Evidence-based practice (EBP) is a particular approach to the relationship between research and evidence, mandating the use of relevant empirical research where such exists. It is a topic to which we will return but there are some lessons to be drawn from specific studies of EBP that are relevant in this context.

Mullen and Bacon's 2004 survey showed that practitioners seldom used research findings in practice decisions, were largely unfamiliar with EBP guidelines and manuals, and only rarely read reports of relevant research studies (Mullen, Shlonsky, Bledsoe, & Bellamy, 2005, p. 63). Most respondents in a study of field instructors agreed that EBP is a "useful" practice idea, but 43 percent indicated they only sometimes found and critically appraised the best scientific evidence, and seven percent did not do so at all (Edmond, Megivern, Williams, Rochman, & Howard, 2006, p. 385). In a survey of social work faculty in MSW programs throughout the United States, over 40 percent of respondents held that almost any form of research evidence was sufficient to justify an intervention as evidence-based. Only 25 percent of the survey respondents "defined EBP exclusively as 'a process that includes locating and appraising credible evidence as a part of practice decisions'" (Rubin & Parrish, 2007, p. 417). And a study of social workers in Australia by Gray, Joy, Plath, and Webb (2014), although finding "largely positive and welcoming support for EBP" (p. 26), showed empirical research to be understood "predominately in generic terms or as a single source," with only six percent of the respondents stating that they appraised a range of research to inform practice changes (p. 34).

There has been some recent evidence of change in this reserve towards the use of empirical research evidence. Sundell, Soydan, Tengvald, and Anttila (2010) have noted changing attitudes toward evidence within the Swedish social work community, with greater sympathy being shown for the use of randomised or quasi-experimental design studies than previously (pp. 717, 719). Parrish and Rubin (2012) have found that 38 percent of their sample of Texas social workers use research evidence "often or very often" in practice decisions. Although low, they believe these figures are encouraging because they contrast with studies that indicate that practitioners "rarely use research to guide their practice" (p. 208). Morago (2010) reports that 74.8 percent of respondents reported "a good knowledge of EBP," and 95.5 percent stated that "good quality research findings" should form the basis for making professional decisions (pp. 460-461). In a sample drawn from the United Kingdom and United States, Pope, Rollins, Chaumba, and Risler (2011) showed that many social workers are knowledgeable about EBP and 87 percent of respondents used research findings in their practice at least sometimes (pp. 361).

These results may contrast to an extent with the low and sporadic use of empirical research evidence reported in other studies, but even these recent studies suggest that use of empirical research is variable and that, whilst perhaps positive about the principles of EBP, social workers are less inclined to implement research findings in their practice. If the uptake of empirical research has largely been low, where have social workers been turning for guidance on practice issues? They have been relying on intuition and practice experience. They further rely heavily upon consultation, frequently drawing on the judgement of respected colleagues, agency traditions, professional consensus, and the authority of consultants and supervisors (Edmond et al., 2006, p. 388; Gray et al., 2014, p. 25; Mullen & Bacon, 2003, p. 227; Rubin & Parrish, 2007, p. 405).

## EXPLAINING THE SPORADIC UPTAKE OF EMPIRICAL RESEARCH EVIDENCE

A number of reasons have been cited for the modest and sporadic uptake of empirical research demonstrated in many studies. Perhaps the most provocative is the explanation given by Rosen (2003). He proposes that since the issues addressed by social workers are often encountered by lay people, social work practitioners may bring into their professional lives "lay understandings, perceptions, and conceptions of helping" that have already been established outside that role. Their lay understanding may intrude on their professional habits of thought and skills (p. 199).

Although practitioner's failure to use research is seen as a result of their lack of "research-mindedness," Marsh, Fisher, Mathers, and Fish (2005) suggest that the inadequate uptake of research may be attributed to researchers failing "to engage with the way practitioners use knowledge in practice, or to build collaborative partnerships with the practice community" (p. 15). Additionally, practitioners may not make full use of research due to the belief that such research over-simplifies reality. Social work activity occurs in "open conditions" which cannot be captured easily in research (Kjorstad, 2008, p. 145).

In light of these considerations, it is understandable that social workers might be more comfortable with their own intuition based on experience and lay judgement. This might certainly explain situations in which practitioners simply see no need to look beyond their personal experience and possibly a confirmatory discussion with colleagues.

In addition to such factors, however, are more pragmatic reasons. Lack of time has been cited as an obstacle to consistent use of empirical research in studies by Edmond et al. (2006, p. 388) and Beddoe (2011, p. 572). Resourcing is also a significant obstacle to social workers accessing the research literature. Lack of funding means that social workers and social agencies are often not able to afford access to the peer-reviewed research literature (Holden et al., 2012, p. 487). Morago's (2010) survey of UK social care and social work agencies found that lack of time, resources, information, and training were specific barriers to EBP implementation (pp. 458-459, 461-462).

## SOCIAL WORK'S LONG LEGACY OF EMPIRICAL RESEARCH

In spite of studies largely indicating a poor uptake of research, an examination of social work's history reveals an interest in employing empirical research to guide practice that can be traced back to the 1890s. This was spurred in part by criticism that it lacked a scientific literature (Gibbons, 2001, pp. 4-5; Gibbs, 2003, p. 17; Leighninger, 2012, p. 20; Nothdurfter & Lorenz, 2010, para 2; Thyer, 2010, p. 3; Witkin & Harrison, 2001, p. 293). Thyer and Myers (2011) have traced views from a number of sources over 80 years regarding this need to firmly attach social work to a scientific approach (pp. 11-12). Gellis and Reid (2004) have referred to the "ideal" existing in the early part of the twentieth century that practitioners were to act as scientists making and testing hypotheses about clients and utilising the results of scientific studies in their practice, although they admit that "there was a rather large gap between the professed ideal and the actual reality" (p. 156).

Attempts to test the efficacy of social work intervention in the 1970s, however, did not at that time provide much grounds for encouragement. In 1973, Joel Fischer published a review of social casework studies appearing in major social work journals, dissertations, or agency reports from the 1930s to 1973. This study and a number of others emerging during this period caused significant dismay in the profession for they failed to provide empirical support for the effectiveness of social casework (Fortune, 2010, p. 24; Gellis & Reid, 2004, p. 156; Gibbons, 2001, p. 7; Orcutt, 1990, pp. 160-161; Roberts, Yeager, & Regehr, 2006, p. 13).

These findings spurred an effort amongst those supportive of the scientific practitioner and empirical clinical practice models to encourage practitioners to more rigorously evaluate their practice especially through single-case design and to encourage research in practice (Adams, Matto, & LeCroy, 2009, p. 166; Fortune, 2010, p.

24; Trinder, 2000b, pp. 141-142). Orcutt (1990) describes major research studies of social work practice from the earlier part of the twentieth century through to the 1970s (pp. 153-172), and she confirms that during the 1970s and 1980s "an aggressive movement in the direction of empirically based practice" emerged (p. 5). In 1969, for instance, William Reid employed a rigorous experimental study design which set a standard for his subsequent work developing social work practices based on an empirical demonstration of effectiveness (Videka & Blackburn, 2010, pp. 183, 186).

A number of studies in the period since have described the use of research in addressing social problems and in evaluating social interventions and the efficacy of programs, and they have produced encouraging results (Batista, 2010, p. 51; Catalano, Hill, Haggerty, Fleming, & Hawkins, 2010, pp. 73-78; Combs-Orme, 1988; Gibbons, 2001, p. 6; Hopps, Lowe, & Rollins, 2010, pp. 115-117; Pritchard 2004a; 2004b). Reid and Fortune (2003) surveyed evaluations of 130 social work programs reported in the literature during the period 1990 to 1999 and found that the "great majority" showed "positive results" (pp. 59, 69), and in a further study, Reid, Kenally, & Colvin (2004) indicated that 77 percent of the interventions they surveyed between 1990 and 2001 demonstrated "significant differences" at post-test or follow-up and these usually on important measures (pp. 74, 77).

It would appear, therefore, that in spite of some success in measuring social work interventions and some positive results, at the practice level research evidence has not been consistently utilised. This has been in part due to a gap between the researcher and the practitioner, in part due to pragmatic considerations such as time constraints, in part due to the perception that empirical research is not critical, in part due to the belief that ethical obligations can be met by conferring with colleagues and consulting authorities.

In short, then, calls for making social work more scientific have had less impact than its proponents occupying key roles in the profession have envisioned. Otto, Polutta, and Ziegler (2009) have noted that "there is hardly any controversy about whether Social Work should be studied scientifically, and there is also a board consensus that Social Work practice should be founded on empirically valid knowledge" (p. 10). As is so often the case, there exists a gap between the principle and the practice.

## NO ROOM FOR COMPLACENCY ABOUT THE ROLE OF RESEARCH

Social work cannot be complacent about the role of research in professional practice. Given that social workers have a very responsible community role, their motivation should be to ensure that their practice is informed by "reliable research evidence" (Chalmers, 2005, p. 228). Indeed, a number of writers have stressed the ethical responsibility of social workers to ensure that interventions and outcomes are as beneficial as possible for clients. Client confidence in social worker aptitude is only well-placed if social workers are sufficiently informed about the evidentiary status of the interventions they are employing. Clients expect social workers to be able to justify their decisions especially where such decisions have profound implications (Crawford, 2011a, p. 127; 2011b, pp. 5-7; Gambrill, 2003, p. 49; 2011, pp. 38-39; 2013, p. 2; Marsh et al., 2005, pp. 3-4; Otto et al., 2009, p. 11; Plath, 2006, p. 59; Rosen, 2003, p. 198; Rubin & Parrish, 2007, p. 419; Williams & Sherr, 2013, p. 109).

Social workers also have obvious obligations to a number of other groups. They need to be able to justify their ethical use of funds in practice services to their funding providers and they have a professional responsibility to supervisors, agency directors, and their colleagues (Rosen, 2003, p. 198; Williams & Sherr, 2013, p. 109). Most significantly, they have an obligation to strengthen the profession's status. Social work practice gains increased credibility from other professions if it is understood to be drawing on a solid core of research-based rationales. Social workers are often required to justify their actions in court and other formal settings, so they are obliged to draw upon compelling evidence if they are to be taken seriously (Crawford, 2011a, pp. 127-128; 2011b, p. 6). Use of research evidence is an effective counter to perceptions that social work activity is arbitrary and ill-informed.

## THE EMERGENCE OF EVIDENCE-BASED PRACTICE

Social work has in recent decades been influenced by a form of practice hailed as a means of bringing practice and research together in a way that strengthens the empirical base of social work. Based on evidence-based medicine (EBM), which was formulated in the early 1990s by a group at McMaster University in Canada (Sackett, Straus, Richardson, Rosenberg, & Haynes, 2000, p. 2), evidence-based practice (EBP) has in the past two decades been introduced into a number of disciplines, including education, psychiatry, clinical psychology, and nursing (Reynolds, 2000, p. 17), but it has also had an impact on a wide range of social work contexts (Rice, Hwang, Abrefa-Gyan, & Powell, 2010, p. 158). And having begun as an "Anglo-Saxon phenomenon," it has found roots in such places as the Scandinavian countries and the Netherlands (Morago, 2006, p. 468), although, as discussed earlier, its empirical roots can be traced back to the early days of the profession.

Sackett et al. (2000) defined evidence-based medicine as "the integration of best research evidence with clinical expertise and patient values" (p. 1). They were convinced that this approach would optimise clinical outcomes and quality of life. The EBM process comprises steps which social work scholars have adapted (Gray, Joy, Plath, & Webb, 2013, p. 158; Morago, 2006, p. 462; Mullen, Bledsoe, & Bellamy, 2008, p. 327;

Thyer, 2010, p. 7). Gibbs and Gambrill (2002) unpack the process in some detail:

1. Convert information needs into answerable questions. Such questions are stated specifically enough to guide a computer search, concern the client's welfare, relate to a problem that has some chance of a solution, and, ideally, formed in collaboration with the client. A well-formed question describes the client, course of action, alternate course(s) of action, and intended result.
2. Track down with maximum efficiency the best evidence with which to answer the question. (This requires electronic access to bibliographic databases and skill in searching them efficiently and quickly enough to guide practice.)
3. Critically appraise the evidence for its validity and usefulness. (This entails applying a hierarchy of evidence relevant to several question/evidence types.)
4. Apply the results of this appraisal to policy/ practice decisions. This requires deciding whether the evidence applies to the decision at hand based on whether a client is similar enough to those studied, access to interventions described in the literature, weighing anticipated outcomes relative to concerns such as number needed to treat, practical matters, and client's preferences.
5. Evaluate outcome. This may entail record keeping including single-case designs (steps described in Sackett et al., 1997, p. 3). (pp. 453-454)

There are clearly four elements involved in this definition of EBP: 1) the best available research evidence, 2) the practitioner's expertise and experience, 3) the client's circumstances, 4) the client's preferences and values. Roberts, Yeager, and Regehr (2006) have also added another element.

The nature of the organisation or agency in which the social worker works, resource constraints, and organisational mandate, must also be factored into the process (p. 8).

## EVIDENCE-BASED PRACTICE: WINNING ENDORSEMENT

Trinder (2000c) has attributed the appeal of EBP to its resonance with such contemporary concerns as risk management and the confidence that a rigorous application of science may bring security, in addition to the emergence of managerialism and its focus on effectiveness, transparency, and accountability, as well as empowerment (pp. 5-13).

Evidence-based practice, therefore, enjoys strong support amongst many in social work academia (Roberts et al., 2006, p. 12). Nothdurfter and Lorenz (2010) have suggested that the promotion of EBP is part of social work's long history of establishing social work practice on a scientific footing (para. 2), and there have accordingly been a range of arguments used by proponents of EBP in its support.

A key reason for support has been increased recognition that the professional literature has often contained "unrigorous reviews, misrepresentations of disliked (or misunderstood) approaches, and inflated claims of knowledge" (Gambrill, 2011, p. 28). Gambrill (2011) cites studies that demonstrate the lack of rigor and questionable reliability of a number of reviews and practice guidelines which have led to continued use of interventions which are either harmful or ineffective (pp. 28, 30). She is suspicious of "authority-based decision-making" which she describes as decisions based on criteria such as "consensus, anecdotal experience, or tradition," and she perceives EBP as an alternative to such practices (p. 27). Sheldon (2001) insists that EBP serves to discourage social workers from accepting ideas simply because they are based in authority. He refers to the child sexual abuse scandal in Britain in the 1980s. He sees this as a failure to employ evidence-based practices (pp. 803-804).

EBP has also been seen as a means of meeting ethical obligations to involve clients as informed participants sharing in the decision-making. EBP is thought to promote transparency and encourage greater integration of ethical and evidentiary issues and identify knowledge gaps (Gambrill, 2006, pp. 339-340; 2008, pp, 425, 432-435; 2013, pp. 12-14). Thyer and Pignotti (2011) express enthusiasm over the congruence between social work values and the idea that the practitioner should identify the "best available research evidence" when seeking an appropriate intervention (p. 329). This also means sharing with the client that evidence is not available when such is the case. In discussing this need for candidness, Gambrill (2006) explains that EBP, as understood by its originators, "is essentially a way to handle uncertainty in an honest and informed manner, sharing ignorance and knowledge....The uncertainty associated with decisions is acknowledged, not hidden" (p. 340).

## EVIDENCE-BASED PRACTICE: CONTENTION AND CONTROVERSY

EBP has not, however, won universal acceptance either amongst practitioners, as we have already noted, or social work academics (Batista, 2010, p. 45; Roberts et al., 2006, p. 12). There are a number of reasons for EBP having come under intense criticism and these will be explored below.

A number of writers have detected different emphases within EBP in social work (Aisenberg, 2008, pp. 297-298; Gambrill, 2006, pp. 341-342; Gray & Mcdonald, 2006, p. 10; Morago, 2006, p. 469). Bergmark, Bergmark, and Lundstrom (2012) refer to "major disagreements" and a "contradiction" within EBP (pp. 599). That some of these different emphases in EBP are reconcilable will become clear but it is inevitable that examples of

deviations from an original will be found and critics have critiqued these. It appears, however, that whilst making sound criticisms of these departures, which are effectively more narrow conceptions of EBP practice, some critics have overlooked the fact that they are not necessarily interacting with EBP as originally conceived.

The idea that EBP has not always been accurately represented has been argued rather forcefully. Gambrill (2011) refers to "the steady misrepresentation of the process and philosophy of evidence-based practice (EBP)" (p. 26). She further responds that "the process and philosophy of evidence-based practice as described in original sources is not presented in the majority of publications in social work" (p. 26). And similarly, "the professional literature abounds with distorted descriptions and misrepresentations of this process and philosophy" (p. 28). Thyer and Pignotti (2011) also heatedly protest that "a rampant problem" in social work critiques of EBP is a reliance on "third or fourth-hand interpretations which have successively deviated from the original description" which leads to "mischaracterizations and straw-person portrayals" (p. 331).

There is some merit to these complaints. Avby, Nilsen, and Dahlgren's (2013) study yielded five qualitative different understandings of EBP. Rubin and Parrish (2007) document that even social work educators are unclear about the definition of EBP (p. 417). In addition, Gray et al. (2014) found an "unsophisticated" application of evidence-based practice even amongst those showing positive support (p. 37).

Not all criticism of EBP, however, results from misunderstandings or misperceptions. Criticism of EBP ranges from perceived material and organisational obstacles impeding proper EBP implementation to what are believed to be systemic and fundamental flaws. It is hardly possible to explore the full gamut of criticisms but it is possible to look at some of the more significant concerns. The following section will, therefore, identify concerns aimed at the EBP model itself and determine the validity of that criticism. It will also look at legitimate criticisms which have been targeted at departures from that model in the hope of further clarifying the model itself.

## EBP: An Approach which is Managed by Management?

Webb (2001) has made the point that the emphasis on evidence and effectiveness in evidence-based practice legitimises managerial values associated with the optimisation of performance and cost effectiveness (pp. 58, 60, 74). Plath (2006) has made similar comments (p. 66).

This is a legitimate concern but Grady and Drisko (2014) have demonstrated the extent to which the EBP process can instead be *negatively* impacted by external demands for cost efficiency and speedy assessment processes. They highlight the risk associated with the practitioner engaging in the EBP process without a thorough assessment of the client and situation (pp. 9-10). There can be a real clash between the EBP decision-making process and the manner in which it is implemented at the policy level if client values and professional expertise are ignored. Rather than EBP being an ally of the managerialist agenda it can all too readily suffer at its hands. It should also be kept in mind that EBP could, in fact, be successfully employed to challenge managerial control and decision-making and to bolster professional autonomy (Sheldon, 2001, pp. 807). Ultimately, as Bantry White (2010) has observed, "arguably, some of the critique of evidence-based-practice can be construed as 'guilty by association', for its use (or misuse) by the managerialist agenda" (p. 133). This criticism does not, therefore, indicate an inherent flaw in the model itself.

## EBP: An Approach which is Lacking Evidentiary Support?

A number of critics have highlighted the fact that there is no empirical evidence that EBP is more effective than alternative forms of practice in spite of its basic assumptions regarding the value of empirical support. This irony is not lost on its critics (Bouffard & Reid, 2012, p. 9; Trinder, 2000a, p. 213; Upshur & Tracy, 2004, p. 199).

This is a surprising criticism, however, for it would seem particularly meritorious for any approach that seeks to integrate credible research evidence, client values and preferences, professional experience and expertise, and the need for strong self-critical evaluation. But if, indeed, EBP cannot be *proved* effective, clients' outcomes can still be measured and these at a more specific level can give insight into the value of the EBP model. The face validity of EBP is, therefore, strong (Mullen et al., 2005, p. 68; Thyer, 2004, p. 168).

## EBP: An Approach which Requires Too Much Time and Skill?

Critics of EBP believe it is impractical to expect the average social worker to implement the process of EBP. They are concerned that practitioners do not have the time to perform the level of searching and appraisal required by the EBP process (Yunong & Fengzhi, 2009, p. 179). Adams, Matto, and LeCroy (2009) have also argued that social workers cannot be expected to respond to the vast range of client problems and become proficient in all the empirically supported interventions (p. 177).

The commitment in terms of time and resources for evidence-based practice is, in the words of Barber (2012), a "formidable" obstacle and a "tall order" especially given the average social worker's workload. Access to online journals, the need for skills in electronic searching of databases, and skills in statistical and research methods are additional barriers (p. 199). Some proponents of EBP do admit that this is a significant issue for social work. They, therefore, urge that practitioners be trained appropriately for EBP, that is, that they possess the skills to assess the information needs, search for evidence, assess information quality, engage with clients, and evaluate and use results (Mullen et al., 2005, pp. 70).

Mullen and Streiner (2004) have observed that with increasing access to resources searching for evidence is becoming easier (p. 116). Batista (2010) is, in fact, quite confident that "simple searches" of the appropriate databases are potentially within the capacity of any practitioner (p. 52), and Shlonsky and Gibbs (2004) are even convinced that "high-quality searches" of such resources can be performed in minutes in the hands of someone who has developed basic searching skills which, they note, can only improve further with practice (p. 148). Drisko and Grady (2012) are similarly assured that "the necessary skills can be updated and refined with a little practice" (p. 39).

Some authors have suggested that practitioners, agencies, and schools of social work seek collaborative opportunities to reduce pressures and support EBP principles of research and decision-making. They have advocated a university-agency partnership model in which universities provide the research expertise and agencies provide the knowledge which comes from direct engagement with clients (Barber, 2012, pp. 199-200; Fortune, McCallion, & Briar-Lawson, 2010, pp. 285-286; Richman, 2010, p. 271). Grady (2010) identifies specific strategies which schools of social work can adopt to support practitioners (pp. 402-408). Jones and Sherr (2014) have also identified strategies which social work faculty can adopt to cultivate relationships with practitioners and which the profession more widely can use to promote that relationship (pp. 143-146).

Admittedly, social workers cannot be expected to master the whole array of empirically supported interventions but as Rubin (2011) has noted, this is an argument for reducing practitioner caseload not against EBP. He also responds that when the practitioner lacks the necessary skills in a particular treatment, the EBP process does not preclude them from referring the client to a practitioner who has the requisite training. If this is not practicable, the practitioner can provide an intervention with which they themselves are skilled even if it does not enjoy the same empirical support (p. 71).

## EBP: An Approach which is Fixed and Inflexible?

Nevo and Slonin-Nevo (2011) object to the procedural steps characteristic of EBP. They are convinced that the EBP process hamstrings progress between the practitioner and client because the client is unable to move from one issue to another (p. 1187). They point out that if the client is, indeed, at the centre but there are changing goals, conditions, and preferences, applying a single protocol is not possible (pp. 1190-1191). They feel that EBP is inflexible, that once an intervention is selected most if not all of the intervention has to be applied. They observe that "in research, we are committed to strict protocols in order to keep our variables controlled. In treatment, however, the situation is dynamic" (pp. 1191). Arnd-Caddigan and Pozzuto (2010) also assert that important treatment goals cannot always be identified until the treatment is underway and first goals may lose their relevancy (p. 48).

These are important considerations but in the therapeutic relationship practitioners are not always engaged in an experiment requiring controlled variables. They are engaged in applying or adapting the research (if such exists). They are, thus, in a position to abandon a strategy and start the process afresh, that is, rethink and renegotiate the intervention, apply the intervention, and evaluate results. Of course, if the practitioner does find that the whole protocol can be successfully applied, then the results can be added to the research base to be drawn on later. And, as has been well observed, evidence gathered by practitioners engaged with clients can itself be used to test and supplement existing research (Gellis & Reid, 2004, pp. 157-158, 161).

There is no reason, then, to view the EBP steps as requiring a fixed, inexorable order. Bellamy, Bledsoe, and Mullen (2009), for instance, provide an example of an application of the EBP steps (pp. 23-26) but point out that they may not be followed in the typical order that they set out

(p. 23). They urge that "at each step in the process the practitioner's expertise, experience, and constraints (e.g., practical, financial, ethical) are considered together with practitioner and client values and preferences" (p. 26). Rosen (2003) also believes that steps may need to be reconsidered throughout the practitioner-client relationship. He proposes that EBP be "enhanced" by incorporating systematic planned practice (SPP) and single-system designs (SSD) (p. 202). He describes how the "master plan…is subject to modifications in response to reconsideration and to new case-relevant information" (p. 203). This is aided by adopting "limited-range plans for different segments of treatment (for example, phases, sessions, weeks)…specifying the outcomes to be attained during the segment in question, specifying the interventions to be used," providing rationales and evaluating outcomes. He refers to "flexible implementation of interventions, informed by ongoing feedback from evaluation of outcome attainment" (p. 203).

Clearly, proponents of EBP do not necessarily envisage a linear process that is unable to accommodate the vicissitudes and new insights associated with the unfolding practitioner-client relationship.

## EBP: An Approach which is Lacking in Quality Research Studies?

The EBP process has been facilitated by developments in information technology which have increased online access to full-text research articles, systematic reviews of studies, and practice guidelines. Since systematic reviews summarise randomised controlled trials (RCTs), practitioners are not faced with the task of searching for and then evaluating their effectiveness (Batista, 2010, p. 51).

In spite of this improved access to resources, a common criticism is the shortage of quality research studies in many areas of social work and

for many populations (Berger, 2010, pp. 176, 181-183). This shortage is a serious challenge. Admittedly, empirical support for practice is strongest in the mental health field but the research base is far more uneven outside this area. This has been described as a "major limiting factor" for EBP in social work (Gellis & Reid, 2004, p. 158), and some proponents have been compelled to admit that many decisions are still made for which good evidence does not exist (Mullen & Streiner, 2004, p. 115).

In response to the shortage of quality studies, a number of social work academics have pointed out that because social work is multidisciplinary, evidence from related disciplines can and should be used (Marsh et al., 2005, p. 12; Mullen et al., 2005, p. 73; Rosen & Proctor, 2003, p. 9; Thyer, 2008, p. 344; Thyer & Myers, 2011, p. 23). Moreover, when dealing with populations which have been understudied, it would appear that proponents of the EBP process do not *insist* on the existence of sufficient evidence to guide practice. In fact, ethical codes obligate social workers to inform their clients when the data is lacking (Gibbs & Gambrill, 2002, pp. 462-463). What EBP proponents instead *require* is that the practitioner search for and appraise whatever evidence does exist, looking to the final step of the EBP process – outcome evaluation – to provide constructive data. Particular caution is then required in monitoring outcomes (Mullen et al., 2005, p. 74; Mullen & Streiner, 2004, p. 115).

Practitioners work with whatever is available and in time the shortages will be addressed. Knowledge gaps simply point to the need for research (Mullen et al., 2005, p. 74), and they may be somewhat addressed through collaborative relationships between researchers and practitioners (Beddoe, 2011, p. 572; Berger, 2010, p. 184-185). And, as indicated above, some writers have, in fact, suggested a number of strategies in which schools of social work and individual faculty can be integral in supporting social work agencies and practitioners as they attempt to implement EBP (Grady, 2010, pp. 402-408; Jones & Sherr, 2014, pp. 143-146).

## EBP: An Approach which Overrides Client Voice?

Regarding EBM, Upshur and Tracy (2004) suggest that "patients do not become relevant until Step 4. In fact, patients are seen as passive objects that have evidence applied to them after the information has been extracted from them" (p. 198). This criticism is similarly aimed at EBP. Trinder (2000a), for instance, feels the "potential danger" of EBP is that it can tend to focus on what is to be done and divert attention away from hearing the client's story although the client's story is a crucial evidence source in establishing course of action (p. 234).

Clients, however, are relevant from the beginning. They drive the question! Gray et al. (2014) believe that EBP is a "goal worth pursuing" because it is a "client-focused, clinical decision-making process" in which the searching for evidence and its analysis "is driven by the individual client's situation, values, preferences, and interests" (p. 26). EBP is, therefore, an integration of expertise (practitioner) with values and needs (client). Admittedly, the EBP process requires that the client clearly state their values and preferences in the initial assessment and throughout the intervention, and when this is not done the EBP process is compromised (Grady & Drisko, 2014, pp. 10-11), but client cooperation or lack thereof is not an issue of concern for EBP alone. Nor is the concern raised by some that the result of any assessment may primarily represent the perspective not of the client but of the practitioner who constructs their own narrative of the situation (Crisp, Anderson, Orme, & Lister, 2005, p. 18). Indeed, if the client does have a "pivotal role" in assessment (Grady & Drisko, 2014, p. 10) and is offered the opportunity to review the assessment, such risks diminish. Crisp, Anderson, Orme,

and Lister (2003) note the increased recognition that clients should be as involved as possible in the assessment process (p. 2). This is congruent with the EBP requirement that the client's voice be at the fore. Broadhurst et al. (2010) have, for instance, insisted that assessment in child welfare practices in some areas of England and Wales has been compromised by a managerial culture of performance necessitating quick solutions and short-cuts (pp. 365-367). But if such an analysis is accurate, the clients (the families and children) have, in fact, not been placed at the centre as would be mandated by EBP. Also undermined, for that matter, is the EBP practitioner's role in conscientious decision-making.

Client circumstances and needs are, therefore, considered throughout the process. Indeed, they are given equal emphasis with the other elements in the current definition of EBP. Shlonsky and Gibbs (2004) indicate the importance of each element. They argue that "action is not dictated by current best evidence operating in a vacuum. None of the three core elements can stand alone; they work in concert" (p. 138). Drisko and Grady (2012) also argue that "informed, shared decision-making by the client is a co-equal component in EBP" (p. viii). Elsewhere, Drisko (2014) notes that EBP "weighs equally the preferences of the client, clinical expertise and the best research evidence" (p. 124).

Other proponents of EBP have made similar observations. Mullen et al. (2005) state that there is a "synergistic combination" of all elements and that reliance upon any one of these single elements without integration of the whole would not be considered EBP (p. 65). They describe what they call the "hallmarks" of evidence-based social work, and it is clear that the client has been placed at the core (p. 67). Gambrill (2013) also insists that one of the "hallmarks" of EBP is the involvement of clients as informed participants (p. 2). Gambrill (2006) writes that "the philosophy and process of EBP as described by its originators is a deeply participatory antiauthoritarian paradigm"

(p. 352). Cautioning that social workers must avoid imposing ideas on clients, Gilgun (2005) states that they must "be ready, willing, and even *eager* [emphasis added] for clients to falsify their ideas and assumptions" (p. 59).

Clearly, the client is paramount throughout the process. And, just as clearly, evidence is not passively applied. It is significantly dynamic in the hands of the motivated practitioner and client. In short, as Barber (2012) observes, EBP is "an intensely consultative procedure" between practitioner and client (p. 200) and again, EBP "is ultimately about informed consent...and it is also about treating the client as a collaborator rather than a recipient" (p. 194).

## EBP: An Approach which Side-Lines Practitioner Skill?

A rather prominent argument railed against EBP is that it is best characterised as a formulaic, mechanistic, "cookbook," decision-making process. It dictates to practitioners, ignores their expertise and professional judgement, overrides reflective judgement, dictates to clients, and ignores their preferences and values (Webb, 2001, pp. 57, 67, 71-74, 76). In contrast to EBP, Webb suggests that in real practice "cognitive heuristic devices are the determinants of decision making and not evidence" (p. 57), and that practitioners tend to rely more on "common sense" than scientific rational processes (pp. 64-65). He suggests that social workers cannot be assumed to make decisions on the basis of empirical research data (p. 65) and that "motivational and cognitive interests will determine how people evaluate evidence rather than objective information processing strategies" (p. 67).

The concern that EBP encourages mechanistic "cookbook" interventions overlooks the definition of EBP. Expertise is not belittled. It is part of the equation. Without a thorough and thoughtful assessment the EBP process will not achieve the benefits it claims for itself (Grady & Drisko,

2014, p. 6). The practitioner is obliged to use their expertise to determine whether evidence in the literature applies to the individual client bearing in mind their circumstances and values, and, if so, how that research evidence should be implemented in negotiation with the client (Batista, 2010, p. 50; Gibbs, 2003, p. 19; Mullen & Streiner, 2004, p. 117; Thyer & Myers, 2011, p. 20). Practitioner discretion is, therefore, essential. Even Rosen and Proctor (2003), who argue strongly for the use of practice guidelines, recognise "the need for creativity and innovation, and the exercise of professional judgment and practice wisdom" (p. 7). In discussing practice guidelines for intervention (PGIs), Rosen (2003) elsewhere says that employing PGIs, whilst integrating such elements as systematic planned practice and recursive evaluation, "would not only require practitioners' theoretical and technical competence, it would also call forth and use their best clinical judgment, creativity, and innovative ability – qualities that have been claimed by detractors of EBP to be underutilised in empirically guided practice" (p. 205).

Observations regarding cognitive bias in decision-making and the tendency to rely on "heuristic devices" (Webb, 2001, p. 57, 65) are well taken. But given the potential of social workers to cause harm, social workers have a moral and professional obligation "to think harder, more systematically, and more conscientiously" (Smith, 2004, p. 12). In fact, this is precisely the reason why EBP emphasises the role of critical thinking, values, knowledge, and skills. As we will see below, it is critical that we examine our own biases, and this is best done in interaction with others.

EBP, therefore, employs professional judgement and expertise in integrating information regarding the client's situation, preferences, and research findings. Epstein (2009) suspects a lack of enthusiasm amongst practitioners for EBP as it is frequently implemented because it gives no room for the practitioner's contribution to knowledge (pp. 221-222). This is a reasonable criticism where such instances are found but it is not implicit in

EBP (Gellis & Reid, 2004, pp. 157-158). Smith (2004) points out that if "leading figures in the evidence-based movement in health care" uphold the practitioner's role and experience, there is no reason to insist that social work adopt a "recipe approach to practice" in which that very role is diminished (p. 9). EBP is not, therefore, a substitute for professional competence. Professional skills are an essential component (Morago, 2006, p. 470). Drisko and Grady (2012) put it well when they write that "the professional expertise of the clinician is the 'glue' that combines and integrates all the elements of the EBP process. It is the cement that holds the other parts of the model together" (p. 8).

## EBP: An Approach which Merely Provides Lists of Treatments?

Thyer and Pignotti (2011) suggest that one source of resistance to EBP within social work may be attributable to confusion between EBP and the promulgation of empirically supported treatments (p. 332). A number of writers have helpfully distinguished these conceptualisations of EBP by delineating between EBP as a verb and EBP as a noun (Gray et al., 2013, p. 158; Thyer & Myers, 2011, p. 8). Williams and Sherr (2013), for instance, observe that the originators of EBP envisioned EBP as a verb, a decision-making process involving several interactive steps between practitioner and client. But they also state that the term EBP is employed as a noun to designate an "empirically validated treatment" (p. 101). Regarding these distinctions, Gray et al. (2014) indicate that the "mainstream view" is that EBP is "a clinical decision-making process" arising from evidence-based medicine and is distinct from "empirically supported interventions" (ESIs) and "empirically supported treatments" (ESTs) employed in psychology (p. 24), although Gray et al. (2013) note elsewhere that many studies fail to make any distinctions (p. 158).

Drisko and Grady (2012) explain that ESTs or "evidence-based interventions" (EBIs) although "similar" to EBP involve different definitions and logic. They argue that ESTs identify the effectiveness of specific treatments in specific contexts whilst EBP is a decision making-process focusing on specific clients (p. 10). They elsewhere affirm that EBP is often "confused" with ESIs and ESTs, and explain that "ESIs are *distinct treatment models*, whereas EBP is a *decision-making process* that may or may not result in the implementation of an ESI" (Grady & Drisko, 2014, p. 6). In this regard, Mullen et al. (2008) suggest that EBP and ESIs are complementary inasmuch as the search process associated with EBP should locate ESIs when such exist (p. 327).

Thyer and Myers (2011) also point out that in contrast to "best practices" and ESIs, EBP guides decision-making. It does not tell practitioners what to do (p. 20). Similarly, Thyer and Pignotti (2011) assert that EBP does not involve lists of treatments. In EBP the practitioner decides what services to provide by appraising the research evidence and integrating this with elements such as client preferences and values, professional expertise, and availability of resources. They observe that these elements are not included in the lists of ESTs (p. 332). They, therefore, feel that it is quite contrary to EBP for the practitioner to decide how to treat a client only on the basis of the scientific evidence. The other elements comprising the EBP model need to be factored in (p. 333). They insist that if a client, therefore, refused an empirically supported intervention, "a practitioner could still remain true to EBP by offering alternative treatments" (pp. 332). It is interesting to observe the consistency of this position with earlier commentary on EBM: "without clinical expertise, practice risks becoming tyrannised by evidence, for even excellent external evidence may be inapplicable to or inappropriate for an individual patient" (Sackett, Rosenberg, Muir Gray, Haynes, & Richardson, 1996, p. 72).

## EBP: An Approach which Favours Specific Evidence Hierarchies?

Gray, Plath, and Webb (2009) point out that advocates of EBP argue that the most reliable grounds on which to base practice are those which derive from empirical or scientific research. They complain that the hierarchical approach to evidence and emphasis on a "gold standard" of evidence entails "a definition of evidence that is too narrow and a research methodology that does not match with the realities of the real world and human behaviour" (p. 48). Loughlin (2006) also thinks the epistemic hierarchy has effectively declared some sources of knowledge as "illegitimate or at least inferior," and he claims further that there is an "absence of any sound arguments explaining why we should regard some sources of knowledge as inherently superior to others" (p. 289). This criticism is echoed by others. Epstein (2009) insists that the "hierarchies of evidence" are relied upon "unquestionably" (p. 221). Bouffard and Reid (2012) also assert that "the rationale behind them is never presented in detail" (p. 7). Upshur and Tracy (2004) describe the rationale as an "an unargued epistemological stance" (p. 200).

More specifically, the complaint relates to an apparent prominence being given quantitative methods of evaluation, such as randomised controlled trials, at the expense of qualitative methods that provide more specific information about service-users' values, preferences, and needs. This is one of the key objections raised against evidence-based practice. What constitutes evidence for practice in an evidence-based framework?

There is no doubt that EBP prefers certain methodologies. Indeed, hierarchies of evidence have been established in which study designs are ranked according to their susceptibility to bias and capacity to accurately predict intervention efficacy. Every methodology has it biases and limitations. EBP has simply sought to reduce bias where possible by selecting the appropriate methodology (Batista, 2010, p. 50). In fact, there is "widespread agreement" regarding the best methods to minimise bias and threats to validity (Mullen et al., 2005, p. 71).

Randomised controlled trials (RCTs), a topic to which we will return in greater detail, may be preferred when dealing with effectiveness and prevention questions but other research methods are required contingent on the research question (Gibbs & Gambrill, 2002, p. 464). Interestingly, although Otto et al. (2009) have observed that there are EBP proponents who believe that only experimental designs can really provide validly informative answers on effectiveness (p. 12), and Trinder (2000a) has suggested that in practice EBP often only seems to count RCTs and meta-analysis (p. 237), he does agree that EBP "*theoretically* [emphasis added] supports the matching of research designs to questions" (pp. 236-237).

Thyer (2010) brings clarity to this issue by explaining that "best evidence" does not entail "so-called gold-standard studies such as randomized controlled trials or meta-analyses...but simply the best available relevant evidence" (p. 7). He advises that "if there are no studies of superlative quality, then you locate and assess those of lesser quality....There is *always* evidence for a social worker to consult, even if it is not evidence of the highest quality" (p. 7). Gambrill (2006) also suggests that if there are no RCTs available "then we may consult a hierarchy of evidence and move down the list" (p. 348). She observes that this will be necessary in social work because most of the practices and policies it draws on have not been critically tested (p. 348). After observing that EBP does, indeed, give "greater weight" to systematic reviews and RCTs because they offer greater internal validity, Webber (2014) states that "all forms of evidence" will need to be considered when these are unavailable (p. 173).

Acknowledging the primacy of RCTs in the EBP research hierarchy for learning about the effectiveness of particular interventions, Rubin and Parrish (2012) also affirm that qualitative studies could well appear at the top of the hierarchy when looking at subjective experiences of treatment or to generate hypotheses (p. 216). Elsewhere, Rubin (2011) suggests that qualitative studies rather than experiments would be used, for instance, in determining why homeless clients do not use a particular shelter or why clients prematurely cease treatment (p. 76). He states that although EBP may involve trying to find the best evidence, the fact is that "interventions with less than the best evidence might be a better choice in light of client characteristics, practitioner skills, and feasibility issues" (p. 71).

Since there is clearly a role for qualitative studies, it is no surprise that Thyer (2012) suggests that in the history of social work the idea that quantitative research has been "epistemologically privileged" and qualitative methods "inherently deficient" is a "myth" (p. 115). He suggests that "qualitative methods can provide social workers with rich insights into the lives of clients and other participants in social work research," and "quantitative research is not particularly well-suited to create hypotheses or to develop theories" (p. 120). He concludes that "qualitative research has always formed an important element of mainstream scientific methodology and this approach has had a dominant influence in social work's disciplinary literature" (p. 123).

Indeed, evidence in EBP can be broadened to include not only evidence obtained from research studies but also evidence derived from social work practitioners in practice with clients. In this context, Gellis and Reid (2004) refer to the "scientifically oriented practitioner" who employs single-subject methods to test and guide interventions. They consider that integration of the two kinds of evidence (from research and from practice) strengthens the scientific base for practice (pp. 157-158).

If client preferences and values are to be assigned a key role, as they are in EBP, then client notions of evidence will also need to be factored in. The cultural belief systems of the client must be taken seriously and attempts made to incorporate these in order to engage the client. A failure to do so may compromise success (Zayas, Drake, & Jonson-Reid, 2011, p. 404).

Granted that there are differing cultural definitions of evidence, that what constitutes evidence in one culture may not do so in another, it becomes clear that the ability to interpret soft data (qualitative evidence from non-scientific sources) becomes a valuable part of the social worker's skill set.

Murdach (2010) examines the main sources of soft data encountered in social work practice, which are taken from the verbal and behavioural responses of clients and collaterals and which she indicates are derived from interviews, formal and informal observation, clinical documents and reports, official sources, and facts drawn from the case itself (p. 309). She identifies five principal types of soft evidence: Accounts (clients' "stories"), Explanations (statements clarifying what problem or condition exists), Interpretations ("efforts to make sense of events"), Arguments (client's justifications for decisions or plans), and Nonverbal Communication ("'situational' or 'environmental' evidence," e.g., dress and body language) (pp. 310-311).

Evidence of this kind boosts the practitioner's craft and gives added insight to Thyer's (2010) observation that "augmenting practice wisdom, insight, and art *with* the findings of science would merely seem to be the hallmark of professional practice, not a threat to these traditional sources of guidance" (p. 15).

The role of societal and environmental factors in shaping clients' experiences and in requiring careful negotiation between practitioner and client has been highlighted by Simmons (2012). She points out that in EBP experimental evidence may be privileged over the PiE (Person in Environment) model which acknowledges such factors in assessment and intervention (pp. 13-14). She offers three clinical vignettes from her practice that depict situations which, in her judgement, required deviation from standard EBP interventions for the presenting diagnosis (pp. 9-13). Such tailoring to fit the demands of the practice situation is, in principle, readily accommodated within the EBP process. If prominence is given to the client voice, and the practitioner utilises their judgement and experience in assessment, and if the intervention is researched and negotiated only in the light of such contexts, then there is room to accommodate a PiE model. As Simmons (2011) elsewhere says, "thorough assessment that accounts for the client's biopsychosocial-spiritual functioning and needs is a necessary first step in the process of EBP" (p. 265).

In essence, then, there is a clear hierarchy of evidence with regard to questions of effectiveness. When good evidence exists, practitioners will need to use their professional judgement in determining its applicatory value in the given context; where it is lacking practitioners will be obliged to use that same judgement. Where questions other than effectiveness are being addressed, there are an array of methodologies that are fit for purpose. And where client preferences, values, and interpretations of the evidence are not congruent with practitioner understanding or knowledge of the evidence, the practitioner will need to critically and creatively negotiate solutions in collaborative discussion with the client.

Batista (2010) explains that EBP provides a method for comparing competing interventions and the means to make informed decisions. Over time, new interventions and evaluative methods will emerge and supplant existing best practices (pp. 52-53). He says confidently, "EBP is not perfect, but when used correctly, it has tremendous potential to provide clients with information, options, and programs that work" (p. 53).

Barber (2012) believes that the quantitative-qualitative "polemic" often appears to possess "a moral overtone, as if some methods were somehow liberal, empowering, and good while others were conservative, oppressive, and bad" (p. 193). He suggests that this is but a "tiresome

and unnecessary debate" for rather the most appropriate methodological approach should be entirely contingent on the research question being asked (p. 193). Trinder (2000b) also urges that "polarised debates about methodology" be abandoned. Evidence ranging from meta-analysis and RCTs to qualitative studies are required (p. 157). Plath (2006) refers to "a general agreement in the literature that appropriate methods must be chosen for the social work research questions being asked" (p. 63). Thyer (2012) puts it succinctly: "a researcher's methodological tools should be selected to fit the task at hand" (p. 123). With this it is impossible to logically disagree.

## EBP: An Approach which Favours Randomised Controlled Trials?

As indicated above, the status assigned RCTs within evidence-based practice and their utility when applied to social work is strongly contested. The fact is, however, that RCTs, and especially systematic reviews of randomised trials, are considered the "gold standard" not without reason. Random allocation and the use of control groups are geared to establish greater transparency and reliability of results (Batista, 2010, pp. 48-49). Interestingly, Hutchison and Rogers (2012), whilst raising a number of cautions regarding RCTs, still acknowledge that RCT methodology "more reliably eliminates bias, and is more likely to establish a causal connection between two variables" (p. 988).

Nevertheless, although RCTs are, in principle, ideal when applied to questions concerning causality and effectiveness, there are clear limitations to their use in social work practice (Adams et al., 2009, p. 171; Batista, 2010, p. 49; Gray et al., 2009, p. 32; Otto et al., 2009, pp. 12-13; Trinder, 2000a, pp. 229-231; 2000b, pp. 150-154). The fact that it would clearly be unethical for participants in a trial to be exposed to an intervention suspected of being harmful has been seen as a feature limiting the usefulness of RCTs (Morago, 2006, p. 467).

And more generally, the value of RCTs has been challenged with the detection of common types of bias believed to inflate RCT results (Gellis & Reid, 2004, pp. 158-159).

Some exponents of EBP do appear to have recognised the strength of these concerns. Mullen (2006), for instance, feels that the "highly controlled, artificial contexts" in which RCTs are usually conducted fail to provide clear insight into the effectiveness of interventions in "real-world contexts" (p. 87). Rubin and Parrish (2007) agree that RCTs can have limited external validity and that there is a scarcity of RCTs in many social work practice areas (pp. 412, 414). Although Rubin and Parrish do believe that RCTs are "evolving" to make them more meaningful for minority populations, they do concede there is a long way to go before social work practitioners can feel assured about generalising the findings of RCTs to clients (p. 412). Morago (2006), therefore, points to a number of authors who, whilst upholding the importance of RCTs, consider that other research designs may be better when dealing with disadvantaged or vulnerable individuals (pp. 471-472). A single experiment might be of greater value than RCTs if it involved adequate sampling and factored in "culturally sensitive procedures" lacking in an RCT (Fraser, 2003, p. 27).

Ironically, although EBP has been negatively critiqued for placing RCTs near the top of the research hierarchy, the EBP process itself provides an in-built compensatory mechanism. Since RCTs can only yield probabilistic findings, since they typically exclude clients with co-morbidity, and granted that practitioners may have to modify empirically-supported interventions in light of unique client concerns and interests, the evaluative step in the EBP process takes on particular importance. If the results of RCTs are employed in a particular case, they are not blindly applied if the practitioner is truly engaged in EBP and RCTs may, indeed, give way to other methods. Methods need to be fit for purpose.

Interestingly, Aisenberg (2008) takes the view that a more narrow rendering of EBP which prioritises evidence derived from RCTs was not the original intent of EBP (pp. 297-298), and Morago (2006) adds that the emphasis on RCTs has itself since shifted towards greater recognition of broader concepts of evidence and research designs contingent on the purpose of enquiry (p. 473). Mullen and Streiner (2004) summarise the situation by affirming that the earlier ideas "that practice *must* be based on the conclusions of RCTs and only RCTs have been softened in the face of reality to the use of the best *available* evidence" (p. 119).

## EBP: An Approach which Disadvantages Minority Groups?

Exclusion of ethnic minority populations from RCTs, or at best small sample sizes of these groups in such trials, raises concerns about generalisability and applying such studies to ethnic populations. This is a particular concern given the commitment to marginalised and ethnically diverse minorities characterised by social work (Aisenberg, 2008, pp. 299-300; Berger, 2010, pp. 181-182).

Critics assert that EBP privileges scientific knowledge over cultural ways of knowing. Employing EBP without incorporating indigenous ways of knowing may rob ethnic minority communities of treatments which promote their resilience and well-being (Aisenberg, 2008, p. 301). In addition, research-generated evidence characterised by homogeneous subjects may lack clear application amongst diverse patient populations often possessing co-morbid conditions (Aisenberg, 2008, p. 301).

Clearly, cultural differences should not be disregarded when generalising the results of an RCT. The intervention might need to be modified to render it culturally competent. But there will be instances where qualitative methods will be placed at the top of the research hierarchy when gauging subjective experiences. Ethnographic methods, for instance, might be more useful than RCTs in influencing policy changes regarding inhumane living conditions (Rubin & Parrish, 2012, p. 216). Rubin (2011) says it is "critical" that empirically supported treatments not be applied "mechanistically or blindly" to disadvantaged clients. Interventions with less empirical support should be chosen if they better fit the client's circumstances or attributes (p. 77).

Although referring to this issue of exclusion as a "prominent" weakness of EBP, Aisenberg (2008) does not think it is insurmountable (p. 302). For him "the original perspective of evidence-based medicine (EBM)...can serve as a crucial example for social work" (p. 303). He suggests that its "original vision and philosophy" would resolve issues which might otherwise emerge from over-reliance on empirical studies (pp. 303-304). He notes that an "inclusive approach" would enable providers "to integrate the best science available" with professional expertise, client culture, and preferences (p. 304).

## EBP: An Approach which by Using Practice Guidelines Threatens Professional Autonomy and Ignores the Individual Client?

Rosen and Proctor (2003) define practice guidelines as "a set of systematically complied and organized statements of empirically tested knowledge and procedures to help practitioners select and implement interventions that are most effective and appropriate for attaining the desired outcomes" (p. 1). The guidelines may be based on research evidence but in the absence of such evidence, they are based on professional consensus (Mullen & Bacon, 2003, p. 226; Mullen, Bledsoe, & Bellamy, 2008, pp. 327-328). Since practitioners usually do not have access to the vast amount of information available, practice guidelines become very useful in EBP (Fraser, 2003, pp. 19).

The guidelines are valued in EBP because they are designed to ensure that practitioners conform to desirable and consistent standards, promote effectiveness of practice, and assure clients that professional standards are being met (Rosen & Proctor, 2003, p. 1). Guidelines also contribute to "rapprochement" between researchers and practitioners (Howard & Jenson, 1999, p. 297). They are further valued because when applicable to all they have the potential to reduce service disparities by standardising treatments provided to underserved, ethnic, or racial groups. Those guidelines that are culturally specific, on the other hand, should improve services for targeted groups (Peebles-Wilkins & Amodeo, 2003, pp. 209-210).

Those cautious of the evidence-based practice movement, however, believe that evidence-based guidelines cannot adequately deal with the complex and unique situations in which social work practice engages (Nothdurfter & Lorenz, 2010, para. 1). Witkin and Harrison (2001) argue that human beings are characterised by complexity and fluidity, thus rendering pre-formulated interventions difficult (p. 294).

Practice guidelines can, indeed, be used to prescriptively dictate which intervention to use, to override professional judgment, and to ignore the uniqueness and unpredictability of the client or situation (Shlonsky, Noonan, Littell, & Montgomery, 2011, p. 363). This is why Epstein (2009) suggests that "practice guidelines are often perceived by practitioners as a threat to their professional autonomy and individual creativity" (p. 222).

Some proponents of EBP have also shown hesitation over the use of reviews and guidelines. Rubin and Parrish (2007) take the view that reliance upon such tools suggests a dependence on authority and fails to pay sufficient attention to the particularity of client needs (p. 411). Gambrill (2006) has also expressed concern, contrasting "the broad philosophy and evolving process of EBP, envisioned by its originators" with "narrow views of EBP such as use of empirically based guidelines and treatment manuals" (p. 338). She feels that the use of such tools does not fully regard the role of professional expertise. She asserts that decision-making regarding clients is "much more complex" than selecting and using guidelines and requires other considerations, such as attention to individual client circumstances and characteristics, in addition to research findings. She notes that guidelines are often inadequate since existing research may not apply to a particular client (p. 341, 344).

In fact, Bergmark, Bergmark, and Lundstrom (2012) perceive the use of guidelines as one of the "major disagreements" regarding how EBP in social work is to be accomplished. They refer to the "contradiction" between what they label the "Sackett position," which its advocates think is "a way of empowering social workers and clients by bringing social work closer to research," and the "guidelines model," in which "guidelines and interventions are presented to social workers who 'merely' do the work" (p. 599).

The fact is, however, that the specific example cited by Bergmark et al. (2012, p. 599) in support of the guidelines model (Rosen) does acknowledge that the "proper use of practice guidelines requires and encourages the practitioner to adopt an active, critical, and innovative stance" (Rosen & Proctor, 2003, p. 8). Rosen and Proctor (2003) do recognise that human behaviour is "complex and multi-determined," and that "interventions cannot be viewed as or expected to be uniformly applicable or universally effective" (p. 3). They readily acknowledge that although guidelines alert the practitioner to the decisions that need to be made and provide the information to support such decisions, practitioners are still faced with the issue of client particularity. The use of guidelines, they explain, requires "creativity and innovation, and the exercise of professional judgment and practice wisdom" (p. 7). In addition, they proffer that because empirical evidence is often unavailable, practitioners are obliged to "critically exercise considerable choice and creativity in combining knowledge from theory, research, and personally acquired practice wisdom to address client needs properly" (p. 7).

Writing within an EBP context, Mullen and Bacon (2003) state that no guideline can anticipate all the variables operating in a complex clinical situation. "Moving from practice guidelines to individual case situations will always require professional judgement and skill, drawing from accumulated clinical experience" (p. 229). They further advise that because guidelines are not always consistent, practitioners will be required to exercise judgement (p. 229). Howard and Jensen also do not feel that guidelines displace professional judgement. They assert that practice guidelines "increase practice effectiveness in a manner that does not impose additional burdens on practitioners" and can provide direction "without unduly limiting their professional autonomy." They add that "guidelines do allow for justifiable deviations from accepted practice" (p. 296).

Clearly, then, there is a place for guidelines in EBP. Although indicating that the inappropriate use of guidelines identifies a narrow conception of EBP, Gambrill (2006) does acknowledge a role for them by admitting that "practice guidelines are but one component of EBP" (p. 341) Neither professional expertise nor the particularities of client needs are compromised by the judicious use of guidelines.

## EBP: An Approach which is Founded on an Outmoded Positivism?

A frequently recurring complaint with EBP is that it is entrenched in a positivist-empirical paradigm which can only deal with social phenomena that are observable and measurable (Alvesson & Sköldberg, 2009, p. 17; Gray & Mcdonald, 2006, p. 14; Nothdurfter & Lorenz, 2010, para. 3). Positivism assumes an objective view of the world, "an objective reality governed by laws and mechanisms that can be identified" (Morris, 2006, p. xviii).

The fact is that positivism has been the dominant view in the philosophy of both natural and social sciences (Alvesson & Sköldberg, 2009, p. 15; Thyer, 2010, p. 11). Social work itself has from the beginning possessed a positivist orientation (Thyer, 2008, p. 341; 2010, pp. 11-12; Thyer & Myers, 2011, pp. 12-13). Indeed, it is a paradigm which underlies most of the books on research methodology in social work (Morris, 2006, p. xvii). Gray and MacDonald (2006) have suggested that the adoption of positivism gave "academic respectability" to social work within educational institutions in the past (p. 14).

That was, however, in the past and new paradigms such as postmodernism, social constructivism, and critical realism have emerged in recent decades to challenge the traditional positivist paradigm. Fook (2004), for instance, explains that postmodernism has challenged the idea that professional and specialist knowledge "is necessarily 'objective' and unchangeable" in light of the "*interpretive*" and "*reflective*" nature of knowledge (p. 33). Seeing that concepts such as culture, spirituality, and relationship are now widely viewed as part of the evidentiary equation, although they are not easily measured, Witkin and Iversen (2012) have suggested a more social constructionist orientation (pp. 232-233, 244). Positivism, therefore, sustains criticism because it is felt that any claim to objective truth and reason excludes other voices and marginalises the vulnerable by scripting them out of the story. It fails to recognise and value interpretations and subjective experiences. This is thought to undermine social work's principle of respecting diverse individual and cultural experiences.

Further criticism has been levelled at positivism because of its suspected sidelining of qualitative studies. Epstein (2009) thinks the hierarchies of evidence privileges positivism (p. 221). In the opinion of Morris (2006), qualitative data is not appropriate within a positivist paradigm (pp. xx, 12). This opinion is strong enough for Alvesson

and Skolberg (2009) to submit that a recognition of the value of qualitative studies has been tied to a rejection of positivism (p. 49).

It would appear, however, that many of the criticisms leveled at positivism and its alleged off-spring, EBP, are robbed of their force. This is because EBP proponents grant the validity of many of the points made but insist that they do not apply because it is not what they are suggesting.

EBP proponents Rubin and Parrish (2012) freely acknowledge that "pure scientific objectivity is impossible to attain, that we all are influenced by our prior experiences and biases no matter how hard we try to use impeccable scientific methods and designs" (p. 207). They further concede that "there is no escaping the fact that we all have our own unique internal subjective realities that interfere with our ability to know an external objective social reality" (p. 207). They explain that "contemporary positivism" recognises that a social worker can be influenced by their own biases, predilections, and experiences (p. 208).

Although labelled a "positive purist" (Gray et al., 2009, p. 170), Thyer (2008) readily states that positivism "does not imply, as is commonly construed, the development of definitive, complete, or absolutely certain answers to questions" (p. 340). Accurately distinguishing positivism from the long discredited logical positivism, Thyer (2010) says that "positivism does not mean that scientific research is the *only* way in which to discover useful knowledge" (p. 12). Thyer (2012) also suggests that "positivism's contention that there is an objective external reality need not conflict with the position that much of the world of human beings is a social construction" (p. 118).

"Certainty in science," Thyer (2010) further tells us, "is relative, provisional, and fallible, with any given findings always susceptible to being overturned by new and better data" (p. 13). Discussing the human predisposition to see what we want to see and to sometimes miss the obvious, Sheldon (2001) says "we need to take extraordinary observational, cognitive, and behavioural precautions" against such tendencies. He concludes, "this is all that science is: epistemological paranoia in a good cause. We cannot, through its procedures ever be *sure,* but we can be *surer for now*" (p. 806). Indeed, the concept of "best available evidence" itself suggests that evidence is provisional.

Gambrill (2006) has argued that "contrary to the claim that EBP seeks for and assumes that certainty about knowledge is possible," EBP, instead, recognises that there is an element of uncertainty and bias in decision-making and "attempts to give helpers and clients the knowledge and skills to handle this honestly and constructively" (p. 345). More recently, in response to the criticism that EBP embraces the idea that social work interventions need to be squarely based "on proven knowledge" of effectiveness founded on empirical research (Otto et al., 2009, p. 9), Gambrill (2011) points out that the term "proven" suggests that proponents of EBP assume certainty is possible, a view which she then firmly rejects (p. 39). She agrees that whilst science is designed to give us answers this does not mean that we can have "certain knowledge" (p. 42).

Rubin and Parrish (2012) refer to the "common misperception" that "researchers are either positivistic 'quants' or anti-positivistic 'quals'" (p. 209). They counter that "some of the most highly respected qualitative methodologists actually are contemporary positivists who reject epistemological attacks on the pursuit of objectivity" (p. 209). They then make the point that subjective insights drawn from independent sources will aid the investigator committed to assessing the accurate depiction of subjective experiences. Moreover, triangulation and prolonged engagement help to improve standards of objectivity and accuracy in measuring subjective observations and interpretations (p. 209). In their response, Rubin and Parrish are adopting the kind of post-positivist approach described by Morris (2006). According to Morris,

this takes the view that objective reality exists but can never be fully comprehended. The researcher should, however, "strive for objectivity" by being conscious of personal biases and by "attending to the observations and judgements of key players through peer feedback" (p. 71).

There can be no doubt that all observations are theory-laden (including this one). Assumptions, values, and world views influence both observations and interpretations (Gambrill, 2011, p. 42; Gilgun, 2005, p. 55). This explains why Rubin and Parrish (2012) suggest triangulating across multiple fallible perspectives (p. 209). This should provide a better idea of reality. In other words, the best way for us to discover truth is to do so within the context of a broader community of individuals intent on interaction. Views are held tentatively, subject to further investigation and discovery, as we progress towards greater approximation to the truth. This is explained by Solomon and Draine (2010) who propose that "true objective reality cannot be known" and quantitative researchers do acknowledge that individuals have their own subjective understandings of phenomenon based on personal experiences but that "through the process of conceptualizing the phenomenon, an objective (or, more precisely, an intersubjective) reality can be created" (p. 29). To deny that closer approximation to the truth is attainable through interaction is to remove substantive grounds for dialogue and any meaningful rationale for convincing anyone of another point of view.

It is clear that these proponents of EBP reject the view that EBP is reliant on an epistemology which fails to fully engage with social work practice. Whatever one's view of their attempts to clarify positivism, it would appear that these proponents have responded to a number of epistemological criticisms by recognising the weight of their critics' concerns but without seeing a need to abandon the EBP model.

## REFLECTING ON CRITICAL REFLECTION AND EVIDENCE-BASED PRACTICE

Plath (2006) observes that evidence-based practice ("scientific", "positivist") and critical reflective practice ("interpretive") have been considered "somewhat conflicting approaches" to social work. She thinks that social workers may wonder whether research findings or critical reflection should inform their practice (p. 57). She explains that critical reflective approaches in social work "emphasise the importance of continually analysing the impact of values, relationships, context, past experiences and feelings in seeking to understand individuals and society" (p. 67). She does not believe that this sits well with "rigid theoretical frameworks" in decision-making, but she does see as "simplistic" the perceived divide between evidence-based practice and critical reflective practice. In fact, Plath recognises that within EBP, critical analysis has been deemed "integral" to the use and interpretation of research evidence in practice (p. 67).

Although Plath (2006) thinks that "in abstract theoretical terms the positivist and interpretive paradigms are distinct" (p. 68), this characterization is, as we established earlier, based on a particular view of positivism which is rejected by leading proponents of EBP. What is important, however, is that even given her understanding of EBP and positivism, she does not feel that EBP and critical reflection are alien in daily practice.

Plath (2006) explains that the concept of evidence in critical reflective practice "incorporates research findings as a source of evidence to inform practice decisions in social work, but also includes other forms of evidence" (p. 68). She recognises that "definitive evidence" sometimes exists, but that "interpretive research findings and practice experience" are also significant. She insists that both "rational processes" and "reflective insights" have an important place (p. 68). Smith (2004) also

affirms that, in addition to other evidence, the reflective social worker utilises their own personal experience as an evidence source drawing on past experience and being sensitive to cues about how the client(s) perceives themself (pp. 13-14).

Describing the integration of a critically reflective approach with an evidence-based practice approach, Plath (2006) identifies the skills required: a readiness to creatively consider different approaches, the ability to assess research methodologies, to evaluate multiple sources of evidence, and to determine applicability to the particular practice context (p. 69). Determining applicability requires sensitivity to contextual information. Fook (2004), for instance, has remarked upon the need for "responsive and *responsible* practice – this includes the use of evidence, but it also includes the imperative to match professional practice and knowledge with the situation at hand" (p. 34).

Interestingly, Plath (2006) takes the view that "a critical reflective approach to evidence-based practice in social work....fits more closely with the ethics, values and traditions of social work than does a rule-based or prescriptive approach to evidence-based practice" (p. 70). That some practitioners may practice prescriptively may well be so. This is not, however, a criticism that can be placed at the door of evidence-based practice which at the first does not seem to have countenanced that approach. Indeed, EBP proponents insist that those who engage in this way are not practicing EBP (Mullen et al., 2005, p. 69). Still, the virtue of Plath's point is that she clearly articulates the need for a critical reflective element in practice.

Plath (2006) refers to the "challenge" of integrating evidence-based practice and critical reflective practice (p. 70), but it is not clear that there is anything in EBP as originally conceived that, in principle, renders critical reflection difficult to accommodate. Pack (2013) is also convinced that a "synthesis" between the two is possible (p.

65). Gilgun (2005) states with some assurance that "EBP promotes a high degree of practitioner reflection and mindfulness" (p. 59).

## IT'S ALL IN A WORD: EVIDENCE-BASED PRACTICE VS. EVIDENCE-INFORMED PRACTICE

Although Adams et al. (2009) refer to "EBP, or the sometimes preferred term, *evidence-informed practice*" (p. 166), thereby implying they are essentially the same, Nevo and Nevo-Slonim (2011) do not believe this to be the case. To these authors, the terms "based" and "informed" are not interchangeable terms. They have different nuances suggesting different relationships between evidence and practice (p. 1179).

Recognising that EBP proponents do not consider empirical evidence to be the only element in the EBP model, Nevo and Nevo-Slonim (2011) ask how the term "based" in the phrase "evidence-*based* practice" should, in fact, be understood? (p. 1179). They point out that if practice is adapted to client preferences and practice experience, if evidence does not have any priority over the experience and values of the practitioner and client, then practice cannot be understood to be *based* on empirical evidence (pp. 1185).

Given that in EBP practitioners factor in client values when applying empirical findings to practice, Nevo and Nevo Slonim-Nevo (2011) ask what role such values have? What if the client refuses a recommended intervention? Should the practitioner attempt to convince the client or should they suggest an alternative intervention which possesses less evidentiary support? Is the term "evidence-based" in such circumstances justified? They point out that the practitioner should give precedence to the client's preferences and values, and the evidence will be simply "one factor" to consider (p. 1184). Although the originators of EBP would be unmoved by such examples, for they did hold that evidence is only one factor,

Nevo and Nevo-Slonim are correct to say that "evidence-informed" more clearly reflects the dynamics in such cases.

Observing that EBP requires practitioners who are competent in evaluating current research, Nevo and Slonin-Nevo (2011) suspect that practitioners will rely on the credentials of the researchers or upon the practices they are most comfortable with and not upon the merits of the evidence (p. 1189). This may well be the case, but that is not a criticism of the model itself but upon a failure to practice it.

Nevo and Nevo-Slonim (2011) do, however, make a very telling point. Even if the practitioner does find the "best" evidence, that is, an intervention which shows the highest success rate in *relevant* cases, the practitioner's judgment and clinical expertise is required to assess the relevance of that evidence and its similarity to the *specific* case. If the practitioner cannot simply apply but is obliged to adapt the evidence to the circumstances, then once again the term "evidence-based" is conceptually misleading (pp. 1191-1192). Otto et al. (2009) have also observed that evidence is not necessarily sufficient for decision-making. They, too, recognise the importance of professional expertise and experience in applying evidence to clients (p. 14).

In short, given that proponents of EBP do require practitioners to use their clinical skills and judgment in appraising the appropriate evidence, that evidence is just one factor in establishing practice and does not alone provide adequate basis for practice nor a fixed protocol for action, then it would appear that the phrase "evidence informed practice" more clearly characterises the role that evidence plays in the equation.

It seems reasonable, then, for Epstein (2009) to acknowledge that "informed" is a "more nuanced term…because it implies that practice knowledge and intervention decisions might be *enriched* by prior research but not *limited* to it" (p. 224). He explains that "in this way, EIP is more inclusive than EBP" (p. 224). Shlonsky et al. (2011) are also convinced that "evidence-informed better conveys that decisions are guided or informed by evidence rather than based solely upon it, and that clients themselves are informed consumers of services" (p. 363).

Although Nevo and Nevo-Slonim (2011) and Epstein (2009) convincingly establish that the terms "evidence-based" and "evidence-informed" do have different nuances, in terms of the model itself, EBP need not be understood to differ from EIP. Shlonsky et al. (2011) say simply, "EIP is not a practice model that differs from EBP. Rather, EIP can be seen as a more fitting name for the same process" (p. 363). Interestingly, Sackett et al. (1996) long ago noted that "external clinical evidence can inform, but can never replace, individual clinical expertise" (p. 72).

It is certainly preferable to employ the language of "evidence-informed" since it is unambiguous in rendering the original intent of EBP (that is, placing the client at the centre and recognising that evidence can inform but never replace individual professional expertise) rather than "based" which is misleading. It is notable that Gambrill (2008, 2010, 2013), who is a strong defender of evidence-based practice, has herself used the term interchangeably with "evidence-informed practice."

## CONCLUSION

Although there is dispute regarding the role that empirical evidence should properly have in effective social work practice, social workers do recognise the importance of evidentiary support. Even when, for either epistemological or pragmatic reasons, social workers do not perceive the need for empirical research they do draw on other sources of evidence. In order to make effective practice decisions, however, the practitioner is required to consider *all* sources of evidence including empirical research evidence and is required to examine and modify both personal and professional assumptions and actions in light of the research evidence and client responses. And although empirical research may hold an important place, recognising cultural (and therefore disparate) definitions of evidence is a part of valuing the client's needs and perspectives.

In daily practice, then, the social worker should integrate contributions from multiple sources of evidence including from professional expertise and judgement (their own and that of colleagues), client's cultural preferences, personal values, the context of intervention, *and* empirical research. The phrase "evidence-informed" seems to more clearly articulate the relationship between these elements.

Evidence must be used in a critically reflective way if it is to be used effectively. Evidence-informed practice or a critical reflection approach to EBP in social work seeks to value evidence gained from experience and other contextual factors as well as research evidence. Where specific research is lacking, the effective social worker will be required to draw on theory with a research basis and knowledge derived from practice experience.

In short, the practitioner is required to use the "best available" evidence. For practice to be maximally effective in the client-centred world of social work, evidence is crucial, but more will be required than what is available in the empirical research evidence – certainly nothing less, *if* that evidence is available, but more.

## REFERENCES

Adams, K. B., Matto, H. C., & LeCroy, C. W. (2009). Limitations of evidence-based practice for social work education: Unpacking the complexity. *Journal of Social Work Education, 45*(2), 165–186. doi:10.5175/JSWE.2009.200700105

Aisenberg, E. (2008). Evidence-based practice in mental health care to ethnic minority communities: Has its practice fallen short of its evidence? *Social Work, 53*(4), 297–306. doi:10.1093/sw/53.4.297 PMID:18853666

Alvesson, M., & Sköldberg, K. (2009). *Reflexive methodology: New vistas for qualitative research* (2nd ed.). London: SAGE.

Arnd-Caddigan, M., & Pozzuto, R. (2010). Evidence-based practice and the purpose of clinical social work. *Smith College Studies in Social Work, 80*(1), 35–52. doi:10.1080/00377310903504965

Avby, G., Nilsen, P., & Dahlgren, M. A. (2013). Ways of understanding evidence-based practice in social work: A qualitative study. *British Journal of Social Work*, 1–18. doi:10.1093/bjsw/bcs198

Bantry White, E. (2010). Review: H. U. Otto, A. Polutta, and H. Zieglar (eds): Evidence-based practice: Modernising the knowledge base of social work? Voluntas, 21(1), 132-134. doi:10.1007/s11266-009-9114-z

Barber, J. G. (2012). Putting evidence-based practice into practice. In C. N. Dulmus & K. M. Sowers (Eds.), *The profession of social work: Guided by history, led by evidence* (pp. 191–202). Hoboken, NJ: John Wiley.

Batista, T. (2010). A case for evidence based practice. *Columbia Social Work Review, 1*, 45–53.

Beddoe, L. (2011). Investing in the future: Social workers talk about research. *British Journal of Social Work, 41*(3), 557–575. doi:10.1093/bjsw/bcq138

Bellamy, J. L., Bledsoe, S. E., & Mullen, E. J. (2009). The cycle of evidence-based practice. In H.-U. Otto, A. Polutta, & H. Ziegler (Eds.), *Evidence-based practice: Modernising the knowledge base of social work?* (pp. 21–29). Opladen, Germany: Barbara Budrich.

Berger, R. (2010). EBP: Practitioners in search of evidence. *Journal of Social Work, 10*(2), 175–191. doi:10.1177/1468017310363640

Bergmark, A., Bergmark, Å., & Lundstrom, T. (2012). The mismatch between the map and the terrain: Evidence-based social work in Sweden. *European Journal of Social Work, 15*(4), 598–609. doi:10.1080/13691457.2012.706215

Bouffard, M., & Reid, G. (2012). The good, the bad, and the ugly of evidence-based practice. *Adapted Physical Activity Quarterly, 29*, 1-24. Retrieved from http://journals.humankinetics.com/apaq

Broadhurst, K., Wastell, D., White, S., Hall, C., Peckover, S., & Thompson, K. et al. (2010). Performing "initial assessment": Identifying the latent conditons for error at the front-door of local authority children's services. *British Journal of Social Work, 40*(2), 352–370. doi:10.1093/bjsw/bcn162

Catalano, R. F., Hill, K. G., Haggerty, K. P., Fleming, C. B., & Hawkins, J. D. (2010). Social development interventions have extensive, long-lasting effects. In A. E. Fortune, P. McCallion, & K. Briar-Lawson (Eds.), *Social work practice research for the twenty-first century* (pp. 72–80). New York: Columbia University Press.

Chalmers, I. (2005). If evidence-informed policy works in practice, does it matter if it doesn't work in theory? *Evidence & Policy: A Journal of Research, Debate and Practice, 1*(2), 227–242. doi:10.1332/1744264053730806

Combs-Orme, T. (1988). Infant mortality and social work: Legacy of success. *The Social Service Review, 62*(1), 83–102. doi:10.1086/603662

Crawford, K. (2011a). Conclusion: Why is it necessary to consider the evidence and knowledge that underpins practice? In I. Mathews & K. Crawford (Eds.), *Evidence-based practice in social work* (pp. 115–130). Exeter, UK: Learning Matters.

Crawford, K. (2011b). What underpins social work practice? In I. Mathews & K. Crawford (Eds.), *Evidence-based practice in social work* (pp. 3–21). Exeter, UK: Learning Matters.

Crisp, B. R., Anderson, M. R., Orme, J., & Lister, P. G. (2003). *Knowledge review 1: Learning and teaching in social work education: Assessment.* Retrieved from Social Care Institute for Excellence website: http://www.scie.org.uk/publications/knowledgereviews/kr01.pdf

Crisp, B. R., Anderson, M. R., Orme, J., & Lister, P. G. (2005). *Knowledge review 9: Learning and teaching in social work education: Textbooks and frameworks on assessment.* Retrieved from Social Care Institute for Excellence website: http://www.scie.org.uk/publications/knowledgereviews/kr09.asp

D'Cruz, H., & Jones, M. (2014). *Social work research in practice: Ethical and political contexts* (2nd ed.). London: SAGE.

Drisko, J. (2014). Research evidence and social work practice: The place of evidence-based practice. *Clinical Social Work Journal, 42*(2), 123–133. doi:10.1007/s10615-013-0459-9

Drisko, J. W., & Grady, M. D. (2012). *Evidence-based practice in clinical social work.* New York: Springer. doi:10.1007/978-1-4614-3470-2

Edmond, T., Megivern, D., Williams, C., Rochman, E., & Howard, M. (2006). Integrating evidence based practice and social work field education. *Journal of Social Work Education, 42*(2), 377–396. doi:10.5175/JSWE.2006.200404115

Epstein, I. (2009). Promoting harmony where there is commonly conflict: Evidence-informed practice as an integrative strategy. *Social Work in Health Care, 48*(3), 216–231. doi:10.1080/00981380802589845 PMID:19360527

Fook, J. (2004). What professionals need from research: Beyond evidence-based practice. In D. Smith (Ed.), *Social work and evidence-based practice* (pp. 29–46). London: Jessica Kingsley.

Fortune, A. E. (2010). Empirical practice in social work. In A. E. Fortune, P. McCallion, & K. Briar-Lawson (Eds.), *Social work practice research for the twenty-first century* (pp. 23-30). New York: Columbia University Press.

Fortune, A. E., McCallion, P., & Briar-Lawson, K. (2010). Building evidence-based intervention models. In A. E. Fortune, P. McCallion, & K. Briar-Lawson (Eds.), *Social work practice research for the twenty-first century* (pp. 279–295). New York: Columbia University Press.

Fraser, M. W. (2003). Intervention research in social work: A basis for evidence-based practice and practice guidelines. In A. Rosen & E. K. Proctor (Eds.), *Developing practice guidelines for social work intervention: Issues, methods, and research agenda* (pp. 17–36). New York: Columbia University Press.

Gambrill, E. (2003). Evidence-based practice: Implications for knowledge development and use in social work. In A. Rosen & E. K. Proctor (Eds.), *Developing practice guidelines for social work intervention: Issues, methods, and research agenda* (pp. 37–58). New York: Columbia University Press.

Gambrill, E. (2006). Evidence-based practice and policy: Choices ahead. *Research on Social Work Practice, 16*(3), 338–357. doi:10.1177/1049731505284205

Gambrill, E. (2008). Evidence-based (informed) macro practice: Process and philosophy. *Journal of Evidence-Based Social Work, 5*(3-4), 423–452. doi:10.1080/15433710802083971 PMID:19042875

Gambrill, E. (2010). Evidence-informed practice: Antidote to propaganda in the helping professions? *Research on Social Work Practice, 20*(3), 302–320. doi:10.1177/1049731509347879

Gambrill, E. (2011). Evidence-based practice and the ethics of discretion. *Journal of Social Work, 11*(1), 26–48. doi:10.1177/1468017310381306

Gambrill, E. (2013). Evidence-informed practice. In B. A. Thyer, C. N. Dulmus, & K. M. Sowers (Eds.), *Developing evidence-based generalist practice skills* (pp. 1–24). Hoboken, NJ: John Wiley.

Gellis, Z., & Reid, W. J. (2004). Strengthening evidence-based practice. *Brief Treatment and Crisis Intervention, 4*(2), 155–165. doi:10.1093/brief-treatment/mhh012

Gibbons, J. (2001). Effective practice: Social work's long history of concern about outcomes. *Australian Social Work, 54*(3), 3–13. doi:10.1080/03124070108414328

Gibbs, L. E. (2003). *Evidence-based practice for the helping professions: A practical guide with integrated multimedia.* Pacific Grove, CA: Brooks/Cole-Thomson Learning.

Gibbs, L., & Gambrill, E. (2002). Evidence-based practice: Counterarguments to objections. *Research on Social Work Practice, 12*(3), 452–476. doi:10.1177/1049731502012003007

Gilgun, J. F. (2005). The four cornerstones of evidence-based practice in social work. *Research on Social Work Practice, 15*(1), 52–61. doi:10.1177/1049731504269581

Grady, M. D. (2010). The missing link: The role of social work schools and evidence-based practice. *Journal of Evidence-Based Social Work, 7*(5), 400–411. doi:10.1080/15433711003591101 PMID:21082470

Grady, M., & Drisko, J. W. (2014). Thorough clinical assessment: The hidden foundation of evidence-based practice. *Families in Society, 95*(1), 5–14. doi:10.1606/1044-3894.2014.95.2

Gray, M., Joy, E., Plath, D., & Webb, S. A. (2013). Implementing evidence-based practice: A review of the empirical research literature. *Research on Social Work Practice, 23*(2), 157–166. doi:10.1177/1049731512467072

Gray, M., Joy, E., Plath, D., & Webb, S. A. (2014). Opinions about evidence: A study of social workers' attitudes towards evidence-based practice. *Journal of Social Work, 14*(1), 23–40. doi:10.1177/1468017313475555

Gray, M., & Mcdonald, C. (2006). Pursuing good practice?: The limits of evidence-based practice. *Journal of Social Work, 6*(1), 7–20. doi:10.1177/1468017306062209

Gray, M., Plath, D., & Webb, S. A. (2009). *Evidence-based social work: A critical stance.* New York, NY: Routledge.

Holden, G., Tuchman, E., Barker, K., Rosenberg, G., Thazin, M., Kuppens, S., & Watson, K. (2012). A few thoughts on evidence in social work. *Social Work in Health Care, 51*(6), 483–505. doi:10.1080/00981389.2012.671649 PMID:22780700

Hopps, J. G., Lowe, T. B., & Rollins, L. S. (2010). Evidence-based services to children in a conservative environment. In A. E. Fortune, P. McCallion, & K. Briar-Lawson (Eds.), *Social work practice research for the twenty-first century* (pp. 108–127). New York: Columbia University Press.

Howard, M. O., & Jenson, J. M. (1999). Clinical practice guidelines: Should social work develop them? *Research on Social Work Practice, 9*(3), 283–301. doi:10.1177/104973159900900302

Hutchison, K. J., & Rogers, W. A. (2012). Challenging the epistemological foundations of EBM: What kind of knowledge does clinical practice require? *Journal of Evaluation in Clinical Practice*, *18*(5), 984–991. doi:10.1111/j.1365-2753.2012.01905.x PMID:22994996

Jones, J. M., & Sherr, M. E. (2014). The role of relationships in connecting social work research and evidence-based practice. *Journal of Evidence-Based Social Work*, *11*(1-2), 139–147. doi:10.1080/15433714.2013.845028 PMID:24405138

Kjorstad, M. (2008). Opening the back box: Mobilising practical knowledge in social research – Methodological reflections based on a study of social work practice. *Qualitative Social Work: Research and Practice*, *7*(2), 143–161. doi:10.1177/1473325008089627

Leighninger, L. (2012). The history of social work and social welfare. In C. N. Dulmus & K. M. Sowers (Eds.), *The profession of social work: Guided by history, led by evidence* (pp. 1–34). Hoboken, NJ: John Wiley.

Loughlin, M. (2006). The future for medical epistemology? Commentary on Tonelli (2006), Integrating evidence into clinical practice: An alternative to evidence-based approaches. *Journal of Evaluation in Clinical Practice*, *12*(3), 289–291. doi:10.1111/j.1365-2753.2006.00589.x PMID:16722910

Marsh, P., Fisher, M., Mathers, N., & Fish, S. (2005). *Developing the evidence base for social work and social care practice*. Retrieved from Social Care Institute for Excellence website: http://www.scie.org.uk/publications/reports/report10.pdf

Morago, P. (2006). Evidence-based practice: From medicine to social work. *European Journal of Social Work*, *9*(4), 461–477. doi:10.1080/13691450600958510

Morago, P. (2010). Dissemination and implementation of evidence-based practice in the social services: A UK survey. *Journal of Evidence-Based Social Work*, *7*(5), 452–465. doi:10.1080/15433714.2010.494973 PMID:21082474

Morris, T. (2006). *Social work research methods: Four alternative paradigms*. Thousand Oaks, CA: Sage.

Mullen, E. J. (2006). Choosing outcome measures in systematic reviews: Critical challenges. *Research on Social Work Practice*, *16*(1), 84–90. doi:10.1177/1049731505280950

Mullen, E. J., & Bacon, W. F. (2003). Practitioner adoption and implementation of practice guidelines and issues of quality control. In A. Rosen & E. K. Proctor (Eds.), *Developing practice guidelines for social work intervention: Issues, methods, and research agenda* (pp. 223–235). New York: Columbia University Press.

Mullen, E. J., Bledsoe, S. E., & Bellamy, J. L. (2008). Implementing evidence-based social work practice. *Research on Social Work Practice*, *18*(4), 325–338. doi:10.1177/1049731506297827

Mullen, E. J., Shlonsky, A., Bledsoe, S. E., & Bellamy, J. L. (2005). From concept to implementation: Challenges facing evidence-based social work. *Evidence & Policy: A Journal of Research. Debate and Practice*, *1*(1), 61–84. doi:10.1332/1744264052703159

Mullen, E. J., & Streiner, D. L. (2004). The evidence for and against evidence-based practice. *Brief Treatment and Crisis Intervention*, *4*(2), 111–121. doi:10.1093/brief-treatment/mhh009

Murdach, A. D. (2010). What good is soft evidence? *Social Work*, *55*(4), 309–316. doi:10.1093/sw/55.4.309 PMID:20977054

Nevo, I., & Slonim-Nevo, V. (2011). The myth of evidence-based practice: Towards evidence- informed practice. *British Journal of Social Work*, *41*(6), 1176–1197. doi:10.1093/bjsw/bcq149

Nothdurfter, U., & Lorenz, W. (2010). Beyond the pro and contra of evidence-based practice: Reflections on a recurring dilemma at the core of social work. *Social Work & Society, 8*. Retrieved from http://www.socwork.net/sws/article/view/22/62

Orcutt, B. A. (1990). *Science and inquiry in social work practice*. New York: Columbia University Press.

Osmond, J., & O'Connor, I. (2006). Use of theory and research in social work practice: Implications for knowledge-based practice. *Australian Social Work*, *59*(1), 5–19. doi:10.1080/03124070500449747

Otto, H.-U., Polutta, A., & Ziegler, H. (2009). Struggling through to find what works: Evidence-based practice as a challenge for social work. In H.-U. Otto, A. Polutta, & H. Ziegler (Eds.), *Evidence-based practice: Modernising the knowledge base of social work?* (pp. 9–16). Opladen, Germany: Barbara Budrich.

Pack, M. (2013). What brings me here? Integrating evidence-based and critical-reflective approaches in social work education. *Journal of Systemic Therapies*, *32*(4), 65–78. doi:10.1521/jsyt.2013.32.4.65

Parrish, D. E., & Rubin, A. (2012). Social workers' orientations toward the evidence-based practice process: A comparison with psychologists and licensed marriage and family therapists. *Social Work*, *57*(3), 201–210. doi:10.1093/sw/sws016 PMID:23252312

Peebles-Wilkins, W., & Amodeo, M. (2003). Performance standards and quality control: Application of practice guidelines to service delivery. In A. Rosen & E. K. Proctor (Eds.), *Developing practice guidelines for social work intervention: Issues, methods, and research agenda* (pp. 207–220). New York: Columbia University Press.

Plath, D. (2006). Evidence-based practice: Current issues and future directions. *Australian Social Work*, *59*(1), 56–72. doi:10.1080/03124070500449788

Pope, N. D., Rollins, L., Chaumba, J., & Risler, E. (2011). Evidence-based practice knowledge and utilization among social workers. *Journal of Evidence-Based Social Work*, *8*(4), 349–368. doi:10.1080/15433710903269149 PMID:21827303

Pritchard, C. (2004a). Effective social work: A micro approach – Reducing truancy, delinquency and school exclusions. In D. Smith (Ed.), *Social work and evidence-based practice* (pp. 61–86). London: Jessica Kingsley.

Pritchard, C. (2004b). The extremes of child abuse: A macro approach to measuring effective prevention. In D. Smith (Ed.), *Social work and evidence-based practice* (pp. 47–60). London: Jessica Kingsley.

Reid, W. J., & Fortune, A. E. (2003). Empirical foundations for practice guidelines in current social work knowledge. In A. Rosen & E. K. Proctor (Eds.), *Developing practice guidelines for social work intervention: Issues, methods, and research agenda* (pp. 59–79). New York: Columbia University Press.

Reid, W. J., Kenaley, B. D., & Colvin, J. (2004). Do some interventions work better than others? A review of comparative social work experiments. *Social Work Research*, *28*(2), 71–81. doi:10.1093/swr/28.2.71

Reynolds, S. (2000). The anatomy of evidence-based practice: Principles and methods. In L. Trinder (with S. Reynolds) (Eds.), *Evidence-based practice: A critical appraisal* (pp. 17-34). Oxford, UK: Blackwell.

Rice, K., Hwang, J., Abrefa-Gyan, T., & Powell, K. (2010). Evidence-based practice questionnaire: A confirmatory factor analysis in a social work sample. *Advances in Social Work, 11*, 158-173. Retrieved from http://advancesinsocialwork.iupui.edu/

Richman, J. M. (2010). Building capacity for intervention research. In A. E. Fortune, P. McCallion, & K. Briar-Lawson (Eds.), *Social work practice research for the twenty-first century* (pp. 269–278). New York: Columbia University Press.

Roberts, A. R., Yeager, K., & Regehr, C. (2006). Bridging evidence-based health care and social work: How to search for, develop, and use evidence-based studies. In A. R. Roberts & K. R. Yeager (Eds.), *Foundations of evidence-based social work practice* (pp. 3–20). New York: Oxford University Press.

Rosen, A. (2003). Evidence-based social work practice: Challenges and promise. *Social Work Research, 27*(4), 197–208. doi:10.1093/swr/27.4.197

Rosen, A., & Proctor, E. K. (2003). Practice guidelines and the challenge of effective practice. In A. Rosen & E. K. Proctor (Eds.), *Developing practice guidelines for social work intervention: Issues, methods, and research agenda* (pp. 1–14). New York: Columbia University Press.

Rubin, A. (2011). Teaching EBP in social work: Retrospective and prospective. *Journal of Social Work, 11*(1), 64–79. doi:10.1177/1468017310381311

Rubin, A., & Parrish, D. (2007). Challenges to the future of evidence-based practice in social work education. *Journal of Social Work Education, 43*(3), 405–428. doi:10.5175/JSWE.2007.200600612

Rubin, A., & Parrish, D. E. (2012). Improving the scientific base of social work practice. In C. N. Dulmus & K. M. Sowers (Eds.), *The profession of social work: Guided by history, led by evidence* (pp. 203–223). Hoboken, NJ: John Wiley.

Sackett, D. L., Rosenberg, W. M. C., Muir Gray, J. A., Haynes, R. B., & Richardson, W. S. (1996). Evidence based medicine: What it is and what it isn't: It's about integrating individual clinical expertise and the best external evidence. *BMJ (Clinical Research Ed.), 312*(7023), 71–72. doi:10.1136/bmj.312.7023.71 PMID:8555924

Sackett, D. L., Straus, S. E., Richardson, W. S., Rosenberg, W., & Haynes, R. B. (2000). *Evidence-based medicine: How to practice and teach EBM* (2nd ed.). Edinburgh, UK: Churchill Livingstone.

Sheldon, B. (2001). The validity of evidence-based practice in social work: A reply to Stephen Webb. *British Journal of Social Work, 31*(5), 801–809. doi:10.1093/bjsw/31.5.801

Shlonsky, A., & Gibbs, L. (2004). Will the real evidence-based practice please stand up? Teaching the process of evidence-based practice to the helping professions. *Brief Treatment and Crisis Intervention, 4*(2), 137–153. doi:10.1093/brief-treatment/mhh011

Shlonsky, A., Noonan, E., Littell, J., & Montgomery, P. (2011). The role of systematic reviews and the Campbell Collaboration in the realization of evidence-informed practice. *Clinical Social Work Journal, 39*(4), 362–368. doi:10.1007/s10615-010-0307-0

Simmons, B. M. (2011). The complexity of evidence-based practice: A case study. *Smith College Studies in Social Work*, *81*(2-3), 252–267. doi:10.1080/00377317.2011.589352

Simmons, B. M. (2012). Evidence-based practice, person-in-environment, and clinical social work: Issues of practical concern. *Smith College Studies in Social Work*, *82*(1), 3–18. doi:10.1080/00377317.2011.638889

Smith, D. (2004). Introduction: Some versions of evidence-based practice. In D. Smith (Ed.), *Social work and evidence-based practice* (pp. 7–27). London: Jessica Kingsley.

Solomon, P., & Draine, J. (2010). An overview of quantitative research methods. In B. A. Thyer (Ed.), *The Handbook of Social Work Research Methods* (2nd ed., pp. 26–36). Thousand Oaks, CA: SAGE.

Sundell, K., Soydan, H., Tengvald, K., & Anttila, S. (2010). From opinion-based to evidence-based social work: The Swedish case. *Research on Social Work Practice*, *20*(6), 714–722. doi:10.1177/1049731509347887

Thyer, B. A. (2004). What is evidence-based practice? *Brief Treatment and Crisis Intervention*, *4*(2), 167–176. doi:10.1093/brief-treatment/mhh013

Thyer, B. A. (2008). The quest for evidence-based practice?: We are all positivists! *Research on Social Work Practice*, *18*(4), 339–345. doi:10.1177/1049731507313998

Thyer, B. A. (2010). Introductory principles of social work research. In B. A. Thyer (Ed.), *The handbook of social work research methods* (2nd ed., pp. 1–24). Thousand Oaks, CA: SAGE.

Thyer, B. A. (2012). The scientific value of qualitative research for social work. *Qualitative Social Work: Research and Practice*, *11*, 115–125. doi:10.1177/1473325011433928

Thyer, B. A., & Myers, L. L. (2011). The quest for evidence-based practice: A view from the United States. *Journal of Social Work*, *11*(1), 8–25. doi:10.1177/1468017310381812

Thyer, B. A., & Pignotti, M. (2011). Evidence-based practices do not exist. *Clinical Social Work Journal*, *39*(4), 328–333. doi:10.1007/s10615-011-0358-x

Trinder, L. (2000a). A critical appraisal of evidence-based practice. In L. Trinder (with S. Reynolds) (Eds.), *Evidence-based practice: A critical appraisal* (pp. 212-241). Oxford, UK: Blackwell.

Trinder, L. (2000b). Evidence-based practice in social work and probation. In L. Trinder (with S. Reynolds) (Eds.), *Evidence-based practice: A critical appraisal* (pp. 138-162). Oxford, UK: Blackwell. doi:10.1002/9780470699003.ch7

Trinder, L. (2000c). Introduction: The context of evidence-based practice. In L. Trinder (with S. Reynolds) (Eds.), *Evidence-based practice: A critical appraisal* (pp. 1-16). Oxford, UK: Blackwell.

Upshur, R. E. G., & Tracy, C. S. (2004). Legitimacy, authority, and hierarchy: Critical challenges for evidence-based medicine. *Brief Treatment and Crisis Intervention*, *4*(3), 197–204. doi:10.1093/brief-treatment/mhh018

Videka, L., & Blackburn, J. A. (2010). The intellectual legacy of William J. Reid. In A. E. Fortune, P. McCallion, & K. Briar-Lawson (Eds.), *Social work practice research for the twenty-first century* (pp. 183–194). New York: Columbia University Press.

Webb, S. A. (2001). Some considerations on the validity of evidence-based practice in social work. *British Journal of Social Work*, *31*(1), 57–79. doi:10.1093/bjsw/31.1.57

Webber, M. (2014). From ethnography to randomized controlled trial: An innovative approach to developing complex social interventions. *Journal of Evidence-Based Social Work*, *11*(1-2), 173–182. doi:10.1080/15433714.2013.847265 PMID:24405141

Williams, N. J., & Sherr, M. E. (2013). Oh how I try to use evidence in my social work practice: Efforts, successes, frustrations, and questions. *Journal of Evidence-Based Social Work*, *10*(2), 100–110. doi:10.1080/15433714.2011.597299 PMID:23581804

Witkin, S. L., & Harrison, W. D. (2001). Editorial: Whose evidence and for what purpose? *Social Work*, *46*(4), 293–296. doi:10.1093/sw/46.4.293 PMID:11682970

Witkin, S. L., & Iversen, R. R. (2012). Contemporary issues in social work. In C. N. Dulmus & K. M. Sowers (Eds.), *The profession of social work: Guided by history, led by evidence* (pp. 225–259). Academic Press.

Yunong, H., & Fengzhi, M. (2009). A reflection on reasons, preconditions, and effects of implementing evidence-based practice in social work. *Social Work*, *54*(2), 177–181. doi:10.1093/sw/54.2.177 PMID:19366166

Zayas, L. H., Drake, B., & Jonson-Reid, M. (2011). Overrating or dismissing the value of evidence-based practice: Consequences for clinical practice. *Clinical Social Work Journal*, *39*(4), 400–405. doi:10.1007/s10615-010-0306-1

## ADDITIONAL READING

Anastas, J. W. (2004). Quality in qualitative evaluation: Issues and possible answers. *Research on Social Work Practice*, *14*(1), 57–65. doi:10.1177/1049731503257870

Arnd-Caddigan, M. (2011). Toward a broader definition of evidence-informed practice: Inter-subjective evidence. *Families in Society*, *92*(4), 372–376. doi:10.1606/1044-3894.4160

Asgary-Eden, V., & Lee, C. M. (2011). So now we've picked an evidence-based program, what's next? Perspectives of service providers and administrators. *Professional Psychology: Research and Practice*, *42*(2), 169–175. doi:10.1037/a0022745

Atherton, C. R., & Bolland, K. A. (2002). Postmodernism: A dangerous illusion for social work. *International Social Work*, *45*(4), 421–433. doi:10.1177/0020872802045004020 1

Auslander, W., Fisher, C., Ollie, M., & Yu, M. (2012). Teaching master's and doctoral social work students to systematically evaluate evidence-based interventions. *Journal of Teaching in Social Work*, *32*(4), 320–341. doi:10.1080/08841233.2012.707170

Barber, J. G. (1996). Science and social work: Are they compatible? *Research on Social Work Practice*, *6*(3), 379–388. doi:10.1177/104973159600600308

Belchamber, R. (1997). Re-evaluating social work's debt to the scientific tradition. *Social Work & Social Sciences Review*, *7*, 13–25. Retrieved from http://www.whitingbirch.net/cgi-bin/scribe?showinfo=ip003

Bolland, K., & Atherton, C. (2002). Heuristics versus logical positivism: Solving the wrong problem. *Families in Society*, *83*(1), 7–13. doi:10.1606/1044-3894.38

Crisp, B. R. (2000). A history of Australian social work practice research. *Research on Social Work Practice*, *10*, 179–184. Retrieved from http://rsw.sagepub.com/

Dore, I. J. (2006). Evidence-focused social care: On target or off-side? *Social Work & Society, 4*, 232-255. Retrieved from http://www.socwork.net/sws

Drisko, J. W. (1997). Strengthening qualitative studies and reports: Standards to promote academic integrity. *Journal of Social Work Education*, *33*, 185–197. Retrieved from http://www.tandfonline.com/toc/uswe20/current

Faul, A. C., McMurtry, S. L., & Hudson, W. W. (2001). Can empirical clinical practice techniques improve social work outcomes? *Research on Social Work Practice*, *11*(3), 277–299. doi:10.1177/104973150101100301

Fischer, J. (1973). Is casework effective? A review. *Social Work, 18*(1), 5–20. doi:10.1093/sw/18.1.5

Fischer, J. (1994). Empirically-based practice: The end of ideology? *Journal of Social Service Research*, *18*(1-2), 19–64. doi:10.1300/J079v18n01_03

Gambrill, E. (1999). Evidence-based practice: An alternative to authority-based practice. *Families in Society*, *80*(4), 341–350. doi:10.1606/1044-3894.1214

Geddes, J. (2000). Evidence-based practice in mental health. In L. Trinder (with S. Reynolds) (Eds.), *Evidence-based practice: A critical appraisal* (pp. 66-88). Oxford: Blackwell.

Gibbs, L. E. (1991). *Scientific reasoning for social workers: Bridging the gap between research and practice*. New York: Merrill.

Gomm, R., & Davies, C. (2000). *Using evidence in health and social care*. London: SAGE.

Gossett, M., & Weinman, M. L. (2007). Evidence-based practice and social work: An illustration of the steps involved. *Health & Social Work*, *32*(2), 147–150. doi:10.1093/hsw/32.2.147 PMID:17571649

Gould, N. (2010). Integrating qualitative evidence in practice guideline development: Meeting the challenge of evidence-based practice for social work. *Qualitative Social Work: Research and Practice*, *9*(1), 93–109. doi:10.1177/1473325009355623

Haynes, R. B., Devereaux, P. J., & Guyatt, G. H. (2002). Clinical expertise in the era of evidence-based medicine and patient choice. *Evidence-Based Medicine*, *7*(2), 36–38. doi:10.1136/ebm.7.2.36

Kirk, S. A., & Reid, W. J. (2002). *Science and social work: A critical appraisal*. New York: Columbia University Press.

Lilienfeld, S. O. (2007). Psychological treatments that cause harm. *Perspectives on Psychological Science, 2*(1), 53–70. doi:10.1111/j.1745-6916.2007.00029.x

Littell, J. H., Corcoran, J., & Pillai, V. (2008). *Systematic reviews and meta-analysis.* New York: Oxford University Press. doi:10.1093/acprof:oso/9780195326543.001.0001

Lubove, R. (1965). *The professional altruist: The emergence of social work as a career, 1880-1930.* Cambridge: Harvard University Press. doi:10.4159/harvard.9780674420939

Manuel, J. I., Mullen, E. J., Lin Fang, , Bellamy, J. L., & Bledsoe, S. E. (2009). Preparing social work practitioners to use evidence-based practice: A comparison of experiences from an implementation project. *Research on Social Work Practice, 19*(5), 613–627. doi:10.1177/1049731509335547

Murphy, A., & McDonald, J. (2004). Power, status and marginalisation: Rural social workers and evidence-based practice in multidisciplinary teams. *Australian Social Work, 57*(2), 127–136. doi:10.1111/j.1447-0748.2004.00127.x

Nutley, S., Walter, I., & Davies, H. T. O. (2009). Promoting evidence-based practice: Models and mechanisms from cross-sector review. *Research on Social Work Practice, 19*(5), 552–559. doi:10.1177/1049731509335496

O'Hare, T. (2005). *Evidence-based practices for social workers: An interdisciplinary approach.* Chicago: Lyceum Books.

Otto, H.-U., Polutta, A., & Ziegler, H. (Eds.), *Evidence-based practice: Modernising the knowledge base of social work?* Opladen, Germany: Barbara Budrich.

Payne, M. (2007). Performing as a "wise person" in social work practice. *Practice: Social Work in Action, 19*(2), 85–96. doi:10.1080/09503150701393577

Pignotti, M., & Thyer, B. A. (2009). Use of novel unsupported and empirically supported therapies by licensed clinical social workers: An exploratory study. *Social Work Research, 33*(1), 5–17. doi:10.1093/swr/33.1.5

Proctor, E. K., & Rosen, A. (2006). *Concise standards for developing evidence-based practice guidelines.* Chicago: Lyceum Books.

Reed, G. M., Kihlstrom, J. F., & Messer, S. B. (2006). *What qualifies as evidence of effective practice.* Washington, DC: American Psychological Association. doi:10.1037/11265-001

Richmond, M. E. (1917). *Social diagnosis.* Philadelphia: Russell Sage Foundation.

Roberts, A. R., & Watkins, J. M. (2009). *Social workers' desk reference* (2nd ed.). New York: Oxford University Press.

Rosen, A. (1994). Knowledge use in direct practice. *The Social Service Review, 68*(4), 561–577. doi:10.1086/604084

Rubin, A. (1985). Practice effectiveness: More grounds for optimism. *Social Work, 30,* 469–476. doi:10.1093/sw/30.6.469

Rubin, A., & Parrish, D. (2007). Problematic phrases in the conclusions of published outcome studies: Implications for evidence-based practice. *Research on Social Work Practice, 17*(3), 334–347. doi:10.1177/1049731506293726

Shaw, I. (2010). Qualitative social work practice research. In A. E. Fortune, P. McCallion, & K. Briar-Lawson (Eds.), *Social work practice research for the twenty-first century* (pp. 31–48). New York: Columbia University Press.

Shaw, I., & Ruckdeschel, R. (2002). Qualitative social work: A room with a view. *Qualitative Social Work: Research and Practice, 1*(1), 5–23. doi:10.1177/147332500200100101

Sheldon, B. (1986). Social work effectiveness experiments: Review and implications. *British Journal of Social Work*, *16*, 223–242. Retrieved from http://bjsw.oxfordjournals.org/

Stern, S. B., Alaggia, R., Watson, K., & Morton, T. R. (2008). Implementing an evidence-based parenting program with adherence in the real world of community practice. *Research on Social Work Practice*, *18*(6), 543–554. doi:10.1177/1049731507308999

Stevens, M., Liabo, K., Frost, S., & Roberts, H. (2005). Using research in practice: A research information service for social care practitioners. *Child & Family Social Work*, *10*(1), 67–75. doi:10.1111/j.1365-2206.2005.00346.x

Stevens, M., Liabo, K., & Roberts, H. (2007). A review of the research priorities of practitioners working with children in social care. *Child & Family Social Work*, *12*(4), 295–305. doi:10.1111/j.1365-2206.2006.00482.x

Thyer, B. (2001). *Single-case designs*. Thousand Oaks, CA: Sage.

Thyer, B. A., & Kazi, M. (Eds.). (2004). *International perspectives on evidence-based practice in social work*. London: Venture Press.

Thyer, B. A., & Pignotti, M. (2011). Clinical social work and evidence-based practice: An introduction to the special issue. *Clinical Social Work Journal*, *39*(4), 325–327. doi:10.1007/s10615-011-0359-9

Wells, K., & Littell, J. H. (2009). Study quality assessment in systematic reviews of research on intervention effects. *Research on Social Work Practice*, *19*(1), 52–62. doi:10.1177/1049731508317278

White, B. W. (Ed.). (2008). *Comprehensive handbook of social work and social welfare: The profession of social work*. Hoboken, New Jersey: John Wiley.

Wike, T. L., Bledsoe, S. E., Bellamy, J. L., & Grady, M. D. (2013). Examining inclusion of evidence-based practice on social work training program websites. *Journal of Social Work Education*, *49*, 439–450. doi:10.1080/10437797.2013.796791

## KEY TERMS AND DEFINITIONS

**Empirical:** Evidence gathered through observation or experiment and capable of being replicated (i.e. reproduced and verified) by others.

**Epistemology:** A term describing the branch of philosophy concerned with the origin, nature, and limits of human knowledge and how knowledge relates to truth, belief, and justification.

**Evidence-Based Practice:** A systematic process that integrates available best evidence, client preferences and values (wherever possible), client's circumstances, and professional expertise, resulting in services that are individualised to the client.

**Practice Guidelines:** Systematically complied and organised statements of empirically tested knowledge and procedures to help practitioners select and implement the most effective and appropriate interventions.

**Randomised Controlled Trial (RCT):** A trial designed to test the efficacy or effectiveness of various types of medical intervention. It must include a control group and participants are randomly allocated to receive one or other of the alternative treatments under study to eliminate allocation bias.

**Reflective Practice:** The capacity for individuals to learn from professional experience, to reflect on action and to understand one's motives, attitudes, and values, using that insight to add to one's existing knowledge base.

# Chapter 2
# Finding the Evidence for Practice in Social Work

**Justin Cargill**
*Victoria University of Wellington, New Zealand*

## ABSTRACT

*The revolution in information technologies, in particular the growth of the Internet and greater access to computers, has given social workers unprecedented access to information resources. Researching such resources is crucial and it needs to be done efficiently. Planning an efficient search requires knowing which databases and other resources to use, knowing how to formulate an answerable question, identifying terms that inform the question, selecting the appropriate methodological filters, and being able to critically appraise evidence for its quality and relevance. This chapter, therefore, outlines some of the research sources available to social workers, it looks at some principles for finding information for practice in social work, and it outlines some criteria for evaluating the quality of that information.*

## INTRODUCTION

In 2001, a 24-year-old woman died from lung and kidney complications in a clinical trial. She died because the investigators performed inadequate preliminary research on the chemical she inhaled as part of the trial. Their search strategy failed to find material which would have cautioned them against its use (John Hopkins University, 2001; Perkins, 2001; Savulescu & Spriggs, 2002).

Although the investigators used an appropriate database (PubMed), their search strategy was poorly constructed and they did not retrieve those records which would have alerted them to potential difficulties. They also did not search widely

enough. They used textbooks on pharmacology and pulmonary medicine and they used search engines such as Google and Yahoo, but there were other online databases they should have searched, in addition to a range of other resources (Perkins, 2001).

This sober illustration depicts a case in which someone may have literally died from a poor search strategy. It provides the caution that social workers also could, in principle, do more harm than good in their research. With this thought as background, this chapter will do three things. It will outline some of the research sources available to social workers (Sources); it will look at some principles for finding information for practice in

DOI: 10.4018/978-1-4666-6563-7.ch002

social work (Searching); and it will outline some criteria for evaluating the quality of that information (Selection).

As observed in the previous chapter, there are multiple sources of evidence available to the social worker. This includes empirical evidence, in addition to evidence derived from qualitative studies, professional expertise, judgement, and experience, theoretical knowledge, organisational guidelines, critical reflection, and evidence that arises from the particular practice situation, such as the client's cultural values, problems, situation, and strengths. This chapter focuses upon finding the research evidence (quantitative and qualitative) and, in particular, the searching of electronic databases and how the quality of such evidence is evaluated.

## SOURCES

Rapidly evolving information technologies have given social workers unprecedented access to information resources. At some point, the social work practitioner will be faced with determining which sources will provide access to the most useful material. Squandering time and energy searching in the wrong place is disheartening.

There is little point listing in this chapter a comprehensive range of sources in social work available through the Internet. It is an interesting but discouraging exercise to explore such lists only to find that the organisations and groups no longer exist or the web addresses have changed. There is little that dates a text which includes such a list, so much as this.

Having said all this by way of qualification, below is something akin to a list. It also, however, provides some explanatory material describing the context and the utility of these sources and it has the virtue of identifying websites that are not likely to disappear. It includes sources for systematic reviews and bibliographic databases and concludes with some comment about grey

literature. Many of these resources may be familiar and well-utilised. This list does not pretend to be comprehensive. It is presented merely to give an idea of the range of sources available.

## Prominent Search Engines

The advent of the Internet has given social workers access to a plethora of resources and types of evidence upon which to base practice. Search engines, such as Google, Alta Vista, and Yahoo, search across the Internet, although no one engine searches the entire Internet, there are no controls over quality, and authorship and currency are not always easy to determine. Using a general search engine is not, therefore, ideal. In fact, Szuchman and Thomlison (2011) take the view that "the Internet sometimes does contain suitable sources, but doing a Google or Yahoo search is likely to waste your time" (p. 64). They then comment on the results of a search on Google for the phrase "healthy aging" and advise that it would be better to have spent the time searching a database, such as PsychInfo, being assured that the material came from "legitimate sources" (p. 64). Nevertheless, one particularly well known Internet search engine is suitable: Google Scholar.

### Google Scholar (www.google.com/scholar)

Released in 2004, this freely accessible web search engine indexes the full text of scholarly literature. It also includes selected web pages that are deemed to be scholarly. The full texts of articles in Google Scholar are not necessarily available freely to all searchers, however. Searchers with access through an institution may be able to freely access material and some records provide links to subscription or purchase options.

Google Scholar does not offer the searching, limiting, and filtering features available in databases such as PubMed (Boeker, Vach, & Motschall, 2013; Bramer, Giustini, Kramer, & Anderson,

2013; Shultz, 2007, p. 444). But because Google Scholar possesses an easy user interface it is a good place for an initial search for potentially useful material. Google Scholar also provides access to grey literature (i.e. preprints, conference proceedings, and institutional repositories) (Shultz, 2007, p. 444). In addition, its "cited by" feature provides access to other material that has cited the item, and its "Related articles" feature expands the field of related material.

## Systematic Reviews

A systematic review will summarise data from the results of a number of individual studies which meet the review's eligibility criteria and will, therefore, enable readers to draw conclusions about the totality of research in a specific area. A systematic review uses a clear, reproducible methodology to find, evaluate, and synthesise the results of relevant research. If there are sufficient studies using similar methods measuring similar entities, a statistical method (called a meta-analysis) is used to combine the results from the individual studies. This will establish trends and differences across the studies (Shlonsky, Noonan, Littell, & Montgomery, 2011, pp. 363-364).

Systematic reviews are valued, in principle, because they can be used to identify or refine hypotheses, they may highlight the pitfalls of previous work, they can help formulate guidelines, and they increase the statistical power of the studies because they involve many studies and increased sample size (Mulrow, 1995, pp. 2-5). Littell (2010) asserts that "the synthesis of results across studies is essential to evidence informed practice....since empirical knowledge is not static, we need periodic syntheses of ever-expanding bodies of evidence" (p. 162). Nevertheless, systematic reviews and meta-analyses vary in quality and credibility. Clearly, the value of a systematic review will only be as strong as the studies it incorporates

and as strong as the critical appraisal conducted by reviewers. Systematic reviews themselves, therefore, require evaluation (see below).

Some of these evaluative issues are addressed by the Cochrane and Campbell Collaborations, two reviewing organisations which occupy a particularly prominent place in the creation of systematic reviews.

## The Cochrane Collaboration (www.cochrane.org)

Founded in 1992, the Cochrane Library is a subscription-based database but in many countries it has been made freely available to all residents by their respective governments. All countries, however, have free access to the abstracts of all Cochrane Reviews and to short plain-language summaries of selected articles.

The Cochrane Library includes access to all the peer-reviewed systematic reviews and protocols prepared by the Cochrane Review Groups, quality-assessed abstracts of systematic reviews by non- Cochrane groups, details of controlled trials and other healthcare interventions from bibliographic databases and other published and unpublished sources, and details of completed and ongoing health technology assessments from around the world.

The Cochrane Collaboration is useful to social workers interested in learning about the most up-to-date information pertaining to the assessment and treatment of various health matters, including mental health issues.

## The Campbell Collaboration (www.campbellcollaboration.org)

Founded in 2000, this is a voluntary network of scholars, educators, practitioners, policy-makers, and consumers producing systematic reviews in the social sciences. It focuses on three major fields:

social welfare, criminal justice, and education. All titles, protocols, reviews, and user abstracts are freely available. Like Cochrane, the Campbell Collaboration encourages researchers to update their respective reviews to maintain relevancy. The Campbell Library includes research on psychosocial treatments like family therapy and mentoring programs, as well as research on issues such as juvenile delinquency and substance abuse.

## Databases

Resources addressing practice questions are not always available in a summarised form. In such cases, practitioners must seek individual research articles to address practice needs. This material is locatable in databases. Most databases have certain advantages over Internet search engines. They employ subject headings, they possess search builders for incrementally conducting a search, and they provide a search history facility which enables comparison and combination of search sets. They also have the ability to search in a much wider range of fields beyond author and title.

Gray, Joy, Plath, and Webb (2014) have found in their survey of social work practitioners that the databases most frequently searched were Medline (40%), Social Work Abstracts (17%), and the Cochrane Collaboration (15%) (p. 34), and Shlonsky, Baker, and Fuller-Thomson (2011) are convinced from their study that PsycINFO "is the best database for finding rigorous studies in social care" (p. 398). But of course there are many more databases. Below is a list of some useful databases with brief annotations.

## Cinahl

The Cumulative Index to Nursing and Allied Health Literature (CINAHL) is an index of English-language and selected other-language journal articles about nursing but also allied health, including social work.

## EMBASE

This database is similar in scope and content to Medline but provides greater coverage of European and non-European language publications. It also has a broader coverage of such topics as psychiatry and alternative medicine.

## PsychInfo

International in scope, this is an indexing and abstracting database of peer-reviewed literature in the behavioral sciences and mental health.

## PubMed

This U.S. government website provides access to Medline, the U.S. National Library of Medicine's bibliographic database of journals published in the United States and beyond. Medline is the largest subset of PubMed and includes material on the delivery of health care, nutrition, psychiatry, and psychology.

PubMed contains citations and abstracts with links to freely accessible material where available. But it also contains PubMed Central (PMC), a repository of freely accessible, full text, peer reviewed articles. Although for many, there is no functional difference between PubMed and Medline the appearance of an item in PMC does not mean the journal has been accepted for indexing in Medline.

One of the significant benefits of searching PubMed is the ability to utilise the MeSH (Medical Subject Headings). Subject headings enable more precise searching. In a comparison of PubMed and Google Scholar, Scholar did not retrieve a number of records appearing in PubMed because PubMed used appropriate MeSH terms, although these terms might not have appeared in the title or abstract of the records. Also even if the word was not searched as a MeSH term, PubMed automatically mapped it to a MeSH term (Shultz, 2007, p. 443).

## Social Services Abstracts

This database provides bibliographic coverage of current research focused on social work education, practice and policy, community and mental health services, and social welfare and social policy.

## Social Work Abstracts

Produced by the National Association of Social Workers (NASW), SWAB provides extensive indexing and abstracting coverage of social work and human services journals.

## Sociological Abstracts

This resource abstracts the international literature in the social and behavioural sciences.

## Professional Organisational Websites

This is but a small sample of professional and organisational websites on the Internet including clearinghouses and guidelines.

## California Evidence-Based Clearinghouse for Child Welfare (CEBC) (http://www.cebc4cw.org/)

The primary goal of this website is to provide a searchable database of programs that can be utilised by professionals who serve children and families involved with the child welfare system.

## ClinicalTrials.gov (http://www.clinicaltrials.gov/)

This is a service of the U.S. National Institutes of Health. It provides access to information on publicly and privately supported clinical studies on a wide range of diseases and conditions. Information is provided and updated by the sponsor or principal investigator of the clinical study. Each record includes details regarding the disease or condition, intervention (medical product, behaviour, or procedure), and outcomes of the study.

## Information for Practice (IP) (http://ifp.nyu.edu/)

IP began in 1993 and is a freely accessible international resource for social work and related professionals. It focuses on aggregating news and new scholarship for professional practice and it is constantly updated, although it does not pretend to be exhaustive. A "primary focus" is to provide access to the full text of documents in the grey literature (Holden, Barker, Rosenberg, & Cohen, 2012, p. 168).

## Inter-Center Network for Evaluation of Social Work Practice (http://www.intsoceval.org)

This network, which began in 1997, is currently made up of research centres attached to governments or universities from Denmark, England, Finland, the Netherlands, Scotland, Sweden, and Switzerland, as well as two U.S. based centres (the Center for the Study of Social Work Practice at Columbia University; the Hamovitch Center for Science in the Human Services at University of Southern California). The network is a forum for the members of these centres to exchange information, discuss each centre's research-related ideas and activities, and encourage international collaboration through research projects and exchange visits.

## Joanna Briggs Institute (JBI) (http://joannabriggs.org/)

This is an international research and development arm of the School of Translational Science at the University of Adelaide, South Australia.

The Institute collaborates internationally with over 70 entities across the world supporting the use of evidence to assist in the improvement of healthcare outcomes.

## National Guideline Clearinghouse (NGC) (http://www.guideline.gov/)

An initiative of the U.S. Department of Health and Human Services, this is a publicly available resource for evidence-based clinical practice guidelines and information on medication and concerns about medications.

## SAMHSA Registry of Evidence-Based Programs and Practices (www.nrepp.samhsa.gov/)

The Registry is a searchable online database of mental health and substance abuse interventions. Its purpose is to make available information on evidence-based programs and practices to help inform decision-making. NREPP rates the quality of the research supporting intervention outcomes and the quality and availability of training and implementation materials. It does not provide an exhaustive list of interventions or endorsements of specific interventions.

## Grey Literature

The Third International Conference on Grey Literature (GL '99) in Washington, DC, in 1999, defined grey literature as that which is "produced on all levels of government, academics, business, and industry in print and electronic formats, but which is not controlled by commercial publishers" (Farace, 1998, p. iii).

The primary benefit of using electronic databases is the ease of searching and recovering material. It also seems intuitive to restrict searching to peer-reviewed journal articles. But relying solely on electronic database searches to find relevant published studies risks what has been termed "publication bias." Studies have demonstrated that journals are less likely to publish statistically non-significant results, researchers are less inclined to submit for publication statistically non-significant results, and published studies are more likely to conclude that an intervention is effective. This can artificially inflate results and conclusions (Bronson & Davis, pp. 33, 35; The Cochrane Collaboration, 2002; Littell, 2010, p. 165; Wilson, 2009, pp. 431-432). This means that important information regarding efficacy may be missed if sole reliance is placed on published literature. In fact, "a large number" of trials presented at conferences and scientific meetings never reach full publication (Hopewell, McDonald, Clarke, & Egger, 2008, p. 6).

The assumption that an unpublished study must have been rejected by the peer-review process is precisely that, an assumption. Many studies are simply not submitted for publication because the authors deem the results uninteresting or non-significant, or for a whole host of pragmatic reasons. Since studies may be rejected for reasons which are entirely unrelated to methodology and quality, their non-publication status tells us nothing about methodological status (Wilson, 2009, pp. 435-436). To present an accurate picture, then, it is necessary to go beyond the published literature. In fact, the contribution from grey trials is particularly important when there have only been a few intervention trials involving small samples (Hopewell et al., 2008, p. 7).

Grey literature is not always easily locatable, although with the advent of the Internet this problem is increasingly less significant (Luzi, 2000, p. 106). Libraries themselves have had difficulty acquiring and making accessible grey literature. The New York Academy of Medicine has, however, made an effort to acquire materials from various organisations producing grey literature. The Grey Literature Report http://www.greylit.org/ is an effort to collect these items for the Academy's collection and provides lists of organisations producing grey literature.

Grey literature can also be located in conference proceedings. The British Library (Boston Spa) is probably the most comprehensive and easily accessible collection of conference publications in the world and is found at: http://www.bl.uk/reshelp/atyourdesk/docsupply/collection/confs/index.html

In addition, grey literature can be found by contacting relevant organisations and perusing the websites of government or state agencies, research centres, and reports from non-governmental organisations. Some of the sources described earlier in this section provide access to grey literature.

## SEARCHING

This section will look at how to construct what is generally called the "search strategy." Databases will invariably include guides on how to search and since most searches, however, poorly constructed will retrieve results of some sort, simple searches of most databases are always possible. But the quality and relevance of results is important, as is clear from the earlier reference to the John Hopkins University trial.

The intent of this section is, therefore, to lay down some important principles behind creating effective searches which once understood can be applied to most databases. These principles can be grouped into three main steps: formulating the search question, identifying the appropriate search terms, and constructing the search strategy.

### Formulating the Search Question

The first issue confronting the researcher involves that of formulating the search question. This involves converting the information need into a specific, answerable question. Gibbs (2003) explains that "if you can learn to pose a specific question, you have hope of finding a specific answer" (p. 53). Shlonsky and Gibbs (2004) point out that posing a question that can be answered

by a database requires that the "database must be given information in a format and language that it can interpret" (p. 142).

Sackett, Richardson, Rosenberg, and Haynes (1997) have suggested that a "well-built" clinical question designed to search for the best available research evidence consists of four elements (pp. 27-29). These elements are often referred to by the acronym PICO with each letter representing an aspect of the practice question. In many cases the PICO components will be present without being labelled as such.

- 'P' identifies the patient or population and their particular problem(s), that is, their condition or need.
- 'I' stands for intervention. This refers to treatments or preventative measures.
- 'C' represents comparison. Are there alternative treatments or interventions that would fit the client's needs? This enables the practitioner to suggest a range of options to the client assuming research-supported alternatives are located. This is important because it allows clients to voice any concerns about the intervention and to select among options when they are available.
- 'O' stands for outcomes. What are the specific outcomes or goals sought by the practitioner and client?

Sometimes a further acronym 'T' is used. It variously stands for type of problem or question being asked, for example, diagnosis, treatment, or prevention (Drisko, 2014, p. 125; Drisko & Grady, 2012, pp. 35; Schardt, Adams, Owens, Keitz, & Fontelo, 2007, Background), best type of study design for the question (Schardt et al., 2007, Background), or time-frame associated with the question (Fineout-Overholt, & Johnston, 2005, p. 158).

Gibbs (2003) has referred to this structure as "Client-Oriented, Practical, Evidence-Search

Questions (COPES)" (p. 57). Gibbs points out that the COPES framework renders the question specific enough to find answers in an electronic search (pp. 57-58). He also observes that COPES questions fall into five types: "effectiveness, prevention, risk, assessment, and description" (p. 58). He suggests that each one of these question types meets the "four elements in a well-formulated question": "client type and problem," "what you might do," "alternate course of action," and "what you want to accomplish" (p. 59).

Shlonsky and Gibbs (2004) have found that many practitioners struggle with posing answerable questions. They have delineated what they term "common pitfalls" (p. 142). Among these they include asking questions involving interventions which are unavailable or which would be rejected by the client; asking vague questions in which the concepts, intervention, or outcomes are not clearly defined; failing to label the problem or intervention correctly; or "asking two or more questions within one question….making it unwieldly" (pp. 142, 144).

## Identifying the Appropriate Search Terms for the Electronic Search

Having established the search question and the key concepts comprising that question, the next step is to consider the search terms.

The value of the PICO (or COPES) framework is the ability it gives to set out clearly the information need. The framework serves to steady and control the researcher's thinking. In creating a search strategy, it becomes necessary to think about the words or phrases that represent elements in the structure. It is important to keep in mind, however, that some questions are not naturally accommodated in a PICO structure, such as questions seeking information on the possible causes of a condition. It is also frequently not possible to complete every aspect of the structure. Comparison may not be relevant in some questions. In fact, many qualitative questions consist of but two components: the population and their cir-

cumstances or experiences. Pearson and Hannes (2013) point out that in qualitative questions the 'I' would denote "interest" or "issue" rather than intervention (p. 227)

It also may not always be possible to search on every element of the structure even if the question lends itself naturally to doing so. The particular populations, settings, or outcomes may not be well described in the title or abstract of an article and they may not be well indexed with subject headings. Very specific questions may not as yet produce quality research results. Nevertheless, none of this can be known until the search has been tried and results canvassed. Therefore, it is best to define practice questions in detail and search in light of that. Only then is the researcher in a position to determine whether they should search on fewer concepts and are, therefore, obliged to search more broadly.

There are a number of approaches which can be taken when searching a database. It is possible to search for a specific author, or title, or publication source. It is also possible to use these as a basis for further searching. This is often called "citation pearl searching" and involves using a known relevant item(s) as a basis for tracking further material, perhaps more material by the same author(s), or even more commonly, using the reference list or the keywords found in known relevant items (De Brun & Pearce-Smith, 2009, p. 95-99). There are, however, two main approaches taken when looking more widely for material to address a question: free text searching and subject heading (controlled vocabulary) searching.

### Searching with Free Text

This first approach is called "free text searching." It is also often called "natural language" searching. The database will search across records for the particular term or phrase that is entered. Google, for instance, uses free text searching.

To guide free text searching, it is necessary to develop a list of terms which are expected to appear in material of relevance. Free text searching gives scope to introduce alternative words or phrases for the concepts. These are called *synonyms* but they are not what could be labelled "dictionary synonyms." They might include singular and plural words, alternative terms, spelling variations, possible hyphenation, but even in some cases, antonyms. Of course, not all the appropriate "synonyms" may come to mind until after an initial search.

Truncation and wildcards are used in free text searching. These expand search options and speed up the search process. The truncation symbol is usually an asterisk but the database help facility will provide that information. Taking the stem or root of a word and adding the truncation symbol will retrieve variant endings of words. *Alcohol\** will yield *alcohol, alcoholic* and *alcoholism*. This would circumvent the need to search for all these separate options. Clearly, care is needed about where the term is truncated. If the stem is too short it will retrieve too many irrelevant records. The search for *alco\** would also retrieve *alcove*.

The wildcard symbol which is often a question mark (?) is useful when faced with different spelling. It can be inserted into the word when an extra letter is sometimes used. *Behavio?r* will search for *behaviour* (British English) and *behavior* (American English). Of course, the truncation symbol (ie. *behavio\**) could be used but that would yield *behaviourism, behaviorism, behavioural, behavioral* as well and those terms may not be required, The wildcard symbol cannot be used at the start of a word, which means that words such as *etiology* would require entering both spellings (*etiology* and *aetiology*).

## Searching with Subject Headings (Controlled Vocabulary)

The second main approach to searching is to use subject headings or thesaurus searching. Databases describe subject headings in different ways. The Medline and Cochrane databases, for instance, use

the term MeSH (Medical Subject Headings), but subject headings may be described as "Descriptors" or even simply "Subject Terms." Some databases will describe them as "Keywords," which can be a little confusing because when constructing a free text search the researcher thinks in terms of key words to describe their information need. Subject headings are technically called "controlled vocabulary."

Subject headings are designed to identify the subject(s) of the article. In principle, material which covers the same subject matter will be assigned the same subject terms even if those terms do not themselves appear anywhere in the material. Subject headings are valuable because search results are not contingent on the researcher thinking of the right free text terms for the search, and they have the potential to retrieve articles that may use different words to describe the same concept.

There are two ways to establish the appropriate subject headings for a topic of interest. The first is to conduct a free text search, find a record that is useful, and use the subject headings assigned that record as a basis for a fresh search. The alternative is to locate the appropriate headings by searching through the database thesaurus. Searching the thesaurus is valuable because it often suggests other terms that would also inform the search and it overcomes problems associated with different spelling and terminology. Databases use different subject headings, so subject headings need to be adapted to suit each database. Fortunately, PubMed users do not need to be familiar with the MeSH terms that are the basis of MEDLINE searching. PubMed contains a sophisticated search engine that maps entered terms to the MeSH.

Many databases offer the option to "explode" subject headings to also include more specific or narrower terms in the search. This expands the search options. Below is an example from PubMed showing part of the MeSH structure in which the MeSH term *Alcoholism* appears:

```
Substance-Related Disorders
   Alcohol-Related Disorders
      Alcoholism
```

In PubMed the MeSH terms are automatically exploded unless that option is turned off. Using the example above, this means that a search for the MeSH term *alcohol-related disorders* would explode to also include a search for the MeSH term *alcoholism.*

It is important when employing subject headings to determine the year when the heading was introduced. This was one of the failings in the preliminary research for the John Hopkins University trial. The MeSH for the chemical was introduced in 1995. By using that MeSH (and not others also), the investigators missed material that was published prior (Perkins, 2001). If it is not otherwise clear, the year can be determined by looking at the search results for that heading and checking for the oldest dates. Even if the records have been retrospectively assigned headings these earlier records will be a useful guide.

There is a caveat regarding the use of subject headings, however. They are not always adequately or consistently applied. The indexing in Medline, for instance, has undergone criticism in the past (Dickersin, Scherer, & Lefebvre, 1995, p. 28), although there have been improvements in the period since (Glanville, Lefebvre, Miles, & Camosso-Stefinovic, 2006, pp. 131-132, 135), and as a general rule Medline indexing surpasses that found elsewhere. It can be frustrating, however, to look for the subject headings assigned a relevant article in the hope of finding precisely the search terms that might recover similar material only to find that the subject headings so allocated are not helpful. Indexers are not always expert in the subject area or methodological aspects of the articles they are indexing, and authors themselves do not always make their research methods or objectives sufficiently clear for indexers to assign subject terms at an appropriate level.

Searches only using subject headings are, therefore, dependent on the indexing of the databases and since this might not be comprehensive there is a risk of missing relevant material. This risk can be estimated by conducting sample searches using free text and subject headings together and then sample searches using subject headings only and comparing the results. If using subject headings only sees a marked decrease in relevant results, then clearly a search using subject headings alone may be a liability. In light of these various considerations, it is usually best to select a combination of free text words and also subject headings when identifying search terms.

## Selecting the Appropriate Methodology Filters

Methodological search filters enable the researcher to select the most useful evidence for each question type (effectiveness, prevention, risk/prognosis, assessment, and description) into which a search can be categorised. These filters should search for studies with the most rigorous methodology (Gibbs, 2003, p. 99; Shlonsky & Gibbs, 2004, pp. 141, 146). Gibbs (2003) uses the label MOLES ("Methodology-orienting locators for an evidence search") to describe these filters (p. 98), and he has provided a table listing in descending order of utility the filter terms for each question type (p. 100). The same table is also conveniently listed in his book's website: http:www.evidence.brookscole.com

If, for instance, the researcher were looking for material addressing effectiveness or prevention questions, then adding MOLES terms such as *random\**, OR *controlled clinical trial\**, OR *control group\**, OR *evaluation stud\**, OR *study design*, OR *double blind*, OR *placebo* would be appropriate. If looking for synthesis studies, such terms as *meta-anal\**, OR *meta anal\**, OR *systematic review\** would be suitable (Gibbs, 2003, p. 100).

These MOLES terms are designed for free text searching. With the exception of Medline, which has a policy of carefully indexing research methodologies, indexing is often variable and imprecise. It is better, therefore, not to rely solely on a search of methodological terms in the subject headings but to use a free text strategy. Such a search will then detect these terms in the title, or abstract, or subject headings (if they are indeed indexed), or in the full text of the document (if the full text is searchable). Of course, an article's title or abstract may not contain methodological terms either. Shlonsky, Baker, et al. (2011) found in their study that when the use of methodological terms did not retrieve an article this was often because the subject headings, title, and abstract lacked those terms. They do note that such terms are occurring with greater frequency in more recent publications (p. 397) so this will become less of a concern but clearly this does mean that employing methodological terms in a search may still sometimes miss relevant material. It is, therefore, best to experiment.

Methodological search terms can also be used to search for qualitative studies. These can be described according to the method used to collect data (e.g. *interview*, *audio-recording*, *focus group*, *participant observation*), or according to the methodology that was used (e.g. *grounded theory*, *ethnography*, *phenomenology*, or *action research*). Adding these terms to the keywords that identify the question may home in on qualitative studies. And, of course, adding such terms as *experience\**, or *attitude\**, or the word *qualitative* itself should locate qualitative studies.

## Constructing the Search Strategy

Once the researcher has established the search question, identified the search terms (key concepts and their synonyms, although the search itself may suggest more search terms), and selected the methodological filters, they are in a position to construct a search strategy.

This section will focus on how to construct a search strategy so that it can be interpreted by a database. Databases provide their own easily accessible tutorials and guides on the mechanics of searching their interfaces. There is no need to duplicate that information here and since databases undergo interface changes from time to time it becomes even less necessary to do so. This, then, will serve as a guide to principles of searching which can be applied across databases. Although this section will be largely familiar to skilled searchers, it may still serve as useful revision in some cases.

Constructing a search strategy involves pulling together the search terms and methodological filters (should these be used). This involves combining the search terms using the terms AND, OR, and NOT. These are called Boolean operators.

- AND is used to connect concepts. These are the ideas that must be present in the document for it to be relevant. AND requires that all the search terms appear in the same record. The more concepts connected using AND, the smaller the search result will be because of the requirement that the records contain *all* the concepts.

- OR is used to connect synonyms. OR requires that at least one of the search terms appears in the record. The more synonyms linked using OR, the larger the search result will be because of the requirement that the records contain *any* of the synonyms. The OR search need not merely be used for retrieving precise synonyms. If, for instance, the researcher were searching for material on two different interventions, they could conduct two separate searches but they could rather search for them both in the one search by linking them with the OR operator.

- NOT requires that the term not appear at all in any of the records, although clearly this operator needs to be used with caution.

Invariably, if the Boolean operator is not being used the system will default to AND. This means that a search for *alcohol abuse* will be interpreted as *alcohol* AND *abuse*. It is probably better, though, to enter the AND operator so that the relationships between the search terms are explicit.

Databases will also frequently offer proximity operators. This enables the searching of words within a certain range of each other or in the same paragraph. The operator NEAR in the Cochrane Library database, for instance, will find the search terms within six words of each other. This provides more control over the search strategy than use of the AND operator.

It is important when searching an unfamiliar database to check the help file. This will establish what Boolean operators are available and whether they must be in upper case, although it would appear that consistent use of the upper case regardless of the database is safe. The help files will also explain what the truncation and wildcard symbols are and whether the database provides for proximity searching.

The principles considered thus far can now be put in a structured search in a database.

## Applying a Search Strategy to a Case Scenario: Some Examples

Let us assume a 16 year old male presents, suffering from alcohol addiction. We are faced with looking for studies which might suggest a suitable intervention. We might consider cognitive behavioural therapy. We may understand from previous reading or from comments from colleagues that this therapy has been successfully applied but we wish to know what its current status is. We may also consider that studies of its efficacy may suggest other (better?) interventions. We could frame the question in this way:

*If an adolescent male suffering from alcohol addiction undergoes cognitive behavioural therapy or not, then will they reduce their drinking?*

This is an effectiveness question. It is framed in an *if/then* format which Gibbs (2003) suggests for effectiveness questions. These kinds of questions can be answered through a process of testing or verification (p. 67). As an aside, we may have found that the adolescent is suffering from depression and after interviewing or investigation of the background, we may have reason to think either that the depression is alcohol-induced or that the depression is itself the cause of the addiction. We have, then, become aware of other issues which we might consider building into our search. But we do need to be careful about utilising too many concepts because of the risk of reducing our search result too markedly. Such complexity in a case scenario brings to the fore the fact that social work is a complex activity and ready solutions in the literature which can be directly applied will only sometimes be forthcoming. The literature may give insights and prompts, but the practitioner will need to bring their skills and experience to bear in interpreting the usefulness of the literature.

There are clearly five concepts in our scenario: adolescent, male, alcohol addiction, cognitive behavioural therapy, and treatment. If we were using the PICO framework to structure our question, the concepts *adolescent, male,* and *alcohol addiction* would inform our P (population) search. *Cognitive behavioural therapy* would appear as the I (intervention). We have no specific concept(s) for the C (Comparison). O (outcome) would be defined by terms suggesting efficacy.

Our first task is to consider synonyms for these concepts.

The first concept is *adolescent* and the synonyms are *adolescents, adolescence, youth, youths, teenager, teenagers.* But we could express the variant endings as adolescen*, youth* and teenager* (assuming an asterisk is the truncation symbol in the database we are using), thereby removing the need to enter all these options.

The second concept is *male*. We will not include this concept in our search. The kind of health and social science databases we would be using usually permit us to select gender as a filter. We can apply that filter (or enter the term itself) only once we have conducted our search and we have seen the number of search results. This strategy refers to our principle of not building too many concepts into our search.

The third concept is *alcohol addiction*, so this would also suggest the terms *alcohol abuse*, *alcoholic*, *alcoholism*. Once again, the truncation symbol (*alcohol\**) will retrieve these options.

The fourth concept is *cognitive behavioural therapy*. The synonyms would translate as *cognitive behavioral therapy, cognitive behaviour therapy*, or *cognitive behavior therapy*. But we could express these variations as *cognitive behavio\* therapy*. Clearly, the truncation symbol saves time. We could also consider using *CBT*, although invariably when an acronym or abbreviation is used in a record the full term appears at least once in a prominent place in that record, so it would probably be unnecessary. But to err on the side of caution we will also include the acronym in our search. Acronyms can, of course, represent more than one entity, but the acronym may be informed by other terms in the search.

The fifth concept is *treatment* and there are a host of synonyms we could use, including such terms as *effective, efficacy, rehabilitation, recovery*. It would probably be unnecessary to include this concept in our search since we can assume that most records including the terms *adolescents, alcohol addiction*, and a therapy, such as *cognitive behavioural therapy*, will be looking at treatment outcomes.

We could set out our search terms as a sentence or a "search string," combining each concept with its synonyms and enclosing them in brackets, and then connecting the bracketed sets with AND. This is how that would look:

(adolescen\* OR youth\* OR teenager\*) AND (alcohol\*) AND ("cognitive behavio\* therapy" OR cbt)

This would combine each individual word with its variant endings from the first bracketed set with the word *alcohol* and its variant endings from the second set and with the therapy option from the third set, thereby producing a very large number of combinations.

The advanced search facility in most databases will enable us to produce complex search sequences like this by providing a series of search boxes into which we can place our synonyms, whilst joining each box with AND. A portion of our search is below to serve as an example. Note that placing keywords in quote marks (i.e. "cognitive behavio\* therapy") will search for the terms as a phrase.

```
adolescen* OR youth* OR teenager*
AND
alcohol*
AND
"cognitive behavio* therapy" OR cbt
```

Thus far, the search has been constructed using free text searching, considering concepts and synonyms and how these are best combined. We will, however, wish to consider subject headings. To do this we will use PubMed as our example because this database is one that is freely accessible to all.

In PubMed the subject heading (MeSH) for *adolescent* is indeed *adolescent*. We learn this by entering the term *adolescent* into the search box and selecting the MeSH option from the drop down menu. In examining the description for *adolescent* we also discover that *adolescent* will search for other terms such as *teens, teenagers, youth*, and *adolescence*. A key point to note is that if we are doing a free text search in PubMed and truncate a term which happens to be a MeSH term, the search will retrieve that MeSH term but not explode that term to include more specific or narrower MeSH terms in the search result. If, then, we entered the term *adolescent* as a free text search, PubMed would retrieve this term as a MeSH heading along with narrower terms (if such exist) and it would also search for this term in the title and abstract. If, however, we truncated the term (i.e. *adolescen\**) it would retrieve the term *adolescent* from the MeSH but not explode the term to include narrower terms. In this case, however, that is not a concern since there are no narrower terms under *adolescent*.

The MeSH for *alcohol addiction* is *alcoholism*. We learn this by entering the term *alcohol addiction* into the search box and selecting the MeSH option. Examining the description for *alcoholism* shows that *alcoholism* covers the terms *alcohol abuse*, *alcohol dependence*, and *alcoholic intoxication* amongst others. We are given a choice of almost 50 subheadings (under *adolescent* there are 13 subheadings). These are terms used to find frequently discussed aspects of a subject. The subheadings in this case include *diagnosis*, *drug effects*, *psychology*, *rehabilitation*, and *therapy*. This means we could narrow our search by looking for records assigned the specific subject heading *alcoholism-therapy*. We could certainly limit our search to such options, but it is usually wiser not to limit to specific subheadings until we see the results for the subject headings themselves, which in this case is simply *alcoholism*.

The MeSH heading for *Cognitive behavioural therapy* is *Cognitive Therapy*. It sits in the MeSH structure under a broader subject heading *Behavior Therapy* (see below):

```
Psychotherapy
   Behavior Therapy
      Cognitive Therapy
            Acceptance and Commit-
                ment Therapy
         Mindfulness
```

*Cognitive Therapy* includes two narrower MeSH terms, *Acceptance and Commitment Therapy* and *Mindfulness*. Searching on *Cognitive Therapy* will explode to include these narrower terms.

In common with many other databases, a free text search on PubMed will also search subject headings. This means a free text search for *alcoholism* will search for subject headings in which *alcoholism* appears. But PubMed's indexing, however, is particularly sophisticated and automatically maps to MeSH headings which may not even contain the free text term that was used. If we entered the phrase *cognitive behavioural therapy*, it would search for this phrase but it would also map to *Cognitive Therapy* as a MeSH and retrieve records assigned that heading. Since the MeSH function is complex, it is wise to read the help files to ensure that maximum use is made of this facility.

Below is another example.

Assume we are tasked with managing the return of a 12 year old Australian Aboriginal boy from foster care to his family of origin. We have seen instances of re-entry to foster care following unsuccessful reunification, and we wish to know what strategies exist to avert this. Our question is

*… if an Australian Aboriginal child has been returned to their family of origin what factors will prevent successful reunification?*

Rephrasing the question can yield different search terms and this may add to our pool of results. Another way of stating the question, then, is to ask: what are the strategies to mitigate re-entry to foster care of an Australian Aboriginal child? Or perhaps, what are the causes and risks of re-entry to foster care of an Australian Aboriginal child?

This is different from our previous example because we do not have a specific intervention in mind. And as in the previous example there is no specific comparison. But even without an intervention component, we still have a population (Aboriginal foster child) and an issue (causes of re-entry). Thinking about concepts and synonyms, our search could appear as follows:

aborigin\* AND ("foster child\*" OR "foster care") AND (re-entry OR reentry OR reunification OR return) AND (risk\* OR permanency OR stability OR "parent child relations" OR "family relations")

There are a number of observations to make about this search:

- The term *Aboriginal* does not solely apply to Australia's indigenous population. Adding the term *Australian* to the search would, therefore, make the results immediately more relevant. But to do so would be to omit a number of records which refer to Australian Aboriginals but which do not use the term *Australian*, so it becomes necessary to omit this term from the search.
- This is a free text search, although if we were to look at some of the search results we would find that some of the terms appear as subject headings as well.
- The term *re-entry* has an alternative spelling, so this is also included in the search.
- The words and phrases in each bracketed set are not necessarily synonyms. This is particularly marked in the last set but for the purposes of the question and given the terms appearing in the other sets they will have similar implications.
- In this example there is not necessarily a direct match between each of the PICO components and each of the bracketed sets, although some of the PICO components are represented.

- If no such studies involving Aboriginal ethnicity exist, then other studies more generally on risk of re-entry might provide the next best guidance on how to proceed.

## Building the Search Incrementally

In the examples above, we constructed search strings of free text terms using a range of concepts and synonyms. Constructing the search in this way has the advantage of speed, although it may become confusing if it is a complex search requiring multiple groupings. But such a search also conceals important information about our search. It does not show where precisely the results are coming from. If our search retrieves few results, we do not know which terms are responsible for the low yield and which may require reconsideration.

We can avoid this difficulty if we build the search incrementally. Most databases enable the user to track the search history. This means we can conduct a search in manageable segments, and by viewing the search history we can see a list of the previous searches. We can then combine the results of the search sets as appropriate. Systematic reviews provide good examples of the manner in which reviewers search multiple combinations of free text truncated terms, subject terms, and sub-headings, in addition to filtering by methodology, publication type, gender, date range, and so on.

## Finding Too Many or Too Few Results

If the search retrieves an unmanageably large number of records, it becomes necessary to revisit the free text search terms and the subject headings. This may involve adopting more specific free text terms or even relying upon the subject headings alone for the search. If the database assigns sub-headings to its subject headings, employing these would make the search more precise. Limiting the search by date range is also a possibility. This might, however, have the effect of omitting earlier seminal studies, although it might be hoped that these would appear in the reference lists of the more recent relevant items.

If, on the other hand, an insufficient number of records has been retrieved to satisfy the need, then it becomes necessary to widen or expand the search. This would entail greater use of synonyms or perhaps even broadening the search question. "Exploding" the subject headings to include other narrower subject terms is a possibility, and if the subject headings have been refined with subheadings these headings might need to be removed.

## Searching Broadly Versus Narrowly

In constructing a search strategy, it is necessary to find a balance which provides comprehensive results without also retrieving too many irrelevant items (Higgins & Green, 2011, 6.4.4 Sensitivity versus precision). The terms "sensitivity" and "specificity' (or "precision"), used in other contexts in statistics, have been used to describe this feature of database searching. Clinical Queries in PubMed has sensitivity and specificity filters. So also does the database Cinahl. These are search formula which will further inform the search.

Sensitivity refers to "high recall, low precision" searching (De Brun & Pearce-Smith, 2009, p. 59). A highly sensitive search will retrieve a larger amount of relevant material but also a lot of material which is irrelevant. It is more inclusive and is used to avoid the risk of omitting relevant material (pp. 59-60).

Specificity (or precision) means "lower recall, higher precision" searching (De Brun & Pearce-Smith, 2009, p. 59). A highly specified search will mean a higher portion of the results will be relevant, but some of the relevant material will be omitted (pp. 59-60).

Sensitivity searching requires greater time to sift through the results. Wilczynski, Haynes, and Hedges (2006) pointedly state that "researchers... will best be served by the most sensitive search strategy *when they have time* [emphasis added]

to sort through articles" (p. 5). Time, however, is not necessarily something that social workers have at their disposal. These authors found that specificity was "enhanced" when they combined methodological search terms with content appropriate keywords, thereby decreasing the number of articles that needed to be sorted through to find relevant material (p. 6).

The *Cochrane Handbook* (Higgins & Green, 2011) also endorses a sensitive search where practicable, recommending "the sensitivity-maximizing version in combination with a highly sensitive subject search" (6.4.11.1 The Cochrane Highly Sensitive Search Strategies for identifying randomized trials in MEDLINE). The handbook suggests that if this retrieves too many results, "the sensitivity- and precision-maximizing version" should rather be used. Interestingly, it then adds this comment, "It should be borne in mind that MEDLINE abstracts can be read quite quickly as they are relatively short and, at a conservative estimate of 30 seconds per abstract, 1000 abstracts can be read in approximately 8 hours" (6.4.11.1). Whilst reading 1000 abstracts may be necessary when writing a systematic review, it is less likely that the busy practitioner will be able to engage with the literature at this level. But the point does establish that broad searching does not necessarily imply careless searching.

In sum, whether the researcher chooses to adopt a broad or more narrow search will ultimately be contingent on the amount of time available, the amount of material available, and the reason for the search.

## Documenting the Search

It is a good idea to document the search listing the date and the databases or other sources used, detailing the search strategy, the number of results, and any ideas that the search may have generated. This may be valuable information which could inform another separate search or provide useful information at a future date.

## Summarising Key Points

These points below serve as a checklist for searching:

1. Try to use subject headings (exploded if appropriate) and free-text terms for concepts, ensuring a wide range of synonyms.
2. Avoid too many different concepts, but use a wide variety of synonyms and related terms (both free text and subject headings) for the concepts that are used.
3. Combine different concepts with AND; synonyms must be combined with OR.
4. Avoid use of the NOT operator in combining search sets, unless there is little risk of inadvertently missing something.
5. Use truncation to ensure maximum use of free text terms.
6. Avoid language limiters. Although the article may be in another language and an English abstract may be all that is available, key parts of an article can be translated.
7. It is not always possible to search for every aspect of a question. The concepts may not be well described in the title or abstract and may not be well indexed with subject headings.
8. Ideally aim for high sensitivity to reduce the chance of missing something, although in a practice context where time is at a premium this may not be possible.
9. Avoid limiting searches to keywords in the title and abstract. In many databases not all the records possess abstracts. In addition, the researcher cannot be confident that the terms they have selected for their search are used by the abstractor. Authors and searchers often use different vocabulary to describe the same concept. As an example, a search for the phrase "quality of life" in PubMed retrieves over ten thousand citations where quality of life was deemed a major topic of the article by the indexer, but the term, "quality of life," did not appear in either the title or abstract.
10. Examine the subject headings and abstracts of useful material with a view to locating other search terms.
11. Query several relevant databases before deciding that there is sufficient material. That decision is usually only justified if sufficient material has been located satisfactorily addressing the question or if the same literature is recurring yielding nothing new in which case further investment of time is not worth the effort.
12. Avoid beginning with a conclusion and only searching for supporting evidence ("backward reasoning") (Gibbs, 2003, p. 7). Searching only for material that supports a favoured position is to engage in what has been labelled "an artfully concealed lie" (Gibbs, 2003, p. 89; Shlonsky and Gibbs, 2004, p. 142). Shlonsky and Gibbs (2004) advise the researcher "to search as diligently for *dis*confirming evidence as they do for evidence that supports their hunches" (p. 142).
13. Recheck the search strategy and perhaps broaden it if the search retrieves nothing of relevance. There may be little or no research available. Gibbs (2003) observes that "a well-planned and executed search that finds nothing *is* a finding — it means we may not now know given the state of existing knowledge!" (p. 93). But assurance is first necessary that there really is no evidence and that results are not simply being compromised because of failure to use the appropriate databases, or most appropriate keywords, or subject headings.

## SELECTION

Once the search has been conducted, the next task is to sift through the records for those that will be most relevant.

Thomas and Hodges (2010) advise reading the clearly relevant material in some detail to clarify the ideas and arguments. Once that is done "possibly relevant" material is more easily identified (p. 116). This may seem obvious but it avoids stewing over a record unsure of its value and then making an almost arbitrary decision to retain or discard it.

What makes an article or study "relevant"? Clearly, material which addresses the question or provides insights which will inform a practice context, but once identified this material will require appraisal. The purpose of appraisal is to answer three questions: What are the results of the study? Are the results valid? How will these results help? (De Brun & Pearce-Smith, 2009, p. 103; Gibson & Glenny, 2007, p. 97). It is to establish which articles or studies are the most valid and applicable.

There are some basic criteria which will help in the initial appraisal of relevant material. This is a first level of evaluation. If methodology filters are used, homing in on research material, it is less likely that some of this evaluative criteria will be required.

### First Level of Evaluation

- Is the author(s) identified and are the contact details available? Is the author(s) credentialed in the area? If the author is not an expert in the area they may draw extensively from authors who are, thus making the item of some use. Nevertheless, if the content appears useful, it will still be necessary to read the original authors to ensure they have been interpreted correctly.
- Has the author(s) a bias? Perhaps the study is compromised by its funders? Perhaps the writer has a particular ideology or experience which has unduly influenced them? Bias, however, does not necessarily mean the material is without merit.
- Is the article/report published in a refereed journal or from a well-known publisher? Even if it is not, the material can still be significant as is clear from the comments above regarding grey literature. Grey literature will require the same scrutiny as published literature.
- Is the material well referenced? Are sources cited credible? Can the information be verified elsewhere in credible sources? Even so, perhaps the references only support points which no one disputes, although the overall conclusion may remain unsupported.
- Is the material recent or is it dated? It may not be recent but it may still be valuable. After all, seminal studies only become seminal because they have been around for a while.
- How is the argument developed? Gibbs (2003) has helpfully described a number of fallacies: "uncritical documentation," "appeal to authority," (p. 28), "appeal to experience" (p. 29), "vague" or "poorly formulated" questions (p. 30), "vague quantifying adjectives" or terms (such as "generally," "most likely," "probably") (pp. 30-31), "appealing to tradition" or "precedent" (p. 31). Evidence of these shortcomings in a document is certainly grounds for discarding, although the material may prompt a particular research direction.

These criteria provide initial conditions that need to be met. As is clear, they cannot be applied in a knee-jerk manner for they each require qualification on a case-by-case basis. If, however, material fails the nuanced application of these criteria then, indeed, the material can probably be safely put aside without the need for closer scrutiny.

Crisp (2004) has also suggested nine questions which she encourages researchers to use when selecting research evidence. One question in particular, "Is the basis of this evidence methodologically sound?" (p. 81) requires rather close scrutiny of the content, so the issues this raises will appear in a discussion of second level criteria.

- "Why am I using this evidence?" (p. 81). If the evidence is being used to support an argument or practice decision, it must be relevant.
- "Am I only using this evidence because it is readily available to me or because I believe it to be credible?" (p. 81). Evidence needs to be credible, not merely available.
- "Am I using this evidence without considering how apt it is for the context because it comes from an eminent source?" (p. 81).
- "To what extent do personal factors impinge on my evaluation of this evidence?" (p. 81). Being conscious of how one's own experiences, background, and biases might shape the interpretation of research findings is important.
- "Will others be convinced by this evidence?" (p. 81). Research evidence needs to be perceived to be credible.
- "Is it possible that there is more appropriate evidence? If so, do I have the resources (including time) to search for other evidence?" (p. 82).
- "Are there reasons why this evidence cannot be applied?" (p. 82). Cultural or other contexts may raise issues of generalisability.
- "Is it possible that this evidence has been superseded?" (p. 82). New research evidence may confirm earlier evidence but it might also contradict it.

What is notable about this set of questions is that, although as in the first list it includes some external criteria, it also includes questions which probe the researcher's attitudes and motivations and has the effect of making the researcher more self-conscious about how they are evaluating the material and whether decisions are transparent. That makes this criteria very useful.

Material located on the Internet should be subjected to these different sets of criteria as well. But there is an additional evaluative filter available when encountering material on the Internet. The website's domain name which appears in the URL (web address) gives added information to aid evaluative decisions.

The domain name occurs before the first backslash (/). It will appear as edu, org, com, net, gov, govt, or a country code. Truncating the URL back to the domain name will establish the nature of the source. Domain names which include edu, org (they may be professional or charitable organisations), and gov are more likely to have scholarly content (Szuchman & Thomlison, 2011, p. 65), although even in the case of an edu address the site may be the personal website of a lecturer or professor and, therefore, not have undergone peer review.

Google searchers can search for specific domains by adding the word *site* to the search. This command instructs Google to search only in the specified domain. This means that a search for *youth "alcohol abuse" site.gov* would search U.S. government websites for the term *youth* and the phrase *"alcohol abuse."* Similarly, *youth "alcohol abuse" site:gov.uk* would search government websites from the United Kingdom. Searching within domains, therefore, is a useful evaluative filter which also serves to reduce the search result.

## Second Level of Evaluation

Once various combinations of the above criteria have been applied, the remaining material can be subjected to a second level of evaluation. This is in effect to ask whether the information or argument in the article or study is unambiguous and rigorously-derived and whether the conclusions follow logically from the rest of the content.

Pawson, Boaz, Grayson, Long, and Barnes (2003) have developed a set of helpful principles which can be used to appraise material at this deeper level. They label these principles "TAPUPA," based on the quality dimensions which they have suggested.

- **T**ransparency – is it open to scrutiny?
- **A**ccuracy – is it well grounded?
- **P**urposivity – is it fit for purpose?
- **U**tility – is it fit for use?
- **P**ropriety – is it legal and ethical?
- **A**ccessibility – is it intelligible? (p. 40)

The TAPUPA framework is designed to assess the quality of social care knowledge more widely, but it also has the virtue of capturing many of the characteristics of social work research. Although Pawson et al. (2003) point out that these are "basic questions" in the sense that they are "generic" and "elemental" (p. 37), they do require careful content analysis. "Transparency", for instance, requires that the material provide detail regarding the theoretical framework, rationale, and process of analysis (pp. 38, 42). "Accuracy" requires that assertions, conclusions, and recommendations are solidly based on data (p. 38). "Purposivity" requires experience at judging appropriate methodologies (pp. 38-39).

The generic nature of these principles gives them wide application and this is their value. But, of course, questions regarding the nature of the argument or study, its clarity and rigour, will be rendered more specific contingent on the nature of the material.

Such questions clearly undergird the checklist below for appraising systematic reviews which has been adapted from Oxman (1995). Amongst the evaluative criteria for evaluating systematic reviews are the following:

- Is the question which the review seeks to address clearly stated?

- Is the search strategy clearly set out? Is it systematic and thorough so that the relevant studies are identified?
- Are the inclusion criteria adopted by the reviewers made explicit, and are they appropriate or is there evidence of selection bias?
- Is the validity of the studies adequately appraised?
- Are the conclusions or recommendations supported by the data? (p. 78).

The diversity of problems, contexts, and interventions associated with social work activity means that statistical comparisons are difficult to achieve. There are too many variables and results may have limited transferability to other contexts. Not only does a systematic review, therefore, require evaluation on its own merits (as above), but its applicability to a specific case scenario can, of course, only be determined on a case-by-case basis after careful practitioner scrutiny.

Gibbs (2003) discusses the usefulness of the Quality of Study Rating Form (QSRF), which had earlier undergone several iterations and was revised again by Gibbs for his 2003 text (pp. 157-158). He observes that it had been designed for use by students to evaluate the relative merits of studies and treatments. In this context, he also notes that it is particularly valuable for evaluating randomised controlled trials but it can be used to rate any effectiveness study (p. 158). This set of questions below has been adapted from criteria (there are 22 in total) that Gibbs sets out in detail (pp. 160-164):

- Does the study describe the subject(s) clearly and the presenting problems?
- Is the treatment clearly specified so that it could be replicated?
- Does the study identify where the treatment occurred and over how long, and provide contact details of those at the facility?

- Does the study explain the rationale for the interventions used or cite literature that can be followed up?
- Were the subjects randomly selected for inclusion in the study, and once selected were they randomly assigned to the control or treatment groups?
- Were subjects in the control and treatment groups treated equally prior to treatment?
- Were subjects unaware of whether they were in the control or treatment groups?

Gibbs includes a range of other criteria which involve statistical analysis (pp. 161-164) and which require rather more detail than can be set out here. Nevertheless, the criteria above give some guidance regarding what to look for, and only once there is assurance on these points is there any obligation to subject the studies to statistical scrutiny.

These criteria address the question of whether the results are internally valid. In the typical format as laid out in most published reviews and studies, there are key places where determinative information to inform evaluation can be expected. The *Title*, *Abstract* or *Introduction/background* should clearly state the question. Failure to do so may raise a red flag regarding further weaknesses in the paper. The *Methods* or *Methodology* and *Results* sections should provide information to address the criteria suggested above. These sections will, therefore, provide the data to inform whether an explanation of the findings as set out in the *Discussion* and *Conclusions* are accurately represented or if there are other ways of interpreting that data.

In addition to meeting this criteria for internal validity, a study will also need to satisfy external validity to be deemed relevant. This is a question of applicability and asks whether the results will help in a particular practice context. These are the questions which require answering before study results can be applied:

- Is the client(s) and their situation sufficiently similar to those in the study to make the results applicable?
- Is the intervention feasible? Are the resources available to pursue the intervention or recommended course of action?
- Does the client support this intervention or recommended course of action?
- Will the potential benefits outweigh any identifiable harms?

A range of appraisal instruments and frameworks is available for use in the assessment of qualitative research. Some are generic, being applicable to almost all qualitative research designs; others have specifically been developed for use with certain methods or techniques. Hannes (2011) has noted that tools for the appraisal of qualitative research usually share some basic criteria. These include the requirement for ethical research, relevance to practice or policy, rigorous methodology, and equally rigorous reporting (Section 1: Core criteria for quality assessment). But he also notes there is debate regarding whether such concepts as validity and reliability can be applied to qualitative research. He takes the view that validity, reliability, and objectivity can be established, and that researcher bias is the "core criterion" to be evaluated. The researcher needs to be able to make their "influence and assumptions clear and to provide accurate information on the extent to which the findings of a research report hold true" (Introduction).

Commenting on the difficulty associated with developing universal standards for qualitative studies, Gibbs (2003) specifically discusses the Qualitative Study Quality (QSQ) form. This has been created based on other qualitative study rating forms and on extensive discussions on qualitative study quality (p. 228). Gibbs sets out the 22 evaluative criteria which comprise the form (pp. 228-234). Below is a set of questions adapted from that form which will give an idea of the detailed contents of the QSQ, whilst also providing sufficient criteria to make evaluative assessments of some qualitative studies:

- Is the research question clear and stated before the study began? This may not entail a very specific question, but there should at least be a general statement about what the study was designed to show.
- Is the methodology identified and appropriate? Does the study specify why a particular methodology was selected, and are there references to literature that define the methodology?
- Does the study explain from where the subjects were selected or from where their records for observation were derived?
- Is the time frame of the study specified?
- Does the study record the number of refusals to participate or respondents dropping out of the study and the reasons?
- What criteria was used for selecting subjects or records for observation? Does the study provide sufficient information to permit replication of the procedure?
- Do the authors state that they selected subjects or records according to a random selection procedure, and is there sufficient detail to allow replication?
- Does the study rely on one single observer or preferably two or more independent observers?
- Does the study make clear how much agreement existed between observers once their assessments were compared, and what procedure was used to check this?
- Does the study supply information which would suggest that the author(s) ensured respondents gave accurate responses and that their known participation in the study did not influence their responses?
- Is there a clear link between the observations and the conclusions?

- Are the transcripts of interviews or the records available so that the data could be checked?
- Is an independent assessor of the observations identified to confirm that they also drew the same conclusions as the study's authors?
- Does the study avoid unwarranted extrapolation? If the sample was not randomised, do the authors refrain from extrapolating the results beyond those in the sample?

Lincoln and Guba (1985) discuss four "trustworthiness criteria" to evaluate qualitative research findings: "credibility," "transferability," "dependability," and "confirmability." They suggest that these four terms are loosely equivalent to the terms "internal validity," "external validity," "reliability," and "objectivity" used in reference to quantitative studies (p. 300). Lincoln and Guba's detailed discussion provides multiple suggestions of how these criteria can be met along with caveats and pitfalls (pp. 301-327). Drawing on Lincoln and Guba, these criteria are described in brief below to give an idea regarding their focus and intent.

- **Credibility:** Was the inquiry carried out in such a way that the findings would be approved by the participants who are the subject of the inquiry? (p. 314). This would include efforts made by the researchers for respondents to be able to review transcripts to confirm or clarify interpretations (pp. 301, 314). It would also include triangulation using "multiple and different *sources*, *methods*, *investigators* and *theories*" (p. 305).
- **Transferability:** To what extent can the findings be applied to similar settings? Can hypotheses be developed which have application in different settings? The researcher is "responsible for providing the widest possible range of information for

inclusion" so that the reader can make an informed decision about whether transfer is possible (p. 316).

- **Dependability:** How dependable are the accounts given that changes to the entity being studied may occur during fieldwork? This criterion evaluates whether the process of research is logical and clearly documented. This involves keeping clear and detailed records (e.g. transcriptions and recordings) which can be subjected to an audit trail (pp. 316-318).

- **Confirmability:** Does the study indicate the extent to which the research findings are determined by the participants in the study and not the researcher? This would entail researchers reflecting on the impact they may have had on the research and providing information on their background and perspective. An audit process examining the data, findings, interpretations, and recommendations, and attesting that it is supported by data would establish confirmabilty. So would keeping a reflective journal (pp. 318-319).

Although Litva and Jacoby (2007) do not wish to be seen to be creating a "rigid checklist" (p. 162), they acknowledge the value of these same four criteria (p. 163). Hannes (2011) also believes this criteria suggests the methodological standard that a qualitative study should be able to attain, although he recognises that a study may follow appropriate procedures and yet the data be poorly interpreted, and conversely a study may lack clarity in its methodology and yet still provide valuable insight (Section 1: Core criteria for quality assessment: What indications are we looking for in an original research paper?)

The various criteria outlined in this section contain the basic questions necessary for assessing the quality of quantitative and qualitative research studies and is admittedly a brief survey. Further

more detailed resources for learning these sort of appraisal skills can be found in Gibbs (2003) who devotes four chapters on how to appraise studies that evaluate the effectiveness of treatment, how to appraise systematic reviews and meta-analyses, assessment and risk/prognosis studies, and descriptive and qualitative studies (pp. 147-236). Resources can also be found at the book's website: http://www.evidence.brookscole.com

There are also a number of appraisal instruments that are available on the Internet. Two commonly used critical appraisal tools are the Qualitative Assessment and Review Instrument (QARI) Instrument and the Critical Appraisal Skills Programme (CASP) instrument. Both contain ten quality criteria. Pearson and Hannes (2013) compare the differences between the two (pp. 229-237). These tools are listed below along with other checklists and tools that are easily accessible on the Internet. They clearly define what is meant by each individual criterion, making it easier for practitioners who may have less confidence in appraising qualitative research.

## Qualitative Assessment and Review Instrument (QARI) (http://joannabriggs.org/sumari.html)

The QARI software tool from the Joanna Briggs Institute (JBI) is designed for appraising, extracting and synthesizing qualitative research. Although subscription is required to gain full benefits, the appraisal forms can be found on various websites.

## The University of Oxford Centre for Evidence Based Medicine (http://www.cebm.net/index.aspx?o=1157)

This site provides critical appraisal sheets for systematic reviews and randomised controlled trials, setting out what questions to ask and what to look for.

## Critical Appraisal Skills Programme (CASP) (http://www.casp-uk.net/)

This programme includes eight critical appraisal tools which are free to download and can be used by anyone under the Creative Commons License.

## CONCLUSION

Developments in information technology have facilitated evidence-based practice (Gambrill, 2006, p. 341; Gibbs, 2003, p. 15). But the tools available to the practitioner need to be fully harnessed if there is not to be risk of significantly relevant information being overlooked. It is, therefore, necessary to be familiar with the information resources and to know when the use of any one of them is appropriate. It is also necessary to master the basic principles and practices of searching for and selecting material which is useful in practice. This chapter has sought to summarise some of the resources that are available, to set out the principles of searching, and to summarise some useful criteria for evaluating sources. The potential benefits associated with the vast plethora of material available need to be maximised so that the social work practitioner's efforts are informed by the best available research evidence.

## REFERENCES

Boeker, M., Vach, W., & Motschall, E. (2013). Google Scholar as replacement for systematic literature searches: Good relative recall and precision are not enough. *BMC Medical Research Methodology*, *13*(1), 131. doi:10.1186/1471-2288-13-131 PMID:24160679

Bramer, W. M., Giustini, D., Kramer, B. M. R., & Anderson, P. F. (2013). The comparative recall of Google Scholar versus PubMed in identical searches for biomedical systematic reviews: A review of searches used in systematic reviews. *Systematic Reviews*, *2*(1), 115. doi:10.1186/2046-4053-2-115 PMID:24360284

Bronson, D. E., & Davis, T. S. (2011). *Finding and evaluating evidence: Systematic reviews and evidence-based practice*. Oxford, UK: Oxford University Press. doi:10.1093/acprof:oso/9780195337365.001.0001

The Cochrane Collaboration. (2002). Publication bias: What is publication bias? Retrieved from http://www.cochrane-net.org/openlearning/html/mod15-2.htm

Crisp, B. R. (2004). Evidence-based practice and the borders of data in the global information era. *Journal of Social Work Education*, *40*, 73–86. doi:10.1080/10437797.2004.10778480

De Brun, C., & Pearce-Smith, N. (2009). *Searching skills toolkit: Finding the evidence*. Chichester, UK: Wiley Blackwell. doi:10.1002/9781444303599

Dickersin, K., Scherer, R., & Lefebvre, C. (1995). Identifying relevant studies for systematic reviews. In I. Chalmers & D. G. Altman (Eds.), *Systematic Reviews* (pp. 17–36). London: BMJ.

Drisko, J. (2014). Research evidence and social work practice: The place of evidence-based practice. *Clinical Social Work Journal*, *42*(2), 123–133. doi:10.1007/s10615-013-0459-9

Drisko, J. W., & Grady, M. (2012). *Evidence-based practice in clinical social work*. New York: Springer. doi:10.1007/978-1-4614-3470-2

Farace, D. J. (1998). Foreword. In *Perspectives on the design and transfer of scientific and technical information. Third international conference on grey literature, 13-14 November 1997.* Luxembourg. GL'97 proceedings (p. iii). Amsterdam: TransAtlantic GreyNet.

Fineout-Overholt, E., & Johnston, L. (2005). Teaching EBP: Asking searchable, answerable clinical questions. *Worldviews on Evidence-Based Nursing, 2*(3), 157–160. doi:10.1111/j.1741-6787.2005.00032.x PMID:17040536

Gambrill, E. (2006). Evidence-based practice and policy: Choices ahead. *Research on Social Work Practice, 16*(3), 338–357. doi:10.1177/1049731505284205

Gibbs, L. E. (2003). *Evidence-based practice for the helping professions: A practical guide with integrated multimedia.* Pacific Grove, CA: Brooks/Cole-Thomson Learning.

Gibson, F., & Glenny, A.-M. (2007). Critical appraisal of quantitative studies 1: Is the quality of the study good enough for you to use the findings? In J. V. Craig & R. L. Smyth (Eds.), *The evidence based practice manual for nurses* (2nd ed., pp. 95–126). Edinburgh, UK: Churchill Livingstone.

Glanville, J. M., Lefebvre, C., Miles, J. N. V., & Camosso-Stefinovic, J. (2006). How to identify randomized controlled trials in MEDLINE: Ten years on. *Journal of the Medical Library Association: JMLA, 94,* 130–136. Retrieved from http://www.mlanet.org/publications/jmla/ PMID:16636704

Gray, M., Joy, E., Plath, D., & Webb, S. A. (2014). Opinions about evidence: A study of social workers' attitudes towards evidence-based practice. *Journal of Social Work, 14*(1), 23–40. doi:10.1177/1468017313475555

Hannes, K. (2011). Critical appraisal of qualitative research. In J. Noyes, A. Booth, K. Hannes, A. Harden, J. Harris, S. Lewin, & C. Lockwood (Eds.), *Supplementary guidance for inclusion of qualitative research in Cochrane systematic reviews of interventions: Version 1.* Cochrane Collaboration Qualitative Methods Group. Retrieved from http://cqrmg.cochrane.org/supplemental-handbook-guidance

Higgins, J. P. T., & Green, S. (Eds.). (2011). *Cochrane handbook for systematic reviews of interventions: Version 5.1.0.* Retrieved from http://handbook.cochrane.org/

Holden, G., Barker, K., Rosenberg, G., & Cohen, J. (2012). Information for clinical social work practice: A potential solution. *Clinical Social Work Journal, 40*(2), 166–174. doi:10.1007/s10615-011-0336-3

Hopewell, S., McDonald, S., Clarke, M. J., & Egger, M. (2008). Grey literature in meta-analyses of randomized trials of health care interventions. *Cochrane Database of Systematic Reviews,* (2). doi:10.1002/14651858.MR000010.pub3 PMID:17443631

John Hopkins University. (2001). *Report of internal investigation into the death of a volunteer research subject.* Retrieved from http://www.hopkinsmedicine.org/press/2001/july/report_of_internal_investigation.htm

Lincoln, Y. S., & Guba, E. G. (1985). *Naturalistic inquiry.* Newbury Park, CA: SAGE.

Littell, J. H. (2010). Pulling together research studies to inform social work practice: The science of research synthesis. In A. E. Fortune, P. McCallion, & K. Briar-Lawson (Eds.), *Social work practice research for the twenty-first century* (pp. 162–180). New York: Columbia University Press.

Litva, A., & Jacoby, A. (2007). Qualitative research: Critical appraisal. In J. V. Craig & R. L. Smyth (Eds.), *The evidence based practice manual for nurses* (2nd ed., pp. 153–183). Edinburgh, UK: Churchill Livingstone.

Luzi, D. (2000). Trends and evolution in the development of grey literature: A review. *International Journal on Grey Literature, 1*(3), 106–116. doi:10.1108/14666180010345537

Mulrow, C. D. (1995). Rationale for systematic reviews. In I. Chalmers & D. G. Altman (Eds.), *Systematic Reviews* (pp. 1–8). London: BMJ.

Oxman, A. D. (1995). Checklists for review articles. In I. Chalmers & D. G. Altman (Eds.), *Systematic Reviews* (pp. 75–85). London: BMJ.

Pawson, R., Boaz, A., Grayson, L., Long, A., & Barnes, C. (2003). *Knowledge review 3: Types and quality of knowledge in social care.* Retrieved from Social Care Institute for Excellence website: http://www.scie.org.uk/publications/knowledgereviews/kr03.pdf

Pearson, A., & Hannes, K. (2013). Evidence about patients' experiences and concerns. In T. Hoffmann, S. Bennett, & C. Del Mar (Eds.), *Evidence-based practice across the health professions* (2nd ed., pp. 221–239). Sydney: Churchill Livingstone.

Perkins, E. (2001). Johns Hopkins' tragedy: Could librarians have prevented a death? Retrieved from http://newsbreaks.infotoday.com/nbreader.asp?ArticleID=17534

Sackett, D. L., Richardson, W. S., Rosenberg, W., & Haynes, R. B. (1997). *Evidence-based medicine: How to practice and teach EBM.* Edinburgh, UK: Churchill Livingstone.

Savulescu, J., & Spriggs, M. (2002). The hexamethonium asthma study and the death of a normal volunteer in research. *Journal of Medical Ethics, 28*(1), 3–4. doi:10.1136/jme.28.1.3 PMID:11834748

Schardt, C., Adams, M. B., Owens, T., Keitz, S., & Fontelo, P. (2007). Utilization of the PICO framework to improve searching PubMed for clinical questions. *BMC Medical Informatics and Decision Making, 7*(16). doi:10.1186/1472-6947-7-16 PMID:17573961

Shlonsky, A., Baker, T. M., & Fuller-Thomson, E. (2011). Using methodological search filters to facilitate evidence-based social work practice. *Clinical Social Work Journal, 39*(4), 390–399. doi:10.1007/s10615-010-0312-3

Shlonsky, A., & Gibbs, L. (2004). Will the real evidence-based practice please stand up? Teaching the process of evidence-based practice to the helping professions. *Brief Treatment and Crisis Intervention, 4*(2), 137–153. doi:10.1093/brief-treatment/mhh011

Shlonsky, A., Noonan, E., Littell, J. H., & Montgomery, P. (2011). The role of systematic reviews and the Campbell Collaboration in the realization of evidence-informed practice. *Clinical Social Work Journal, 39*(4), 362–368. doi:10.1007/s10615-010-0307-0

Shultz, M. (2007). Comparing test searches in PubMed and Google Scholar. *Journal of the Medical Library Association: JMLA, 95*(4), 442–445. doi:10.3163/1536-5050.95.4.442 PMID:17971893

Szuchman, L. T., & Thomlison, B. (2011). *Writing with style: APA style for social work* (4th ed.). Australia: Brooks/Cole, Cengage Learning.

Thomas, D. R., & Hodges, I. D. (2010). *Designing and managing your research project: Core knowledge for social and health researchers*. Los Angeles, CA: SAGE.

Wilczynski, N. L., Haynes, R. B., & Hedges, T. (2006). Optimal search strategies for identifying mental health content in MEDLINE: An analytic survey. *Annals of General Psychiatry*, 5(4). doi:10.1186/1744-859X-5-4 PMID:16556313

Wilson, D. B. (2009). Missing a critical piece of the pie: Simple document search strategies inadequate for systematic reviews. *Journal of Experimental Criminology*, 5(4), 429–440. doi:10.1007/s11292-009-9085-5

## ADDITIONAL READING

Anastas, J. W. (2004). Quality in qualitative evaluation: Issues and possible answers. *Research on Social Work Practice*, 14(1), 57–65. doi:10.1177/1049731503257870

Atkins, D., Best, D., Briss, P. A., Eccles, M., Falck-Ytter, Y., & Flottorp, S. et al. (2004). Grading quality of evidence and strength of recommendations. *BMJ (Clinical Research Ed.)*, 328(7454), 1490–1494. doi:10.1136/bmj.328.7454.1490 PMID:15205295

Beaven, O., & Craig, J. V. (2007). Searching the literature. In J. V. Craig & R. L. Smyth (Eds.), *The evidence-based practice manual for nurses* (2nd ed., pp. 51–94). Edinburgh, UK: Churchill Livingstone.

Berman, Y. (1995). Knowledge transfer in social work: The role of grey documentation. *The International Information & Library Review*, 27(2), 143–154. doi:10.1016/S1057-2317(95)80003-4

Burdett, S., Stewart, L. A., & Tierney, J. F. (2003). Publication bias and meta-analysis. *International Journal of Technology Assessment in Health Care*, 19(1), 129–134. doi:10.1017/S0266462303000126 PMID:12701945

Cline, R. J. W., & Haynes, K. M. (2001). Consumer health information seeking on the Internet: The state of the art. *Health Education Research*, 16(6), 671–692. doi:10.1093/her/16.6.671 PMID:11780707

Dixon-Woods, M., Shaw, R. L., Agarwal, S., & Smith, J. A. (2004). The problem of appraising qualitative research. *Quality & Safety in Health Care*, 13(3), 223–225. doi:10.1136/qshc.2003.008714 PMID:15175495

Drisko, J. W. (1997). Strengthening qualitative studies and reports: Standards to promote academic integrity. *Journal of Social Work Education*, 33, 185–197. Retrieved from http://www.tandfonline.com/toc/uswe20/current

Eysenck, H. J. (1995). Problems with meta-analysis. In I. Chalmers & D. G. Altman (Eds.), *Systematic Reviews* (pp. 64–74). London: BMJ.

Gilgun, J. F. (1994). A case for case studies in social work research. *Social Work*, 39, 371–380. doi:10.1093/sw/39.4.371

Lee, E., Mishna, F., & Brennenstuhl, S. (2010). How to critically evaluate case studies in social work. *Research on Social Work Practice*, 20(6), 682–689. doi:10.1177/1049731509347864

Littell, J. H., Corcoran, J., & Pillai, V. (2008). *Systematic reviews and meta-analysis*. New York: Oxford University Press. doi:10.1093/acprof:oso/9780195326543.001.0001

Martin, J. L., Perez, V., Sacristan, M., & Alvarez, E. (2005). Is grey literature essential for a better control of publication bias in psychiatry? An example from three meta-analyses of schizophrenia. *European Psychiatry, 20*(8), 550–553. doi:10.1016/j.eurpsy.2005.03.011 PMID:15994063

Mays, N., & Pope, C. (2000). Qualitative research in health care: Assessing quality in qualitative research. *BMJ (Clinical Research Ed.), 320*(7226), 50–52. doi:10.1136/bmj.320.7226.50 PMID:10617534

Morse, J. M., Barrett, M., Mayan, M., Olson, K., & Spiers, J. (2002). Verification strategies for establishing reliability and validity in qualitative research. *International Journal of Qualitative Methods, 1*(2), 13–22. Retrieved from http://www.iiqm.ualberta.ca/en/International-JournalofQualitat.aspx

Mullen, P. D., & Ramirez, G. (2006). The promise and pitfalls of systematic reviews. *Annual Review of Public Health, 27*(1), 81–102. doi:10.1146/annurev.publhealth.27.021405.102239 PMID:16533110

Richardson, W. S., Wilson, M. C., Nishikawa, J., & Hayward, R. S. A. (1995). The well-built clinical question: A key to evidence-based decisions. *ACP Journal Club, 123*(3), A12–A13. Retrieved from http://acpjc.acponline.org/ PMID:7582737

Sandars, S., & Del Mar, C. (2005). Clever searching for evidence: New search filters can help to find the needle in the haystack. *BMJ (Clinical Research Ed.), 330*(7501), 1162–1163. doi:10.1136/bmj.330.7501.1162 PMID:15905232

Silberg, W. M., Lundberg, G. D., & Musacchio, R. A. (1997). Assessing, controlling, and assuring the quality of medical information on the Internet: Caveant lector et viewor – Let the reader and viewer beware. *Journal of the American Medical Association, 277*(15), 1244–1245. doi:10.1001/jama.1997.03540390074039 PMID:9103351

Smyth, R. L. (2007). Systematic reviews: What are they and how can they be used? In J. V. Craig & R. L. Smyth (Eds.), *The evidence-based practice manual for nurses* (2nd ed., pp. 185–207). Edinburgh, UK: Churchill Livingstone.

Soydan, H., Mullen, E. J., Alexandra, L., Rehnman, J., & Li, Y.-P. (2010). Evidence-based clearinghouses in social work. *Research on Social Work Practice, 20*(6), 690–700. doi:10.1177/1049731510367436

Thompson, S. G. (1995). Why sources of heterogeneity in meta-analysis should be investigated. In I. Chalmers & D. G. Altman (Eds.), *Systematic Reviews* (pp. 48–63). London: BMJ.

Thyer, B. A. (Ed.). (2001). *Handbook of social work research methods*. Thousand Oaks, CA: Sage. doi:10.4135/9781412986182

Yeager, K. R., & Roberts, A. R. (2006). A practical approach to formulating evidence-based questions in social work. In A. R. Roberts & K. J. Yeager (Eds.), *Foundations of evidence-based social work practice* (pp. 47–58). Oxford, UK: Oxford University Press.

## KEY TERMS AND DEFINITIONS

**Boolean Operators:** Words that combine search terms to either broaden or reduce a search result.

**Controlled Vocabulary:** Another term for subject headings.

**Database:** A searchable electronic system that stores and indexes the abstracts (and sometimes full text) of published and unpublished records.

**Descriptors:** A term assigned by some databases to controlled vocabulary.

**Free Text:** Words that are entered into a database as they would if they were spoken.

**Index:** Another term for thesaurus. "Index term" is a synonym for controlled vocabulary.

**Search Strategy:** A combination of selected free text and subject heading terms which are used when searching for material to address a question.

**Subject Headings:** Used to standardise the indexing in a database. This enables the searcher to select and search for synonyms or related and preferred terms and also to see descriptions of the terms. Subject headings identify the content of the item and are added to the thesaurus or index.

**Text Word:** Words that have not been individually indexed in the database, i.e. they do not appear in the database thesaurus.

**Thesaurus:** Many databases employ subject headings to standardise the indexing in the database. This enables the searcher to select and search for synonyms or related and preferred terms and also to see descriptions of the terms. This is also known as controlled vocabulary.

# Chapter 3
# Applying Evidence in Practice:
## Isn't that Straight-Forward?

**Ian Dore**
*University of Brighton, UK*

## ABSTRACT

*Judgement and decision-making lie at the heart of practice and are feats that practitioners perform under conditions that are complex and uncertain, the attainment of positive outcomes for service-users dependent upon the aptitude of those charged with the task and the scaffolding provided by their employing organisations. Faced with such a challenge, social workers somehow avoid paralysis and take action to support and protect those with whom they work, drawing on experience, skill, information, and intervention evidence. The way they negotiate, orientate, interpret, and apply this knowledge is often through unconscious thought processes that require illumination and balance. This chapter considers how practitioners make sense of the situations that they come into contact with and discusses the intuitive-analytical reasoning continuum integral to this. Attention is given to the role of value as an influence upon perception and subsequent interpretation, together with the role played by cognitive processes.*

## INTRODUCTION

### Inherent Intuition

Social work's multi-faceted nature makes it unique in many ways, the sphere of practice comprising an interplay of person-in-environment phenomena which the practitioner must orientate in order to realise positive change: emancipation, justice, or well-being. To do so, the individual worker travels alongside, within, and between the lives and experiences of individuals, attending to the idiosyncratic characteristics they encounter, unearthed as they move between indeterminate psychosocial worlds. To reach their destination, the positive outcome, the practitioner must make sense of that which confronts them, to make links between the worlds they discover (Schofield, 1998) and arrive at a judgement or decision capable of attaining that which first appears beyond comprehension. Social workers perform this task day in, day out, drawing on innate decision-making processes, often computed intuitively without conscious thought (Helm, 2011; Kirkman & Melrose, 2014; Munro, 2011). In tandem with this, practitioners, to a lesser or greater extent, apply external knowledge

DOI: 10.4018/978-1-4666-6563-7.ch003

to the situations they face, endeavouring to build a picture which attains a level of comprehension permitting judgement formation.

## APPLYING EVIDENCE IN PRACTICE

Decision-making is clearly a fallible activity, yet when faced with high levels of uncertainty individuals do not necessarily attend to information which might offer insight or prove enlightening (Webb, 2006), our hardwired biases seemingly dismissive. With the backdrop set, this chapter considers the application of evidence in practice, centring on the concept of evidence-based practice as a decision-making process, affiliated with Sackett, Rosenberg, Muir Gray, Haynes, & Richardson's (1996) definition of evidence-based medicine which sees it as "the conscientious, explicit, and judicious use of current best evidence in making decisions about the care of individual patients"; where best evidence is viewed as "clinically relevant research" (p. 71). Attention is, therefore, given to patterns of thinking, perception, and the influences which drive these processes. As the conduit for decision-making, the individual holds the key to the realisation of good practice and, therefore, efforts to foster their decision-making capabilities form part of the discussion.

Research indicates that biases cloud our ability to make decisions (Broadhurst et al., 2010; Kirkman & Melrose, 2014; Munro, 1999, 2011) and that effort and challenge is needed if they are to be in some way guarded against (Turney, 2009; Webb, 2006), often aided by the support of others (Helm, 2011; Kirkman & Melrose, 2014; Munro, 2011). For the purposes of utility, the role played by others will provide the foundations for a link to direct practice, as depicted in the following case study. This is positioned here as a thinking point, to be later used as an anchor for practice development.

## Case Study

Jake is a newly appointed Practice Manager within a front-line child protection team responsible for the supervision of six social workers, each with varying degrees of experience. The team's remit is the initial screening and, if appropriate, assessment of referrals related to possible incidents of child abuse or neglect. A recent inspection process has drawn attention to analysis as an area for development within the assessments completed by the team. Mindful of his new responsibilities with regard to practice standards and team development, Jake is keen to identify ways to improve this area of identified need. Understanding the importance of maintaining currency, Jake is currently signed up to bulletins from the government department responsible for children's services, a professional magazine dedicated to developments in social care, and other key organisations, such as charities, who undertake work and research across the sector. While not expansive, these external knowledge sources offer insight and are likely to inform his mentoring of the team. Additionally, Jake retains access to literature accumulated from various training courses attended over the past six years when he first joined the department as a newly qualified social worker.

Situated in England, Jake has read the recent review of child protection by Munro (2011), identifying the importance of supervision in balancing practitioner reasoning, and also research from the National Society for Prevention of Cruelty to Children (NSPCC), concerned with common shortcomings that feature in the initial stage of assessment (Broadhurst et al., 2010). Armed with this information, Jake's objective is to enhance the judgement-making capabilities of his supervisees, integral to which is the need to increase their alertness to evidence and skills in critical decision-making. His starting point is to gather together pertinent knowledge; that related to use of evidence, decision-making, and supervision.

## Accessing Literature and Evidence: Where Is It?

For many social workers access to literature poses a challenge. Internet databases vary in scope and frequently act to sign-post rather than provide full access to articles. Irrespective of your theoretical perspective, whether, for instance, you pragmatically apply information to the practice context or more fervently seek definitive answers (see Plath, 2013, pp. 235-237), it is likely that as a social worker attempts to actively seek out and interpret up-to-date evidence will be met with various hurdles. In England, the development of organisations such as the Social Care Institute for Excellence (SCIE), predicated on the dissemination of knowledge about what works, represents an attempt to share and impart knowledge between those working within the profession. While a worthy cause, unless practitioners have full access to databases, such as when studying a post-qualifying course delivered by a higher education institution or their employing organisations subscribe to such resources, access limitations remain problematic, presenting themselves as a barrier at an organisational level (Gray, Joy, Plath, & Webb, 2013).

The accessing of material also endures the influence of practitioner value, later discussed in relation to judgement and decision-making, suffice to say here that the selection of information is dependent on that which the practitioner seeks, duly shaped by their ontological position. Hence, this chapter does not claim in any sense to be value free; it has been written from material that has stimulated thought, shaped by an interpretivist perspective, much of which has commonalities with the case study cited above in terms of accumulation. That aside, database searches were employed to generate new sources of information, particularly with regard to *heuristics* and *decision-making*, both of which were deployed as search terms combined with *"social work"* or *"evidence-based practice"* in various combinations. While research results appeared promising,

a manual trawl was necessary in order to tease out work which could be assimilated within the piece, attending to intuition as a source of bias. This proved to be something of a slow process, perhaps mirroring the findings of others that little is known about how practitioners in certain fields make judgements in practice (Helm, 2011) and that decision-making in social work is rarely a focus for research (Taylor, 2012). As a largely applied subject, the knowledge-base for social work is far reaching so, although it is beyond the scope of this chapter to explore decision-making more fully, other subject areas will undoubtedly have much to contribute.

## Evidence in Use

Social work terrain often feels intangible, often insurmountable, operating within specific time and space contingencies, where the act of knowing flickers esoterically before being extinguished by contextual winds which render the once perceptible unrecognisable. Within such places sensemaking is the dance which the practitioner must master to demonstrate, drawing on Schon's notions of practice wisdom, "the ability to find the familiar in the unique" (Fisher & Somerton, 2000, p. 391) and to make links between perception and reflection by means of interpretation. As Gray and Webb (2013b) posit, "to understand diversely shaped cultures, experiences, actions and beliefs – and to make their significance apparent in spoken and written forms – is the core of interpretation and it is indispensable to social work" (p. 3).

What informs interpretation, in this sense envisaged as solution-focused and thus understood as a conduit manifesting in good professional judgement, is an interplay of phenomena both internal and external to the practitioner; a process which Webb (2006) captures as an ability to marshal both concept-driven and practice-driven patterns of thinking together with intuitions primed by repeated reframing of the situation presenting (p. 219). While this premise assumes that the practitioner's moral imperative is to demonstrate best practice and is, therefore, contingent upon the practitioner's ethical virtue, it conveys a complexity of sensemaking which avoids surface and one dimensional understandings; a short-coming detrimental to practice at both an individual and collective level (Howe, 1996; Ruch, 2010).

Formulating a judgement, therefore, involves use of information provided or provoked by some form of stimulus or active thought process, one which embodies a "commitment to thinking" (Webb, 2006, p. 219). Specific to a given time and space, it is this available information which constitutes the practitioner's knowledge base, an element of which may, or may not, merit the classification of evidence. Here is where attention must first fall, with an interest in knowledge types; for example, see Pawson, Boaz, Grayson, Long, & Barnes (2003), briefly suspended. Evidence, the understanding of which has been broadened by numerous authors (Plath, 2013), at this juncture, is comprehended from a scientific positivist perspective, within which knowledge generation occurs via an empirical research process; its subsequent application determined by a decision-making process which integrates the research evidence with clinical expertise and patient values (Gray et al., 2013). Interest in the adoption of EBP as a mode of practice, as employed by social workers in the field, indicates that its realisation faces a number of challenges. Organisational resource constraints, significantly linked to access issues, and a lack of necessary practitioner skill, including that related to the critical appraisal of research, were amongst those challenges identified in a literature review undertaken by Gray et al. (2013). Notably, a lack of critical appraisal skills has been cited as one of the key areas of deficit in relation to the aptitudes of individual practitioners more generally: Common themes have been observed in social workers not being able to fully synthesise or analyse information which they themselves generate during the process of assessment (Helm, 2011; Turney, 2009); that they can be "verificationist", display-

ing a bias for selecting information that supports early ideas (Holland, 2011, p. 169); and the low self-perceptions held by some practitioners, in terms of their abilities to appraise literature (Pope, Rollins, Chaumba, & Risler, 2011), illustrates the lack of confidence held by some in relation to this area. These findings point towards the difficulty in forming decisions in conditions of complexity and uncertainty, the very fabric of social work (for example, see Munro 2011), and are perhaps indicative of a wider issue in social work education and training.

Bestowed with a task bordering on the realms of poison chalice territory, practitioners are charged with making decisions that ensure the safety of service-users. While this represents a systemically fallible position, where, sadly, harm can never be totally prevented (Munro, 2011), social work agencies and their political masters retain a tendency to lurch towards simplistic and reductionist conceptions of risk which seek to avoid "the worst case" scenario (Parton, 2010, p. 869); yet it is questionable whether the deployment of any calculation of risk probability is capable of accurately depicting the phenomena to which it claims to pertain and predict (Dore, 2006; Smith, 2001). Accepting the inherent fallibility of the task in hand, decision-making moves towards a standpoint of reaching a conclusion that is "least wrong" (Holland, 2011, p. 182). Under such conditions one might expect to see practitioners openly embrace the use of evidence in practice in order to help craft a lucid picture of the situation that they must strive to comprehend. Indeed, for many workers an openness and familiarity to pertinent evidence databases and utilization of research in clinical decision-making has been found (Pope et al., 2011), in other literature attitudes are less favourable with practitioners doubting the accuracy and validity of research findings (Gray et al., 2013, p. 164). It should be noted that in a follow-up exploratory study of the attitudes held by Australian social workers, Gray, Joy, Plath, & Webb (2014) reported largely, though not necessarily generalisable, positive perspectives. Unsurprisingly these were shaped, as acknowledged by the authors, by the practice context. They also noted that this was supportive of broader research linked to embedding EBP as a function of organisational culture (p. 37).

From the swirling milieu that constitutes the practice context, social workers do battle not just with competing evidence or attitudes towards such evidence but with a plethora of tensions which exist within themselves, their agency, and a society often conflicted in its sense of becoming; oscillating between the provision of care and control, caught in a revolving "dilemma of difference" where the act of defining disadvantage to in some way empower, creates disadvantage and disempowerment (Fook, 2012, p. 59). For practitioners seeking to uphold the key values of social justice and human well-being, the use of evidence possesses a glimmer of dual utility: a route to value realisation through the attainment of positive change. Indeed, attention has been given to the way in which elements of the EBP process can cogently fit with ethical practice (Pope et al., 2011; Williams & Sherr, 2013) with some registering bodies, such as the Health and Care Professions Council in England, specifying the requirement that practitioners maintain currency of their knowledge base, as outlined within their *Standards of Conduct, Performance and Ethics* (Health and Care Professions Council, 2012). While some of the tensions between the practitioner and their external loci may not be so susceptible to such airbrushing, with the enactment of human well-being instead relying upon subversive acts of discretion directed against organisational protocols (Lipsky, 2010), it is possible to see the beginnings of tessellation towards something resembling a coherent whole.

What gives practice any semblance of coherence? This might first appear like a glib question to pose. While the short answer provides us with the individual, it is the mechanisms and processes, which the individual practitioner employs, draws

upon, enacts, and demonstrates, that offer illumination. It is their use of self which has potential to serve as both their anchor and sensemaker, yet this demands effort and exposure to the endemic tensions described above: "It is through learning how to handle this sort of tension that new social workers start to learn about use of self" (Ward, 2010, p. 46). By bringing differing worlds together, the practitioner is better situated to gain an understanding, to understand meaning behind action and patterns in behaviour (Schofield, 1998), necessary components for any intervention. Seated here is the relationship between the worker and the client. Effective use of self has an intimate connection with this relationship and can provide a platform for authentic practice (Ruch, 2010; Ward, 2010). Such relationship-based practice enables further exploration of the different worlds in play, for, as Ferguson (2011) notes, "it is a psychosocial approach, which focuses on the interaction between the external factors that influence people's life chances and the social conditions they live in and their internal emotional worlds and capacities to be loving, safe, caring individuals" (p. 8).

Thus it increases the sensemaking opportunities available to the practitioner, equipped now with a decision-making field featuring generative mechanisms. Faced with tides of uncertainty, practitioners undoubtedly find themselves confronted with a multitude of hypothetical conclusions, each warranting a "least wrong" response; in applying evidence to aid understanding and outcomes, practitioners are not introducing a silver bullet, for such a remedy does not exist. Truths and values are "relative to time and place, culture and people" (Howe, 1996, p. 85), seated within the precepts of the individual who brings their unique, value-based lens to bear in the situations they encounter, subsequently shaping interpretation and, therefore, practice (Banks, 2012; Clark, 2006). To stay above water the practitioner needs to look towards themselves, to think reflectively about their feelings. To do so, as Ruch (2012) suggests, enables them to embrace critical thinking as "it seeks to unsettle assumptions about how we experience the world, a core characteristic of the critical thinker" (p. 77). The practitioner must, then, challenge themselves, analyse their practice footprint and, crucially, be open and flexible in their thinking, for, as intimated by some, a hypothesis should not necessarily last for long (Holland, 2011, p. 170). Again, effort is demanded, decisions stemming from poor application, gut feeling, bias, or neglectful synthesis take active effort to avoid; often aided by the critical challenge from others (Munro, 2011).

## How Do We Decide?

Shrouded by competing knowledge claims, incorporating semantical and epistemological deliberation, EBP is presented as a decision-making process (Gray et al., 2013; Pope et al., 2011; Thyer & Pignotti, 2011) resting upon a protocol of empirical research generation that supports interventions or treatments (Gray et al., 2013; Williams & Sherr, 2013); a historically congruent incarnation which avoids conceptions of EBP as evidence-based practices (Gambrill, 2008) or empirically supported interventions (ESIs) (Gray et al., 2013; Pope et al., 2011; Thyer & Pignotti, 2011). Active engagement on the part of the decision-maker is a prerequisite, as is the existence of evidence; hence agency is seated within the actions of the practitioner, notably in relation to the appraisal and subsequent application of relevant evidence. In order to reach a conclusion, the process posits that one must observe the following five steps:

1.  Identify answerable questions.
2.  Locate evidence to answer the question posed.
3.  Critically appraise the evidence in terms of its validity and usefulness.
4.  Integrate this appraisal with possessed clinical expertise and the client's values.
5.  Evaluate the effectiveness and efficiency of the previous steps, making necessary adjustments (Gray et al., 2013; Pope et al., 2011).

Focusing a question within a complex system may be hard enough, crisis can occur almost instantaneously with no prior warning even when the patterns of the past are conscious; family systems swing from being open to closed, with often one small change tipping the stasis, however fluid, into a new dimension. Yet within this mix, social workers do and must make decisions for the benefit and safety of the service-users with whom they work. Accepting the premise of EBP, applying evidence in such circumstances requires the practitioner to be a rational agent, capable of producing consistent preferences and consistent predictions (Taylor, 2012, p. 556), with access to research evidence which may well not exist (Plath, 2013), and fully equipped with the skills of critical analysis. Should all three determinants come together in the same time and space, feasible formulations sound like a possible consequence; yet is the landscape not just a little more colourful?

The practice context can resemble a resource vortex, pushing and consuming physical boundaries, mental effort, and emotional availability. The emotional impact can be high, manifesting in negative affect and, if inadequately supported, can lead to emotional exhaustion and practitioner burnout (Carpenter, Webb, Bostock, & Coomber, 2012). Unsurprisingly, this powerful force that is emotion effects direct practice, impacting upon how practitioners reason and act. Anxiety may distort judgement and communication (Ruch, 2010), exerting an unconscious influence "on where attention is focused and how information is interpreted" (Munro, 2011, p. 91). Our experiences of emotion and our emotional responses to such experiences shape and guide future thoughts and behaviour, often eliciting a recognition-primed decision-making model. If familiarity is recognised then an expectedness of what comes next is primed (Kirkman & Melrose, 2014). Initially, this is not a conscious process but an intuitive one, automatic and unconscious, influenced by what has gone before, as Helm (2011) posits: "Intuition is formed upon personal experiences and on processes of social development and acculturation that provide rules and beliefs to guide judgement" (p. 900).

Beneath this stratus, a level of filtering has already taken place within memory. Phenomena are more memorable if they arouse emotion and are either the first or most recent (Munro, 1999, p. 754). Heightened degrees of emotional arousal experienced during the time of the experience can increase the likelihood of future recall as a consequence of an amygdala agitated by stress hormones, such as adrenaline and noradrenaline, causing subsequent stimulation of the connections between the amygdala and parts of the brain associated with memory functioning (Curran & Gilbert, 2008). Given that an individual's experiences do not take place in the sterile world of a clinical laboratory, memories are cloaked in a milieu specific to their birth comprising a host of experiential representations: emotional, factual, auto-biographical, perceptual, somatic, and behavioural; all effecting retrieval (Siegel, 2012) and thus our intuition. What is more, it has been contended that feelings experienced at the time of remembering will "profoundly influence which elements become associated with this complexly bound representation during retrieval" (Siegel, 2012, p. 50), potentially accelerating the rate of diversion and distortion.

In the fast-paced environment of practice, workers must then consciously strive to mitigate perception distortion. This requires time, a resource coveted by many, which, when in short supply, lures the practitioner towards intuitive modes of decision-making (Helm, 2011; Kirkman & Melrose, 2014; van de Luitgaarden, 2009) away from analytical processes situated at a later interval on the decision-making continuum. It is not that intuition is fundamentally flawed; indeed, such thinking allows actions to take place with speed and accuracy (Munro, 2011) and is arguably a necessary product of the practice context, especially when faced with high uncertainty (Helm, 2011); rather there is a need for practitioners, together with their employing organisations, to be alert to the error potential that lies within. Naturally some biases or mental-short cuts, heuristics, will be more vivid, lending themselves more readily to countermeasures; common examples include availability heuristics and confirmation-bias. The former, as already observed, relates to the ease at which situations come to mind, encompassing emotionally potent recall and the likelihood that more recent experiences will be recalled over earlier ones with the exception of first impressions. The latter pertains to the retention of intuitive beliefs in the face of contradictory evidence (Kirkman & Melrose, 2014) evident in situations where practitioners tie themselves to original assessment positions (Broadhurst et al., 2010; Holland, 2011; Munro, 1999, 2011).

The rationality embodied in EBP then is counter-intuitive, running against in-built and evolved (Munro, 2011) predispositions that enable us to navigate our various existences free from paralysis and indecision, for as Webb (2006) posits,

*research on heuristics undermines the model of social work practice as data-driven information flows, whereby valid and reliable decisions are reached on the basis of empirical research data. People simply do not act or behave in this way, even when they have evidence at their disposal. (p. 160)*

Emerging from an individual's unique person-in-environment configuration, intuition becomes established through pattern-recognition (Munro, 2011, p. 91) which is then drawn upon when seeking a conclusion. Within a recognition-primed decision-making model, essentially a matching exercise, and accepting the premise of bounded-rationality, noting the aforementioned limitations to truth (Howe, 1996) and the fallibilities inherent in knowing and prediction (Dore, 2006), an individual assesses the situation and then mentally simulates possible courses of action in succession before arriving at one which resembles a "good enough option" (Kirkman & Melrose, 2014, p. 45). Under this model, propositions originally offered by Simon assert that this search is bounded by the individual's quest for a satisfactory option; they are "satisficing", rather than seeking the optimum outcome level (see Helm, 2011; Kirkman & Melrose, 2014; Webb, 2006). The level sought is aspirational, nuanced by the individual and the decision-making field (Taylor, 2012), where competing cues play a kind of hide and seek with the gaze of the individual charged with sensemaking.

Thus it follows that a focus on how to improve the intuitive awareness of the practitioner is a necessity if efforts are to be made to reduce bias in judgement formulation and decision-making, perhaps pushing attainment more confidently towards what is least wrong. Both Kirkman and Melrose (2014, pp. 47-48) and Munro (2011, p. 88) draw on Klein's ideas, proposing that intuitive expertise and learning can be enhanced through four steps:

1. Engaging in practice, setting specific goals and criteria for evaluation.
2. Gathering experience.
3. Obtaining timely, diagnostic feedback.
4. Participating in reflection of prior experiences.

The need for a critical stance appears as a constant buffer, via questioning (Kirkman & Melrose, 2014) and reflection (Munro, 2011); common, too, is the involvement of others, either through the conduit of supervision or less formal group processes, thereby, offering an opportunity to enhance the scope of feedback available to practitioners, if of appropriate quality, sufficiently provocative, and motivational.

In order for this feedback to possess utility, practitioners must first be able to hear it. This requires an openness and tolerance to being wrong (Turney, 2009) and an ability to allow oneself to become vulnerable; thereby, permitting an exploration of areas of perceived weakness, an early step towards understanding, necessary if such areas are to be prevented from distorting one's view of the world (Ward, 2010, p. 50). It also commands that supervisors demonstrate rigour and curiosity, for instance, they should "motivate workers to question their own views and interpretations, seek disconfirming evidence and test their hypothesis'" (Helm, 2011, p. 906). In this sense, supervision affords practitioners, in this case learners, as surely we all are, the opportunity to encourage them "to deepen his or her understanding of the multiplicity of understandings (and misunderstandings) present in a challenging practice scenario" (Davys & Beddoe, 2009, p. 919).

Within these spaces practitioners can, indeed must, confront the muddied waters of practice and question their questioning if they are to protect against themselves as contaminants to their own perception, multi-layered as it is (van de Luitgaarden, 2009). The much extolled aptitude of self-awareness is integral here, particularly in light of recent research suggesting that "*how* we think about and interpret information is tied to *what* kinds of stimuli capture and hold our attention" (Lagattuta & Sayfan, 2013, p. 2107). It is in reflective spaces, like supervision, that this awareness is brought to life, giving breath to the transformational quality of learning (Davys & Beddoe, 2009, p. 921), the active engagement with which can help temper pattern-confirming thought processes: processes invariably contorted by external ideological worlds seeking measurement of the immeasurable, comprised of expectant calls for certainty and objectivity (Ruch, 2012), which, if some are to be believed, can be elicited through the imposition of actuarial processes designed to make the elusively invisible, visible (Helm, 2011; van de Luitgaarden, 2009). Under a modernist quest, such as it is, validity is awarded through revelation, the premise being that for something to be it must be disclosed (Gray & Webb, 2008, p. 189), a somewhat compromising position for social work.

## The Performance

Social work is lucidly enigmatic: "it is not a precise activity" (England, 1986, p.77). It is interpretive (Gray & Webb, 2013a; Helm, 2011), resting on the perceptions of perception (van de Luitgaarden, 2009). Between the lines of perception lie blindspots, sometimes rendering our sensemaking fallible; on other occasions, it is our perceptions themselves which conspire against us in our task. Much effort and application is needed to craft a picture that is a best fit or the least wrong, to select and synthesise information of salience and utility. This is often achieved through an intuitive process, with deliberate, analytical thinking playing a subservient role. This reality first appears out-of-kilter with the EBP process, yet that is not to say that through processes of critical reflection, for instance, alignment could not be sought, nor is it the case that practitioners will negate to use empirically produced evidence in practice; for instance, as has been recognised, the individual is multi-faceted and their choice of information selected will, to some extent, be guided by their "formal learning of relevant knowledge" as well as "ideology and philosophy" (England, 1986, p. 29). In the multitudinous space of social work, competing continuums abound, to be wrestled and grappled with, in order to proceed with some semblance of ethical coherence. Evidential hierarchies and technical competence verses interpersonal skill are other prime examples.

Who does the wrestling and grappling? Who is the sensemaker upon which this mighty task falls? Irrespective of the practitioner's epistemological perspective or ontological stance, it is they who formulate conclusions in conditions of systemic high uncertainty and focus is, therefore, rightly bestowed upon them and their ability to exercise what has been demanded of them. While many celebrate EPB as a model for ethically informed practice (Pope et al., 2011; Williams & Sherr, 2013), permitting clients protection from authority-based care built on criteria such as "anecdotal experience, tradition, or popularity" (Gambrill, 2008, p. 425), caution is called for. Narrowness and rigidity in application could limit the practitioner's room for manoeuvre, curtailing the execution of good professional judgement (Dore, 2006, p. 248). Desires to improve interventions should be welcomed. Certainly, the premise of drawing on outside knowledge has merit, particularly when striving to balance the inner, immediate, raw-subjectively born of the unique practitioner-in-context configuration; it provides, or has the potential to, a provocation of thought. Again, we are led back to the thought processes of the individual: their perception, synthesis, and ability to analyse, all of which are dependent upon value and their use of self.

In musing on social work's uniqueness as a caring profession, England (1986) sees good social work as contingent on the individual social worker, an artist, whose practice is based on the "intuitive use of self" (p. 32). In situating social work as art bordered and influenced by science, evident within references to the use of formal knowledge and theory as a means to inform understanding (pp. 35-37) and his view that a confinement to the social sciences would function as an impediment (p. 76), England acknowledges and emphasises its constituent nature, distilled in his view that both art and science are "integral and essential parts of the whole" (p. 115). Given the divergent forces which circle practice, social work should make no apology and be broad and bold in its embrace. It has been argued elsewhere that an inclusive, "knowledge-aware" position be adopted (Dore 2006, p. 249), one which does not "neglect sources of knowledge that are tacit, that currently lack prestige and seem less compelling" (Pawson et al., 2003, p. viii). Efforts as to how to best marshal this manifest indeterminacy not only have a practical dimension but also an ethical one. Here we must pick up the notion of ethical virtue as a means to realise good practice.

As a consequence, questions like "what makes a good social worker?" take centre stage, for this is an ethics which resists moral imperatives, apparent in deontological ethics; instead the focus is on the character and dispositions of the individual, viewed, as they are, as a moral agent. In adopting this stance, interest in the manifestation of abstract obligations and duties for action (Banks, 2012) is set aside, granting freedom to consider the values within the individual's inner character, such as perception and judgement (Webb, 2006), honesty and integrity (Banks, 2012), as a guide both for, and of, action. The attraction to social work is captured thus:

*The integrity of the social worker is not found in consistent action across cases, nor in carrying out agency policy or the law accurately, rather it is found in the consistency of a fundamental orientation of good-will towards those whom one works for and works with, and towards the activities in which one engages. (Webb, 2006, pp. 220-221)*

Motivationally, the virtuous character is an exemplar for social work, perhaps essential, in terms of fitness to practice (Clark, 2006, p. 83). Guided by virtue, they seek conclusions that are ethically just, based on an understanding shaped by ethically primed perception. Interpretations guided by virtue hold the potential for positive outcomes, congruous to those of society within a set time and space, for virtue is, in part, a phenomenon of culture (McBeath & Webb, 2002, p.

1018) and, as such, possesses a degree of fluidity. This inherent malleability is intimately linked to the systemic symbiosis that surrounds practice. At the level of direct practice, these relationships represent spaces of possibility for loss and gain. Availed with transformative qualities, they offer themselves as "the vehicle through which interventions are mediated, as well as potentially being of intrinsic value as an intervention in its [their] own right" (Ruch, 2010, p. 22).

Notable by its absence, the unseen reality of human change in relation to a specific intervention context, the "why" of "why do some interventions work and others do not?" (Dore, 2006, p. 246) is likely to be found within these relationships. It is beyond the scope of this chapter to duly attend to this connection, yet it is essential that one is alert to the subjective experiences of the relationship as a catalytic power within the process of the intervention, framed, for example, in ideas of "Critical-Best Practice" within which Ferguson (2003, 2013) captures this fundamental requisite, stressing the need to attend to "'practice-based evidence' which relates to experiential knowledge and the social actions and processes that go to make up the very nature of social work in practice" (Ferguson, 2003, p. 1007). As a solution-focused and constructive approach, Ferguson (2003) astutely identifies the need for fluidity with regard to the dynamics in motion, citing human agency, power, and creativity amongst them (p. 1009), shining a light on the impact of where social work takes place (Ferguson, 2013, p. 118). Within this model, relationships and understandings of what worked, what went well, how, and why are co-constructed between the client and other pertinent players. In this sense, meaning making is evolutionary, yet unavoidably tied to the context within which it is forged.

Best efforts to understand are the fabric of social work and it is effort, rather than understanding, which is tangible in a sea that is tacit and opaque. We stand on the borders of perception, with understanding distant from the event (Gray & Webb,

2008, p.192), our perceptions always inadequate (Rossiter, 2011). Efforts to understand are based on our limited notions of knowing and we need to be attuned to this, alert to the necessity for representation alongside the oppressive potential of totality. Values depend on the former, such as our conception of social justice, yet our definitions of clients and disadvantage may actually jeopardise emancipation (Fook, 2012; Rossiter, 2011). Social work's orientation towards understanding should, therefore, be cautious (Rossiter, 2011, p. 991) and accompanied with a healthy level of humility (Dore, 2006, p. 251), where practitioners embrace the bounded nature of understanding and aim, perhaps more appropriately, to understand alongside clients "how the difficulties are being experienced" (Holland, 2011, p. 173).

Attempts to mould judgements from information pitted with black-holes tempt public service agencies towards the black and white, where, in the event of tragedy, a bigger, better, procedural manual is sought (for example, see Munro, 2011). In these circumstances it is too often forgotten that it is people, rather than bureaucratised-systems, who keep other people safe. While the "why?" will continue to challenge the profession as it always has, glimmers of insight and inspiration abound; all, however practically small, require effort and application of thought. In England, following a recent review of child protection services, use of systems methodology has been employed in an effort to not just look at what went wrong but to consider why (Department for Education, 2013; Munro, 2011). Practical tools, such as the use of "fast and frugal decision trees" and case closure check-lists, have been encouraged as a way to support a more analytical thought process (Kirkman & Melrose, 2014) and purposeful critical thinking promoted as a way to provoke self-curiosity, which

*... takes a questioning (and self-questioning) attitude towards the issue or problem at hand and examines the information, ideas, assumptions,*

*concepts and so on associated with it and considers how they act to support a particular view or interpretation of the situation. (Turney, 2009, p. 4)*

Organisations have a key-role to play in supporting practitioners in their judgement-making roles, from fostering access to resources (Gambrill, 2008) to providing supervision which questions the questioning of practitioners (Helm, 2011), ever mindful of the dangers inherent in the subscription to an unbounded-rationality.

## On the Ground

Returning to our thinking point registered at the outset of this chapter, how might Jake attain his objective of enhancing the judgement-making capabilities of his supervisees, attending to the need to increase their alertness to evidence and skills in critical decision-making? Furnished with the knowledge reviewed within this chapter, it is apparent that Jake's primary task is to facilitate an awareness of that which is invisible, to provoke and unsettle thinking in order to embed curiosity as a virtue, thereby, creating a healthy level of open-mindedness and an interest in the invisible dynamics that might shape thinking (Ruch, 2012). Jake's starting point may well be to synthesise common themes in the literature, perhaps using a tangible piece of pertinent research as a framework and platform that he can incorporate into practice, using it to inform his practice within supervision sessions, for instance. Having assessed the literature, Jake might then seek to enhance the reflective nature of supervision. Drawing on themes associated with questioning, curiosity, and challenge, exploration emerges as a key activity which he might seek to foster.

In utilizing a reflective learning model which features exploration space, such as that proposed by Davys and Beddoe (2009), both the impact and implications of a given issue are given space. The practitioner is first encouraged to locate themselves in the event and to consider their responses and associated meanings before being guided towards the consideration of external frameworks, including theory, legislation, intervention protocols, and ethics. In doing so, they reveal what knowledge they possess and what knowledge they may need (p. 927). Accepting what is known about common heuristics, such as availability heuristics, confirmation-bias, and affect heuristics (Kirkman & Melrose, 2014; Munro, 1999), Jake should consider using targeted questions to illuminate these specific areas in order to lance their potential as perennial blind-spots. Questions to pose to the practitioner might include these below:

- Are any qualifications needed regarding the strength of evidence contained in this assessment and the implications for decision-making?
- What puzzles you about what you are seeing and assessing?
- What is the most striking feature of this situation and if it were removed, would there still be concerns?
- Have you carefully examined a case history or have you been tempted to ignore it? (see Broadhurst et al., 2010).

Questions are also needed of managers; for instance, they too will need to challenge their responses to their supervisees and question the extent to which supervision is being driven by the reactions of supervisees, rather than being balanced and appropriately led by themselves as an external regulator. Questions about organisational culture, openness, and a critical analysis of what practitioners attend to in their assessments, such as pulling out significant life events, are also a necessity, as is attention to the administrative systems that surround practice (Broadhurst et al., 2010).

Both within supervision and at an organisational level more widely, efforts should also be made to improve the feedback given to practitioners; while time is often in short supply, instant feedback has been shown to greatly enhance learning (Kirkman & Melrose, 2014) and can help individuals recognise areas to be addressed in order to attain a successful outcome (Davys & Beddoe, 2009). Feedback is not dependent upon the supervisor alone and Jake might establish group supervision sessions, as there is some evidence indicating that such forums can increase critical thinking amongst participants (Carpenter et al., 2012). Mindful of the potential for groupthink to limit divergent discussion (Kirkman & Melrose, 2014), use of a "Critical Best Practice" framework could be harnessed, built around the sharing of case examples rooted in "what social workers actually do" (Ferguson, 2013, p. 124). In doing so, the tacit elements of meaning, gut feelings, and intuition may be brought into the open and offered space for critical, analytical appraisal.

## CONCLUSION

Within this chapter, judgement and decision-making have been explored in relation to the context in which practice takes place, encompassing the psychosocial worlds of the practitioner and that which surrounds them. Contained within these worlds is information which forms the basis for action. What the individual attends to is, it is suggested, value-laden and vulnerable to distortion by means of evolved thought processes. Rather than seeking to eradicate these processes and revert to a prescriptive procedural position, which may actually hinder professional learning (Munro, 2011), social workers should be encouraged to bring them into the light. Through the enhancement of critical thinking that which is previously unseen becomes less opaque, better enabling individuals to identify blind spots, consequentially creating greater opportunities for these to be addressed; perhaps through the seeking of new or additional knowledge, some of which may, or may not, take the form of empirical evidence. Within this dynamic, the role of others and organisations has been shown to be an essential component in developing social work practice, a key element of which involves acceptance, openness, and a preparedness to work with the self within the confines of vacillating, and ultimately limited, truths.

# REFERENCES

Banks, S. (2012). *Ethics and values in social work* (4th ed.). Basingstoke, UK: Palgrave Macmillan.

Broadhurst, K., White, S., Fish, S., Munro, E., Fletcher, K., & Lincoln, H. (2010). *Ten pitfalls and how to avoid them: What research tells us*. Retrieved from National Society for the Prevention of Cruelty to Children website: http://www.nspcc.org.uk/Inform/publications/downloads/tenpitfalls_wdf48122.pdf

Carpenter, J., Webb, C., Bostock, L., & Coomber, C. (2012). *Effective supervision in social work and social care* (Research Briefing 43). Retrieved from Social Care Institute for Excellence website: http://www.scie.org.uk/publications/briefings/files/briefing43.pdf

Clark, C. (2006). Moral character in social work. *British Journal of Social Work, 36*(1), 75–89. doi:10.1093/bjsw/bch364

Curran, A., & Gilbert, I. (2008). *The little book of big stuff about the brain: The true story of your amazing brain*. Carmarthen: Crown House.

Davys, A. M., & Beddoe, L. (2009). The reflective learning model: Supervision of social work students. *Social Work Education, 28*(8), 919–933. doi:10.1080/02615470902748662

Department for Education. (2013). *Working together to safeguard children: A guide to inter-agency working to safeguard and promote the welfare of children*. Retrieved from http://media.education.gov.uk/assets/files/pdf/w/working%20together.pdf

Dore, I. (2006). Evidence focused social care: On target or off-side? *Social Work and Society, 4*, 232-255. Retrieved from http://www.socwork.net/sws

England, H. (1986). *Social work as art: Making sense for good practice*. London: Allen and Unwin.

Ferguson, H. (2003). Outline of a critical best practice perspective on social work and social care. *British Journal of Social Work, 33*(8), 1005–1024. doi:10.1093/bjsw/33.8.1005

Ferguson, H. (2011). *Child protection practice*. Basingstoke: Palgrave Macmillan.

Ferguson, H. (2013). Critical best practice. In M. Gray & S. Webb (Eds.), *The new politics of social work* (pp. 116–127). Basingstoke, UK: Palgrave MacMillan.

Fisher, T., & Somerton, J. (2000). Reflection on action: The process of helping social work students to develop their use of theory in practice. *Social Work Education, 19*(4), 387–401. doi:10.1080/02615470050078384

Fook, J. (2012). *Social work: A critical approach to practice* (2nd ed.). London: Sage.

Gambrill, E. (2008). Evidence-based (informed) macro practice: Process and philosophy. *Journal of Evidence-Based Social Work, 5*(3-4), 423–452. doi:10.1080/15433710802083971 PMID:19042875

Gray, M., Joy, E., Plath, D., & Webb, S. A. (2013). Implementing evidence-based practice: A review of the empirical research literature. *Research on Social Work Practice, 23*(2), 157–166. doi:10.1177/1049731512467072

Gray, M., Joy, E., Plath, D., & Webb, S. (2014). Opinions about evidence: A study of social workers' attitudes towards evidence-based practice. *Journal of Social Work, 14*(1), 23–40. doi:10.1177/1468017313475555

Gray, M., & Webb, S. A. (2008). Social work as art revisited. *International Journal of Social Welfare*, *17*(2), 182–193. doi:10.1111/j.1468-2397.2008.00548.x

Gray, M., & Webb, S. A. (2013a). Critical social work. In M. Gray & S. A. Webb (Eds.), *Social work theories and methods* (2nd ed., pp. 99–109). London: Sage.

Gray, M., & Webb, S. A. (2013b). Introduction. In M. Gray & S. A. Webb (Eds.), *Social work theories and methods* (2nd ed., pp. 1–10). London: Sage.

Health and Care Professions Council. (2012). *Standards of conduct, performance and ethics*. Retrieved from http://www.hcpc-uk.org/assets/documents/10003B6EStandardsofconduct,performanceandethics.pdf

Helm, D. (2011). Judgements or assumptions? The role of analysis in assessing children and young people's needs. *British Journal of Social Work*, *41*(5), 894–911. doi:10.1093/bjsw/bcr096

Holland, S. (2011). *Child and family assessment in social work practice* (2nd ed.). London: Sage. doi:10.4135/9781446288580

Howe, D. (1996). Surface and depth in social-work practice. In N. Parton (Ed.), *Social theory, social change and social work* (pp. 77–97). London: Routledge.

Kirkman, E., & Melrose, K. (2014). *Clinical judgement and decision-making in children's social work: An analysis of the "front door" system*. Retrieved from Department for Education website: https://www.gov.uk/government/uploads/system/uploads/attachment_data/file/305516/R337_-_Clinical_Judgement_and_Decision-Making_in_Childrens_Social_Work.pdf

Lagattuta, K. H., & Sayfan, L. (2013). Not all past events are equal: Biased attention and emerging heuristics in children's past-to-future forecasting. *Child Development*, *84*(6), 2094–2111. doi:10.1111/cdev.12082 PMID:23480128

Lipsky, M. (2010). *Street-level democracy: Dilemmas of the individual in public services* (Updated Edition). New York: Russell Sage Foundation.

McBeath, G., & Webb, S. A. (2002). Virtue ethics and social work: Being lucky, realistic, and not doing ones duty. *British Journal of Social Work*, *32*(8), 1015–1036. doi:10.1093/bjsw/32.8.1015

Munro, E. (1999). Common errors of reasoning in child protection work. *Child Abuse & Neglect*, *23*(8), 745–758. doi:10.1016/S0145-2134(99)00053-8 PMID:10477235

Munro, E. (2011). *The Munro review of child protection: Final report – A child-centred system*. London: TSO. Retrieved from Department for Education website: https://www.gov.uk/government/uploads/system/uploads/attachment_data/file/175391/Munro-Review.pdf

Parton, N. (2010). Child protection and safeguarding in England: Changing and competing conceptions of risk and their implications for social work. *British Journal of Social Work*, *41*(5), 854–875. doi:10.1093/bjsw/bcq119

Pawson, R., Boaz, A., Grayson, L., Long, A., & Barnes, C. (2003). *Knowledge review 3: Types and quality of knowledge in social care*. Retrieved from Social Care Institute for Excellence website: http://www.scie.org.uk/publications/knowledgereviews/kr03.pdf

Plath, D. (2013). Evidence-based practice. In M. Gray & S. A. Webb (Eds.), *Social work theories and methods* (2nd ed., pp. 229–240). London: Sage.

Pope, N. D., Rollins, L., Chaumba, J., & Risler, E. (2011). Evidence-based practice knowledge and utilization among social workers. *Journal of Evidence-Based Social Work*, 8(4), 349–368. doi:10.1080/15433710903269149 PMID:21827303

Rossiter, A. (2011). Unsettled social work: The challenge of Levinas's ethics. *British Journal of Social Work*, 41(5), 980–995. doi:10.1093/bjsw/bcr004

Ruch, G. (2010). The contemporary context of relationship-based practice. In G. Ruch, D. Turney, & A. Ward (Eds.), *Relationship-based social work: Getting to the heart of practice* (pp. 13–28). London: Jessica Kingsley.

Ruch, G. (2012). Two halves make a whole: Developing integrated critical, analytic and reflective thinking in social work practice and education. In J. Lishman (Ed.), *Social work education and training* (pp. 69–83). London: Jessica Kingsley.

Sackett, D. L., Rosenberg, W. M. C., Muir Gray, J. A., Haynes, R. B., & Richardson, W. S. (1996). Evidence based medicine: What it is and what it isn't: It's about integrating individual clinical expertise and the best external evidence. *BMJ (Clinical Research Ed.)*, 312(7023), 71–72. doi:10.1136/bmj.312.7023.71 PMID:8555924

Schofield, G. (1998). Inner and outer worlds: A psychosocial framework for child and family social work. *Child & Family Social Work*, 3(1), 57–67. doi:10.1046/j.1365-2206.1998.00062.x

Siegel, D. J. (2012). *The developing mind: How relationships and the brain interact to shape who we are* (2nd ed.). New York: The Guildford Press.

Smith, C. (2001). Trust and confidence: Possibilities for social work in "high modernity". *British Journal of Social Work*, 31(2), 287–305. doi:10.1093/bjsw/31.2.287

Taylor, B. (2012). Models for professional judgement in social work. *European Journal of Social Work*, 15(4), 546–562. doi:10.1080/13691457.2012.702310

Thyer, B. A., & Pignotti, M. (2011). Evidence-based practices do not exist. *Clinical Social Work Journal*, 39(4), 328–333. doi:10.1007/s10615-011-0358-x

Turney, D. (2009). *Analysis and critical thinking in assessment*. Devon: Research in Practice.

van de Luitgaarden, G. M. J. (2009). Evidence-based practice in social work: Lessons from judgment and decision-making theory. *British Journal of Social Work*, 39(2), 243–260. doi:10.1093/bjsw/bcm117

Ward, A. (2010). The use of self in relationship-based practice. In G. Ruch, D. Turney, & A. Ward (Eds.), *Relationship-based social work: Getting to the heart of practice* (pp. 46–65). London: Jessica Kingsley.

Webb, S. A. (2006). *Social work in a risk society: Social and political perspectives*. London: Palgrave Macmillan.

Williams, N. J., & Sherr, M. E. (2013). Oh how I try to use evidence in my social work practice: Efforts, successes, frustrations, and questions. *Journal of Evidence-Based Social Work*, 10(2), 100–110. doi:10.1080/15433714.2011.597299 PMID:23581804

## ADDITIONAL READING

Bisman, C. (2004). Social work values: The moral core of the profession. *British Journal of Social Work*, 34(1), 109–123. doi:10.1093/bjsw/bch008

Gambrill, E. (2007). Views of evidence-based practice: Social workers' code of ethics and accreditation standards as guides for choice. *Journal of Social Work Education, 43*(3), 447–462. doi:10.5175/JSWE.2007.200600639

Gambrill, E. (2011). Evidence-based practice and the ethics of discretion. *Journal of Social Work, 11*(1), 26–48. doi:10.1177/1468017310381306

Gigerenzer, G. (2007). *Gut feelings: The intelligence of the unconscious*. London: Viking.

Hammond, K. (1996). *Human judgment and social policy: Irreducible uncertainty, inevitable error, unavoidable injustice*. Oxford: Oxford University Press.

Healey, K. (2008). Critical commentary on "Social work as art revisited". *International Journal of Social Welfare, 17*(2), 194–195. doi:10.1111/j.1468-2397.2007.00565.x

Holden, G., Tuchman, E., Barker, K., Rosenberg, G., Thazin, M., Kuppens, S., & Watson, K. (2012). A few thoughts on evidence in social work. *Social Work in Health Care, 51*(6), 483–505. doi:10.1080/00981389.2012.671649 PMID:22780700

Manuel, J. I., Mullen, E. J., Fang, L., Bellamy, J. L., & Bledsoe, S. E. (2009). Preparing social work practitioners to use evidence-based practice: A comparison of experiences from an implementation project. *Research on Social Work Practice, 19*(5), 613–627. doi:10.1177/1049731509335547

McAuliffe, D. (2010). Ethical decision-making. In M. Gray & S. A. Webb (Eds.), *Ethics and value perspectives in social work* (pp. 41–50). New York: Palgrave Macmillan.

Moseley, A., & Tierney, S. (2005). Evidence-based practice in the real world. *Evidence and Policy, 1*(1), 113–119. doi:10.1332/1744264052703212

Munro, E. (2012). Risk assessment and decision making. In M. Gray, J. Midgley, & S. A. Webb (Eds.), *The Sage handbook of social work* (pp. 224–235). London: Sage. doi:10.4135/9781446247648.n15

Ruch, G. (2007). Reflective practice in contemporary child-care social work: The role of containment. *British Journal of Social Work, 37*(4), 659–680. doi:10.1093/bjsw/bch277

Schon, D. (1983). *The reflective practitioner: How professionals think in action*. London: Temple Smith.

Shaw, I. (2013). Ways of knowing. In M. Gray & S. A. Webb (Eds.), *Social work theories and methods* (2nd ed., pp. 241–252). London: Sage.

Strough, J., Karns, T. E., & Schlosnagle, L. (2011). Decision-making heuristics and biases across the life span. *Annals of the New York Academy of Sciences, 1235*(1), 57–74. doi:10.1111/j.1749-6632.2011.06208.x PMID:22023568

Taylor, B. (2010). *Professional decision making in social work*. Exeter: Learning Matters.

Thompson, S., & Thomson, N. (2008). *The critically reflective practitioner*. Basingstoke: Palgrave Macmillan.

Timmermans, S., & Berg, M. (2003). *The gold standard: The challenge of evidence-based medicine and standardization in health care*. Philadelphia: Temple University Press.

Webb, S. A. (2001). Some considerations on the validity of evidence-based practice in social work. *British Journal of Social Work, 31*(1), 57–79. doi:10.1093/bjsw/31.1.57

White, S. (2009). Arguing the case in safeguarding. In K. Broadhurst, C. Grover, & J. Jamieson (Eds.), *Critical perspectives on safeguarding children* (pp. 93–110). Chichester: Wiley-Blackwell.

## KEY TERMS AND DEFINITIONS

**Critical Thinking:** A self-questioning stance which provokes self-curiosity and an unsettling of that which is believed to be known, both about the self and the outside world. It involves reflexivity, considering the practitioner's impact upon the situation presenting and the impact of the situation upon the practitioner.

**Heuristics:** Decision-making short cuts that are based on prior experiences which allow decisions to be made quickly, often based on incomplete information: components of intuitive responses. These, in the main, perform well, but are prone to biases, susceptible as they are to distortions via emotion, recognition, and recall.

**Intuition:** An automatic and unconscious thought process which has evolved over time, influenced by personal, social and cultural experiences, specific to the context of the individual's lived experiences.

**Knowledge-Aware Practice:** A holistic approach to the use of information in practice, encompassing a continuum of knowledge from that based on empirical evidence to that gained overtime through practice experiences.

**Sensemaking:** The practitioner's task of attempting to best understand the practice scenario which confronts them, permitting them to arrive at a judgement or decision.

**Virtue Ethics:** Ethics concerned with the character of the individual as a moral agent. Key virtues include perception, judgement, honesty, and integrity. These virtues act as a guide and internal motivator for action.

# Chapter 4
# Navigating Practice–Informed Evidence and Evidence–Based Practice:
## Balancing Multiple Discourses and Competing Claims to Knowledge

**Margaret Pack**
*Australian Catholic University, Australia*

## ABSTRACT

*This chapter explores social workers' application of practice evidence in their everyday work in team and agency contexts. Practice evidence concerns the practitioner seeking the best available knowledge, accessed, adapted, and applied to guide practice with clients. How social workers decide which sources to draw from and which are appropriate sources of evidence for practice is based on many considerations. These include the social worker's values and ethics for practice, legislative and policy requirements, professional standards of practice, and the range of theories applied to any case or situation encountered in practice. Practice wisdom, or the experience gained in the repetition of seeing the same kind of client presentations across time, produces a further source which is drawn upon within the social worker's repertoire of knowledge. In this sense, there are multiple knowledge frameworks within which social workers operate, balancing contradictory and competing discourses about "what works" in any practice situation.*

## INTRODUCTION

Evidence-based practice has been defined in various ways in social work internationally. A British definition drawing from a child protection context sees the approach relying at its foundation on

*... a combination of practitioner expertise and knowledge of the best external research, and evaluation based evidence. It involves a careful, clear and thoughtful use of up-to-date evidence when making decisions about how to work with individual parents and families. (Lifelong Learning UK, 2011, p.7)*

DOI: 10.4018/978-1-4666-6563-7.ch004

As social workers operate from an appreciation of the relevance of context and culture, they are concerned with the way in which evidence is defined, gathered, and applied in relation to competing knowledge claims. The need to identify where the gap in knowledge exists is the first step when social workers identify their information needs in order to meet these needs accurately (Howard, McMillen, & Pollio, 2003). The dimensions of age, life stage of development, ethnicity, gender, and sexuality are important in defining what evidence is appropriate for social work and also guides the practitioner in the application of evidence. Social workers, as other professionals, work with clients across a broad range of contexts. Whose knowledge claims are dominant and the relative power positioning behind the various claims is analysed in anti-oppressive social work practice. This anti-oppressive critique, therefore, informs social workers' choice and application of diverse knowledge sources to practice.

Social workers have an appreciation of the importance of practice wisdom and the oral traditions in Indigenous cultures. From within the predominant culture, social workers explore how evidence becomes marginalised knowledge by the colonising or predominant cultures. By casting a critical eye on Western methods, the practice of social work itself can be seen as being a form of imperialism. A "de-colonising" approach suggests that no practice is value free, therefore, all "evidence" is reflective of the practitioner's worldview (Smith, 1999). In the Australasian context, this appreciation of alternative ways of knowing has elevated narrative as a primary means of meaning-making and as being directly constitutive of identity. As a consequence, narrative and "yarning" are acknowledged as the cornerstones of this oral tradition and are valued by social work as a profession as sources of "evidence" (Bennett, Green, Gilbert, & Bessarab, 2013). Core knowledge for practice is passed on during narrative discussions, social workers' conversations with one another in case meetings, and in clinical supervision sessions, where practice dilemmas and themes within a social worker's caseload are deliberated upon and directions identified.

Sources of practice evidence in the widest sense can, therefore, include discussions with key advisors, colleagues, clients and their families, and peer and clinical supervisors. Reference to what is traditionally considered authoritative sources of evidence through reference guidelines, indexing, research studies, and electronic journal databases are other ways in which social workers glean knowledge for practice. The individual social worker's own discovery of what has worked over time with particular clients who present with similar issues is a further storehouse of knowledge derived more directly from review of their practice within peer review and from evaluations with clients after the work is completed. Clients' evaluations of their experience of therapy is evidence in a primary sense which aligns with the term "practice wisdom" (Crockett, Drewery, McKenzie, Smith, & Winslade, 2004; Dulwich Centre Publications, 2004). This source of evidence may not be ranked according to sample size and research design. Further, the generalisability of findings across populations of clients may not be possible. However, the issue of quality in this scientific sense may not be the primary consideration of the social worker.

Social workers may make a pragmatic decision to apply lessons learned from what has worked in the past to a similar practice situation in the present. In this sense, each client contact is a test of evidence of how to form and maintain the therapeutic relationship effectively to support the client's growth and healing. Through repeating of the therapeutic process with each client or family, group, or community, the efficacy of the social worker's framework for practice is tested (Pack, 2004). Every client, family, group, and community the social worker engages with is a test of the application of theory and how integrated and coherent the social worker's framework for practice is (Pack, 2004). This "evidence" and how to apply it, therefore, may be contextually specific and defined taking into account differing circumstances. In turn, these circumstances may be dependent upon the client's background, goals, presenting issues, and type of therapeutic relationship established. These variables include work with particular groups of clients who present with differing needs to health and welfare organisations in statutory and not-for-profit settings.

## Social Work Fields of Practice

The fields or specialisations within social work practice can involve particular skill sets and competencies that are associated with specific contexts of practice. For example, the use of practice guidelines to inform and guide practice in mental health is a customary part of training of mental health social workers and other mental health professionals. Mental health is one of the fields of practice in which evidence can be accessed directly through reference to practice guidelines which are themselves based on systematic reviews of the evidence-based literature, for example, New Zealand Guidelines Group Reports. These sources of evidence for practice are very helpful when time-poor social workers are practising with clients who have differing DSMV diagnoses, such as schizophrenia, bipolar affective disorder, or who are at risk of harm to self (suicide prevention guidelines), as specific approaches and interventions are recommended for client diagnoses and issues. Such guidelines provide an up-to-date appraisal of the recommended treatment approaches based on a range of peer reviewed research studies, including systematic reviews and findings from the empirical research literature. The use of guidelines can usefully be applied to a particular presenting issue, ethical dilemma, or diagnosis, enabling social workers to think more deeply about the issue and apply evidence for practice in the moment. When referring to practice guidelines, a knowledge-base then becomes very accessible

to the practitioner who may not feel confident in undertaking their own research independently.

The use of evidence-based guidelines is a contested area of social work with debate centring on the appropriateness of a "what works" also known as a pragmatic approach (Dore, 2006). Furthermore, there are concerns that distilling down complexity in organisations employing risk-averse policies is falsely creating an ethos of certainty where the opposite is in reality closer to the lived experience of social workers on the job (Dore, 2006).

## BACKGROUND: PRACTICE-INFORMED EVIDENCE

Given these concerns, many social workers have preferred to use the softer term "evidence-informed practice". This term encompasses a wider range of sources including the following:

- The individual social worker's skills, knowledge, and the use of self in the practitioner's role.
- Inter and intra-agency policy, legal frameworks, and eligibility to access and use services.
- Evidence-based guidelines.
- Embodied ethics based in an application of standards of practice and codes of professional ethics.
- The best available evidence of what works based on reflection on theory, clinical supervision, narratives of clients', colleagues' and own experiences which are processed through peer review and clinical supervision (i.e. practice wisdom).
- Empirical research, including qualitative research designs, action research, and practice research, involving client and family or community narratives.

- The practitioner's own unique framework for practice which draws upon the multi-theoretical approaches to working in an integrated way with clients and the overarching personal and professional philosophies to practice.

Given that evidence-informed practice is defined as both a process and an underlying philosophy, the underpinning values of the individual social worker and those of the profession also need to be identified. Gambrill (2007), for example, proposes that the Social Workers' Code of Ethics and the accreditation standards of social work education programmes mediate the social worker's choices. When the social worker selects among different perspectives or evidence-based approaches, a code of professional ethics assists in navigating potential ethical and application dilemmas. A systemic view of how evidence can be applied on multiple levels to encompass the micro, meso, and macro dimensions of people's lives is recommended (Gitterman & Germain, 2008). This approach, drawing on ecological systems theory, is recommended in approaching the application of evidence in social work in fields such as sexual abuse recovery (for instance, Pack, 2013). Howard et al. (2003) suggest that the practitioner who is familiar with the unique circumstances of the individual, family, community, and society is the most appropriate person to work in partnership to apply the knowledge within a collaborative relationship of trust and respect. This person-in-environment perspective is itself embedded in how evidence is applied. Sources of evidence can be both systemically and reflexively considered by social workers who work with their clients within the wider systems to which both belong to influence change. An example of this occurs when social workers witness individual problems over a number of client presentations and in this process connect the public issues within these individual presentations. This provides social workers with a knowledge source to be used to lobby for changes in the social, political, and economic structures which surround the individual and also the systems within which the social work service is provided.

Social workers who advocate practice informed evidence rely on the following steps which are cyclical rather than linear:

1. Identifying information needs in the moment.
2. Moving from the dilemma to the formulation of key question(s) that are answerable or at least able to be informed by evidence.
3. Discovering the best available evidence to address the questions.
4. Assessing the quality and applicability of the evidence found.
5. Applying the evidence in relation to the specific situation to guide the selection of approaches and modalities/interventions in partnership with the client, family, group, or community.
6. Evaluating the process of applying the evidence using the dual lens of the practitioner's need for guidance and the client's need for effective process/outcomes from their contact with the social worker (Howard et al., 2003).

The question arises then as to why is it that evidence for practice is not more widely consulted by social workers? There are several practical impediments to which I will now turn in the following section.

## INTEGRATING THEORY WITH PRACTICE

Most social workers lack the reflective space and time to undertake research in a structured, comprehensive way but they wish to ensure that they are being careful, clear, and considered about what they are doing with their clients for the safety and well-being of themselves, their clients, colleagues, and their employing organisation. Because social workers are often required to "think on their feet", particularly in fields such as child protection and in acute health settings, practice guidelines, decision-making trees and flow charts, and agency policies are used routinely to break down complex everyday decisions into the most appropriate next steps to take. Following such guides for action can ensure that, as far as possible, social workers are integrating their own professional skills and knowledge with what is known from evaluative studies. Integration of differing sources of knowledge and applying these central tenets to practice can ensure that social workers are following the most effective way of assisting their clients through the most up-to-date, best quality information. The second part of this process is how the social worker decides which key findings to integrate into their ethical and professional knowledge-base.

The professional use of self and the personal values, skills, and ethical principles are critical concerns in the use and application of evidence for practice. If the social worker lacks the skills, qualities, and knowledge-base for applying the best evidence to practice, then the intervention or programme is unlikely to have effective outcomes. Some of the skills, qualities, and knowledge-base needed for social work are clear from the Australian Association of Social Workers (AASW, 2013) which identifies the following "indicators" that practice standards are being demonstrated:

1.  *Practices within a social justice and human rights framework.*
2.  *Facilitates people's empowerment and works to eliminate all violations of human rights.*
3.  *Identifies social systems and structures that preserve inequalities and injustices and advocates for change.*
4.  *Challenges policies and practices that are oppressive and fail to meet international standards of human rights, social inclusion and social development. (p. 9)*

The values underpinning these standards are "respect for persons", "social justice", and "professional integrity" (AASW, 2013, p. 7). Human rights and social justice, therefore, are fundamental values and principles that guide the application of evidence in social work.

## EXPLORING THE ROLE OF PRACTICE-INFORMED EVIDENCE IN SOCIAL WORK: A BRIEF REVIEW OF LITERATURE

In previous studies (for instance, Fook, 2004; Howard et al, 2003; Webb, 2001), evidence-based practice has often been contrasted with reflective and psychodynamic approaches in social work. Webb (2001) argues that evidence-based practice espouses a deterministic view of rationality in which all dilemmas can be reduced, solved, or "answered" when this is untrue for many of the complex situations social workers' are faced with. Gambrill (2007) views clinical expertise as determining how evidence informs practice, including client evaluation and values, information about risk management, and the effective use of professional judgement.

As most social work research studies are not systematic reviews, which are considered to be the "gold standard" in the evidence-based literature, case studies and smaller qualitative studies may be considered as lacking rigour methodologically. Therefore, most social work research studies might have internal consistency in the researched population but lack generalisability across whole populations.

Although there is an assumption that medical practitioners search for evidence more systematically, there is evidence to the contrary; for example, information searching amongst general practitioners in a medical context has been likened to an act of "foraging", an ecological metaphor, which describes the diverse range of methods for gleaning information (Dwairy, Dowell, & Stahl, 2011). In the medical provider literature, the most sought method of dealing with practice dilemmas was found to be talking to colleagues for advice and secondly, referring to books to "scavenge" relevant information quickly with the purpose of applying it to one's practice with patients (Dwairy et al., 2011). This advice and knowledge from colleagues may itself be drawn from a wide range of sources, including training and professional education, practice wisdom, and case conferences. The process of applying multi-theoretical approaches and peer-reviewed research and guidelines needs to take into account the values that social workers hold, both to guide the search for evidence and the application of findings to practice (Edmond, Megivern, Williams, Rochman, & Howard, 2006; Howard et al., 2003).

Clinical supervision is the major forum within which social workers appraise evidence for practice through a process of critical self-reflection within an established relationship with a more experienced peer. Clinical supervision of practice is a requirement of professional associations of social workers in Australia and New Zealand reflecting its importance and connections to quality in practice. When social workers encounter challenging aspects of their work, they can be jettisoned into unknown or unfamiliar territory. Making decisions in this space is important to workforce retention and worker satisfaction as well as to positive outcomes for the client (Pack, 2004, 2011, 2014). I now turn to consider the process of critical reflection as a means by which social workers assess the relevance and quality of evidence for practice as well as how to apply it.

## ALTERNATIVE SOURCES OF EVIDENCE: REFLECTIVE PRACTICE

Fook and Askeland's (2007) model of critical reflection aims to challenge cultures, that is, the preconceived ideas which are embedded in

practices, in order to examine and change them if they do not fit with the stated ideals of individual professionals. Gardner (2009) similarly recommends educating social workers to critique their agency policies and structures that impact upon service delivery and clients.

Social workers also need to listen to the experience of clients and their families, as this source of evidence provides another way of seeing ourselves as others do (Fook & Askeland, 2007). These narratives have the potential for creating a co-created space in which service-users can discuss their hopes and dreams for their lives and for the future. This strengths-based assessment to identify the client's preferences and motivation enables social workers to critically reflect on their own practice which means giving the client greater choice and autonomy for deriving their own recovery or healing process. It also enables social workers to cast a critical eye on their own actions in practice and the underlying power dynamics of "client" and "worker".

Reflecting and critically appraising evidence for relevance and validity (otherwise referred to as "closeness to truth") and applicability (usefulness in moving clinical practice forward) are identified as mediating the social worker's decision to use evidence to guide practice (Gambrill, 2007). Ruch (2007) discusses in relation to the child protection social work field the ways in which a critical reflective process can guide complex decision-making taking into account multiple roles, legal frameworks, and ethical guidelines, alongside the individual social worker's values and frameworks for practice. The process is informed by the ongoing reflection on the agency and society in which abuse occurs and what is happening to the social worker in the agency. In a similar way, Rossiter (2011) advocates an orientation to social work practice that she refers to as involving "unsettling" practices. This concept refers to the fact that the social worker, the team, the agency, and the knowledge being applied all exist in a tension which is grounded in the taken for granted assumptions we have about concepts and theories in social work practice. This is a tension that exists continuously as a dynamic within social work practice and so is never resolved. Rossiter concludes that we need to put our ethics and values as social workers ahead of this knowledge in practice to guide all that social workers do. The consequence of this is that we need to regard the ethics for practice as involving this core tension and contradiction which she sees as being derived in the uncertainty of social work as a profession and, therefore, the authority with which it can assert its knowledge claims. On the basis of the ethics of Emmanual Levinas, a philosopher, Rossiter asserts that ethics must precede knowledge generation. This proposal can be usefully applied to social work practice in terms of how evidence is applied by the ethical practitioner. The implications of Rossiter's thesis is that ethics for social work need to be the primary consideration in applying knowledge to practice and therefore that no evidence can be applied without the application of personal and professional ethics by each social work practitioner.

## FUTURE RESEARCH DIRECTIONS

### Strengths-Based Theories and the Recovery Paradigm: Practitioners/Service-User Perspectives

The "unsettling" of social work practice (Rossiter, 2011) and the challenging of professional knowledge-base for practice is behind the current movement which represents a paradigm shift away from the expert-knows best discourses to survivor narratives of healing and transcending oppression. These narratives critique what social workers do in new and revealing ways based in the Recovery Paradigm (see, for instance, Pack, 2013).

Recovery is considered to be a process of returning to a quality of life that enables the person affected by illness to continue to live well with a long-term condition (Starnino, 2009). For example, inspiring hope and a positive self-concept are aspects of what is considered to be conducive to staying well in the face of mental illness (Russinova, Rogers, Ellison, & Lyass, 2011). The process of recovery is considered as a means of re-authoring self-identity through addressing social stigma, support, autonomy, self-determination, and decision-making power over one's life (Carpenter, 2002). Essential in this process is the need to move beyond mere symptom management. Components of recovery involve fulfilling employment, sustaining relationships, and a sense of belonging and participating with an equal voice in community. Returning to an integrated belonging in community is pivotal in this recovery process (Starnino, 2009). Other aspects increasing hope for the future, personal creativity, and spiritual fulfilment, feature prominently in the research literature about recovery. These less tangible aspects of life may cause social workers discomfort when they may not have explored these aspects of practice in relation to their own lives (Fallot, 2007). Therefore, the evidence-based practice literature highlights that mental health social workers should receive specific training and education at the tertiary level (Razzano et al., 2010).

The literature on recovery emphasises the concept of "empowerment" (Starnino, 2009) which some consumer and peer networks dispute as being appropriate as no one is devoid of personal decision-making and personal resources; for example, contradictions are apparent in the goals of evidence-based practice and those of the recovery movement. These tensions are also evident in the social work practice research literature. Practice needs to encompass a more holistic vision of what recovery is, involving co-created conversations between service-users, their caregivers, and their families (Rapp & Goscha, 2006). Supporting the service-user to develop a quality of life in relation to his or her social environment is an example of an application of the recovery literature to guide practice (Rapp & Goscha, 2006). Prominent in the literature on recovery is the strengths-perspective where the social worker aims to capture the hopes and aspirations of the service-user in their intervention. Strengths-based models are characterised as a collaborative endeavour with service-users and their families (Saleebey, 2005). Due to their position in the multidisciplinary team and involvement in discharge planning and follow-up services in the community, social workers have found a synergy with an integrative approach comprising strengths-based, narrative, and service-user led movements. These theories in action guide practice in fields such as mental health (Saleebey, 2005) and sexual abuse recovery (Pack, 2013).

## SOLUTIONS AND RECOMMENDATIONS

In the recovery process, social workers as part of their assessment ask how the diagnosis has influenced the service-user's life to explore the "sparkling events" (White & Epston, 1990) or exceptions to the "problem", where people transcend the "problem" to areas of personal success and fulfilment.

An example of this process of working in a strengths-based paradigm appears in the following case study involving Billy. This case illustration describes both the major narrative of the youth justice system, in which the social worker operates with all its contradictions, and the client, Billy's personal narrative of wanting to belong in his peer group as a young man of migrant parents who is unemployed. Therefore, there are many complex contextual factors to consider and little empirical research to guide the social worker in justifying that Billy should not be sent into the adult criminal justice system as a first offender.

## Case Study

Billy is an unemployed 16 year old whose parents are Armenian migrants, resettled in Australia. Billy is currently serving two years in a juvenile detention centre and will soon be moved to an adult prison to serve a remaining three years in custodial care. He assaulted and robbed a corporate employee having lunch in a park to get money to support his drug habit, as he is a regular user of the drug "P" belonging to the methamphetamines. A police officer tackled Billy, who was under the influence of drugs, and during the scuffle Billy assaulted the police officer. In gathering evidence for his continued sentence in the community, whilst under probation and a community care sentence, his social worker discussed the research finding and her experience professionally that violence is typically associated with addiction to P. In her defence of Billy, she pointed out that as a 16 year old, his physical prowess is a source of self-esteem and a "badge of honour" within his peer group which begets friendship and kudos from others. In this same group, "group think" has created pressure on Billy to act out in ways that are socially unacceptable but valued within the peer group. Within his circle of friends, physical violence is associated with being "manly" and "cool." Anger is often expressed physically rather than verbalised, due to men and boys' socialisation to be "manly" and not to express emotion openly. Billy felt empathy for his victim and chose a man likely to have money to rob but felt sorry for his actions and ran off before taking the man's wallet. When police tackled Billy to the ground he made a rational choice to fight; he remembered feeling afraid and intimidated so he did not surrender to being physically restrained but rather lashed out. Billy's narrative attributes meanings to young men's violence that challenges the predominant discourses that make assumptions about young men's violence as being anti-social behaviour, having at its base a lack of empathy for others.

The case study illustrates that young men's violence is both complex and dynamic and its origins are often misunderstood, necessitating a multi-theoretical and narrative analysis to guide the approach to assessment and intervention. A narrative analysis of Billy's behaviour reveals hidden meanings and suggests ways in which young men can be guided and supported into pro-social ways of being. Theories such as the "Good Lives Model" of offender rehabilitation suggest the importance of comprehensive assessment based in the individual's life goals, including ways of reaching these goals that are socially acceptable and avoid infringing the rights of others. Goals, such as having sufficient money to live on, employment, and sustaining relationships to have a sense of belonging, are encompassed within such strengths-based models of assessment and intervention (Clark, 2013; Ward, 2002; Ward & Gannon, 2006; Wilson & Yates, 2009).

This nuanced understanding of the complexity of being human, the multi-faceted nature of practice, and the interdependence of professional knowledge, ethics, skills, and values, as well as personal and professional experiences, all shape social work practice. This is its evidence-base that can enable social work to become more aware of its own strengths and limitations as a profession. Evidence needs to be informed by the meanings and experiences service-users give to their health and welfare providers. Thus, the values espoused by the profession would be better serviced by a "knowledge-aware approach" where differing sources of evidence are combined to provide new directions (Dore, 2006). This concept allows uncertainty and fallibility into the mix and thus distinguishes evidence-informed from evidence-prescribed approaches to social work practice (Dore, 2006).

## CONCLUSION

The common meanings and experiences service-users give to their health and welfare providers contend against the dominant knowledge of "expert-knows-best". From the recovery paradigm, what counts as evidence can be questioned and the knowledge-base for practice expanded. Open inquiry is, therefore, needed when searching, analysing, and deciding what is "appropriate" evidence and applying where the practitioner views this evidence as relevant to practice. This decision-making needs also to recognise that significant gaps may exist in the theoretical models of explanation, as was exemplified in the interpretation of Billy's move to the adult criminal justice system on the basis of his age. These gaps in understanding inevitably lead to a divide between theory assessment and intervention approaches, while the practitioner may find they are practising in an "unknown zone" or "liminal space" (Myerhoff, 1982, 1992). In this space, social workers are engaged in actively constructing new theories of practice. In many situations, therefore, social workers require an appreciation that their power and authority does not derive from a clear evidence-base, as this body of knowledge with theoretical underpinning does not yet exist or exists in a partial form but needs to be brought into a coherent whole. This chapter, drawing on the case study of Billy, an adolescent enmeshed in the youth justice system, demonstrates a common challenge in an applied field of practice. The dilemma is how to navigate between the practice-based evidence involving the use of professional self, embodied ethics, and practice wisdom, alongside the service-user narrative, and to use these as primary sources of knowledge to be applied in practice. Evidence from more traditionally considered sources, such as practice guidelines, decision-making trees, systematic reviews of literature, and randomised controlled trials, may or may not be part of the knowledge sources used by social workers. That is because that evidence may not exist or may exist only in parts that the social worker needs to bring together for practice. This evidence must, however, be triangulated with the other forms of evidence mentioned throughout this chapter, including service-users' and their families' perspectives.

# REFERENCES

Australian Association of Social Workers. (2013). *Practice standards 2013*. Retrieved from http://www.aasw.asn.au/document/item/4551

Bennett, B., Green, S., Gilbert, S., & Bessarab, D. (Eds.). (2013). *Our voices: Aboriginal and Torres Strait Islander social work*. South Yarra, Australia: Palgrave Macmillan.

Carpenter, J. (2002). Mental health recovery paradigm: Implications for social work. *Health & Social Work*, *27*(2), 86–94. doi:10.1093/hsw/27.2.86 PMID:12079172

Clark, M. D. (2013). The strengths perspective in criminal justice. In T. D. Saleebey (Ed.), *The strengths perspective in social work practice* (6th rev. ed., pp. 129–148). Pearson Education.

Crocket, K., Drewery, W., McKenzie, W., Smith, L., & Winslade, J. (2004). Working for ethical research in practice. *International Journal of Narrative Therapy and Community Work*, *3*, 61–66. Retrieved from http://www.dulwichcentre.com.au/e-journal.html

Dore, I. J. (2006). Evidence-focused social care: On target or off-side? *Social Work & Society*, *4*, 232-255. Retrieved from http://www.socwork.net/sws

Dulwich Centre Publications. (2004). Narrative therapy and research. *International Journal of Narrative Therapy and Community Work*, *2*, 29–36. Retrieved from http://www.dulwichcentre.com.au/e-journal.html

Dwairy, M., Dowell, A. C., & Stahl, J.-C. (2011). The application of foraging theory to the information searching behaviour of general practitioners. *BMC Family Practice*, *12*(1), 90. doi:10.1186/1471-2296-12-90 PMID:21861880

Edmond, T., Megivern, D., Williams, C., Rochman, E., & Howard, M. (2006). Integrating evidence-based practice and social work field education. *Journal of Social Work Education*, *42*(2), 377–396. doi:10.5175/JSWE.2006.200404115

Fallot, R. D. (2007). Spirituality and religion in recovery: Some current issues. *Psychiatric Rehabilitation Journal*, *30*(4), 261–270. doi:10.2975/30.4.2007.261.270 PMID:17458450

Fook, J. (2004). What professionals need from research: Beyond evidence-based practice. In D. Smith (Ed.), *Social work and evidence-based practice* (pp. 29–46). London: Jessica Kingsley.

Fook, J., & Askeland, G. A. (2007). Challenges of critical reflection: "Nothing ventured, nothing gained. *Social Work Education*, *26*(5), 520–533. doi:10.1080/02615470601118662

Gambrill, E. (2007). Views of evidence-based practice: Social workers' code of ethics and accreditation standards as guides of choice. *Journal of Social Work Education*, *43*(3), 447–462. doi:10.5175/JSWE.2007.200600639

Gardner, F. (2009). Affirming values: Using critical reflection to explore meaning and professional practice. *Reflective Practice*, *10*(2), 179–190. doi:10.1080/14623940902786198

Gitterman, A., & Germain, C. B. (2008). *The life model of social work practice: Advances in theory and practice* (3rd ed.). Chichester, UK: Columbia University.

Howard, M. O., McMillen, C. J., & Pollio, D. E. (2003). Teaching evidence-based practice: Toward a new paradigm for social work education. *Research on Social Work Practice*, *13*(2), 234–259. doi:10.1177/1049731502250404

Lifelong Learning UK. (2011). *Work with parents: National occupational standards.* Retrieved from https://www.gov.uk/government/uploads/system/uploads/attachment_data/file/175555/NOS-PARENTS.pdf

Myerhoff, B. (1982). *Number our days: A triumph of continuity and culture among Jewish old people in an urban ghetto.* New York: Simon and Schuster/Touchstone Books.

Myerhoff, B. (1992). *Remembered lives: The work of ritual, storytelling, and growing older.* Ann Arbor, MI: University of Michigan Press.

Pack, M. (2004). Sexual abuse counsellors' responses to stress and trauma: A social work perspective. *Aotearoa New Zealand Social Work Review, 16*, 19-25. Retrieved from http://anzasw.org.nz/about/topics/show/207-aotearoa-nz-social-work-review

Pack, M. (2011). Discovering an integrated framework for practice: A qualitative investigation of theories used by social workers working as sexual abuse therapists. *Journal of Social Work Practice, 25*(1), 79–93. doi:10.1080/02650533.2010.530646

Pack, M. (2013). Vicarious traumatisation and resilience: An ecological systems approach to sexual abuse counsellors' trauma and stress. *Sexual Abuse in Australia and New Zealand, 5,* 69-76. Retrieved from http://www.anzatsa.org/index.php?page=SAANZ&PHPSESSID=NXlr8FauuICTIxqV%2CK2Wu2

Pack, M. (2014). Vicarious resilience: A multilayered model of stress and trauma. *Affilia: Journal of Women & Social Work, 29*(1), 18–29. doi:10.1177/0886109913510088

Rapp, C. A., & Goscha, R. J. (2006). *The strengths-model: Case management with people with psychiatric disabilities* (2nd ed.). New York, NY: Oxford University Press.

Razzano, L., Jonikas, J., Goelitz, M., Hamilton, M., Marvin, R., & Jones-Martinex, N. et al. (2010). The recovery education in the academy program: Transforming academic curricula with the principles of recovery and self-determination. *Psychiatric Rehabilitation Journal, 34*(2), 130–136. doi:10.2975/34.2.2010.130.136 PMID:20952366

Rossiter, A. (2011). Unsettled social work: The challenge of Levinas's ethics. *British Journal of Social Work, 41*(5), 980–995. doi:10.1093/bjsw/bcr004

Ruch, G. (2007). Reflective practice in contemporary child-care social work: The role of containment. *British Journal of Social Work, 37*(4), 659–680. doi:10.1093/bjsw/bch277

Russinova, Z., Rogers, E. S., Ellison, M. L., & Lyass, A. (2011). Recovery-promoting professional competencies: Perspectives of mental health consumers, consumer-providers and providers. *Psychiatric Rehabilitation Journal, 34*(3), 177–185. doi:10.2975/34.3.2011.177.185 PMID:21208856

Saleebey, D. (2005). *The strengths perspective in social work practice* (4th ed.). Boston: Pearson/Allyn & Bacon.

Smith, L. T. (1999). *Decolonising methodologies: Research and Indigenous peoples.* London: Zed Books.

Starnino, V. R. (2009). An integral approach to mental health recovery: Implications for social work. *Journal of Human Behavior in the Social Environment, 19*(7), 820–842. doi:10.1080/10911350902988019

Ward, T. (2002). Good Lives and the rehabilitation of offenders: Promises and problems. *Aggression and Violent Behavior, 7*(5), 513–528. doi:10.1016/S1359-1789(01)00076-3

Ward, T., & Gannon, T. A. (2006). Rehabilitation, etiology, and self-regulation: The comprehensive good lives model of treatment for sexual offenders. *Aggression and Violent Behavior*, *11*(1), 77–94. doi:10.1016/j.avb.2005.06.001

Webb, S. A. (2001). Some considerations on the validity of evidence-based practice in social work. *British Journal of Social Work*, *31*(1), 57–79. doi:10.1093/bjsw/31.1.57

White, M., & Epston, D. (1990). *Narrative means to therapeutic ends*. New York: Norton.

Wilson, R. J., & Yates, P. M. (2009). Effective interventions and the Good Lives Model: Maximising treatment gains for sexual offenders. *Aggression and Violent Behavior*, *14*(3), 157–161. doi:10.1016/j.avb.2009.01.007

## ADDITIONAL READING

Argyris, C., & Schon, D. A. (1976). *Theory in practice: Increasing professional effectiveness*. San Francisco, CA: Jossey Bass.

Arnd-Caddigan, M. (2011). Toward a broader definition of evidence-informed practice: Intersubjective evidence. *Families in Society*, *92*(4), 372–376. doi:10.1606/1044-3894.4160

Asgary-Eden, V., & Lee, C. M. (2011). So now we've picked an evidence-based program, what's next? Perspectives of service providers and administrators. *Professional Psychology: Research and Practice*, *42*(2), 169–175. doi:10.1037/a0022745

Atherton, C. R., & Bolland, K. A. (2002). Postmodernism: A dangerous illusion for social work. *International Social Work*, *45*(4), 421–433. doi:10.1177/00208728020450040201

Barber, J. G. (1996). Science and social work: Are they compatible? *Research on Social Work Practice*, *6*(3), 379–388. doi:10.1177/104973159600600308

Belchamber, R. (1997). Re-evaluating social work's debt to the scientific tradition. *Social Work & Social Sciences Review*, *7*, 13–25. Retrieved from http://www.whitingbirch.net/cgi-bin/scribe?showinfo=ip003

Crisp, B. R. (2000). A history of Australian social work practice research. *Research on Social Work Practice*, *10*, 179–184. Retrieved from http://rsw.sagepub.com/

Drisko, J. W. (1997). Strengthening qualitative studies and reports: Standards to promote academic integrity. *Journal of Social Work Education*, *33*, 185–197. doi:10.1080/10437797.1997.10778862

Faul, A. C., McMurtry, S. L., & Hudson, W. W. (2001). Can empirical clinical practice techniques improve social work outcomes? *Research on Social Work Practice*, *11*(3), 277–299. doi:10.1177/104973150101100301

Gambrill, E. (2003). Evidence-based practice: Implications for knowledge development and use in social work. In A. Rosen & E. K. Proctor (Eds.), *Developing practice guidelines for social work intervention: Issues, methods, and research agenda* (pp. 37–58). New York: Columbia University Press.

Gambrill, E. (2006). Evidence-based practice and policy: Choices ahead. *Research on Social Work Practice*, *16*(3), 338–357. doi:10.1177/1049731505284205

Gambrill, E. (2008). Evidence-based (informed) macro practice: Process and philosophy. *Journal of Evidence-Based Social Work*, *5*(3-4), 423–452. doi:10.1080/15433710802083971 PMID:19042875

Gambrill, E. (2010). Evidence-informed practice: Antidote to propaganda in the helping professions? *Research on Social Work Practice*, *20*(3), 302–320. doi:10.1177/1049731509347879

Gambrill, E. (2011). Evidence-based practice and the ethics of discretion. *Journal of Social Work*, *11*(1), 26–48. doi:10.1177/1468017310381306

Gambrill, E. (2013). Evidence-informed practice. In B. A. Thyer, C. N. Dulmus, & K. M. Sowers (Eds.), *Developing evidence-based generalist practice skills* (pp. 1–24). Hoboken, New Jersey: John Wiley.

Kondrat, D. C., & Teater, B. (2009). An anti-stigma approach to working with persons with severe mental disability: Seeking real change through narrative change. *Journal of Social Work Practice*, *23*(1), 35–47. doi:10.1080/02650530902723308

Manuel, J. I., Mullen, E. J., Fang, L., Bellamy, J. L., & Bledsoe, S. E. (2009). Preparing social work practitioners to use evidence-based practice: A comparison of experiences from an implementation project. *Research on Social Work Practice*, *19*(5), 613–627. doi:10.1177/1049731509335547

McAuliffe, D. (2010). Ethical decision-making. In M. Gray & S. A. Webb (Eds.), *Ethics and value perspectives in social work* (pp. 41–50). Basingstoke: Palgrave Macmillan.

Moseley, A., & Tierney, S. (2005). Evidence-based practice in the real world. *Evidence and Policy*, *1*(1), 113–120. doi:10.1332/1744264052703212

Munro, E. (2012). Risk assessment and decision making. In M. Gray, J. Midgley, & S. A. Webb (Eds.), *The Sage handbook of social work* (pp. 224–235). London: Sage. doi:10.4135/9781446247648.n15

Pilgrim, D. (2009). Recovery from mental health problems: Scratching the surface without ethnography. *Journal of Social Work Practice*, *23*(4), 475–487. doi:10.1080/02650530903375033

Schon, D. A. (1983). *The reflective practitioner: How professionals think in action*. London: Temple Smith.

Smith, D. (Ed.). (2004). *Social work and evidence-based practice*. London: Jessica Kingsley.

Strough, J., Karnes, T. E., & Schlosnagle, L. (2011). Decision-making heuristics and biases across the life span. *Annals of the New York Academy of Sciences*, *1235*(1), 57–74. doi:10.1111/j.1749-6632.2011.06208.x PMID:22023568

Taylor, B. J. (2010). *Professional decision making in social work*. Exeter: Learning Matters.

Thompson, S., & Thompson, N. (2008). *The critically reflective practitioner*. Basingstoke: Palgrave Macmillan.

Thyer, B. A. (2004). What is evidence-based practice? *Brief Treatment and Crisis Intervention*, *4*(2), 167–176. doi:10.1093/brief-treatment/mhh013

Thyer, B. A. (2008). The quest for evidence-based practice?: We are all positivists! *Research on Social Work Practice*, *18*(4), 339–345. doi:10.1177/1049731507313998

Thyer, B. A. (2010). Introductory principles of social work research. In B. A. Thyer (Ed.), *The handbook of social work research methods* (2nd ed., pp. 1–24). Thousand Oaks, California: SAGE.

Thyer, B. A. (2012). The scientific value of qualitative research for social work. *Qualitative Social Work: Research and Practice*, *11*, 115–125. doi:10.1177/1473325011433928

Thyer, B. A., & Myers, L. L. (2011). The quest for evidence-based practice: A view from the United States. *Journal of Social Work*, *11*(1), 8–25. doi:10.1177/1468017310381812

Thyer, B. A., & Pignotti, M. (2011). Evidence-based practices do not exist. *Clinical Social Work Journal*, *39*(4), 328–333. doi:10.1007/s10615-011-0358-x

Timmermans, S., & Berg, M. (2003). *The gold standard: The challenge of evidence-based medicine and standardization in health care.* Philadelphia: Temple University Press.

White, M. (1995). *Re-authoring lives: Interviews and essays.* Adelaide, South Australia: Dulwich Centre Publications.

White, S. (2009). Arguing the case in safeguarding. In K. Broadhurst, C. Grover, & J. Jamieson (Eds.), *Critical perspectives on safeguarding children* (pp. 93–109). Oxford: Wiley-Blackwell.

## KEY TERMS AND DEFINITIONS

**Critical-Reflective Practice:** A form of practice which challenges cultures, that is, the preconceived ideas which are embedded in practices, in order to examine and change them.

**Decolonising Methodologies:** A framework developed by Smith (1999) to explain the process by which colonisation occurs. Contextual histories, politics, and cultural considerations reveal how Indigenous people are disenfranchised by the imposition of Western models of research and practice. Thus research is viewed as a form of imperialism.

**Liminal Spaces:** A concept developed by Myerhoff (1982) to describe a place of reflection where the practitioner deliberates on an unknown situation from what is already known or familiar.

**Recovery Paradigm:** Service-users' accounts of their healing journey from trauma, health, and mental health issues which is a source of evidence for social work practice.

**Service-Users:** People who use social work and social welfare services, their caregivers, and families.

# Section 2
# Social Work Fields of Practice

*Evidence-informed practice is explored in relation to differing fields and contexts of social work practice. These fields of practice include refugee resettlement, mental health, youth justice, neurosurgery, social workers in schools, sexual abuse recovery, fathering, and art therapy.*

# Chapter 5
# Refugee Women:
## Resilient and Reluctant Users of Social Work Services

**Mary Nash**
*Massey University, New Zealand*

**Antoinette Umugwaneza**
*New Zealand Red Cross Refugee Services – Palmerston North, New Zealand*

## ABSTRACT

*This chapter approaches the topic of resettlement social work with women refugees portrayed as resilient yet reluctant users of social work services. While the field of social work with refugees has already been widely introduced and discussed, less attention has been paid to resettlement work with women refugees. In order to contextualise this discussion, key terms are briefly defined, and relevant legislation together with demographic features are covered. The chapter includes a case study presented by one of the authors, an expert by experience. Research relating to this field of practice is presented and ethical issues discussed. Practical applications and cultural concerns derived from the research suggest how practitioners and refugee women may work together, drawing on the strengths and experience of the refugee women to achieve goals that are consistent with those set out by the United Nations High Commissioner for Refugees (UNHCR).*

## INTRODUCTION

Mary and Antoinette have worked together to write this chapter. Mary has previously researched the experiences of social workers in New Zealand working with refugees and migrants. Antoinette came to New Zealand as a refugee and is now working as a caseworker supporting refugee resettlement.

DOI: 10.4018/978-1-4666-6563-7.ch005

The International Federation of Social Workers (IFSW, 2012) reminds us that the "issues surrounding refugees are matters of justice and peace. Social workers in the vast majority of countries will be required to address the problems facing refugees in their practice" (para. 4). Potocky-Tripodi (2002) has argued that "social work practice with refugees and immigrants requires specialised knowledge of the unique issues of these populations" (p.

3). Without this knowledge we consider that resettlement support will be jeopardised. There is a broad consensus in the statistics cited by the United Nations High Commissioner for Refugees (UNHCR, 1990) that

*... refugee women represent, either as single women or with their dependents, approximately 80 per cent of the UNHCR's target population and that programmes can be effective only if they are planned with an adequate understanding of, and consultation with, this group. (p. 7)*

While the field of social work with refugees has already been widely introduced and discussed, less attention has been paid to resettlement work with women refugees. This chapter, therefore, approaches the topic of resettlement social work with a focus on women refugees and their rights to citizenship and participation in society and through the case study portrays them as resilient yet reluctant users of social work services. It moves, therefore, from a macro human rights perspective to a micro and applied perspective in which women refugees and their daily concerns as new settlers are considered.

In order to contextualise this discussion for an international audience, key terms are briefly defined and relevant legislation together with demographic features are covered. The chapter includes a case study presented by one of the authors, herself an expert by experience. Research relating to this field of practice is presented and ethical issues discussed. The *Indicators of Refugee Integration* framework (Ager & Strang, 2004) assists the discussion.

Key words and phrases used in the literature search included *refugees*, *"women refugees"*, *"social work with refugees"*, *"women and human rights"*, *"refugee resettlement"*, and *resilience*. It was interesting to note how often, when searching documents on-line, the word *women* failed to turn up, suggesting that it is timely to focus on women refugees and how they manage the issues

involved in, and the processes of, resettlement. Much of the research we have drawn on is based on qualitative and narrative methods designed to give voice to refugee women themselves. We found that practical applications and cultural concerns derived from the research and guided by experience suggest how practitioners and clients may work together, drawing on their strengths and resilience, to achieve goals which are consistent with those set out by the UNHCR, as recognised in Australia and New Zealand. Many of the information sources for this chapter are derived from open access sites on the internet, particularly policy statements, UNHCR research, and NGO websites. This means that readers without access to libraries (and, therefore, without on-line access to academic journals) will, nevertheless, be able to follow up some valuable sources of information on their own behalf.

## WOMEN REFUGEES

According to the Convention Relating to the Status of Refugees (1951), a refugee is a person who

*... owing to well-founded fear of being persecuted for reasons of race, religion, nationality, membership of a particular social group or political opinion, is outside the country of his nationality and is unable or, owing to such fear, is unwilling to avail himself of the protection of that country. (Article 1(A)2)*

The severity of the situation of women refugees, in particular, is contextualised by the Women's Refugee Commission (WRC, n.d.) which is concerned with the particular vulnerabilities and needs of women refugees, including their safety and reproductive health care. The Commission is a solution-focused organisation which advocates for women refugees and displaced women at the highest levels and bases its arguments on its own research and work with women in the field.

Although the actual numbers and proportions of the women refugee population are hard to determine, the numbers of refugee women and children cited appear high in proportion to the number of refugee men (WRC, n.d. para. 1). The UNHCR conducts and sponsors valuable research with regard to making known the experiences of women refugees and what they say about their refugee experiences. From its research findings, the UNHCR (n.d.) seeks to build

*… upon women's resilience and strength to support their empowerment and strengthen their protection, and promotes their full participation in all decisions affecting their lives. Despite the many challenges, displacement can enable women to take on new roles and instigate positive change. With the appropriate support, refugee women can improve their lives and the lives of their children, families and communities. (para. 4)*

This contextualising quote presents a picture in which a constructive approach is being encouraged, where the particular and critical needs of women are recognised and presented in ways that indicate that women have the abilities and inner resources necessary to overcome their difficulties and rebuild their own and their dependents' lives, provided they receive the appropriate and empowering support to which they have every right. Our contextualisation of women refugee resettlement is based on a brief but, in our view, representative review of literature which is drawn from current international and Australian information, as well as a selection of indicative academic research publications. This review focuses on key and ongoing conditions for women refugees facing resettlement and this influences the resettlement process, its challenges, and its opportunities. It also highlights popular research methodology in this field, for example, the use of narrative and oral history techniques. Relevant ethical issues that social workers encounter in their work with women coping with displacement, new customs,

and living conditions, include taking responsibility for being sensitive to the world of the other and finding ways to use a person-centred approach that is empowering for people with different cultural norms. As Antoinette says: "It is not only about my condition in my country of origin but the condition of my own personal culture, of being a woman and my way of living in Rwanda" (for a wealth of further information and useful links, we recommend a visit to Refworld: Gender, equality and women at http://www.refworld.org/cgi-bin/texis/vtx/rwmain?page=women).

## International Policies

The UNHCR is the undisputed international authority leading the field where intervention on behalf of refugees is concerned. It develops policy based on human rights informed by both research and experience in the field. This it regularly evaluates and updates, providing goals for improving refugee well-being. In 1987, the UNHCR Executive Committee formally recognised that "refugee women had protection and assistance needs which necessitated special attention" (UNHCR, 1990, p. 3) and since then it has consistently recognised the requirements of refugee women.

In 2000, the UN Security Council Resolution on Women, Peace, and Security (S.C. Res. 1325, 2000) was adopted unanimously. This resolution focused on the needs of women and girls involved in the various stages of the refugee journey from displacement to resettlement or repatriation. From a social work point of view, it is encouraging in that it drew attention to women's resilience, strength, and ability to make essential contributions to peace negotiations, which can only occur when women are allowed and encouraged to fully participate in all peace negotiations and efforts at rebuilding broken societies. On the 10th anniversary of this Resolution, the WRC (2010) issued a statement on its progress to date, talking about "high hopes" and "unmet expectations" and making a number of recommendations. These were grouped under three headings and concerned ways of, firstly, promoting the meaningful participation of women and girls in, for example, both the planning and implementation stages of humanitarian assistance programmes; secondly, improving ways of protecting and preventing, as well as responding to violence against women and girls; and thirdly, addressing the particular challenges that displaced women and girls face when conflict ends. The Non-Government Working Group on Women, Peace and Security (n.d.) monitors the implementation of UN Security Council Resolution 1325 and describes itself as serving "as a bridge between women's human rights defenders working in conflict-affected situations and policy-makers at U.N. Headquarters" (para. 2).

Also of significance in this context is the UNHCR Age, Gender and Diversity policy (UNHCR, 2011c). The stated objective for this policy is

*... through the systematic application of an Age, Gender and Diversity (AGD) approach in its operations worldwide, UNHCR seeks to ensure that all persons of concern enjoy their rights on an equal footing and are able to participate fully in the decisions that affect their lives and the lives of their family members and communities. (para. 1)*

This policy explicitly recognises that women and men experience being a refugee differently, and it seeks to ensure that the implications of age, gender, and diversity are fully acknowledged by UNHCR staff. The UNHCR also monitors policy and service provision to ensure, where possible, that the most vulnerable refugees have their rights and their dignity protected.

In 2001, a dialogue with refugee women was held in Geneva to respect women refugees' rights and work towards their equality. Expressing both hope and respect, the women challenged the UNHCR to make a difference as a result of what they were telling the world (UNHCR, 2001). Ten years later, the same difficulties are facing women refugees, hence the *Survivors, Protectors,*

*Providers* dialogues project (UNHCR, 2011b), a research project partnered by the UNHCR and the Centre for Refugee Research at the University of New South Wales in Australia, designed to give voice to women refugees themselves. There are seven dialogues from groups of women in Delhi, Colombia, Jordan, Uganda, Zambia, Finland, and Thailand, spanning five continents. Together, they have provided insights into the world of women refugees that show resilience, competence, and determination to survive and build new and rewarding lives for women and their families. Overall, one of the women participants' strongest messages was that service provision aimed at assisting refugee integration has to be grounded in a deep understanding of the impact of these experiences on their lives. Many of the women commented that racist and xenophobic behaviour and language served to keep the horror of these experiences alive. Another key message has been the women's desire to take up leadership roles and to participate as equal citizens in their new countries of residence. The reports offer a politically aware, gendered analysis, with practical recommendations for ways of working with refugee women. They also model excellent and innovative research methods with many links to other research, together with a set of excellent recommendations for social workers in this field.

This brings us to what is happening in Australia, where in 2012-13 refugee resettlement amounted to 12,012 people under the HCR quota. There were over 7,000 other on shore-applicants (Australian Government, Department of Immigration and Border Protection, 2013). A further publication, *Getting Settled: Women Refugees in Australia* (Australian Government, Department of Social Services, 2013), has supplied official information about government services and systems available to women refugees in the resettlement process. According to this report, "Australia is one of only a few countries in the world that specifically offers a Woman at Risk visa subclass and provides dedicated refugee settlement programs for women and their families" (p. 7). When reading material supplied by government agencies or groups with a particular mission in relation to the topic being covered, it is essential for social workers to critically interrogate the text and to consider how the information presented compares with their own experience.

The UNHCR defines "women at risk" as women or girls who "have protection problems particular to their gender and *lack effective* protection normally provided by male family members. They may be: single heads of families" (UNHCR, 2011a, p. 263). This report includes a synopsis of the research on vulnerable refugee women carried out over recent years by the Centre for Refugee Research at the University of New South Wales and the Australian National Committee on Refugee Women (ANCRW, n.d.) which is "a lobbying, advocacy and research group which works with and for refugee women and their families in order to bring about change in the refugee system and to enhance their ability to rebuild their lives" (para. 1). Over 500 women participated in the research and the findings are consistent with those from the dialogues with women research mentioned above. The report quotes powerful statements from some of the women, highlighting how much trauma and suffering they have experienced and, indeed, continue to experience. It stresses how strongly the women felt and that those working with them must know and understand how their terrible experiences stay with them and affect them. This point was also made by Weaver and Burns (2001) who argued that

*… understanding that some refugee clients "shout with fear at night" can help us to appreciate the lasting impact trauma can have and can guide our work with this vulnerable yet resilient population. Helping professionals are challenged to become better versed in the at-risk position of asylum seekers and engage in advocacy to encourage greater protection of this population. (p. 147)*

In short, one can see that the research literature covers a wide spectrum of issues relating to the resettlement experiences and requirements of women refugees and their rights to gender equality. It is widely recognised that social workers must function on micro, meso, and macro levels (Al-Qdah, & Lacroix, 2010; Potocky-Tripodi, 2002). As one social work respondent in a New Zealand research project aptly put it:

*You have got to be able to have a structural analysis, you have got to be able to have a global analysis….Because in this sector…if you only have casework skills, you only have…a micro-base approach to your work, it is not going to work, it will be very soul destroying. (Nash, Wong, & Trlin, 2006, p. 352)*

With greater experience in working with refugees settling into new countries, there is increased emphasis at the macro level on citizenship (Pittaway & Van Genderen Stort, 2011; Yasmeen, 2007) and participation (Al-Qdah & Lacroix, 2010; Kreitzer, 2002; Pavlish, 2005; Valtonen, 2002), as well as advocacy and monitoring of programmes by academic researchers and agencies which support refugees in resettlement, including organisations run by former refugees themselves (Al-Qdah, & Lacroix, 2010; Australian National Committee on Refugee Women, n.d.; University of New South Wales Centre for Refugee Research, n.d.).

On a micro level, research into ways of engaging and working with refugees in the resettlement field highlights the importance of knowing about and being willing and strong enough to listen to women's stories of their pre-settlement experiences and recognising their strength and resilience and their capacity for successful resettlement. For example, data from the Nash and Trlin (2001) nationwide postal surveys indicated a need for more training, particularly in cross-cultural knowledge and skills for social workers and other people.

Senior staff from a range of non-government agencies were asked for their views on this and several made comments which are relevant and useful for this chapter. For example, one person reflected on the importance of cultural awareness:

*I think it is important to be culturally aware, to know a lot about their notion of family, their traditional roles. I mean we have to spend time letting people understand that you can't deal with individuals as individuals; they are members of a family, and the husband's idea of a suitable role for the wife will have a huge impact on them for instance, and that can be a big learning curve for western women who have had the ability to be self-determined. (Nash & Trlin, 2001, n.p.)*

Antoinette's case study, below, illustrates this point very clearly. The Western women social workers certainly struggled to find the right path between recognising resilience and building on it and working within the family setting in a culturally perceptive and accepting manner. The question then arises, how can social workers know the right way to approach women and men from the diversity of cultures now being encountered? In the Nash and Trlin (2001) survey this was recognised as a real challenge by staff at one organisation where there was considerable experience to draw upon. They suggested that

*… what people need, though, is the confidence to ask the right questions of the clients, and that is not what they have been trained in. They have been trained in needing to have enough background to know, and when they don't have that they feel disempowered, vulnerable….*

*What we have to get into our training institutions is knowledge about the respectful way to inquire….*

*It may be as simple as saying "is it appropriate in your culture to shake hands?"….*

*One of the things our agency tries to do, and everything it does is to re-empower, and to enquire of somebody "teach me about your culture, teach me what I could do that would be helpful, what I could do that would be non-helpful". It is such a respectful empowering thing to do. (n.p.)*

These two points are endorsed by Hutchinson and Dorsett (2012) where Hutchinson generously provides an example from her own practice and discusses its implications for cross-cultural learning, once she had realised the cultural etiquette she had just broken and its potential risks:

*At times I find it hard to sit with such cultural difference and I find myself reflecting on my Western ideals, values and beliefs. I reflect on what it means to be a woman in my family, and in broader society. I also reflect from a feminist perspective that strongly upholds gender equality and women having a voice. Importantly, I reflect on how cultural differences impact on my practice with my clients and how they influence my interaction. I recall a time when my values and beliefs impacted on the discussion with a client regarding a family issue. The father, the head of the family, had made a decision regarding one of the children. I remember asking his wife, the mother, what she felt about the decision that had been made. She gave me such an intense look of disbelief [as if I should have known better than to have not asked her that question, or put her in such a position]. Through the interpreter she explained that her husband is the one that makes such decisions. I quickly withdrew any further focus of probing her view and learnt a valuable lesson that day. (p. 72)*

Hutchinson and Dorsett (2012) explain that

*… what may at first appear to be inclusive practices from a Western point of view, may be construed by refugee clients to be seen as disrespectful,*

*exclusionary and discriminatory practice that could prevent clients from seeking assistance or accessing services in the future. Furthermore, practitioners need to be alert to the dominant and powerful role their culture plays in "making some worldviews valid, while making others invalid" (Hick, Fook, & Pozzuto, 2005, p. 92). In practice, our attention needs to be focused on our communication with clients leaving our own values and belief systems "at the door and respecting differences" (Meares, 2007, p. 88). Cultural sensitivity involves an acknowledgment of cultural differences, having respect and valuing differences. (p. 72)*

One staff member interviewed by Nash and Trlin (2001) recounted a story which paints a vivid picture of how easily things well-meant can go so badly wrong:

*It is often hard to find the right professional people who understand about the cultural thing. Often, I mean we could have a health worker from the city council. I had that once, come to an orientation – after all, we would like to talk about safety in the home, talking to Somali women who came straight from the refugee camp, and he was a very, very white skinned male, looked very British, a lovely guy, but he came in front of all my Somali women and started to talk about safety in the home, and why we keep meat in the fridge, and where you put it and all these sorts of things. He demonstrated with a big kitchen fridge, and it created an uproar on these Somali women. They were all sitting in this big hostel where we were, and they had a stand up fight, they thought although we had an interpreter, that we were accusing them of…having meat juices dripping everywhere, they were quite hot and bothered. And here was this very white male from the city council in a tie and a suit; he couldn't cope! (n.p.)*

These three points (the need for more cross-cultural training, understanding and working with different perceptions of the different roles of husbands and wives, and learning how to ask for cultural guidance in a respectful manner) identify very simple and practical ways of working with women refugees. They illustrate not only the importance of working with women and their families in culturally appropriate ways but also suggest how this can be done and how easily mistakes can occur.

The presentation on how to manage meat in a fridge, while well-meant, clearly showed no recognition of the women refugees' resilience and capacity for adapting quickly to new ways of managing the tasks of everyday life. Recent literature on women refugees and their resilience points to the processes by which resilience is practiced and demonstrated. Hutchinson & Dorsett (2012) argue that resilience can more helpfully be viewed as a fluid, dynamic series of processes or interactions between the person in their environment, than as a static or measurable trait (p. 60). Similarly, for Lenette, Brough and Cox (2013) "it is in the dynamic space of everyday life-worlds of refugee women that a more complex set of possibilities become enacted, which gives meaning to the *processes* rather than the *traits* of resilience" (p. 639).

## Case Study

Antoinette has prepared the following case study drawing on her years of experience.

All my life, I have been in extreme admiration for my mum. Words cannot describe her resilience and her determination to live and raise her ten young children on her own. My father was killed when I was only six years old and left my mum with ten children. The oldest was 19 years old and the youngest was only five days old. I am the seventh in my family.

Becoming a refugee was the hardest life experience, despite the fact that I had grown up in such a resourceful environment. I believe no one can imagine it if they have not been a refugee themselves.

I left my home on the 9 April 1994 around 12pm. It was after three days that the plane carrying the Rwandan President was shot and the President and everyone else in the plane were killed. I was an ordinary citizen but hearing that breaking news of the death of the President, I knew in my heart that there will be tragic consequences. Straight after, we started to hear gunshots everywhere and could see through the night sky flashes of fire like lightning, blazing across the city. The national radio asked people to keep calm and not to leave their homes.

For three days we were unable to leave home, we were running out of food, and we were feeling apprehensive from not knowing what was going on. With our nearest neighbours we decided to leave our homes for a safer location. It is from that day I became a refugee.

From that first day I realised how a woman has a challenging role and a difficult responsibility once she becomes a refugee. From my experience, these roles and response\abilties were highlighted by three different periods. The first one was at the time of leaving our home; the second one was when I left my country and realised that I had become a refugee; and finally, the third one is when I was resettled in a third country.

When we were leaving our home, I had to think about what I would have to take for our immediate needs. My first thought was to take food, clothes, and blankets for my children. A man may have thought about something else, such as transport and accommodation. We didn't have time to pack and take any bags. I put on the children as much clothes as they could support and got them in the car, threw on them a couple of blankets I grabbed from the beds, took a bowl of rice from the stove, milk for my 15 months old baby, and we ran for our lives. That is where the mother instinct and the resilience of a woman kick in. As a mother you know that you need to stay strong for the children.

The second period I found difficult was when I had left my home, my country, my mum, and my siblings, and found myself living with around 100 people under the same roof. Some of them I had never met before and others I knew but had never lived with them before. While I was trying to adjust to a new environment, I realised that there are these everyday new tasks which I was not used to. I needed to carry on doing them no matter what. These tasks are cooking, feeding your children, and trying to keep them healthy and clean as you can, and then the washing. Some of these tasks I have never done before. Some women were mocking, teasing me about my cooking and I didn't always cope well with this.

At several times I was exhausted and emotionally and physically drained. Some days, the backs of my fingers were bleeding from rubbing them when I was washing the clothes. During this period, I was wondering how long I will be able to cope, wondering if there was anyone who cared about our situation and could help in any way whatever. When you realise that there is not much hope and you are about to give up, you then realise that you have five children to feed and look after. That is when your strength and resilience to survive come into play. It is really a survival instinct.

The third period I found challenging was when I was resettled in a third country by which I mean not the country of original asylum but the resettlement country, which is New Zealand. My family and I were overjoyed when we landed in our current home country. It was like "The Promised Land". We were safe. We had financial support, our children could get education, we had our own home, and there was modern equipment, such as a washing machine. There were no more piles of clothes to wash by hand. And, mostly, we had a wonderful social worker to support us in this resettlement process, but unfortunately the social support we were offered was not always culturally suitable.

For example, I have five young children to look after and I came with my mother-in-law who was 79 years old at that time. She was critically ill when we came and at some stages required 24 hour care. So the "honeymoon" feeling did not last. I soon became extremely home sick, stressed, and depressed. I was so aggressive and everybody in the family was so intense. My social worker, although she lacked understanding of how things worked in my country of origin, recognised my qualifications (a BA in Social and Economic Studies) and my capacity for employment, and she wanted to empower me. She wanted to encourage me to look for a job, as I had mentioned to her I had worked for fifteen years in a national bank.

In her assessment, I was overwhelmed by looking after my family, learning a new language, just finding my way around my new situation, so she recommended that I see my GP who prescribed me anti-depressants and referred me to mental health services. But I didn't take the medication and refused to go to mental health because I had a strong sense of stigma about such a service.

I told my social worker I needed time out and to rest, as I was so stressed at home. My social worker, therefore, booked me into Women's Refuge. I was excited about going to Women's Refuge, away from my family to rest and relax. The social worker from Women's Refuge rang to come and pick me up and I told her that my husband was dropping me off. The social worker could not believe it. She said that I should not have told him. So Women's Refuge was then not an option for me. In my culture, even if I was being beaten up by my husband, there was no way I could go anywhere at all without telling my husband. In my culture you would do that only if you want to end your relationship.

Another case was when the social worker suggested that my mother-in-law, who was in constant need for care, go into residential care. She did not understand that this was also not an option for our family. My daughters were growing up and were able to help me to look after her. Of course,

there were a lot of "sacrifices" from them, as they had to give up some of the opportunities they had outside the city in which we were living in order to be available to look after their grandma. She died at home at 92 years of age.

## Discussion

Effective social work practice depends on insightful assessment followed by appropriate intervention. Assessment necessitates, amongst other qualities, a degree of cultural sensitivity, together with sound theoretical knowledge. For many women refugees, family life will function on collective and patriarchal values and customary acceptance of different but complementary roles for men and women. For the women, values may vary and those working with them in their country of resettlement need to be sensitive to how they may have conducted life in their country of origin and what, if any, changes in role can be considered or worked towards without causing more harm than good in the new country.

In discussing this case study, the authors of this chapter recognise the potential for tensions to arise between the professional social worker's stance and that of many women from refugee backgrounds. For the qualified social worker, the principles of a person-centred approach, empowerment, and equal rights for women are embedded in her practice, just as traditional, often patriarchal cultural practices inform many women refugees. When the two come into contact and need to work together, these different world views may result in misunderstandings, lost opportunities, and conflict. The social worker who has a professional social work qualification may, therefore, face an ethical dilemma when confronted with the need to accept women's aspirations to be self-determining about how they settle and to ensure that they maintain their cultural and collective ways of living family life. Her professional code of ethics with its individualistic values may seem to be in conflict with the traditional values she now encounters. It is in recognition of these sensitivities that this chapter describes women refugees as both resilient and reluctant users of social work services.

For Antoinette, a crucial facilitator in enabling her family to settle and achieve employment, housing, education, and health (the four key factors identified by Ager and Strang, 2004, as indicators of successful resettlement) has been the cultural knowledge (or lack thereof) of the social workers she and her family encountered. In this case study, the social workers were inclined to assess her needs as a mother, without necessarily understanding her earlier life experiences or cultural norms. Without this recognition of cultural difference, traumatic lived experiences, and the strains of transition from one set of social norms to another, assessment of her situation and of the strengths she could draw on in response to new circumstances was likely to be less acute than it needed to be.

As an example, social workers tended to see Antoinette as facing a series of burdens in looking after her family. So the social worker, who recognised the stresses facing Antoinette as she cared for her family, saw her work as a burden of care. Similarly, the time spent caring for grandma was seen as a "burden" to be lifted from the family. Neither Antoinette nor the family saw these situations as a burden but simply an unquestionable duty of care to be fulfilled with love. Of course, there were stresses and strains but in assessing them the social workers were inclined to focus on resolving individual stresses but failed to see solutions in collective strengths. Social workers are encouraged to develop their sensitivity to cultural differences. Antoinette sensed the frustration of her social workers as they struggled to work with her in partnership and with shared understandings. Although these were difficult to achieve, over time and with good will they were able to succeed. Time is a crucial element in the building of the relationship between practitioner and client and when working with refugees who are settling into a new environment it becomes particularly important.

Ager and Strang (2004) identify as the foundation of the whole settlement process the single domain of "rights and citizenship". The refugee, who is still in the early stages of resettlement, may be challenged by the concepts embedded in rights discourse, especially if they have fled persecution for holding opinions which diverged from what was politically acceptable. This connects at once to much of the early review of research and literature in this chapter. It protects the principles and values of the refugee seeking safety and respect, belonging, and independence. It also places the social worker and refugee in a domain where they must apply with the greatest respect their understandings of freedom of expression and freedom to work out how to settle into a new community, how to obtain satisfactory housing, employment, education, and health, without betraying their innermost values. When these values express themselves outwardly in different and seemingly conflicting ways, wisdom as well as professionalism must come into play.

The more comfortable the social worker is with collective approaches to practice, such as can be found in community development work, the more opportunity there can be for her to work successfully with women refugees, drawing on their strengths which are often derived from a collective approach to organising their lives. Such approaches to practice encourage client self-determination in which it is the client, not the social worker, whose values and cultural practices will usually take precedence.

We consider that settlement work with women refugees lends itself to community development work which provides for collective types of intervention while not precluding one-on-one casework. Community development work is informed by an ecological framework of macro, meso, and micro levels of analysis and provides the practitioner with a wide-ranging set of tools for assessment and intervention. An ecological framework that informs practice provides a foundation for structural analysis and in working with refugee settlement this is enabling for both the practitioner and those they work with, particularly where the agency builds on the resilience of their client group. Both Valtonen (2002) and George (2002) argue that community development and self-help policies are effective in the pursuit of successful resettlement. Their research particularly emphasises the importance of self-help and ethnic groups for supporting new settlers as they adapt and integrate into their new communities. The research we have drawn on in the first part of this chapter, particularly where we hear the voices of women refugees themselves, encourages this approach to settlement and respects the strength and resilience of women refugees.

Table 1 summarises our developing model for working with women refugees in their country of

*Table 1. Model for working with women refugees in their country of settlement, drawing on an ecological framework*

| Ecological Level | Knowledge and Understanding | Skills for Implementation |
|---|---|---|
| Macro | International overview of diverse causes of forced migration leading to gendered structural analysis. | Political and economic literacy, knowledge of reasons for forced migration in countries of client origin, including importance of histories. |
| Meso | Identifying national policies concerned with management of intake of women refugees. Knowledge of organisations and social networks related to settlement of women refugees. | Gendered analysis of relevant social policies. Strong networks with national, regional, and community resources for women refugees as they settle into their new environments. |
| Micro | Competency in working with and for refugee women as they settle into their new home and take up new citizenship. Ethical awareness and commitment to working with people whose ethical principles challenge one's own. | Awareness of and respect for different cultural approaches to male and female relationships. Ability to adapt strengths based practice and community development work accordingly. |

settlement, drawing on an ecological framework. It is derived from Antoinette's experiential expertise, together with her counselling and practice knowledge, complemented with Mary's research findings, and their combined knowledge of the social work literature in this field of practice.

## CONCLUSION

In the contextualising part of this chapter, we cited the UNHCR (n.d.) which states that "despite the many challenges, displacement can enable women to take on new roles and instigate positive change. With the appropriate support, refugee women can improve their lives and the lives of their children, families and communities" (para. 4).

These are encouraging words yet they need to be interpreted with care, as we hope we have illustrated through the case study. The UNHCR can make encouraging suggestions and observations at an international level, but it does not make national policy and, in fact, may have little or no influence on domestic policy in some countries. While it is acknowledged that research may produce good models and recommendations, their implementation and fruits are slow to emerge. There are many useful sources of information concerning women refugees, their experiences of resettlement, and the issues that confront them in becoming integrated (as opposed to assimilated) and participating citizens. It is important that social workers are informed at this macro level when engaging with women refugees.

At a meso level, practitioners are encouraged to intervene at a community level so that community development work takes place. At the micro level, refugees and practitioners will work together, and one hopes they will be supported in their employing agencies by the foundation principles of human rights legislation. Practitioners need, however, to be sensitive to the tensions and dilemmas that inevitably occur as people with different customs and understandings try to achieve what they consider to be for the best. Women refugees have too much at stake to risk losing the little they have left which may be of immeasurable worth to them but invisible to the host community. What they bring with them, above all, are their treasured beliefs, relationships, and histories, as precious to them as those of the host country are to its people.

## REFERENCES

Ager, A., & Strang, A. (2004). *Indicators of refugee integration: Final report – Report to the Home Office Immigration Research and Statistics Service*. Retrieved from Home Office website: http://www.homeoffice.gov.uk/rds/pdfs04/dpr28.pdf

Al-Qdah, T., & Lacroix, M. (2010). Iraqi refugees in Jordan: Lessons for practice with refugees globally. *International Journal of Social Work*, *54*(4), 521–534. doi:10.1177/0020872810383449

Australian Government, Department of Immigration and Border Protection. (2013). *Fact Sheet 60: Australia's refugee and humanitarian programme*. Retrieved from http://www.immi.gov.au/media/fact-sheets/60refugee.htm

Australian Government, Department of Social Services. (2013). *Getting settled: Women refugees in Australia*. Retrieved from http://www.dss.gov.au/sites/default/files/documents/01_2014/sc_update_women_at_risk.pdf

Australian National Committee on Refugee Women. (n.d.). ANCORW Mission Statement. Retrieved May 10, 2014, from http://www.ancorw.org/mission.htm

Convention Relating to the Status of Refugees, July 28, 1951, 189 U.N.T.S. 137.

George, U. (2002). A needs-based model for settlement service delivery for newcomers to Canada. *International Social Work*, *45*(4), 465–480. doi:10.1177/00208728020450040501

Hutchinson, M., & Dorsett, P. (2012). What does the literature say about resilience in refugee people? Implications for practice. *Journal of Social Inclusion*, *3*(2), 55–78. Retrieved from https://www104.griffith.edu.au/index.php/inclusion/index

International Federation of Social Workers. (2012). Refugees. Retrieved from http://ifsw.org/policies/refugees/

Kreitzer, L. (2002). Liberian refugee women: A qualitative study of their participation in planning camp programmes. *International Social Work*, *45*(1), 45–58. doi:10.1177/0020872802045001319

Lenette, C., Brough, M., & Cox, L. (2013). Everyday resilience: Narratives of single refugee women with children. *Qualitative Social Work: Research and Practice*, *12*(5), 637–653. doi:10.1177/1473325012449684

Nash, M., & Trlin, A. (2001). *Research into non-government/not for profit agencies and organizations providing services to immigrants and refugees in New Zealand*. Palmerston North, NZ: New Settlers Programme, Massey University.

Nash, M., Wong, J., & Trlin, A. (2006). Civic and social integration: A new field of social work practice with immigrants, refugees and asylum seekers. *International Social Work*, *49*(3), 345–363. doi:10.1177/0020872806063407

Non-Government Working Group on Women. Peace and Security. (n.d.). About us. Retrieved from http://www.womenpeacesecurity.org/about/

Pavlish, C. (2005). Refugee women's health: Collaborative inquiry with refugee women in Rwanda. *Health Care for Women International, 26*(10), 880–896. doi:10.1080/07399330500301697 PMID:16263661

Pittaway, E., & Van Genderen Stort, A. (2011). *Protectors, providers, survivors: A dialogue with refugee women in Finland.* Retrieved from United Nations High Commissioner for Refugees website: http://www.unhcr.org/4ec3d7606.pdf

Potocky-Tripodi, M. (2002). *Best practices for social work with refugees and immigrants.* New York: Columbia University Press.

S.C. Res. 1325, U.N. Doc. S/RES/1325 (Oct. 31. 2000).

United Nations High Commissioner for Refugees. (n.d.). Women: Particular challenges and risks. Retrieved from http://www.unhcr.org/pages/49c3646c1d9.html

United Nations High Commissioner for Refugees. (1990). *UNHCR policy on refugee women.* Retrieved from http://www.unhcr.org/3ba6186810.html

United Nations High Commissioner for Refugees. (2001). *Respect our rights: Partnership for equality – Report on the dialogue with refugee women – Geneva, Switzerland 20-22 June 2001.* Retrieved from http://www.unhcr.org/3bb44d908.pdf

United Nations High Commissioner for Refugees. (2011a). *Resettlement handbook: Division of international protection.* Retrieved from http://www.unhcr.org/4a2ccf4c6.html

United Nations High Commissioner for Refugees. (2011b). *Survivors, protectors, providers: Refugee women speak out.* Retrieved from http://www.unhcr.org/4ec5337d9.html

United Nations High Commissioner for Refugees. (2011c). *UNHCR age, gender and diversity policy: Working with people and communities for equality and protection – Women, 1 June.* Retrieved from http://www.unhcr.org/4e7757449.html

University of New South Wales Centre for Refugee Research. (n.d.). Welcome to CRR. Retrieved from http://www.crr.unsw.edu.au/

Valtonen, K. (2002). Social work with immigrants and refugees: Developing a participation-based framework for anti-oppressive practice – Part 2. *British Journal of Social Work, 32*(1), 113–120. doi:10.1093/bjsw/32.1.113

Weaver, H. N., & Burns, B. J. (2001). "I shout with fear at night": Understanding the traumatic experiences of refugees and asylum seekers. *Journal of Social Work, 1*(2), 147–164. doi:10.1177/146801730100100203

Women's Refugee Commission. (n.d.). How we work. Retrieved from http://www.womensrefugeecommission.org/about/how-we-work

Women's Refugee Commission. (2010). *UN Security Council Resolution 1325 on women, peace and security: High hopes, unmet expectations.* Retrieved from http://womensrefugeecommission.org/programs/women-peace-and-security/research-and-resources

Yasmeen, S. (2007). Muslim women as citizens in Australia: Diverse notions and practices. *The Australian Journal of Social Issues*, *42*, 41–54. Retrieved from http://www.acoss.org.au/publications/magazines/

## ADDITIONAL READING

All about resilience. (n.d). Retrieved from http://www.psychologytoday.com/basics/resilience

Allotey, P. (1999). Travelling with "excess baggage": Health problems of refugee women in Western Australia. *Women & Health*, *28*(1), 63–81. doi:10.1300/J013v28n01_05 PMID:10022057

Bartolomei, L. A. (2009). *Struggling against the silences: Exploring rights based responses to the rape and sexual abuse of refugee women and girls.* (Unpublished doctoral dissertation). Social Sciences & International Studies, Faculty of Arts & Social Sciences, University of New South Wales.

Benson, G. O., Sun, F., Hodge, D. R., & Androff, D. K. (2012). Religious coping and acculturation stress among Hindu Bhutanese: A study of newly-resettled refugees in the United States. *International Social Work*, *55*(4), 538–553. doi:10.1177/0020872811417474

Bond, S. (2010). *Women on the move: Evaluating a refugee mentoring pilot project.* Fitzroy, Vic: Brotherhood of St Laurence. Retrieved from http://www.bsl.org.au/pdfs/Bond_Women_on_the_Move_evaluation_2010.pdf

Casimiro, S., Hancock, P., & Northcote, J. (2007). Isolation and insecurity: Resettlement issues among Muslim refugee women in Perth, Western Australia. *The Australian Journal of Social Issues*, *42*, 55–69. Retrieved from http://www.acoss.org.au/publications/magazines/

Cousens, J. (2003). *My life in a new state: An exploration of the major challenges to settlement identified by Tamil Sri Lankan women refugees during their first years in Sydney.* Kensington, NSW: Centre for Refugee Research, School of Social Work, University of New South Wales; Retrieved from http://www.crr.unsw.edu.au/media/File/My_Life_In_A_New_State_June04.pdf

Este, D., & Ngo, H. V. (2011). A resilience framework to examine immigrant and refugee children and youth in Canada. In S. Chuang & R. Moreno (Eds.), *Immigrant children: Change, adaptation, and cultural transformation* (pp. 27–49). Lanham, MD: Lexington Books.

Gallegos, D., Ellies, P., & Wright, J. (2008). Still there's no food! Food insecurity in a refugee population in Perth, Western Australia. *Nutrition and Dietetics*, *65*(1), 78–83. doi:10.1111/j.1747-0080.2007.00175.x

Gwatirisa, P. (2009). *National issues for immigrant and refugee women.* Surry Hills, NSW: Settlement Council of Australia.

Hagelund, A., & Kavli, H. (2009). If work is out of sight: Activation and citizenship for new refugees. *Journal of European Social Policy*, *19*(3), 259–270. doi:10.1177/0958928709104741

Khakbaz, M., & Faye, D. B. (2011). We are here, now what? Practice reflection on working with refugee women and their settlement journey. *International Journal of Diversity in Organisations, Communities & Nations*, *10*(5), 3-19. Retrieved from http://ijd.cgpublisher.com/

McMichael, C., & Manderson, L. (2004). Somali women and well-being: Social networks and social capital among immigrant women in Australia. *Human Organization*, *63*, 88–99. Retrieved from http://www.sfaa.net/publications/human-organization

Muslim Women Support Centre of WA Inc. (2001). Services. Retrieved May 5, 2014, from http://www.muslimtents.com/mwscwa/page/services.html

Nash, M. (2005). Responding to settlement needs: Migrants, refugees and community development. In M. Nash, R. Munford, & K. O'Donoghue (Eds.), *Social work theories in action* (pp. 140–154). London: Jessica Kingsley.

Nash, M. (2011). Self-reflexive student research and its implications for social work education. *Social Work Education*, *30*(3), 331–344. doi:10.1080/02615479.2010.482984

Nash, M., & Trlin, A. D. (2006). *A survey of non-government/not for profit agencies and organisations providing social services to immigrants and refugees in New Zealand*. Palmerston North, N.Z: New Settlers Programme, Massey University.

Pepworth, J., & Nash, M. (2009). Finding "a safe place to cry": A review of research and evidence informing social work with refugees and new settlers in Aotearoa New Zealand. *Aotearoa. New Zealand Social Work Review*, *21*, 48-59. Retrieved from http://anzasw.org.nz/about/topics/show/207-aotearoa-nz-social-work-review

Phillmore, J. (2011). Refugees, acculturation strategies, stress and integration. *Journal of Social Policy*, *40*(03), 575–593. doi:10.1017/S0047279410000929

Refugee Week. (2013). Statistics at a glance. Retrieved from http://www.refugeeweek.org.au/resources/stats.php

Sainsbury, D. (2006). Immigrants' social rights in comparative perspective: Welfare regimes, forms of immigration and immigration policy regimes. *Journal of European Social Policy*, *16*(3), 229–244. doi:10.1177/0958928706065594

Schweitzer, R., Greenslade, J. H., & Kagee, A. (2007). Coping and resilience in refugees from the Sudan: A narrative account. *The Australian and New Zealand Journal of Psychiatry*, *41*(3), 282–288. doi:10.1080/00048670601172780 PMID:17464710

Tilbury, F., & Rapley, M. (2004). "There are orphans in Africa still looking for my hands'": African women refugees and the sources of emotional distress. *Health Sociology Review*, *13*(1), 54–64. http://pubs.e-contentmanagement.com/loi/hesr doi:10.5172/hesr.13.1.54

United States Institute of Peace. (n.d.). What is U.N. Security Council Resolution 1325 and why is it so critical today? Retrieved May 15, 2014, from http://www.usip.org/gender_peacebuilding/about_UNSCR_1325

## KEY TERMS AND DEFINITIONS

**Refugee:** A person who, due to a well-founded fear of persecution in relation to race, religion, nationality, membership in a particular social group, or adherence to a political opinion, is outside their home country and is either unable or unwilling to avail him or herself of the protection of that country.

**Refugee Resettlement:** The settlement of people who have fled their country for fear of persecution and who have arrived at a destination where they are permitted to settle and put down roots.

**Resilience:** A term defined in many ways. In this chapter "resilience" is viewed as evidenced through everyday processes and describes the quality in a person which enables them to overcome misfortunes and other challenges or barriers rather than be drained of resolve. A positive attitude, optimism, and an ability to regulate emotions are clear strengths of the resilient person.

**Social Work with Refugees:** Social work in its broadest sense as a field of practice with a specialist client group, namely, refugees.

# Chapter 6
# More than Pills and Beds:
## Contemporary Challenges in Social Work Practice and Mental Healthcare

**Sebastian Rosenberg**
*University of Sydney, Australia*

**Fiona McDermott**
*Monash University, Australia*

## ABSTRACT

*Contemporary models of mental healthcare emphasise the importance of multi-disciplinary approaches in supporting recovery for consumers. There is growing evidence of the key role to be played by social workers derived from both the principles of recovery and those underpinning social work theory and practice, particularly a focus on person-in-environment. However, pressures on the way mental healthcare is provided in Australia are threatening this confluence. These pressures are much more concerned with the needs of funders than professionals, consumers, and their families. The aim of this chapter is to explore the evidence to support social work as an integral element in mental health recovery and to better understand these emerging challenges. The role of social work in good mental healthcare is too important to become marginalized; yet this prospect is real. Better understanding of the contemporary landscape of social work can help ensure this does not occur.*

## INTRODUCTION

Promising evidence regarding the benefits of multi-disciplinary collaborative approaches to mental healthcare continues to accrue. The role of social workers as part of such collaborations is clear. This is particularly the case when applying largely consumer-driven concepts like recovery to such collaborative processes. This is because there is a strong accord between the emergent concepts of recovery and the social work perspective. Both centre on a need to move away from a limited focus on bio-medical issues in mental health.

Many consumers are seeking more than stabilisation of symptoms and medication – more than pills and beds. Instead, many consumers see the keys to proper mental healthcare and their recovery being in better consideration of

DOI: 10.4018/978-1-4666-6563-7.ch006

broader psychosocial concerns, such as housing, employment, social inclusion, and friendship. This broader perspective regarding recovery fits well with social work practice.

However, new and emerging pressures on the way mental healthcare is provided in Australia are threatening this confluence. Flat fee for service payment arrangements are administratively simple but fail to engender the desired multi-disciplinary approach. These payment systems are driving unwanted outcomes, picking professional winners and losers. At this stage, it is hard not to see social work as losing out under existing payment systems. Other important issues include the advent of new, personalised packages of care, with individual fundholding, such as to be established under Australia's National Disability Insurance Scheme (NDIS). These will place new pressures on consumers to find services that meet their needs. The advent of Activity Based Funding also threatens to reward hospital-focused approaches to service delivery over community-based approaches. Finally, there is a fundamental weakness in relation to the overall mental health workforce, including social workers, particularly in relation to community mental health.

Together these challenges suggest a paradox. While evidence for the effectiveness of social work as part of recovery-based models of care has never been stronger, the infrastructure to support such models appears weak or obscure. This chapter aims to explore this paradox, to inform contemporary thinking about policy and service design, and to highlight opportunities for closer and greater engagement of social work in mental health.

## SEARCH STRATEGY

There were two key approaches to the search strategy used in the preparation of this chapter. First, multiple searches were conducted using library catalogues and journal and statistical databases (Australian Institute of Health and Welfare, Australian Bureau of Statistics). All identified documents were examined and those that were relevant were retrieved for inclusion. Other documents were searched and included where appropriate, such as technical reports and working papers. Internet searches were also carried out, using the key words *recovery*, *"collaborative mental healthcare"*, *"community mental health"*, *"social work"*, *and "peer support"*. Second, references were traced in literature already known to the authors. The scope of the searches was broad to ensure maximum retrieval and minimise the exclusion of items of interest.

## BACKGROUND

It is worth providing a brief context in relation to Australia's current mental health system. Mental illness is common. One in five people will experience a mental illness in any year and almost half the population will experience a mental illness in their lifetime (Australian Bureau of Statistics [ABS], 2008).

Australia's mental health system has a very limited penetration of services with only 35% of people with a mental illness receiving care (ABS, 2008). Depressingly, this rate of access is largely unchanged over the past decade (ABS, 1998). This may have improved since the advent of the Better Access Program in 2006, to be discussed later in this chapter, though this is not verifiable.

It is widely regarded that mental health is underfunded in Australia (and worldwide) (World Health Organisation, 2003). While mental illness accounts for 13% of the burden of disease in Australia (Mathers, Vos, & Stevenson, 1999), it accounts for only around 5% of total health spending (Australian Institute of Health and Welfare [AIHW], 2012). Mental health spending has increased over recent years by an average of 4.8% but has failed to keep pace with the increase in overall health spending over the past decade

(5.3%) (AIHW, 2012). In other words, mental health's share of total health spending is waning not waxing.

Perhaps as a consequence of this situation, across Australia mental health has been subject to regular review and scrutiny, with regular parliamentary and other inquiries revealing substantial inadequacies in both access to and the quality of mental healthcare available in this country (Mental Health Council of Australia, 2005; Senate Community Affairs Reference Committee, 2010; Senate Select Committee on Mental Health, 2006).

Mental illness is a disease that particularly affects adolescents and young adults, with 75% of all mental illness manifest before the age of 25 (Kessler et al., 2005). It is a significant problem, therefore, that service access rates are particularly low among youth, with only 13% of young men with a mental illness receiving any care in the past 12 months.

The impact of mental illness is profound, affecting individuals, the community, and the economy. It has been estimated that Australia spends at least $28.6 billion per year, excluding capital expenditure, supporting people with mental illness. This is equivalent to 2.2% of Australia's Gross Domestic Product and does not include indirect costs, such as lost productivity (Medibank Private and Nous Group, 2013). An Australian study has suggested that anxiety and affective disorders alone are associated with more than 20 million work impairment days annually (Lim, Sanderson, & Andrews, 2000).

Australia has led the world with regard to the development of plans and strategies in relation to mental health reform. There have been four national plans, two national policies, several intergovernmental agreements, one Council of Australian Governments (CoAG) Action Plan, plus myriad state plans. The problem has been and remains one of implementation.

While evidence about good practice in mental healthcare continues to accumulate, Australia's many plans for mental health reform have not yielded significant change to the way services are provided. The experience of care for people seeking mental healthcare remains generally poor and is often the subject of intense criticism (Mendoza et al., 2013) and, as stated earlier, the overall rate of access to mental health services remains low, particularly among vulnerable groups.

It is in this context that we can now explore the rationale for engaging social work in good mental health and recovery practice.

## THE SYNERGY BETWEEN MENTAL HEALTH, RECOVERY, AND SOCIAL WORK

Recovery principles have become increasingly enshrined in mental health policy in Australia (Fossey et al., 2012; McGeorge, 2012; Oades & Anderson, 2012). The *Fourth National Mental Health Plan* (2009) includes "social inclusion & recovery" as a priority area and the *National Standards for Mental Health Services* (2010) advocates that mental health services incorporate recovery principles into practice and service delivery. These standards identify the importance of consumer and carer participation (standard 2), the importance of a high standard of evidence-based assessment (standard 7), and continuity of care (standard 8) characterised by integrated partnerships and collaboration amongst consumers, carers, family members, and health service providers.

The concept of recovery derives from a consumer base in which the discourse of illness, treatment, and cure is substituted by one which incorporates all domains of human life and a holistic understanding of mental health as reflective of bio-psychosocial elements. While the notion of recovery comprises a range of different theoretical positions, the underpinning values and goals of recovery-oriented services work from principles of empowerment through choice and self-management; an emphasis on strengths; the provision of services to meet individual needs;

the importance of family and community; and the centrality of respect, hope and meaning-making (Bland, Renouf, & Tullgren 2009; Oades & Anderson 2012; Slade, Adams, & O'Hagan, 2012). As such, recovery principles represent a shift in power relationships from paternalism to partnership. Australian enthusiasm for the application of recovery principles to mental healthcare is demonstrated by the development of the *National Framework for Recovery-Oriented Mental Health Services*, issued by all Australian Health Ministers in 2013 (Australian Health Ministers' Advisory Council, 2013).

Importantly, however, while definitions of recovery place emphasis on relationships, the valuing of the lived experience of illness, the importance of hope, empowerment and strengths, the criteria from which measures have been derived for demonstrating the evidence base of recovery are rarely those acknowledged by consumers as representing their understanding of what recovery entails.

The philosophy of recovery has always sat well with the principles underpinning social work theory and practice, namely a focus on person-in-environment, and an emphasis placed on the relationship between social worker and service-user as essential to effective practice. Bland et al. (2009) note that

*... the recovery paradigm offers a coherent set of principles to guide social work practice in mental health. The emphasis on relationships, valuing the lived experience of illness, and the importance of hope, empowerment and strengths are principles familiar to social workers. (p. 47)*

But these authors also note the tension between evidence-based practice and recovery principles, noting the philosophical differences between scientific evidence and lived experience as placing the practitioner in a potentially conflicting position needing to decide which should be relied upon to shape practice. These factors may account for

apprehension amongst consumers that recovery may have been hijacked by mental health policy makers operating as a stalking horse for reductions in services. This could be described as the adoption or colonisation of a new rhetoric without genuinely changed practice, potentially impacting negatively on service-users themselves. As Tullgren (Bland et al., 2009) has commented:

*... because of the centrality of outcome measures in service delivery, people with mental illness who fail to recover, or who backslide, or who don't recover in the permitted time, can be blamed for poor results of programs....Recovery, then, becomes a get-out-of-gaol-free card...to explain poor outcomes. (p. 47)*

Thus, it would appear that there remains a significant challenge to ensure the rhetoric of recovery translates to practical changes at the service level, helping to drive the transition away from crisis-driven clinical services to a network of supports, resources, and opportunities which facilitate recovery.

## Evidence for the Recovery Approach

Determining what the nature of evidence will be for deciding on the effectiveness of recovery programmes is in itself problematic. Williams et al. (2012) in their systematic review of measures of recovery-oriented services found no measure was a good fit with the conceptual framework of recovery. These researchers noted gaps in knowledge regarding how to measure the recovery orientation of services due to the fact that recovery outcome measures were seen not to have evolved to a stage where a gold standard measure of recovery orientation has emerged.

While Gordon and Ellis (2013) noted 12 domains that consumers identified as important to recovery, it was the clinician-rated, symptom-focused, standardised outcome measures which predominated in studies of treatment interventions for mental health conditions. When consumers critique these they argue that existing measures do not support what is important from a consumer-recovery perspective, perhaps largely because consumers had provided minimal input into these studies. Consumers have stated that the use of such measures is akin to the hotel manager rating the guests! From a social work perspective, it is also the case that the interaction between social workers and clients, recognised as intrinsic to intervention – and also to recovery – has rarely been studied (Stanhope & Solomon, 2008).

We, therefore, face a contradiction. On the one hand, mental health policy claims recovery principles and practices as central to the delivery of services; on the other hand, what constitutes evidence for interventions relies in large part on research designs and methodologies (often randomised controlled trials) which are inimical to recovery philosophy and practice.

It is, therefore, unsurprising that funding mechanisms deriving from current Australian mental health policy indicate that programmes, such as Better Access and Access to Allied Psychological Services (ATAPS), reveal little take-up by social workers, the majority of whom work within public mental health services and community mental health programmes.

However, this also alerts us to considerations of the extent to which it is these services which require a re-think of the ways in which recovery principles and practices might transform service delivery, making it genuinely recovery-driven. Such a re-think may promote a move away from the so-called medical model and towards the establishment of a model in which service providers "must pay more attention to the process of care and ensure that they genuinely engage and collaborate with their clients" (Stanhope & Solomon, 2008, p. 886).

However, it would be mistaken to believe that there exists no evidence for the effectiveness of recovery-based services. Indeed, two recent studies have used randomised control trial methodology to evaluate the effectiveness of using peer support and found it was a "promising intervention for reducing psychiatric hospitalization for patients at risk of readmission" (Sledge et al., 2011, p. 541).

## Evidence from Consumers

More importantly, and more in-line with recovery philosophy, evidence exists from consumers themselves as to the effectiveness of recovery-based services. The delivery of recovery-based services through collaborative interdisciplinary teams, which include consumer or peer support workers, have increasingly demonstrated positive outcomes, reinforcing Gordon and Ellis's (2013) argument regarding the need to use outcome methods and findings from consumer evaluations in order to expand the standards of evidence in research of consumer recovery models.

There is also increasing evidence for the value of peer-led and peer-supported mental health programmes. For example, research by Davidson, Belamy, Guy, and Miller (2012) describes the unique contribution peers make to service provision and outcomes. Bologna and Pulice (2011) demonstrate from their findings that trained consumer professionals and paraprofessionals can provide a range of effective and valued services to consumers. Cook et al. (2010) provide evidence that Wellness Recovery Action Planning (WRAP), a programme of self-management of mental illness taught by peers, can lead to significant positive change in skills, attitudes, and behaviour. The Australian-based Centre for Excellence in Peer Support also provides numerous evaluations and accounts of the benefits of such initiatives from within Australia and internationally.

## Evidence from Collaborative Models of Mental Health Service Delivery

A study by Evans et al. (2012) concluded that an adequately skilled mental health multidisciplinary workforce with professional diversity (including social workers) is associated with greater effectiveness. The benefits of collaborative, multidisciplinary teamwork include: minimising user and carer distress, avoiding service fragmentation, integrated service delivery, and continuity of care by harnessing a mix of professional skills (see also Belling et al., 2011; Newhouse & Spring, 2010).

This is similarly endorsed by Ng, Herrman, Chiu, and Singh (2009) who report on the place of Prevention and Recovery Care (PARC) services in Australia which address the need for a comprehensive and flexible mental health service that includes inpatient, community outreach, rehabilitation, and home-based care. Such services have been found to reduce inpatient admissions and facilitate early discharge. They are clearly reliant on a coordinated, multidisciplinary team approach where team members collectively participate in delivering care. Salyers and Tsemberis (2007) have also demonstrated how the strong evidence to support multidisciplinary Assertive Community Treatment can sit well within a recovery approach.

Thinking about collaborative practice takes us into the developing world of interdisciplinary practice. The trans or interdisciplinary approach strives to grasp the complexity of a problem, taking into account the diverse perceptions of problems, making links between abstract and case-specific knowledge, and developing descriptive, normative, and practical knowledge for the common interest (Fenwick, 2012; Hadorn, Pohl, & Bammer, 2010). Such collaborative models for service delivery in health demonstrate the benefits of "coordinated and coherent linkages between disciplines resulting in reciprocal interactions that overlap discipline boundaries, generating new common methods, knowledge and perspectives" (Newhouse & Spring, 2010, p. 309).

In relation to recovery principles, such models of interdisciplinary practice must include peer or consumer workers in order to ensure, from a consumer perspective, that such services are "knowledge based and recovery focused" (Oades & Anderson, 2012; Stanhope & Solomon, 2008).

As early as 2002, consumers, carers, and NGOs contributed their views on interdisciplinary teamwork at a symposium organised by the RANZCP Professional Liaison Committee at the TheMHS conference of Australia and New Zealand. Participants concluded that the achievement of effective and responsive partnerships with consumers and carers meant an expanded notion of who should comprise membership of an interdisciplinary team if "an outcome of effective service delivery" was to be attained (Macdonald, Herrman, Hinds, Crowe, & McDonald, 2002, p.126). As the Evaluation of the Delivery for Mental Health Peer Support Worker Pilot Scheme in Scotland (set up in 2006 and evaluated in 2011) demonstrated, the inclusion of peer workers on mental health teams was beneficial for all parties.

The culture of the mental health team changed from one of "us and them" to one in which the principles of recovery remained at the forefront, intrinsic to the development of practice strategies. The study concluded that what mattered was the character of the team rather than the organisation in which it was based and that the peer support workers were seen to offer a unique and distinctive role which complemented and strengthened the team, despite the team's initial scepticism. Not surprisingly, the integration of peer support workers into the team and the organisation needed strong support from senior management (see also Cabot & Cronin, 2013). A further example of peer workers as integral to interdisciplinary teams delivering recovery-driven interventions is the Personal Helpers and Mentors Programs (see Cabot and Cronin, 2013, for a descriptive account in which a rural NSW service employed consumers in a professional capacity as part of the mental health team).

## Issues Impacting Social Work and Collaborative Mental Healthcare

While the preceding sections have clearly demonstrated the merit of social work engagement in models of multi-disciplinary mental healthcare, there are contemporary challenges impeding the emergence of these models. This section aims to describe these challenges.

The advent of the Better Access Program from November 2006 changed the way Australians seek assistance for mental healthcare by making visits to psychologists rebatable under Medicare (Howard, 2006). In the 2013 financial year, Australia spent almost $612m on 6.43m services provided under this programme. This is $12m per week, by far the largest single mental health programme operating in Australia. The merit of this spending is the subject of debate. There has been one Government-funded evaluation which suggested the Program was meeting its goals and was lifting the rate of access to care (Pirkis et al., 2011). However, others have provided evidence to indicate that this massive programme is only actually providing better access to some groups, with others continuing to miss out (Hickie, Rosenberg, & Davenport, 2011).

What is clear is that the existing Medicare approaches are clearly favouring some professions over others. Table 1 shows the Better Access Program services provided in 2013 (Medicare

*Table 1. Better access program: 2013 activity summary*

| Service Type | Services (n) | MBS Fees Paid $ |
|---|---|---|
| GP Services | 2,430,746 | 196,166,299 |
| Clinical Psychology Services | 1,613,176 | 205,973,187 |
| Registered Psychology Services | 2,138,320 | 189,156,562 |
| Occupation Therapy Services | 47,708 | 4,008,739 |
| Social Work Services | 207,811 | 16,610,314 |
| **Totals** | **6,437,761** | **611,915,101** |

Australia Statistics, 2014). The GP items are grouped together. Social work items accounted for only 2.8% of all the services provided and 2.3% of the total spending. By this account, then, social work appears as a minor, peripheral element of the most significant change to mental health funding in Australia over recent years.

More detailed investigation of the Better Access service profile indicates that group therapy is also a very minor element in service provision with the vast majority of services provided as "in office" appointments (Medicare Australia Statistics, 2014). Only 177,303 out of the total of 6.43m services provided under the Better Access Program in 2013 were provided out of office. Clinical psychologists provided less than 2% of their services as out of office appointments, registered psychologists 5.5% (Medicare Australia Statistics, 2014).

Social workers provided nearly 12% of their services out of office with occupational therapists providing nearly 20%. These figures are quite out of proportion with social work's overall contribution to the Program and strongly indicate the difficulties associated with trying to work within a flat fee for service structure. Such payment systems encourage office-based practice, making clients come to the providers. This is efficient from the provider's perspective and is administratively simple. Yet it is clearly out of step with the way some social workers (and occupational therapists) conduct their practice. Clearly, there are also questions as to the extent to which the Better Access Program is delivering inter-disciplinary collaboration when practically the entire programme is being provided by individual practitioners in their rooms. There have already been concerns raised that such fees for service approaches are anathema to collaborative care, particularly in relation to reaching groups or people not currently receiving services (Headspace, 2010; Scott et al., 2009). There are also other big shifts in relation to funding and policy that could drive activity in directions away from the evidence-based collaborative models of care described earlier.

A key focus of mental health reform is to drive the establishment of new models of genuinely community-based mental healthcare. However, in reality, the vast bulk of mental health services in Australia are still delivered from hospitals as either inpatient services or as ambulatory (outpatient) services. Most jurisdictions have run down their community outreach mental health teams and funding for non-government organisations remains a small element of overall spending (around 7%) (Department of Health and Ageing, 2013).

It is, in fact, precisely in this area of community mental healthcare where governance of the system is most oblique. The states and territories still fund some community-based psychosocial rehabilitation services, though in many jurisdictions the services offered here are now being swept up as state jurisdictional contributions to the NDIS. The Federal government also funds several related community mental health programmes, such as Personal Helpers and Mentors (PHaMs). They further looked to establish Medicare Locals as new players in this field through the new Partners in Recovery Program.

It is problematic that it is in precisely the area of most concern to mental health reform, the development of a vibrant genuine community mental health sector, where governance is at its most confused. There is a lack of clarity regarding where responsibility falls to grow this part of the mental health service landscape. Again, it is potentially social workers and the organisations for which they work that could be negatively affected by this confusion.

Another element is the introduction of Activity Based Funding (ABF) for mental health, already in place in hospitals but slated for broader application from 2016. ABF and its mandating financial agreements threaten to provide new incentives for hospital-based care over community models (Rosenberg & Hickie, 2013). This is not due to any intrinsic flaw in ABF. Rather it is due to the fact that investment in the necessary casemix infrastructure to support community mental health

has simply not occurred. The most mature casemix systems, Diagnosis-related Groups (DRGs), do not work well in mental health and have been used and deployed only in hospital settings. There is no classification system currently available to support the judicious application of ABF to mental health, not in Australia or anywhere else.

A further contemporary challenge relates to the NDIS. This scheme promises a new level of autonomy and service to people covered, based largely on the implementation of individualised packages of care. The concept is that each person will have greater control in decision-making regarding the construct of their own package rather than relying on a set of one size fits all government disability service providers. Exciting in theory and demonstrated to be effective for people with permanent impairments, particularly physical disabilities, this approach is poorly understood in terms of its application to people with a mental illness. In its recent position paper, the Mental Health Council of Australia (2013) outlined several important issues. First there remains doubt regarding the number of people to be covered and, more importantly, excluded under the rules to be imposed by the NDIS. With so many programmes being included by state and federal governments under the rubric of the NDIS, it is reasonable to be concerned about the funds and services that will remain for those not lucky enough to be deemed eligible for NDIS care. The key issue from a social work perspective though must be the extent to which individual packages will be used to buy the evidence-based multi-disciplinary care in which social work plays an important role. New empowered consumers will need to understand their options and the evidence if judicious choices are to be made.

There is also an issue about compatibility of the NDIS with a recovery philosophy. If people with a mental illness recover under their NDIS package, will the system permit flexible, episodic exit and re-entry for those clients? There is also concern about the actual shape and construct of an individualised package of care for a person with severe mental illness. What are the components of care, who can provide these services, and by what measures is it reasonable to assess their impact? These issues are yet to be resolved but threaten to make the establishment of sound models of collaborative mental healthcare more complex due to the bureaucratic primacy afforded to clarification around eligibility and funding rules.

A final but key issue impacting on social workers is the poor state of workforce planning. The AIHW keeps track and reports on the state of the health workforce, but in relation to the mental health workforce data are only available for psychiatrists, nurses, and registered psychologists. The AASW (2011) estimates that social workers comprise one third of the public mental health sector workforce and are the fourth largest professional group after nurses, medical staff, and psychologists.

Australia is poorly equipped to understand existing roles for social workers and to plan for the future. Healy and Lonne (2010) state plainly that this means it will be difficult to determine how national needs will be met in areas such as mental health and child protection. They call for a national workforce and curriculum plan, a critical piece of planning infrastructure currently unavailable in Australia in relation to social work. Adding to the potential confusion here is the likely development of a much larger consumer or peer workforce as part of mental health reforms across Australia (Mental Health Commission of New South Wales, 2013).

## SOLUTIONS AND RECOMMENDATIONS

Given the real and potential problems cited above, how should social work practice respond? Rather than remaining somewhat on the periphery of mental health service provision, there are at least three important areas in which social work-ers may work to promote knowledge-based and recovery-focused service delivery models in the mental health field: through advocacy, practice leadership, and research.

## Advocacy

Social workers working with a recovery focus reflect the argument that there is a need to move away from traditional practice models (Slade et al., 2012). Social workers place particular emphasis on advocacy as constituting a key value and skill. They are centrally placed to advocate for the introduction of a recovery focus in services. This may mean arguing for a paradigm shift in philosophy and practice towards one which promotes collaborative models of care. Such a strategy will recognise and enlist consumer expertise as having an intrinsic role in tackling this contradiction between mental health policy and funding changes.

Clearly, there is also a role for social work to advocate for itself. Through its peak bodies and related organisations, the voice of social workers must be clear and strong if evidence-based approaches are to be pursued. Funding and policy decisions are too important to be left to those with merely the strongest professional or industrial voices.

## Practice Leadership

As we have noted earlier, social workers are frequently members of interdisciplinary teams in public and community mental health services. Given their philosophical and value orientation and its close "fit" with recovery principles and practices, great potential exists for social workers to consider how the team itself may exemplify a recovery-focus.

This requires adoption of informed leadership roles within teams, familiarity with knowledge and research evidence about the effectiveness of such endeavours, and a willingness to work with mental health consumers to develop recovery-driven models of interdisciplinary teamwork. While this might require entry into less familiar territory, some examples may be worth examining.

Newhouse and Spring (2010) advance their Evidence Based Behaviour Program which uses an ecological framework reminiscent of social work's commitment to a person-in-environment view of the social and material world. Their argument is that to promote change, actors must influence multiple levels – interpersonal, organisational, community, and public policy. To do so, they outline an interdisciplinary model of collaborative practice, primarily located within health, which supports evidence-based shared decision-making on interprofessional healthcare teams.

What is so far missing from Newhouse and Spring's (2010) formulation, if translated into the mental health field, is the presence of consumers or peer workers. The team engages in a five step process ("1) Ask, 2) Acquire, 3) Appraise, 4) Apply, and 5) Analyze and Adjust") whereby team members synthesise evidence-based research as a guide for decision-making and action (p. 313). The potential to adapt such a process, including expanding on the evidence base to include consumer knowledge-informed evidence, holds potential for leading a recovery-focused interdisciplinary mental health team which includes consumers.

Others advocating for the development of interdisciplinary team capacities, such as Ling (2012), describe the use by such a team of "contribution stories" which aim to surface and outline how those involved in decision-making understand the causal pathways connecting the intervention to its intended outcomes (p. 87). The purpose of sharing contribution stories is to capture the narratives of practitioners and consumers, assisting them to describe how their activities can produce intended and unintended outcomes. Contribution stories are drawn from those more abstract and perhaps rarely evoked "theories of change" which practitioners and consumers might hold and which explain (to them) how they connect resources and actions to

outcomes (p. 87). Articulating these theories of change provides a starting point for team reflection and action. As the team listens to its members' analysis of the case, the contribution stories and theories of change which motivate members, a plan emerges. The uncertainties and areas of ignorance, ambiguity, or limited evidence become apparent. Hypotheses or hunches are generated about likely outcomes, perhaps with reference to the patterns discernable in other similar cases.

## FUTURE RESEARCH DIRECTIONS

As we have noted, the kinds of outcome measures that matter to consumers are those which are generally the focus of social work interventions, for example, the centrality of a trusting relationship, the importance of ensuring day-to-day needs are met and sustained, an acceptable quality of life attained, and so on. Social work has an increasingly confident research presence in the mental health field and demonstrated understanding and utilisation of research designs and methodologies which parallel the epistemology and methodology underpinning a recovery perspective. This relates to their shared interest in a focus on process and a commitment to "understanding social interactions and methods which can capture the complexity of human processes at the micro level" (Stanhope & Solomon, 2008, p. 895).

In relation to research approaches, there is clearly a need to expand the repertoire of methods to enable the establishment of, and evidence base for, the kinds of psychosocial interventions synonymous with recovery principles. The adoption of constructivist (or interpretivist) as well as critical epistemologies, which rely on qualitative, interpretive, participatory, and mixed quantitative and qualitative methods, sit well with social work's research and value orientation (Gordon & Ellis, 2013; McDermott, 1996; Stanhope & Solomon, 2008).

Other commentators offer valuable suggestions for social workers wishing to research and promote recovery focused models. For example, McGeorge (2012) identified strategies for developing recovery-focused mental health studies in Australia and the South Pacific region. Of the fourteen strategies noted, four are of particular relevance: the involvement of service-users, families and carers; developing expertise and commitment to models of collaborative care; increasing understanding of community work and the processes necessary to engage community support; and establishing broad based coalitions involving consumers, family members, NGOs, clinicians, and administrators to guide and support the collaborative processes involved.

## The Role of Social Workers: A Case Study

Mary is a 45 year old woman who suffers from schizophrenia. She was first diagnosed in her early 20s and over the next two decades spent considerable periods of time in psychiatric hospitals, usually prompted by severe psychotic episodes. She is the mother of three children, all of whom have been either adopted or placed in long-term foster care. She has some contact with her eldest daughter and is desperate to maintain this fragile connection. Mary's family history reveals serious problems, most notably in regard to her mother's suicide. Mary retains contact with her older brother who has remained a significant source of practical assistance and support.

Mary's mental health fluctuates considerably with frequent changes being made to her medication in order to achieve stability. She is an outpatient of a Community Mental Health service which she attends irregularly. Mary also receives occasional visits from a community mental health team but only when neighbours in her public housing estate become concerned at signs of her deteriorating mental well-being. Mary experiences considerable isolation and loneliness, ameliorated somewhat by her devotion to her two cats.

When Mary resumed contact with her daughter she became extremely motivated to improve her health. Her brother engaged a private psychologist to see her on a weekly basis and for a brief period this brought her some relief (and social contact) and her mental health seemed stable. However, after about 2 months, Mary experienced a severe psychotic episode, inflicting serious injuries on herself. She was again hospitalised. The psychologist attempted to follow-up Mary's situation with the Community Mental Health service but found that, due to the pressures on staff and the frequent changes in personnel, there was no one who had established an ongoing relationship with Mary.

The psychologist then contacted the social worker in the psychiatric unit where Mary was still an inpatient. The mental health team in the psychiatric unit, which included two consumer consultants and a nurse, were working collaboratively to plan for Mary's eventual discharge. The team had identified that Mary's needs were multiple, including medication stability, emotional well-being, and social and relational connection. The nurse could also assist in attending to Mary's physical health needs.

As her health improved, the social workers encouraged Mary to become involved in planning and arranging her own care. A bed was to become available for her in new supported accommodation close to the suburb where Mary had lived, and she had been assessed as a suitable patient. The nature of the support provided through her new housing included a range of service providers (social work, occupational therapy, psychiatric nursing). It also had a creative programme of daily living skills, relaxation and meditation, and excellent links with community education and employment programmes for residents. Some of the psychosocial services were provided by a non-government organisation which operated on recovery principles, including an innovative Peer Support Programme. From her new accommodation and with regular support from services, Mary began to participate in activities and gain confidence. She is now part of a peer-run structured group support programme and has begun some vocational training with a view to getting a job. Mary's mental health has improved and she has had several mutually satisfactory meetings with her daughter. The social workers in the support team are able to check in on Mary from time to time. Mary's need for hospitalisation has diminished.

## CONCLUSION

This chapter has attempted to set out the evidence for social work as part of a recovery-based approach to mental healthcare. This evidence looks strong. Yet important changes in the landscape of mental health policy and funding are sending, at best, mixed signals as to their support for these evidence-based models of care. At worst, it is possible to see social work at risk of becoming a more marginal player in contemporary Australian mental healthcare. This would be a significant and retrograde step in the provision of high quality services.

Social work practitioners need to consider carefully how they can contribute to addressing this risk. This will be critical if people with a mental illness are going to have access to a skilled, professional social work workforce into the 21st century.

## REFERENCES

Australian Association of Social Workers. (2011). *Submission to the Senate Community Affairs Committee into commonwealth funding and administration of mental health services.* August. Retrieved from http://www.aasw.asn.au/document/item/2265

Australian Bureau of Statistics. (1998). *National survey of mental health and wellbeing 1997.* Canberra: Author.

Australian Bureau of Statistics. (2008). *National survey of mental health and wellbeing 2007.* Canberra: Author.

Australian Health Ministers' Advisory Council. (2013). *A national framework for recovery-oriented mental health services: Policy and theory.* Retrieved from Commonwealth of Australia Department of Health website: http://www.health.gov.au/internet/main/publishing.nsf/Content/B2CA4C28D59C74EBCA257C1D0004A79D/$File/recovpol.pdf

Australian Institute of Health and Welfare. (2012). *Australia's health 2012.* Canberra: Author.

Belling, R., Whittock, M., McLaren, S., Burns, T., Catty, J., Rees Jones, I., & Wykes, T. (2011). Achieving continuity of care: Facilitators and barriers in community mental health teams. *Implementation Science*, 6(1), 23. doi:10.1186/1748-5908-6-23 PMID:21418579

Bland, R., Renouf, N., & Tullgren, A. (2009). *Social work practice in mental health: An introduction.* Crows Nest, NSW: Allen & Unwin.

Bologna, M. J., & Pulice, R. T. (2011). Evaluation of a peer-run hospital diversion program: A descriptive study. *American Journal of Psychiatric Rehabilitation, 14*(4), 272–286. doi:10.1080/15487768.2011.622147

Cabot, W., & Cronin, B. (2013, April). *Recovery: The journey within three rural communities in NSW.* Paper presented at the 12th National Rural Health Conference, South Australia.

Cook, J. A., Copeland, M. E., Corey, L., Buffington, E., Jonikas, J. A., & Curtis, L. C. et al. (2010). Developing the evidence base for peer-led services: Changes among participants following Wellness Recovery Action Planning (WRAP) education in two statewide initiatives. *Psychiatric Rehabilitation Journal, 34*(2), 113–120. doi:10.2975/34.2.2010.113.120 PMID:20952364

Davidson, L., Belamy, C., Guy, K., & Miller, R. (2012). Peer support among persons with severe mental illnesses: A review of evidence and experience. *World Psychiatry: Official Journal of the World Psychiatric Association (WPA), 11*(2), 123–128. doi:10.1016/j.wpsyc.2012.05.009 PMID:22654945

Department of Health and Ageing. (2013). *National mental health report 2013: Tracking progress of mental health reform in Australia 1993-2011.* Retrieved from Commonwealth of Australia Department of Health website: http://www.health.gov.au/internet/ main/publishing.nsf/Content/ B090F03865A7FAB9CA257C1B0079E198/$File/ rep13.pdf

Evans, S., Huxley, P., Baker, C., White, J., Madge, S., Onyett, S., & Gould, N. (2012). The social care component of multidisciplinary mental health teams: A review and national survey. *Journal of Health Services Research & Policy, 17*(Suppl. 2), 23–29. doi:10.1258/jhsrp.2012.011117 PMID:22572713

Fenwick, T. (2012). Complexity science and professional learning for collaboration: A critical reconsideration of possibilities and limitations. *Journal of Education and Work, 25*(1), 141–162. doi:10.1080/13639080.2012.644911

Fossey, E., Cuff, R., Ennals, P., Grey, F., McKenzie, P., & Meadows, G. ... Zimmerman, A. (2012). Supporting recovery and living well. In G. Meadows, J. Farhall, E. Fossey, M. Grigg, F. McDermott, & B. Singh. (Eds.), *Mental health in Australia: Collaborative community practice* (3rd ed., pp. 502-528). Sydney, Australia: Oxford University Press.

*Fourth national mental health plan: An agenda for collaborative government action in mental health 2009-2014.* (2009). Retrieved from Commonwealth of Australia Department of Health website: http://www.health. gov.au/internet/main/publishing.nsf/Content/ 9A5A0E8BDFC55D3BCA257BF0001C1B1C/ $File/plan09v2.pdf

Gordon, S. E., & Ellis, P. M. (2013). Recovery of evidence-based practice. *International Journal of Mental Health Nursing, 22*(1), 3–14. doi:10.1111/ j.1447-0349.2012.00835.x PMID:22830603

Hadorn, G. H., Pohl, C., & Bammer, G. (2010). Solving problems through transdisciplinary research. In R. Frodeman, J. T. Klein, & C. Mitcham (Eds.), *The Oxford handbook of interdisciplinarity* (pp. 431–452). New York, NY: Oxford University Press.

Headspace. (2010, May 17). *Headspace concern over exclusion of key workers from mental healthcare* [Press release]. Retrieved from http://www.headspace.org.au/about-headspace/media-centre/media-release-archive/headspace-concern-over-exclusion-of-key-workers-from-mental-health-care

Healy, K., & Lonne, B. (2010). *The social work and human services workforce: Report from a national study of education, training and workforce needs.* Strawberry Hills, Australia: Australian Learning and Teaching Council.

Hickie, I. B., Rosenberg, S., & Davenport, T. A. (2011). Australia's Better Access initiative: Still awaiting serious evaluation? *The Australian and New Zealand Journal of Psychiatry, 45*(10), 814–823. doi:10.3109/00048674.2011.610744 PMID:21980930

Howard, J. (2006, May 9). *Better mental health services for Australia* [Press release]. Retrieved from http://pandora.nla.gov.au/pan/10052/20061221-0000/www.pm.gov.au/news/media_releases/media_Release1858.html

Kessler, R. C., Berglund, P., Demler, O., Jin, R., Merikangas, K. R., & Walters, E. E. (2005). Lifetime prevalence and age-of-onset distributions of DSM-IV disorders in the National Comorbidity Survey Replication. *Archives of General Psychiatry, 62*, 593-602. doi:10.1001/archpsyc.62.6.593

Lim, D., Sanderson, K., & Andrews, G. (2000). Lost productivity among full-time workers with mental disorders. *The Journal of Mental Health Policy and Economics, 3*(3), 139–146. doi:10.1002/mhp.93 PMID:11967449

Ling, T. (2012). Evaluating complex and unfolding interventions in real time. *Evaluation, 18*(1), 79–91. doi:10.1177/1356389011429629

Macdonald, E., Herrman, H., Hinds, P., Crowe, J., & McDonald, P. (2002). Beyond interdisciplinary boundaries: Views of consumers, carers and non-government organizations on teamwork. *Australasian Psychiatry, 10*(2), 125–129. doi:10.1046/j.1440-1665.2002.00420.x

Mathers, C., Vos, T., & Stevenson, C. (1999). *The burden of disease and injury in Australia.* Canberra: Australian Institute of Health and Welfare.

McDermott, F. (1996). Social work research: Debating the Boundaries. *Australian Social Work, 49*(1), 5–10. doi:10.1080/03124079608411156

McGeorge, P. (2012). Lessons learned in developing community mental healthcare in Australasia and the South Pacific. *World Psychiatry: Official Journal of the World Psychiatric Association (WPA), 11*(2), 129–132. doi:10.1016/j.wpsyc.2012.05.010 PMID:22654946

Medibank Private and Nous Group. (2013). *The case for mental health reform in Australia: A review of expenditure and system design.* Retrieved from https://www.medibankhealth.com.au/files/editor_upload/File/Mental%20Health%20Full%20Report.pdf

Medicare Australia Statistics. (2014). Medicare item reports. Retrieved April 5, 2014, from https://www.medicareaustralia.gov.au/statistics/mbs_item.shtml

Mendoza, J., Bresnan, A., Rosenberg, S., Elson, A., Gilbert, Y., Long, P.,…Hopkins, J. (2013). *Obsessive hope disorder: Reflections on 30 years of mental health reform in Australia and visions for the future.* Sippy Downs, Australia: ConNetica.

Mental Health Commission of New South Wales. (2013). *Living well in our community: Towards a strategic plan for mental health in NSW.* Sydney, Australia: Author.

Mental Health Council of Australia. (2005). *Not for service: Experiences of injustice and despair in mental healthcare in Australia*. Canberra: Author.

Mental Health Council of Australia. (2013). *Mental health and the National Disability Insurance Scheme, position paper, November 2013*. Canberra: Author.

*National standards for mental health services 2010*. (2010). Retrieved from Commonwealth of Australia Department of Health website: http://www.health.gov.au/internet/main/publishing.nsf/Content/CFA833CB8C1AA178CA257BF0001E7520/$File/servst10v2.pdf

Newhouse, R. P., & Spring, B. (2010). Interdisciplinary evidence-based practice: Moving from silos to synergy. *Nursing Outlook*, *58*(6), 309–317. doi:10.1016/j.outlook.2010.09.001 PMID:21074648

Ng, C., Herrman, H., Chiu, E., & Singh, B. (2009). Community mental healthcare in the Asia-Pacific region: Using current best-practice models to inform future policy. *World Psychiatry: Official Journal of the World Psychiatric Association (WPA)*, *8*(1), 49–55. Retrieved from http://www.world-psychiatry.com/ PMID:19293961

Oades, L. G., & Anderson, J. (2012). Recovery in Australia: Marshalling strengths and living values. *International Review of Psychiatry*, *24*(1), 5–10. doi:10.3109/09540261.2012.660623 PMID:22385421

Pirkis, J., Ftanou, M., Williamson, M., Machlin, A., Spittal, M. J., Bassilios, B., & Harris, M. (2011). Australia's Better Access initiative: An evaluation. *The Australian and New Zealand Journal of Psychiatry*, *45*(9), 726–739. doi:10.3109/00048674.2011.594948 PMID:21888609

Rosenberg, S. P., & Hickie, I. B. (2013). Making activity-based funding work for mental health. *Australian Health Review*, *37*(3), 277–280. doi:10.1071/AH13002 PMID:23731959

Salyers, M. P., & Tsemberis, S. (2007). ACT and recovery: Integrating evidence-based practice and recovery orientation on assertive community treatment teams. *Community Mental Health Journal*, *43*(6), 619–641. doi:10.1007/s10597-007-9088-5 PMID:17514503

Scott, E., Naismith, S., Whitwell, B., Hamilton, B., Chudleigh, C., & Hickie, I. (2009). Delivering youth-specific mental health services: The advantages of a collaborative, multi-disciplinary system. *Australasian Psychiatry*, *17*(3), 189–194. doi:10.1080/10398560802657322 PMID:19296265

Senate Community Affairs Reference Committee. (2010). *The hidden toll: Suicide in Australia*. Canberra: Commonwealth of Australia.

Senate Select Committee on Mental Health. (2006). *A national approach to mental health: From crisis to community*. Canberra: Commonwealth of Australia.

Slade, M., Adams, N., & O'Hagan, M. (2012). Recovery: Past progress and future challenges. *International Review of Psychiatry*, *24*(1), 1–4. doi:10.3109/09540261.2011.644847 PMID:22385420

Sledge, W. H., Lawless, M., Sells, D., Wieland, M., O'Connell, M. J., & Davidson, L. (2011). Effectiveness of peer support in reducing readmissions of persons with multiple psychiatric hospitalizations. *Psychiatric Services*, *62*(5), 541–544. doi:10.1176/appi.ps.62.5.541 PMID:21532082

Stanhope, V., & Solomon, P. (2008). Getting to the heart of recovery: Methods for studying recovery and their implications for evidence-based practice. *British Journal of Social Work*, *38*(5), 885–899. doi:10.1093/bjsw/bcl377

Williams, J., Leamy, V., Bird, C., Harding, J., Larsen, C., & LeBoutillier, L. et al. (2012). Measures of the recovery orientation of mental health services: Systematic review. *Social Psychiatry & Epidemiology*, *47*(11), 1827–1835. doi:10.1007/s00127-012-0484-y PMID:22322983

World Health Organisation. (2003). *The mental health context. (The mental health policy and service guidance package)*. Retrieved from http://www.who.int/mental_health/resources/en/context.PDF

## ADDITIONAL READING

Australian Association of Social Workers. (2008). *Practice standards for mental health social workers*. Canberra: Author.

Bland, R., & Epstein, M. (2008). Encouraging principles of consumer participation and partnership: The way forward in mental health practice in Australia. In S. Taylor, M. Foster, & J. Fleming (Eds.), *Healthcare practice in Australia: Policy, context and innovations* (pp. 239–254). South Melbourne, Vic., Australia: Oxford University Press.

Boston Consulting Group. (2006). *Improving mental health outcomes in Victoria: The next wave of reform*. Retrieved from http://www.health.vic.gov.au/mentalhealth/publications/boston-report060706.pdf

Bradstreet, S. (2006). Harnessing the "lived experience": Formalising peer support approaches to promote recovery. *Mental Health Review*, *11*(2), 33–37. doi:10.1108/13619322200600019

Cameron, N., & McDermott, F. (2007). *Social work and the body*. Basingstoke, Hampshire: Palgrave MacMillan.

Crosbie, D. W. (2009). Mental health policy: Stumbling in the dark? *The Medical Journal of Australia*, *190*, S43–S45. Retrieved from https://www.mja.com.au/journal/ PMID:19220174

Davidson, L., Rakfeldt, J., & Strauss, J. (2010). *The roots of the recovery movement in psychiatry: Lessons learned*. Chichester, UK: Wiley-Blackwell. doi:10.1002/9780470682999

Department of Health and Ageing. (2010). *National mental health report 2010: Summary of 15 years of reform in Australia's mental health services under the national mental health strategy 1993-2008*. Canberra: Commonwealth of Australia.

Ife, J. (2001). *Human rights and social work: Towards rights-based practice*. Cambridge, UK: Cambridge University Press. doi:10.1017/CBO9781139164689

Jorm, A. F. (2011). Australia's Better Access initiative: Do the evaluation data support the critics? *The Australian and New Zealand Journal of Psychiatry*, *45*(9), 700–704. doi:10.3109/00048674.2011.604302 PMID:21888607

Meadows, G., Farhall, J., Fossey, E., Grigg, M., McDermott, F., & Singh, B. (Eds.). (2012). *Mental health in Australia: Collaborative community practice* (3rd ed.). Sydney, NSW: Oxford University Press.

National Advisory Council on Mental Health. (2010). *Fitting together the pieces: Collaborative care models for adults with severe and persistent mental illness – Final project report*. Retrieved from http://www.health.gov.au/internet/main/publishing.nsf/Content/0ABBFD239D790377CA257BF0001C6CBC/$File/colsev.pdf

National Mental Health Commission. (2013). *A contributing life: The 2013 national report card on mental health and suicide prevention*. Retrieved from http://www.mentalhealthcommission.gov.au/media/94321/Report_Card_2013_full.pdf

Pilgrim, D. (2005). *Key concepts in mental health-care*. London: SAGE.

Rapp, C. A. (1998). *The strengths model: Case management with people suffering from severe and persistent mental illness*. New York, N.Y: Oxford University Press.

Rosen, A., Gurr, R., & Fanning, P. (2010). The future of community-centred health services in Australia: Lessons from the mental health sector. *Australian Health Review, 34*(1), 106–115. doi:10.1071/AH09741 PMID:20334766

Rosenberg, S., & Hickie, I. (2013). Managing madness, mental health and complexity in public policy. *Evidence Base, 3,* 1-19.Retrieved from http://journal.anzsog.edu.au/

Rosenberg, S. P., Mendoza, J., & Russell, L. (2012). Well meant or well spent?: Accountability for $8 billion of mental health reform. *The Medical Journal of Australia, 196*(3), 159–161. doi:10.5694/mja11.11553 PMID:22339513

Saleeby, D. (2001). Commentary: The diagnostic strengths manual? *Social Work, 46*(2), 183–187. doi:10.1093/sw/46.2.183 PMID:11329647

Whiteford, H. A., & Buckingham, W. J. (2005). Ten years of mental health service reform in Australia: Are we getting it right? *The Medical Journal of Australia, 182,* 396–400. Retrieved from https://www.mja.com.au/journal PMID:15850436

## KEY TERMS AND DEFINITIONS

**Collaborative Mental Healthcare:** The needs of service-users identified as central to the work of a team of multidisciplinary mental health service providers, including consumers, who address the problems, goals, and issues presented by the service-user, with emphasis on the creation of equal relationships amongst all participants and recognition of the service-user's right to autonomy and choice.

**Community Mental Health:** In Australia, the vast majority of mental healthcare is provided in institutions, most commonly public hospitals but also private hospitals, psychiatric specialist hospitals, and prisons. Community mental health refers to services and care provided in non-hospital (or other institutional) settings. It includes services provided in or accessible from the home. Community mental health services help people with a mental illness to live independently and manage their recovery and wellness.

**Peer Support:** In mental health, peer support is a form of consumer participation in which peers, that is, people with expertise by experience, assist fellow consumers.

**Recovery:** As used in mental health, this is a concept which privileges lived experience-based knowledge, emphasising the potential for a satisfying life beyond symptoms where supports are available to enable people to live well in spite of them.

**Social Work:** The social work profession facilitates social change and development, social cohesion, and the empowerment and liberation of people. Principles of social justice, human rights, collective responsibility, and respect for diversity are central to social work. Underpinned by theories of social work, social sciences, humanities, and indigenous knowledge, social work engages people and structures to address life challenges and enhance well-being.

# Chapter 7
# Child Protection, "Dirty Work," and Interagency Collaboration

**Annette Flaherty**
*Centre for Remote Health, Flinders University, Australia*

## ABSTRACT

*Working in partnership is considered a key mechanism for effective delivery of services to children and families. However, child protection system inquiries in Australia and internationally repeatedly highlight strained relationships and poor collaboration within the child protection service system. Despite organisational, technological, legislative, and procedural changes to enhance and facilitate interagency working, these interventions have generally failed to realise this goal. Trust and shared values are considered integral to effective interagency working. Developing trust and thus effective working relationships is fraught when one group of workers in the service system is perceived to be "dirty workers." This chapter explores the concept of "dirty work." It suggests that the way in which failure to attend to belief systems at the organisational, professional, and community level, particularly as they relate to the professional stigma which attaches to the practice of child protection work, inhibits the ability of agencies to work successfully together.*

## INTRODUCTION

Child protection work necessarily involves "examining a family's private habits" (Morris, 2005, p. 135) and it holds up to scrutiny secrets and practices that someone has assessed as harmful to children. It is perhaps about airing a family's "dirty laundry". The work challenges norms about the privacy and autonomy of the family and exposes family members to shame, humiliation and, at times, criminal proceedings. Child protection work also attracts considerable media attention,

typically when things go wrong. In such cases, the workers are perceived to have either failed in their mandate to protect children or used their coercive powers to intervene in a family inappropriately.

In order to go about their work of investigating and ensuring the safety and well-being of children, child protection workers perform what might be called "necessary evils", that is, they "must knowingly and intentionally" risk causing harm to another "in the service of achieving some greater good or purpose" (Margolis & Molinsky, 2008, p. 847). The harm may result to the adults

DOI: 10.4018/978-1-4666-6563-7.ch007

through the exposure of "private" family business or to the children; for example, removing children, whilst necessary to ensure their safety, will also cause them distress.

Performing necessary evils can result in powerful and disruptive emotions in the person undertaking such tasks (Margolis & Molinsky, 2008), in part because such activities pose a threat to the person's self-assessment that they are moral and just. Failing to perform such activities when required may threaten their assessment of themselves as a responsible professional (Margolis & Molinsky, 2008). As well as these potential threats to the child protection worker's personal and professional identity, child protection work can be understood as "dirty work": work that is important but physically, socially, or morally tainted (Hughes, 1951, 1962).

The performance of dirty work impacts on occupational identity; ineffectively dealing with the stigma of job related taint is thought to result in lower job commitment and performance and to influence high turnover of workers engaged in such work (Ashforth & Kreiner, 1999). It can also affect the relationships which dirty workers have with others. Internal strategies to manage taint and enhance professional self-esteem may result in dirty workers growing cautious in their dealing with others and relationships can be marked by hostility and defensiveness (Ashforth & Krenier, 1999). This has important consequences for multi-agency working which requires relationships of professional trust and respect to be effective (Freeth & Reeves, 2004; Newell & Swan, 2000).

This chapter explores the impact of the dirty work label on the achievement of effective interagency working in child and family work. In doing so, it draws on the findings from a research study which involved in-depth interviews with child protection workers in the Northern Territory. The study found that these workers were aware of their dirty work label and that this had a negative impact on the development of strong inter-agency collaborations. The chapter will,

firstly, describe what is meant by dirty work and consider whether child protection work is dirty work. Secondly, the chapter will explore issues relating to interagency collaboration. The chapter will then consider a case study of child protection practice in the Northern Territory which found that practitioners were aware of their stigmatised professional identity and that this identity had a negative impact on their ability to develop trusting relationships with other workers. Finally, the chapter makes recommendations for education, practice, and future research.

## DIRTY WORK

The concept of dirty work was first used in 1951 by Hughes to refer to those occupations that are physically, socially, or morally tainted but that are necessary for the survival of society. Hughes (1951) suggested that work could be dirty because "it may be simply disgusting. It may be a symbol of degradation, something that wounds one's dignity. Finally it may be dirty work in that it in some way goes counter to the more heroic of our moral conceptions" (p. 319). He noted that when society delegates dirty work to groups who "act as agents on society's behalf", society then stigmatises those groups, "effectively disowning and disavowing the work it has mandated" (Drew, Mills, & Gassaway, 2007, p. 4). Hughes (1962) argued that it is because dirty workers do the dirty work that others can continue to regard themselves as clean and, therefore, superior. Ashforth and Kreiner (1999) argue that "the taint affects people's relationships with the 'dirty workers' even while they may applaud the workers" (p. 416).

Ashforth and Kreiner (1999) provide criteria for each of the three forms of taint. Firstly, *physical* taint results when an occupation is directly associated with rubbish or death (e.g. cleaner or funeral director) or is thought to be performed under particularly noxious or dangerous conditions (e.g. soldier or factory worker). Secondly, *social* taint results when the work brings the worker into regular contact with people who are themselves stigmatised (social worker or corrections officer) or where the worker appears to have a servile relationship to others (personal care worker or maid). Finally, *moral* taint results when an occupation is seen as sinful or of questionable virtue (prostitute or tattoo artist) or where the worker is thought to employ methods that are deceptive, intrusive, or confrontational (tabloid journalist or police officer). The key question about dirty work is, "How can you do it?" (Ashford & Kreiner, 1999, p. 91). Psychiatric nursing (Godin, 2000) is an example of a tainted profession both as a result of close association with people who routinely transgress social ideals of right behaviour and because there is the use of coercive force to ensure patient compliance. Some occupations, such as psychiatric nursing, may be considered "dirty work" on multiple dimensions.

Kreiner, Ashforth and Sluss (2006) argue that dirty work occupations vary according to the breadth and depth of their dirtiness. Breadth refers to the proportion of work that is dirty or to the centrality of the dirt to the occupational identity, and depth refers to the intensity of the dirtiness and the extent to which a worker is directly involved in the dirtiness. They suggest that the breadth and depth of dirtiness tends to be greater in occupations tainted on multiple dimensions, although there are many occupations that have high breadth or depth because of a single or predominant dimension, and they cite the social taint of welfare workers as an example of this.

## IS CHILD PROTECTION WORK DIRTY WORK?

From its beginnings in the 1800s, child protection work concerned itself with pollution: children who were "ragged and dirty and surrounded by moral and physical pollution" and exposed to vice, idleness, and crime in morally dangerous homes (Scott & Swain, 2002, p. 20). Such children and families were perceived to pose a threat to social stability. By the 1960s, child protection work was faced with critics who "alleged child saving derived from the middle class desire to control the 'dangerous and perishing classes'; the push from middle class professions to improve their status and expand the scope of their work; and the desire of middle class women to widen their sphere of influence" (Scott & Swain, 2002, p. 7). Child saving, it was suggested, had less to do with the children and more to do with remaking the working class so that it adopted middle class child rearing norms to satisfy the demand of monopoly capitalism. Although middle class children may also have been abused or neglected, such children were able to be presented as "clean and well clothed, leaving inspectors nothing to object to" (Scott & Swain, 2002, p. 78). Child abuse and neglect, critics asserted, was a symptom of oppression and poverty, and individual level intervention was at best paternalistic, a "band-aid", and at worst, social control and the policing of disempowered families. From this perspective, working class families need to be protected from the oppressive use of State power enacted by the activities of child protection workers; child protection work is, therefore, morally suspect.

Despite changes to practice which draw on strengths based approaches to working with families, current criticisms of child protection systems, particularly in the United Kingdom and Australia, show continuity with these earlier concerns. Critics assert that the growth in and dominance of a managerialist and audit culture which seeks to locate blame has led to an over reliance on procedures to avoid potential risk and a preoccupation with social control rather than the provision of care. It is asserted that child protection work as a result adopts a forensic approach to the detriment of those families needing help which precludes the development of relationships with the families and communities they ostensibly serve (Lonne, Parton, Thomson, & Harries, 2008).

In Australia, there is a potential further source of moral stigma for child protection work. Embedded within the history of child welfare in Australia is the history of the "Stolen Generations", the term used to describe the forcible removal of Indigenous children from their parents to achieve the policy of social assimilation. The *Bringing Them Home Report* (Human Rights and Equal Opportunity Commission, 1997) concluded that the practices of removing Indigenous children under a policy of assimilation was racially discriminatory, a gross violation of human rights, and genocidal. There is considerable national shame associated with this period of Australian history. The continued overrepresentation of Indigenous children among child protection systems has led some commentators to suggest that "there is a risk that much contemporary child welfare law and practice is actually assimilation in a veiled disguise as the values of the dominant group are imposed" (Stanley, Tomison, & Pocock, 2003, p. 20). This view positions current child protection work as not merely inheriting a history which is shameful but as a contemporary organization which enacts a policy of assimilation; a policy linked to genocide. This is especially important in the context of child protection practice in jurisdictions such as the Northern Territory, Australia, where over one-third of the population is Indigenous. Recent work by Ashforth and Kreiner (2013) suggest bigger differences exist between moral dirty work and the other two forms of taint. They argue that moral dirty work poses a greater identity threat to its practitioners, relies on insiders as a social buffer, and that such practitioners have a greater tendency to condemn those who condemn them, thus raising the risk that they may remain locked in defensive postures.

## Media Reporting of Child Protection Work

Whilst it is true that media campaigns in Australia and elsewhere have helped highlight the issue of child abuse and the rights of children (Goddard & Saunders, 2001), a number of studies have explored the way that child protection work is portrayed in the media. Overwhelmingly, this work has illustrated the negative portrayal of those who work in child protection. A study in the United Kingdom by Franklin (1999) found only 30 "positive" stories in a sample of about 2,000 reports. Ayre (2001), writing about the situation in the United Kingdom, asserts that media reporting there is often unbalanced and portrays child protection workers as incompetent and unreliable because they have either been too harsh or too lenient with parents or carers. More recently, the Social Work Task Force (2009) in England found that "social work is under continuous attack" (p. 62) and that in the media social work had largely been reduced to child protection work: "The media focus on harrowing cases of child abuse has also led to worries that social work has been reduced to high-end child protection in popular understanding, thus disregarding other important aspects of social work" (pp. 48-49).

Ayre (2001) suggests the nature of media reporting about child protection work has led to a "climate of mistrust" (p. 889), with child protection workers described in the popular press as "child stealers", "abusers of authority", and "the SAS in cardigans" (p. 890). Further, confidentiality requirements prohibiting child protection workers from speaking to the media can lead to perceptions that workers are stalling or indecisive (Ayre, 2001).

In Australia, Wilczynski and Sinclair (1999), in their analysis of coverage of child protection reporting, found most attention was focused on child abuse horror stories. Mendes (2001), for example, noted that reports about child protection tended to be sensationalist and simplistic, revealing considerable hostility toward the child protection workforce. Mendes detailed Australian newspaper reporting which described child protection workers as "out of control" and "unaccountable", concluding that individual child protection social workers appear to "receive disproportionate attention and criticisms compared to other professionals" (p. 31).

Child protection work, then, has often been criticised for being judgemental, imposing white middle class values on people who are marginalised as a result of class or culture, of being racist, of punishing poor people, and of using power inappropriately. Based on the Kreiner, Ashforth, and Sluss (2006) typology, child protection work would be considered an occupation with *pervasive stigma*. As members of society and consumers of media, child protection workers are aware of their poor portrayal and its impact on community perceptions. It is not surprising that working in statutory child protection work is the least preferred employment option for Australian social work students (Woodcock & Dixon, 2005).

## Interagency Collaboration

The complex needs of vulnerable children and families cannot be satisfactorily responded to by one agency or sector; in order to address the needs of such families, agencies need to work together collaboratively to ensure the safety and well-being of children. The lack of effective interagency working, both at the front line and strategically, has been noted in a series of child protection system inquiries both in Australia and internationally (Bamblett, Bath & Roseby, 2010). Even where the policy and procedural framework exists to support better interagency working, they have not proved sufficient to achieve widespread implementation of collaborative practices (Smith & Mogro-Wilson, 2007).

The literature on collaboration to protect children identifies the complexity of the concept itself; the term describes a range of, or different ways of, working together. Typically, five levels of working together have been identified, existing on a "continuum from informal and local collaboration to formal and whole agency collaboration" (Horwath & Morrison, 2007, p. 56). These different levels of working together have been described as communication, co-operation, co-ordination, coalition, and integration (Horwath & Morrison, 2007). This chapter adopts a broad understanding of interagency collaboration as a process "though which parties who see different aspects of a problem can consistently explore their differences and search for solutions that go beyond their own limited vision of what is possible" (Gray, 1989, p. 5). This broad definition of collaboration stresses the search for shared norms and the interdependent and interactive nature of collaboration. Further, it suggests that for collaboration to evolve "the integrative elements manifest in personal relationships, psychological contracts and informal understandings and commitments need to supplant the aggregative elements manifest in formal organisational roles and legal contracts" (Thomson & Perry, 2006, p. 22). The interactive process of collaboration is not well understood (Thomson & Perry, 2006).

Problems relating to the implementation of interagency working have been identified. These include a lack of shared ownership of the collaboration; organisational structures which do not support working together, for example, they inhibit the sharing of information; conflicting professional ideologies and mistrust; inadequate resources; confusion about different roles and responsibilities; and communication problems (Milbourne, Macrea & Maguire, 2003). In exploring interagency collaboration between child protection and mental health services in Australia, Darlington, Feeney and Rixon (2005) found that inadequate resources, the lack of a procedural framework to support information sharing, professional boundary issues, a poor understanding of each other's role, and unrealistic expectations of each other contributed to poor uptake of collaborative working together.

Collaborative practice is thus influenced by both individual level factors and organisational level factors, although most research focuses on organisational level adoption of policies; there is less research which explores individual level influences (Smith & Mogro-Wilson, 2007). However, beliefs and attitudes of staff influence the ability to engage in collaborative practice (Frambach & Schillewaert, 2002). For example, Cameron, Macdonald, Turner and Lloyd (2007) have indicated that a reluctance to engage, turf warfare, and perceptions of the professionalism or otherwise of the "other" occurring at the statutory-voluntary agency interface are important influences on collaboration. Respecting the role and workers of the other agency is considered fundamental to working together (Scott, 2005).

Whilst working together successfully requires supportive structures and governance arrangements (Huxham & Vangen, 2000), the interactional and relational components of working together is critical. Problems of communication and trust have been a key feature identified in public inquiries into child deaths and child protection systems in Australia and internationally (Bamblett, Bath & Roseby, 2010; Horwath & Morrison, 2007). Bryson, Crosby, and Stone (2006) describe "trust as the lubricant and the glue" of successful working together, both facilitating the work of collaboration and holding the collaboration together (p. 47). Newell and Swan (2000) assert that high levels of trust are necessary because this will facilitate communication, and they note that trust involves both dealing with risk and uncertainty and accepting vulnerability.

Horwath and Morrison (2007) note that under such conditions, trust, a key requisite for working together, "becomes impossible as professionals are drawn into an unthinking and rigid allegiance to their own agency, service or discipline in which 'watching one's back' to avoid responsibility or blame becomes the underlying driver for behaviour" (p. 65). Gask (2005) describes these attitudes and beliefs as the "covert barriers" to successful working together and argues that if change is to occur within organisations it is "essential to acknowledge the covert barriers…thus allowing them to become overt" (p. 1791). The importance of both trust and good communication to interagency collaboration explains why simply putting formal collaboration mechanisms in place does not always lead to *collaborative practice*. According to Newell and Swan (2000) these do not lead to the development of informal integration which underpin the emergence of what they call "companion and competence trust" (p. 1321).

In a review of the literature, Horwath and Morrison (2007) suggest that most studies that look at difficulties with interagency collaboration fail to take account of the wider context of interest group power structures and socio-political processes. These structures and processes include discourses about child protection practice which transcends the local, whilst being at the same time locally reproduced in the interactions between child protection workers and others in the service network. Such discourses include the categorisation of child protection work as dirty work.

## Dirty Work and Interagency Collaboration

There has been little attention paid in the research literature to child protection work as a dirty work occupation, though there has been considerable mention in news reports and inquiries describing child protection workers as defensive, beleaguered, and stigmatised. Where stigma and social work practice are the subject of research the concept of spoiled identity tends to be used with reference to the *consumers* of social work or child protection services.

Research in other practice settings suggests that dirty workers are attuned to how others think of them and the stigma associated with their work (Ashforth & Kreiner, 1999; Bolton, 2005; Tracy, 2004). The difficulty for the dirty worker is that when they look beyond the self for validation it is unlikely to be forthcoming. Moreover, they too will have internalised the messages about their dirty work. Research elsewhere has illustrated that issues of status and professional identity influence social work practice. In the United States, for example, Keiser (2010) found that workers in social security programs are cognizant of the "micro network of vertical and horizontal relationships" (p. 251) which surround them, and their decision-making is influenced by how they understand other workers in the service network to perceive them. In Scotland, Halliday, Burns, Hutton, McNeill and Tata (2009) found that social workers in the criminal justice system perceived they had low status in relation to judges and lawyers and wrote their court reports in a manner they judged would enhance their status as professionals with these other professionals.

Given the importance of social validation to one's sense of self, it should follow that a dirty work label acts to undermine an individual's attempts to identify with their occupation. The work of Ashforth and Kreiner (1999), among others, demonstrates that this is not always the case and that the dirty work label coupled with strong pressures for group formation can foster defence mechanisms (taint management strategies) which transform the meaning of "dirt", moderate the impact of social perceptions of dirtiness, and create strong work cultures. However, contextual factors, such as high staff turnover, can inhibit group formation and thus strong occupational culture, even where dirty workers engage in these taint management defence mechanisms (Ashforth & Kreiner, 1999). Here, dirty work categorisation can affect leadership, teamwork, motivation, and inter group relations and, as a result of a climate of distrust, undermine the cohesiveness, morale, and

effectiveness of a whole organisation (Paetzold, Dipboye & Elsbach, 2008). Research in other contexts has found that the taint management strategies developed by dirty workers to moderate the impact of their status can affect both decision-making and working collaboratively. Workers grow cautious in their dealings with other professionals, focus on those aspects of the job which may increase their status, and dismiss the knowledge and competence of other professionals (Ashforth & Kreiner, 1999).

Blyth and Milner (1990), Butler (1996) and Buckley (2003) argue that the nature of child protection work itself works against effective interagency working because child protection work is considered dirty work. However, there has been little research which explores the impact of dirty work on interagency collaboration in child protection beyond Pithouse's (1998) ethnographic study of child protection workers in England. Pithouse (1998) found that child protection workers believed they were used as a "dustbin" for other agencies' problems; this led to child protection workers questioning the competence of others, minimising or dismissing the concerns expressed by other professionals about families with whom they worked, and telling atrocity stories. The aim of these strategies was to "bolster the occupational self-image" (p. 24). Pithouse (1998) explains that "an espirit de corps of embattled welfare veterans is created as a bulwark against outside groups who must be suffered, manipulated, ignored or subtly educated in the ways of social work" (p. 27).

## Case Study: Dirty work and Child Protection Practice in the Northern Territory, Australia

As identified above, child protection system inquiries frequently cite poor interagency working as contributing to system failures and the inability to achieve the best outcomes for children and families. A recent child protection inquiry in Australia's Northern Territory (Bamblett, Bath &

Roseby, 2010) highlighted that professional relationships between the child protection agency and others in the service network were characterised by hostility, and the child protection service was described by others as secretive, unpredictable, inconsistent, and judgemental. Although this inquiry acknowledged the influence of beliefs and attitudes as contributors to effective working together, ultimately the recommendations focused on legislation and the development of procedures for the sharing of information as the solution to poor working together. Such a focus has been the pattern with many other child protection system inquiries both nationally and internationally.

Despite the commonly "accepted wisdom" that stigma attaches to child protection practice in Australia, particularly in relation to practice with Indigenous peoples (Age Round Table on child protection, 2009), there is negligible research exploring this topic. This case study focuses on the Northern Territory, Australia. The Northern Territory is the least populated state of Australia, with a population of 227,900 and a land mass of 1,352,200 square kilometres. Most of the Northern Territory is described as remote or very remote. In addition to having the youngest population, the Northern Territory also has the highest proportion of Indigenous residents in Australia, with one third of the population being Indigenous compared with approximately two and half percent of the nation's population being Indigenous (Australian Bureau of Statistics, 2011). Reflecting the socio-economic disadvantage of Indigenous children, the child protection service is dominated by practice with Indigenous families, with neglect being the most common reason for notification to the service (Bamblett, Bath & Roseby, 2010).

## The Study

This study set out to understand how child protection workers in the Northern Territory operationalised child neglect; it did not set out to explore professional stigma or dirty work. As part of this study, child protection workers were asked how they viewed their role. In answering this question, the participants spoke about how they believed others in the service network viewed them, and these responses highlighted their sense of isolation and marginalisation within the service network.

The study received ethics approval from the Human Research Ethics Committee of the Northern Territory Department of Health and Menzies School of Health Research; the Central Australian Human Research Ethics Committee; and the Monash University Human Research Ethics Committee.

## The Literature Review and Search Strategy

As an initial step, a literature review was undertaken using the key words *"social work"*, *"child protection"*, and *"dirty work"*. These references were supplemented by useful works appearing in the reference lists of relevant material.

## The Participants

Child protection workers from seven offices of the statutory child protection service across the Northern Territory were invited to participate in this research during 2008 and 2009. Eligible workers were those employed within the statutory child protection service in a professional capacity and whose job required them to assess and/or make decisions about referred cases of child neglect. Excluded from this research were members of the Child Abuse Taskforce whose primary focus is cases of child sexual abuse and, for pragmatic reasons, those who worked in the Mobile Child Protection team. All offices were sent an information sheet outlining the research question and the researcher attended six of the seven offices to answer questions about the research. The office which was not visited had, at the time of the research, only one worker and the cost of visiting this office was prohibitive.

Approximately 70 per cent of participants were women. Half of participants had an undergraduate degree as their highest educational qualification and 30 percent a post graduate degree. Approximately 30 per cent had been employed for less than one year and 50 percent for over three years. Sixteen percent of participants were Indigenous.

Given the lack of available demographic data on the child protection workforce in the Northern Territory, it is not possible to compare those who participated with those who did not in order to conclude whether there were differences in ways that would affect the findings. However, participants were compared to a national survey of the child protection workforce and where possible Northern Territory specific data, and no marked differences were found (Martin & Healey, 2010).

## The Method

In-depth interviews were conducted with the 30 child protection workers who participated in this study. Interviews ranged from between one hour and three hours, with the average time being one and a half hours. Interviews were audio-taped and transcribed by the researcher and transcripts sent back to participants for approval prior to data analysis. Data was analysed using thematic analysis which is a method for identifying, analysing, and reporting patterns or themes within qualitative data; a "theme captures something important about the data in relation to the research question and represents some level of patterned response or meaning within the data set" (Braun & Clarke 2006, p. 82). As noted above, this study did not set out to explore professional stigma; themes relating to stigma were generated inductively from the qualitative data.

## Limitations

This is a small scale exploratory study which was conducted during a period of considerable national media scrutiny of the child protection workforce in the Northern Territory. As a result, child protection workers in this study may have been more sensitive in their assessments of how others viewed them and their practice. Further, it may be that practitioners who were particularly affected by their status in relation to other professionals or who struggled with their work with cases of child neglect may have been more likely to participate in this study, thus resulting in a more pessimistic account of practice than exists more generally.

## Findings

Participants in this study expressed considerable ambivalence about the value of child protection work in cases of child neglect and wondered whether the intervention caused more harm than help:

*I am not sure how to put this but I do question a lot of the time whether half or three quarters of the stuff we are doing is actually necessary or actually achieves anything....I personally think we are guilty of doing more harm than good.*

Moreover, many of the child protection workers understood the work they did as *punishment* and argued that their intervention should only be reserved for those who deserved a punitive response.

Most importantly, the participants expressed the belief that other professionals viewed them negatively. They were acutely aware of their stigmatised professional identify. Child protection workers spoke of the "distrust, but also accusations of blatant lying on (our) part; we are often called liars...and there is a lot of tolerance for that kind of sledging". Others described being "seen as the enemy".

All of the workers spoke of often feeling powerless, although they believed that others perceived them as "all powerful". Child protection workers in this study also believed that other professionals assessed that they used their power capriciously, taking "children away for no reason", that "we all sit in here and make these arbitrary decisions". One participant recalled: "a lawyer said to me outside court, you have the power of the Third Reich".

Overwhelmingly, when the child protection workers talked about child neglect it was practice with Indigenous families which dominated. In this study the child protection workers believed that others assessed their practice as continuing that of "the Welfare" and the history of forced removal of Indigenous children: "Because it has been said to us…with the neglect, you get it thrown in your face. It is said, 'You are doing this again, this is the Stolen Generations'".

Neglect cases embodied the risk that workers would be accused of culturally inappropriate practices. This positioned child protection work as involving the imposition of culturally inappropriate values onto Indigenous people, the inappropriate use of power, punishing a marginalised and disadvantaged group, and allegations of racism.

The child protection workers were also sensitive that the only kind of media reporting they received is "negative": "You are either the awful evil people who have stolen this poor person's child….or you are not doing enough, that baby needs to be removed."

Not surprisingly, when workers talked about how they managed to continue in the role, the support of other child protection workers was critical. Without that support, participants stated, the job would be "unworkable." It was only with other child protection workers that they could develop "trust, absolute trust."

Workers in this study described a world of practice where they felt isolated and defensive, distrustful of others and in turn distrusted by others, perceived as all powerful when they felt helpless, and sensitive to the moral taint associated with being seen as the primary inheritors and current enactors of the forcible removal of Indigenous children. In turn, these workers questioned the referrals made to their service by other health and community service professionals. Similar to the workers in Pithouse's (1998) study, these workers also believed they were *used* by other agencies. In this study, the workers suggested that notifications to the child protection service were inappropriate, and rather than being about child protection concerns the notifications resulted from others not doing their jobs properly: "I am sick of other agencies, education being one and health being another, that when it gets too hard for them, well, let's notify child protection. I am not sure they have done everything they necessarily can do."

Moreover, these referrals were frequently understood to be the result of judgemental practice by others, that is, they accused others of the very things of which they believed themselves accused. Whilst this response served to enhance intragroup allegiance, workers were sceptical that these charges were taken seriously by others or enhanced their status in relation to other professionals.

## Discussion

Front-line workers in health or community services want to see themselves as caring professionals (Rosenthal & Peccei, 2006) and participants in this study were no different. This study found that work with cases of child neglect in particular threatened to challenge the desired self-image of child protection workers. The case study illustrates that issues related to stigma and professional identity negatively impact on child protection practitioners and the development of relationships with other professionals based on trust. As discussed above, trust is considered critical to interagency working. Many of these workers live and work in small towns and the effect of a stigmatised professional identity may be more potent in this setting than in metropolitan settings where there is greater separation between the personal and professional self (Pugh, 2007).

Research which has explored the impact of status on decision-making in the broader community services field has shown that because workers operate in networks of power relationships, decisions are influenced by how workers understand others in the service system to perceive them (Keiser, 2010; May & Winter 2009; Maynard-Moody & Musheno, 2003). Practice may be influenced by the desire to gain credibility and improve relative status in relation to those who possess higher status, for example, criminal justice social workers hoping to impress judges and orienting their court reports to that end (Halliday et al., 2009). Alternatively, where practitioners experience marginalisation and hostility from the wider service system, they may endeavour to protect their self-image by a focus on questioning the legitimacy of other practitioners (Ashforth & Kreiner, 1999; Pithouse, 1998). As a result, they grow increasingly cautious in their dealing with other professionals, with resultant professional relationships marked by hostility and defensiveness as marginalised workers endeavour to enhance their professional self-esteem (Ashforth & Kreiner, 1999).

The participants in this study were well aware of their tainted professional identity. Although this taint may apply to all child protection work in the Northern Territory and elsewhere, it was with cases of child neglect that its stain was most potent. It is in these cases where personal or dominant cultural values threaten to play out in the assessment task, and historically it is cases of child neglect where accusations of the assimilative tendency of the child protection service have occurred (Stanley, Tomison, & Pocock, 2003).

Participants considered that they were perceived by other professionals as the *enemy*; morally tainted by being practitioners working for an agency perceived to be the primary inheritor of the Stolen Generations; and, in cases of child neglect, potentially enacting through the imposition of "white middle class values" culturally insensitive practice and previous policies of assimilation.

Further, participants were conscious of the way that child protection professionals' work in general, and their work with Indigenous families in particular, had been framed and reported in the local and national media. They were sensitive to the way they and their practice were perceived by the broader community and defensive about the possibility of "trial by media". Defensive practice in response to media framing and reporting has previously been documented (Ayre, 2001; Taylor, Beckett, & McKeigue, 2008).

Operating in a context where they perceived their work to be considered dirty work, participants described a practice world where they felt isolated and defensive, distrustful of others, and in turn distrusted. Consequently, as suggested by the dirty work literature (Ashforth & Kreiner, 1999) and demonstrated by Pithouse (1998), strategies were developed to moderate the impact of their status in ways which influenced decision-making and collaborative working. Similar to the practitioners in Pithouse's study, these strategies were primarily designed to "bolster their occupational self-image" rather than to improve their image to others (p. 24).

Firstly, participants focussed on the incompetence of other health and community service workers and the way they "used" the child protection service. Secondly, in focussing on incompetence, participants also questioned the legitimacy of child neglect referrals made by the broader health and community service sector to the child protection service. In rejecting the appropriateness of referrals made by other professionals and narrowing the kinds of families with whom they are involved (that is, those who *deserved* to be involved with the child protection service), the gulf between the child protection service and other professionals is widened. However, this response risks reinforcing practitioners' perceived marginalised professional status, resulting in agency practice not being in synchrony with broader professional or community norms.

Despite their attempts to "bolster their occupational self-image" (Pithouse, 1998, p. 24), the ability of the child protection practitioners in this study to do this successfully in relation to cases of child neglect was fraught. Their ability to manage stigma successfully was related to macro-level discourses about their work, as found in other studies looking at dirty work occupations (Tracey & Scott, 2006). Moreover, participants in this study had to a large extent internalised the view that their work with cases of child neglect was ineffective at best and abusive at worst. They remained confused and uncertain about what was the "right" response in these cases, fearful of creating another Stolen Generation and, at the same time, concerned that children were being left in undesirable care situations which they felt powerless to improve. This ambivalence about the value of child protection practice in cases of child neglect influenced the way it was operationalised and left the workers defensive in their dealings with others.

## Solutions and Recommendations

This chapter has focussed on the interactional and relational dimensions of interagency collaboration; however, it is clear that these occur within an organisational, cultural, and political context. As noted earlier, the practice of child protection challenges deeply held norms about the privacy and autonomy of the family and thus is a contested and politicised area of social work practice. As Lonne, Parton, Thomson and Harries suggest (2008), there is a "significant dispute concerning what exactly the social mandate and functions" of statutory child protection services should be, who the client(s) of these services is (the child, parents/carers or the community?) and "what the work should entail" (investigation or assistance?) (p. 57). As a result

*… their mission, goals and practice approaches are contested among a variety of dependent actors.…their actions and achievements are usually subject to considerable criticisms, which is often couched in the language of "accountability" but is nevertheless tantamount to a pervasive "blame culture." (Lonne et al., 2008, p. 57)*

In response to the realisation that a focus on investigation and detection both fails to protect children and diverts resources away from supportive and preventative services, a number of jurisdictions have endeavoured to enhance family support services and divert families who require support away from the statutory service system toward voluntary service provision (Bamblett, Bath & Roseby, 2010). Within such approaches, the goal is to reserve involvement with the statutory child protection services for families whose children are at high risk. However, whilst such approaches might result in child protection workers endeavouring to work with a "lighter touch", any shift in policy or practice approaches occurs in an organisational and political context where minimising the risk of a fatal case of child abuse, and the public and media blame that accompanies this, still exerts a significant influence on child protection practice (Hayes & Spratt, 2009). Ever increasing notifications to statutory child protection services in Australia suggests this is also influencing the practice of non-statutory health and community service professionals as well (Bamblett, Bath & Roseby, 2010).

In describing child protection as a "wicked problem", that is, a social problem which is difficult to address because there is incomplete or contradictory knowledge, and because of the inter-connected nature of the problems with other social problems, Devaney and Spratt (2009) argue that the current technical rational policy making approach is flawed and results in a focus on short term outcomes such as immediate safety.

Such a focus primarily reflects the outputs of child protection systems rather than longer term outcomes which address the needs of children. How to respond to "wicked problems" and answering questions related to clarifying the nature of the problem and how best to deal with it is the outcome of prevailing cultural and political values, including those related to the nature of the relationship between the State and its citizens. An approach which frames the issue as one of child welfare focuses on participation, partnership, and assistance. However, a framing of the issue as *child protection* shifts the focus to a forensic approach, requiring investigation about who caused harm. The implications of these different frames have been addressed in the research literature, for example, in describing the difference between approaches in Sweden and Canada. Khoo, Hyvonen and Nygren (2003) note that in Sweden statutory child protection workers approach referrals ready to give assistance. In Canada, service is provided only to the most vulnerable and is narrowly focused on protection. These front-line differences reflect broader cultural and political differences about the ways child maltreatment, the needs of children, and the role of the State are framed.

This discussion highlights that in order to influence the context in which statutory child protection practice occurs, including the policy context and thus the way that child protection practice is enacted as workers go about their business and the way their work is viewed by others, organisational, cultural, and political debate is required which explores the best way to understand and respond to the complex and contested issue of child maltreatment. In Australia, this clearly requires a determined effort to engage in proper negotiation and engagement with Indigenous communities and organisations (Bamblett, Bath & Roseby, 2010).

At the level of practice, there are local responses which can assist in responding to the dirty work status of statutory child protection workers. Reder and Duncan (2003) stress the importance of the psychological and interactional dimensions of interagency working, and this study has confirmed that developing trusting working relationships is fraught when one group of workers perceive themselves to be dirty workers and subsequently develop strategies to manage this by undermining the legitimacy of others. Despite organisational and technological changes designed to facilitate better interagency working, such interventions have often failed to realise their goals. It may be that without attending to belief systems at the organisational, professional, and community levels, particularly as they relate to stigma, such efforts will continue to achieve only partial success. Attending to the psychological and interactional dimensions of interagency work, including the ways in which some work is considered dirty work, needs to be included not only in social work education and training but also in that of teachers, doctors, nurses, and allied health professionals.

For those considering work in a dirty work occupation, learning strategies for self-care might usefully form a part of this education and should also be attended to during organisational orientation and staff induction. Orientation should offer the real opportunity for workers from different agencies in the child and family network to learn with, from, and about each other to reduce the likelihood of stereotypical responses.

In addition to exploring and responding to the emotional impact of being a dirty worker on child protection workers, supervisors in child protection and elsewhere should be alert to the impact of professional stigma on decision-making and interagency working during case discussions and professional or clinical supervision. Do workers exhibit strong intragroup allegiance by dismissing the competence and value of others in the service network? If so, this should be explicitly addressed.

Given the complexity of interagency working, time needs to be invested in order for different workers to appreciate potential differences in terms of agency and professional values, philosophies, and mission. Horwath and Morrison (2007) highlight the importance of multi-disciplinary training as a key lever in the facilitation of interagency collaboration. Providing space to learn with, from, and about each other assists in the development of a common language which transcends professional boundaries. Further interagency collaboration is a *practice* and workers require training in "how to do it" well. Such training should attend to both tacit knowledge (underlying beliefs) and explicit knowledge (interpersonal skills and technical knowledge).

Although research indicates that a history of difficulties and conflict can inhibit successful interagency working leading to mistrust and suspicion, frequently insufficient time is given to building up trust between prospective agency partners (Milbourne et al., 2003; Thomson & Perry, 2006). This indicates that attention needs to be paid to nurturing relationships and building trusted networks as key preparatory activities prior to any attempt to formalise joint working. Research exploring failures to implement organisational change identifies that neglecting the "people issues" are a frequent cause of failure (Horwath & Morrison, 2007).

Countering the dirty work designation remains problematic, however. Mendes (2001) suggests the social work response to hostile media reporting of child protection work has "generally been muted or ineffective" and argues that the active involvement of professional associations may assist to reframe the way that the media reports on the issue of child abuse and neglect (p. 32). This approach may open up conversation about child protection practice and practitioners, thus challenging the potency of the dirty work designation. To what degree this can counter societal discomfort relating to the moral taint associated with child protection practice remains questionable.

## FUTURE RESEARCH DIRECTIONS

There is minimal research in the Australian context about the impact of dirty work on social work practice. The findings of this study suggest that further research exploring the way in which professional stigma, or doing the dirty work, impacts on interagency collaboration is warranted.

## CONCLUSION

A number of studies (Blyth & Milner, 1990; Horwath & Morrison, 2007; Reder, Duncan, & Gray, 1993) have highlighted that strained relationships between different agencies and professionals within child protection service networks inhibit effective interagency working. Drawing on the research literature and the findings of a case study of child protection practice in the Northern Territory, Australia, this chapter has argued that child protection work can be considered dirty work: necessary but socially and morally tainted.

Being a dirty worker has important consequences for multiagency working which requires relationships of professional trust and respect to be effective (Freeth & Reeves, 2004; Newell & Swan, 2000). Despite research which explores the importance of the psychological and interactional dimensions of interagency working (Reder & Duncan, 2003), this has not been drawn on generally when solutions to the problem of poor interagency working are developed. Typically, responses favour legislative and procedural interventions. This paper has argued that without explicitly attending to the professional stigma associated with being a dirty worker such interventions will continue to meet with only muted success.

## REFERENCES

Age Round Table on child protection. (2009, November 25). *The Age*. Retrieved from http://www.theage.com.au/national/

Ashforth, B. E., & Kreiner, G. E. (1999). "How can you do it?" Dirty work and the challenge of constructing a positive identity. *Academy of Management Review*, *24*, 413–434. doi:10.5465/AMR.1999.2202129

Ashforth, B. E., & Kreiner, G. E. (2013). Dirty work and dirtier work: Differences in countering physical, social and moral stigma. *Management and Organization Review*, *10*(1), 81–108. doi:10.1111/more.12044

Australian Bureau of Statistics. (2011). *Regional statistics, NT*. Canberra, Australia: Author.

Ayre, P. (2001). Child protection and the media: Lessons from three decades. *British Journal of Social Work*, *31*(6), 887–901. doi:10.1093/bjsw/31.6.887

Bamblett, M., Bath, H., & Roseby, R. (2010). *Growing them strong together: Promoting the safety and wellbeing of the Northern Territory's children. Report of the Board of Inquiry into the Child Protection System in the Northern Territory*. Darwin: Northern Territory Government.

Blyth, E., & Milner, J. (1990). The process of inter-agency work. In M. Langan (Ed.), *Taking child abuse seriously: Contemporary issues in child protection theory and practice* (pp. 194–211). London: Unwin Hyman.

Bolton, S. C. (2005). Women's work, dirty work: The gynaecology nurse as "other". *Gender, Work and Organization*, *12*(2), 169–186. doi:10.1111/j.1468-0432.2005.00268.x

Braun, V., & Clarke, V. (2006). Using thematic analysis in psychology. *Qualitative Research in Psychology*, *3*(2), 77–101. doi:10.1191/1478088706qp063oa

Bryson, J. M., Crosby, B. C., & Stone, M. M. (2006). The design and implementation of cross-sector collaborations: Propositions from the literature. *Public Administration Review*, *66*(s1), 44–55. doi:10.1111/j.1540-6210.2006.00665.x

Buckley, H. (2003). *Child protection workforce: Beyond the rhetoric*. London: Jessica Kingsley.

Butler, S. (1996). Child protection or professional self-preservation by the baby nurses? Public health nurses and child protection in Ireland. [PubMed]. *Social Science & Medicine*, *43*(3), 303–314. doi:10.1016/0277-9536(95)00378-9

Cameron, A., Macdonald, G., Turner, W., & Lloyd, L. (2007). The challenges of joint working: Lessons from the supporting People Health Pilot evaluation. [PubMed]. *International Journal of Integrated Care*, *7*, 1–10. Retrieved from https://www.ijic.org/index.php/ijic

Darlington, Y., Feeney, J. A., & Rixon, K. (2005). Interagency collaboration between child protection and mental health services: Practices, attitudes and barriers. [PubMed]. *Child Abuse & Neglect*, *29*(10), 1085–1098. doi:10.1016/j.chiabu.2005.04.005

Devaney, J., & Spratt, T. (2009). Child abuse as a complex and wicked problem: Reflecting on policy developments in the United Kingdom in working with children and families with multiple problems. *Children and Youth Services Review*, *31*(6), 635–641. doi:10.1016/j.childyouth.2008.12.003

Drew, S. K., Mills, M., & Gassaway, B. M. (2007). *Dirty work: The social construction of taint*. Waco, TX: Baylor University Press.

Frambach, R. T., & Schillewaert, N. (2002). Organisational innovation adoption: A multi-level framework of determinants and opportunities for future research. *Journal of Business Research*, *55*(2), 163–176. doi:10.1016/S0148-2963(00)00152-1

Franklin, B. (1999). *Social policy, the media and misrepresentation*. London: Routledge.

Freeth, D., & Reeves, S. (2004). Learning to work together: Using the presage, process, product (3P) model to highlight decisions and possibilities. [PubMed]. *Journal of Interprofessional Care*, *18*(1), 43–56. doi:10.1080/13561820310001608221

Gask, L. (2005). Overt and covert barriers to the integration of primary and specialist mental health care. [PubMed]. *Social Science & Medicine*, *61*(8), 1785–1794. doi:10.1016/j.socscimed.2005.03.038

Goddard, C., & Saunders, B. (2001). *Child abuse and the media*. Canberra: Australian Insitute of Family Studies.

Godin, P. (2000). A dirty business: Caring for people who are a nuisance or a danger. [PubMed]. *Journal of Advanced Nursing*, *32*(6), 1396–1402. doi:10.1046/j.1365-2648.2000.01623.x

Gray, B. (1989). *Collaborating: Finding common ground for multi-party problems*. San Francisco: Jossey-Bass.

Halliday, S., Burns, N., Hutton, N., McNeill, F., & Tata, C. (2009). Street-level bureaucracy, interprofessional relations, and coping mechanisms: A study of criminal justice social workers in the sentencing process. *Law & Policy*, *31*(4), 405–428. doi:10.1111/j.1467-9930.2009.00306.x

Hayes, D., & Spratt, T. (2009). Child welfare interventions: Patterns of social work practice. *British Journal of Social Work*, *39*(8), 1575–1597. doi:10.1093/bjsw/bcn098

Horwath, J., & Morrison, T. (2007). Collaboration, integration and change in children's services: Critical issues and key ingredients. [PubMed]. *Child Abuse & Neglect*, *31*(1), 55–69. doi:10.1016/j.chiabu.2006.01.007

Hughes, E. C. (1951). Work and the self. In J. H. Rohrer & M. Sherif (Eds.), *Social psychology at the crossroads* (pp. 313–323). New York: Harper and Brothers.

Hughes, E. C. (1962). Good people and dirty work. *Social Problems*, *10*(1), 3–11. doi:10.2307/799402

Human Rights and Equal Opportunity Commission. (1997). Bringing them home: Report of the National Inquiry into the Separation of Aboriginal and Torres Strait Islander Children from their Families. Sydney, Australia: Author.

Huxham, C., & Vangen, S. (2000). Ambiguity, complexity and dynamics in the membership of collaboration. *Human Relations*, *53*(6), 771–806. doi:10.1177/0018726700536002

Keiser, L. R. (2010). Understanding street-level bureaucrats' decision making: Determining eligibility in the social security disability program. *Public Administration Review*, *70*(2), 247–257. doi:10.1111/j.1540-6210.2010.02131.x

Khoo, E. G., Hyvonen, U., & Nygren, L. (2003). Gate keeping decisions in child welfare: A comparative study of intake decision making in Canada and Sweden. [PubMed]. *Child Welfare*, *82*, 507–525. Retrieved from http://www.ncbi.nlm.nih.gov/pubmed/14524423

Kreiner, G. E., Ashforth, B. E., & Sluss, D. M. (2006). Identity dynamics in occupational dirty work: Integrating social identity and system justification perspectives. *Organization Science*, *17*(5), 619–636. doi:10.1287/orsc.1060.0208

Lonne, B., Parton, N., Thomson, J., & Harries, M. (2008). *Reforming child protection*. London: Routledge.

Margolis, J. D., & Molinsky, A. (2008). Navigating the bind of necessary evils: Psychological engagement and the production of interpersonally sensitive behaviour. *Academy of Management Journal, 51*(5), 847–872. doi:10.5465/AMJ.2008.34789639

Martin, B., & Healey, J. (2010). *Who works in community services: A profile of Australian workforces in child protection, juvenile justice, disability services and general community services*. Adelaide: National Institute of Labour Studies, Flinders University.

May, P. J., & Winter, S. C. (2009). Politicians, managers, and street-level bureaucrats: Influences on policy implementation. *Journal of Public Administration Research and Theory, 19*(3), 453–476. doi:10.1093/jopart/mum030

Maynard-Moody, S. W., & Musheno, M. C. (2003). *Cops, teachers, counselors: Stories from the front lines of public service*. University of Michigan Press.

Mendes, P. (2001). Blaming the messenger: The media, social workers and child abuse. *Australian Social Work, 54*(2), 27–36. doi:10.1080/03124070108414321

Milbourne, L., Macrea, S., & Maguire, M. (2003). Collaborative solutions or new policy problems: Exploring multiagency partnerships in education and health work. *Journal of Education Policy, 18*(1), 19–35. doi:10.1080/268093032000042182

Morris, J. (2005). For the children: Accounting for careers in child protective services. *Journal of Sociology and Social Welfare, 32*, 131–140. Retrieved from http://www.wmich.edu/socialwork/journal/

Newell, S., & Swan, J. (2000). Trust and inter-organisational working. *Human Relations, 53*, 1287–1328. Retrieved from http://hum.sagepub.com/

Paetzold, R. L., Dipboye, R. L., & Elsbach, K. D. (2008). A new look at stigmatization in and of organizations. *Academy of Management Review, 33*(1), 186–193. doi:10.5465/AMR.2008.27752576

Pithouse, A. (1998). *Social work: The social organisation of an invisible trade* (2nd ed.). Aldershot, England: Ashgate.

Pugh, R. (2007). Dual relationships: Personal and professional boundaries in rural social work. *British Journal of Social Work, 37*(8), 1405–1423. doi:10.1093/bjsw/bcl088

Reder, P., & Duncan, S. (2003). Understanding communication in child protection networks. *Child Abuse Review, 12*(2), 82–100. doi:10.1002/car.787

Reder, P., Duncan, S., & Gray, M. (1993). *Beyond blame: Child abuse tragedies revisited*. London: Routledge.

Rosenthal, P., & Peccei, R. (2006). The social construction of clients by service agents in reformed welfare administration. *Human Relations, 59*(12), 1633–1658. doi:10.1177/0018726706073194

Scott, D. (2005). Inter-organisational collaboration in family-centred practice: A framework for analysis and action. *Australian Social Work, 58*(2), 132–141. doi:10.1111/j.1447-0748.2005.00198.x

Scott, D., & Swain, S. (2002). *Confronting cruelty: Historical perspectives of child protection in Australia*. Melbourne: Melbourne University.

Smith, B. D., & Mogro-Wilson, C. (2007). Multi-level influences on the practice of interagency collaoboration in child welfare and sustance abuse treatment. *Children and Youth Services Review*, *29*(5), 545–556. doi:10.1016/j.childyouth.2006.06.002

Social Work Task Force. (2009). *Building a safe and confident future*. London: Department of Children, Schools and Families. Retrieved from http://www.cscb-new.co.uk/downloads/reports_research/D_Report%20of%20SW%20Task%20Force%202009.pdf

Stanley, J., Tomison, A. M., & Pocock, J. (2003). *Child abuse and neglect in Indigenous Australian communities*. Melbourne: National Child Protection Clearinghouse, Australian Insitute of Family Studies.

Taylor, H., Beckett, C., & McKeigue, B. (2008). Judgements of Solomon: Anxieties and defences of social workers involved in care proceedings. *Child & Family Social Work*, *13*, 23–31. doi:10.1111/j.1365-2206.2007.00507.x

Thomson, A. M., & Perry, J. L. (2006). Collaborative process: Inside the black box. *Public Administration Review*, *66*(s1), 20–32. doi:10.1111/j.1540-6210.2006.00663.x

Tracy, S. J. (2004). The construction of correctional officers: Layers of emotionality behind bars. *Qualitative Inquiry*, *10*(4), 509–533. doi:10.1177/1077800403259716

Tracy, S. J., & Scott, C. (2006). Sexuality, masculinity, and taint management among firefighters and correctional officers: Getting down and dirty with "America's heroes" and the "scum of law enforcement". *Management Communication Quarterly*, *20*(1), 6–38. doi:10.1177/0893318906287898

Wilczynski, A., & Sinclair, K. (1999). Moral tales: Representations of child abuse in the quality and tabloid media. *Australian and New Zealand Journal of Criminology*, *32*(3), 262–283. doi:10.1177/000486589903200305

Woodcock, J., & Dixon, J. (2005). Professional ideologies and preferences in social work: A British study in global perspsective. *British Journal of Social Work*, *35*(6), 953–997. doi:10.1093/bjsw/bch282

## ADDITIONAL READING

Boyas, J., Wind, L. H., & Kang, S.-Y. (2012). Exploring the relationship between employment-based social capital, job stress, burnout, and intent to leave among child protection workers: An age-based path analysis model. *Children and Youth Services Review*, *34*(1), 50–62. doi:10.1016/j.childyouth.2011.08.033

Burns, K. (2011). "Career preference", "transients" and "converts": A study of social workers' retention in child protection and welfare. *British Journal of Social Work*, *41*(3), 520–538. doi:10.1093/bjsw/bcq135

Goddard, C., & Hunt, S. (2011). The complexities of caring for child protection workers: The contexts of practice and supervision. *Journal of Social Work Practice*, *25*(4), 413–432. doi:10.1080/02650533.2011.626644

Mansell, J., Ota, R., Erasmus, R., & Marks, K. (2011). Reframing child protection: A response to a constant crisis of confidence in child protection. *Children and Youth Services Review*, *33*(11), 2076–2086. doi:10.1016/j.childyouth.2011.04.019

Meyers, J. (Ed.). (1994). *The backlash: Child protection under fire*. London: Sage.

Mills, S. M. (2012). Unconscious sequences in child protection work: Case studies of professionals' experiences of child removal. *Journal of Social Work Practice*, *26*(3), 301–313. doi:10.1080/02650533.2011.562603

Munro, E. (1999). Common errors of reasoning in child protection work. [PubMed]. *Child Abuse & Neglect*, *23*(8), 745–758. doi:10.1016/S0145-2134(99)00053-8

Sandfort, J. (1999). The structural impediments to human service collaboration: The case of welfare reform. *The Social Service Review*, *73*(3), 314–339. doi:10.1086/514426

Shin, J. (2011). Client violence and its negative impacts on work attitudes of child protection workers compared to community service workers. [PubMed]. *Journal of Interpersonal Violence*, *26*(16), 3338–3360. doi:10.1177/0886260510393002

Stevenson, S. (2012). Inside the lion's den: The risks to experts entering into child protection court proceedings. *Journal of Social Work Practice*, *26*(3), 315–326. doi:10.1080/02650533.2011.599489

## KEY TERMS AND DEFINITIONS

**Child Protection Workers:** A term denoting those who work in the statutory child protection system, which in Australia is the responsibility of the state and territory governments. The workers in the statutory child protection system are responsible for responding to notifications about children who have been, or are at risk of, experiencing child abuse and neglect.

**Dirty Work:** A phrase referring to those occupations which are physically, socially, or morally tainted, but which are necessary for the survival of society.

**Interagency Collaboration:** This phrase describes the process of agencies coming together and sharing resources and knowledge in order to improve effectiveness, efficiency, and outcomes for children and families.

**Social Stigma:** A concept denoting the disapproval expressed towards an individual or group as a result of a perception by the wider society that the indvidual or group possesses certain characteristics which deviate from acceptable cultural norms.

**Social Work:** The profession of social work. Using the best available research evidence, theories of human behaviour and social systems, social workers work with indvidiuals, groups, communities, and structures to enhance individual and collective well-being.

# Chapter 8
# Social Work and Youth Justice in a Global Context:
## Practising in Shifting and Conflicting Paradigms

**Bill Whyte**
*University of Edinburgh, UK*

## ABSTRACT

*Social work in youth justice is directed by international standards based on an implied socio-educative paradigm that conflicts with the dominant criminal justice paradigm in operation in most jurisdictions. This creates global challenges in establishing "child-centred" policy and practice for dealing with young people under the age of 18 years in conflict with the law. Social work practitioners, directed by international imperatives and professional ethics, operate between shifting and often conflicting paradigms. It is essential they are familiar with international obligations and operate as "culture carriers" providing an ongoing challenge to systems of youth justice. This chapter examines these issues and, in the absence of consensus or of a shared paradigm for social work practice across jurisdictions, considers what a socio-educative paradigm for practice might look like.*

## INTRODUCTION

International standards set by the United Nations Convention on the Rights of the Child (UNCRC, G.A. Res. 44/25, 1989) and its associated guidance and more recently the *Guidelines of the Committee of Ministers of the Council of Europe on Child-Friendly Justice* (Group of Specialists on Child-Friendly Justice, 2010) and the *Recommendation of the Committee of Ministers to Member States on the European Rules for Juvenile Offenders Subject to Sanctions or Measures* (Comm. of Ministers, 2008) have highlighted global challenges that apply to all jurisdictions in establishing "child-centered" policy and practice for dealing with young people under the age of 18 years who are in conflict with the law. This is particularly the case for those young people involved in serious and violent offending whether they are dealt with within or outside of criminal processes.

The requirements of UNCRC and its associated guidance focus on the best interests of the child

DOI: 10.4018/978-1-4666-6563-7.ch008

as a paramount consideration and extra judicial solutions as the norm for dealing with young people in trouble with the law; and they place an emphasis on socio-educative rather than punitive interventions. This is an implied rather than an outlined practice paradigm (here, paradigm is being used to mean a model or set of assumptions, concepts, values, and practices that constitute a way of viewing social reality). As yet, there is no consensus or shared paradigm for social work practice across jurisdictions, and few, if any, have achieved the ambition set by UNCRC and its associated standards. As a consequence, social work practitioners operate between shifting and often conflicting paradigms and systems within their locality.

As a profession, social work is directed by international imperatives and professional ethics (International Association of Schools of Social Work [IASSW], n.d.; International Federation of Social Workers [IFSW], 2012). Whatever social workers' abilities to change and influence local systems, it is crucial that they are familiar with international obligations and operate as "culture carriers" providing an ongoing challenge to systems of youth justice which fail to recognise that the status of children and young people requires an approach in which responsibility is shared between young people, their family/community, and the state.

## BACKGROUND

Approaches to dealing with children and young people who break the law vary much more widely across jurisdictions than the equivalent justice systems for adults. In addition to cultural and institutional differences, youth systems vary in their structures and age jurisdiction, as well as in the underlying normative and value assumptions underpinning policy and practice. Many western countries pursued youth crime policies

during much of the 20th century which eroded the distinction between the young person or child in need and the delinquent youth. This is despite the growing evidence over generations that the differences between children in need and young people coming to the attention of authorities for breaking the law are far outweighed by their similarities (Committee on Children and Young Persons, 1964; Whyte, 2009).

In the early 21st century, welfare oriented approaches were often superseded by punitive law and order ideologies driven by politicians under pressure to be seen to be tough on crime (Brown, 2005). The predominance of "punishment" as a cultural response, for example, has often meant that the public framing of provision for responding to youth crime has been dominated by a language of punishment without consideration of how best to respond to the characteristics and circumstances of the young people in ways that are likely to result in positive change, contributing to the well-being and safety of the young person, victims, and the community as a whole (Whyte, 2009).

## Aims and Objectives

The objectives of this chapter are to examine these issues in detail and, in the absence of a consensus or of a shared paradigm for social work practice across jurisdictions, consider the implications for social work and explore what a socio-educative paradigm for practice might look like.

## Search Strategy

The literature used in this chapter is based on accumulated knowledge gathered through literature searches of United Nations documents relating to *"juvenile justice"* and *"delinquency"* and database searches on keywords such as *"juvenile justice"*, *"youth justice"*, *"youth crime"*, *"desistence"*, and *"social work"*.

# YOUTH JUSTICE IN A GLOBAL CONTEXT

## Justice and Welfare: Children First?

The combination of two concepts, special responses to children and young people and equal rights under the law, creates tension in practice on how best to reconcile the competing claims of the law, judicial process, and punishment, with the need to consider the best interests and the rights of the child or young person, while responding effectively to the needs of victims and communities and to reducing offending.

Systems dealing with young people who offend are often differentiated along the broad dimensions of justice and welfare. As with all ideal-types, models are seldom found in a pure form. All countries remain uncomfortable with a rigid distinction between youth justice and child welfare/protection and, in practice, most combine elements of the different approaches based on age thresholds that have little empirical justification. Legislation tends to maintain a separation between systems dealing with the care and protection of children and young people (child welfare) and responses to offending by children and young people (youth justice).

With respect to young people in their teens who are in conflict with the law, the second half of the 20th century saw a swing away from welfare approaches to systems associated more with access to due process, particularly in English speaking jurisdictions, directed by principles of proportionality and accountability and with greater recognition of the place of victims. Nonetheless, all countries allow for varying degrees of overlap and convergence between child welfare and youth justice systems with the age of transition to the justice system (from shared responsibility to individual criminal responsibility) ranging from 7 to 18 years with the norm around 14; 12 for English speaking countries (Goldson & Muncie, 2012). The definition of "youth" in western jurisdictions,

for purposes other than prosecution, can extend to 24. "The United Nations, for statistical purposes, defines 'youth' as those persons between the ages of 15 and 24 years, without prejudice to other definitions by Member States" (United Nations Department of Economic and Social Affairs, 1981).

The philosophy of child protection and a strong sense of collective responsibility for the positive upbringing of children and young people continues to hold sway in Northern European countries up to the mid-teens, in some states to 18 and, exceptionally as in Germany, until 21. However, because the peak age for offending is typically in the mid to late teens, the majority of young people who offend, notwithstanding child protection or diversionary measures, are commonly dealt with by youth or adult criminal courts.

These circumstances present real day-to-day challenges for social work practitioners concerned with effectiveness, values, rights, and with ethical practice, whether they are indirectly or directly involved in youth justice. They must contend with variable definitions and statutes on what constitutes "a child" and "a youth" and demarcations between those who are and are not deemed solely and criminally responsible for their action and its consequences or between those considered best dealt with in criminal proceedings (youth or adult) and those not.

The legitimacy of criminal justice and public conviction can only exist if the person is viewed, in principle, as singly, solely, and fully responsible for his/her actions, and the criminal justice paradigm, no matter how it is modified, is incompatible with the objectives of prevention and of shared responsibility for dealing with children and young people up to age 18, the norm for children's legislation and international standards. The criminal justice paradigm requires no adult or other party to accept any share in the responsibility/guilt for a young person's action. Indeed, it can be argued that the criminalisation and conviction of children and young people absolves adults, service providers, the community, and the state as a whole from collective responsibility and accountability for the "failure" in the young person's upbringing. In this regard many, if not most, jurisdictions stand accused by the UN Committee on the Rights of the Child (UNComRC) of poor child-centred and children's rights approaches to youth crime and of high levels of criminalisation and detention of young people, many of whom have a public care background (Whyte, 2009).

## International Standards

The near universal ratification of the UNCRC has placed importance on establishing a level playing field for all children and young people through delivery of progressive universal provision and early social intervention measures aimed at positive upbringing. In relation to youth crime, the UNCRC has produced a number of standards and guides: the *United Nations Standard Minimum Rules for the Administration of Juvenile Justice – "The Beijing Rules"* (G.A. Res. 40/33, 1985); the *UN Guidelines for the Prevention of Juvenile Delinquency – "The Riyadh Guidelines"* (G.A. Res. 45/112, 1990); the *UN Rules for the Protection of Juveniles Deprived of their Liberty – "The "Havana Rules"* (G.A. Res 45/113,1990); the *UN Standard Minimum Rules for Non-Custodial Measures – "The "Tokyo Rules"* (G.A. Res. 45/110, 1990); and the *UN Economic and Social Council Guidelines for Action on Children in the Criminal Justice System – "The Vienna Guidelines"* (E.S.C. Res. 1997/30, 1997). The UNCRC and its associated guidance has stressed the importance of

- well-being as a paramount consideration;
- an age of criminal responsibility based on maturity;
- socio-educative interventions rather than punitive ones;
- extra judicial solutions;
- deprivation of liberty only as a last resort; and
- safeguards for the use of alternatives to custody.

Benchmarks for Social Work and other professional practice have, in effect, been set by international agreements and regulations. The UNCRC (G.A. Res 44/25, 1989) requires that in "all actions concerning children, whether undertaken by public or private social welfare institutions, courts of law, administrative authorities or legislative bodies, the best interests of the child shall be a primary consideration" (Article 3).

The qualification of the key principle as *a* primary rather than *the* primary consideration can find expression in quite different practices in different jurisdictions, often invoking the public interest as "trumping" and over-riding the interests of the child when it comes to criminal matters, even for relatively minor or persistent offending.

The principle of universal human rights was consolidated by the creation of the United Nations and the adoption of the Universal Declaration of Human Rights in 1948, but it was not until the UNCRC (G.A. Res 44/25, 1989) came into force that a universal instrument focused specifically and exclusively on protecting and promoting children's rights. At the heart of the Convention is Article 1 which provides, unequivocally, that the term "child" refers to "every human being below the age of eighteen years"; something to which English speaking jurisdictions, in particular, have paid scant recognition until recently.

The UNCRC (G.A. Res 44/25, 1989) sets out the terms in which children and young people due to "physical and mental immaturity" require "special safeguards and care, including appropriate legal protection" (Preamble). The associated guidance has gradually clarified the expectations and set standards for signatory countries. These include the *United Nations Standard Minimum Rules for the Administration of Juvenile Justice* (G.A. Res. 40/33, 1985) which provide guidance and set standards for the protection of children's human rights through the development of separate and specialist youth justice systems with a minimum age of criminal responsibility based on "emotional, mental and intellectual maturity" (Rule 4.1) and the adoption of socio educative responses to youth crime rather than punitive (criminal) ones "within a comprehensive framework of social justice for all juveniles" (Rule 1.4). This does not suggest or imply that children and young people should be seen to have no responsibility for their actions. It recognises that accountability and responsibility should be modified according to their maturity, implying that, at least up to the age of 18, their responsibility should be shared by adults and that the community and state is responsible for positive upbringing.

The *UN Guidelines for the Prevention of Juvenile Delinquency* (G.A. Res. 45/112, 1990) stress the value of child-centred early intervention, shared responsibility for the upbringing of young people, and the promotion of non-criminogenic attitudes through multidisciplinary approaches to crime prevention. The *Guidelines* stress that "the successful prevention of juvenile delinquency requires efforts on the part of the entire society to ensure the harmonious development of adolescents" (Guideline 2); utilising formal agencies of social control only as a "last resort" (Guideline 6). The *Guidelines* focus on the collective responsibility ("the entire society") for the whole child, which includes children and young people who may or may not be in conflict with the law and "who are abandoned, neglected, abused, exposed to drug abuse, in marginal circumstances and who are at general social risk" (Marshall, 2007, p. 7). They promote a progressive universalism signalling a major overlap in provision between children and young people in adversity and for those in conflict with the law and that meeting needs and building human and social capital is a priority to avoid escalating offending.

The *UN Rules for the Protection of Juveniles Deprived of their Liberty* (G.A. Res 45/113, 1990) identify core principles including the independence of prosecutors and their role in promoting diversion from criminal proceedings for young people up to the age of 18. Deprivation of liberty should be a "last resort" and only "for the minimum necessary period" (Rule 2). It is very difficult

to conclude from available data, particularly in English speaking jurisdictions, that these rules hold much sway over prosecution practice. *The UN Standard Minimum Rules for Non-Custodial Measures* (G.A. Res. 45/110, 1990) are intended to promote greater community involvement, responsibility, and community based responses to crime, again reinforcing youth crime as a collective and shared rather than simply an individual responsibility.

*The Guidelines for Action on Children in the Criminal Justice System* (E.S.C. Res. 1997/30, 1997), stress the "interdependence and indivisibility of all rights of the child" (Guideline 10) outlined in UNCRC. Guideline 11(a) specifically encourages the development of "a child-oriented juvenile justice system". Guideline 15 explicitly supports prevention, the diversion from criminal systems, and the importance of dealing with underlying social causes. It requires countries to provide "a broad range of alternative and educative measures" at all stages. One of its operating tenets in youth crime prevention and youth justice is that long-term change is brought about "when root causes are addressed" (Guideline 41). The preamble to UNCRC stresses the dynamic nature of the framework and that it expects it to be continually developed on the basis of research and practice-related evidence. The international practice model recommended is one of diversion, as far as possible, from criminal proceedings up to the age of 18, stressing the value of early preventive intervention.

Whether or not UNCRC is incorporated into local legislation, international law requires that signatories should adhere to the spirit and principles of the Convention, and the UNCRC should represent the standard for measuring any appropriate system of youth justice. As a consequence, social work is challenged to use these international standards to direct practice and also to use its influence in local jurisdictions. In most instances, it is difficult to argue on the basis of UNComRC's concerns over the levels of criminalisation and detention of young people up to the age of 18 that international obligations have featured greatly as a priority in regard to young people who break the law.

## Social Work and Youth Justice

The United Nations International Children's Emergency Fund (UNICEF, 2013) acknowledges the variety of experiences of, and approaches to, social work in different jurisdictions and suggests that this makes it all the more essential for social work to be aware of the internationally agreed scope and forms of its action and intervention when considering its role in relation to youth justice. It notes that article 40 of UNCRC requires that a child in conflict with the law has the right to treatment which takes their age into account and promotes their reintegration into society and that this, in turn, requires "tailored support" for each child and his/her family throughout the different stages of youth justice including after release in the case of detention (p. 1).

The IFSW (2012) emphasises that the social work profession should draw on theories of human development, social theory, and social systems to facilitate individual, organisational, social, and cultural change, founded on the principles of human rights and social justice. The IFSW identifies three key action areas for social work: promoting social change, problem-solving in human relationships, and empowering people to enhance their own well-being.

The IASSW (2014) has proposed a revised international and global definition of social work as

*... a practice-based profession and an academic discipline that promotes social change and development, social cohesion, and the empowerment and liberation of people. Principles of social justice, human rights, collective responsibility and respect for diversities are central to social work. Underpinned by theories of social work, social sciences, humanities and indigenous knowledges,* *social work engages people and structures to address life challenges and enhance wellbeing. (para. 1)*

UNICEF (2013) identifies three overarching roles for social work in youth justice. These comprise working alongside, but independently from, the youth justice system, involving primary and secondary prevention through largely voluntary engagement; working at the interface with the justice system, providing primary and secondary preventive measures for young people and families coming into contact with the system; and working within the justice system, providing secondary and tertiary prevention aimed at reducing re-offending and re-integration from the moment of the young person's apprehension or arrest through to disposal and, where appropriate, follow-up.

Social work roles in youth justice will vary between jurisdictions and may include involvement from the time of apprehension or arrest; being present with the child during police questioning; involvement in pre and post trial "solutions"; providing emotional and possibly paralegal and other advice, assistance, and support to the young person and their family; and maintaining contact with the child throughout the pre-trial period in order to provide assistance and advice as required. Social work is likely to be required to prepare reports on the child's circumstances and characteristics and on all aspects of the family situation and on the developmental needs of the child; to examine the crime or offence as a social phenomenon with consequences for the young person, the family, the victim, and the community as a whole; and to formulate a view and plan on how best to respond.

## A Dilemma for Social Work?

Two years after a "State Party" ratifies the UNCRC the country is obliged to submit an initial report to the UNComRC outlining how it is applying the convention and each state is required, thereafter, to provide periodic reports at five-yearly intervals. The Committee, which monitors the application of the UNCRC into law, policy, and practice within national borders, meets around three times a year in Geneva, Switzerland. It has two principal functions; firstly, to issue "General Comments" on the application of UNCRC and secondly, to examine how each "State Party" is implementing the convention and complying with it in law, policy, and practice. On both counts the Committee attempts to identify institutionalised obstructions to the implementation of the UNCRC in general and, more specifically, serious breaches and violations of the human rights of children within particular youth justice systems (Goldson & Muncie, 2012).

In the vast majority of jurisdictions, the Committee's "General Comment" in respect of youth justice concludes that implementation of the UNCRC is often piecemeal and that the human rights obligations frequently appear as little more than afterthoughts (U.N. Committee on the Rights of the Child, 2007). The repetitive nature of the Committee's findings stem at least in part from the fact that the UNCRC is ultimately permissive and breaches attract no formal sanction. In this sense, Goldson and Muncie (2012) suggest it may be the most ratified of all international human rights instruments but it also appears to be the most violated, particularly with regard to youth justice.

The persistent recurrence of human rights violations is further compounded by evidence of the racialisation of youth justice practice (Goldson, 2009). Muncie (2008) reported that 15 of 18 western European jurisdictions studied were explicitly criticised by the UNComRC for negatively discriminating against children from minority ethnic communities and migrant children seeking asylum. The Committee's reports on the UK and British Commonwealth countries, such as Australia (U.N. Committee on the Rights of the Child, 2005) and Canada (U.N. Committee on the Rights of the Child, 2003) have expressed concerns, inter alia,

over the high levels of criminal prosecutions; the high number of youths in custody; juvenile and adult offenders being kept together in detention; public access being available to youth records; the over-representation of Indigenous children and children from ethnic minority backgrounds in criminal proceedings; and children with mental health or learning difficulties being involved in criminal proceedings. Mandatory sentencing similarly features in monitoring reports.

Jurisdictions have tended to respond to the Committee's reports through partial reforms, often by bolting apparent "child friendly" responses and other informal methods, such as restorative approaches, onto otherwise retributive and punitive youth justice systems, with little direct impact on the dominant practice paradigm.

UNComRC published a list of concerns and criticisms regarding the UK's performance in 1995, along with a comprehensive set of recommendations on how better to meet practice obligations and protect children's rights. In revisiting these concerns in 2002, it remained highly critical of UK practices and expressed disappointment that the majority of the recommendations from 1995 had not been acted on (Harvey, 2002). The UK delegation, for example, argued in 2002 that the low age of criminal responsibility in all UK jurisdictions allowed for early intervention while recognising children's responsibility for their crime. It also argued that children's legislation, although providing protection and guarantees of services for children up to the age of 18, did not apply to children in detention.

However, signal judgments of the High Court in England, following a judicial review instigated by the Howard League in 2002, confirmed that English and by extension other UK jurisdictions (or for that matter any) cannot designate young people under 18 as "ex" children simply by their entrance into the criminal justice system and detention. The High Court held that the *Children Act* 1989 did apply to children held in custody and indicated that the Howard League had "performed a most useful service in bringing to the public attention matters which, on the face of it, ought to shock the conscience of every citizen" (*R (on the application of the Howard League for Penal Reform) v. Secretary of State for the Home Department*, 2002, paragraph 175).

Moreover, in July 2007, the Howard League brought a judicial review against the Home Secretary, arguing that the Children Act 1989 applied to children in prison. The appeal decision resulted in three English Law Lords confirming that local authorities should provide the young person with the care due under s20 of the *Children Act* 1989. In effect, this confirmed that local authorities have the same duties to children up to 18 who leave custody as to "children in need". The wording of the 1989 Act in England and Wales is almost identical in Scots law. Assistant Director and head of the legal team at the Howard League for Penal Reform, Chris Callender, noted that

*... local authorities across the country are failing to provide proper assessments and care plans for vulnerable children leaving custody....children are in danger of returning to precisely the same situations that led to their crimes and imprisonment in the first place. (Howard League for Penal Reform, 2007)*

In 2006, R (on the application of K) v. Manchester City Council established important details about the ways in which children leaving custody should be assessed, namely, that assessments should be carried out by local authority social services departments and not Youth Offending Team workers and that the assessments should explicitly cover the future needs of the child on release. As a result of these cases, the Prison Service has rewritten Prison Service Order 4950, which deals with the regime for juveniles, so that a range of child protection measures could be incorporated.

These decisions confirm that young people involved in serious crime, even if dealt with in criminal processes, still fall within a children services and child protection (social work) policy

framework and are entitled to aftercare support to ensure their personal and social well-being, integration, and long-term desistence from crime.

The most recent contribution to this discussion in the UK (*R (on the application of HC) v. Secretary of State for the Home Department*, 2013; hereafter, *HC*) saw an English High Court decision confirm that young people up to the age of 18 (not under 17 as in certain circumstances in England and Wales) are entitled to special protection or measures for similar reasons. The decision, which was not appealed by the UK government, clearly states that young people under 18 are entitled to special consideration and cannot be treated as adults. The basis for the judgment was, in large measure, because of the duties conferred on young people by ratification of the UNCRC. The Court ruling highlighted that "there can, accordingly, be no question but that the treatment of 17 year-olds as adults when arrested and detained...is inconsistent with the UNCRC and the views of the United Nations Committee of the Rights of the Child" (*HC*, paragraph 47). Further, "it is not only international law and international expert opinion which advocate special protection for 17 year-olds in detention. There is a substantial body of domestic opinion as to the need not to treat such detainees as adults" (*HC*, paragraph 51). And stated elsewhere, "ignoring the special position of children in the criminal justice system is not acceptable in the modern civil society" (*Regina v. G*, 2003/2004, paragraph 53).

These decisions confirm that local authorities, at least in England (which probably is applicable to most jurisdictions), retain a statutory duty to safeguard the welfare of children even if they are in detention, no matter what harm they may have done. It could be argued from this that entering the criminal justice system may itself be grounds for social work and child protection activity even if alongside rather than as an alternative to criminal processes for young people up to the age of 18. This undoubtedly raises paradigmatic questions and dilemmas for social work practice. It challenges those responsible for child welfare and child protection, in particular social work, to consider how social work should respond when young people under 18 are caught up in criminal processes and, in particular, detention.

The *Guidelines of the Committee of Ministers of the Council of Europe on Child-Friendly Justice* (Group of Specialists on Child-Friendly Justice, 2010) and the *Recommendation of the Committee of Ministers to Member States on the European Rules for Juvenile Offenders Subject to Sanctions or Measures* (Comm. of Ministers, 2008) have attempted to further strengthen the need for a child-centred approach to practice for young people involved in offending. In particular, they stress the importance of desistence and social integration and avoiding (adult) criminal proceedings irrespective of the gravity of their crime and that, with some exceptions for serious crimes, records should not be disclosed on reaching the age of majority.

These developments driven by the UNCRC challenge social work in all jurisdictions to promote and deliver child-centred welfare provision, whatever the local youth justice practices are. However, giving practice expression to these duties is a difficult matter without local multi-disciplinary protocols and shared resources between criminal justice corrections and probation, youth justice, children's services, housing, education and employment, leisure and health-related provision; in other words without an integrated "whole" systems approach to child care, child protection, and to youth justice. The lack of an established practice paradigm for social work reflects the dilemmas facing practitioners caught between the conflicting paradigms in operation. These dilemmas are illustrated in the case study of Shane, a young man facing the possibility of secure care.

## Case Study

Shane (nearly 16) first came to the attention of social workers when he was six because his parents were having difficulty controlling him. Social work records show a history of early physical and emotional abuse and neglect, domestic violence, poor parental supervision, and peer difficulties. There were concerns about sexual abuse but no direct evidence. Shane has a history of poor school attendance and achievement. He also has a history of interpersonal violence, vandalism, assault, and numerous petty offences that have brought him to the attention of the youth justice system. He is facing charges relating to a young woman who was unknown to him when he approached her in an alleyway and used violent and sexual threats towards her. He ran away when he saw someone else entering the alleyway. Shane is facing the possibility of detention or other secure care.

## Questions for Reflection from the Case Study

1. What kind of challenges does Shane present for social work in supervising him in the community or during and after a period of detention?
2. What steps can be taken to ensure his developmental needs can be met in line with the UNCRC standards while safeguarding the community and potential victims?

## FUTURE DIRECTIONS

## Social Education: A Paradigm for Social Work Practice?

In recent years, growing pressure from the UNCRC and the development of European standards and rules, has resulted in some serious attempts in the UK, particularly in Scotland and Wales, and to a lesser extent in England, to find an appropriate practice expression to the UNCRC for young people involved in crime and to recognise children's rights alongside considerations for victims and the community. It could be argued that Scotland has been more progressive in doing this in that in 1971 it replaced its national probation service with local authority criminal justice social work services and its youth courts with welfare based tribunals, Children's Hearings. These civil tribunals, staffed by trained lay representatives of the community with safeguards of appeal to the courts, symbolized a shared collective responsibility for finding solutions for children, young people, and families in difficulty.

In the real world, however, good principles, values, and even structures do not in themselves guarantee good practice and, in reality, youth justice practice in Scotland until 2007 similarly struggled to find a consistent platform in the context of conflicting political influences reflecting the dominance of a criminal justice paradigm in the UK. As a consequence most young people over 15 were routinely prosecuted and youth detention rates were high.

Scotland has stepped forwards and backwards over the years depending on the colour of politics in Westminster. However the establishment of a Scottish Parliament in 1997 and the election in 2007 of an SNP government with an overall majority has allowed for a re-exploration of Scotland's European traditions. With this, there has been growing support for the exploration and application of the socio-educative or pedagogical paradigm, which was the basis for radical change in post-war Scotland (Smith & Whyte, 2008), through the promotion of a whole systems approach to youth crime as part of Scotland's national child development strategy, *A Guide to Getting It Right for Every Child* (The Scottish Government, 2008).

Recent legislation (Children's Hearings Act 2011 and the Children and Young Person's Act 2014) support an attempt to return to a fundamental principle that the default position should be to decriminalise all young people up to age 18 appearing in a Children's Hearing for offending. This was the original intention of the system but it was modified by UK legislation in 1974. The launch of the whole system approach, led mainly by social work and police, has seen the prosecu-

tion and detention rates of young people under 18 halved in a few years and the lowest for a decade (The Scottish Government, 2013).

Similar trends are emerging in other jurisdictions which may reflect the impact of the UNCRC or other local political and economic factors. The re-emergence of support for a socio-educative approach to youth crime in Scotland, for example, may be less reflective of a major shift in public or political attitudes towards the UNCRC or youth crime and much more part of a government driven cultural project re-emphasising Scottish identity and its distinctive traditions in the run up to a referendum on Scottish independence in September 2014. Nonetheless, as a case study, it illustrates that social work does not operate in a vacuum. Notwithstanding international standards, government policy needs to reflect a strong sense of collective and inclusive responsibility for children's upbringing and provide mechanisms to support a shift in the practice paradigm.

Historical developments in Scotland were recognised by academics at the time not just as making adjustments to a flawed youth justice system but as a paradigm shift in the way of thinking about and responding to children in need, particularly those in trouble with the law (Bruce, 1985). In essence, this socio-educative paradigm shift was viewed as a means to individual improvement and social cohesion driving a "well developed sense of human mutual obligation" (Paterson, 2000, p. 9). At its foundation is a collectivist belief that educational success and failure cannot be understood only in formal educational terms but must be related to the social and economic circumstances faced by children and young people. Contemporary writers have similarly suggested that social education "has a key role in tackling a range of social problems and in promoting cohesion in a growingly diverse society" (Bloomer, 2008, p. 32). The paradigm is by definition collective and social, that is, society's policy and practices reflect collective responsibility for the upbringing of children as at the core of a mature civil society.

Social education or pedagogy in this European sense is grounded in opposition to individualistic approaches that fail to consider the social dimensions of human existence (Smith & Whyte, 2008) and is consistent with the objectives of youth justice practice based on international standards and international principles directing social work. It offers possibilities for the development of practice methods within an integrative approach to social well-being consistent with research on desistence from crime, without over-focusing on the young person as an offender or denying the young person's shared responsibility to the community as a whole and to individual victims, which may require adjudicated control mechanisms. Social education provides a positive alternative to deficit-based and correctional models of practice that often serve only to highlight tensions in philosophies of justice and welfare and amplify difficulties.

Social and educational perspectives are rooted in education and social sciences respectively which in coming together can provide a better integrated theoretical framework for youth justice practice directed by the UNCRC principles, children's services, and children's rights (Hämäläinen, 2003). The language of social education, if somewhat underdeveloped, has found its way into children's policy discourses (Cameron, 2004; Moss & Petrie, 2002). In some jurisdictions, the return to systemic family work and wrap around approaches reflect this notion of locating a young person within a positive community of interest to support personal and social change on behalf of the community and victims.

There isn't scope in this paper to outline or rehearse the growing body of literature on effective practice in youth justice from the "what works?" movement of the 1990s through to a greater understanding of pathways to desistence (see Whyte, 2009), save to note that specialist social workers in this field need to have criminological and child development knowledge. They need to exercise authority in ways that acknowledge and address, in so far as is possible, the harm done to victims.

They equally need skills in working with young people and their families in a systemic way, as well as mobilising more traditional skills of social work as brokers and advocates in assisting young people and their families to overcome structural barriers and achieve their change goals through co-productive means.

Theoretical and empirical developments point to the need for a paradigmatic shift ultimately aimed at social well-being – social and individual integration – that supports young people to view themselves not as criminals but as having a sense of personal agency and control, gaining opportunities to establish social bonds which will help them develop a positive personal identity to the future benefit of the community.

The question of what the practice paradigm should look like is part of a longstanding debate in the world of youth and adult criminal practice. In the 1960s medical analogies in relation to individual change and concepts of treatment, diagnosis, and dependent need tended to dominate the social work practice discourse. This gave rise to thinking and practices which seemed to imply that when wider psychological and personal needs were met, individual criminality would somehow disappear. This failed to give sufficient weight to crime itself and its consequences as a social phenomenon existing in time, space, and social relations within which individual choices and opportunities operate. The late 1970s and early 1980s saw a rise in pessimism reflected in a "nothing works" or "prison works" mind set. From the mid-1980s onwards research reviews on effectiveness began, slowly, to re-establish the evidential basis for optimism that people can and do change. However, the associated "what works?" or "RNR" (risks, need, responsivity) model (Andrews et al., 1990), as it came to be known, tended to over-focus on individuals, their cognitive abilities, and their criminality, i.e. it tended to reinforce an offender identity.

The slow but steady growth of research and accumulated experience in the early part of this decade on what helps people desist from crime has re-established the importance of personal change within a social context in which positive (non-offender) identity, having a sense of personal control or agency, and positive social relations and opportunities, are seen as crucial in supporting sustained change. Nonetheless, the desistence debate still tends to view people through the lens of "offender" in tension with the evidence and experience which suggests that when people (are allowed to) stop seeing themselves as offenders they are more likely to sustain positive change as long as social opportunities and supports are there to assist them. While this discourse has largely related to adults, the empirical work underpinning it has often been drawn from studies on young people who by definition are still developing their adult social identity.

Critiques of RNR have emerged providing a better perspective on the strengths and limitations of these empirically based directing principles in guiding practitioners in their efforts to assist young people to develop a positive sense of self and in fulfilling their own ambitions for a "good life" (Ward & Maruna, 2007). The "good lives" approach draws on the analogy of acquiring social goods and capital (Ward & Gannon, 2006).

Alongside these approaches, there has been a developing debate about the kind of practitioner required to support effective practice both in youth and adult justice – a development from "what works?" towards "who works?" This shows signs of returning to concepts of community and collective well-being, promoting social, family, and personal integration as legitimate objectives, certainly of youth justice under the UNCRC standards. There is greater support than ever from the literature to refocus existing practice towards social education and welfare as a means of achieving effective outcomes for children and young people who offend, for their families, and for victims, and for the community as a whole.

Over 30 years ago, Bottoms and McWilliams' (1979) "non-treatment paradigm" challenged

practice to move away from correctionally-driven "treatment" ideas based on medical analogies toward a model based on help and mutuality, traced back to founding principles of probation (advise, assist, and befriend). The paradigm proposed a shift from treatment to a focus on help and assistance and from diagnosis to shared assessment seeking collaborative advantage. This was supported by a growing body of empirical evidence from crime surveys showing that breaking the law was more normal than atypical and was not exclusive to a disadvantaged criminal class. It was similarly clear from the evidence that poverty did not in any simplistic or individualist way cause crime or only the poor and all of the poor would be criminals. The empirical evidence showed that this was not the case as highlighted by data on white and blue collar crime and other evidence, only too apparent more recently, relating to finance and banking, and to clergy and celebrity abuse. Yet in reality, most individuals processed through justice systems, particularly youth, are typically poor and disadvantaged and possess multiple difficulties, highlighting social and structural barriers to change and progress. While social and economic disadvantage and other structural barriers do not fully explain nor justify crime or its consequences for victims, it sets the context for a journey of personal and social change which has to be recognised and somehow factored into any system serious about promoting reductions in re-offending, particularly for young people who are the concern of social work.

Bottoms and McWilliams' (1979) "non-treatment" paradigm (see Table 1) was revised by Raynor (1985) and further by Raynor and Vanstone (1994) to focus more specifically on the emerging "what works?" evidence and its consequences, to create an evidence-based framework for the further development of ethical practice. More recently, McNeill (2006) attempted to explore what a desistence paradigm might look like based on the potential implications of emerging desistence research on practice.

*Table 1. Summary of crime-related practice in four paradigms*

| Non-Treatment Paradigm | Revised Paradigm | What Works? Paradigm | Desistance Paradigm |
|---|---|---|---|
| **Treatment** becomes help. | Help consistent with a commitment to the reduction of harm. | Intervention required to reduce re-offending and protect the public. | Help in navigating towards ending and reducing re-offending, to reduce harm, and to make good to offenders and victims. |
| **Diagnoses** becomes shared assessment. | Explicit dialogue and negotiation offering opportunities for consensual change. | Professional assessment of risk and need governed by structured assessment instruments. | Explicit dialogue and negotiation assessing risks, needs, strengths, and resources, and offering opportunities to make good. |
| Client's **dependent need** as the basis for action becomes a collaboratively defined task as the basis for action. | Collaboratively defined task relevant to criminogenic need and potentially effective in meeting need. | Compulsory engagement in structured programmes and case management processes as required; elements of legal orders imposed irrespective of consent. | Collaboratively defined tasks which tackle risks, needs, and obstacles to desistance by using and developing the offender's human and social capital. |
| *Source:* Adapted from Bottoms and McWilliams (1979), McNeill (2006), Raynor (1985), and Raynor and Vanstone (1994). | | | |

Whyte (2009) attempted to develop Bottom's and McWilliams' (1979) paradigm in line with UNCRC practice standards for young people as a socio-educative or pedagogical paradigm for youth justice (see Table 2). The socio-educative paradigm requires more from social work than the technical management of offence-focused programmes and the disciplined management of compulsory orders as a key to engagement. The paradigm places a high premium on collabora-tion, involving young people and their families or "communities of interest" in the process of establishing shared objectives and co-designing interventions to meet these. A necessary ethical and practical corollary is that interventions should be equally preoccupied with overcoming structural barriers. This requires supporting young people to make good to victims and the community, where appropriate, but also making good *to* the young people, themselves often victims, to enable them

*Table 2. Youth crime practice paradigm*

| Non-Treatment Paradigm | Socio-Educative Paradigm |
|---|---|
| **Treatment** becomes help. | Help to overcome structural barriers and intervention to acquire and sustain personal and social "capital", build resilience and a positive personal identity to support change towards reducing and desisting from offending, reducing harm, and making good to victims, where appropriate, with the support of family and community. |
| **Diagnoses** becomes shared assessment. | Explicit dialogue and negotiation with young people and their families through a collaborative systemic assessment of their social and developmental needs, risks, strengths, and resources, assisted and directed by the formulation of a structured professional assessment (including the use of instruments) and explicit corporate or community planning to identify and direct opportunities for positive change. |
| Client's **dependent need** as the basis for action becomes a collaboratively defined task as the basis for action. | Collaboratively defined tasks through voluntary, or as a last resort, compulsory engagement, which tackle risks, needs, and obstacles to change by using structured approaches, relational, case/risk management, and child protection processes, as required to develop the young person's human and social capital, positive personal identity, and social integration; maintained change through community resources. Source: adapted from Whyte (2009, p.18) |

to achieve security, better personal and social integration and inclusion, and with it the progressive and positive reframing of their identities essential to personal maturation, social integration, and maintaining desistance from crime.

## CONCLUSION

The wider social context of behaviour and the impact of structural factors, such as poverty and community fragmentation, have become marginalised in social work and youth justice practice. The role of social work is to promote well-being and safety through broadly based social education strategies and to find educational solutions to social problems (Hämäläinen, 2003). While practice is generally concerned with direct work with children and young people and their families, socio-educative principles can be applied to wider questions of social integration in different phases of the lifespan. This is based on the belief that social circumstances and social change can be influenced through social education. This is not an alternative but should complement political action to affect the external "power" issues of society's structures, institutions, and legislation. Socio-educative action, like social work, aspires to change society by influencing the personal in society: people, morals, and culture.

## REFERENCES

Andrews, D. A., Zinger, I., Hoge, R. D., Bonta, J., Gendreau, P., & Cullen, F. T. (1990). Does correctional treatment work? A clinically relevant and psychologically informed meta-analysis. *Criminology*, *28*(3), 369–404. doi:10.1111/j.1745-9125.1990.tb01330.x

Bloomer, K. (2008). Modernising Scotland's teaching workforce. In K. Bloomer (Ed.), *Working it out: Developing the children's sector workforce* (pp. 32–35). Edinburgh, UK: Children in Scotland.

Bottoms, A. E., & McWilliams, W. (1979). A non-treatment paradigm for probation practice. *British Journal of Social Work*, *9*, 159–202. Retrieved from http://bjsw.oxfordjournals.org/

Brown, S. (2005). *Understanding youth and crime: Listening to youth?* Maidenhead, UK: Open University Press.

Bruce, N. (1985, April). *Juvenile justice in Scotland: A historical perspective?* Paper presented at a Franco-British workshop, The Best Interests of the Child. Edinburgh, UK.

Cameron, C. (2004). Social pedagogy and care: Danish and German practice in young people's residential care. *Journal of Social Work*, *4*(2), 133–151. doi:10.1177/1468017304044858

Comm. of Ministers, *Recommendation*, 1040th Meeting, Doc. No. CM/Rec(2008)11 (2008).

Committee on Children and Young Persons. (1964). *The Kilbrandon report: Children and young persons: Scotland*. Edinburgh, Scotland: Scottish Home and Health Department, Scottish Education Department. Retrieved from http://www.scotland.gov.uk/Publications/2003/10/18259/26879

E.S.C. Res. 1997/30, U.N. Doc. E/RES/1997/30 (July 21, 1997).

G.A. Res. 40/33, U.N. Doc. A/RES/40/33 (Nov 29, 1985).

G.A. Res 44/25, U.N. Doc. A/RES/44/25 (Nov. 20, 1989).

G.A. Res. 45/110, U.N. Doc. A/RES/45/110 (Dec. 14, 1990).

G.A. Res. 45/112, U.N. Doc. A/RES/45/112 (Dec. 14, 1990).

G.A. Res. 45/113, U.N. Doc. A/RES/45/113 (Dec. 14, 1990).

Goldson, B. (2009). Counterblast: "Difficult to understand or defend" – A reasoned case for raising the age of criminal responsibility. *Howard Journal of Criminal Justice*, *48*(5), 514–521. doi:10.1111/j.1468-2311.2009.00592.x

Goldson, B., & Muncie, J. (2012). Towards a global "child friendly" juvenile justice? *International Journal of Law, Crime and Justice*, *40*(1), 47–64. doi:10.1016/j.ijlcj.2011.09.004

Group of Specialists on Child-Friendly Justice (CJ-S-CH). (2010). *4th draft of the Council of Europe guidelines on child-friendly justice.* Strasbourg, France: Council of Europe.

Hämäläinen, J. (2003). The concept of social pedagogy in the field of social work. *Journal of Social Work*, *3*(1), 69–80. doi:10.1177/1468017303003001005

Harvey, R. (2002). The UK before the UN Committee on the Rights of the Child. *Child-RIGHT, 10*(190), 9-11. Retrieved from http://www.childrenslegalcentre.com/index.php?page=childright_archive

Howard League for Penal Reform. (2007, July 26). *Press release: Howard League hails Court of Appeal victory.* London: Author.

International Association of Schools of Social Work. (n.d.). Global definition of the social work profession. Retrieved March 14, 2014, from http://www.iassw-aiets.org/uploads/file/20140303_IASSW%20Website-SW%20DEFINITION%20approved%20IASSW%20Board%2021%20Jan%202014.pdf

International Federation of Social Workers. (2012, March 3). Statement of ethical principles. Retrieved March 14, 2014, from http://ifsw.org/policies/statement-of-ethical-principles/

Marshall, K. (2007). The present state of youth justice in Scotland. *The Scottish Journal of Criminal Justice Studies: The Journal of the Scottish Association for the Study of Delinquency*, *13*, 4–19. Retrieved from http://www.sastudyoffending.org.uk/journal

McNeill, F. (2006). A desistance paradigm for offender management. *Criminology & Criminal Justice*, *6*(1), 39–62. doi:10.1177/1748895806060666

Moss, P., & Petrie, P. (2002). *From children's services to children's spaces: Public policy, children and childhood. London.* Falmer Routledge.

Muncie, J. (2008). The "punitive" turn in juvenile justice: Cultures of control and rights compliance in Western Europe and the USA. *Youth Justice*, *8*(2), 107–121. doi:10.1177/1473225408091372

Paterson, L. (2000). Scottish democracy and Scottish utopias: The first year of the Scottish Parliament. *Scottish Affairs, 33*, 45-61. Retrieved from http://www.euppublishing.com/journal/scot

R (on the application of HC) v. Secretary of State for the Home Department, [2013] EWHC (Admin) 982, [2013] W.L.R. (D) 157 (Eng).

R (on the application of K) v. Manchester City Council, [2006] EWHC (Admin) 3164.

R (on the application of the Howard League for Penal Reform) v. Secretary of State for the Home Department, [2002] EWHC (Admin) 2497, [2003] 1 F.L.R. 484 (Eng).

Raynor, P. (1985). *Social work, justice and control.* Oxford, UK: Blackwell.

Raynor, P., & Vanstone, M. (1994). Probation practice, effectiveness and the non-treatment paradigm. *British Journal of Social Work, 24*, 387–404. Retrieved from http://bjsw.oxfordjournals.org/

Regina v. G, [2003] UKHL 50, [2004] 1 A.C. 1034 (appeal taken from Eng.).

The Scottish Government. (2008). *A guide to getting it right for every child.* Edinburgh, UK: Author.

The Scottish Government. (2013). *The Scottish policing performance framework: Annual report 2012-2013.* Edinburgh, UK: Author.

Smith, M., & Whyte, B. (2008). Social education and social pedagogy: Reclaiming a Scottish tradition in social work. *European Journal of Social Work, 11*(1), 15–28. doi:10.1080/13691450701357174

U.N. Committee on the Rights of the Child, 34th Sess., U.N. Doc. CRC/C/15/Add.215 (Oct. 3, 2003).

U.N. Committee on the Rights of the Child, 40th Sess., U.N. Doc. CRC/C/15/Add.268 (Oct. 20, 2005).

U.N. Committee on the Rights of the Child, 44th Sess., U.N. Doc. CRC/C/GC/10 (April 25, 2007).

United Nations Department of Economic and Social Affairs. (1981). Definition of youth. Retrieved from http://www.un.org/esa/socdev/documents/youth/fact-sheets/youth-definition.pdf

United Nations International Children's Emergency Fund. (2013). *The role of social work in juvenile justice.* Retrieved http://www.unicef.org/ceecis/UNICEF_report_ on_the_role_of_social_work_in_juvenile_justice.pdf

Ward, T., & Gannon, T. A. (2006). Rehabilitation, etiology, and self-regulation: The comprehensive good lives model of treatment for sexual offenders. *Aggression and Violent Behavior, 11*(1), 77–94. doi:10.1016/j.avb.2005.06.001

Ward, T., & Maruna, S. (2007). *Rehabilitation: Beyond the risk paradigm.* London: Routledge.

Whyte, B. (2009). *Youth justice in practice: Making a difference.* Bristol, UK: Policy Press.

## ADDITIONAL READING

Abramson, B. (2006). Juvenile justice: The "unwanted child" – Why the potential of the Convention on the Rights of the Child is not being realized, and what we can do about it. In E. L. Jensen & J. Jepsen (Eds.), *Juvenile law violators, human rights and the development of new juvenile justice systems* (pp. 15–38). Oxford: Hart.

Andrews, D., & Bonta, J. (1998). *The psychology of criminal conduct.* Cincinnati, OH: Anderson.

Cameron, C. (2013). Cross-national understandings of the purpose of professional-child relationships: Towards a social pedagogical approach. *International Journal of Social Pedagogy, 2*, 3–16. Retrieved from http://www.internationaljournalofsocialpedagogy.com/

Defence for Children International. (2007). *From legislation to action? Trends in juvenile justice systems across 15 countries.* Retrieved from https://www.defenceforchildren.org/files/DCI-JJ-Report-2007-FINAL-VERSION-with-cover.pdf

Goldson, B., & Muncie, J. (2006). Rethinking youth justice: Comparative analysis, international human rights and research evidence. *Youth Justice*, 6(2), 91–106. doi:10.1177/1473225406065560

Lockyer, A., & Stone, F. H. (1998). *Juvenile justice in Scotland: Twenty five years of the welfare approach*. Edinburgh: T. & T. Clark.

Lorenz, W. (2008). Paradigms and politics: Understanding methods paradigms in an historical context – The case of social pedagogy. *British Journal of Social Work*, 38(4), 625–644. doi:10.1093/bjsw/bcn025

McAra, L., & McVie, S. (2010). Youth crime and justice: Key messages from the Edinburgh study of youth transitions and crime. *Criminology & Criminal Justice*, 10(2), 179–209. doi:10.1177/1748895809360971

Pratt, J. (2008). Scandinavian exceptionalism in an era of penal excess: Part I – The nature and roots of Scandinavian exceptionalism. *The British Journal of Criminology*, 48(2), 119–137. doi:10.1093/bjc/azm072

Stephens, P. (2013). *Social pedagogy: Heart and head*. Bremen: EHV.

Storø, J. (2012). The difficult connection between theory and practice in social pedagogy. *International Journal of Social Pedagogy*, 1, 17–29. Retrieved from http://www.internationaljournalofsocialpedagogy.com/

## KEY TERMS AND DEFINITIONS

**Child:** Anyone who has not yet reached their 18th birthday.

**Criminal Responsibility:** The age at which a child becomes responsible for his or her actions and can be legally prosecuted as a juvenile.

**Delinquent Act:** Any act committed by a child or young person that is a criminal offence if committed by an adult.

**Juvenile Delinquency:** A youth who has been found by a judge in juvenile court to have committed a violation of the criminal law.

**Juvenile/Youth justice:** The system for dealing with crimes committed by children or adolescents.

**Practice Paradigm:** A model or set of assumptions, concepts, values, and practices that constitutes a way of viewing social reality.

**Social Pedagogy:** An approach to caring for children which combines education and care, emphasising that bringing up children is the shared responsibility of parents and society. The term *pedagogy* originates from the Greek *paidagogeo*, meaning "a child's guide" based on principles around holistic education and well-being.

**Youth:** As defined by the United Nations anyone between 15 and 24 years of age.

# Chapter 9
# Social Work Practice Outcomes:
## Making a Measurable Difference

**Colin Pritchard**
*Bournemouth University, UK*

**Richard Williams**
*Bournemouth University, UK*

## ABSTRACT

*The key issue in all human services is outcome. The authors report on a series of four mixed methods research studies to conclude that good social work can bring about positive measurable differences to inform policy and practice. The first focuses on how effective Western nations have been in reducing Child Abuse Related Deaths (CARD); the second explores a three-year controlled study of a school-based social work service to reduce truancy, delinquency, and school exclusion; the third examines outcomes of "Looked After Children" (LAC); the forth re-evaluates a decade of child homicide assailants to provide evidence of the importance of the child protection-psychiatric interface in benefiting mentally ill parents and improving the psychosocial development and protection of their children. These studies show that social work has a measurable beneficial impact upon the lives of those who had been served and that social work can be cost-effective, that is, self-funding, over time.*

## INTRODUCTION

### The Need for Evaluation

Social work is a discipline found in all Western democracies and, despite variations in service delivery, all social workers are concerned with the pursuit of social justice. Social work is involved with the care and protection of children and adults, the rehabilitation of offenders, and care and support of the mentally ill, to name but some of the main contexts of practice. In every country, irrespective of its current political ethos, social work has considerable statutory powers as social workers are often charged to "control because we care". This frequently means facing the dilemma of balancing conflicting human rights – classically, those between a vulnerable child and their neglecting parent, or safeguarding the mentally ill from predations of either family or society. Consequently, the social worker walks the tightrope of serving either the client or the state.

DOI: 10.4018/978-1-4666-6563-7.ch009

Social work, like medicine, is a science-based art, drawing upon the social and cognitive sciences as well as the biological sciences and neurosciences. Social work's model of human behaviour recognises a constant interaction and interplay between biological-psychological-social factors that align best with the person-in-environment perspective. In brief, this model assumes that human beings are bio-psycho-social entities. Sometimes the biological "leads" while at other times the psychosocial is key, with each of the elements continually interacting.

Classically, medicine is concerned with life-promoting and life-saving outcomes; so, too, is social work. Social workers' decisions can lead to the enforced separation of a child from its parents, compulsory admission to a hospital, return of an offender to prison, or separation of elderly partners from each other. Such social work decisions are as life-affecting as any decisions that a medical doctor might make in relation to patients. Hence the significance of these questions: when do social worker know they have been effective, and can social workers show that they have benefited their clients and society?

## GOOD SOCIAL WORK WORKS

A clinical supervisor at the start of each supervision session might begin with the words: "What have you done for your client today? What ease, comfort, change, and support have you brought about?" The rather truncated Hippocratic oath of medicine is "do thou no harm", an ethical statement to which most social workers would aspire. However, a far better ideal would be to ask, "are you part of the solution or part of the problem?" If we offer our client inadequate social work care and support, this may leave them more vulnerable than before our involvement. Therefore, we have an ethical imperative to assess accurately our clients' needs and intervene appropriately, based on the evidence-informed approaches available.

All social workers will wonder on reflection whether they could have done better when things have gone wrong, a situation which one of us has previously described (Pritchard, 1995). However, this chapter brings together a series of studies which show that good social work works and can make a measurable positive difference both to the individual, their families, and more generally to the wider society. This first example below describes social work's role in the prevention of child abuse related deaths.

## Has the Media "Got it Wrong" about Child Abuse Related Deaths (CARD)?

We begin with a large scale quantitative research study of what, in the early 1960s, shocked the Western world. People thought battered baby syndrome (Kempe, Silverman, Steele, Droegemueller, & Silver, 1962) could not occur in the affluent context of North America, as it involved the extremes of child neglect and abuse, often resulting in child deaths.

In 1962, one of us worked as a Principal Psychiatric Social Worker in the UK and shared the common sceptical reaction to Kempe's battered baby syndrome. However, in 1973 the reporting of a high profile child abuse case resulting in death (Maria Colwell) made the UK realise that Kempe and his colleagues had made us think the unthinkable. As a consequence of reporting the death of Maria Colwell, the UK, along with other Western countries, began to place child protection far higher up the policy agenda than hitherto. The UK did not have its Children's Department until 1948, a service with relative minimal powers to remove children from the home and take them into public care. But when the rate of CARD became recognised, various Western countries started to develop their child protection services in earnest.

The first international comparative study of the frequency of CARD explored how effective the nations were in reducing CARD and found that in

1973 the UK had the fourth highest CARD rate in the international league table (Pritchard, 1992). This was based upon the simple measurement of confirmed child homicides, i.e. it was known that there was an assailant so the death was not considered "accidental" or self-inflicted. Data for this study was drawn from WHO statistics for babies (<1 year) and infants (1-4 years) to calculate a 0-4 year old rate. The study demonstrated that, in contrast to the impression given by the media in many countries, CARD is relatively rare. Moreover, since the 1970s when most Western countries began to respond to CARD, there have been major reductions in most, if not all, countries (Pritchard, 1992; Pritchard & Sharples, 2008; Pritchard & Williams, 2011).

For this chapter, rather than dwell on what might be considered a historical 1970s baseline, we offer an original analysis from the latest WHO (2013) mortality data and compare a new three-year average, 1979-81, with the index years of 2008-10. We compare baseline rates of CARD per million (pm) with the outcomes for index years 2008-10 in the 21 Western countries or the countries latest index years available. Countries with earlier index years are indicated in Table 1.

One problem with using only confirmed homicides, it has been argued, is that the assailants, who are predominately parents or those in a parent role (90%), would seek to hide the offence (Creighton, 1993; Newton & Vandeven, 2006). The key WHO mortality category which most likely contains under-reported CARD is Undetermined Death (UnD). UnD always includes a degree of violence but is used when the authorities cannot determine whether the causes of death result from accident or self-infliction, the result of third party actions, or are simply unknown. The death would consequently be categorised as undetermined because it is unclear whether the death was accidental or self-inflicted, the latter being highly unlikely for children under five. Perhaps in the 1980s and early 1990s, before the development and strengthening of child protection procedures, the possibility that

UnD would contain a "hidden" CARD might have been more likely. However, the present concern about the extremes of abuse, a UnD containing a CARD, whilst still possible is probably now less likely.

We report confirmed CARD deaths for 0-4 year olds and a third of all UnD deaths, and then sum the confirmed CARD and a third of UnD as combined deaths to counter any suggestion we have under-estimated the incidence and frequency of CARD. Table 1 shows the results. By the nature of the crime, these figures can never be totally accurate given efforts by the perpetrators to conceal such an event, but it is the best established evidence available at a national level.

The first point to note is that the highest CARD for the most vulnerable group, 0-4 years, is currently at 51 per million (pm) in the USA, followed by Belgium and New Zealand at 24pm, and Switzerland at 20pm, indicating that the actual numbers are very small. For example, for the period 2008-10, in the USA out of 60.79 million children aged from 0-14, there was an annual average of 1,068 confirmed CARD, and in the UK out of 10.74 million children aged from 0-14, there was only an annual average of 13 confirmed CARD (WHO, 2013). These figures were far exceeded by road deaths in both countries (Pritchard, 2002; Pritchard & Williams, 2011; WHO, 2013). The CARD rates in Belgium (24pm), Greece (5pm), the Netherlands (16pm), and Switzerland (20pm) have increased since the 1979-81 period; conversely, nine countries reduced their confirmed CARD by more than 50% over the period.

The four countries with the highest rates of current Undetermined Deaths (UnD) were New Zealand at 18pm, followed by Portugal and the USA at 15pm, and Belgium at 13pm, whilst twelve countries had UnD at fewer than 5pm.

In regard to the Combined CARD and UnD rates, again the USA was highest at 66pm, followed by New Zealand 42pm, Belgium 37pm, and Germany at 25pm. Eight countries had current Combined rates of <10pm. These were the

*Table 1. Child abuse related deaths (CARD) & Undetermined deaths (UnD) rates per million plus Combined CARD & 33% UnD: Countries ranked by highest Combined rates*

| Country 1989-91 v Latest year | 0 – 4 years CARD – UnD | 0 – 4 years Combined |
|---|---|---|
| 1. USA 2005-07 Ratio | 65 – 23 51 – 15 0.78 – 0.65 | 88 66 0.75 |
| 2. New Zealand 2008-08 Ratio | 28 – 0 24 – 18 0.86 – 18x | 28 42 1.50 |
| 3. Belgium 2004-06 Ratio | 7 – 17 24 – 13 3.43 – 0.76 | 24 37 1.54 |
| 4=. Canada 2002-04 Ratio | 19 – 5 16 – 9 0.84 – 1.80 | 24 25 1.00 |
| 4=. Germany 2008-10 Ratio | 21 – 8 17 – 8 0.81 – 1.0 | 29 25 0.86 |
| 6. Japan 2007-09 Ratio | 19 – 13 10 – 12 0.53 – 0.92 | 32 22 0.69 |
| 7. Switzerland 2005-07 Ratio | 11 – 3 20 – 0 1.82 – 0x | 14 20 1.43 |
| 8=. Finland 2008-10 Ratio | 19 – 12 8 – 11 0.42 – 0.92 | 31 19 0.61 |
| 8=. Netherlands 2008-10 Ratio | 8 – 1 16 – 3 2.0 – 3 | 9 19 2.11 |
| 10. Austria 2008-10 Ratio | 38 – 4 10 – 8 0.26 – 2 | 42 18 0.43 |
| 11. Portugal 2008-10 Ratio | 18 – 40 2 – 15 0.11 – 0.38 | 58 17 0.29 |
| 12. France 2006-08 Ratio | 14 – 12 11 – 3 0.79 – 0.25 | 26 15 0.54 |
| 13. Australia 2004-06 Ratio | 21 – 4 10 – 1 0.48 – 0.25 | 25 11 0.45 |
| 14. UK 2008-10 Ratio | 14 – 18 5 – 4 0.36 – 0.22 | 32 9 0.28 |
| 15=. Denmark 2004-06 Ratio | 25 – 2 4 – 3 0.16 – 1.50 | 27 7 0.26 |

*continued in next column*

*Table 1. Continued*

| Country 1989-91 v Latest year | 0 – 4 years CARD – UnD | 0 – 4 years Combined |
|---|---|---|
| 15=. Sweden 2008-10 Ratio | 15 – 2 6 – 1 0.40 – 0.50 | 17 7 0.41 |
| 17. Italy 2006-08 Ratio | 4 – 2 5 – 1 1.20 – 0.50 | 6 6 1 |
| 18. Greece 2007-09 Ratio | 1 – 0 5 – 0 5 – 1 | 1 5 5 |
| 19=. Norway 2008-10 Ratio | 13 – 0 3 – 0 0.23 – 1 | 13 3 0.23 |
| 19=. Spain 2007-09 Ratio | 3 – 1 3 – <1 1 – 0.75 | 4 3 1 |
| 19=. Ireland 2007-09 Ratio | 2 – 0 0 – 3 xx – 3x | 2 3 1.50 |

UK (9pm), Denmark and Sweden (7pm), Italy (6pm), Greece (5pm), and Norway, Spain, and Ireland (3pm).

There were, however, some countries with relatively big ratio increases over the period: Netherlands 1:2.11, Ireland and New Zealand 1:1.50, and Switzerland 1:1.43; though it must be remembered these rates indicate quite small numbers of actual deaths. Conversely, seven countries had comparative falls of equivalent of more than 50% with ratios of 1:0.50 over the period; Austria 1:0.43, Australia 1:0.45, Sweden 1:0.41, Portugal 1:0.29, the UK 1:0.28, Denmark 1:0.26, and Norway 1:0.23; all of whom might be considered to be especially successful in reducing CARD.

Incidentally, as has been shown elsewhere (Pritchard & Williams, 2011), the UK was only one of two countries whose CARD rates fell significantly more than the general Child-

Mortality-Rates (CMR), indicating that British child protection underwent a greater improvement than its general paediatric services (Pritchard, Davey, & Williams, 2013). Perhaps surprisingly, five English-speaking countries (UK, Australia, Canada, New Zealand, USA) had the highest CMR in 21 Western countries (Pritchard & Wallace, 2014) which suggests another avenue for social work research.

Admittedly, the Combined CARD rates probably overestimate possible hidden CARDS, as child abuse in the late 1970s and early 1980s was not the major policy and political concern it has become today. It might once have been easier to "hide" a CARD than would be the case today, but it is perhaps better to over-estimate the problem than be accused of under-estimating it.

In the next section, we will be turning our focus to a practice-based research project to examine its application to direct social work intervention.

## A Longitudinal Prospective Controlled Outcome Study of a School-Based Social Work Service (Mixed Qualitative and Quantitative Methodology)

One reason why medicine has progressed and why most medical schools teach evidence-based practice is because they have developed prospective, controlled, longitudinal studies of comparative treatments for a range of conditions to measure outcome. Studies exist in every speciality, including those closest to social work, i.e. medical treatment of the elderly, paediatrics, and psychiatry. This research approach identifies two groups/samples of respondents, with one group receiving a particular form of intervention whilst the other either has current standard care or another form of treatment; thus comparing intervention A with intervention B. After measuring the groups at the start of the intervention, the baseline, their progress is then measured over time from the same baseline to see which produces the better results for the patient.

This model is perfectly feasible for social work, as was shown in a three-year longitudinal, controlled prospective study of a school-based social work service compared with standard education social work service (Pritchard, Cotton, Bowen, & Williams, 1998; Pritchard & Williams, 2001; Williams & Pritchard, 2006). The study is not widely known, in part because the Home Office of the day was embarrassed by the results. One of us was told that his own report on the study (Pritchard, 2001) gave the wrong message. It seemed to be recommending a "soft" stance on crime, whereas the official message was to be "tough" on crime and "tough" on the causes of crime. So, after a two-year delay following the official end of the project and a restricted internal publication, the author's report on the study was virtually hidden on the Home Office website under "miscellaneous" and it has since been removed. The report clearly demonstrated that adequately funded basic front-line social work was highly effective, but it was thought that offering problematic teenagers a social work service might be seen as a "soft" approach.

This research project consisted of one full-time senior educational social worker assigned to linked primary and secondary schools, with a potential case-load of nearly 1,000 children aged 5-16 from a severely disadvantaged socio-economic area. The primary school was based in the county's most disadvantaged estate, carrying the highest rate of child protection referrals, proportionately more people on the books of social services and probation, the highest concentration of crime in the county, and having amongst the worst chronic unemployment in the whole region with 44% of fathers unemployed! Typically, in what are generally thought to be affluent areas, there are pockets of severe social deprivation which are invisible to the general public. In one sense, the poor in southern English cities are relatively worse off than in many inner-city metropolitan areas because they are concentrated and, being unrecognised, they remain socially isolated. The secondary school, adjacent to the primary school, was based in the third worst estate in the county. The project schools were matched with two other schools from other severely disadvantaged areas but not quite as under-resourced as the project schools.

At the beginning of the project, all the children aged 7-16 completed a self-reported questionnaire about their behaviour and attitude to education; this established a base-line range of behaviours and attitudes, both in and outside school. Because the questionnaire was designed to be simple and of interest to children, all four schools produced a 90%+ response rate from the primary school children aged 7-10 and the secondary school children aged 11-16.

At the start, the project schools had a worse profile on virtually everything, including truancy, theft (both in and out of the school), vandalism, fighting, smoking, drug misuse, and negative attitudes about education. However, the control schools were only a little better and both secondary schools had some of the worst General Certificate of Secondary Education (GCSE) results in the region, as well as having the highest school exclusion rates in the county. The latter meant either expensive, but often ineffective, "home tuition" or the even more expensive option of "pupil referral units" (PRU), which bring together some of the most disruptive children in the system. Perhaps not surprisingly, on testing the teachers' morale in the four schools, there was a very high rate of work-related stress and absenteeism.

The project's aims were educational and centred upon the child. Truancy was not to be tolerated, though it was recognised that truancy occurred either because of problems with the child, the family, the school, or a combination of all three. The zero-tolerance policy regarding truancy was not punitive but rather taken as a serious indicator that the child and/or their family needed immediate help.

The project was independently monitored throughout by one of us (Pritchard) who was the "counter" and had the easier task; the social work practitioner, the "doer", was the other (Williams). Williams' approach was to engage the child and the family in a positive child-focused relationship and to reduce stress and problems of communication in an effort to (re)engage the child with their education and, thereby, facilitate their integration into society to maximise the child's potential. Whilst the project had the active co-operation of both head-teachers, not all the teachers welcomed the intervention, some thinking it was colluding with "neglectful parents". Indeed, there were two teacher respondents who were particularly unreceptive and thus proved to be an invaluable baseline to compare progress three years on.

Williams' initial opening in the first week of the project convinced the evaluator that the initiative would not last out the term. He eschewed having a separate office in the schools, and, through his attendance in the staff room, invited the staff of each school to refer their ten most "problematic" children! It proved to be an excellent move as within months the teachers could see a positive change in some of their most troublesome children. In gaining teacher confidence, he encouraged earlier and earlier referrals, including children with any unexplained absence from school (Pritchard & Williams, 2001).

At the end of the first year, there were slight improvements in the project schools compared with the controls which were also surveyed annually. Regular visits were made to remind the schools that they were being "assessed". By the second year, these improvements were now significantly better on many of the measures, and by the end of the third year, the project schools had measurably transformed the children's behaviour in and out of school, not least by reducing crime and drug misuse on their estates.

Half way through, we became concerned about measuring the degree of pupil engagement. We, therefore, undertook a county wide survey with a random sample of children and young people on the case load of the Education Social Work Service. These children and young people were a serious challenge in the schools, often in danger of being excluded or their parents were being prosecuted because of their children's persistent non-attendance at school.

From the case load of the 28 full-time equivalent education social workers, the sample consisted of a total of 112 children. We found that where the social worker had "engaged" the child, based upon the child's confidential anonymous perception, positive results had occurred. In the county, 8% of the children were definitely not engaged, 76% were; the remaining children did not report either way. In the case of the project school, 3% of the children remained non-engaged, 5% unsure and 92% responded extremely positively about their education social worker (Pritchard et al., 1998). This was a vitally important finding as the social worker's approach was essentially based upon establishing and sustaining supportive counselling and, therefore, improving relationships with children and invariably the family.

The results at the end of the third year were remarkable. The secondary school had its best GCSE results ever. The project school teachers' stress rate fell dramatically, and as one of the unreceptive group said in their final interview:

*I still don't really hold with this soft approach. Parents should be made to be responsible but I'll say this for the project, it got the parents off my back so I could do the job I'm paid to do: teach the children. (Anonymous, personal communication, October 2000)*

This teacher was very committed and child-focused, but she could never quite understand why she found it difficult to reach some of the disruptive children and especially their parents. Nevertheless, she cared and she did find that the children responded once the pressures had been lessened at home.

A minimal Cost-Benefit-Analysis was carried out, based upon reduced cost of crime and the savings from reduced cost of exclusion from school and entry into Pupil Referral Units (PRU). Based upon the Home Office's own figures, the typical cost of offences and court appearances for the 14-16 year olds was at the time £2,700, but the annual cost of PRU places was then £14,000. We were so surprised at the cost saved that we erred on the side of caution. We focussed *only* upon the cost of those teenagers from the project estate and the comparable disadvantaged estate of the control school, rather than the whole three year cohort between first and third years, to calculate any savings obtained; this was because it was the youngsters in these especially deprived areas who initially had the higher rate of delinquency and were considered to be at most risk.

Overall, there was an annual saving equivalent of a minimum £87,000 p.a. *over and above* the cost of the project, including evaluation costs. This was an equivalent of 111% return on the "investment", demonstrating that the approach was cost-effective and self-funding. This figure did not include any savings to the health service related to reduced drug misuse, or any estimated cost to those homes which were not burgled or property not vandalised, nor did it consider the hidden cost of the benefit of improved staff morale in the project schools. Significantly, it did not attempt to estimate the long term contributions to the economy made by the young people who left school with improved attainment levels.

Perhaps the most remarkable finding was that in the final year of project secondary school, all parents had visited the school at least once for a non-disciplinary reason, indicating the growing identification with the school and its educational aspirations, better preparing these young people for a more effective future (Pritchard & Williams, 2001). Highly significant was the finding that child protection referrals fell to below the county average and each one of these involved self-referral; a development that readily conforms with the spirit of the recommendation for partnership in working with families made by Munro (2011).

Fortunately, the school-based-social work service did not end after the Home Office funding ceased, as the project secondary school elected to continue with the approach. Indeed, it was further developed, becoming an integral part of the school's inclusion initiative (Williams & Pritchard, 2006).

A key feature of the project's evaluation was that it used an integrated methodology. Qualitative methods for in-depth interviews were used with teachers and some children. Quantitative methods were employed for in-depth analysis of case records, education, police, and social services data, and the annual children's questionnaires; this last questionnaire aimed to elicit demographic backgrounds, attitudes to education, and their behaviour in and out of school.

The ongoing success of this project led to a study of the outcomes of some of the most disadvantaged children in society, that is, children who need to be taken into care. A study focusing on such children is reported below.

## Looked After Children: A Controlled Retrospective Outcome Study

Legislation to protect children will vary in every country but all have some form of statutory powers to remove children from their family home. In the UK, such children are described as "Looked After Children" (LAC). Stein and colleagues (Biehel, Clayden, & Stein, 1995) first alerted us to the major issue of poor outcomes for LAC in the UK. Despite improvements over the last decade, Stein (2012) has still found relatively poorer psychosocial outcomes of former LAC compared with young people from the general population who have never been in care. However, we offer in this chapter a more meaningful comparative measure of outcome for LAC than comparison of this group to the general population of children and young people.

Following the Home Office funded study described above, the issue of what happened to "educational failures", those Excluded-from-School (EFS), was raised. This led to an examination of the records of the county's five year cohort of young people who had been permanently excluded-from-school. These were all young men now aged 16-24 years.

We initially found that 10% of the 215 young EFS men had also been in the care of the local authority as LAC. Thinking of the work of Stein (2012) and others, we had assumed that, being *both* former LAC and EFS, this group would have had a doubly worse outcome. To our pleasant surprise, the doubly disadvantaged sub-group had a statistically significant better outcome than those who were only EFS, as based upon police and social service records. The apparent difference between the young men was that the former LAC had ongoing social work support after leaving care, whereas the "ordinary" former EFS young men had virtually no follow-up service until they came into contact with the police. Initially, it was thought this result may have been an artefact of a relatively small sample size but the Local Authority went on to ask us to examine a matched five-year cohort of their former LAC and EFS young men.

The uniqueness of this study came from contrasting the LAC outcomes with another disadvantaged group, EFS young men. The LAC cohort would initially have been more disadvantaged than the EFS, otherwise the EFS would also have been in care, as were the sub-group of youngsters being both LAC and EFS. Thus, we had a natural control group which was studied longitudinally as each group could serve as a basis for comparison with the other, albeit retrospectively.

The results were surprising. In virtually all areas, we found that the former LAC (n=438) men now aged 16-24 had measurable better outcome benefits compared to the EFS (n= 215). The LAC men had statistically significantly far fewer post-care criminal convictions, far lower re-conviction rates than the official Home Office's prediction, and significantly lower criminality with LAC at 36% to EFS at 64%. The LAC who were offenders had far fewer crimes than the EFS and crucially, the LAC had far fewer convictions for violence than the EFS men with 9% compared to 25%. The unsupported former EFS had a conviction rate more than 1000 times higher than this age group in the general population.

Currently, to randomly find one murderer aged between 16-24 years in the UK would require more than 78,000 young men; the EFS had three from the group of 215 young men. Also, the former LAC had no suicides, whilst the EFS had a suicide rate 100 times the rate of their age peers in the general population with two in 215 young men; randomly finding one suicide of this age would require more than 14,000 young men. However, the one area where LAC did slightly less well than the EFS was as victims of crime, 24% to 22%, with one former LAC being a murder victim. It should be noted that both groups, therefore, had a relatively high rate of being victims of crime, although they did live in areas of high density criminality. Although 12% of the former LAC continued to lead disruptive lives, having committed an offence in the previous year, the majority did not, resulting in a saving of hundreds of thousands of pounds of public finances compared to the EFS men.

This study showed that the long-term support by front-line social workers to young people, who are likely to be carrying a continued degree of psychosocial disadvantage, was cost-effective.

Social work follow-up services were not just of benefit to the public purse but also helped these young people create a better life for themselves than might otherwise have been the case.

## Identifying a "Disregarded" Disadvantaged Group

An important yet overlooked finding was that this study identified another disadvantaged group, namely former EFS. Although a significant majority of men in British prisons had experienced exclusion from school, agencies and politicians do not appear to recognise the needs of these young people. To be excluded in practical terms is to be seen as "undeserving". Teenagers, so defined, are given the message that society has rejected them, making them virtually unemployable and stigmatised. Conversely, society rightly sees former LAC as victims and "deserving young people" who merit society's care. To illustrate this point the following example is offered.

Recently, we met a group of former London-based EFS young people at the National Children's Bureau. All expressed extreme bitterness at their treatment by the education system and the phrases they constantly used when describing their personal circumstances included the following comments: "we were kicked out", "nobody cared", "nobody was interested".

The inevitable educational under-achievement of these former EFS young men results in a high degree of social isolation. This under-achievement leaves crime, drugs, or welfare benefit lifestyles as an almost rational economic response to their plight. Education social work in the UK is singularly under-resourced, but it should be an area given highest importance and priority, as maintaining the link with a highly vulnerable group of young people through social workers based in schools might well be the last opportunity to prevent a long-term criminal career.

## THE CHILD PROTECTION-PSYCHIATRIC INTERFACE: A FUTURE POLICY

We now turn to an admittedly controversial section based upon a study of a decade of child homicide assailants from a 4% sample of the UK population, which in social science terms is a large scale sample. This study led us to argue for the need to prioritise the child protection-psychiatric interface as we seek more accurately to determine the risk to children whose parents have diagnosed psychiatric disorders.

Perhaps the biggest issue for most Western world social workers is that of the extremes of child abuse which result in the death of a child. There are various models of assessment which are generally too broad to yield confidence in their predictive powers, classically because they produce too many false positives.

### National Incidence of CARD

It is important to note how relatively few CARD assailants there are. In the UK general population in 1990 there were 10,469,000 men aged the same as our assailants in the Wessex study, with an annual average of 43 child (0-14) murders. Thus, to randomly find one murderer would require 243,465 men, assuming that all the 43 homicides were committed by men, when in fact under five-year old child homicides (0-5) are more often committed by women. However, by 2008-10 confirmed CARD in the UK averaged only 13 per annum (WHO, 2013), with a male population of 12,672,000. This incidence could be extrapolated to predict that there would be one CARD murderer in 974,769 men. Despite the media reporting of such events, this highlights just how statistically rare such tragic events are. However, we now move from a quantitative perspective because qualitative experience has shown that re-analysis of earlier statistical analysis is required.

### Qualitative Insights

Doctors, nurses, and social workers can become desensitised to the human tragedies with which they deal; so too can academic researchers. One needs to remain "detached" when examining a decade of child homicides and the records of a further two years of cases of convicted sex abuse records with a large sample (n=238). But such detachment can blind one to the enormity of what has happened. When one of us was bathing his grandson, then aged three years and who was thus contemporaneous with Peter Connelly (known in the media as "Baby P", a high-profile media case in which the child was killed by brutal step-fathers), he remarked to himself: "Look at him. He looks like a skinned rabbit but his personality fills our home with joy". And speaking not as an academic psychiatric social worker but as a father and grand-father, he asked, "How can anybody persistently be cruel to a child?"

This revelation led to a major re-evaluation of the data on the study of a decade of child homicides and focused upon who killed children, not their comparative frequency (Pritchard et al., 2013). The data to be analysed was drawn from police records and the incidence of mental illness within the general population (Jenkins et al., 1998; Metzler, Gill, Pettigrew, & Hinds, 1995).

There were 13,419 mentally ill men estimated to be living in the Wessex region. Over a ten year period, one in 3,355 mentally ill men killed a child; whilst of the estimated 8,002 mentally ill women, 8 were assailants. This means that one in 1,003 killed over that ten year period. These statistics are vastly different from the ratios found in the general population. For example, currently there are 16,867 million UK men the same age as our assailants. If we assumed that all UK children (0-14) were killed by men (12 in 2010), then to randomly find one child-killer would need 1,405 million men. Nonetheless, even with such small numbers over the decade these ratios can still be used in the assessment of risk to the child. However, with such big ratios it is far too easy to have false positives when estimating the risk of a child fatality but as will be seen below there are indicators which can aid in a more realistic assessment.

In regard to the violent multi-criminal child sex abusers (VMCCSA), so described because of their previous convictions, assailants were found both within and extra-family. Based upon police records, there were 990 such men in the region. The four within-family and five extra-family perpetrators of abuse yields a ratio of one in 110 of such men who killed children over the decade.

When we looked at other British studies of deaths related to mental disorder and in serious case reviews (Brandon et al., 2008; Falkov 1996), we discovered that, in highlighting the psychiatric diagnosis as a variable in the incidence of child abuse, the two variables strongly correlated which suggests a degree of external validation of our findings.

We estimate that of the Wessex cases, half the children who died may not have done so had adult psychiatrists considered "child protection" and had the child protection social workers thought about "mental illness" in relation to parents. A family-centred treatment could then have been offered. Most important would have been the benefits to the children since they often become "carers" for their parents in times of disturbance. These children need active support during such times and not merely for "child protection" reasons.

## A Need to Rethink?

It is very rare for academics to admit that their previously accepted research was flawed but this was the case with the first published study of a decade of child homicides from the Wessex region of England (Pritchard, 2004; Pritchard & Bagley, 2001). This research yielded a total of 23 assailants who over a decade killed 33 children. Within

this total group, the majority of assailants were from within the murdered child's family. Of the assailants studied, there were 18 parents of whom 12 were diagnosed with a mental illness. Indeed, all the four fathers diagnosed as being mentally ill killed themselves after the tragedy, as did two mothers who had a diagnosed mental illness. A further two of the eight mothers diagnosed with a mental illness, who were included in the study, attempted suicide. These results were disturbing because we did not want to add further stigma to those diagnosed as mentally ill but researchers must report as they find. However, we later realised that we had made the mistake of focusing upon the differential levels of risk of child murder by the "categories" of the assailants. To redress this, we re-analysed the raw data and now report those reworked findings.

Within-family assailants were the most frequent assailants with eight mothers diagnosed as mentally ill, four fathers diagnosed as mentally ill, four step-fathers/de facto partners having had previous convictions for violence, and two mothers having children on the Child Protection Register. We then translated these frequencies into rate per million (pm) to derive some idea of the differential risk. Mentally ill fathers were involved in child deaths by abuse at a rate of 30pm, mentally ill mothers (MIM) 100pm, mothers of children on the Child Protection Register twice the MIM rate, and step-fathers/cohabitees four times the MIM rate.

The minority assailants over the decade were the five extra-family male killers, all of whom were VMCCSA, but these extra-family VMCCSA killed 50 times the MIM rate (Pritchard, 2004). Great stress was made about these VMCCSA being minorities or a rarity. Whilst, clearly, they are extremely dangerous, somewhat controversially we advocated consideration of reviewable sentences for such men, if convicted of a sex and violent crime, before they went on to kill (Pritchard & Sayer, 2006).

## Focusing on the CARD Assailants

Who is responsible for the intentional deaths of children by abuse and neglect? The answer, based upon the evidence, is reasonably simple and clear. The first group consists mainly of the mentally ill parents, that is, those who have a diagnosed mental illness and who neither have access to, nor receive, the integrated family-based treatment they require and who are found to have delusional ideas and thinking that lead to the abuse of their children. The actions of these parents, rather than being intentionally malicious, are generally seen as an act of misguided care, based, paradoxically, in love for the child.

The second major group, based upon their criminal records and previous convictions for violence, consists of the severely personality disordered. Both as parents and as extra-family assailants seen in their earlier and often life-long pattern of violence, they are reported to express "zero degrees of empathy" (Baron-Cohen, 2011). Such men are more likely to be responsible for death by child abuse. Such a finding would hardly surprise a criminologist.

The following vignettes are illustrations from cases involved in the research previously undertaken by us.

## Neglect of a Three-Year-Old

A young mother with borderline learning difficulties went shopping one cold November night in the United Kingdom. Due to her personality, she was always desperate for attention and was seeking this when she met a man in a public bar. She quietly gave her three year old child a nip of spirits so that he went to sleep, concealed the child behind rubbish bins, and then went for sex with the man. Hours later, a distraught mother who had forgotten that her child had been left sleeping outside, went to the police to report her missing child. Unfortunately, it was too late; the child died

of exposure. The mother was grief stricken. She had no previous convictions for violence but was severely personality disordered.

## The Domestically Violent Step-Father

One step-father assailant, with a previous conviction for violence, murdered his stepson following a horrendous act of rape, brutally mutilating his stepson in characteristic rage. He had beaten his wife and fractured the skull of the five year old who had come to his mother's assistance. He blamed his wife, as illustrated by his comment: "She shouldn't wind me up as she knows I have a temper". This man was incapable of expressing any compassion and empathy for others including women and children, a trait common to men with a psychopathic personality structure (Baron-Cohen, 2011).

## The Loving but Deluded Parent

This case involved a successful businessman who was having paranoid delusions. As a Muslim he heard Shatan, the Islamic equivalent of the Christian Devil, saying he would destroy good Muslims by giving their children HIV/AIDS. In order to save his children, in a misguided act of love he killed them. He then killed himself when he became aware of the enormity of what he had done.

## The Depressed Suicidal Mother

A mother, profoundly depressed, apparently responding to her daughter's plea, "don't leave me behind", killed her child in what the mother believed would be a joint suicide. The mother was resuscitated, only to face life-long guilt over what she had done to her daughter.

Apart from the severe personality disordered, although some researchers do claim there are improving outcomes for such men, all the other assailants needed the effective help which would be obtainable if the child protection-psychiatric interface was recognised. In the case of those parents who are diagnosed with mental health conditions, this service provision is feasible and should be available.

So, to conclude this section with a further controversial point, we argue that the child protection focus is wrongly placed upon the extremes of child abuse. It should rather re-focus upon improvements to the development of the child care and protection/psychiatric interface. In addition, when national governments tackle relative poverty, this initiative will sit well with social work's commitment to social justice and, as our research has shown, will also be likely to lead to a further reduction in child abuse related deaths.

## Children of Mentally Ill Parents: A Neglected Group?

It is easy to ignore the psychosocial impact of a parental mental disorder and the influence it can exert upon the child. Imagine what it must be like for children to hear their parents talking of killing themselves in the midst of their profound depression, hearing a mother or father express extreme delusional ideas of alien invasion, or to have parents diagnosed with "severe personality" disorder and being thus incapable of effective parenting which includes the capacity to care, nurture, and demonstrate empathy. A lack of these emotional competencies is often disproportionately found amongst violent offenders and may be factors in the personality structure of those parents who go on to abuse their children (Baron-Cohen, 2011). Therefore, social workers need to remember the impact parental mental illness can have on a child's subsequent mental health (Pritchard, 2004, 2006), which recent research findings would suggest is a relatively neglected area in most Western countries with the exception of Norway and Germany (Mattejat & Remschmidt, 2008; Mechling, 2011; Siegenthaler, Munder, & Egger, 2012; Wiegand-Grefe, Geers, Petermann, & Plass, 2011).

## The Implications for Social Work Practice

A family-centred bio-psychosocial treatment programme would have a built-in preventative element, considerably reducing risk and optimising children's subsequent psychosocial development. We recognise the recommended approach mentioned above is controversial. Therefore, social workers need to be able to provide appropriate, client-specific, considered, evidence-informed judgements. Research findings can be uncomfortable when they contradict our preconceptions and opinions, but when the research evidence changes we must change our minds, practice, and policies to align with new developments. These adjustments are needed, not least in regard to improving the psychosocial development of children of mentally ill parents, where an integrated approach is beginning to have some measurably positive outcomes (Gladstone, McKeever, Seeman, & Boydell, 2014; Gleeson et al., 2010; Ostman & Afzelius, 2011; Siegenthaler, et al, 2012; Van der Gagg et al., 2013; van Santvoort, Hosman, van Doesum, & Janssens, 2013).

We conclude on a positive note by remembering that CARD rates for many countries, including the UK, have never been lower since records began, and these outcomes can be further improved by focusing upon the child protection-psychiatric interface. As practitioners and social work academics, we are not seeking controversy but the research findings reported here produce these contradictions as well as directions for future reflection.

## A Digression: The Poverty Dimension and Re-Thinking CARD?

Child murderers have a very different demographic compared to those who murder adults where the assailants are predominately men. Although this finding surprised us, on reflection it made sense because despite the poor socio-economic circumstances of some assailants, especially where the step-fathers/cohabitees are concerned, the key over-riding factor is the psychological state of the assailant. Here is further, apparently contradictory evidence of our position. In the last analysis, Child-Mortality-Rates (CMR) are an indicator of how well a nation meets the needs of its children, just as mortality rates are more generally the ultimate measure for so many social consequences. For example, it was found that in 20 Western countries, relative poverty, as measured by Income Inequality (Wilkinson & Picket, 2009) and CMR, were strongly linked (Pritchard & Wallace, 2014).

Perhaps the most startling and totally unexpected finding in our re-evaluation of the CARD data emerged when correlating national CARD rates with poverty in 20 Western countries. Counter-intuitively, we found there was no statistical association with poverty and child deaths by abuse (Pritchard et at., 2013). This runs counter to within-nation clinical studies where there are proportionally more murders amongst socio-economically disadvantaged adults.

The five countries with the highest CMR had the worst relative poverty and the four countries with the lowest CMR had the least relative poverty (Pritchard et al., 2013; Pritchard & Wallace, 2014; Pritchard & Williams, 2011). An unexpected finding was that the current highest CMR was found in five of the six English-speaking countries which also had the worst relative poverty; alongside poverty, therefore, there may be cultural factors in operation.

This poverty dimension for total child mortality was suggested by the fact that the USA was ranked first for both relative poverty and CMR but there were marked differences between ethnic groups, with their white children's child mortality rates being the highest in the western world. But African American children died at the rate of 2.2 to one white child. It is noteworthy that there is no correlation between CARD rates and poverty in the USA; a finding which led us to interpret this data as showing that the key to child death by murder is the psychological/psychiatric state of the assailant. While poverty is an important variable to consider, only six of the 16 parents who killed in our regional study were socio-economically disadvantaged.

## CONCLUSION

For any human service, especially in regard to vulnerable and disadvantaged people in society, the question must be: is the service effective, does it bring measurable comfort, support, or change that can be transferred outside the locale of the study? Qualitative research has much to commend it and to do it well is very difficult, but so often it ends at showing interesting developments from a "sample" of 20, 30, or 50 people. The question then remains as to whether such results can be generalised. This almost inevitably means there must be some quantitative measures, not least for policy makers, to justify any public expenditure.

This chapter has shown that both at a macro and micro level good social work works and can contribute to improvements in people's lives and bring about major changes when measured at a national level – in reduced Child Abuse Related Deaths, in helping the relative successful integration of former Looked After Children, in offering a new preventive approach by recognising the child protection-psychiatric interface. At the local school level, adequately resourced social work can produce a cost-effective service for disruptive and disrupted children. This benefits both the wider community and, more importantly, the individual child who might have remained a victim of his or her socio-economically disadvantaged heritage.

It is hoped that an integral part of every social worker's practice will reflect the injunction of Maria Farrow (Pritchard's supervisor): "and what have you done for your client today?", with an integrated client-centred focus, so that most times they can be confident that they are facilitating measurable comfort, support, and change in people's lives.

## REFERENCES

Baron-Cohen, S. (2011). *Zero degrees of empathy: A new theory of human cruelty.* London: Allen Lane.

Biehal, N., Clayden, J., & Stein, M. (1995). *Moving on: Young people and leaving care schemes.* London: HMSO.

Brandon, M., Belderson, P., Warren, C., Howe, D., Gardner, R., Dodsworth, J., & Black, J. (2008). *Analysing child deaths and serious injury through abuse and neglect: What can we learn? A biennial analysis of serious case reviews 2003-2005* (Research Report DCSF-RR023). London: Department for Children, Schools and Families.

Creighton, S. J. (1993). Children's homicide: An exchange [Letter to the editors]. *British Journal of Social Work, 23,* 643–644. Retrieved from http://bjsw.oxfordjournals.org/

Falkov, A. (1996). *Study of working together "Part 8" reports: Fatal child abuse and parental psychiatric disorders: An analysis of 100 area child protection committee case reviews conducted under the terms of part 8 of Working Together Under the Childrens Act 1989* (ACPC Series, Report No.1). London: Department of Health.

Gladstone, B. M., McKeever, P., Seeman, M., & Boydell, K. M. (2014). Analysis of a support group for children of parents with mental illnesses: Managing stressful situations. *Qualitative Health Research, 24*(9), 1171–1182. doi:10.1177/1049732314528068 PMID:24659228

Gleeson, J. F., Cotton, S. M., Alvarez-Jimenez, M., Wade, D., Crisp, K., & Newman, B. et al. (2010). Family outcomes from a randomized control trial of relapse prevention therapy in first-episode psychosis. *The Journal of Clinical Psychiatry, 71*(04), 475–483. doi:10.4088/JCP.08m04672yel PMID:20021994

Jenkins, B., Bebbington, P., Brugha, T. S., Farrell, M., Lewis, G., & Meltzer, H. (1998). British psychiatric morbidity survey. *The British Journal of Psychiatry, 173*(1), 4–7. doi:10.1192/bjp.173.1.4 PMID:9850201

Kempe, C. H., Silverman, F. N., Steele, B. F., Droegemueller, W., & Silver, H. K. (1962). The battered-child syndrome. *Journal of the American Medical Association, 181*(1), 17–24. doi:10.1001/jama.1962.03050270019004 PMID:14455086

Mattejat, F., & Remschmidt, H. (2008). The children of mentally ill parents. *Deutsches Ärzteblatt International, 105,* 413–418. doi:10.3238/arztebl.2008.0413 PMID:19626164

Mechling, B. M. (2011). The experiences of youth serving as caregivers for mentally ill parents: A background review of the literature. *Journal of Psychosocial Nursing and Mental Health Services, 49,* 28–33. doi:10.3928/02793695-20110201-01 PMID:21323266

Metzler, H., Gill, B., Pettigrew, M., & Hinds, K. (1995). *The prevalence of psychiatric morbidity among adults living in private households.* London: The Stationery Office.

Munro, E. (2011). *The Munro review of child protection: Final report – A child-centred system. CM, 8062.* London: The Stationery Office.

Newton, A. W., & Vandeven, A. M. (2006). Unexplained infant and child death: A review of sudden infant death syndrome, sudden unexplained infant death, and child maltreatment fatalities including shaken baby syndrome. *Current Opinion in Pediatrics, 18*(2), 196–200. doi:10.1097/01.mop.0000193296.32764.1e PMID:16601503

Ostman, M., & Afzelius, M. (2011). Children's representatives in psychiatric services: What is the outcome? *The International Journal of Social Psychiatry, 57*(2), 144–152. doi:10.1177/0020764008100605 PMID:19875625

Pritchard, C. (1992). Changes in children's homicide in England and Wales and Scotland 1973-1988 as an indicator of effective child protection: A comparative study of Western European statistics. *British Journal of Social Work, 22,* 663–684.

Pritchard, C. (1995). *Suicide: The ultimate rejection? – A psycho-social study.* Buckingham: Open University Press.

Pritchard, C. (2001). *A family-teacher-social work alliance to reduce truancy and delinquency: The Dorset Healthy Alliance project* (RDS Occasional Paper No 78). London: Home Office, Research, Development and Statistics Directorate.

Pritchard, C. (2002). Children's homicide and road deaths in England and Wales and the USA: An international comparison 1974-1997. *British Journal of Social Work, 32*(4), 495–502. doi:10.1093/bjsw/32.4.495

Pritchard, C. (2004). *The child abusers: Research & controversy.* Maidenhead: Open University Press.

Pritchard, C. (2006). *Mental health social work: Evidence-based practice.* Abingdon: Routledge.

Pritchard, C., & Bagley, C. (2001). Suicide and murder in child murderers and child sexual abusers. *Journal of Forensic Psychiatry, 12*(2), 269–286. doi:10.1080/09585180110057208

Pritchard, C., Cotton, A., Bowen, D., & Williams, R. (1998). A consumer study of young people's views on their educational social worker: Engagement as a measure of an effective relationship. *British Journal of Social Work, 28*(6), 915–938. doi:10.1093/oxfordjournals.bjsw.a011408

Pritchard, C., Davey, J., & Williams, R. (2013). Who kills children?: Re-examining the evidence. *British Journal of Social Work, 43*(7), 1403–1438. doi:10.1093/bjsw/bcs051

Pritchard, C., & Sayer, T. (2006). Exploring potential "extra-familial" child homicide assailants in the UK and estimating their homicide rate: Perception of risk –- The need for debate. *British Journal of Social Work, 38*(2), 290–307. doi:10.1093/bjsw/bcl333

Pritchard, C., & Sharples, A. (2008). "Violent" deaths of children in England and Wales and the major developed countries 1974-2002: Possible evidence for improving child protection? *Child Abuse Review, 17*(5), 297–312. doi:10.1002/car.1016

Pritchard, C., & Wallace, M. S. (2014). Comparing UK and other Western countries' health expenditure, relative poverty and child mortality: Are British children doubly disadvantaged? *Children and Society.* Advance online publication. doi:10:1111/ CHSO12079

Pritchard, C., & Williams, R. (2001). A three-year comparative longitudinal study of a school-based social work family service to reduce truancy, delinquency and school exclusions. *Journal of Social Welfare and Family Law, 23*(1), 23–43. doi:10.1080/01418030121650

Pritchard, C., & Williams, R. (2011). Poverty and child (0-14 years) mortality in the USA and other Western countries as an indicator of "how well a country meets the needs of its children" (UNICEF). *International Journal of Adolescent Medicine and Health*, *23*(3), 251–255. doi:10.1515/ijamh.2011.052 PMID:22191192

Siegenthaler, E., Munder, T., & Egger, M. (2012). Effect of preventative interventions in mentally ill parents on the mental health of the offspring: Systematic review and meta-analysis. *Journal of the American Academy of Child and Adolescent Psychiatry*, *51*(1), 8–17. doi:10.1016/j.jaac.2011.10.018 PMID:22176935

Stein, M. (2012). *Young people leaving care: Supporting pathways to adulthood*. London: Jessica Kingsley.

van der Gaag, M., Smit, F., Bechdolf, A., French, P., Linszen, D. H., & Yung, A. R. et al. (2013). Preventing a first episode of psychosis: Meta-analysis of randomized controlled prevention trials of 12 month and longer-term follow-ups. *Schizophrenia Research*, *149*(1-3), 56–62. doi:10.1016/j.schres.2013.07.004 PMID:23870806

van Santvoort, F., Hosman, C. M., van Doesum, K. T., & Janssens, J. M. (2014). Effectiveness of preventative support groups for children of mentally ill or addicted parents: A randomised controlled trail. *European Child & Adolescent Psychiatry*, *23*(6), 473–484. doi:10.1007/s00787-013-0476-9 PMID:24072523

WHO. (2013). *Annual Mortality Statistics*. Retrieved from http://www.who.int/healthinfo/statistics/mortality/en/

Wiegand-Grefe, S., Geers, P., Petermann, F., & Plass, A. (2011). Kinder Psychisch Kranker Eltern: Merkmale Elterlicher Psychiatrischer Erkrankung und Gesundheit der Kinder aus Elternsicht [Children of mentally ill parents: The impact of parental psychiatric diagnosis, comorbidity, severity and chronicity on the well-being of children]. *Fortschritte der Neurologie-Psychiatrie*, *79*(01), 32–40. doi:10.1055/s-0029-1245623 PMID:21089005

Wilkinson, R., & Pickett, K. (2009). *The spirit level: Why equality is better for everyone*. London: Penguin.

Williams, R. G., & Pritchard, C. (2006). *Breaking the cycle of educational alienation: A multiprofessional approach*. Maidenhead, England: Open University Press.

## ADDITIONAL READING

Axford, N., Little, M., Morpeth, L., & Weyts, A. (2005). Evaluating children's services: Recent conceptual and methodological developments. *British Journal of Social Work*, *35*(1), 73–88. doi:10.1093/bjsw/bch163

Berridge, D. (2007). Theory and explanation in child welfare: Education and looked-after children. *Child & Family Social Work*, *12*(1), 1–10. doi:10.1111/j.1365-2206.2006.00446.x

Briggs, D. (2010). The world is out to get me, bruv': Life after school "exclusion". *Safer Communities*, *9*, 9–19. doi:10.5042/sc.2010.0222

Buckley, H., & O'Nolan, C. (2014). Child death reviews: Developing CLEAR recommendations. *Child Abuse Review*, *23*(2), 89–103. doi:10.1002/car.2323

Butler, I., & Drakeford, M. (2008). Booing or cheering? Ambiguity in the construction of victimhood in the case of Maria Colwell. *Crime, Media, Culture, 4*(3), 367–385. doi:10.1177/1741659008096372

Cooper, A. (2014). A short psychosocial history of British child abuse and protection: Case studies in problems of mourning in the public sphere. *Journal of Social Work Practice, 28*(3), 271–285. doi:10.1080/02650533.2014.927842

Damashek, A., Nelson, M. M., & Bonner, B. L. (2013). Fatal child maltreatment: Characteristics of deaths from physical abuse versus neglect. *Child Abuse & Neglect, 37*(10), 735–744. doi:10.1016/j.chiabu.2013.04.014 PMID:23768940

Devaney, J., Lazenbatt, A., & Bunting, L. (2010). Inquiring into non-accidental child deaths: Reviewing the review process. *British Journal of Social Work, 41*(2), 242–260. doi:10.1093/bjsw/bcq069

Devaney, J., & Spratt, T. (2009). Child abuse as a complex and wicked problem: Reflecting on policy developments in the United Kingdom in working with children and families with multiple problems. *Children and Youth Services Review, 31*(6), 635–641. doi:10.1016/j.childyouth.2008.12.003

Fazel, S., & Grann, M. (2006). The population impact of severe mental illness on violent crime. *The American Journal of Psychiatry, 163*(8), 1397–1403. doi:10.1176/appi.ajp.163.8.1397 PMID:16877653

Francis, J. (2000). Investing in children's futures: Enhancing the educational arrangements of "looked after" children and young people. *Child & Family Social Work, 5*(1), 23–33. doi:10.1046/j.1365-2206.2000.00141.x

Harker, R. M., Dobel-Ober, D., Lawrence, J., Berridge, D., & Sinclair, R. (2003). Who takes care of education?: Looked after children's perceptions of support for educational progress. *Child & Family Social Work, 8*(2), 89–100. doi:10.1046/j.1365-2206.2003.00272.x

Kearney, J. (2013). Perceptions of non-accidental child deaths as preventable events: The impact of probability heuristics and biases on child protection work. *Health Risk & Society, 15*(1), 51–66. doi:10.1080/13698575.2012.749451

Lauritzen, C., Reedtz, C., Van Doesum, K. T. M., & Martinussen, M. (2014). Implementing new routines in adult mental health care to identify and support children of mentally ill parents. *BMC Health Services Research, 14*(1), 58. doi:10.1186/1472-6963-14-58 PMID:24507566

Liabo, K., Gray, K., & Mulcahy, D. (2013). A systematic review of interventions to support looked-after children in school. *Child & Family Social Work, 18*(3), 341–353. doi:10.1111/j.1365-2206.2012.00850.x

Liu, T.-C., Chen, C.-S., & Loh, C. P. A. (2010). Do children of parents with mental illness have lower survival rate?: A population-based study. *Comprehensive Psychiatry, 51*(3), 250–255. doi:10.1016/j.comppsych.2009.07.004 PMID:20399334

Lobbestael, J., Arntz, A., & Bernstein, D. P. (2010). Disentangling the relationship between different types of childhood maltreatment and personality disorders. *Journal of Personality Disorders, 24*(3), 285–295. doi:10.1521/pedi.2010.24.3.285 PMID:20545495

Mawby, R. C., & Gisby, W. (2009). Crime, media and moral panic in an expanding European Union. *Howard Journal of Criminal Justice, 48*(1), 37–51. doi:10.1111/j.1468-2311.2008.00547.x

Parton, N. (2012). The Munro review of child protection: An appraisal. *Children & Society*, 26(2), 150–162. doi:10.1111/j.1099-0860.2011.00415.x

Pirkis, J. E., Burgess, P. M., Francis, C., Blood, R. W., & Jolley, D. J. (2006). The relationship between media reporting of suicide and actual suicide in Australia. *Social Science & Medicine*, 62(11), 2874–2886. doi:10.1016/j.socscimed.2005.11.033 PMID:16387400

Pritchard, C. (2010). The psychiatric-child protection interface: Research to inform practice. In C. Morgan & D. Bhugra (Eds.), *Principles of social psychiatry* (2nd ed., pp. 483–497). London: John Wiley & Son. doi:10.1002/9780470684214.ch37

Pritchard, C. (2012). Family violence in Europe, child homicide and intimate partner violence. In M. C. A. Liem & W. A. Pridemore (Eds.), *Handbook of European homicide research: Patterns, explanations, and country studies* (pp. 171–183). New York: Springer. doi:10.1007/978-1-4614-0466-8_10

Pritchard, C., & King, E. (2004). A comparison of child-sex-abuse-related and mental-disorder-related suicide in a six-year cohort of regional suicides: The importance of the child protection-psychiatric interface. *British Journal of Social Work*, 34(2), 181–198. doi:10.1093/bjsw/bch021

Pritchard, C., & Williams, R. (2009). Does social work make a difference? A controlled study of former "looked-after-children" and "excluded-from-school" adolescents now men aged 16-24: Subsequent offences, being victims of crime and suicide. *Journal of Social Work*, 9(3), 285–307. doi:10.1177/1468017309334903

Pritchard, C., & Williams, R. (2010). Comparing possible "child-abuse-related-deaths" in England and Wales with the major developed countries 1974-2006: Signs of progress? *British Journal of Social Work*, 40(6), 1700–1718. doi:10.1093/bjsw/bcp089

Richardson, J., & Lelliott, P. (2003). Mental health of looked after children. *Advances in Psychiatric Treatment*, 9(4), 249–256. doi:10.1192/apt.9.4.249

Sidebotham, P., Atkins, B., & Hutton, J. L. (2012). Changes in rates of violent child deaths in England and Wales between 1974 and 2008: An analysis of national mortality data. *Archives of Disease in Childhood*, 97(3), 193–199. doi:10.1136/adc.2010.207647 PMID:21525527

Sidebotham, P., Bailey, S., Belderson, P., & Brandon, M. (2011). Fatal child maltreatment in England, 2005–2009. *Child Abuse & Neglect*, 35(4), 299–306. doi:10.1016/j.chiabu.2011.01.005 PMID:21481462

Silver, E., Piquero, A. R., Jennings, W. G., Piquero, N. L., & Leiber, M. (2011). Assessing the violent offending and violent victimization overlap among discharged psychiatric patients. *Law and Human Behavior*, 35(1), 49–59. doi:10.1007/s10979-009-9206-8 PMID:20145985

Singer, J. B., & Slovak, K. (2011). School social workers' experiences with youth suicidal behavior: An exploratory study. *Children & Schools*, 33(4), 215–228. doi:10.1093/cs/33.4.215

Stroud, J., & Pritchard, C. (2001). Child homicide, psychiatric disorder and dangerousness: A review and an empirical approach. *British Journal of Social Work*, 31(2), 249–269. doi:10.1093/bjsw/31.2.249

Ting, L., Jacobson, J. M., & Sanders, S. (2008). Available supports and coping behaviors of mental health social workers following fatal and nonfatal client suicidal behaviour. *Social Work*, 53(3), 211–221. doi:10.1093/sw/53.3.211 PMID:19275117

Vulliamy, G., & Webb, R. (2003). Supporting disaffected pupils: Perspectives from the pupils, their parents and their teachers. *Educational Research*, 45(3), 275–286. doi:10.1080/0013188032000137265

# KEY WORDS AND DEFINITIONS

**Child Abuse Related Deaths (CARD):** A phrase referring to the non-accidental death of children at the hands of an adult.

**Child Mortality Rates (CMR):** A term referring to the death of infants and children per thousand live births under the age of five.

**Longitudinal Study:** A study conducted over a period of time in which health outcomes and risk factors are repeatedly monitored.

**Looked after Children (LAC):** A term generally used to describe children looked after by the state either long or short term.

**Mental Illness:** A term describing a range of states from mild to severe which influences an individual's moods, cognition, and behaviour, and which renders them unable to cope with life's daily routines and demands.

# Chapter 10

# Picking up the Pieces:
## Working with Adult Women Sexual Abuse Survivors

**Margaret Pack**
*Australian Catholic University, Australia*

## ABSTRACT

*This chapter reports the findings from a review of contemporary assessment and treatment approaches with adult women who have experienced Child Sexual Abuse (CSA). The social worker who engages with women recovering from CSA in adulthood needs to address issues of trust, relationship, and safety. Services that provide culturally sensitive and appropriate models of intervention are likely to impact positively on client rapport and engagement with the social worker and, therefore, greater therapeutic gains are possible when a relationship of trust is established. The implications for social work practice are discussed in relation to a multi-systems and multi-theoretical approach involving the client and her social networks from within strengths-based and ecological systems perspectives. Future research is recommended on the impact of the availability of culturally appropriate services for CSA survivors and cultural safety supervision for social workers, as these variables influence the therapeutic outcomes for women survivors of CSA.*

## INTRODUCTION

In this chapter, some of the major debates relating to working therapeutically with women survivors of child sexual abuse (CSA) are outlined. The case is made for social workers to be involved as active researchers in their practice in order to be effective in working with clients in this challenging field. This rationale is followed by a description of the search strategy, inclusion and exclusion criteria, and the results obtained from the sources, including electronic database searches. This information is

reported so that readers can see how the evidence was identified, and the range of journals, books, and other publications that yielded "evidence" for practice. My background as author is also described as this is likely to impact on the way I have approached the search and analysed the literature as a middle-class Pakeha woman (Pakeha is a term used to describe a New Zealander of European descent). Noteworthy also is my identity as a social worker turned academic born in New Zealand where bicultural practice in social work is embedded in the practice standards for social

DOI: 10.4018/978-1-4666-6563-7.ch010

work (Aotearoa New Zealand Association of Social Workers, 2013). Since moving to Australia to live and work, I have become more aware of Aboriginal social work models and ways of thinking. Another influence on my practice is feminist theory and values which inform this review. This feminist worldview developed when I was employed in the health services working alongside adult women survivors as a mental health social worker. An interest in trauma-informed theory as a psychotherapist also informs my practice which I am aware is written from within a largely individual psychological Western framework. In my view, trauma-informed approaches usefully inform practice with adult women who have experienced CSA but need to be balanced with more systemic understandings. For example, human rights and social justice models involving an analysis of power and powerlessness inform my practice. I am interested in the processes by which women become marginalised in their families and society through structural inequality. I am also interested in the ways in which cultures impose social taboos about disclosing sexual abuse and other forms of oppression. These themes are important to me as a social worker and I have developed theory related to my experience of working to address inequality using these models (Pack, 2004, 2008, 2010a, 2010b, 2012). From an analysis of power and powerlessness, the social taboos about disclosing sexual abuse and other forms of oppression which effectively silence women from engaging in seeking help for their issues, are important to consider. With this positioning and background outlined, the results of the search are analysed and the major themes are then presented.

## BACKGROUND

I am mindful in writing this chapter that much of the literature I discovered is derived from a Western paradigm and so I acknowledge that there are many comprehensive Indigenous models of

practice that are under-represented in this literature review. However, the systemic focus of many of the articles reviewed aligns with social work's unique person-in-environment or ecological systems theory perspectives. This understanding of the role of broader systems brings an appreciation of social work's act of witnessing survivor narratives, with witnessing seen as a political activity in which many private troubles inhere in public issues. Individual therapy I see as being an act of witnessing in the way described by Herman (1992) in her theory development for therapy with survivors of trauma.

With this explanation of what is to follow, I wish also to acknowledge the current emphasis on risk and resilience and the disclosure of abuse which are key themes I have discovered in the literature. These themes are to be viewed with some degree of caution as being less relevant to some women and in some cultures due to core assumptions about "recovery" as a concept which is based on Western assumptions. The healing process from CSA is, therefore, to be viewed in a context in which some adult survivors may be silenced due to threats, and felt powerlessness, not allowing them to engage freely in a therapeutic process that is recommended in this chapter. The intention is not to minimise these women's experiences but to emphasise the recommended approaches for those clients who are able to engage with social workers and other helping professionals.

The therapeutic process described in this chapter is not meant to imply that healing from CSA is a linear process. In the models presented, a staged approach is recommended within the tasks and phases of healing. Healing is also viewed as needing to be supported by the survivor's significant others and families in the community; therefore, the individual focus of some studies needs to be tempered with those which provide more systemic understandings of healing from within a person-in-environment perspective. The profession of social work has actively developed an understanding of ecological systems theory

(Germain & Gitterman, 1980). This theoretical underpinning of practice is one that I draw upon and have applied in my work with women survivors of CSA (Pack, 2013, 2014).

## THE LITERATURE SEARCH STRATEGY

This literature search involved searching for *"sexual abuse"* as a subject heading combined with *adult* as a keyword in the Social Services Abstracts database. This obtained 705 results. I selected a date range from 2005 to the present and this limited the records to 256. The abstracts of the 256 were then read for relevance to the scope of the topic on adult survivors of sexual assault. The inclusion criteria required that the abstract referred to women survivors of CSA and the treatment and assessment approaches recommended for working in this field of practice. Studies that were excluded dealt with men who were CSA survivors due to the focus of the article being adult women survivors. The treatment approaches with children who had been abused were excluded as retrospective or historical accounts of sexual abuse were sought amongst adult women. The studies which compared treatment approaches across male and female survivors of CSA were retained. All articles were from scholarly peer-reviewed journals and were available in English. The majority of studies were from Western country journals though an international search was undertaken. There was one article that was unavailable in English translation beyond the abstract and this was excluded as no translation services were available for writing this chapter. Several references to older publications outside the search parameters but which were linked to seminal works in the field and cited from multiple sources were followed up and included in the review. Once every source was read and summarised, the themes noted across the collection were drawn and patterns associated with the most frequently occurring were

reported. Where there were conflicting opinions, these were highlighted and reported. Where there were synergies across approaches, commonalities were reported. Gaps and under-researched areas are included in the final section recommending directions for future research.

Below are the major themes from the literature and these are illustrated by means of a case study.

## RATIONALE FOR REVIEWING CONTEMPORARY APPROACHES TO SOCIAL WORK WITH WOMEN SURVIVORS OF CSA

Contemporary assessment and treatment approaches with adult women survivors who have been sexually abused are important for social workers to become familiar with as inevitably these issues arise when working with women, their partners, children, and within their extended families. Survivors in the course of their contact often feel moved to tell their social worker about their lives when sexual abuse history is neither sought nor intended to be the primary focus of contact. Social workers deal routinely with many situations involving family violence, marginalisation, and abuse in areas such as domestic violence and child protection. Retrospective accounts of historical childhood abuse often emerge across contexts of practice in the course of engagement with women. For example, sexual abuse disclosures are prevalent across many different organisational settings in which social workers are employed, including child protection, the mental health services, in refugee health, and the not-for profit and community work contexts (Pack, 2012). When disclosures are made to the social worker about events in the past, the question arises about how to honour that disclosure and to avoid re-traumatising the woman who is remembering traumatic memories of events in the past. This review has discovered the establishment of safety as being first and foremost an important means to promote healing from historical CSA.

If the social worker and client are of different cultural backgrounds, there is the potential to miss important features of the woman survivor's experience (Fontes & Plummer, 2010). For this reason, culturally appropriate models exist alongside the Western-based trauma-informed models derived from Western psychology (Bennett, Green, Gilbert, & Bessarab, 2013). Social work with adult women survivors of sexual abuse trauma is considered to be an advanced field of practice due to the breadth and depth of theory and approaches needing to inform practice. Specialist skills and competencies are considered necessary prerequisites also due to its longer term nature of work and its inherent complexity (Chouliara et. al., 2011). Part of this complexity is related to trust that has been breached at an earlier life stage, leading to difficulties for the social worker in forging rapport to build the therapeutic relationship in which healing can occur. Therefore, multi-theoretical and systemic approaches are recommended in working with women survivors.

Overlaid with the particular set of theories applied to practice, the approach adopted needs to be sensitive to cultural differences, which include the impact of colonisation and the current governmental policies on health and welfare across generations (Bennett et al., 2013). Sexual abuse severity and the nature of the abuse needs to be assessed as well as the women's support networks to focus the subsequent therapy and to identify which clients are at an increased risk of mental health and health issues (Curtis, 2006). Differing forms of abuse are often interlocking, with childhood neglect being a gateway to other forms of maltreatment, including sexual abuse (Fargo, 2009). Therefore, a full assessment of the needs is recommended.

In some cultures, any disclosure of abuse is surrounded by taboos and disclosure is fraught with shame and so disclosure may be delayed or not be a feature of recovery. In an effort to avoid paternalistic and ethnocentric attitudes, a critical-reflective approach has been suggested by Aboriginal social workers in Australia (Bennett et al., 2013). Bessarab and Crawford (2013) write of the need for social workers to apply a critical perspective to their practice in order to examine the role of white privilege and institutional racism in perpetuating a cycle of violence for Aboriginal people in Australia. They argue for increased funding for trauma-informed care to support individuals and communities with multiple needs. Green (2011, in Bessarab & Crawford, 2013, p. 109) has identified three key concepts of the recovery from trauma for working with Aboriginal people. These concepts, common to Aboriginal social workers' notions of healing from trauma, are: establishing safety, self and collective identity, connectedness, and developing hope. These concepts of Aboriginal healing align with the three core principles of trauma-informed Western psychotherapy which involve ensuring safety; identifying skills, resources and protective factors to build resilience; and finally, facilitating emotional expression through memory work (Herman, 1992). I will go on to explore these three themes in the literature in relation to recommended approaches to working with women survivors with implications for the organisational context in which social workers practice.

## Establishing Safety and Building Rapport

There are three main stages to working with women sexual assault survivors who have experienced historical sexual abuse issues that are identified across the reviewed research studies. The first stage is generally conceptualised in relation to helping women to manage their symptoms and traumatic memories which can assist survivors to feel more in charge of their own healing trajectory (Briere, 1992; Chouliara et al., 2011; Herman, 1992; Lev-Wiesel, 2008). Complex post-traumatic stress symptoms, such as sleep, appetite, and energy difficulties, recurring flashbacks, and troubling memories of abuse, need to be addressed early to ensure immediate safety and well-being (Herman, 1992). Therefore, it is recommended that post-traumatic stress disorder (PTSD) be assessed, as women survivors of CSA are often brought into therapy when re-experiencing symptoms and intrusive memories of their abuse which have been triggered by present life events (Feerick & Snow, 2005). PTSD is a psychiatric diagnosis involving three main sets of symptoms. Cognitive patterns and beliefs within the criteria for PTSD can involve persistent thoughts about re-victimisation or re-experiencing the initial trauma when the time has passed, and secondly, these patterns of thinking have been related to behaviours structured around avoiding triggers to traumatic events. Thirdly, increased arousal, flashbacks of CSA, and attention problems are reported in complex PTSD responses (Feerick & Snow, 2005). The nervous system when triggered heightens anxiety, fight and flight, as well as other responses. CSA survivors, therefore, often need professional help to deal with lowering the hyper-arousal systems physiologically so that they can manage day-to-day to have better quality of life. Interventions, such as relaxation, awareness training, and mindfulness, are discussed as being helpful in this context (Fritch & Lynch, 2008). When survivors have been victimised in childhood they have spent so long living in fear that hyper-arousal and anxiety become hard-wired in the part of the brain which deals with traumatic memory and so can be continuously experienced in the present (Rothschild, 2003). For some survivors, managing these symptoms can take months or even years to gain control of and at certain milestones problems can emerge in the management of these responses. A need to achieve some control of flashbacks and symptoms linked to the re-experiencing of past trauma can drive their decision to present for assistance at the helping services (Reavey & Brown, 2007).

Once the complex post-traumatic and other symptomatology, including hyper-arousal, sleep-lessness, and beliefs, such as fears about security, are addressed and self-harming has abated, the working through of the traumatic memory can more safely be embarked upon through talking therapies (Herman, 1992). Specifically, the focus of the memory work moves to what the abuse meant emotionally for the survivor, what it meant for them in the context of their family and social and relational world, and what they would like to be different about that world which has been forever changed by what has happened (Chouliara et al., 2011). Often survivors have complex PTSD under control and no longer have physical or acute symptoms but are unhappy generally with their lives (Wright, Crawford, & Sebastian, 2007). When they experience periods of sadness for the loss of cherished ideals shattered by lost childhood and innocence, there is a tendency to retreat and isolate as adults. This avoidance and withdrawal is often in contrast to what is considered to assist in protecting survivors (Liang, Williams, & Siegel, 2006). Research on protective factors and resilience recommends that women survivors of CSA connect with fulfilling relationships to forge long-term partnerships and establish ties with friends, associates, and community (Briere, 2004). When these patterns of withdrawal and avoidance are explored with awareness of how they operate in the survivor's world view, together with what the survivor wants for her life in a narrative way, a momentum for positive change is begun (Anderson & Hiersteiner, 2007).

## ASSESSMENT MODELS: PACING THE WORK

Assessment in Western knowledge-based systems is viewed as an ongoing process involving client evaluation that continues throughout each stage of the assessment and therapy from engagement to completion. Brief models of assessment and intervention are thought to pose difficulties due to the need to build trust and relationship carefully with adult survivors who have had their personal boundaries and sense of personal integrity violated at the most intimate level often during formative periods of development, such as early childhood and adolescence. Retrospective assessment of adult women survivors for events that happened 10-30 years ago during childhood and adolescence have inherent problems. These problems include the nature of traumatic memory which can act to block and stymie the remembering process due to dissociation and the processing of traumatic memory (Briere, 2004; Herman, 1992). Secondly, adult women survivors can find their human developmental milestones are delayed due to trust being an affected dimension in forging and maintaining adult relationships (Fargo, 2009). For example, intimate partner violence (IPV) has been associated with CSA experiences, as this history has been connected with an increased risk of re-victimisation as adults (Daigneault, Hebert, & McDuff, 2009; Watson & Halford, 2010).

Current assessment and treatment approaches are prefaced on the immediate need to assess and to establish safety for the client, particularly when suicidality and self-harm can form part of the presentation (Briere, 2004). Ongoing problems with depression and anxiety, for instance, can be experienced by survivors of CSA (Lev-Wiesel, 2008). Assessing the impact of sexual abuse by inquiring about traumatic events in the past can re-trigger painful feelings, flashbacks, and memories that have the potential to re-traumatise and re-injure as well as to jeopardise the therapeutic process and gains (Herman, 1992). Therefore, the principle of ensuring immediate safety from self-harm is needed to be factored into each phase of the therapy (Anderson & Hiersteiner, 2007). Once safety is assessed as being established, the therapeutic goal is to work collaboratively with survivors to build resilience and tolerance of strong emotions prior to exploring traumatic memory (Herman, 1992). This memory work and

integration of traumatic memory at a later stage in contact is strongly recommended (Briere, 2004; Herman, 1992).

Developing rapport in the initial stages of contact with adult survivors of childhood abuse is considered to be difficult or at least tentative due to breaches of trust that have occurred earlier in life (Chouliara et al., 2011). Interpersonal difficulties, including post-traumatic stress, fear, anger, and hostility, can feature (Feerick & Snow, 2005). Therefore, careful pacing in the therapeutic work is suggested to avoid "drop outs" and non-attendance.

## Identity, Narrative, and Establishing New Meanings in Life

Assessment approaches used by Aboriginal social workers in Australia acknowledge the intergenerational trauma arising from the experience of colonisation and the suppression of cultural identity (Bennett et al., 2013). Therefore, Aboriginal and Torres Strait women's healing from CSA has an emphasis on dealing with the community and collective identity. This collective identity is developed through a process of storying or "yarning" which encompasses the spiritual world, the understandings of which have been passed down intergenerationally through healers and leaders, an integral part of the "dreamtime" (Morseu-Diop, 2010, p. 131). These deeply embedded collectivist practices are reflected in rituals of the natural world, such as making offerings and ceremony.

In a similar way, Maori in Aotearoa New Zealand use rituals of narrative, disclosure, and prayer or karakia, which are thought to have a re-authoring effect for adult survivors of CSA (Hunter, 2011). To enable the social worker to access a fuller range of meanings, cultural safety supervision is recommended for all Pakeha social workers who are working biculturally to ensure they are able to suspend imposing their own ethnocentric attitudes which might unintentionally impact upon the client's progress of healing (Eketone, 2012). Collectivist rather than individualist values and spiritual aspects of healing in community are stressed within Maori paradigms which are often unfamiliar to Pakeha, as are understandings of what extended family or whanau means. For social workers who are Pakeha the challenge is to engage with alternative understandings through a process of bracketing one's own responses through engaging in cultural safety supervision with a supervisor who is bicultural or who moves in both the worlds of Maori and Pakeha (Eketone, 2012).

## Service-User Perspectives

Survivors' own accounts of what were helpful include listening to women's narratives of CSA in a holistic way, as a focus on symptoms and diagnosis alone can have the effect of dis-empowering adult women survivors of CSA (Hunter, 2011). In this sense, the healing process is also part of the narrative of regeneration, transforming lives. Listening to women's own words and symbols is thought to illuminate the meaning-making that is part of the recovery process. This process of retelling one's story of survival identifies turning points in the narrative from within a strengths-based emancipatory and feminist paradigm (Anderson & Hiersteiner, 2007, p. 641).

Dealing with the meaning of CSA for individual women survivors of CSA and developing new understandings have been identified among survivors' own accounts of healing from CSA in adulthood. For example, Draucker et al's (2011) study of survivor narratives develops a staged model representing change over time in the healing processes of adult survivors of CSA. This study discovered that all participants were motivated to understand their abuse and to integrate it into their life narratives. To heal from CSA as adults, an understanding of the nature of the abuse, why it happened, and the effects on their lives was discussed by the participants as central to their

healing trajectories. Other variables noted by Draucker et al. as supporting the healing process involve being affirmed by trusted others, knowing they were not to blame for the abuse, disclosure of CSA made to trusted others, spirituality, altruism, and "laying claim to one's life" (p. 456).

## The Organisational Context

These therapeutic goals can be in conflict with the need to assess the nature and extent of the traumatisation which are often requirements by private insurance companies and the social workers' employing agencies. Therefore, treatment is offered within a time-frame. The completion of an assessment and DSM V or ICD10 diagnosis may be required. Making a formal DSM V or ICD10 diagnosis is often specified by the social workers' employing organisation which can conflict with the individual's values and professional codes of ethics for social workers (Pack, 2004, 2008). Where there are time-limited sessions available, the agency requirement is to assess and offer brief or time limited group and individual therapy. For many survivors, however, the work is longer term, conflicting with organisational protocols and policies about the time taken for assessment in light of capped numbers of sessions for therapy, with completion and discharge expected within a prescribed timeframe (Pack, 2008). Juggling the agency and private or public insurance requirements with those of the client's need for carefully paced therapy can be one of the sources of vicarious traumatisation (VT) or vicarious impact for those who work closely with women disclosing CSA (Pack, 2009, 2010b). Originally developed by McCann and Pearlman (1990), VT is conceived of as a process that occurs when the practitioner's sense of self and worldview is negatively transformed through their empathetic engagement with traumatic disclosures from clients (Pearlman & Saakvitne, 1995). The effects of VT are considered to be cumulative, permanent, and irreversible if unaddressed (Pearlman & Saakvitne, 1995).

Social workers who are themselves survivors of CSA have special needs to be attended to as they travel a parallel healing journey to their clients and so may require time to address their own issues before embarking on work with survivor clients (Pearlman & Saakvitne, 1995). The impact of trauma-related work on the social worker's significant others is another consideration in assessing VT (Pack, 2010b). Due to the insidious nature of VT which emerges slowly, unlike burnout which has particular flashpoints, specialised models of clinical supervision are recommended to address the potential for VT for social workers and other helping professionals (Sommer, 2008).

## RESILIENCE: BALANCING RISK AND BUILDING PROTECTIVE FACTORS

Adult women have a higher prevalence for reporting childhood sexual abuse than their male counterparts (O'Leary, Coohey, & Easton, 2010). Women survivors report a range of effects from CSA, including post-traumatic stress symptoms, dissociation, avoidance strategies, trust and relationship/sexual difficulties, depression, anxiety, and suicidality (Easton, Coohey, O'Leary, Zhang & Hua, 2011; O'Leary et al., 2010). Social work has advocated a multi-layered and multi-theoretical approach to assessing and intervening to assist women dealing retrospectively with historical CSA (Zala, 2012). In particular, the social contexts surrounding the abuse and a combination of strengths-based, feminist, and ecological systems approaches are recommended (Jonzon & Lindblad, 2006). An integrated approach to retrospective disclosure of CSA by women is considered to be needed to fully understand the impact of sexual victimisation and the needs and requirements of women for support during the recovery process (Draucker et al., 2011; O'Leary et al., 2010).

Assessing the social context of the individual woman survivor is considered important in planning for positive adaptation following CSA, as there is evidence of the moderating or buffering influence of spousal or partner support as well as other fulfilling relationships for mediating depression and anxiety in adult women who are survivors of CSA (Jonzon & Lindblad, 2006; O'Leary et al., 2010). Spousal and partner support is, therefore, considered important for aiding self-esteem and self-efficacy which flows onto intimacy as well as parenting competency for women survivors. As CSA can perpetuate dysfunction in families across generations if unaddressed, intervening in one generation can have positive impacts for future generations (Jonzon & Lindblad, 2006; O'Leary et al., 2010). These findings suggest the relevance of ecological systems models where the individual is always seen as situated in the wider social environments across the life course (Germain & Gitterman, 1980). Within this model there are different levels in which the social worker operates simultaneously. The first component is the work with the individual survivor, and then the co-created space that is the therapeutic relationship, the support systems that surround the survivor, and the agency context that surrounds the social worker and survivor together. Societal attitudes towards sexual abuse surround the social worker, client, and the therapeutic relationship as different layers of experience, with each working with the next in a spiralling rather than linear cause and effect (Pack, 2013). In this sense, the concept of resilience in relation to risk and protective factors needs to be viewed in a systemic rather than cause and effect way, with each variable impacting upon the next level on the micro, meso, and macro levels of the model (Pack, 2013).

## ASSESSING "RISK" FACTORS

The research literature has pointed to several risk factors for poor outcomes in working with sexual abuse survivors. For example, women abused as adolescents are more likely to blame themselves for sexual victimisation as they believe they should have been able to make their perpetrators' stop their abuse. In tackling such attitudes, social workers engaging with women survivors analyse the power dynamics underlying the exploitative and coercive nature of the relationship in which the abuse occurred (Reid & Sullivan, 2009). Gender differences in disclosure have been found where women tended to delay their disclosure of abuse resulting in greater severity of PTSD symptoms. By contrast, men's symptoms did not vary by the timing of their disclosure of CSA (Ullman & Filipas, 2005). Variables, including severe abuse (i.e. of longer duration, by trusted caregivers or parental figures, older age at the time of the abuse), are associated with poorer mental health outcomes (Ullman & Filipas, 2005). Physical force, closer victim-offender relationship, and other life time traumas were found to be contributing factors to compounding the effects of CSA in adulthood (Ullman & Filipas, 2005). Women who experience abuse at a younger age have been found to have more avoidance behaviours and distress than those abused later in childhood (Feerick & Snow, 2005). Telling someone at the time of the abuse has been identified in positive and negative ways in the empirical research literature. Overall, the consensus of opinion is that disclosure can adversely affect survivors when there is a lack of empathetic response from the person told (Draucker et al., 2011; Easton et al., 2011). For example, in a study on psychosexual functioning across the emotional behavioural domains, when participants were older when they were abused, had been physically injured, or had multiple abusers, they were more likely to experience difficulties in at least one area of sexual functioning as adults (Easton et al., 2011). Therefore, children who are older or adolescent at the time of sexual abuse may be more affected in relation to becoming sexually traumatised, and the response may involve having more intense feelings of fear and guilt around touching and sexual contact (Easton et al., 2011).

## DISCLOSURE, TRUST, AND THE IMPACT ON RELATIONSHIPS

When disclosing sexual abuse, the timing and nature of disclosure, as well as to whom the abuse is disclosed, can all affect the recovery process of adult women survivors of sexual abuse. Thus, social workers supporting adult women who are dealing with CSA need to help clients to enhance their existing interpersonal communication skills and to assess their social networks and resources, all of which can act as protective factors to ensure safety prior to emotional processing and memory work (Jonzon & Lindblad, 2006). Assessing existing skills and strengthening social networks are recommended in research studies to build resilience and as a preliminary step if and when the woman decides to disclose details of her abuse as a goal towards her recovery. Preparation for disclosure is strongly recommended in the counselling relationship to assist survivors to identify accurately those likely to respond positively to the disclosure and to respect their confidentiality (Jonzon & Lindblad, 2006). Timing of disclosure is another variable influencing the outcomes for survivors in relation to mental health and psychosexual functioning. The study by O'Leary et al. (2010) found, for example, that disclosure of abuse to trusted others within one year of the abuse occurring resulted in better mental health that those who delayed disclosure.

The impact on relationships is a theme of the studies relating to age and life stage when the abuse first occurred. For example, Easton et al. (2011) concluded in their research that those survivors who were older or adolescent at the first abuse were more likely to experience problems related to the emotional dimension of sexual functioning when compared with younger participants abused earlier in childhood. For example, being afraid of sexual contact was four times greater for adults who were older when the abuse commenced than it was for adults who were younger when their abuse began (Easton et al., 2011). Disclosure had a negative effect on feelings of guilt which increased the likelihood of feeling guilty during sex for participants (Easton et al., 2011).

Developmental models are considered to usefully inform practice with the age and stage of first abuse being an important variable guiding the approach to the therapy (Collishaw et al., 2007). Lack of trust inevitably impacts on intimacy and relational issues at key moments as well as throughout life, including impacting the therapeutic relationship itself (Briere, 2004; Daigneault et al., 2009).

## FOSTERING CONNECTION AND HOPE FOR THE FUTURE

Whether CSA should be regarded as any other trauma or whether it is unique and thus requires a specialised approach remains controversial in the research literature (Lev-Wiesel, 2008). There is evidence in empirical studies that childhood neglect and other forms of maltreatment serve as a pathway to other forms of victimisation, including sexual abuse (Reid & Sullivan, 2009). For example, those children who experience parental unavailability, emotional withdrawal, and lack of support are increased risk factors for being sexually abused later in life (Reid & Sullivan, 2009). The intergenerational impact of childhood abuse leading to dysfunctional relationships across generations has been reported and the link between adolescent abuse and subsequent re-victimisation in adulthood suggested (Reid & Sullivan, 2009).

There is thought to be more focus needed to identify protective factors, skill-building, and grieving for the loss of childhood, and protection from caregivers when sexual abuse occurs during childhood and adolescence. In later stages of reintegration after memory work, the social work role is often to assist survivors to reconnect with their community and family so that they can fully

participate and reclaim a life that is not limited by the original abuse (Monahan, 2010). Where abuse impacts upon the family and its relationships, social workers are often dealing with survivors who are still coming to terms with the loss of sustained family relationships. For example, in the case of sibling abuse, Monahan's (2010) research with older women dealing with a dying parent where sister-brother CSA occurred found that the task at hand was to grieve for the loss of the potential for support from parents during the abuse, now that the loss of the parent was imminent.

## THE CONCEPT OF RECOVERY: THE ROLE OF SIGNIFICANT OTHERS IN RECOVERY

The recovery movement in which survivors control and direct their own healing is a challenge in the expert-knows-best discourses of therapeutic assessment and intervention. The recovery movement suggests that the counselling process is not there to preach to survivors or to direct but rather to help women survivors of CSA to come up with their own answers to questions about their life and the effects of trauma upon it in an ongoing way (Draucker et al., 2011). Responses to abuse disclosure can impact upon mental health either positively or negatively depending on the feedback from the significant others of the survivor (Ullman & Filipas, 2005). A key factor in the success in dealing with the individual women's issues is the social worker's skill and finesse in working creatively across theoretical domains in assessment and intervention. Assessment is a continuous process rather than a one-step event due to the healing having impacts on a number of domains simultaneously, such as relationships, and the psychological, physical, and emotional dimensions of health (Draucker et al., 2011).

Beyond an individual focus of intervention, partner or couple counselling and support networks are targeted in some forms of assessment and intervention which aim to assess and build resilience. For example, Wright, Fopma-Loy, and Fischer's (2005) study of mothers disclosing a childhood history of sexual abuse discovered that spousal and partner support was a strongly protective factor in buffering the depressive symptoms which impact upon parenting capacity. Their study and the studies they reviewed discovered that looking at interpersonal support more comprehensively across a variety of life domains was important to predicting parenting competence for women disclosing CSA.

CSA perpetrated by siblings is identified in the literature as another specialism within the field of sexual abuse recovery. This area is being explored in relation to adult women survivors in later life and how they come to view their sibling relationships subsequently to enable mourning and moving on to occur (Monahan, 2010).

## AN INTEGRATED APPROACH TO ASSESSMENT AND TREATMENT

A multi-theoretical approach involving attachment theory, emancipatory strengths-based and narrative theory, and informed by new trauma-related theories is advocated. Zala (2012), a clinically trained social worker who researches her own practice, advocates including an assessment and treatment approach that integrates trauma theory, attachment theory, feminist principles, and body-orientated psychotherapy, together with systemic couple counselling. Such an integrative approach raises a number of complexities, however. For example, when the focus of the organisation in which most social workers are employed is on the individual client the question arises as to who is the primary client. This question is often prescribed by referral and intake protocols and is, therefore, defined by the agency's policy and process. How to address systemically issues when most therapeutic models are based on the individual survivor is another key issue for the employing agency of

social workers who deal with women who have CSA histories (Zala, 2012). Psycho-education about the effects of childhood sexual abuse trauma in adulthood within a family, for example, might conflict with these agency policies preferring to see individuals in isolation from partners and families who support women survivors.

There is, however, widespread agreement amongst researchers that a powerful means of healing beyond the therapeutic relationship involves a secure attachment to a partner, spouse, or friend who offers the potential for a sustaining relationship and emotional refuge by their continuing unconditional love and acceptance (Herman, 1992; Zala, 2012). As physical intimacy is impacted often in adulthood by CSA in relation to shame, avoidance, and withdrawal, a survivor's primary relationship may also assist as the woman moves out of dissociation and withdrawal into remembering traumatic experiences physically, with awareness of what is occurring in a moment to moment way (Rothschild, 2003).

## CASE DESCRIPTION

I practised as a social worker in a community mental health clinical setting together with a multi-disciplinary team who were influential in guiding assessment and intervention. My practice involved a process of teamwork and weekly, ongoing clinical supervision. The multi-disciplinary team, of which I was a part, comprised psychologists, psychiatrists, nurses, and occupational therapists. The therapy group for adult women survivors described below was an actual group which was facilitated by two of the team while I remained the individual and primary therapist for the clients on my caseload. This case study itself is fictional based on a composite of many clients I have worked with in my practice; therapeutic suggestions within this case study are those I have chosen to work with across a number of client presentations. Pseudonyms are used to represent the client and her family. I refer to my own social work input as "Kathryn" in the scenario. The dialogue is also wholly fictitious, though based in a composite of cases and so does not represent verbatim direct quotations from any actual client.

Carolyn, a 27 year old single first generation Australian of English parents, presented at her general practitioner's practice and was subsequently referred to the community mental health services with a reactive depressive episode considered by her general practitioner to be due to "family stressors", including a recent disclosure by Carolyn of sexual abuse by a family member (her stepfather) as an 11 year old. Inappropriate fondling had continued until she was 14 years of age. Carolyn presented to the mental health social worker as "frequently tearful, self-blaming and racked with guilt" for disclosing the abuse to her mother. This process of disclosure for Carolyn triggered self-recrimination and ruminating thoughts of her own worthlessness leading to fleeting suicidal ideation and thoughts of self-harm. Her mother, Beverly, knew nothing of her daughter's abuse during childhood and upon the telling, her immediate response was one of shock and denial. Her reaction was immediately to disbelieve Carolyn's story as it was "unthinkable" that her ex-partner would "do such a thing". Beverly was adamant that her ex-partner during his visits had never touched Carolyn inappropriately when he was helping her to get ready for bed.

Carolyn commented at interview,

*I felt on telling my story and my mother's reaction, that I was being denied my own voice that had remained silent too long. I had some days after that disclosure that I didn't want to get out of bed because of the overwhelming guilt I experienced. It's been many years since those incidents and I don't believe I should feel guilty any more for telling the truth about what happened to me as an adolescent. I am sure this history led to a relationship break up two years ago when I became fearful and withdrew when my partner became*

*angry with me and I had a flashback of feeling small and powerless again, as I recalled feeling during the abuse with my stepfather.*

Carolyn agreed to attend ten supportive counselling sessions with her social worker, Kathryn, following the assessment and from there decided to join a women survivors' group that met weekly. During this time, Carolyn felt believed. As she exclaimed:

*It was a matter of dealing with my own guilt and pulling my life together again. I was able to have the reassurance that my feelings of guilt are a normal part of the process of shame I had experienced as an adolescent. The counselling helped but it was one of those things where I had to come to my own decisions. I decided that I didn't have to continue to take responsibility for my stepfather's actions and that what he did was wrong and abusive. Regardless of my family's denial of my experience, I began to feel affirmed. I had to come to that point myself.*

Kathryn, a second generation Australian of Greek origin, assessed Carolyn's history. She took her assessment to her team meeting for advice and consultation. Cultural and clinical supervision enabled her to explore reflectively how her background as a woman of Greek origin impacted when listening to Carolyn's account of her experience as a first generation Australian. From within a strengths-based, feminist framework for social work practice, she viewed Carolyn's healing journey through individual counselling and group work as a process unique to Carolyn's experience as no two healing trajectories from sexual abuse are the same. Kathryn's large extended family, some of whom still lived in Athens, had a collectivist orientation and values towards family and events within an extended family structure. Therefore, she considered carefully Carolyn's role within the family, the importance of being believed, and her relationship to her mother as being crucial to her identity as an adult woman recovering from CSA. Kathryn's employing agency, a community outpatient mental health clinic, saw many women who disclosed abuse, though they were initially referred with family issues or mental health concerns. Kathryn's philosophy and emancipatory approach to the work was that most women she saw were resourceful and were seeking greater control over their lives, including improved health and well-being. From her 20 years of practice with women she had seen with historical sexual abuse issues, she reflected:

*Sometimes I see some survivors getting stuck in a phase of their own healing process so at that point they sometimes need some help and that's what our service can offer. It's about supporting women who want to live a satisfying and fulfilling life and about survivors making this decision to want to begin their own healing from trauma. It's not about teaching people what to feel, it's allowing the survivor to control and guide their own healing.*

At first contact, Carolyn, had presented to her general practitioner in a distressed state, not really knowing what specifically she wanted from the referral which involved contact with a social worker. With the current crisis precipitated by her mother's response to her disclosure of the abuse, at the assessment appointment she discussed her anger as being "the problem". Kathryn empathised with Carolyn's feelings of betrayal and anger and affirmed them by saying that the key task was now to grieve for the lack of support she encountered in her brave and courageous act of telling her story. She discussed with Carolyn the importance of acknowledging openly all of her emotional responses that were arising in the session, including her anger and sadness at her mother's failure to recognise and acknowledge Carolyn's narrative of struggle and survival. At its base, Kathryn's formulation from her assessment was that Carolyn was angry at her mother's

perceived failure to protect her from the actions of her stepfather who abused her. As part of her assessment, Kathryn inquired about the relationship with Carolyn and her mother, as well as the divorce and entry of her stepfather into the family. Sibling relationships were also inquired about as part of the assessment interview due to the fact that Carolyn had received some support from a younger brother, now aged 23 years, to whom as an adult she had confided her story. Carolyn's decision to withdraw emotionally from her adult partner due to abuse flashbacks during love-making meant that eventually her partner also withdrew emotionally, thinking she no longer loved him and so their relationship became impacted.

As Monahan (2010) points out, it is often difficult for social workers who work with adult women survivors to address the issue that one or both parents continue to deny rather than acknowledge their experience of CSA. In this, the survivor needs to come to recognise in her experience of her mother the lack of

*...the capacity to ever give her what she needs most: acknowledgement that she has been wronged, an apology for the lack of protection that she should have been afforded and finally, the genuine expression of sorrow for the trauma along with asking for forgiveness for the harm it created. (p. 365)*

To assist Carolyn in the tasks of grieving for what has been lost in her adolescence, Kathryn, as her social worker, needs to support her to work through this lack of emotional acknowledgement from either her mother or stepfather. This is often a painful step as the survivor reflects on the lack of parental capacity to engage emotionally to support and protect. Within this grieving process, the social worker needs to help the survivor to understand that she might never get what she needs from her family of origin to compensate for the many losses in her life since the abuse first occurred. Recognition of what her idealised family would have looked like is considered important to explore to assist the survivor to understand the underlying ideals she has for her family. This step is needed to facilitate mourning for the loss of cherished ideals of family life and support within the family (Monahan, 2010).

At some later point in time, work in a women survivors of CSA support group and further individual sessions were planned to focus on Carolyn's intimacy and relationship issues in adulthood. The individual work was aimed more generally to identify the other impacts of the abuse and was offered to Carolyn as a future option. These interventions cover several domains to address Carolyn's wider healing from CSA in terms of ongoing meaning-making in order to plan for her future goals from within strengths-based, trauma-informed, life course, and ecological systems perspectives.

## CURRENT CHALLENGES IN WORK WITH ADULT WOMEN WHO HAVE CSA: PROMOTING RESILIENCE

Ultimately trauma informed therapy needs to balance two main tensions in practice: honouring the survivor's healing process whilst balancing this with the requirements to assess accurately and intervene appropriately, informed by the findings of the empirical research about approaches to assessment and treatment.

There is abundant evidence that the identification of coping styles, strengths, and protective factors that bolster social support and self-esteem and that promote self-care are all central to the recovery of adult women of CSA (Kelly & Gates, 2010). Current studies challenge earlier findings about poor mental health outcomes for those adults who disclose a history of CSA. Rojas and Kinder (2009) found evidence in their research with 250 undergraduate students disclosing CSA

that CSA did not place either the men or women surveyed at an increased risk of social anxiety. This surprising finding, which refutes previous studies, may provide researchers with the rationale for investigating resiliency and, specifically, if higher education features as a protective factor in understanding the impact of CSA (Rojas & Kinder, 2009).

Disclosure of CSA as a life-long, dynamic process is seen to be a feature promoting adult resilience (Hunter, 2011). This point is illustrated by the case description of Carolyn and her family. Similarly, Cleverly and Boyle's longitudinal research (2010) discovered that the support of parents and family life were influential variables in militating resilience with survivors' accounts of "improved functioning" at follow up between 1983 and 2003 in relation to "life change for the better" (p. 283). The results also indicated that those exposed to CSA had more child, parent, and family difficulties than in the general population, whilst one in three report "being strengthened by the experience" (p. 283).

Kelly and Gates (2010) suggest that research and practice integrate the strengths-based theories to focus attention on honouring coping strategies of adult survivors. They suggest that negative coping styles, such as avoidance and social withdrawal and isolation, rather than being treated as a deficit in social skills could be alternatively re-framed. Briere (2004) concurs with this view. He suggests that some negative characteristics involving clinical diagnostic categories, such as borderline personality among women abused sexually as children, be reframed and honoured as functional and as a normal response to an inherently traumatic event. Strengths-based theory provides the foundation for recovery through an identification of the inherent strengths and resources of the survivor of CSA within her social networks (Kelly & Gates, 2010).

## SOLUTIONS AND RECOMMENDATIONS: THE IMPLICATIONS FOR SOCIAL WORK PRACTICE

All talking therapies have been found to be useful from adult women survivors' perspectives at some stage in the recovery from CSA (Chouliara et al., 2011). Talking therapies, regardless of the specific underpinning theory, enabled women across the reviewed research studies to feel better about themselves and to develop improved self-care over time (Anderson & Hiersteiner, 2007; Chouliara et al., 2011). Attending to the context of the abuse and maintaining a confidential and trusting relationship was of primary importance to the survivors who were interviewed (Anderson & Hiersteiner, 2007; Chouliara et al., 2011). Group work in which women can obtain and give support to others is also considered to be beneficial in the healing from CSA during adulthood through a reduction of distress, depression, and PTSD (Bergeron & Hebert, 2006; Brown, Reyes, Brown, & Gonzenbach, 2013). In a sample of 26 women participating in a group intervention offered by sexual assault centres in Canada, pre and post test scores indicated positive gains following the group which were maintained three months at follow up (Bergeron & Hebert, 2006). Thus the quality of the therapeutic relationship is considered to be central to the process of adult women's accounts of healing from CSA.

Using a strengths-perspective coupled with current trends in the resiliency research literature fits social work's concern to work with client aspirations and priorities collaboratively and to honour clients' coping and so avoid pathologising (Anderson & Hiersteiner, 2007). Resilience theories indicate that not all adults who are survivors of CSA have negative outcomes in their lives in adulthood (Collishaw et al., 2007; Kelly & Gates, 2010; Leech & Trotter, 2006). For example, in a

longitudinal study of 571 participants, more than one in three individuals reporting CSA had no psychiatric problems in adulthood and coped well in major domains of life (Collishaw et al., 2007). More research is recommended into understanding the process by which relationship competencies are developed to build the resilience of adults with CSA histories (Collishaw et al., 2007).

Resilience is thought to be related to the nature of parental care, adolescent peer relationships, the quality of adult intimate relationships, and personality styles (Collishaw et al., 2007). Strengths-based theories of social work practice suggest that even those who endure the trauma of CSA have the innate ability to bounce-back and lead fulfilling lives (Kelly & Gates, 2010). A strengths-based assessment approach is one way of moving into alternative meaning-making with women survivors which moves beyond a problem-based pathologising approach derived from medical and psychiatric practices (Wright et al., 2007).

## A MULTI-THEORETICAL APPROACH

The literature on strengths-based and narrative theories and applications to working with adult survivors of CSA recommends a number of assessment and therapeutic interventions. For example, strengths-based assessment questions focus on identifying support and resources in the client's environment and dealing with the client's hopes and aspirations for the future (Kelly & Gates, 2010). Facilitating disclosure within a safe therapeutic relationship may be helpful at some stages of the recovery process (Chouliara et al., 2011).

Using a strengths-based narrative approach informed by trauma and resilience theories, questions for Kathryn's assessment with Carolyn would include the following:

- What are the nature of relationships and types of support available to Carolyn and are these reciprocal in terms of sharing, closeness, frequency of interaction, duration, and general trustworthiness?
- Who else might Carolyn wish to approach for support? This focuses on the people in Carolyn's network who would likely believe her disclosure and support her emotionally in its aftermath. This assessment might include household, family, friends, people from clubs, work, or school, organisations, neighbours, and any social service providers she may be working with. Including a social network tool, such as an Eco map and genogram, may be useful in identifying alternative forms of support.
- Does the physical environment in which she lives meet Carolyn's basic needs (income, health care, housing)? Is some change needed? If so, what needs to be altered or revised?
- What areas of her life have worked well in her view before this recent upset? For example, how has she achieved her education and forged an intimate relationship which are both considered to be protective factors?
- What has changed in her beliefs and thinking about herself since the interaction with her mother?
- How do these attitudes function in her day-to-day life?
- What are her goals and dreams now and in the future for her life?
- How does Carolyn see her life moving in the next 5 or 10 years?
- Can she recall a time when she felt proud of something in her life that she had achieved as an adult despite the lack of support from her mother or family members?
- How has relocation from England to Australia in her mother's generation influenced or impacted the family's function-

ing? How has the move impacted Carolyn? What are their individual and collective narratives of coming to a new land to make a new life?

## FUTURE RESEARCH DIRECTIONS

The research studies reviewed suggest that new approaches are needed to document the healing trajectories of survivors of CSA to enable research to guide practice from the survivor's direct accounts of experience (Draucker et al., 2011). In this healing, the assessment of risk and protective factors are considered to be critically important. For example, the role of attachment with caregivers in mediating and ameliorating the connection between CSA and adjustment in adulthood is little reported in empirical studies (Feerick & Snow, 2005) and so is an area recommended for further research. Coercion from the perpetrator, abuse by a close relative or family friend, and abuse by multiple perpetrators in experiences of CSA appear to predict higher levels of social anxiety in adult women based in the available empirical research studies (Feerick & Snow, 2005).

Increasing potential victims' awareness of risk factors for being victimised and promoting strategies and skill building to prevent further abuse experiences without implying responsibility have been suggested in previous research (Lalor & McElvaney, 2010; Reid & Sullivan, 2009). Identifying what the risk and protective factors are would assist women and their therapists to work across domains to assess and identify risks in CSA history alongside protective factors and resources to build resilience. Such interventions could assist in limiting women's self-blame by conveying a reasonable assessment of strengths and vulnerabilities to further abuse in adulthood (Reid & Sullivan, 2009). It is important for social workers to learn from older women survivors how they have created new meaning about the traumatic events in their history of CSA in order to learn how these newly evolved meanings guide their lives (Monahan, 2010). In particular, exploring the positive coping skills and how the non-offending family members are impacted upon are neglected areas that require further research in the future (Monahan, 2010).

Identifying coping strategies based in the research literature on the resiliency of adult women dealing with CSA within the initial assessment phase is now considered a priority (Phanichrat & Townshend, 2010). Specifically identifying when avoidant coping processes are involved and reframing these into problem-focused coping are recommended (Phanichrat & Townshend, 2010). These strategies involve multiple forms of problem-solving prefaced on principles of seeking support, cognitive engagement, and seeking alternative meaning-making, and have been identified as central to survivors' narratives of living a good life in the face of historical CSA (Phanichrat & Townshend, 2010).

Cultural issues surrounding accessing appropriate services is a little researched area as it seems likely that differences in value systems need to guide the kinds of services available and in terms of who is employed in those services (Lalor & McElvaney, 2010). In the Australian context, the needs of Aboriginal Australians are complicated by historical issues surrounding White colonial government policies involving principles of assimilation. The forced removal of children from their families by the Australian Government, referred to as "The Stolen Generation", is another legacy of these polices and a source of intergenerational trauma. As Hunter (2011) points out, institutional racism is a legacy of a colonial past which adds a structural layer to CSA of Aboriginal Australians who were abused after being forcibly taken into "care". These dimensions of intergenerational abuse need to be attended to in the course of therapy.

## CONCLUSION

Women survivors of CSA have been found to experience a range of short and long term cognitive, emotional, psychological, and physical effects as adults (Feeric & Snow, 2005; Lalor & McElvaney, 2010). The severity of the CSA and other variables, such as the age of onset, duration, relationship to the perpetrator, and multiple perpetrators, influence subsequent sexual exploitation and re-victimisation during adulthood (Lalor & McElvaney, 2010). Prevention strategies and a mixture of trauma-informed narrative, feminist, ecological systems, and strengths-based approaches to assessment and intervention are recommended to guide social workers in the pacing and choice of intervention. Combined with these theories are the findings of empirical studies of risk and resilience in adults who have been abused sexually as children (Draucker et al., 2011).

Beyond individual therapy, couple counselling, group work, and community campaigns to raise awareness of the issues of CSA in society are recommended (Chouliara et al., 2011; Lalor & McElvaney, 2010). Disclosure of abuse can be fraught with difficulty as fear, shame, and self-blame can inhibit disclosure. However, the practice research indicates that disclosure can have a positive influence on healing from CSA (Collishaw et al., 2007; Hunter, 2011). Specifically, discussing the abuse can decrease the likelihood of psycho-sexual and mental health problems in adulthood (O'Leary et al., 2010). Theoretical models, such as the staged approach from Draucker et al. (2011), which are based on the processes by which individuals heal from CSA are helpful as they are guided by empirical research from survivors themselves and involve a life course, developmental, and narrative perspective. Such models are prefaced on multiple domains of functioning and informed by trauma-informed and risk and resilience variables. Draucker et al. have identified enabling factors that facilitate the movement from one stage of healing to the next, whilst acknowledging that this process is not linear and each person moves through the stages uniquely.

The case study of Carolyn illustrates that healing from sexual abuse is both complex and dynamic, necessitating a multi-systems and multi-theoretical approach to assessment and intervention from a social work perspective. The social worker dealing daily with these complexities requires assistance with this act of witnessing to view its therapeutic potential as well as witnessing as a political activity from a feminist perspective (Herman, 1992). In this challenging and rewarding work, social workers need to seek appropriate assistance from those skilled in offering relational models of clinical supervision and to obtain regular professional development through training about VT and trauma-informed theories of practice.

## REFERENCES

Anderson, K. M., & Hiersteiner, C. (2007). Listening to the stories of adults in treatment who were sexually abused as children. *Families in Society*, 88(4), 637–644. doi:10.1606/1044-3894.3686

Aotearoa New Zealand Association of Social Workers. (2013). *The code of ethics of the Aotearoa New Zealand Association of Social Workers*. Retrieved from http://anzasw.org.nz/social_work_practice/topics/show/158-summary-of-the-code-of-ethics

Bennett, B., Green, S., Gilbert, S., & Bessarab, D. (Eds.). (2013). *Our voices: Aboriginal and Torres Strait islander social work*. South Yarra: Palgrave Macmillan.

Bergeron, M., & Hebert, M. (2006). Evaluation of a group intervention using a feminist approach for victims of sexual abuse. *Child Abuse & Neglect*, 30, 1143–1159. doi:10.1016/j.chiabu.2006.04.007 PMID:17034852

Bessarab, D., & Crawford, F. R. (2013). Trauma, grief and loss: The vulnerability of Aboriginal families in the child protection system. In B. Bennett, S. Green, S. Gilbert, & D. Bessarab (Eds.), *Our voices: Aboriginal and Torres Strait Islander social work* (pp. 93–113). South Yarra: Palgrave MacMillan.

Briere, J. (1992). *Child abuse trauma theory and treatment of the lasting effects*. Newbury Park, C.A.: Sage Publications.

Briere, J. (Ed.). (2004). *Psychological assessment of adult post-traumatic states: Phenomenology, diagnosis and measurement*. Washington, DC: American Psychological Association.

Brown, D., Reyes, S., Brown, B., & Gonzenbach, M. (2013). The effectiveness of group treatment for female adult incest survivors. *Journal of Child Sexual Abuse*, 22(2), 143–152. doi:10.1080/10538712.2013.737442 PMID:23428148

Chouliara, Z., Karatzias, T., Scott-Brien, G., Macdonald, A., MacArthur, J., & Frazer, N. (2011). Talking therapy services for adult survivors of childhood sexual abuse (CSA) in Scotland: Perspectives of service-users and professionals. *Journal of Child Sexual Abuse*, 20(2), 128–156. doi:10.1080/10538712.2011.554340 PMID:21442530

Cleverley, K., & Boyle, M. H. (2010). The individual as a moderating agent of the long-term impact of sexual abuse. *Journal of Interpersonal Violence*, 25(2), 274–290. doi:10.1177/0886260509334284 PMID:19423747

Collishaw, S., Pickles, A., Messer, J., Rutter, M., Shearer, C., & Maughan, B. (2007). Resilience to adult psychopathology following childhood maltreatment: Evidence from a community sample. *Child Abuse & Neglect, 31*(3), 211–229. doi:10.1016/j.chiabu.2007.02.004 PMID:17399786

Curtis, C. (2006). Sexual abuse and subsequent suicidal behaviour: Exacerbating factors and implications for recovery. *Journal of Child Sexual Abuse, 15*(2), 1–21. doi:10.1300/J070v15n02_01 PMID:16702144

Daigneault, I., Hebert, M., & McDuff, P. (2009). Men's and women's childhood sexual abuse and victimization in adult partner relationships: A study of risk factors. *Child Abuse & Neglect, 33*(9), 638–647. doi:10.1016/j.chiabu.2009.04.003 PMID:19811827

Draucker, C. B., Martsolf, D. S., Roller, C., Knapik, G., Ross, R., & Stidham, A. W. (2011). Healing from childhood sexual abuse: A theoretical model. *Journal of Child Sexual Abuse, 20*(4), 435–466. doi:10.1080/10538712.2011.588188 PMID:21812546

Easton, S. D., Coohey, C., O'Leary, P., Zhang, Y., & Hua, L. (2011). The effect of childhood sexual abuse on psychosexual functioning during adulthood. *Journal of Family Violence, 26*(1), 41–50. doi:10.1007/s10896-010-9340-6

Eketone, A. (2012). The purposes of cultural supervision. *Aotearoa New Zealand Social Work, 24*(3-4), 20-30. Retrieved from http://anzasw.org.nz/en/about/topics/show/207-professional-journal-aotearoa-new-zealand-social-work

Fargo, J. D. (2009). Pathways to adult sexual revictimization: Direct and indirect behavioral risk factors across the lifespan. *Journal of Interpersonal Violence, 24*(11), 1771–1791. doi:10.1177/0886260508325489 PMID:18931368

Feerick, M. M., & Snow, K. L. (2005). The relationships between childhood sexual abuse, social anxiety, and symptoms of posttraumatic stress disorder in women. *Journal of Family Violence, 20*(6), 409–419. doi:10.1007/s10896-005-7802-z

Fontes, L. A., & Plummer, C. (2010). Cultural issues in disclosures of child sexual abuse. *Journal of Child Sexual Abuse, 19*(5), 491–518. doi:10.1080/10538712.2010.512520 PMID:20924908

Fritch, A. M., & Lynch, S. M. (2008). Group treatment for adult survivors of interpersonal trauma. *Journal of Psychological Trauma, 7*(3), 145–169. doi:10.1080/19322880802266797

Germain, C., & Gitterman, A. (1980). *Life model of social work practice*. New York: Columbia University Press.

Herman, J. (1992). *Trauma and recovery: The aftermath of violence from domestic abuse to political terror*. New York: Basic Books.

Hunter, S. V. (2011). Disclosure of child sexual abuse as a life-long process: Implications for health professionals. *The Australian and New Zealand Journal of Family Therapy, 32*(2), 159–172. doi:10.1375/anft.32.2.159

Jonzon, E., & Lindblad, F. (2006). Risk factors and protective factors in relation to subjective health among adult female victims of child sexual abuse. *Child Abuse & Neglect, 30*(2), 127–143. doi:10.1016/j.chiabu.2005.08.014 PMID:16466788

Kelly, B. L., & Gates, T. G. (2010). Using the strengths perspective in the social work interview with young adults who have experienced childhood sexual abuse. *Social Work in Mental Health*, *8*(5), 421–437. doi:10.1080/15332981003744438

Lalor, K., & McElvaney, R. (2010). Child sexual abuse, links to later sexual exploitation/high-risk sexual behavior, and prevention/treatment programs. *Trauma, Violence, & Abuse: A Review Journal*, *11*, 159-177. doi:10.1177/1524838010378299

Leech, N., & Trotter, J. (2006). Alone and together: Some thoughts on reflective learning for work with adult survivors of child sexual abuse. *Journal of Social Work Practice*, *20*(2), 175–187. doi:10.1080/02650530600776889

Lev-Wiesel, R. (2008). Child sexual abuse: A critical review of intervention and treatment modalities. *Children and Youth Services Review*, *30*(6), 665–673. doi:10.1016/j.childyouth.2008.01.008

Liang, B., Williams, L. M., & Siegel, J. A. (2006). Relational outcomes of childhood sexual trauma in female survivors: A longitudinal study. *Journal of Interpersonal Violence*, *21*(1), 42–57. doi:10.1177/0886260505281603 PMID:16399923

McCann, I. L., & Pearlman, L. A. (1990). Vicarious traumatization: A framework for understanding the psychological effects of working with victims. *Journal of Traumatic Stress*, *3*(1), 131–149. doi:10.1007/BF00975140

Monahan, K. (2010). Themes of adult sibling sexual abuse survivors in later life: An initial exploration. *Clinical Social Work Journal*, *38*(4), 361–369. doi:10.1007/s10615-010-0286-1

Morseu-Diop, N. (2010). *Healing in justice: An international study of Indigenous peoples' custodial experiences of prison programs and the impact on their journey from prison to community*. Brisbane, Australia: University of Queensland Press.

O'Leary, P., Coohey, C., & Easton, S. D. (2010). The effect of severe child sexual abuse and disclosure on mental health during adulthood. *Journal of Child Sexual Abuse*, *19*(3), 275–289. doi:10.1080/10538711003781251 PMID:20509077

Pack, M. J. (2004). Sexual abuse counsellors' responses to stress and trauma: A social work perspective. *New Zealand Journal of Counselling*, *25*(2), 1–17. Retrieved from http://www.nzac.org.nz/new_zealand_journal_of_counselling.cfm

Pack, M. J. (2008). Back from the edge of the world: Re-authoring a story of practice with stress and trauma using Gestalt theory and narrative approaches. *Journal of Systemic Therapies*, *27*(3), 30–44. doi:10.1521/jsyt.2008.27.3.30

Pack, M. J. (2009). The body as a site of knowing: Sexual abuse counsellors' responses to traumatic disclosures. *Women's Studies Journal*, *23*, 46-56. Retrieved from http://www.wsanz.org.nz/journal.htm

Pack, M. J. (2010a). Revisions to the therapeutic relationship: A qualitative inquiry into sexual abuse therapists' theories for practice as a mitigating factor in VT. *Social Work Review. Journal of New Zealand Association of Social Workers*, *12*, 73–82. Retrieved from http://anzasw.org.nz/about/topics/show/207-aotearoa-nz-social-work-review

Pack, M. J. (2010b). Transformation in progress: The effects of trauma on the significant others of sexual abuse therapists. *Qualitative Social Work: Research and Practice*, *9*(2), 249–265. doi:10.1177/1473325009361008

Pack, M. J. (2012). Vicarious traumatisation: An organisational perspective. *Social Work Now, 50*, 14-23. Retrieved from http://www.cyf.govt.nz/about-us/publications/social-work-now.html

Pack, M. (2013). Vicarious traumatisation and resilience: An ecological systems approach to sexual abuse counsellors' trauma and stress. *Sexual Abuse in Australia and New Zealand*, *5*(2), 69–76.

Pack, M. (2014). Vicarious resilience: A multi-layered model of stress and trauma. *Affilia*, *29*(1), 18–29. doi:10.1177/0886109913510088

Pearlman, L. A., & Saakvitne, K. W. (1995). *Trauma and the therapist: Countertransference and VT in psychotherapy with incest survivors.* New York: Norton.

Phanichrat, T., & Townshend, J. M. (2010). Coping strategies used by survivors of childhood sexual abuse on the journey to recovery. *Journal of Child Sexual Abuse*, *19*(1), 62–78. doi:10.1080/10538710903485617 PMID:20390779

Reavey, P., & Brown, S. D. (2007). Rethinking agency in memory: Space and embodiment in memories of child sexual abuse. *Journal of Social Work Practice*, *21*(1), 5–21. doi:10.1080/02650530601173508

Reid, J. A., & Sullivan, C. J. (2009). A model of vulnerability for adult sexual victimization: The impact of attachment, child maltreatment, and scarred sexuality. *Violence and Victims*, *24*(4), 485–501. doi:10.1891/0886-6708.24.4.485 PMID:19694353

Rojas, A., & Kinder, B. N. (2009). Are males and females sexually abused as children socially anxious adults? *Journal of Child Sexual Abuse*, *18*(4), 355–366. doi:10.1080/10538710903051112 PMID:19842534

Rothschild, B. (2003). *The body remembers: Unifying methods and models in the treatment of trauma and PTSD.* New York: Norton.

Sommer, C. A. (2008). Vicarious traumatisation, trauma-sensitive supervision and counsellor preparation. *Counselor Education and Supervision*, *48*(1), 61–71. doi:10.1002/j.1556-6978.2008.tb00062.x

Ullman, S. E., & Filipas, H. H. (2005). Gender differences in social reactions to abuse disclosures, post-abuse coping, and PTSD of child sexual abuse survivors. *Child Abuse & Neglect*, *29*(7), 767–782. doi:10.1016/j.chiabu.2005.01.005 PMID:16051351

Watson, B., & Halford, W. K. (2010). Classes of childhood sexual abuse and women's adult couple relationships. *Violence and Victims*, *25*(4), 518–535. doi:10.1891/0886-6708.25.4.518 PMID:20712149

Wright, M. O. D., Crawford, E., & Sebastian, K. (2007). Positive resolution of childhood sexual abuse experiences: The role of coping, benefit-finding and meaning-making. *Journal of Family Violence*, *22*(7), 597–608. doi:10.1007/s10896-007-9111-1

Wright, M. O. D., Fopma-Loy, J., & Fischer, S. (2005). Multidimensional assessment of resilience in mothers who are child sexual abuse survivors. *Child Abuse & Neglect*, *29*(10), 1173–1193. doi:10.1016/j.chiabu.2005.04.004 PMID:16315358

Zala, S. (2012). Complex couples: Multi-theoretical couples counselling with traumatised adults who have a history of child sexual abuse. *The Australian and New Zealand Journal of Family Therapy*, *33*(03), 219–231. doi:10.1017/aft.2012.27

## ADDITIONAL READING

Burgess, A. W., Ramsey-Klawsnik, H., & Gregorian, S. B. (2008). Comparing routes of reporting in elder sexual abuse cases. *Journal of Elder Abuse & Neglect, 20*(4), 336–352. doi:10.1080/08946560802359250 PMID:19042661

Canton-Cortes, D., & Canton, J. (2010). Coping with child sexual abuse among college students and post-traumatic stress disorder: The role of continuity of abuse and relationship with the perpetrator. *Child Abuse & Neglect, 34*(7), 496–506. doi:10.1016/j.chiabu.2009.11.004 PMID:20627388

Chihowski, K., & Hughes, S. (2008). Clinical issues in responding to alleged elder sexual abuse. *Journal of Elder Abuse & Neglect, 20*(4), 377–400. doi:10.1080/08946560802359383 PMID:19042663

Colton, M., Roberts, S., & Vanstone, M. (2009). Child sexual abusers' views on treatment: A study of convicted and imprisoned adult male offenders. *Journal of Child Sexual Abuse, 18*(3), 320–338. doi:10.1080/10538710902918170 PMID:19856736

Davies, M., & Rogers, P. (2009). Perceptions of blame and credibility toward victims of childhood sexual abuse: Differences across victim age, victim-perpetrator relationship and respondent gender in a depicted case. *Journal of Child Sexual Abuse, 18*(1), 78–92. doi:10.1080/10538710802584668 PMID:19197616

Del Castillo, D., & Wright, M. O. D. (2009). The perils and possibilities in disclosing childhood sexual abuse to a romantic partner. *Journal of Child Sexual Abuse, 18*(4), 386–404. doi:10.1080/10538710903035230 PMID:19842536

Forouzan, E., & Van Gijseghem, H. (2005). Psychosocial adjustment and psychopathology of men sexually abused during childhood. *International Journal of Offender Therapy and Comparative Criminology, 49*(6), 626–651. doi:10.1177/0306624X04273650 PMID:16249395

Giglio, J. J., Wolfteich, P. M., Gabrenya, W. K., & Sohn, M. L. (2011). Differences in perceptions of child sexual abuse based on perpetrator age and respondent gender. *Journal of Child Sexual Abuse, 20*(4), 396–412. doi:10.1080/10538712.2011.593255 PMID:21812544

Ginzburg, K., Arnow, B., Hart, S., Gardner, W., Koopman, C., & Classen, C. C. et al. (2006). The abuse-related beliefs questionnaire for survivors of childhood sexual abuse. *Child Abuse & Neglect, 30*(8), 929–943. doi:10.1016/j.chiabu.2006.01.004 PMID:16934330

Godbout, N., Sabourin, S., & Lussier, Y. (2009). Child sexual abuse and adult romantic adjustment: Comparison of single- and multiple-indicator measures. *Journal of Interpersonal Violence, 24*(4), 693–705. doi:10.1177/0886260508317179 PMID:18448862

Gore, M. T., & Black, P. J. (2009). Bachelor of Social Work (BSW) students' prior sexual abuse victimization. *Journal of Teaching in Social Work*, 29(4), 449–460. doi:10.1080/08841230903249786

Griffing, S., Lewis, C. S., Jospitre, T., Chu, M., Sage, R., Primm, B. J., & Madry, L. (2006). The process of coping with domestic violence in adult survivors of childhood sexual abuse. *Journal of Child Sexual Abuse*, 15(2), 23–41. doi:10.1300/J070v15n02_02 PMID:16702145

Grossman, S. F., & Lundy, M. (2008). Double jeopardy: A comparison of persons with and without disabilities who were victims of sexual abuse and/or sexual assault. *Journal of Social Work in Disability & Rehabilitation*, 7(1), 19–46. doi:10.1080/15367100802009715 PMID:19042300

Grossman, S. F., Lundy, M., Bertrand, C., Ortiz, C., Tomas-Tolentino, G., Ritzema, K., & Matson, J. (2009). Service patterns of adult survivors of childhood versus adult sexual assault/abuse. *Journal of Child Sexual Abuse*, 18(6), 655–672. doi:10.1080/10538710903317265 PMID:20183424

Han, S. C., Gallagher, M. W., Franz, M. R., Chen, M. S., Cabrall, F. M., & Marx, B. P. (2013). Childhood sexual abuse, alcohol use, and PTSD symptoms as predictors of adult sexual assault among lesbians and gay men. *Journal of Interpersonal Violence*, 28(12), 2505–2520. doi:10.1177/0886260513479030 PMID:23486851

Hillberg, T., Hamilton-Giachritsis, C., & Dixon, L. (2011). Review of meta-analyses on the association between child sexual abuse and adult mental health difficulties: A systematic approach. *Trauma, Violence, & Abuse: A Review Journal*, 12, 38-49. doi:10.1177/1524838010386812

Hooper, C.-A., & Warwick, I. (2006). Gender and the politics of service provision for adults with a history of childhood sexual abuse. *Critical Social Policy*, 26(2), 467–479. doi:10.1177/0261018306062596

Jespersen, A. F., Lalumiere, M. L., & Seto, M. C. (2009). Sexual abuse history among adult sex offenders and non-sex offenders: A meta-analysis. *Child Abuse & Neglect*, 33(3), 179–192. doi:10.1016/j.chiabu.2008.07.004 PMID:19327831

Jung, K., & Steil, R. (2012). The feeling of being contaminated in adult survivors of childhood sexual abuse and its treatment via a two-session program of cognitive restructuring and imagery modification: A case study. *Behavior Modification*, 36(1), 67–86. doi:10.1177/0145445511421436 PMID:21937567

Katerndahl, D., Burge, S. K., & Kellogg, N. (2006). Factors that predict how women label their own childhood sexual abuse. *Journal of Child Sexual Abuse*, 15(2), 43–54. doi:10.1300/J070v15n02_03 PMID:16702146

Lacelle, C., Hebert, M., Lavoie, F., Vitaro, F., & Tremblay, R. E. (2012). Sexual health in women reporting a history of child sexual abuse. *Child Abuse & Neglect*, 36(3), 247–259. doi:10.1016/j.chiabu.2011.10.011 PMID:22425695

Leclerc, B., Wortley, R., & Smallbone, S. (2010). An exploratory study of victim resistance in child sexual abuse: Offender modus operandi and victim characteristics. *Sexual Abuse*, 22, 25–41. doi:10.1177/1079063209352093 PMID:20133960

Lee, S. J., & Tolman, R. M. (2006). Childhood sexual abuse and adult work outcomes. *Social Work Research*, 30(2), 83–92. doi:10.1093/swr/30.2.83

Littleton, H., Breitkopf, C. R., & Berenson, A. (2007). Sexual and physical abuse history and adult sexual risk behaviors: Relationships among women and potential mediators. *Child Abuse & Neglect, 31*(7), 757–768. doi:10.1016/j.chiabu.2006.12.015 PMID:17631958

Lock, T. G., Levis, D. J., & Rourke, P. A. (2005). The sexual abuse questionnaire: A preliminary examination of a time and cost efficient method of evaluating the presence of childhood sexual abuse in adult patients. *Journal of Child Sexual Abuse, 14*(1), 1–26. doi:10.1300/J070v14n01_01 PMID:15914402

Lutz-Zois, C. J., Phelps, C. E., & Reichle, A. C. (2011). Affective, behavioral, and social-cognitive dysregulation as mechanisms for sexual abuse revictimization. *Violence and Victims, 26*(2), 159–176. doi:10.1891/0886-6708.26.2.159 PMID:21780532

McKillop, N., Smallbone, S., Wortley, R., & Andjic, I. (2012). Offenders' attachment and sexual abuse onset: A test of theoretical propositions. *Sexual Abuse, 24*(6), 591–610. doi:10.1177/1079063212445571 PMID:22645229

Meade, C. S., Kershaw, T. S., Hansen, N. B., & Sikkema, K. J. (2009). Long-term correlates of childhood abuse among adults with severe mental illness: Adult victimization, substance abuse, and HIV sexual risk behavior. *AIDS and Behavior, 13*(2), 207–216. doi:10.1007/s10461-007-9326-4 PMID:17968646

Melville-Wiseman, J. (2011). Professional sexual abuse in mental health services: Capturing practitioner views of a contemporary corruption of care. *Social Work & Social Sciences Review, 15*(3), 26–43. doi:10.1921/095352212X655320

Milner, J. S., Thomsen, C. J., Crouch, J. L., Rabenhorst, M. M., Martens, P. M., & Dyslin, C. W. et al. (2010). Do trauma symptoms mediate the relationship between childhood physical abuse and adult child abuse risk? *Child Abuse & Neglect, 34*(5), 332–344. doi:10.1016/j.chiabu.2009.09.017 PMID:20359748

Paranal, R., Thomas, K. W., & Derrick, C. (2012). Utilizing online training for child sexual abuse prevention: Benefits and limitations. *Journal of Child Sexual Abuse, 21*(5), 507–520. doi:10.1080/10538712.2012.697106 PMID:22994690

Pechtel, P., Evans, I. M., & Podd, J. V. (2011). Conceptualization of the complex outcomes of sexual abuse: A signal detection analysis. *Journal of Child Sexual Abuse, 20*(6), 677–694. doi:10.1080/10538712.2011.627418 PMID:22126110

Roberto, K. A., & Teaster, P. B. (2005). Sexual abuse of vulnerable young and old women: A comparative analysis of circumstances and outcomes. *Violence Against Women, 11*(4), 473–504. doi:10.1177/1077801204274329 PMID:16043559

Rodgers, K. B., & McGuire, J. K. (2012). Adolescent sexual risk and multiple contexts: Interpersonal violence, parenting, and poverty. *Journal of Interpersonal Violence, 27*(11), 2091–2107. doi:10.1177/0886260511432148 PMID:22258079

Romano, E., & De Luca, R. V. (2005). An individual treatment programme for sexually abused adult males: Description and preliminary findings. *Child Abuse Review, 14*(1), 40–56. doi:10.1002/car.880

Romano, E., & De Luca, R. V. (2006). Evaluation of a treatment program for sexually abused adult males. *Journal of Family Violence*, *21*(1), 75–88. doi:10.1007/s10896-005-9006-y

Schilling, E. A., Aseltine, R. H. Jr., & Gore, S. (2007). Young women's social and occupational development and mental health in the aftermath of child sexual abuse. *American Journal of Community Psychology*, *40*(1-2), 109–124. doi:10.1007/s10464-007-9130-3 PMID:17557204

Schoedl, A. F., Costa, M. C., Mari, J. J., Mello, M. F., Tyrka, A. R., Carpenter, L. L., & Price, L. H. (2010). The clinical correlates of reported childhood sexual abuse: An association between age at trauma onset and severity of depression and PTSD in adults. *Journal of Child Sexual Abuse*, *19*(2), 156–170. doi:10.1080/10538711003615038 PMID:20390785

Senn, T. E., & Carey, M. P. (2010). Child maltreatment and women's adult sexual risk behavior: Childhood sexual abuse as a unique risk factor. *Child Maltreatment*, *15*(4), 324–335. doi:10.1177/1077559510381112 PMID:20930181

Senn, T. E., Carey, M. P., & Coury-Doniger, P (2011). Self-defining as sexually abused and adult sexual risk behavior: Results from a cross-sectional survey of women attending an STD clinic. *Child Abuse & Neglect*, *35*(5), 353–362. doi:10.1016/j.chiabu.2011.01.013 PMID:21620162

Sequeira, H. (2006). Implications for practice: Research into the effects of sexual abuse on adults with intellectual disabilities. *The Journal of Adult Protection*, *8*(4), 25–31. doi:10.1108/14668203200600026

Sesar, K. (2009). Child sexual abuse. *Ljetopis socijalnog rada/Annual of Social Work 16*, 615-633. Retrieved from http://hrcak.srce.hr/ljetopis?lang=en

Shakespeare-Finch, J., & de Dassel, T. (2009). Exploring posttraumatic outcomes as a function of childhood sexual abuse. *Journal of Child Sexual Abuse*, *18*(6), 623–640. doi:10.1080/10538710903317224 PMID:20183422

Simmel, C., Postmus, J. L., & Lee, I. (2012). Sexual revictimization in adult women: Examining factors associated with their childhood and adulthood experiences. *Journal of Child Sexual Abuse*, *21*(5), 593–611. doi:10.1080/10538712.2012.690836 PMID:22994695

Simpson, C. L. (2010). Resilience in women sexually abused as children. *Families in Society*, *91*(3), 214–247. http://alliance1.org/fis doi:10.1606/1044-3894.4001

Teitelman, J. (2006). Sexual abuse of older adults: Appropriate responses for health and guman services providers. *Journal of Health and Human Services Administration*, *29*, 209–227. Retrieved from http://www.spaef.com/articleArchives.php?journal=JHHSA PMID:17290813

Ullman, S. E., Najdowski, C. J., & Filipas, H. H. (2009). Child sexual abuse, post-traumatic stress disorder, and substance use: Predictors of revictimization in adult sexual assault survivors. *Journal of Child Sexual Abuse*, *18*(4), 367–385. doi:10.1080/10538710903035263 PMID:19842535

Weisbart, C. E., Thompson, R., Pelaez-Merrick, M., Kim, J., Wike, T., & Briggs, E.,... Dubowitz, H. (2008). Child and adult victimization: Sequelae for female caregivers of high-risk children. *Child Maltreatment, 13,* 235–244. doi:10.1177/1077559508318392 PMID:18502979

Wind, L. H., Sullivan, J. M., & Levins, D. J. (2008). Survivors' perspectives on the impact of clergy sexual abuse on families of origin. *Journal of Child Sexual Abuse, 17*(3-4), 238–254. doi:10.1080/10538710802329734 PMID:19042600

Wood, E., & Riggs, S. (2009). Adult attachment, cognitive distortions, and views of self, others, and the future among child molesters. *Sexual Abuse, 21,* 375–390. doi:10.1177/1079063209340142 PMID:19567918

Zafar, S., & Ross, E. C. (2013). Perceptions of childhood sexual abuse survivors: Development and initial validation of a new scale to measure stereotypes of adult survivors of childhood sexual abuse. *Journal of Child Sexual Abuse, 22*(3), 358–378. doi:10.1080/10538712.2013.743955 PMID:23590355

Zinzow, H., Seth, P., Jackson, J., Niehaus, A., & Fitzgerald, M. (2010). Abuse and parental characteristics, attributions of blame, and psychological adjustment in adult survivors of child sexual abuse. *Journal of Child Sexual Abuse, 19*(1), 79–98. doi:10.1080/10538710903485989 PMID:20390780

## KEY TERMS AND DEFINITIONS

**Adult Survivors:** There is some debate about specific ages of abuse and what constitutes "adulthood". Generally, adult women are considered to be those women aged over 18 years who have endured child sexual abuse before the age of 16 years by a trusted parent, caregiver, or perpetrator five years or older.

**Childhood Sexual Abuse (CSA):** An unwanted sexual act between an adult and a child in which the child is engaged then used for the sexual satisfaction of the perpetrator. This sexual abuse might involve differing forms of contact from the perpetrator with varying severity of impact on the victim. CSA includes unwanted sexual touching, fondling, rape, or attempted rape.

**Healing from CSA:** This concept differs from simply coping with CSA; for example, it is aligned with positive healing beyond a return to pre-trauma functioning.

**Prevalence of the Incidence of CSA:** This is not generally able to be defined easily with statistics, although many studies estimate that one in every three or four children is a victim of CSA in the Western world (Briere, 1996; Lev-Wiesel, 2008).

**Protective Factors:** Factors which foster resilience or the ability to rebound after CSA or other traumas.

**Recovery:** The process of developing a "good" life in the face of trauma or CSA. Elements of a good life refer to the survivor possessing sustaining interests, relationships, and material necessities, such as fulfilling work, enabling them to provide adequate housing, health, and income across the life course.

**Recovery Movement:** A movement described as a paradigm shift which challenges the expert-knows best discourses towards the wisdom of survivors of sexual abuse, giving them control to drive and direct their own healing process.

**Resilience:** The capacity to rebound as an adult after experiencing various traumatic events during childhood, such as CSA, to meet developmental milestones across various life domains, for instance, to establish and sustain supportive relationships and to develop competency in areas such as study, work, and parenting.

**Risk Factors:** Factors which obstruct or confound the healing process for survivors of CSA.

# Chapter 11
# A Social Work Approach in High–Tech Neurosurgery and Social Work Research Approaches in Health Care

**Colin Pritchard**
*Bournemouth University, UK*

## ABSTRACT

*Psychiatric social work is inherently inter-disciplinary with an interactive bio-psycho-social model of behaviour. This chapter mainly focuses upon an innovative study in neurosurgery. Sub-arachnoid haemorrhage (SAH) is a life-threatening condition and survivors are often left with serious cognitive impairment. Patients and their carers led the design of a two-year controlled prospective study of a patient and family support service, using the Specialist Neurovascular Nurse (SNVN) to speed rehabilitation and family readjustment. Cost-effective measures found the SNVN group gained significant psychosocial and fiscal benefits when compared to the control group, thus highlighting the effectiveness of a social work approach in neurosurgery. Other studies in healthcare, including surgical patient safety, effectiveness in reducing mortality, cultural influence on suicide rates and implications for prevention, and the implications of the changing patterns of neurological mortality in Western nations, are briefly described.*

## INTRODUCTION

Psychiatric social work has always considered itself to have an interdisciplinary approach, especially in relation to health care. In part, this is because of the interactive model of the bio-psycho-social approach to the nature of human behaviour. The following studies illustrate the value of such an approach in health care because social work, as a practice-based discipline, is a science-based art which can bring the insights of a psychosocial perspective into different areas of health care. The contexts of health care practice to be explored are hospital and after-care for neurosurgery patients and suicide prevention in mental health. The author's research suggests that it is helpful to have a social work-based service for patients and their caregivers integrated with

DOI: 10.4018/978-1-4666-6563-7.ch011

any health care offered. Ideally, it is recommended that there be at least one social worker in every health care team developing such services. These services are developed using social work principles and practices which by their nature are holistic, collaborative, information sharing, and responsive to patients and their families' needs.

## SOCIAL WORK APPROACH IN HIGH-TECH NEUROSURGERY

This chapter begins with an innovative project in high-tech neurosurgery dealing with patient cohorts of sub-arachnoid haemorrhage (SAH), a life-threatening condition. To understand a person and their family's response to a SAH, some background and discussion of what happens to those involved is necessary.

There are probably few conditions more dramatic than that of a SAH in which, generally without warning and no previous symptoms, an aneurysm on one of the major rings of arteries in the brain bursts. Because the skull is a hard box and the brain a soft vital organ, anything that takes up extra space, be it a tumour or a bleed (haemorrhage) such as a stroke, and SAH is a type of stroke, immediately creates a potential life-threatening or seriously disabling condition. The size and position of the bleed will affect the patient physiologically and, therefore, psychosocially but will be different in virtually every patient. It impacts often dramatically because of the suddenness with which it comes upon an individual's family and their social circumstances.

A little more than 50 years ago, almost 90% of SAH patients died within days, and before modern neurosurgery many of the survivors were left with neurological damage which might include loss of speech or sensation, or paralysis ranging from one to all four limbs. At the worst, it involved a traumatic dementia. Today, whilst about 5-10% of SAH are fatal within days, if the patient is stabilised, one of two treatments is effective. The long-standing treatment is a craniotomy, which involves a surgical opening of the skull, finding the aneurysm, and then clipping it. Whilst this is quite an invasive procedure, this is considered a total cure assuming there are no other aneurysms, although there may be varied degrees of physical weakness and impairment.

A more recent treatment is endovascular in which lines are passed through the femoral artery and up into the brain where a coil is placed within the damaged artery. Since this approach is less invasive it is used more often but as it is not always feasible craniotomies are still performed. Whichever treatment is used, if there are no other aneurysms, the patient's life-threatening condition is cured (Frazer, Ahuja, Watkins, & Cipolitti, 2007; Molyneux et al., 2009). However, mention is seldom made of the fact that 3% of all coiled patients have a re-bleed and die. This suggests that the endovascular approach still requires development as less than 1% of craniotomies have a re-bleed from a failed clip. Nonetheless, in both the retrospective and prospective studies to be described, we found that irrespective of treatment approach, there was no difference in the immediate psychosocial impact on the family of suddenly finding their loved ones in a neurosurgical unit fighting for their lives (Janes et al., 2013; Mezue, Matthew, Draper, & Watson, 2004; Pritchard, Foulkes, Lang, & Neil-Dwyer, 2001, 2004).

Following treatment, many patients develop what is now recognised as a post-traumatic stress disorder (PTSD) reaction (Noble et al., 2011; Visser-Meiley, Rhebergen, Rinkel, van Zandvoort, & Post, 2009), which had long been thought inevitable by virtue of the shock of being confronted with a sudden traumatic life-threatening disease (Buchanan, Elias, & Goplen, 2000). This was summed up by one neurosurgeon in responding to a ward sister's question, "if SAH patients are clinically cured, why do they keep returning to the neurosurgical unit?" He replied,

*Whilst the treatment was life-saving and now after clipping they're cured but of course they'll be knocked-off. They've had a massive assault to the brain [the bleed] requiring major treatment. I tell patients they can expect to be off work months, and some are for years. Some never go back because their confidence is destroyed. (Anonymous, personal communication, February, 2000)*

## Background to the Project

The author was invited by neurosurgical professionals to explore the problems faced by the post-treatment group, but at the time the professionals had not identified what questions were to be addressed. Two groups of twelve former patients were invited to the unit to discuss their experience and in effect became a focus group. The patients all readily agreed but there was still no hypothesis and the author met them with an open mind, although with a degree of irritation because the neurosurgical professionals had not specified the questions to be asked.

The first patient and her husband told such a terrible story of isolation, fearfulness, anxiety, and family tensions, that it did not seem ethical to ask much more but rather offer a listening ear. The next pair (patient and carer) told a similar unhappy story and I realised I was dealing with people in quite severe PTSD states, which at the time was not recognised by those in neurosurgery who rather saw the psycho-cognitive distress as an almost inevitable sequel to the physical impact of the SAH. In brief, I had ceased being a researcher and had moved into a counsellor role as this appeared to be what they needed. It had become clear that the patents and their carers "wanted to tell their story" and it seemed an important story that needed to be told.

In the light of this, it was decided to design a survey about patient and carer experience and the interviewees were invited to comment upon and contribute to a draft questionnaire. All interviewees took an active part, crucially acknowledg-ing that the whole treatment and post-discharge experience would be different for the patient and their carer.

Against the author's judgement, the partici-pants insisted that we included the widest coverage of their experience as well as demographics in the questionnaire. The questionnaire was to be postal and self-administered, aimed at those patients and their families discharged over the previous two years. Former patients and families were asked to indicate a degree of agreement/disagreement on a series of structured statements developed by the patient focus group, using a five-point Lickert Scale which evaluated their experience of the service as inpatients and post-discharge. In effect, the patients and their carers designed the questionnaire from their perspective, rather than from that of the professionals, to include everything they thought important.

There were open-ended qualitative questions giving respondents the opportunity to raise issues important to them. These embraced what was "best" and "worst" about their SAH experience both within and after discharge from hospital. The key question which emerged was: "Based on your experience, what if anything would you teach the doctors and nurses?"

The statements and demographic clinical information together yielded 79 questions. With so many questions it was not expected to attract a good response rate especially because it was retrospective. However, the patient and carer focus groups were pressing and very persuasive so it was important that as much as possible from their own words should be included in the questionnaire.

In the event, the strength and relevance of the essentially patient-family designed questionnaire was reflected in a 77% response rate from a two year cohort of treated SAH patients, yielding 142 paired patient and carer respondents. Their results reflected current and standard care in this and other neurosurgical units and were, therefore, designated the "Treatment-as-Usual" (TAU) group, when we undertook a prospective study.

The reason for the high response rate became clear on reading the open-ended responses as many people wrote reams and often with accompanying letters. It also became apparent that many patients were still in a PTSD state, and the patient-centred questionnaire was obviously more relevant to their experience than any questionnaire designed from the professional's perspective. Whilst the majority of patients had had a very good clinical recovery, even after two years many were still cognitively and psychologically distressed.

Below are three cases that typify SAH patient experiences and the psychological aftermath of their condition even after excellent life-saving surgery, as there was virtually no follow-up care to deal with the psychosocial impact of a SAH. To place these experiences in context, it is noteworthy that 54% of patients were less than 50 years old, meaning that the SAH occurred at the height of their professional and family life when they had responsibilities to partners, children, and employers. The case examples are anonymised.

## The Case of "John"

John was a 35 year old entrepreneur, who had just been awarded a major contract that would double his business from 10 to 20 employees. He had observed that he was well on the way to becoming a millionaire. He rang his wife to tell her the good news and planned a romantic dinner, but whilst driving home he suddenly experienced the most intense headache, at first thinking he had been struck from behind. Fortunately, he was able to steer his car off the motorway before becoming totally unconscious. His first subsequent memory occurred a week later when he found his wife crying beside his bed. He made a very good post-operative recovery and was discharged home in less than two weeks. However, he continued to feel distressed, could not concentrate, experienced panic attacks, feared another stroke, and was unable to face returning to work. His identity centred on his career as he was the business. Because of his

time off work, the business failed and he and his family lost everything. John had seen his general practitioner (GP) but because SAH is relatively rare, the GP had little experience of the condition. As John's wound healed well with virtually no physical disability associated with stroke, the community nurse felt he had no further need of assistance and follow-up care. As a family, John, his wife, and his children (who were aged 10 and 12 years), felt even more isolated.

Continuing and longer-term problems remained, with John experiencing periods of depression and an inability to judge what was "physically normal" along with continued cognitive disruption. After a year facing these issues, the pressure on his relationship with his wife meant that his marriage was faltering. Prior to the SAH, he and his wife had led an active sex life but after the SAH, he began to have sexual difficulties because of alarm at his rising blood pressure. Crucially, no one had explained to him that as there were no other aneurysms he was cured. His anxiety, therefore, remained.

## The Case of "Mary"

Mary was a 48 year old senior social worker. During an argument with her "stroppy teenage" daughter, she suddenly felt a massive blow inside her head. As her vision deteriorated, she felt her daughter was disappearing before her eyes, and as she fell to the ground, the last thing she heard was her daughter screaming, "Mam, mam, I've killed you!" A week later, she remembered becoming aware of being in the neurosurgical unit, terrified by what was going on around her. She made a good clinical recovery and was discharged home but there was little effective follow-up other than being given the standard booklet explaining the nature of SAH. Mary considered this booklet somewhat useful but insufficient as it "told us little of what it meant to our situation". One family consequence was that Mary's husband had to take time off work to look after his wife, causing considerable difficulty at work. Mary had a minor weakness in her left leg though there were no other physical problems. The wound healed well so the community care stopped. Mary thought she was "going mad", whilst her teenage daughter went into depression, convinced she had caused her mother's illness. The daughter began to miss school preferring to stay at home with her mother to ensure her mother was safe. As a result, her education deteriorated. Family tensions also arose, with the threat of either the daughter or the husband leaving. Her husband's employers were unsympathetic and he faced losing his position because of the time he had spent as a carer. After a month, he had no choice but to return to work. Mary felt deserted and quite unable to go back to an emotionally demanding job. Her employers, whilst a little more sympathetic, had to temporarily backfill her position while she was away. This meant that Mary lost the opportunity for a promotion and in despair she resigned, compounding the situation at home.

## The Case of "Margaret"

Margaret, aged 58, was a very successful head teacher in a large secondary school, known for her omni-competence, running her home and family, and meeting the numerous demands of her job. Sitting in the garden one summer evening, she bent down to smell a rose and experienced a painful explosion in her head and lost consciousness. As is typical of the above SAH experience, she recalled, "My world was turned upside down. I came away from neurosurgery a trembling wreck; couldn't distinguish any minor ache from the threat of another attack". After six months of barely improved anxiety and total loss of confidence, though she had virtually no physical disability, Margaret decided to take early retirement from a job to which she was previously passionately committed.

The above case examples typify the title of Wertheimer's (2008) book, *A Dented Image: Jour-*

*neys of Recovery from a Subarachnoid Haemor- rhage*. The book describes what happens to many post-discharged SAH receiving standard TAU. For months or years afterwards, all participants felt that, whilst their lives had been saved, they had been irredeemably shattered.

## Patient and Caregiver Designed Research: TAU Outcomes

The initial TAU results, published in the *British Journal of Neurosurgery* (Pritchard et al, 2001), added to the grim picture surrounding the post-operative SAH experience of other researchers (for example, Buchanan et al., 2000; Mezue et al., 2004). However, the uniqueness of this study was that by identifying the patients and their carers' problems, our open-ended qualitative questions enabled them to recommend a solution based upon what they felt they needed.

On the positive side, 25% of the patients said they only had mild or no stress, but the majority (53%) disclosed having severe socially disabling stress. Nearly half (45%) said that they had poor general health but relatively few reported physical weaknesses associated with stroke, although 10% had speech difficulties and 30% reported memory difficulties. There was an overwhelming complaint regarding the lack of support and sense of isolation. One theme throughout was the high level of anxiety (52%) and depression (38%) and a feeling of not knowing what is normal any more.

The social consequences of SAH were quite drastic. 9% lost their jobs; and of those of working age, 82% of the cohort had time off work, 48% were still off work up to two years post-SAH, and only 20% had returned to work in less than three months post-SAH. The actual cost to the families ran into the tens of thousands of pounds and although many middle-class occupations provide full pay for the first six months of sick leave this was soon exhausted, with the cost of being away from work transferred to the employer and the wider economy. Whilst the cost of high-tech neurosurgery is not borne by British people, since the national publicly funded health scheme (NHS) treats without charge at the point of need, it is often forgotten that there is considerable economic cost to families because of the time off work. At the extreme, patients risk becoming unemployed or being under-employed, a theme to which we shall return.

The results of this research detailing the social costs of the condition shocked the surgeons in the Unit who admitted to not giving thought to the consequences of being off work, simply pleased that the patients made clinical recovery. Clinical recovery is the surgeon's primary goal and provides their major source of job satisfaction (Pritchard, Brackstone, & MacFie, 2010). Fortunately, the neurosurgeons recognised that something had to be done and the answer became apparent from the patients' and carers' replies. They had described how isolated in the community they felt as many general practitioners and community nurses had little experience of SAH, an uncommon condition with a life-time prevalence of 1 in a 100,000 people (Lindsay, Bone, & Fuller, 2010) and in the UK only about 2,200 cases a year (Royal College of Surgeons of England, 2006).

Patients and their caregivers, therefore, needed someone from the unit who understood the condition to respond to their family-specific queries. In other words, they needed someone like the "traditional" hospital social worker, who was well-informed about their particular hospital ward's conditions, and who if they did not know, knew someone who did. They could offer appropriate support and counselling where necessary to assist the patient's rehabilitation, including any necessary family re-integration in the community upon discharge from hospital.

As a result, the unit neurosurgeons, concerned for their patients, pressed the Hospital Trust to provide patients with a family support service in a funded two year prospective study. The ward sister developed her counselling skills and became the specialist neurovascular nurse (SNVN) in a new post to be evaluated in the two year prospective study to see if such a service met the needs of patients and families in a reasonably cost-effective way. The prospective patients' outcomes would be compared against the results from the TAU group to determine any statistically significant differences.

## A Social Work Approach in Neurosurgery: A Comparative Longitudinal Controlled Study

The two year retrospective TAU cohort attracted a response rate of 77% of people posted, but the two year prospective study, which yielded 184 patients and carers, had a remarkable 92% response rate from families who had received help from the neurosurgical unit-based SNVN (Pritchard, Foulkes, et al., 2004).

In terms of clinical background, site of bleed, and on a range of standardised measures, such as the Glasgow Coma Score, there was little to choose between the TAU and SNVN cohorts, although among the SNVN patients there was a small but significantly greater number of larger bleeds than the TAU, suggesting that the SNVN group were slightly more physically damaged. Overall, the cohorts were a good match in terms of age, social class background, number of children, and gender. Participants were predominantly female at 67%.

## Qualitative Findings: TAU vs. SNVN Groups Follow Up

Key statistical significant differences in replies to the structured questionnaire (from a series of chi square tests) concerned patients' stay in hospital as well as post-discharge. Of the TAU patients, 28% said they were discharged too soon to SNVN's 16%; frightened 51% to 24%; in pain 47% to 24%; and crucially with unanswered questions about prognosis, TAU 48% to SNVN 20%. Whilst a fair proportion of the SNVN patient group continued to have some psychosocial problems, these were virtually half the rate of the TAU group, indicating the early accumulative value of the SNVN making contact in the neurosurgical unit prior to discharge.

Patients' post-discharge findings were also markedly different, with SNVN having a significantly more satisfactory outcome than TAU on virtually every psychosocial measure. For example, personal stress 43% (TAU) to 19% (SNVH); stress on the family 77% to 29%; family member off work because of SAH 56% to 32%; making unnecessary calls to the GP 32% to 10%; feeling frightened 40% to 11%; and depressed 35% to 21%. Thus, whilst patients in contact with the SNVN were not without problems, they were markedly less distressed than the TAU group, which as we will see, has practical and economic implications.

The carers' post-discharge findings were even more markedly different between the two groups, although there were differences between patients' and carers' perceptions, indicating the different nature of the burden of the condition and how it affected them differently.

Only 20% of TAU carers said there was no further stress from the SAH compared to 72% of the SNVN carers, and 13% of TAU to 54% of SNVN reported they "had all the support they needed". Moreover, 51% of TAU carers to 11% of SNVN carers made "unnecessary calls to the GP"; and "worries about my relative affected my work", was true for 77% of TAU carers to 39% of SNVN carers. These findings provide another indication of the value of social work input of the SNVN service to the carers as well as patients.

When patients and carers of the SNVN group were asked about the service, 88% said the service was a vital link between home and hospital. Only 9% were critical, 76% being highly satisfied, and 54% said the GP should be more willing to take advice from the SNVN. More than 80% of patients and carers said the SNVN was an "invaluable support to the family".

## The Costs of Being Absent from Work

In terms of patients losing their jobs due to the SAH, this occurred in 11% of TAU patients to 1% SNVN. Whilst 28% of TAU patients were on sick leave less than three months to 41% of SNVN, 47% TAU to 16% SAH carers were off work for six or more months due to their SAH. In regard to carers who had been off work less than a month, the results were: TAU 47% to 74% SNVN carers; being off work more than 17 weeks occurred in 26% of the TAU to only 2% SNVN carers.

Based upon the respondents' type of employment, it was possible to estimate the cost to families of the disruption to employment. For TAU patients, this cost averaged £9,076 compared to £4,011 for SNVN patients. For TAU carers, this cost was £3,193 to £888 for SNVN carers. This loss of income for patients and the families of patients is an issue often forgotten. Serious illnesses can have considerable economic costs to families and the wider economy. Thus, overall the TAU families loss of potential earnings exceeded £748,000 when compared to the SNVN £491,000. This represents a "hidden" saving of £257,000 to the families who received psychosocial support which was more than six times the cost of employing the SNVN over the two years.

These figures above do not include any fiscal estimate of the benefit of the improved psychosocial state of the SNVN families. There were slight but significant reductions in length of stay in hospital, reduced use of consultants in outpatient clinics taken by the SNVN, and reduction in GP time in the SNVN families. The service, therefore, had monetary savings of £4,165 per patient receiving a SNVN service.

The Wessex SNVN service was the first of its kind in neurosurgery. The ground-breaking research relating to the importance of a psychosocial approach to rehabilitation with patients and caregivers was a model for other hospital units to follow. Today, of the 33 neurosurgical units in the UK and Ireland, 13 units now have family support services.

## Commonality of the Role of the SNVN and Hospital Social Worker

The development of the SNVN fitted within the social work tradition of being holistic and patient-centred, viewing the patient and their family within the wider context of their community. This meant that upon the patient's admission, the SNVN made herself available to the patient and their caregivers, although often in the first few days the patient was not able to respond. However, the simple presence of the SNVN and her availability to the carers at this moment of need in the face of traumatic events engendered for the family the beginning of hope. Whilst no false assurances were given, the SNVN began to talk with the family about what would be needed when the patient was discharged from hospital to return home.

Initially, the SNVN did a home visit but being a regional service this quickly became impractical, so both patients and carers were seen on the hospital ward. Regular telephone and internet contact was maintained after discharge. An important feature was that because the families had telephone access, they seldom used the telephone other than by the agreed appointment. Moreover, the SNVN developed a patients' and carers' support and psycho-education group which she facilitated, providing wider and mutual support. Details of this group can be found elsewhere (Pritchard, Lindsay, Cox, & Foulkes, 2011). Typical of effective social work outcomes, it was the quality of the SNVN client/family relationship that was more important to patients and their caregivers. This was the active ingredient that contributed to the significantly better SNVN outcomes.

This theme associated with superior SVNM outcomes was succinctly outlined by a senior military person, aged 48, who returned to full time duties. He said,

*Unusually I remember much of my inpatient experience. I was fortunate to have had surgery at the very highest international level. But the second outstanding feature was the SNVN. She was available to deal with all those little questions which if they had not been dealt with would have become major barriers to my recovery, adding to my family's distress [emphasis added]. (Anonymous, personal communication, January, 2004)*

This comment is a reminder of the constant interaction between the individual patient and their family and how dealing with the sum of the whole improves the quality of life for each individual member.

Whilst the post-operative cognitive deterioration associated with SAH has long been known, it was assumed to be almost inevitable (Baisch, Schenk, & Noble, 2011; Buchanan et al., 2000; Mezue et al., 2004; Noble et al., 2011). This study shows this is not the case and such distress can be substantially reduced in many patients, if not totally avoided. The situation of TAU patients whose PTSD is largely left unaddressed also ignores the impact on the family, but a social work type approach can bring about major measurable positive changes even in a high-tech neurosurgery ward.

## INFLUENCING NATIONAL POLICY FOR SAH PATIENTS AND FAMILIES

### Potential National Impact

The above study led to an invitation from the British Society of Neurological Surgeons to re-evaluate their national data (Royal College of Surgeons of England, 2006) on 2,450 SAH patients and to estimate what the effect would be if every Neurosurgery unit had a SNVN. The clinical and demographic data of TAU and SNVN Wessex cohorts were matched and projected onto the UK cases of SAH yielding a comparative sample of 2,380 patients (Pritchard et al., 2011). The composition of this sample indicates that the Wessex SAH sample was fairly typical of SAH patients in the UK during the period under review.

The results when scaled up nationally were dramatic. The 2,380 matched patients consisted of 66% females. At a national level, the SAH patients aged under 44 years were estimated to have 895 school-aged children, and of patients aged between 45-54 there were a further 1,285 school-aged children who would likely have been affected by their parents life-threatening illness. Estimates of length of stay found the projected TAU group would have had 34,850 hospital days compared with the estimated SNVN 30,685 days, a 13% saving (Pritchard et al., 2011).

In 2008, a neurosurgical bed cost £544 per day but most SAH patients would have spent at least one day/night in the Intensive Therapy Unit at £1000 per day (Pritchard et al., 2011). A cautious estimate of reduced neurosurgical beds alone would, therefore, have yielded a potential "saving" of £2,176,000 to the NHS through provision of a social work service. The "saving" for families was estimated at £6,014 million for patients and £2,083 for carers because of the substantially reduced "time-off" work for those who would have received SNVN support.

When economists and politicians discuss the cost of modern health care provision, such sums seem to be presented as if these costs were an economic loss, albeit for a desirable public and moral good. This ignores the fact that many patients of working age return to full time employment and, therefore, in the case of Britain's NHS continue to pay income tax and social security payments which fund the NHS.

Breaking the national sample down by age and accounting for annual age-related mortality and projecting estimate years of productive work, we found that over their expected life-time, at 2008 prices, former working-aged SAH patients could, if making a good psychosocial recovery as did the SNVN, yield a contribution of £162 million to the wider economy (Pritchard & Hickish, 2011). This

shows that successful integrated neurosurgery not only saves lives and rehabilitates but brings economic benefit.

## Evaluating PTSD in Neurosurgery: Elective and Emergency Surgery and Spin-Off Social Work-Led Research in Surgery

The original study attracted the attention of Ear-Nose-Throat (ENT) surgeons who worked in neurosurgery on a chronic condition known as Acoustic Neuroma (AN), a slow growing benign tumour. They were interested to discover whether their elective AN patients had similar problems to SAH patients as an elective craniotomy is the mode of treating AN.

From the two-year retrospective survey of 102 patients and caregivers, it was found that the AN cohort had substantially fewer psychosocial problems than the SAH patients, even though initially AN patients had slightly more physical problems in the first six-months post-discharge. This led us to conclude that the greater degree of PTSD amongst the retrospective SAH cohort was in part due to the traumatic and acute nature of the SAH (Pritchard, Clapham, Davis, Lang, & Neil-Dwyer, 2004; Pritchard, Clapham, Foulkes, Lang, & Neil-Dwyer, 2004; Pritchard, Foulkes, et al., 2004). These results gave us further confidence in the need for a post-operative psychosocial family centred service to deal with the unresolved PTSD.

## PATIENT-RELATED-OUTCOME-MEASURES (PROM) AND PATIENT SAFETY

This social work led research in neurosurgery coincided with national concerns about patient safety in operating theatres. The Chief Medical Officer (2007) recommended that there should be a revalidation of consultant surgeons every five years and their assessment should include

"Patient-Related-Outcome-Measures" (PROM). The above patient-carer-centred studies were the first of their kind in neurosurgery and led to an invitation to the author to serve on the Research and Peer Review Sub-Committee of the Royal College of Surgeons in the development of the revalidation criteria.

The Committee was an unusual setting for a Research Professor of Psychiatric Social Work who learned much about the expertise and also the often divergent focus of surgeons, recognising that they needed a more holistic focus to include patients, families, and the society in which they live. Because the Chief Medical Officer's (2007) focus was upon "failures" in the operating theatre or when things go wrong, the author challenged the negative media and political portrayal that many surgeons had uncritically appeared to accept. In the discussions, it became apparent that the Chief Medical Officer's criticisms were a little unfair, and as John McVie, professor of surgery at the University of Hull, asked, "How can we hear the voice of the surgeon?" (Personal communication, June, 2008). This led to a quantitative and qualitative anonymous and non-attributable survey of all members of the Association of Surgeons of Great Britain and Ireland on the issues concerned with patient safety in theatre.

A 27% online response rate yielded 549 consultant surgeons and outlined the interaction of problems and resources, staffing theatre teams, and crucially, the dichotomy between surgeons' and managers' priorities (Pritchard & Brackstone, 2009; Pritchard, Brackstone & MacFie, 2010). In the survey, the author and team examined the rate of "Patient Adverse Events", and we had a higher rate than those complained of by the Chief Medical Officer (2007), showing the integrity and honesty of our respondents. Nevertheless, the rates from the Association of Surgeons of Great Britain and Ireland were contrasted against a major systematic analysis from North America

(de Vries, Ramrattan, Smorenburg, Gouma, & Boermeester, 2008) to find that the Association's rates were considerably lower.

Perhaps the most encouraging outcomes emerged from the qualitative open-ended questions on job satisfaction, as 100% of the respondents indicated that their work was about facilitating a positive outcome for patients. The worst aspect of their work was identified as a poor outcome for the patient indicating the strong patient-centeredness of these 549 surgeons. In considering sweeping criticism of the British NHS, however, the nation's health outcomes do need to be judged in the light of comparable countries, something to which I now turn.

## COST-EFFECTIVENESS OF NHS IN REDUCING CANCER DEATHS COMPARED TO OTHER WESTERN COUNTRIES

The author was accused by a consultant surgeon of being an "ivory towered academic", that surgeons, by contrast, "are at the table every day to see the problems". But it was suggested to him that surgeons "don't see the big picture" which is essential for developing evidence-based policy. Two studies compared the UK and twenty "Other-Western-Countries" (OWC) on the ultimate health outcome, Total Adult (15-74) Mortality and, because of specific criticisms of the UK, these were compared with adult Cancer Mortality Rates (Pritchard & Hickish, 2011; Pritchard & Wallace, 2011).

Tables 1 to 3 show the updated results from the study that outline the analysis to 2008. Ten death rates per million indicate a reduction in Total Adult deaths and Cancer Mortality Rates and show that the 21 Western countries have made major achievements. However, in terms of actual falls, divided by the % GDP spent on health to

*Table 1. All-Causes-of- Deaths (15-74 years) UK v OWC 1980-82 to 2008-10, rates per million, ratios of change. UK: OWC Odds Ratio, chi square tests. # indicates UK poorer outcome (ranked by highest current ACD).*

| Country & Ranks. Index v Baseline Years | Reduced ACD - Ratio | UK: OWC Odds Ratio | UK v Others X2 - p Value |
|---|---|---|---|
| 1 – 9. USA 1979-81<br>2005-07 | 8621<br>5832 – 0.68 | 1:1.26 | 70.40<br><0.000 |
| 2 – 8. Denmark 1980-82<br>2004-06 | 8778<br>5475 – 0.62 | 1:1.11 | 13.01<br><0.001 |
| 3 – 4. Germany 1981-83*<br>2008-10 | 9390<br>4978 – 0.53 | 1:1.06 | 6.1144<br><0.025 |
| 4 – 6. Portugal 1980-82<br>2008-10 | 9083<br>4955 – 0.55 | 1:1.10 | 13.03<br><0.001 |
| 5 – 7. Finland 1980-82<br>2008-10 | 9057<br>4875 – 0.54 | 1:1.08 | 9.4021<br><0.005 |
| **6 – 2. UK 1979-81**<br>**2003-05**<br>**2004-06**<br>**2005-07**<br>**2006-08**<br>**2007-09**<br>**2008-10** | **9425**<br>**5364 – 0.57**<br>**5281 – 0.56**<br>**5100 – 0.54**<br>**4998 – 0.53**<br>**4804 – 0.51**<br>**4696 – 0.50** | **N/a** | **N/a** |
| 7 – 5. Belgium 1979-81<br>2005-07 | 9279<br>5017 – 0.54 | 1:1.0 | 0.6595<br>n.sig |
| 8 – 13. Canada 1979-81<br>03-05 | 8092<br>4694 – 0.58 | 1:1.16 | 7.5273<br><0.01 |
| 9 – 1. Ireland 1979-81<br>2007-09 | 9975<br>4615 – 0.46 | 1:0.90 | 21.32 ##<br><0.0001 |
| 10 – 18. Greece 1979-8`<br>2007-09 | 7023<br>4609 – 0.66 | 1:1.29 | 80.73<br><0.0001 |
| 11 – 14. France 1979-81<br>2006-08 | 7963<br>4576 – 0.57 | 1:08 | 5.1716<br><0.025 |
| 12 – 12. New Zealand 1979-81<br>2007-09 | 8125<br>4276 – 0.51 | 1:1.02 | 0.2397<br>n.sig |
| 13 – 19. Spain 1980-82<br>2007-09 | 6925<br>4266 – 0.62 | 1:1.22 | 41.69<br><0.0001 |
| 14 – 17. Netherlands 1979-81<br>2008-10 | 7417<br>4246 – 0.57 | 1:1.14 | 27.98<br><0.0001 |
| 15 – 11. Italy 1979-81<br>2006-08 | 8131<br>4104 – 0.50 | 1:0.94 | 3.6263<br><0.1 trend # |
| 16 – 3. Austria 1979-81<br>2008-10 | 9440<br>4069 – 0.43 | 1:0.86 | 31.32 ##<br><0.0001 |
| 17 – 17. Norway 1980-82<br>2008-10 | 7600<br>3967 – 0.52 | 1:1.04 | 3.0794<br><0.1trend |
| 18 – 18. Switzerland 1979-81<br>2004-06 | 7592<br>3920 – 0.52 | 1:0.93 | 9.7978 ##<br><0.01 |

*continued on following page*

*Table 1. Continued*

| Country & Ranks. Index v Baseline Years | Reduced ACD - Ratio | UK: OWC Odds Ratio | UK v Others X2 - p Value |
|---|---|---|---|
| 19 – 19. Sweden 1979-31 2008-10 | 6345 3884 – 0.61 | 1:1.22 | 57.78 <0.0001 |
| 20 – 20. Australia 1979-81 2004-06 | 8230 3783 – 0.46 | 1:0.82 | 69.19 ## <0.0001 |
| 21 – 21. Japan 1979-81 2007-09 | 6272 3747 – 0.60 | 1:1.18 | 34.06 <0.0001 |
| OWC Average 1979-81 OWC Average 2008-10 | 8167 4494 – 0.55 | 1:1.10 | |

n.sig = not significant

produce a cost-effective ratio, the UK was one of the most effective and efficient in the Western world. The UK had some of the biggest reductions between 1980-2010 in both Total Adult Mortality and Cancer Mortality, indicating that the NHS achieves more with proportionately less (Pritchard & Hickish, 2011; Pritchard & Wallace, 2011).

Readers from the 21 countries will be able to assess the degree of success of their own country. Indeed, some might find it surprising that in terms of money spent on health and reduced deaths, the USA was one of the least effective and efficient.

I will now proceed to a discussion regarding research into social work's role in ameliorating suicide in mental health contexts.

## SOCIAL WORK RESEARCH'S CONTRIBUTION TO SUICIDE STUDIES

Durkheim has been described as the "father of sociology" and his seminal work related to social factors in suicide (Durkheim, 1897). Psychiatric social work, whilst inherently multidisciplinary, is based essentially in the social and behavioural sciences which can be valuable in health care as it builds upon an underlying sociological and empirical approach.

Britain decriminalised suicide in 1962 but the Roman Catholic Church still asserts that suicide is a mortal sin. Islam's Quran is quite explicit – suicide is considered to be an act of murder. The author interviewed a depressed Islamic woman who required a translator but the translator would not translate gently-asked questions about the client's despair and whether she ever thought of "hurting herself". This led to a study with an Islamic colleague to explore the theoretical position that there would be disproportionate high rates of "Undetermined Deaths" (UnD) thought to be the sources of "Under-Reported-Suicides" (Cantor, Leenaars, & Lester, 1997; Stanistreet, Taylor, Jeffrey, & Gabby, 2001).

The author and his team examined reported suicides and UnD in 17 "Islamic" countries where, such as Pakistan, suicide is still a crime. We found that suicide rates in six countries were over 100 per million (pm), five of which had higher rates for males than the UK. Conversely, 10 nations had rates of less than 20pm but 12 countries had UnD rates of more than 130pm, with nine Islamic countries having an odds ratio of more than 3:1 UnD to suicides, strongly indicating a high level of under-reporting (Pritchard & Amanullah, 2007).

After publication, a number of psychiatrists from Islamic countries expressed appreciation that the issue had been raised, for when one researcher

*Table 2. Cancer Mortality (15-74 years) UK v OWC 1979-2010, rates per million, ratios of change. UK: OWC Odds Ratios, chi square tests. # indicates UK poorer outcome (ranked by highest current rates)*

| Country Baseline v Index Years & Ranks | Reduced CD - Ratio | OWC: UK Odds Ratio | UK v Others X2 - p Value |
|---|---|---|---|
| 1 – 1 Denmark 1980-82<br>2004-06 | 2908<br>2312 – 0.80 | 1:1.11 | 5.7406<br><0.025 |
| 2 – 5 France 1979-81<br>2006-08 | 2607<br>2029 – 0.78 | 1:1.10 | 5.4531<br><0.025 |
| 3 – 4 Netherlands 1979-81<br>2008-10 | 2637<br>2021 – 0.77 | 1:1.12 | 6.7442<br><0.01 |
| 4 – 2 Belgium 1979-81<br>2005-07 | 2874<br>2015 – 0.71 | 1:1.00 | 0.1524<br>n.sig |
| 5 – 6 Germany 1981-83*<br>2008-10 | 2585<br>2010 – 0.78 | 1:1.13 | 8.6084<br><0.005 |
| **6-3. UK 1979-81**<br>**2003-05**<br>**2004-06**<br>**2005-07**<br>**2006-08**<br>**2007-09**<br>**2008-10** | **2800**<br>**2128 – 0.76**<br>**2021 – 0.72**<br>**1995 – 0.71**<br>**1977 – 0.71**<br>**1950 – 0.70**<br>**1925 – 0.69** | **n/a** | **N/a** |
| 7 – 12 Canada 1979-81<br>2003-05 | 2456<br>1964 – 0.80 | 1:1.06 | 1.4883<br>n.sig |
| 8 – 9 Ireland 1979-81<br>2007-09 | 2542<br>1937 – 0.76 | 1:1.09 | 4.556<br><0.05 |
| 9 – 8 Italy 1979-81<br>2006-08 | 2574<br>1894 – 0.74 | 1:1.04 | 0.9571<br>n.sig |
| 10 – 19 Portugal 1979-81<br>2008-10 | 1993<br>1875 – 0.94 | 1:1.36 | 51.57<br><0.0001 |
| 11 – 17 Spain 1980-82<br>2007-09 | 2104<br>1861 – 0.88 | 1:1.25 | 30.39<br><0.0001 |
| 12 – 13 USA 1979-81<br>2005-07 | 2372<br>1856 – 0.78 | 1:1.10 | 4.8246<br><0.05 |
| 13 - 7 Austria 1979-81<br>2008-10 | 2584<br>1832 – 0.71 | 1:1.03 | 0.5830<br>n.sig |
| 14 – 10 New Zealand 1979-81<br>2007-09 | 2525<br>1823 – 0.72 | 1:1.03 | 0.7155<br>n.sig |
| 15 – 18 Greece 1979-81<br>2007-09 | 2076<br>1787 – 0.86 | 1:1.23 | 23.51<br><0.0001 |
| 16 – 11 Switzerland 1979-81<br>2004-06 | 2510<br>1652 – 0.66 | 1:0.92 | 21.34 ##<br><0.05 |
| 17 – 15 Norway 1980-82<br>2008-10 | 2272<br>1649 – 0.73 | 1:1.06 | 1.5276<br>n.sig |
| 18 – 14 Australia 1979-81<br>2004-06 | 2295<br>1624 – 0.71 | 1:0.99 | 0.2062<br>n.sig |
| 19 – 18 Japan 1979-81<br>2007-09 | 2020<br>1601 – 0.79 | 1:1.13 | 8.4088<br><0.005 |
| 20 – 21 Sweden 1979-81<br>2008-10 | 1967<br>1575 – 0.80 | 1:1.16 | 11.51<br><0.001 |
| 21 – 16 Finland 1980-82<br>2008-10 | 2145<br>1516 – 0.71 | 1:1.02 | 0.3812<br>n.sig |
| OWC Average 1979-81<br>OWCAverage 2008-10 | 2402<br>1842 – 0.77 | 1:1.12 | |

n.sig = not significant

*Table 3. Cost-effectiveness ratios GDP expenditure-on-health expenditure to Reduced Cancer Mortality (15-74) rates per million p.a. (ranked by greatest cost-effective ratio)*

| Country & Years | Reduced rpm | Cost - Effective Ratio |
|---|---|---|
| **1. UK 2003-05** | **672** | **1:92** |
| **2004--6** | **779** | **1:107** |
| **2005-07** | **805** | **1:110** |
| **2006-08** | **823** | **1:113** |
| **2007-09** | **856** | **1:116** |
| **2008-10** | **875** | **1:120** |
| 2. Switzerland 2004-06 | 858 | 1:93 |
| 3. Belgium 2005-07 | 859 | 1:98 |
| 4=. New Zealand 2007-09 | 702 | 1:89 |
| 4=. Ireland 2007-09 | 648 | 1:89 |
| 6. Australia 2004-06 | 671 | 1:87 |
| 7. Italy 2006-08 | 680 | 1:83 |
| 8. Finland 2008-10 | 629 | 1:82 |
| 9. Austria 2008-10 | 752 | 1:79 |
| 10. Norway 2008-10 | 623 | 1:77 |
| 11. Netherlands 2008-10 | 616 | 1:72 |
| 12. Denmark 2004-06 | 596 | 1:68 |
| 13=. France 2006-08 | 578 | 1:60 |
| 13=. Germany 2008-10 | 575 | 1:60 |
| 15. Japan 2007-09 | 419 | 1:57 |
| 16. Canada 2003-05 | 492 | 1:55 |
| 17. Sweden 2008-10 | 392 | 1:45 |
| 18. USA 2005-07 | 516 | 1:39 |
| 19. Greece 2007-09 | 289 | 1:36 |
| 20. Spain 2007-09 | 243 | 1:33 |
| 21. Portugal 2008-10 | 118 | 1:15 |
| Average OWC | 562 | 1:66 |

highlighted the impact of untreated mental illness (Khan & Hyder, 2006), he, like the Islamic author, was then severely criticised for bringing Islam into disrepute. To this came the reply taken from the Prophet in the Hidith: "the most important men in the world are men of knowledge and the best are those who seek new knowledge" (Fadiman & Frager, 1997, p. 157).

These results led us to ask about those Catholic countries where religious doctrine still condemns suicide. We recognised that countries such as Ireland and Portugal have only relatively recently reported more realistic suicide rates, whilst in the more traditional Catholic countries in Latin America the stigma associated with suicide still exists (Cantor et al., 1997; Curlin, Nwodim, Vance, Chin, & Lantos, 2008). We, therefore, adopted a feminist perspective, recognising that countries that have relatively limited women's rights in the form of restricted access to family planning add significant additional pressures to women's lives (Carrol, 2007; Langer, 2002; Sedgh, Henshaw, Singh, Ahman, & Shah, 2007).

The study focused on suicide in Latin America amongst female youths (aged 15-24) compared with the older female age bands to find strong indicative evidence of major under-reporting of suicide (Pritchard & Hean, 2008; Pritchard, Roberts & Pritchard, 2013). Crucially, quite unlike Western European Catholic countries, young women in most Latin American countries had disproportionately higher suicide UnD rates and far higher suicide and UnD rates than in older women. Another important association was the higher Latin American rate of suicides or UnD with higher birth rates. This perhaps is not surprising as most Latin American countries have restricted access to family planning (Carroll, 2007; Langer, 2002).

These studies indicate the influence of cultural factors even between countries who nominally share the same Catholic doctrine. The one Latin American exception, Cuba, whose suicide rates were found to be considerably higher than their UnD, matched the pattern found in both Western and European Catholic countries. This cultural influence is linked to another issue, namely the legality and social acceptance of family planning which is general throughout Catholic Western countries, although Ireland and Portugal, which are the latest European Catholic countries to accept contraception, do have the highest rate of female youth suicide in Europe (Pritchard, Roberts, & Pritchard, 2013).

This pervasive cultural influence on suicide (Kelleher, Chambers, Corcoran, Williamson, & Keeley, 1998) was recently demonstrated in a study that used Durkheim's 1878 original suicide data in 11 European countries. This showed that whilst suicide rates moved up and down, often related to unemployment, in the periods 1972-74, 1984-86, and 2004-06, the differential rates between the countries during the period 1878-2006 hardly altered. This shows that there was a consistency in suicide rates over more than a 100 years (Hansen & Pritchard, 2008).

I now turn to a research study of changing patterns of mortality due to social changes.

## IDENTIFYING CHANGING MORTALITY INDICATING IMPACT OF SOCIAL CHANGES

During a clinical review, it was realised that there were four recorded cases of Motor Neurone Disease (MND) within a three year period. Whilst it could have been a statistical artefact, it was surprising as the textbooks suggest a mortality of about 1 in 100,000, the equivalent of 10 per million annually (Lindsay et al., 2010). At the same time the Department of Psychiatry at the University of Southampton was dealing with the relatively new phenomena of early-onset-dementia.

This led to two studies of the changing patterns of neurological mortality in the Western world, based upon WHO (2013) data, to find that compared with all causes of deaths, there

were major disproportionate increases in adults under 74 years and in effect the dementias were starting 10 years earlier (Pritchard & Hean, 2008; Pritchard, Mayers, & Baldwin, 2013).

Some argued that the reason for these increases might be due to the Gompertzian hypothesis that people are now living longer to develop diseases they previously would not have developed (Chio, Magnani, & Schiffer, 1995; Riggs & Schochet, 1992). Whilst there may be an element of truth in this, we and others demonstrated that this was not the main cause, not least because of the variation between the countries and the sexes. In most countries, women's health outcomes have worsened compared to men's. This is linked to the fact that women's life styles have changed considerably over the past 30 years as they have increasingly entered the workplace in areas which had been a male preserve. Thus, they have been relatively more exposed to the major multi-environmental changes found across the world (Callaghan B., Feldman, D., Gruis, K., & Feldman, 2011; Johansen, 2004; Pritchard & Hickish, 2011; Pritchard, Mayers, & Baldwin, 2013; Retsky, Swartzendruber, Bame, & Wardwell, 1994)

A new analysis for this chapter (Table 4) shows comparison of All Causes of Deaths (ACD) and Combined Neurological Deaths for the 55-74 year olds, with Odds ratios calculated the Combined Neurological deaths have increased proportionate to ACD. Spain has the biggest change 1:3.39, followed by the USA 1:2.75, with Germany, Italy, and the UK on 1:2.69. Only the Netherlands, France, and Japan did not double their Odds ratio, and the smallest change, Japan at 1:1.67, is the equivalent of neurological deaths increasing by 67% over ACD.

When the latest paper was published (Pritchard, Mayers, & Baldwin, 2013), the CEO of a new charity, "Young-Dementia UK", rang to express appreciation that the study was raising the issue. When asked the age of the majority of the charity's

*Table 4. All Causes Deaths, Combined Neurological Deaths by sex rates per million [rpm] and Final Odds Ratios of ACD to Combined Neurological Deaths 1979-81 v 2008-10. 55-78 years old. Ranked by highest Combined Gender Odds Ratio. Significantly Female ratios higher than Males ***

| Country, Latest Years & 79-81 Latest Combined Rank | Total Deaths Males | Total Deaths Females | Combined Neurological Males | Combined Neurological Females | Odds Ratios ACD: Neuro Both Sexes |
|---|---|---|---|---|---|
| 1. Spain 1979-81 2006-08 | 22469 14571 | 11746 6164 | 283 510 | 204 424 | |
| Ratio of change | 0.65 | 0.52 | **1.80** | **2.08 *** | **1:3.39** |
| 2. USA 1979-81 2005-07 | 26981 16288 | 14370 10635 | 360 595 | 261 530 | |
| Ratio of change | 0.60 | 0.74 * | **1.65** | **2.03 *** | **1:2.75** |
| 4=. UK 1979-81 2008-10 | 31146 14005 | 17153 9131 | 425 518 | 327 461 | |
| **4=. Ratio of change** | 0.45 | 0.53 * | **1.22** | **1.41 *** | **1:2.69** |
| 4=. Germany 1990-92 2008-10 | 25734 16360 | 17926 7191 | 444 457 | 247 333 | |
| Ratio of change | 0.64 | 0.40 | **1.03** | **1.35 *** | **1:2.69** |
| 4=. Italy 1979-81 2006-08 | 27257 13522 | 13669 7044 | **359 454** | **245 362** | |
| Ratio of change | 0.50 | 0.52 * | **1.26** | **1.48 *** | **1:2.69** |
| 7=. Canada 1979-81 2002-2004 | 24799 14278 | 12696 8845 | 411 510 | 300 461 | |
| Ratio of change | 0.58 | 0.69 * | **1.24** | **1.54 *** | **1:2.18** |
| 7=. Australia 1979-81 2004-06 | 26087 12061 | 13286 7092 | 403 397 | **290 338** | |
| Ratio of change | 0.46 | 0.53 * | 0.99 | **1.17 *** | **1:2.18** |
| 8. Netherlands 1979-81 2008-10 | 25615 13017 | 12092 8375 | 424 422 | **318 389** | |
| Ratio of change | 0.51 | 0.69 * | 1.00 | **1.22 *** | **1:1.87** |
| 9. France 1979-81 2006-08 | 26049 14776 | 11948 6651 | 599 542 | 421 416 | |
| Ratio of change | 0.57 | 0.56 | 0.90 | 0.99 * | 1:1.68 |
| 10. Japan 1979-81 2007-09 | 20066 12700 | 11018 5501 | 243 226 | 159 138 | |
| Ratio of change | 0.63 | 0.50 | 0.93 | 0.87 | 1:1.67 |
| **Average** 1979-81 2008-10 | 25620 14158 | 13591 6195 | 395 463 | 277 383 | |
| Ratio of change | 0.55 | 0. 46 | **1.17** | **1.38 *** | **1:2.13** |

caseload, she pointed to those mainly in their late 40s and early 50s. A finding of dementia being a disease of midlife would have been unthinkable 30 or more years ago.

When considering clinical studies, a contributory cause of these increases at national levels is indicative of environmental factors. A micro study, triggered by social work practitioners in a rural English country of a cluster of MND, found a local rate four times that of the country and double that of the UK rates (Pritchard & Silk, 2014). This hypothesis-stimulating study was of a village with under 5000 people aged 55+, a village next to a busy airport and surrounded by significantly high Electro-Magnetic-Fields from radar and mobile phone masts on the downs surrounding the village. Again, this finding indicates a possible environmental impact upon human health. Despite reductions in cancer deaths in the Western countries, the incidence of cancer continues to rise, albeit slower than in the past but again pointing to the influence of environmental factors, strongly suggesting epigenetic factors (Pritchard & Hickish, 2011).

## SOME METHODOLOGICAL CONSIDERATIONS

In our earlier chapter, Richard Williams and I discussed the relative paucity of quantitative outcome studies in British social work, and a brief perusal of the last three years of the *British Journal of Social Work* shows quantitative outcomes were very much in the minority, most research studies being "qualitative" in research design. As the above studies demonstrate, those that started from a qualitative research design were able to be triangulated with quantitative methods, allowing the results to be more widely generalised across larger populations. We urge a melding of research methods where appropriate, so that valuable social work perspectives can contribute to the wider field of health.

## CONCLUSION

Is this chapter a long way from social work research and practice? I do not think so. All social work theory as it is translated into practice draws heavily upon social science, but it does not become too detached and "ivory towered" because social workers rarely lose sight of the individual or the vulnerable person, be they consultant surgeon, or surgical patient.

It is argued that social work practitioners should have greater confidence in social work outcomes as they are skilled at working at the interface of complex and often conflicting margins and boundaries of different health and welfare agencies and departments. We believe that we need to have more quantitative findings to support this view, as Richard Williams and I have indicated in our earlier chapter on social work outcomes. Ultimately, there is only one question that matters in the human services, whether it be social work, medicine, or some other agency. That question is, "has the intervention or policy made a positive contribution to the individual and society?"

The social work discipline, built upon a passion for social justice, is one of the few to see the individual within the context of their family and society and is, therefore, uniquely placed to contribute to other disciplines. Social work practitioners should have the confidence in their work to demonstrate its worth.

## REFERENCES

Baisch, S. B., Schenk, T., & Noble, A. J. (2011). What is the cause of post-traumatic stress disorder following subarachnoid haemorrhage? Post-ictal events are key. *Acta Neurochirurgica*, *153*(4), 913–922. doi:10.1007/s00701-010-0843-y PMID:20963450

Buchanan, K. M., Elias, L. J., & Goplen, G. B. (2000). Differing perspectives on outcome after subarachnoid hemorrhage: The patient, the relative, the neurosurgeon. *Neurosurgery*, *46*, 831–838. Retrieved from http://journals.lww.com/neurosurgery/pages/default.aspx PMID:10764256

Callaghan, B., Feldman, D., Gruis, K., & Feldman, E. (2011). The association of exposure to lead, mercury, and selenium and the development of amyotrophic lateral sclerosis and the epigenetic implications. *Neurodegenerative Diseases*, *8*(1-2), 1–8. doi:10.1159/000315405 PMID:20689252

Cantor, C. H., Leenaars, A. A., & Lester, D. (1997). Under-reporting of suicide in Ireland 1960-1989. *Archives of Suicide Research*, *3*(1), 5–12. doi:10.1080/13811119708258251

Carroll, R. (2007, October 8). Killer law. *Guardian*. Retrieved from http://www.theguardian.com/society/2007/oct/08/health.lifeandhealth

Chief Medical Officer. (2007). *Towards a safer surgery*. London: HMSO.

Chio, A., Magnani, C., & Schiffer, D. (1995). Gompertzian analysis of amyotrophic lateral sclerosis mortality in Italy, 1957-1987: Application to birth cohorts. *Neuroepidemiology*, *14*(6), 269–277. doi:10.1159/000109802 PMID:8569998

Curlin, F. A., Nwodim, C., Vance, J. L., Chin, M. H., & Lantos, J. D. (2008). To die, to sleep: US physicians' religious and other objections to physician-assisted suicide, terminal sedation, and withdrawal of life support. *The American Journal of Hospice & Palliative Medicine*, *25*(2), 112–120. doi:10.1177/1049909107310141 PMID:18198363

de Vries, E. N., Ramrattan, M. A., Smorenburg, S. M., Gouma, D. J., & Boermeester, M. A. (2008). The incidence and nature of in-hospital adverse events: A systematic review. *Quality & Safety in Health Care*, *17*(3), 216–223. doi:10.1136/qshc.2007.023622 PMID:18519629

Durkheim, E. (1897). *Suicide: A study in sociology* (J. A. Spaulding & G. George Simpson, Trans.). New York: Free Press.

Fadiman, J., & Frager, R. (1997). *Essential Sufism*. San Francisco: Harper Collins.

Frazer, D., Ahuja, A., Watkins, L., & Cipolitti, L. (2007). Coiling versus clipping for the treatment of aneurysmal subarachnoid hemorrhage: A longitudinal investigation into cognitive outcome. *Neurosurgery*, *60*(3), 434–441. doi:10.1227/01.NEU.0000255335.72662.25 PMID:17327787

Hansen, L., & Pritchard, C. (2008). Consistency in suicide rates in twenty-two developed countries by gender over time 1874-78, 1974-76, and 1998-2000. *Archives of Suicide Research*, *12*(3), 251–262. doi:10.1080/13811110802101153 PMID:18576206

Janes, F., Gigli, G. L., D'Anna, L., Cancelli, I., Perelli, A., Canal, G.,…& Valente M. (2013). Stroke incidence and 30-day and six-month case fatality rates in Udine, Italy: A population-based prospective study. *International Journal of Stroke*, *8*(Suppl. A100), 100-105. doi:10.1111/ijs.12000

Johansen, C. (2004). Electromagnetic fields and health effects: Epidemiological studies of cancer, diseases of the central nervous system and arrhythmia-related heart disease. *Scandinavian Journal of Work, Environment & Health*, *30*(Suppl. 1), 1–30. Retrieved from http://www.sjweh.fi/ PMID:15255560

Kelleher, M. J., Chambers, D., Corcoran, P., Williamson, E., & Keeley, H. S. (1998). Religious sanctions and rates of suicide worldwide. *Crisis*, *19*(2), 78–86. doi:10.1027/0227-5910.19.2.78 PMID:9785649

Khan, M. M., & Hyder, A. A. (2006). Suicides in the developing world: Case study from Pakistan. *Suicide & Life-Threatening Behavior*, *36*(1), 76–81. doi:10.1521/suli.2006.36.1.76 PMID:16676628

Langer, A. (2002). El embarazo no deseado: Impacto sobre la salud y la sociedad en América Latina y el Caribe [Unwanted pregnancy: Impact on health and society in Latin America and the Caribbean]. *Revista Panamericana de Salud Pública*, *11*(3), 192–205. doi:10.1590/S1020-49892002000300013 PMID:11998185

Lindsay, K. W., Bone, I., & Fuller, G. (2010). *Neurology & neurosurgery illustrated*. Edinburgh: Churchill Livingstone.

Mezue, W., Matthew, B., Draper, P., & Watson, R. (2004). The impact of care on carers of patients treated for aneurysmal subarachnoid haemorrhage. *British Journal of Neurosurgery*, *18*(2), 135–137. doi:10.1080/02688690410001680984 PMID:15176554

Molyneux, A. J., Kerr, R. S., Birks, J., Ramzi, N., Yarnold, J., Sneade, M., & Rischmiller, J. (2009). Risk of recurrent subarachnoid haemorrhage, death, or dependence and standardised mortality ratios after clipping or coiling for intracranial aneurysm in the international subarachnoid aneurysm trial (ISAT): Long-term follow-up. *Lancet Neurology*, *8*(5), 427–433. doi:10.1016/S1474-4422(09)70080-8 PMID:19329361

Noble, A. J., Baisch, S., Covey, J., Mukerji, N., Nath, F., & Schenk, T. (2011). Subarachnoid hemorrhage patients' fears of recurrence are related to the presence of posttraumatic stress disorder. *Neurosurgery*, *69*(2), 323–332. doi:10.1227/NEU.0b013e318216047e PMID:21415779

Pritchard, C., & Amanullah, S. (2007). An analysis of suicide and undetermined deaths in 17 predominately Islamic countries contrasted with the UK. *Psychological Medicine*, *37*(3), 421–430. doi:10.1017/S0033291706009159 PMID:17176500

Pritchard, C., & Brackstone, J. (2009). "The voice of the surgeon" on patient safety: The ASGBI survey. *Newsletter (Association of Surgeons of Great Britain & Ireland)*, *28*, 34-36.

Pritchard, C., Brackstone, J., & MacFie, J. (2010). Adverse events and patient safety in the operating theatre: Perspectives of 549 surgeons. *Bulletin of the Royal College of Surgeons of England*, *92*(6), 1–4. doi:10.1308/147363510X507972

Pritchard, C., Clapham, L., Davis, A., Lang, D. A., & Neil-Dwyer, G. (2004). Psycho-socio-economic outcomes in acoustic neuroma patients and their carers related to tumour size. *Clinical Otolaryngology and Allied Sciences*, *29*(4), 324–330. doi:10.1111/j.1365-2273.2004.00822.x PMID:15270817

Pritchard, C., Clapham, L., Foulkes, L., Lang, D. A., & Neil-Dwyer, G. (2004). Comparison of cohorts of elective and emergency neurosurgical patients: Psychosocial outcomes of acoustic neuroma and aneurysmal sub arachnoid hemorrhage patients and carers. *Surgical Neurology*, *62*(1), 7–16. doi:10.1016/j.surneu.2004.01.018 PMID:15226061

Pritchard, C., Foulkes, L., Lang, D. A., & Neil-Dwyer, G. (2001). Psychosocial outcomes for patients and carers after aneurysmal subarachnoid haemorrhage. *British Journal of Neurosurgery, 15*(6), 456–463. doi:10.1080/02688690120097679 PMID:11813996

Pritchard, C., Foulkes, L., Lang, D. A., & Neil-Dwyer, G. (2004). Two year prospective study of psychosocial outcomes and a cost-analysis of "treatment-as-usual" versus an "enhanced" (specialist liaison nurse) service for aneurysmal sub arachnoid haemorrhage (ASAH) patients and families. *British Journal of Neurosurgery, 18*(4), 347–356. doi:10.1080/02688690400004993 PMID:15702833

Pritchard, C., & Hean, S. (2008). Suicide and undetermined deaths among youths and young adults in Latin America: Comparison with the 10 major developed countries – A source of hidden suicides? *Crisis, 29*(3), 145–153. doi:10.1027/0227-5910.29.3.145 PMID:18714911

Pritchard, C., & Hickish, T. (2011). Comparing cancer mortality and GDP health expenditure in England and Wales with other major developed countries from 1979 to 2006. *British Journal of Cancer, 105*(11), 1788–1794. doi:10.1038/bjc.2011.393 PMID:21970877

Pritchard, C., Lindsay, K., Cox, M., & Foulkes, L. (2011). Re-evaluating the national subarachnoid haemorrhage study (2006) from a patient-related-outcome-measure perspective: Comparing fiscal outcomes of treatment-as-usual with an enhanced service. *British Journal of Neurosurgery, 25*(3), 376–383. doi:10.3109/02688697.2011.566379 PMID:21513445

Pritchard, C., Mayers, A., & Baldwin, D. (2013). Changing patterns of neurological mortality in the 10 developed countries: 1979-2010. *Public Health, 127*(4), 357–368. doi:10.1016/j.puhe.2012.12.018 PMID:23601790

Pritchard, C., Roberts, S., & Pritchard, C. E. (2013). "Giving a voice to the unheard"? Is female youth (15-24 years) suicide linked to restricted access to family planning? Comparing two Catholic continents. *International Social Work, 56*(6), 798–815. doi:10.1177/0020872812441645

Pritchard, C., & Silk, A. (2014). A case-study survey of an eight-year cluster of motor neurone disease (MND) referrals in a rural English village: Exploring possible aetiological influences in a hypothesis stimulating study. *Journal of Neurological Disorders, 2*, 147. doi:10.4172/2329-6895.1000147

Pritchard, C., & Wallace, M. S. (2011). Comparing the USA, UK and 17 Western countries' efficiency and effectiveness in reducing mortality. *Journal of the Royal Society of Medicine Short Reports, 2*(60), 1–10. doi:10.1258/shorts.2011.011076 PMID:21847442

Retsky, M. W., Swartzendruber, D. E., Bame, P. D., & Wardwell, R. H. (1994). Computer model challenges breast cancer treatment strategy. *Cancer Investigation, 12*(6), 559–567. doi:10.3109/07357909409023040 PMID:7994590

Riggs, J. E., Schochet, S. S., Jr. (1992). Rising mortality due to Parkinson's disease and amyotrophic lateral sclerosis: A manifestation of the competitive nature of human mortality. *Journal of Clinical Epidemiology, 45*, 1007-1012. doi: 10.1016/0895-4356(92)90116-5

Royal College of Surgeons of England. (2006). *The national subarachnoid haemorrhage evaluation study: Final report of an audit carried out in 34 neurosurgical units in the UK and Ireland between 14 September 2001 to 13 September 2002*. London: British Society of Neurological Surgeons, Royal College of Surgeons. Retrieved from http://www.rcseng.ac.uk/publications/docs/nat_study_subarachnoid_haem_feb2006.html

Sedgh, G., Henshaw, S., Singh, S., Ahman, E., & Shah, I. H. (2007). Induced abortion: Estimated rates and trends worldwide. *Lancet*, *370*(9595), 1338–1345. doi:10.1016/S0140-6736(07)61575-X PMID:17933648

Stanistreet, D., Taylor, S., Jeffrey, V., & Gabby, M. (2001). Accident or suicide? Predictors of coroners' decisions in suicide and accident verdicts. *Medicine, Science, and the Law*, *41*, 111–115. doi:10.1177/002580240104100205 PMID:11368390

Visser-Meiley, J. M. A., Rhebergen, M. L., Rinkel, G. J. E., van Zandvoort, M. J., & Post, M. W. M. (2009). Long-term health-related quality of life after aneurysmal subarachnoid haemorrhage: Relationship with psychological symptoms and personality characteristics. *Stroke*, *40*(4), 1526–1529. doi:10.1161/STROKEAHA.108.531277 PMID:19095984

Wertheimer, A. (2008). *A dented image: Journeys of recovery from a subarachnoid haemorrhage*. London: Routledge.

WHO. (2013) *Annual mortality statistics*. Retrieved from http://www.who.int/healthinfo/statistics/mortality/en/

## ADDITIONAL READING

Ai-Khindi, T., Macdonald, R. L., & Schweizer, T. A. (2010). Cognitive and functional outcome after aneurysmal subarachnoid hemorrhage. *Stroke*, *41*(8), e519–e536. doi:10.1161/STROKEAHA.110.581975 PMID:20595669

Alonso, A., Logroscino, G., Jlick, S. S., & Hernan, M. A. (2009). Incidence and lifetime risk of motor neurone disease in the United Kingdom: A population based study. *European Journal of Neurology*, *16*(6), 745–751. doi:10.1111/j.1468-1331.2009.02586.x PMID:19475756

Baldi, I., Coureau, G., Jaffré, A., Gruber, A., Ducamp, S., & Provost, D. et al. (2011). Occupational and residential exposure to electromagnetic fields and risk of brain tumors in adults: A case–control study in Gironde, France. *International Journal of Cancer*, *129*(6), 1477–1484. doi:10.1002/ijc.25765 PMID:21792884

Berry, E. (1998). Post-traumatic stress disorder after subarachnoid haemorrhage. *The British Journal of Clinical Psychology*, *37*(3), 365–367. doi:10.1111/j.2044-8260.1998.tb01392.x PMID:9784890

Beseoglu, K., Pannes, S., Steiger, H. J., & Hänggi, D. (2010). Long-term outcome and quality of life after nonaneurysmal subarachnoid hemorrhage. *Acta Neurochirurgica*, *152*(3), 409–416. doi:10.1007/s00701-009-0518-8 PMID:19784546

Chen, Y.-Y., Wu, K. C.-C., Yousuf, S., & Yip, P. S. F. (2012). Suicide in Asia: Opportunities and challenges. *Epidemiologic Reviews*, *34*(1), 129–144. doi:10.1093/epirev/mxr025 PMID:22158651

Cook, C. C. (2014). Suicide and religion. *The British Journal of Psychiatry*, *204*(4), 254–255. doi:10.1192/bjp.bp.113.136069 PMID:24692751

Covey, J., Noble, A. J., & Schenk, T. (2013). Family and friends' fears of recurrence: Impact on the patient's recovery after subarachnoid haemorrhage. *Journal of Neurosurgery*, *119*(4), 948–954. doi:10.3171/2013.5.JNS121688 PMID:23876000

Day, T. G., Scott, M., Perring, R., & Doyle, P. (2007). Motor neurone disease mortality in Great Britain continues to rise: Examination of mortality rates 1975–2004. *Amyotrophic Lateral Sclerosis: Official Publication of the World Federation of Neurology Research Group on Motor Neuron Diseases*, *8*(6), 337–342. doi:10.1080/17482960701725455 PMID:18033591

Gearing, R. E., & Lizardi, D. (2009). Religion and suicide. *Journal of Religion and Health, 48*(3), 332–341. doi:10.1007/s10943-008-9181-2 PMID:19639421

Goldacre, M. J., Duncan, M., Griffith, M., & Turner, M. R. (2010). Trends in death certification for multiple sclerosis, motor neurone disease, Parkinson's disease and epilepsy in English populations 1979–2006. *Journal of Neurology, 257*(5), 706–715. doi:10.1007/s00415-009-5392-z PMID:19946783

Heros, R. C. (2013). Fear of recurrence. *Journal of Neurosurgery, 119*(4), 943–945. doi:10.3171/2013.2.JNS13252 PMID:23875959

Katati, M. J., Santiago-Ramajo, S., Pérez-García, M., Meersmans-Sánchez Jofré, M., Vilar-Lopez, R., & Coín-Mejias, M. A., ...Arjona-Moron, V. (2007). Description of quality of life and its predictors in patients with aneurysmal subarachnoid haemorrhage. *Cerebrovascular Diseases, 24*(1), 66–73. doi:10.1159/000103118 PMID:17519546

Lodhi, L. M., & Shah, A. (2005). Factors associated with the recent decline in suicide rates in the elderly in England and Wales, 1985-1998. *Medicine, Science, and the Law, 45*(1), 31–38. doi:10.1258/rsmmsl.45.1.31 PMID:15745271

Marcilio, I., Gouveia, N., Pereira Filho, M. L., & Kheifets, L. (2011). Adult mortality from leukemia, brain cancer, amyotrophic lateral sclerosis and magnetic fields from power lines: A case-control study in Brazil. *Revista Brasileira de Epidemiologia, 14*(4), 580–588. doi:10.1590/S1415-790X2011000400005 PMID:22218657

Mercy, L., Hodges, J. R., Dawson, K., Baker, R. A., & Brayne, C. (2008). Incidence of early onset dementia in Cambridgeshire, United Kingdom. *Neurology, 71*(19), 1496–1499. doi:10.1212/01.wnl.0000334277.16896.fa PMID:18981371

Milner, A., Spittal, M. J., Pirkis, J., & LaMontagne, A. D. (2013). Suicide by occupation: Systematic review and meta-analysis. *The British Journal of Psychiatry, 203*(6), 409–416. doi:10.1192/bjp.bp.113.128405 PMID:24297788

Noble, A. J., & Schenk, T. (2008). Posttraumatic stress disorder in the family and friends of patients who have suffered spontaneous subarachnoid hemorrhage. *Journal of Neurosurgery, 109*(6), 1027–1033. doi:10.3171/JNS.2008.109.12.1027 PMID:19035715

Passier, P. E. C. A., Visser-Meily, J. M. A., Van Zandvoort, M. J. E., Post, M. W. M., Rinkel, G. J. E., & Van Heugten, C. (2010). Prevalence and determinants of cognitive complaints after aneurysmal subarachnoid hemorrhage. *Cerebrovascular Diseases, 29*(6), 557–563. doi:10.1159/000306642 PMID:20375498

Powell, J., Kitchen, N., Heslin, J., & Greenwood, R. (2002). Psychosocial outcomes at three and nine months after good neurological recovery from aneurysmal subarachnoid haemorrhage: Predictors and prognosis. *Journal of Neurology, Neurosurgery, and Psychiatry, 72*(6), 772–781. doi:10.1136/jnnp.72.6.772 PMID:12023423

Pritchard, C. (1988). Suicide, unemployment and gender in the British Isles and European Economic Community (1974-1985): A hidden epidemic? *Social Psychiatry and Psychiatric Epidemiology, 23*(2), 85–89. doi:10.1007/BF01788426 PMID:3133784

Pritchard, C., Cox, M., Foulkes, L., & Lindsay, K. (2011). The patient's voice in neuro-surgery: Psycho-socio-economic benefits of a patient-designed versus standard service following treatment for a subarachnoid haemorrhage. *Social Care and Neurodisability, 2*(2), 80–96. doi:10.1108/20420911111142759

Rinkel, G. J. E., & Algra, A. (2011). Long-term outcomes of patients with aneurysmal subarachnoid haemorrhage. *Lancet Neurology, 10*(4), 349–356. doi:10.1016/S1474-4422(11)70017-5 PMID:21435599

Viner, R. M., Coffey, C., Mathers, C., Bloem, P., Costello, A., Santelli, J., & Patton, G. C. (2011). 50-year mortality trends in children and young people: A study of 50 low-income, middle-income, and high-income countries. *Lancet, 377*(9772), 1162–1174. doi:10.1016/S0140-6736(11)60106-2 PMID:21450338

Wermer, M. J. H., Kool, H., Albrecht, K. W., & Rinkel, G. J. E. (2007). Subarachnoid hemorrhage treated with clipping: Long-term effects on employment, relationships, personality, and mood. *Neurosurgery, 60*(1), 91–98. doi:10.1227/01.NEU.0000249215.19591.86 PMID:17228256

Wong, G. K. C., Poon, W. S., Boet, R., Chan, M. T. C., Gin, T., Ng, S. C. P., & Zee, B. C. Y. (2011). Health-related quality of life after aneurysmal subarachnoid hemorrhage: Profile and clinical factors. *Neurosurgery, 68*(6), 1556–1561. doi:10.1227/NEU.0b013e31820cd40d PMID:21311383

## KEY TERMS AND DEFINITIONS

**Acoustic Neuroma (AN):** A growth on the auditory (hearing nerve) usually benign but causing increasing deafness and affecting balance. The condition usually requires both an ear, nose, and throat surgeon's intervention as well as neurosurgical intervention through the performance of a craniotomy (surgery to the brain).

**Post-Traumatic Stress Disorder (PTSD):** A set of responses that often develop following a traumatic event, such as a life-threatening stroke. The disorder may involve re-living the traumatic event through recurring memories involving intrusive images and nightmares; physical symptoms, such as panic attacks and heart palpitations; increased startle response; emotional numbing; and avoidance behaviours.

**Specialist Neurovascular Nurse (SNVN):** A nurse who provides specialised psycho-social and psycho-education support to patients following sub-arachnoid haemorrhage. The nurse works systemically with patients and their partners, caregivers, and families.

**Sub-Arachnoid Haemorrhage (SAH):** An aneurysm on one of the major arteries of the brain. A type of stroke.

# Chapter 12
# Recruiting and Engaging Men as Fathers in Social Work Practice

**Joseph Fleming**
*Deakin University, Australia*

**Andrew King**
*Groupwork Solutions, Australia*

**Tara Hunt**
*Groupwork Solutions, Australia*

## ABSTRACT

*Evidence in the research literature suggests that men are usually not engaged by social workers, particularly in child welfare and child protection settings. Mothers also tend to become the focus of intervention, even when there is growing evidence that men can take an active and important role in a child's development in addition to providing support to the mother and family. Whilst there have been some promising developments in including men in social work practice internationally, there remains a gap in the research regarding the engagement of men as fathers in Australia. Given the growing relevance of the topic of fathers, the purpose of this chapter is to add to the current knowledge base, to support social work students and practitioners to engage with men in their role as fathers, and to offer an evidence-based practice model that may assist social workers in their work with men as fathers.*

## INTRODUCTION

Parents today live in lesbian, gay, bisexual, and transgender relationships, within extended and reconstituted families, or are single parent families. This chapter is written as a suggested guide for social workers which focuses on engaging fathers in community services, health contexts, and programmes, who would otherwise be less involved for a variety of social and cultural reasons. Ideas about men and families have historically been constructed and shaped in society by sexual divisions in law and gendered assumptions (Collier, 2009). The concept of "father" is now more complex than it was and, as Scourfield and Drakeford (2002) have suggested, ideas about men and masculinity are positioned in different ways and are often not complimentary. As a result, some

DOI: 10.4018/978-1-4666-6563-7.ch012

of this information is relevant to non-biological fathers, mothers, and lesbian, gay, bisexual, and transgender couples. However, these groups may require specific information not presented in this chapter (Power et al., 2012). In the case of gay and lesbian parents, there is a dearth of research in engagement and practice which is an area requiring attention in its own right. However, many of the tools used in this chapter are applicable to working with fathers in gay relationships or are very similar to those tools used when working with women from marginalised communities. The authors take the position that every person has the capacity to be an excellent and effective parent and that fathers, in particular, need to be given the opportunity to be involved in their children's lives. In fact, the growing diversity of life course and residency patterns for men and children has fostered a new awareness of the roles of both mother and father in contemporary society (Marsiglio, Day, & Lamb, 2000).

As authors of this chapter, we agree and acknowledge that gender is of central importance in understanding family dynamics and the occupational culture within the social work profession. We also acknowledge that gender construction in practice and education can be problematic. However, to understand the interplay between masculinity, social work, and women's subordination (Parker & Ashencaen Crabtree, 2014) is a discussion that simply lies beyond the scope of this chapter.

In contemporary society, a father can be both biological and social and described as the significant male role model in a child's life. Men, who are a significant role model in a child's life, can serve as fathers in different kinds of relationships. For example, they may be fathering in intact relationships, separated, or single, and while many men are biological fathers they may also be grandfathers, step-fathers, uncles, another member of the family, or even unrelated, but still act in the role of a caregiver or parental figure.

Over many generations, most cultures have developed with traditional role expectations for men to be "hunters and gatherers" and women to be "nurturers and carers" who support families. In the past, both parents had concrete expectations of the role they played in the family, their relationship, and the broader community. Contemporary society, by contrast, has seen a greater sharing of employment roles across both genders. Today, both men and women can earn comparatively equal wages and women are fulfilling the same paid roles as men across many employment sectors (Baxter & Smart, 2011). Also, the changing employment landscape has seen a decline in the "manual labour" or "blue collar" contexts of employment that has levelled the employment playing field, with more men and women competing for employment with greater equity. This is especially common in regional communities, emerging business sectors, and the service sector. Often without training related to working with diversity, social workers, as is so with other professionals, have to re-evaluate their approach to dominant gender-based roles within the family unit.

Fathers' roles have changed dramatically in recent decades. Not only are more fathers present at the birth of their children than in previous generations, many of them are trying to be more active and engaged fathers in a variety of ways. Many families have navigated this change at a pragmatic level without much discussion and role reflection.

Many women may now have a dual role of provider and nurturer, a role which many men have embraced, whilst other men maintain a role of primary provider. These changes now reflect the flexibility of men's roles in contemporary society – adapting to changing social mores, expectations, and challenges. Social workers, as with other health professionals working with men, learn to practise in the face of some pervasive negative stereotypes about men's supposed inflexibility and unwillingness to change, and they learn to critique their own relative power positions within their relationships with their male clients.

## BACKGROUND

### The Challenge of Involving Fathers in Family and Child Welfare Services

The way society views fathers and the way that a man views himself as a father is constantly changing and fluid (Collier & Sheldon, 2008). Within the family and child welfare services, there is a certain degree of ambiguity surrounding the relationship between men and social work. Whilst the nature of family and child welfare services and in particular social work may be fluid, the social construction of men in society is also constantly changing (Christie, 2001). Of the many social constructs used to describe fathers, recurrent themes involve fathers often being seen as invisible, irrelevant, and a threat. These ideas can persist even when the father is the best option for child placement (Scourfield, 2001). Scourfield (2001) conducted a United Kingdom-based ethnographic research of gendered occupational culture and found that

*... there is a certain exasperation expressed about men's incompetence as carers and as clients. They are variously described as unable to cope, childlike, deluded, obsessive, and stubborn. They are seen as difficult to work with....They are regarded as of little practical use in terms of family life. (p. 81)*

These perceptions of male clients were used as a rationale for not working with them as fathers (Scourfield, 2001). As a result, the responsibility of family welfare is placed in the hands of female clients with men relegated to the periphery of practice, particularly when they are perceived as a risk to children and families (Baum & Negbi, 2013; Clapton, 2009; Coady, Hoy, Cameron, & Hallman, 2013; Parent, Saint-Jacques, Beaudry, & Robitalle, 2007; Storhaug & Oien, 2012; Zanoni, Warburton, Bussey, & McMaugh, 2013). Ultimately, these workplace mentalities serve to protect and reinforce gender-role stereotypes.

Family and child welfare services in general are directed at supporting and monitoring parenting practices according to societal norms. As parenting, family, and child welfare has traditionally been the domain of women, fathers are often excluded as the term "mother" has become analogous with "parent" (Daniel & Taylor, 2001; Zvara, Schoppe-Sullivan, & Kamp Dush, 2013). It has been noted that as a result, within social work practice a heavy emphasis has been placed on mothers at the expense of fathers or father figures (Fletcher & Visser, 2008; Milner, 2004; O'Hagan, 1997). Interest in fathers and social work practice has emerged from the authors' own separate yet similar journeys in practice and research. The central theme in these two journeys so far has been the strong belief that engaging with men as fathers, provided it is safe to do so, is a key element for effective social work practice. This is because fathers potentially can and do make important contributions to a child's development as well as later adult development. As Scourfield (2001) stated:

*... if injustice in social work provision is to be addressed, gendered constructions of clients have to be made explicit and their implications understood. Social workers need to be reflective about their own practice and the gendered discourse of their office culture. (p. 86)*

The core business of social work is concerned with addressing the barriers and inequities that exist in society, and the profession works towards changes in practices that assist each individual, group, and community to reach their full potential

(Australian Association of Social Workers, 2003). Additionally, social work practice encompasses many traditional fields of practice which include mental health, child protection, and health, as well as new emerging fields, such as work with asylum seekers, disaster recovery, green social work, and even veterinary social work (Dulmus & Sowers, 2012). Yet, despite these developments, there is still evidence that we have a long way to go in making the rhetoric about engaging with men as fathers a reality.

There is no shortage of research to suggest that fathers tend to be avoided by social workers and other professionals and possibly vice versa. This is due, in part, to uncertainty about how to approach fathers and work with them effectively (Ashley, Featherstone, Roskill, Ryan, & White, 2006; Daniel & Taylor, 2001; Featherstone, Rivett, & Scourfield, 2007). This task is made more difficult as child and family welfare services are often slow to adapt to the changing realities of family life and even slower to take an active role in promoting change in the families, particularly in the area of child protection (Featherstone, 2006; Fletcher, Silberberg, & Baxter, 2001; O'Hagan, 1997). As discussed, Scourfield (2001) identified the differing perceptions of male and female clients in child protection work. In his ethnographic study, he recognised that notions of masculinity, femininity, and family experience are socially constructed. Even though the assessment of men is essential when there are allegations of physical or sexual abuse, the generalised portrayal of all men as a threat is problematic. The mother in the relationship is often expected to make a choice between her partner and the child(ren). If she does not make this choice, this is viewed by social workers as her failing to protect herself or her child(ren). Scourfield (2003) found that a father's lack of involvement in the child protection process was usually considered negatively by the social worker.

Gaps in knowledge and information about fathers and how to work with them can significantly impact on social work practice (Karpetis, 2010). Furthermore, if we are unable to engage with fathers effectively, as the literature suggests, then how can we be effective in our practice, particularly with children and families? There is clear and growing evidence that a fathers' engagement with children is associated with positive outcomes in all areas of life span development (Coakley, 2013; Cowan, Cowan, Pruett, Pruett & Wong, 2009; Fletcher, 2011; Holmes, Galovan, Yoshida, & Hawkins, 2010; Tamis-LeMonda & Cabrera, 2002).

The remainder of this chapter explores both *why* and *how* social workers can involve fathers in their work and service provision to improve outcomes for families, drawing upon the research literature to guide practice (Featherstone, 2009).

## WHY CONSIDER FATHERS?

### Aims and Objectives of the Literature Review

*Fatherhood is no simple phenomenon, but a complex tapestry of many things. Contemporary fatherhood is both diverse in its manifestations and subject to contradictory qualities, forces, and trends....the reality [is] that fatherhood is not a static phenomenon, but more like a moving target, only some of which has constant meaning. (Peterson & Steinmetz, 2000, p. 315)*

The literature review for this chapter was originally conducted as part of a doctoral research degree by one of the authors (Fleming, 2010). The purpose of the review was to provide evidence about social work practice with fathers and to identify what types of evidence-based intervention were found to be most effective. It has been suggested that fathers, compared to mothers, receive little attention within social work literature (Strug & Wilmore-Schaeffer, 2003). Accordingly, the review was guided by the following two research questions: why involve fathers, and how can fathers become involved in social work practice? Over the last decade a number of commentators have sought to find answers to these important questions to challenge the assumptions of motherhood versus fatherhood in social work practice settings (Bunston, 2013; Curran, 2003; Gordon, Watkins, Walling, Wilhelm, & Rayford, 2011; Milner, 1993, 2004; O'Donnell, Johnson, D'Aunno, & Thornton, 2005; O'Hagan, 1997).

## Search Strategy

Building on this doctoral research (Fleming, 2010), a further review was undertaken in November 2013. Summon (a Proquest search engine) was used to locate the data. This search engine indexes content from a wide range of databases and so ensures coverage across a wide range of sources. Most of the articles retrieved were found to derive from either the Social Services Abstracts or Web of Knowledge databases.

The search strategy was broad involving the search terms *father** and *"social work"* and was limited to English language material with a publication date range of 2000 to 2013. Relevant sources for the search were supplemented by the use of citation follow-up, entailing the review of the reference lists in relevant publications. Studies known to the authors but which did not emerge from the initial searches were also included. Research-based books known to the authors were also used in the review.

## Common Views of Fathering

The role that fathers are playing in postmodern society is still in its infancy and is not reflected within social work practice or within the media. The role has significantly changed due to lower marriage rates and rising divorce rates, new reproductive technologies, and political consequences of the second-wave feminist movement (Collier & Sheldon, 2008). In the field of social work and child protection practice, there have been many developments in practice frameworks, particularly those that focus on both the risks and strengths in child assessments and selected interventions (Fleming, 1998; Turnell & Edwards, 1999). The involvement of fathers in social services is closely dependent on the varying attitudes, behaviours, and personal biographies of social workers, as well as the wider societal influences of fatherhood in public policy discussion (Marsiglio et al., 2000). These directions in public policy can be traced back to the legal frameworks and diverse institutional practices developed since the post-war decades of the 1950s and 1960s (Fletcher, Fairbairn, & Pascoe, 2003; Ghate, Shaw, & Hazel, 2000; Haskett, Marziano, & Dover, 1996).

Societal influences, reflected in policy and legislation, are pertinent to the field of child protection, family law, and family and child welfare settings. Here, the abusers or perpetrators of abuse are still considered to be predominantly men (Brown & Tyson, 2012). In such cases, the fathers in the child protection system are most visible, but it is not always clear how the child protection system is managing these men and fathers as risks to children and mothers. Even men who are not the abusers and who wish to care for their children (where the mother is unable to care) are frequently overlooked by professionals who struggle to see these fathers as capable of nurturing and providing resources (Ashley et al., 2006; Storhaug & Oien, 2012; Zanoni et al., 2013).

There is evidence that fathers now spend more time caring for their children than they did a few decades ago (Bianchi, 2000), even though for many men the role of breadwinner is seen as the key to being a "good father" (Winslow, 2005). Having to meet these dual roles in a new social context, not historically demanded, has resulted in men reporting an increasing level of conflict between their work and family demands (Nomaguchi, 2009; Townsend, 2002). Once thought to be separate social spheres, work and family are now viewed as interconnected (Coltrane, 1996; Kanter, 1977).

Understanding how fathers' work and family role experiences are connected can importantly inform social workers about how to better accommodate all their clients. Integrating work and family roles is an issue relevant to all social workers; it is not solely a women's issue. A case example is the mining industry in Australia which has experienced an increase in both men and women employed. Employment in the mining sector brings substantial economic gain for men and women. However, miners can face a number of stressors on the job, including long work hours, rotating shifts, time away from family and children, and risks at work. These factors place those in the mining industry at higher risk for negative parenting outcomes (Kwek, 2013). However, the occupational conditions inherent in the mining industry have only recently been identified as particularly problematic for workers and their families (Gallegos, 2006; Taylor & Simmonds, 2009).

In recent studies, there is growing evidence that Australian men are becoming more vocal about their need to be more involved with parenting, even though the nature and shape of this role may differ. What is occurring is conceptualised as a quiet men's revolution (King, 2005). This men's revolution is not as vocal as the women's movement but it is noticed as men talk about achieving a better balance between work and family demands (King, 2005). The change is evidenced by the way men will now walk hand-in-hand with their children and proudly push a pram. Some men indicate that the reason for attending a fathering programme is because they want to father their children differently from how they were themselves fathered. The birth of a child is now a "wake-up call" for many men and an opportunity for them to review the choices they make in life and to provide the motivation to develop stronger

relationships (King, 2005). These societal changes have resulted in many contested understandings about what constitutes fatherhood, which is the concern of professionals, researchers, and policy makers alike (Berlyn, Wise, & Soriano, 2008; Fletcher et al., 2003; Huebner, Werner, Hartwig, White, & Shewa, 2008; Stahlschmidt, Threlfall, Seay, Lewis, & Kohl, 2013).

Whilst there is an emerging trend internationally to understand fatherhood (Featherstone, 2006; Gordon, Oliveros, Hawes, Iwamoto, & Rayford, 2012; Marsiglio et al., 2000; Milner, 1993; O'Hagan, 1997; Scourfield, 2003, 2006), little evidence-based research has been undertaken in Australia which seeks the views of professionals about fathers, their input into family life, and in particular the views about fathers who are absent from practice. Collier and Sheldon (2008) argue that decades of social, cultural, and legal change mean that fatherhood is open-ended, fluid, and fragmented. The lives of men cannot be comprehended through the deployment of binaries of good and bad dads, new and traditional fathers. Moreover, they argue that "traditional fatherhood" is persistent in its continued hold over social and cultural expectations of fathers, creating tensions for some men to choose between employment breadwinner roles versus family and childcare commitments. Their framework of fragmenting fatherhood is useful to social workers and other professionals in this respect, as it offers a new way of seeing fathers beyond the traditional frame of reference.

Seeing fatherhood within a traditional role can encourage the exclusion of fathers from social work practice. Concern about this issue was reflected within articles obtained from the literature search, as a persistent theme which emerged is the dilemma of how to involve the peripheral father (Maxwell et al., 2012). For fathers to become involved requires effective engagement strategies to not only invite fathers into services but to also keep them involved. Relationships between parents and social workers play a more integral role during the period of early childhood development than at any other time in a child's life (Cabrera, Tamis-LeMonda, Bradley, Hofferth, & Lamb, 2000; Lamb & Tamis-LeMonda, 2004). The availability of services, both private and public, that are external to the home environment allows the opportunity to engage with and develop relationships with both parents regardless of their social context (married, divorced, separated, single, same-sex couples, and so on). Creating a culture of father-involvement in service delivery is a long-term process but one which is potentially beneficial (Fletcher, 2011).

Other factors that can prevent the effective engagement of fathers are practice barriers (Fleming, 2010). These barriers can include: operating times of the agency or services (i.e. 9am-5pm); practitioners' lack of knowledge or skills of how to involve fathers, especially with vulnerable and at risk families; fathers who do not show up for appointments being perceived by practitioners as disinterested; and working with the mothers and the children being seen as core business, whilst fathers are seen as an adjunct or third wheel (Cosson & Graham, 2012). Fleming (2010), however, also showed that whilst practitioners were grappling with the issue of how to involve fathers, they were also very keen to work with fathers in their service.

If practitioners are aware of these factors, they are in a better position to identify some of the barriers or likely problems encountered by fathers when they seek a particular service or services (Cullen, Cullen, Band, Davis, & Lindsay, 2011). The central practice dilemma which consistently emerges from the research is how to include fathers who are described by social workers as being physically absent or non-resident, or who have abusive social histories. In these situations, it was often the social workers who appeared not to possess the necessary skills and knowledge to include fathers in case planning discussions. This lack of attention to fathers (particularly in the social work education and curriculum) leaves frontline practice in a vulnerable state and one which is at

risk of criticism from other disciplines (Featherstone et al., 2007; Milner, 1993). Child and family welfare and other related services thus need to be responsive to fathers and mothers equally, with an emphasis on the caring relationships significant to children regardless of whether this caring occurs in a heterosexual family or other family types (Collier & Sheldon, 2008).

## INVOLVEMENT OF FATHERS IN SOCIAL WORK PRACTICE

Social work has involved practitioners engaging with a diverse range of families for a very long time and crossing ages, genders, and cultures (Scott & Arney, 2010; Scott & Swain, 2002). The very nature of the work involves a number of players, including the mother, child or children, the social worker, foster carers, and others significant in the welfare of the child or children. Despite the good practice that occurs with families, there still tends to be relatively poor engagement of men as fathers in social work with families. There are many reasons behind this gap in practice with fathers (Berlyn et al., 2008; Bunston, 2013; McPhail, 2004; Tamis-LeMonda, & Cabrera, 2002; Walters, 2011; Zvara et al., 2013), however, the most dominant of all the discourses is that some men are perceived as resources, some as potential risks, and some are seen as both (Strega et al., 2008). Fathers can be difficult to locate, recruit, and retain in social work practice, as research has shown over the last decade (Brown, Callahan, Strega, Walmsley, & Dominelli, 2009; Ferguson & Hogan, 2004; Fleming, 2010; Fleming & King, 2010; Fronek, 2013a; Strega et al., 2008). There are several reasons for this phenomenon that emerged in this literature review: men often pose more of a risk to women and children (Featherstone & Fraser, 2012; Scott & Crooks, 2004); men can be intimidating to social workers (O'Donnell et al., 2005); men are harder to engage or are reluctant recipients of services (Featherstone, 2009; O'Hagan, 1997); and social workers focus on the mothers and often blame them for not protecting the child, even though the mother herself may be a victim of violent abuse (Brown et al., 2009; Featherstone, 2010).

An in-depth ethnographic study was conducted by Fleming (2010) to explore and understand methods of involving fathers in social work practice. Analysis of the data revealed a number of key themes emerging in regard to how social workers and other professionals view the role of men as fathers in their practice. These themes included social workers' definition of the term "parent" and understanding of what constituted a "good" relationship.

Firstly, social work practice with men as fathers focused only on the mothers. The term "parent" was being used by social workers to describe the primary caretaker for bringing up children but the term only applied in their practice to the mother and often did not make reference to the father. Despite the existence of a father, mothers were the ones most often expected and held to be responsible by participants for addressing and resolving problems in the family. The social workers frequently appeared in their practice to find it very difficult to locate fathers and overall were unable to see that involving fathers would lead to a more balanced and inclusive practice. It was perceived by the participants that involving fathers was complex and that attempts from their own experiences with the work they undertook with families had met with little success. Yet inversely, there was an absence of the same level of complexity when they made reference to mothers in their practice. Secondly, the results showed that social workers were more successful with involving fathers if the family was intact, that is, both mother and father were present. However, a father's presentation at an agency was dependent upon the mother's view of the father. Fathers were more likely to be included in a worker's practice if the mother had a good relationship with the father (Fleming, 2010). A

"good" relationship according to social workers would consist of stability within the couple relationship, a high degree of emotional support, and the absence of intimate partner violence, or other undesirable behavioural issues, such as alcohol or drug abuse (Fleming, 2010). A father's inclusion in services would also be more beneficial to workers if the father was also physically available, usually translated as residing in the same household. The more a father was physically unavailable, or distant through work or other commitments, the less likely he would be included in case planning or clinical appointments for the family. Finally, the social workers viewed men as fathers to be more a risk than a resource (Fleming, 2010).

The social workers in the study had limited understanding of diverse family types (for example, parents who were sole parents, same gender, divorced, and/or separated) and often held beliefs that did not support the reality of contemporary family life. These findings from the research regarding the avoidance of fathers, irrespective of whether they are labelled risks or resources (Fleming, 2010), were found to be congruent with other studies of social work practice with fathers summarised in the international literature (Berlyn et al., 2008; Featherstone et al., 2007; Maxwell, Scourfield, Featherstone, Holland, & Tolman, 2012; Walmsley, Strega, Brown, Dominelli, & Callahan, 2009).

## Solutions and Recommendations

### Practice Implications

Whilst not underestimating the fact that some workplaces can enable, or simply overlook, or exclude a father's involvement (Russell & Hwang, 2004), social workers need to identify which features of working with men as fathers can affect their experiences and enable effective engagement to take place. Often services are comfortable recruiting fathers but have trouble understanding how to maximise service impact (Fronek, 2013b). There are also significant differences among fathers in their willingness to engage with social workers. Fathers are a heterogeneous group and one size does not fit all fathers. A local approach needs to be part of an effective model of service delivery. Effective service delivery with fathers will only work if the fathers are genuinely involved and report that they feel connected to the service (King, 2005).

Men's involvement in fathering, no matter what family type these fathers identify with, has the potential to positively affect men's health and well-being. It can also foster personal growth and create opportunities for men to be more involved in their communities, increasing social capital and social inclusion (Palkovitz, 2002). If social work practice is to move forward in developing ways to include fathers, it must address current practices, practice frameworks, and gender discourses (Collier & Sheldon, 2008; Ghate et al., 2000; Sabla, 2009).

This change in focus begins with an acknowledgement that social work has concentrated upon women rather than men (Brown et al., 2009; O'Hagan & Dillenberger, 1995). At its most basic level, the majority of fathers have been satisfied with the health care professionals they encountered when the following factors were achieved: (1) inclusive interactions with the physician and health care staff, (2) perception of receiving quality care, and (3) clear explanations provided (Garfield & Isacco, 2006). Additionally, many of the fathers enjoyed being complimented by health care staff and perceived that they were receiving the same quality service as mothers. At a more sophisticated level, it is useful for services to insist that referrals to their programme make reference to the role of the father in the family. This makes the father's role more present and allows the programme to better assess the father's strengths and weaknesses. It also results in programmes having a higher level of father engagement.

## Social Work Approaches to Assessment and Intervention with Fathers

The following suggestions provide a practice guide and framework for best practice when working with fathers (Cowan et al., 2009; Cullen et al., 2011; Huebner et al., 2008; Knox, Cowan, Cowan, & Bildner, 2011):

- Visit fathers at home and telephone them if they are not at home when the mother is visited and reflect back to them useful observations regarding their family.
- Be persistent and have clear expectations of them as fathers.
- Consult with fathers as to what services they require.
- Employ male staff where possible to ensure gender balance and choice of worker.
- Promote programmes in alternate locations, such as sports clubs, employment training programmes, or workplaces.
- Display positive images of fathers and their children (see Father Inclusive Practice Logos: http://groupworksolutions.com.au/FatherInclusivePractice_logo).
- Use gender specific language. Referring to "fathers" and "dads" as opposed to "parents" should be adopted (although it has been recognised in research that some men would be less self-conscious about attending a programme for all parents rather than one specifically for fathers, Cowan et al., 2009).
- Offer flexible hours of services for working fathers where possible.
- Highlight the positive gains to children of father involvement.
- Use activity-based interventions where fathers can spend time with their children and where their strengths are built upon to positively enhance their fathering skills.
- Emphasise "Teamwork Parenting".

Amongst all these suggestions, "Teamwork Parenting" (Cowan et al., 2009) is particularly important for it involves both parents in working collectively in partnership. It has been shown to have unique effects on parent well-being.

Cowan et al. (2009) conducted a randomised control evaluation of an intervention to increase fathers' engagement, focusing on the impact of training in teamwork parenting. Participants were randomly assigned to either a 16-week group for fathers, a 16-week group for couples, or a one-time informational meeting. Results from an 18-month follow-up demonstrated that both intervention conditions produced superior effects for fathers' engagement with their children, couple relationship quality, and children's behaviour, as compared to the control condition. The results indicated that parenting stress only declined when both parents were involved in the couples' group.

When possible the inclusion of both parents in any parenting intervention is very important. It is important to emphasise that social workers need to be cautious in working with couples when domestic violence is occurring. However, best-practice indicates that it is essential to provide a range of choices for engaging fathers that include working individually with both parents, providing groups that target the parents as a couple, and also providing fathers' groups (King, 2005).

The social work practitioner's awareness of his or her own interactions with fathers is the first step towards supporting involved fathering. The following questions are meant to be a useful guide for social workers to self-assess their interactions with fathers:

- How do you acknowledge the presence of a father on your first interaction?
- Do you include fathers in the conversation when both caregivers are present?
- What is your body language saying that indicates inclusion?
- Do you have eye contact with the father or is it directed at the mother/other caregiver?

- Do you include fathers in discussions about their children or respond to father's questions about their child or children?
- What are your own beliefs (personal biographies) about fathers and their ability to take on child care tasks?

Each setting is different and programmes and organisations need to acknowledge how they may already be effectively engaging men and fathers (Ladbrook, 2003). When a man makes an initial contact with a programme, the immediate environment and openness of staff towards him will influence his level of trust. Most men enter new situations suspicious about what will be expected of them, and they rely on visual cues that suggest they can relax and feel included (King, Sweeney, & Fletcher, 2004).

## What Works for Fathers?

This question has changed significantly over the last decade and has moved from asking if men are interested in accessing family relationship and parenting programmes to how organisations can promote best practice and cater for men's needs. It is now recognised that many men identify fathering as something which is active, challenging, creative, irreplaceable, hard work, and a central part of their life, regardless of their family situation (King, 2005).

According to attachment theory, a secure relationship is essential for a child's healthy development into adulthood (Bowlby, 1988). In the past, studies surrounding the development of children have focused almost exclusively on a child's relationships with their mother. Today, fathers play a unique and crucial role in nurturing and guiding the child's development. Many researchers now believe that fathers can be just as nurturing and sensitive with their babies as mothers (Berk, 2006; Fletcher, 2011), even though this may be expressed differently. Healthy child development relies on the roles played by both the mother and father respectively, whether they live together or apart. The early years of bonding and attachment are crucial to the developing pathways in the child's brain which sets the blueprint for relating to others for the rest of their lives. Traditionally, attachment theory has emphasised the significance of safety, comfort, and security as key factors in a child's development. It is now recognised that "risk and exploration" are equally important factors and are often undervalued.

Bogels and Phares (2008) contend that attachment theory has two streams of expression: the development of safety and security and also risk and exploration. Due to biological and social causes, mothers have a stronger expression of safety and security towards the care and protection needs of young children. This requires the development of close interpersonal relationships. Fathers have a stronger expression of risk and exploration towards the play and challenge needs of young children. This enables them to enter the larger social world and develop greater risk taking and independence. As the child moves towards adolescence and makes a transition into the outside world, mothers have a greater challenge of letting them go and fathers have a greater challenge to stay close. Both experiences in life enable children to best cope with anxiety. According to Paquette (2004), children's involvement in play and challenge experienced with their fathers supports the development of independence, risk taking, and the skills required for development throughout childhood and into the larger social world.

## Fathers and Rough and Tumble Play

A key focus in understanding the skills required for development throughout childhood into the larger social world today is the experience of "rough and tumble play" (RTP) (Paquette, 2004). RTP is not equivalent to fighting between children. All mammals on the planet, especially the juveniles, have some form of RTP. In experiments, when rats are deprived of the experience of RTP, they are much more anxious and likely to socially isolate (Fletcher et al., 2001; Fletcher, Morgan, May, Lubans, & St George, 2011). There is strong evidence that RTP is highly beneficial to children's development, including competency with peers (Parke et al., 2002) and healthy brain development (Pellis & Pellis, 2007). These models are consistent with the literature indicating that father-child physical play is also related to the child's social competencies with peers (Parke et al., 2002). Furthermore, the frequency of these interactions peak in the pre-school years (Pellegrini & Smith, 1998), a period of significant change in a child's psychological, behavioural, and self-regulatory abilities (Séguin, Parent, Tremblay, & Zelazo, 2009; Zelazo, Carter, Reznick, & Frye, 1997).

Whilst there is evidence for the benefit of RTP, some commentators are cautions since the play behaviours of RTP so often mimic aggressive play (Paquette & Dumont, 2013). Others, such as Scott and Panksepp (2003), recognise that RTP encourages children to learn and to develop pro-social behaviours.

As a human services sector, we need to recognise that RTP does not necessarily involve aggression but is fundamental to the child's development of emotional self-regulation, social skills, and cooperation. Recent research has shown that the more fathers have hands-on contact with their children in toddlerhood, the more they engage in RTP with them at the age of three years (Paquette & Dumont, 2013).

RTP may involve the following:

- wrestling, grappling, kicking, and tumbling;
- few rules;
- a clear distinction between RTP and fighting;
- enjoyment as the key emotion, not anger;
- dominance swapping (different people take turns in "winning");

- the parent (often the father) teaching the skill of winning/losing with effort; and
- the development of emotional self-regulation in children.

Fathers' play with their children seems to promote an active, competitive, autonomous, and curious attitude in children that is beneficial to the child's cognitive and social development. It also buffers early separation, stranger, and social anxiety (Bogels & Phares, 2008). While the involvement of fathers has been associated with the rearing of boys, it is equally important for the girls, and while fathers may be seen to have a natural tendency to play with their children, they need to be more conscious of the important opportunity they have to actively develop more quality play experiences with their children. This is a key role that health professionals need to consider in working with the family. An equally important measure is the amount of sole-time play the fathers have with their children in which they can develop their own confidence without the mother being present. Researchers and other professionals recognise that men, as well as women, can be engaged in caring for children and can have healthy relationships with children. This usually is referred to as "non-deficit perspectives" to fathering, where men take an active role in family life and the care of children (King, 2005).

## The Implications for Social Work Practice

Social work practitioners at all levels can be very instrumental in helping fathers to develop attachments to their children. This may be facilitated by

- including information on fathers' roles in child development and child development in general;

- helping fathers to create a baseline checklist of their involvement activities with their children, so that they can see how their children are progressing in their development;
- identifying and providing "emotional space" to address loss (for example, death of a child, pregnancy loss, or miscarriage, or loss of access through separation, or integrating step-children into re-constituted families); and
- including one-to-one sessions or "turning-point moments" at any time with fathers when facilitating parent education groups (Staines & Walters, 2007).

In summary, it is important to encourage fathers to develop strong attachments with their children, as it will benefit not only the child but also the mother, the father, and connections to society in general. Whilst societal expectations of fathers have changed over the last decade in regard to their roles in child care tasks, understanding how this role is conceptualised has remained unchanged (McKeering & Pakenham, 2000). Therefore, it is imperative that social workers address the need to widen their theoretical base to include gender perspectives (O'Hagan, 1997). Generativity is an alternative framework which offers promise to social work practice with the concepts of fatherhood and fathering.

## Generative Fathering

The generative connection in people's lives is the best way of understanding the natural and long standing desire to have children (Hawkins & Dollahite, 1997; King, 2005; Snarey, 1993). Generativity involves the capacity to care for the next generation and demands the ability to give something of oneself to another person. Its greatest and strongest expression is in relation to children. Generativity is equally important in men and women's lives, however, it is expressed differently as the research has indicated (McKeering & Pakenham, 2000). Generativity was developed by Erik and Joan Erikson as part of the eight life stages of development (Erikson, 1964). The generative stage (seventh) occurs when people focus on the greater impact they have on their immediate world and find practical ways in which this is fulfilled. In women's lives, it is discussed and practiced much more from childhood and is strongly expressed in nurturing and intimacy. In men's lives, it is less spoken about from a younger age but is strongly expressed in how they are viewed within their community (those people with whom they significantly deal), in their workplace, and in their connection to their children. Generativity is expressed in the following ways:

- **Biological:** Caring for a young infant that has been brought into the world.
- **Parental:** Caring for the child's longer term developmental needs over the fullness of childhood.
- **Societal:** Caring and supporting others in society. This may entail involvement in Service Clubs, Lifeline, State Emergency Service, and the Rural Fire Service; or instructing apprentices; acting as guides; or mentoring or coaching children, young people, or adults (see Snarey, 1993).

Men's level of societal generativity is strongly linked to parental generativity. Women's parental generativity, unlike that of the fathers', is not significantly related to societal generativity. However, mothers' level of intimacy is a significant predictor of societal generativity, suggesting that their level of intimacy may be a factor in their attainment of societal generativity.

This case study below highlights the importance of generative connections in men's lives (family, employment, and community contexts) and how it can be used to support change.

## Case Study: Charlie and Clare

This reflective story, as recounted below from a case worker at a family relationship centre, has a strong theme of generativity.

During a psycho-educational group for fathers, I identified this man, Charlie (fictitious name), who seemed pretty angry with his wife, Clare (fictitious name). Charlie was in the military. He had a young family and was separated from his wife. He spoke of Clare failing to understand the importance of his role in the military. He made reference to the three young Australian soldiers killed last year in Afghanistan. He became righteous in his tone when he spoke of how they gave their life fighting for their country. Charlie demonstrated a strong sense of patriotism and camaraderie for his fallen countrymen. His conviction was strong. He explained that he, too, was going overseas and appeared quite proud of that fact.

As Charlie spoke of his relationship with Clare and their children, there seemed to be a disconnection from them. He spoke angrily of Clare, stating that she controlled when he saw the kids, that "she was screwed up", and that she didn't understand the importance of his role. Clare was the target of his blame. I acknowledged the importance of his role in the military. I asked him what he meant by insisting that Clare did not understand his role. He said she wanted him to "get out" and that was the source of much of their arguments. I suggested that it made him angry because Clare seemed to have misunderstood his intentions and the importance of his role within the family. He agreed.

I explored what was going on with Clare and Charlie. I suggested to Charlie that his wife might be scared of losing a husband and the father of her children by his serving in a combat zone. I asked if he had discussed her fears with her and found he hadn't. I directed the topic to loyalty and patriotism. I said the patriotism he had for his country was admirable but asked about his patriotism to his family. "I'm not sure what you mean", he replied. I elaborated, explaining that Clare was perhaps fearful of her husband and children's father being killed in combat and that this was very real for her as there were constant reminders on the television, newspapers, and the internet. I added, "You are very patriotic to your country, but there is also patriotism, loyalty, and honour owed to your family. They look at you to keep them safe and secure and Clare is fearful if you're thousands of kilometres away in some foreign country with God knows what going on. Step into her shoes!" He didn't respond. I discussed later with my colleague regarding what he thought. We considered Charlie was an angry man and we felt we hadn't managed to get through to him. He gave positive feedback in the evaluation form but as for putting things into practice we were doubtful.

A few weeks later, I was doing a telephone intake. As I spoke with the woman, she revealed that her co-parent had changed since coming to the centre. She reported a side she had never seen before in the several years they had been together. She told me he was not acting in anger but was spending more time with the children and with her. She told me they were even considering reconciliation. She said they were talking and discussing things really well. I looked down at the file and recognised the name. It was Clare. She was talking about her husband, Charlie. I asked her again, "So in all the years you and he have been together you have never seen him like this before?" "No", she said. I asked her how she felt. She said she liked it and spoke of what a good man he had become. She said, "Before he would get very angry with me and the kids and yell, but now we talk!"

## Working with Fathers: A Checklist for Social Workers

As authors, we developed the list below based on the findings of our research and from our practice as social workers and therapists. This summarised knowledge is also based on our understanding of the evidence-informed literature regarding how generative connections are forged and maintained.

Generative connections are best enhanced in the lives of fathers when the social worker

- finds out how many children they have, the children's age and special interests;
- builds a connection around how their own work context is relevant to fathers and the context of their children (remember the fathers are not likely to express a need for support, help, etc.);
- assumes and discusses with the men as fathers how they demonstrate care (Hawkins & Dollahite, 1997; King, 2000). This can be achieved by the social worker taking note of how the father exhibits the following attributes:
  - **commit:** The capacity of the father to provide for the physical and ongoing support for the child; his awareness and involvement with the child;
  - **choose:** The capacity to make day to day decisions for the child that meets the child's needs;
  - **care:** The ability to attend to the important transitions in a child's life and to provide the optimal conditions that maximise their growth;
  - **change:** The ability to adapt as the child grows older and the father matures in his relationship with the child;
  - **create:** The creation of resources for material comfort and the resolution of problems that allow opportunities for the development of emotional well-being;

- **connect:** The ability to form lasting and healthy attachments with the child. These attachments will change over time to meet the child's evolving needs;
- **communicate:** The capacity to relate with the child by sharing meaningfully with them, both verbally and non-verbally.

- explores opposites or tensions – what helps or blocks and what is valuable or is a distraction to achieving the above;
- normalises the experiences fathers have and validates the strengths they bring to parenting;
- amplifies the significance of the positive choices which fathers make in their child's life;
- discusses what the role of fathering means today and what parts of the role fathers consider important to them;
- utilises the metaphor of walking alongside fathers in the work that the social worker does and finding out how this may be helpful to them;
- uses generative perspective questioning. This type of questioning uses key words (i.e. "influence", "impact", "responses", "respond", "value", "respect", and "significant hopes and dreams or challenges") to explore people's focus on three dimensions: past, present, and future. This entails asking fathers questions that focus on past observations, present context, and future possibilities or hopes. Below are sample questions for each dimension.

Generative perspective questions – Focus on *past* context:
- How would you describe your childhood?
- What is your strongest memory of your father while growing up? What stood out most?

Generative perspective questions – Focus on *present* context:
- Are you aware of how this impacts on your child?
- How would your child describe you?

Generative perspective questions – Focus on *future* context:
- What type of parent would you like your child to be?
- What can you see yourself doing with your child in 10 years time?

Generativity is best enhanced when the father is focused on vulnerability in a key relationship in his life (often the relationship with the children). Due to this vulnerability, the father must decide how he can best respond to what is required. This slows him down and enables him to be more purposeful. One example involves asking the father to recount the story of the birth of one of his children. This story tunes him into expressing an important time when his child was most vulnerable to illustrate how he responded to his child's need for care.

Further examples involve asking fathers questions about how they influence, have an impact on, or make a difference for others, and asking them who had had an influence or impact on, or made a difference for them? The following questions, if relevant, can also be an effective way to gauge a father's level of generativity:

1. Who or how do you protect others in your life?
2. Who do you keep safe?
3. What happens when the protection of others is misused?
4. What is the difference between keeping someone safe and controlling them?
5. When does protecting someone become intrusive/abusive?
6. How do you keep yourself safe?

## FUTURE RESEARCH DIRECTIONS

Gender discourses are constrained only by the social world in which they exist. For example, a biological resident father status is an important aspect of hegemonic masculinity and, therefore, represents the dominant discourse on fatherhood and social work practice. This argument then results in other forms of fathering, such as step-fathering or non-resident father types, being relegated to a less important position and often rendered invisible to practice. Whilst social workers may often be reluctant to admit that they have certain gender biases, this chapter has demonstrated that under certain conditions professionals can find ways to engage men (if safe to do so) as fathers. This engagement has important implications for researchers and social workers, possibly opening up new ways of seeing men as fathers beyond the heavily infused notions of risk and danger (which has often been a dominant theme in the literature) by assisting professionals to look more deeply into the basis of father's identity as men and as parents.

A major criticism of past research has been that many studies looking at mothers and fathers have relied on the perspective of the client who is usually the mother (Tamis-LeMonda & Cabrera, 2002). As a result of this emphasis, efforts were made in this chapter to provide an alternative perspective and to help social workers keep fathers in mind in their work, raising awareness, and encouraging their presence.

In summary, this chapter has attempted to address a gap in the parenting literature by seeking to elucidate how men as fathers are described, discussed, and constructed by social workers. It has attempted to demonstrate that contemporary fathering is increasingly diverse and more complex than it was three decades ago. Consequently, the Australian social work profession would benefit greatly from the funding of practice-based research and changes to social work education to build a knowledge-base for engaging with fathers more effectively.

In particular, there is a greater need for practice-based research into successful interventions with fathers, who are often described as vulnerable or hard to reach, as well as male caregivers, who have perpetrated family violence and are still involved with families. Thus far, there have been gaps in this type of research in Australia, leaving social workers without evidence-based practice frameworks to draw upon in their work. In terms of future research directions, it would be beneficial for social workers to apply the generativity concepts to their practice with fathers and evaluate the results.

## CONCLUSION

This chapter has identified the complexity and ambiguities involved in understanding the roles fathers play in contemporary social work practice in Australia. The literature review undertaken offered an important insight into the current issues faced by social workers and other professionals working with fathers in their practice.

The review has also suggested that neglecting fathers and their role in families can compound problems for mothers and children, particularly in the area of child protection and family violence. According to the evidence, it can no longer be accepted practice that fathers are ignored or excluded. This chapter has sought to build upon previous studies about men as fathers specifically in the context of social work practice, based upon gender and its impact on fields of practice such as child protection. It has offered an opportunity to explore how notions of fathers and of fathering in an Australian context are constructed by different professionals in the human services. In addressing the need to effectively work with men as fathers, it is important for social workers to continue their work with mothers and to keep in mind their wider engagement with families that include fathers.

## ACKNOWLEDGMENT

In discussing general trends in this chapter on how fathers and fatherhood are perceived, we further extend ideas which have been developed by other researchers in the field of fatherhood and gender. We gratefully acknowledge the ability to draw from their work. Given the limited scope of this chapter, we will comment only briefly on the specific social processes and interest group politics surrounding the fatherhood terrain. Thus, for the purpose of this chapter, the term "father" will pertain to both the social and biological aspects of the term.

We would like to express our gratitude to the many people who saw us through this chapter; to all those who provided support, talked things over, read, wrote, offered comments, allowed us to quote their remarks and assisted in the editing, proofreading, and design. Special thanks are due the following: John van der Giezen and Emeritus Professor Thea Brown.

## REFERENCES

Ashley, C., Featherstone, B., Roskill, C., Ryan, M., & White, S. (2006). *Fathers matter: Research findings on fathers and their involvement with social care services*. London: Family Rights Group.

Australian Association of Social Workers. (2003). *Practice standards for social workers: Achieving outcomes*. Retrieved November 17, 2013, from http://svc037.bne242p.server-web.com/adobe/publications/Practice_Standards_Final_Oct_2003.pdf

Baum, N., & Negbi, I. (2013). Children removed from home by court order: Fathers' disenfranchised grief and reclamation of paternal functions. *Children and Youth Services Review*, *35*(10), 1679–1686. doi:10.1016/j.childyouth.2013.07.003

Baxter, J., & Smart, D. (2011). *Fathering in Australia among couple families with young children* (Occasional Paper Series No. 37). Canberra: Department of Families, Housing, Community Services and Indigenous Affairs.

Berk, L. (2006). *Child development* (7th ed.). Boston: Pearson Publishing.

Berlyn, C., Wise, S., & Soriano, G. (2008). *Engaging fathers in child and family services: Participation, perceptions and good practice* (Occasional Paper No. 22). Sydney: National Evaluation Consortium.

Bianchi, S. (2000). Maternal employment and time with children: Dramatic change or surprising continuity. *Demography*, *37*(4), 401–414. doi:10.1353/dem.2000.0001 PMID:11086567

Bogels, S., & Phares, V. (2008). Fathers' role in the etiology, prevention and treatment of child anxiety: A review and new model. *Clinical Psychology Review*, *28*(4), 539–558. doi:10.1016/j.cpr.2007.07.011 PMID:17854963

Bowlby, J. (1988). *A secure base: Clinical applications of attachment theory*. London: Routledge.

Brown, L., Callahan, M., Strega, S., Walmsley, C., & Dominelli, L. (2009). Manufacturing ghost fathers: The paradox of father presence and absence in child welfare. *Child & Family Social Work*, *14*(1), 25–34. doi:10.1111/j.1365-2206.2008.00578.x

Brown, T., & Tyson, D. (2012). An abominable crime: Filicide in the context of parental separation and divorce. *Children Australia*, *37*(04), 151–160. doi:10.1017/cha.2012.36

Bunston, W. (2013). What about the fathers? Bringing "dads on board" with their infants and toddlers following violence. *Journal of Family Studies*, *19*(1), 70–79. doi:10.5172/jfs.2013.19.1.70

Cabrera, N., Tamis-LeMonda, C. S., Bradley, R. H., Hofferth, S., & Lamb, M. E. (2000). Fatherhood in the 21st century. *Child Development, 71*(1), 127–136. doi:10.1111/1467-8624.00126 PMID:10836566

Christie, A. (Ed.). (2001). *Men and social work: Theories and practices.* Basingstoke: Palgrave.

Clapton, G. (2009). How and why social work fails fathers: Redressing an imbalance, social work's role and responsibility. *Practice, 21*(1), 17–34. doi:10.1080/09503150902745989

Coady, N., Hoy, S. L., Cameron, G., & Hallman, L. S. (2013). Fathers' experiences with child welfare services. *Child & Family Social Work, 18*(3), 275–284. doi:10.1111/j.1365-2206.2012.00842.x

Coakley, T. M. (2013). The influence of father involvement on child welfare permanency outcomes: A secondary data analysis. *Children and Youth Services Review, 35*(1), 174–182. doi:10.1016/j.childyouth.2012.09.023

Collier, R. (2009). *Men, law and gender: Essays on the "man" of law.* Abingdon: Routledge.

Collier, S., & Sheldon, S. (2008). *Fragmenting fatherhood: A socio-legal study.* Oxford: Hart.

Coltrane, S. (1996). *Family man: Fatherhood, housework, and gender equity.* New York: Oxford Press.

Cosson, B., & Graham, E. (2012). "I felt like a third wheel": Fathers' stories of exclusion from the "parenting team". *Journal of Family Studies, 18*(2-3), 121–129. doi:10.5172/jfs.2012.18.2-3.121

Cowan, P. A., Cowan, C. P., Pruett, M. K., Pruett, K., & Wong, J. J. (2009). Promoting fathers' engagement with children: Preventive interventions for low-income families. *Journal of Marriage and the Family, 71*(3), 663–679. doi:10.1111/j.1741-3737.2009.00625.x

Cullen, S. M., Cullen, M. A., Band, S., Davis, L., & Lindsay, G. (2011). Supporting fathers to engage with their children's learning and education: An under-developed aspect of the parent support adviser pilot. *British Educational Research Journal, 37*(3), 485–500. doi:10.1080/01411921003786579

Curran, L. (2003). Social work and fathers: Child support and fathering programs. *Social Work, 48*(2), 219–227. doi:10.1093/sw/48.2.219 PMID:12718417

Daniel, B., & Taylor, J. (2001). *Engaging with fathers: Practice issues for health and social care.* London: Jessica Kingsley.

Dulmus, C., & Sowers, K. (Eds.). (2012). *Social work fields of practice: Historical trends, professional issues, and future opportunities.* New Jersey: Wiley.

Erikson, E. H. (1964). *Insight and responsibility.* New York: Norton.

Featherstone, B. (2006). Why gender matters in child welfare and protection. *Critical Social Policy, 26*(2), 94–314. doi:10.1177/0261018306062587

Featherstone, B. (2009). *Contemporary fathers: Theory, policy and practice.* Bristol: Policy Press.

Featherstone, B. (2010). Writing fathers in but mothers out!!! *Critical Social Policy, 30*(2), 208–224. doi:10.1177/0261018309358290

Featherstone, B., & Fraser, C. (2012). Working with fathers around domestic violence: Contemporary debates. *Child Abuse Review, 21*(4), 255–263. doi:10.1002/car.2221

Featherstone, B., Rivett, M., & Scourfield, J. (2007). *Working with men: Theory and practice in health and social welfare.* London: Sage.

Ferguson, H., & Hogan, F. (2004). *Strengthening families through fathers: Issues for policy and practice in working with vulnerable fathers and their families.* Dublin: Department of Social, Community and Family Affairs.

Fleming, J. (1998). Valuing families in statutory practice. *Child Abuse Prevention, 6,* 1-4. Retrieved from http://www.aifs.org.au

Fleming, J. (2010). *The absence of fathers in child and family welfare practice* (Doctoral dissertation). Retrieved from http://arrow.monash.edu.au/vital/access/manager/Repository/monash:80105

Fleming, J., & King, A. (2010). A road less travelled: Working with men as fathers in family based services. *Developing Practice, 26,* 40-51. Retrieved from: http://www.acwa.asn.au/developing_practice11.html

Fletcher, R. (2011). *The dad factor: How the father-baby bond helps a child for life.* Warriewood, Australia: Finch Publishing.

Fletcher, R., Fairbairn, H., & Pascoe, S. (2003). *Fatherhood research in Australia.* Newcastle, Australia: The Family Action Centre.

Fletcher, R., Morgan, P. J., May, C., Lubans, D. R., & St George, J. (2011). Fathers' perceptions of rough-and-tumble play: Implications for early childhood services. *Australian Journal of Early Childhood, 36,* 131–138. Retrieved from http://www.earlychildhoodaustralia.org.au/australian_journal_of_early_childhood/

Fletcher, R., Silberberg, S., & Baxter, R. (2001). *Fathers' access to family-related service.* Newcastle, Australia: The Family Action Centre.

Fletcher, R. J., & Visser, A. L. (2008). Facilitating father engagement: The role of family relationship centres. *Journal of Family Studies, 14*(1), 53–64. doi:10.5172/jfs.327.14.1.53

Fronek, P. (Host). (2013a, February 2). Involving fathers: In conversation with Joseph Fleming [Episode 42]. Podsocs. Podcast retrieved November 18, 2013, from http://www.podsocs.com/podcast/involving-fathers/

Fronek, P. (Host). (2013b, March 16). *Working with fathers from a strengths perspective: In conversation with Andrew King* [Episode 46]. Podsocs. Podcast retrieved November 24, 2013, from http://www.podsocs.com/podcast/working-with-fathers-from-a-strengths-perspective/

Gallegos, D. (2006). *Fly-in fly-out employment: Managing the parenting transitions.* Perth, Australia: Centre for Social and Community Research.

Garfield, C. F., & Isacco, A. (2006). Fathers and the well-child visit. *Pediatrics, 117*(4), 637–645. doi:10.1542/peds.2005-1612 PMID:16585280

Ghate, D., Shaw, C., & Hazel, N. (2000). *Fathers and family centres: Engaging fathers in preventive services.* York, UK: York Publishing Services.

Gordon, D. M., Oliveros, A., Hawes, S. W., Iwamoto, D. K., & Rayford, B. S. (2012). Engaging fathers in child protection services: A review of factors and strategies across ecological systems. *Children and Youth Services Review, 34*(8), 1399–1417. doi:10.1016/j.childyouth.2012.03.021 PMID:25232202

Gordon, D. M., Watkins, N. D., Walling, S. M., Wilhelm, S., & Rayford, B. S. (2011). Adolescent fathers involved with child protection: Social workers speak! *Child Welfare, 90,* 95–114. Retrieved from http://www.cwla.org/ PMID:22533056

Haskett, M. E., Marziano, B., & Dover, E. R. (1996). Absence of males in maltreatment research: A survey of recent literature. *Child Abuse & Neglect, 20*(12), 1175–1182. doi:10.1016/S0145-2134(96)00113-5 PMID:8985608

Hawkins, A. J., & Dollahite, D. C. (1997). *Generative fathering: Beyond deficit perspectives.* Thousand Oaks, CA: Sage.

Holmes, E. K., Galovan, A. M., Yoshida, K., & Hawkins, A. J. (2010). Meta-analysis of the effectiveness of resident fathering programs: Are family life educators interested in fathers? *Family Relations, 59*(3), 240–252. doi:10.1111/j.1741-3729.2010.00599.x

Huebner, R. A., Werner, M., Hartwig, S., White, S., & Shewa, D. (2008). Engaging fathers: Needs and satisfaction in child protective services. *Administration in Social Work, 32*(2), 87–103. doi:10.1300/J147v32n02_06

Kanter, R. (1977). *Work and family in the United States: A critical review and agenda for research and policy.* New York, NY: Russell Sage Foundation.

Karpetis, G. (2010). Psychodynamic clinical social work practice with parents in child and adolescent mental health services: A case study on the role of the father. *Journal of Social Work Practice, 24*(2), 155–170. doi:10.1080/02650531003741629

King, A. (2000). Working with fathers: The non-deficit perspective. *Children Australia, 25*(3), 23-27. Retrieved from http://journals.cambridge.org/action/displayJournal?jid=CHA

King, A. (2005). The quiet revolution amongst men: Developing the practice of working with men in family relationships. *Children Australia, 30*(2), 33-37. Retrieved from http://journals.cambridge.org/action/displayJournal?jid=CHA

King, A., Sweeney, S., & Fletcher, R. (2004). A checklist for organisations working with men. *Developing Practice, 11,* 55-66. Retrieved from http://www.acwa.asn.au/developing_practice11.html

Knox, V., Cowan, P., Cowan, C. P., & Bildner, E. (2011). Policies that strengthen fatherhood and family relationships: What do we know and what do we need to know? *The Annals of the American Academy of Political and Social Science, 635*(1), 216–239. doi:10.1177/0002716210394769

Kwek, G. (2013, December 30). Miner dies at Fortescue's Christmas Creek Mine in WA. *Sydney Morning Herald.* Retrieved January 28, 2014, from http://www.smh.com.au/business/mining-and-resources/miner-dies-at-fortescues-christmas-creek-mine-in-wa-20131230-302bo.html#ixzz2rg1Bq900

Ladbrook, D. (2003). *Being dad to a child under two: Exploring images and visions of fatherhood, evolving expectations in a changing society.* Perth, W.A.: Ngala Family Resource Centre. Retrieved from http://www.ngala.com.au/For-Professionals/Being-Dad-to-a-Child-Under-Two

Lamb, M., & Tamis-LeMonda, C. (2004). The role of the father. In M. E. Lamb (Ed.), *The role of the father in child development* (4th ed., pp. 222–271). Hoboken, NJ: Wiley.

Marsiglio, W., Day, R. D., & Lamb, M. E. (2000). Exploring fatherhood diversity: Implications for conceptualizing father Involvement. *Marriage & Family Review, 29*(4), 269–293. doi:10.1300/J002v29n04_03

Maxwell, N., Scourfield, J., Featherstone, B., Holland, S., & Tolman, R. (2012). Engaging fathers in child welfare services: A narrative review of recent research evidence. *Child & Family Social Work, 17*(2), 160–169. doi:10.1111/j.1365-2206.2012.00827.x

McKeering, H., & Pakenham, K. I. (2000). Gender and generativity issues in parenting: Do fathers benefit more than mothers from involvement in child care activities? *Sex Roles, 43*(7/8), 459–480. doi:10.1023/A:1007115415819

McPhail, B. A. (2004). Setting the record straight: Social work is not a female-dominated profession. *Social Work, 49*(2), 323–326. doi:10.1093/sw/49.2.323 PMID:15124974

Milner, J. (1993). A disappearing act: The differing career paths of fathers and mothers in child protection investigations. *Critical Social Policy, 38*(38), 48–63. doi:10.1177/026101839301303803

Milner, J. (2004). From "disappearing" to "demonised": The effects on men and women of professional interventions based on challenging men who are violent. *Critical Social Policy, 24*(1), 79–101. doi:10.1177/0261018304241004

Nomaguchi, K. (2009). Change in work-family conflict among employed parents between 1977 and 1997. *Journal of Marriage and the Family, 71*(1), 15–32. doi:10.1111/j.1741-3737.2008.00577.x

O'Donnell, J. M., Johnson, W. E. Jr., D'Aunno, L. E., & Thornton, H. L. (2005). Fathers in child welfare: Caseworkers' perspectives. *Child Welfare, 84*, 387–414. Retrieved from http://www.questia.com/library/p435256/child-welfare PMID:15984170

O'Hagan, K. (1997). The problem of engaging men in child protection work. *British Journal of Social Work, 27*(1), 25–42. doi:10.1093/oxfordjournals.bjsw.a011194

O'Hagan, K., & Dillenberger, K. (1995). *The abuse of women within child care work*. Buckingham, UK: Open University Press.

Palkovitz, R. (2002). *Involved fathering and men's adult development*. New Jersey: Erlbaum.

Paquette, D. (2004). Theorizing the father–child relationship: Mechanisms and developmental outcomes. *Human Development, 47*(4), 193–219. doi:10.1159/000078723

Paquette, D., & Dumont, C. (2013). Is father-child rough-and-tumble play associated with attachment or activation relationships? *Early Child Development and Care, 183*(6), 760–773. doi:10.1080/03004430.2012.723440

Parent, C., Saint-Jacques, M.-C., Beaudry, M., & Robitalle, C. (2007). Stepfather involvement in social interventions made by youth protection services in step-families. *Child & Family Social Work, 12*(3), 229–238. doi:10.1111/j.1365-2206.2007.00494.x

Parke, R. D., McDowell, D. J., Kim, M., Killian, C., Dennis, J., Flyr, M. L., & Wild, M. N. (2002). Fathers' contributions to children's peer relationships. In C. S. Tamis-LeMonda & N. J. Cabrera (Eds.), *Handbook of father involvement: Multidisciplinary perspectives* (pp. 141–167). New Jersey: LEA.

Parker, J., & Ashencaen Crabtree, S. (2014). Fish need bicycles: An exploration of the perceptions of male social work students on a qualifying course. *British Journal of Social Work, 44*(2), 310–327. doi:10.1093/bjsw/bcs117

Pellegrini, A. D., & Smith, P. K. (1998). Physical activity play: The nature and function of a neglected aspect of play. *Child Development, 69*(3), 577–598. doi:10.1111/j.1467-8624.1998.tb06226.x PMID:9680672

Pellis, S. M., & Pellis, V. C. (2007). Rough-and-tumble play and the development of the social brain. *Current Directions in Psychological Science, 16*(2), 95–98. doi:10.1111/j.1467-8721.2007.00483.x

Peterson, G. W., & Steinmetz, S. K. (2000). The diversity of fatherhood. *Marriage & Family Review, 29*(4), 315–322. doi:10.1300/J002v29n04_05

Power, J. J., Perlesz, A., Brown, R., Schofield, M. J., Pitts, M. K., McNair, R., & Bikerdike, A. (2012). Bisexual parents and family diversity: Findings from the work, love, play study. *Journal of Bisexuality*, *12*(4), 519–538. doi:10.1080/15299716.2012.729432

Russell, G., & Hwang, C. (2004). The impact of workplace practices on father involvement. In M. Lamb (Ed.), *The role of the father in child development* (4th ed., pp. 476–501). New York: John Wiley & Sons.

Sabla, K.-P. (2009). *Fatherhood and parenting support: Lifeworld perspectives and aspects of a successful cooperation*. Munich: Juventa-Verl.

Scott, D., & Arney, F. (Eds.). (2010). *Working with vulnerable families: A partnership approach*. New York: Cambridge.

Scott, D., & Swain, S. (2002). *Confronting cruelty, historical perspectives on child protection*. Melbourne: Melbourne University Press.

Scott, E., & Panksepp, J. (2003). Rough and tumble play in human children. *Aggressive Behavior*, *29*(6), 539–551. doi:10.1002/ab.10062

Scott, K. L., & Crooks, C. V. (2004). Effecting change in maltreating fathers: Critical principles for intervention planning. *Clinical Psychology: Science and Practice*, *10*(1), 95–111. doi:10.1093/clipsy.bph058

Scourfield, J. (2001). Constructing men in child protection work. *Men and Masculinities*, *4*(1), 70–89. doi:10.1177/1097184X01004001004

Scourfield, J. (2003). *Gender and child protection*. London: Palgrave MacMillan.

Scourfield, J. (2006). The challenge of engaging fathers in the child protection process. *Critical Social Policy*, *26*(2), 440–449. doi:10.1177/0261018306062594

Scourfield, J. B., & Drakeford, M. (2002). New labour and the "problem of men". *Critical Social Policy*, *22*(4), 619–640. doi:10.1177/026101830220040401

Séguin, J. R., Parent, S., Tremblay, R. E., & Zelazo, P. D. (2009). Different neurocognitive functions regulating physical aggression and hyperactivity in early childhood. *Journal of Child Psychology and Psychiatry, and Allied Disciplines*, *50*(6), 679–687. doi:10.1111/j.1469-7610.2008.02030.x PMID:19298475

Snarey, J. (1993). *How fathers care for the next generation: A four decade study*. Cambridge, MA: Harvard University Press. doi:10.4159/harvard.9780674365995

Stahlschmidt, M. J., Threlfall, J., Seay, K. D., Lewis, E. M, & Kohl, P. L. (2013). Recruiting fathers to parenting programs: Advice from dads and fatherhood program providers. *Children and Youth Services Review*, *35*(10), 1734–1741. doi:10.1016/j.childyouth.2013.07.004 PMID:24791035

Staines, J., & Walters, J. (2007). *Evaluation of a fathers group within a child and family consultation service in East London* [Unpublished report]. Retrieved from groupworksolutions.com.au

Storhaug, A. S., & Oien, K. (2012). Fathers' encounters with the child welfare service. *Children and Youth Services Review*, *34*, 296–303. doi:10.1016/j.childyouth.2011.10.031

Strega, S., Fleet, C., Brown, L., Dominelli, L., Callahan, M., & Walmsley, C. (2008). Connecting father absence and mother blame in child welfare policies and practice. *Children and Youth Services Review*, *30*(7), 705–716. doi:10.1016/j.childyouth.2007.11.012

Strug, D., & Wilmore-Schaeffer, R. (2003). Fathers in the social work literature: Policy and practice implications. *Families in Society*, *84*(4), 503–511. doi:10.1606/1044-3894.145

Tamis-LeMonda, C., & Cabrera, C. (Eds.). (2002). *Handbook of father involvement*. Mahway, NJ: Lawrence Erlbaum Associates.

Taylor, J. C., & Simmonds, J. G. (2009). Family stress and coping in the fly-in fly-out workforce. *Australian Community Psychologist, 21*(2), 23-36. Retrieved from http://www.groups.psychology. org.au.com/publications/

Townsend, N. (2002). *The package deal: Marriage, work, and fatherhood in men's lives*. Philadelphia, PA: Temple University Press.

Turnell, A., & Edwards, S. (1999). *Signs of safety: A safety and solution oriented approach to child protection casework*. New York: Norton.

Walmsley, C., Strega, S., Brown, L., Dominelli, L., & Callahan, M. (2009). More than a playmate, less than a co-parent: Fathers in the Canadian BSW curriculum. *Canadian Social Work Review, 26*, 73–96. Retrieved from http://caswe-acfts.ca/cswr-journal/

Walters, M. (2011). *Working with fathers: From knowledge to therapeutic practice*. UK: Palgrave Macmillan.

Winslow, S. (2005). Work-family conflict, gender, and parenthood, 1977-1997. *Journal of Family Issues, 26*(6), 727–755. doi:10.1177/0192513X05277522

Zanoni, L., Warburton, W., Bussey, K., & McMaugh, A. (2013). Fathers as "core business" in child welfare practice and research: An interdisciplinary review. *Children and Youth Services Review, 35*(7), 1055–1070. doi:10.1016/j.childyouth.2013.04.018

Zelazo, P. D., Carter, A., Reznick, J. S., & Frye, D. (1997). Early development of executive function: A problem-solving framework. *Review of General Psychology, 1*(2), 198–226. doi:10.1037/1089-2680.1.2.198

Zvara, B. J., Schoppe-Sullivan, S. J., & Kamp Dush, C. (2013). Fathers' involvement in child health care: Associations with prenatal involvement, parents' beliefs, and maternal gatekeeping. *Family Relations, 62*(4), 649–661. doi:10.1111/fare.12023

## ADDITIONAL READING

Allen, S., & Daly, K. (2007). *The effects of father involvement: An updated research summary of the evidence*. Centre for Families, Work, and Wellbeing: University of Guelph. Retrieved from http://www.fira.ca.cms/documents/29/Effects_Father_Involvement.pdf

Bellamy, J. L. (2009). A national study of male involvement among families in contact with the child welfare system. *Child Maltreatment, 14*(3), 255–262. doi:10.1177/1077559508326288 PMID:18984807

Buckley, H. (2002). *Child protection work: Beyond the rhetoric*. London: Jessica Kingsley.

Burgess, A. (2009). *Fathers and parenting interventions: What works?* Marlborough, UK: The Fatherhood Institute.

Daniel, B., & Taylor, J. (1999). The rhetoric versus the reality: A critical perspective on practice with fathers in child care and protection work. *Child & Family Social Work, 4*(3), 209–220. doi:10.1046/j.1365-2206.1999.00117.x

Department for Education and Skills. (2007). *Every parent matters*. London: The Stationery Office.

Department of Families. Housing, Community Services and Indigenous Affairs. (2009). *Father inclusive practice guide*. Retrieved March 26, 2013, from http://www.fahcsia.gov.au/sa/families/pubs/Pages/Father-inclusive_practice_guide.aspx

Doherty, W. J., Kouneski, E. F., & Erickson, M. F. (1998). Responsible fathering: An overview and conceptual framework. *Journal of Marriage and the Family*, *60*(2), 277–292. doi:10.2307/353848

Dubowitz, H. (2006). Where's dad? A need to understand father's role in child maltreatment. *Child Abuse & Neglect*, *30*(5), 461–465. doi:10.1016/j.chiabu.2006.04.002 PMID:16707159

Dugmore, P., & Cocker, C. (2008). Legal, social and attitudinal changes: An exploration of lesbian and gay issues in a training programme for social workers in fostering and adoption. *Social Work Education*, *27*(2), 159–168. doi:10.1080/02615470701709600

Dunk-West, P. (2013). Gender, agency and the sexual self: A theoretical model for social work. *Advances in Social Work and Welfare Education*, *15*, 32-47. Retrieved from http://www.anzswwer.org/

Fagan, J., & Palm, G. (2004). *Fathers and early childhood programmes*. Clifton Park, NY: Delmar Learning.

Farmer, E. (1997). Paradox in child protection practice: Regulated mothers and protected fathers. In P. Saunders & T. Eardley (Eds.), *States, markets, communities: Remapping the boundaries* (pp. 57–68). Sydney, NSW: National Social Policy Research Centre.

Featherstone, B. (2010). Engaging fathers: Promoting gender equality. In B. Featherstone, C. Hooper, J. Scourfield, & J. Taylor (Eds.), *Gender and child welfare in society* (pp. 173–194). Hoboken, NJ: Wiley. doi:10.1002/9780470684771.ch7

Fletcher, R., & Silberberg, S. (2006). Involvement of fathers in primary school activities. *Australian Journal of Education*, *50*(1), 29–39. doi:10.1177/000494410605000103

Iversen, A. E., Esbjørn, B. H., Christensen, E., & Hansen, N. S. (2012). Exploring the impact of involving fathers in the treatment of their children: A study using interpretative phenomenological analysis (IPA). *Qualitative Studies*, *3*, 22-39. Retrieved from http://ojs.statsbiblioteket.dk/index.php/qual/index

King, A. (2013). The Newpin inside fathers program in Australia. *Developing Practice*, *34*, 67-80. Retrieved from http://www.acwa.asn.au/developing_practice11.html

King, L. (2012). *Hiding in the pub to cutting the cord?* Warwick, UK: Warwick Knowledge Centre. Retrieved from http://www2.warwick.ac.uk/knowledge/culture/fatherhood

Lamb, M., & Tamis-LeMonda, C. (2004). The role of the father. In M. E. Lamb (Ed.), *The role of the father in child development* (4th ed., pp. 222–271). Hoboken, NJ: Wiley.

Lamb, M. E. (1977). Father-infant and mother-infant interaction in the first year of life. *Child Development*, *48*(1), 167–181. doi:10.2307/1128896

Lapierre, S. (2009, April). Towards an ideal of gender equity? Child protection practices in cases involving domestic violence. Paper presented at the 3rd Gender and Child Welfare Interdisciplinary Conference, Cardiff University, UK.

Malm, K., Murray, J., & Green, R. (2006). *What about the dads? Child welfare agencies' efforts to identify, locate and involve non-resident fathers*. Washington, DC: US Department of Health and Human Services, Office of the Assistant Secretary for Planning and Evaluation.

Maxwell, N., Scourfield, J., Featherstone, B., Holland, S., & Lee, J. (2012). The benefits and challenges of training child protection social workers in father engagement. *Child Abuse Review*, *21*(4), 299–310. doi:10.1002/car.2218

Nettle, D. (2008). Why do some dads get more involved than others? Evidence from a large British cohort. *Evolution and Human Behavior, 29*(6), 416–423. doi:10.1016/j.evolhumbehav.2008.06.002

Newland, L. A., & Coyl, D. D. (2010). Fathers' role as attachment figures: An interview with Sir Richard Bowlby. *Early Child Development and Care, 180*(1-2), 25–32. doi:10.1080/03004430903414679

Perry, L. (2010). *Cheers to childbirth*. Turramurra, NSW: Pure Publishing.

Peterson, L. M., Butts, J., & Deville, D. M. (2000). Parenting experiences of three self-identified gay fathers. *Smith College Studies in Social Work, 70*(3), 513–521. doi:10.1080/00377310009517608

Pleck, J., & Masciadrelli, B. (2004). Paternal involvement by U.S. residential fathers: Levels, sources and consequences. In M. E. Lamb (Ed.), *The role of the father in child development* (4th ed., pp. 222–271). Hoboken, N.J.: Wiley.

Pruett, K. (1987). *The nurturing father*. New York: Warner Books.

Pruett, K. (2000). *Father-need*. New York: Broadway Books.

Roberts, E. (2012, 23 December). Fathers play such an important role. Let's not keep mum about dads. *The Observer*. Retrieved March 22, 2013, from http://www.guardian.co.uk/commentisfree/2012/dec/23/fathers-important-role

Robinson, B. (2001). *Fathering from the fast lane: Practical ideas for busy dads*. Australia: Finch.

Robson, S. (2006). Parent perspectives on services and relationships in two English early years centres. *Early Child Development and Care, 176*(5), 443–460. doi:10.1080/03004430500039721

Ryan, M. (2000). *Working with fathers*. Abingdon: Radcliffe Medical Press.

Scourfield, J. (2008, April). Real men, real women: A rounded view of gendered practice in child protection. Paper for the Canadian Gender and Child Welfare Network inaugural meeting at McGill University School of Social Work, Montreal, Quebec.

Scourfield, J. (2014). Improving work with fathers to prevent child maltreatment: Fathers should be engaged as allies in child abuse and neglect prevention. *Child Abuse & Neglect, 38*(6), 974–981. doi:10.1016/j.chiabu.2014.05.002 PMID:24873732

Smit, R. (2004). Involved fathering: Expanding conceptualisations of men's paternal caring. *Koers, 69*(1), 101–120. doi:10.4102/koers.v69i1.299

Spandler, H., Roy, A., & Mckeown, M. (2014). Using football metaphor to engage men in therapeutic support. *Journal of Social Work Practice: Psychotherapeutic Approaches in Health. Welfare and the Community, 28*, 229–245. doi:10.1080/02650533.2013.853286

Staines, J., & Walters, J. (2008). The fathers group: A shoulder to cry on. *Context: The Magazine for Family Therapy and Systemic Practice in the UK, 96*, 15-20. Retrieved from http://www.aft.org.uk/about/view/about-context.html?tzcheck=1

Theophilou, N. (2013). *Ten stories about what men are doing well*. [Kindle edition]. Retrieved from http://www.amazon.com/Stories-about-what-Doing-Well-ebook/dp/B00FIV1XZC

Tiedje, L. B., & Darling-Fisher, C. (2003). Promoting father-friendly healthcare. *American Journal of Maternal/Child Nursing, 28*, 350-357. doi:10.1097/00005721-200311000-00004

White, N. R. (1994). About fathers: Masculinity and the social construction of fatherhood. *The Australian and New Zealand Journal of Sociology, 30*(2), 119–131. doi:10.1177/144078339403000202

## KEY TERMS AND DEFINITIONS

**Child Welfare:** The child welfare system is a group of public and private services that are focused on ensuring that all children live in safe, permanent, and stable environments that support their well-being. In Australia the child welfare system and legislation is different for each State and Territory.

**Father:** A term which has come to identify a form of social, rather than biological, relationship. There can be no single concept that encapsulates fathering. For the purposes of this chapter, the word "father" pertains to both the social and biological aspects of the term.

**Fatherhood:** A status attained by having a child and which remains unchanged – unless an only child dies. The term "fatherhood" is used interchangeably with the term "fathering" which includes, beyond the procreative act itself, all the childrearing roles, activities, duties, and responsibilities that fathers are expected to perform and carry out.

**Generativity:** A concept involving the capacity to care for the next generation and demanding the ability to give something of oneself to another person.

**Social Work:** A human service profession which uses theories of human behaviour and social systems to improve the well-being and quality of life of individuals and groups by addressing social disadvantages such as poverty, and mental and physical illness or disability. Human rights and social justice are integral components in social work.

# Chapter 13
# Art Therapy:
## A Social Work Perspective

**Shiri Hergass**
*Clinical Social Worker, Australia*

## ABSTRACT

*Art therapy is universally practiced and has proven to be a successful intervention for trauma. This chapter focuses on how art therapy can be used to heal transgenerational trauma in Aboriginal Australians with a particular focus on children. The effects of trauma in general and transgenerational trauma more specifically on one's brain, physiology, and physical, emotional, and behavioural health are discussed. Promising practices of why art therapy works are outlined, challenges and cultural considerations for working with Aboriginal populations are identified, and solutions and future research are recommended.*

## INTRODUCTION

Art is an important, universal facet of human expression as old as human civilization. Creating art is an innate human tendency that has been likened to speech and tool making for defining our species (Dissanayake, 1992). Expressive arts (e.g. dancing, drawing, play or drama, creative writing, painting, poetry, music, sculpting, and photography) have long been used with children to promote psychological health and social support.

Currently, art therapy is diversely practiced in a range of countries, cultures, and contexts (Rubin, 2005). In this paper, I investigate the use of art therapy for healing the effects of trauma in today's Australian Aboriginal society. More specifically, I review the benefits, considerations, and challenges for using art therapy as a therapeutic intervention for Aboriginal children experiencing transgenerational stress and trauma, with a particular focus on early childhood.

I discuss different art therapy approaches, as well as the factors influencing the effectiveness of various art therapy programmes. The objectives are to provide: (1) a comprehensive overview of the impact of transgenerational trauma; and (2) future directions for research and art therapy design. The strongest recommendations are to: (1) include Aboriginals in the design of art therapy programmes; and (2) to consider how to best

DOI: 10.4018/978-1-4666-6563-7.ch013

include the caregivers of children in art therapy programmes, particularly since the caregivers have often also experienced transgenerational trauma.

## BACKGROUND

I have worked as an art therapist and group facilitator for the past 15 years in both the private and public sectors. I began my social work experience in a developing town near the northern border of Israel. It was a town that had a large number of vulnerable complex families who also had to deal with the daily reality of living in a war zone. Working with very young children in extreme trauma conditions, I felt that talk therapy was not sufficient or appropriate. Instead, with a small suitcase full of art materials, I started exploring different approaches whilst simultaneously studying art therapy.

I worked with Ethiopian immigrants, Bedouins, and with women and children who survived different forms of trauma. I found that art filled the gaps words could not. Art gave colour and shape to the unmentionable and created a bridge that allowed me to cross and meet people of different cultures. It was non-threatening and allowed healing to occur, especially with the children.

Eight years ago, I immigrated to Australia and opened a private practice working with vulnerable, complex families who are often referred from the Department of Child Services, Sydney Children Services, and Foster Care services. I also manage a rural project for a non-profit organisation called "Gunawirra" where we work with 43 Aboriginal preschool children in the New South Wales outback. Through Gunawirra I work with traumatised educators and therapists who themselves work with vulnerable, traumatised families.

The work is two-fold. It involves designing programmes that can make a real and lasting improvement to the lives of traumatised children and their parents, and it involves helping the facilitators of these programmes to work through their own trauma, so that they are in a space to care for others. Using art as a therapeutic medium helps to create a foundation upon which both carers and families can express themselves. It helps to open up topics that are painful and gives a language for deep traumatic experiences to be expressed and processed.

We work in partnership. I learn about their culture by what they share and show me and this helps me to shape the therapy in contrast to previous imperialistic models which, in practice, were irrelevant for this culture. This is an ever-evolving model which is as much their design as mine. The key success factor is the relationship that is created between the staff and me. Utilising art as therapy has been key in working with the trauma experienced by the childcare centre staff and is also central to the programmes that we create together for the children and their parents as a necessary on-flow.

Throughout my work over the years, I have seen that art is a wonderful tool in which children and adults can communicate a vast variety of feelings in a non-threatening way in order to gain self-esteem, improved communication, empowerment, and emotional health. This experience, in addition to my research, has largely informed this paper.

## THE DEVELOPMENTAL IMPORTANCE OF EARLY CHILDHOOD

The first years of life are critical for brain, social, and emotional development. During early childhood (birth to age four), brain development peaks and its growth is faster than at any other developmental stage (Pally & Olds, 2000). Trauma experienced during early childhood may also alter the brain's biology and functions and have long-term negative consequences. Early experiences have a great impact on an infant's physiological systems because they are so unformed and easily influenced. Stress responses, emotional systems, and even the growth of the brain itself may not progress adequately if the infant lacks the necessary environmental and social conditions.

A child's emotional environment and caregiver experiences in early childhood are developmentally important. A safe environment with loving caregivers is important to children's developing sense of safety and trust in the larger world. A secure attachment to one or more caregivers in early childhood can affect behaviour and relationships into adulthood (Bowlby, 1979). Stressors and traumatic experiences in children's early years can significantly affect their emotional and psychological development, physiology, physical health, and social and coping skills.

## Early Social Environment and Neurobiology

The genetically timed emergence of brain circuits during infancy means it is especially important to experience healthy relationships and attachments in order for the brain to develop normally (Pally & Olds, 2000; Schore, 2003). From birth to two years of age is a crucial time for emotional development. The systems that manage our emotions, stress responses, the responsiveness of neurotransmitters in the brain, and other brain processes (e.g. the neural pathways that encode our implicit understanding of how relationships work) develop during this time.

The psychological and physiological coping strategies established in infancy and toddlerhood tend to persist through life. Both are developed in response to our earliest relationships. The earliest relationships shape our nervous systems which influence future emotional well-being and determine how we respond to stress as a consequence.

Many aspects of our physiology and emotional behaviours are shaped by our social interactions. The brain itself has been called a "social organ". Our minds and our emotions become organised through engaging with other people (Gerhardt, 2004). Research shows that genes provide the raw ingredients for our minds, but early relationships are what create our tendencies and personalities and help shape our developing nervous system and capacity to respond to future stress. For example, when an infant looks at her parent smile, she is pleasurably aroused and her heart rate increases. Neuropeptides and dopamine are released and reach the prefrontal cortex, helping new tissue growth in the prefrontal brain (Gerhardt, 2004). Early positive experiences with other people produce brains with more neuronal connections, i.e., more richly networked brains and better brain performance. On the other hand, a negative look can also trigger a biochemical response. A parent's disapproving face can trigger stress hormones, such as cortisol, which halt endorphins and dopamine neurons and the pleasurable feelings they generate.

## Effects of Trauma

Everyone responds to trauma differently. Despite individuals' great capacity to adapt, it is well established that childhood experiences of trauma can have severe and long-lasting effects (van der Kolk, 2008). The systems of the brain responsible for thinking and processing information have shown signs of sensitivity and vulnerability to traumatic experiences; and they may lead to developmental challenges, such as problematic speech, impulsivity, attention deficit disorders, difficulty in school, relationship hardships, and struggles with work later in life (Perry, 2001), as well as many physical ailments.

## Effects of Trauma on Early Brain Development

The majority of the brain's neurobiology processes happen early in life. If these processes are disrupted by trauma, abnormal behaviour and cognition may occur. Children whose brains and body systems are still in the process of development are especially vulnerable to trauma. Current research shows that experiences of stress and trauma early in life can affect brain development. The architecture of the brain is constructed through a process that begins before birth and continues into adulthood; experiences – positive and negative – shape critical features of the brain architecture. The effect of an experience will vary depending on the brain development stage occurring at the time.

Traumatic experiences affect brain development in children and adults differently. Because a child's brain is developing, the effects can be more profound. For example, for adults, trauma alters a mature brain in which neurological connections have already been made. Although re-organisation of these connections can cause difficulties for adults, the impact on a developing brain (that is, a child's brain) is comparatively worse.

If the experience occurs during a critical period of development (that is, the brain is on an accelerated growth curve and neural networks are being built), the effect can be significant. For example, between the ages of three and five the frontal cortex is in a critical period of development. The frontal cortex is the area responsible for planning, organising, paying attention to, and remembering details. If children experience trauma during this critical development period of the frontal cortex, their life-long functions in these areas can be diminished (Perry, 2001; van der Kolk, 2008). Because a child's brain is so malleable (receptive to environmental input), changes to the brain architecture manifest more quickly and more deeply. A child's development can be impaired or slowed down (van der Kolk, 2008). Further, if traumatic states become the primary organising experience for a child's brain, then neurological systems can be distorted for the long term (Perry 2009; van der Kolk & McFarlane 1996).

Traumatic memories activate the emotional right brain but decrease activity in the verbal left-brain. The right brain becomes highly aroused, while the left frontal brain is unable to make sense of the experience and verbalise. Without the verbalising activities of the left frontal brain,

Broca's area and the hippocampus, it becomes difficult to process and evaluate feelings. These left-brain activities normally put experiences into a context and sequence. Without them, one cannot get into the past and, therefore, is unable to let go of the traumatic experience and its memories. Instead they leap into the present as flashbacks.

Recovery may depend on activating the appropriate parts of the left-brain to put the traumatic experience into context and heal (Pennebaker, 1993). This is not an option for the small child as the hippocampus is not fully functional until age three. Without a fully developed prefrontal cortex, there is little chance of overriding the subcortical system with the orbitofrontal cortex and, therefore, a child under age three who experiences trauma may get stuck in a constant appraisal of threat.

When previously traumatised patients were exposed to re-experiencing their trauma using their imagination, there was a heightened activity only in the right hemisphere – the area responsible for most emotional arousal (van der Kolk & McFarlane, 1996). This state of heightened arousal hinders healthy brain development. Moreover, the part of the left hemisphere (Broca's area), which is responsible for making experience known as language, was "turned off"; this is exemplified by the frozen watchfulness often observed in traumatized children (van der Kolk & McFarlane, 1996).

## Effects of Stress and Trauma on Physiology

Human babies are born with the expectation of having stress managed for them. As long as a caring adult maintains their equilibrium through touch, stroking, feeding, and rocking they tend to have low levels of cortisol (Levine, 2001). But their immature systems are very unstable and reactive and can plunge into very high cortisol levels if no one responds to them (Gunnar & Donzella, 2002).

The normal response to traumatic experience is to be afraid, initiating a fight or flight response. The sympathetic nervous system releases adrenaline, heart rate and blood pressure increase, and cortisol is produced. These things usually return to normal after a few hours, but when trauma is extreme or chronic this might not happen and it may take a year or more to recover.

Cortisol is useful as a short-term mobiliser to support the fight or flight reflex. When the stressful situation is over, the body returns to normal. However, research shows that if stress persists and high levels of cortisol remain in the body over longer periods of time, this leads to many emotional dysfunctions, such as depression, anxiety, and suicidal tendencies in adulthood, as well as eating disorders, alcoholism, obesity, and sexual abuse (Colomina, Albina, Domingo, & Corbella, 1997). Moreover, high cortisol levels due to fear can damage the hippocampus leading to neuron loss, thereby affecting its capacity to retrieve information and an ability to learn and remember. The ability of the prefrontal cortex to think and manage behaviour can also be affected (Schulkin & Rosen, 1998). In addition, high cortisol levels over prolonged periods can damage other parts of the body, such as the lymphocytes of the immune system. This can even lead to decrease in muscle mass and osteoporosis and it may also play a part in diabetes and hypertension through increased blood glucose and insulin levels.

The brain's system that responds to stress may cause children who experience trauma to be on constant high alert, to become impulsive, and it may lead to a decline in their overall health. Serious and long-term psychiatric damage into adulthood may occur and can cause damage to physical health and vulnerability to stress throughout life (Felitti, 1998; Pynoos, Ritzmann, Steinberg, Goenjian, & Prisecaru, 1996). The hippocampus and corpus callosum inhibit the exchange of information between hemispheres and prevent emotional experience being processed into language (O'Brien, 2004).

## Effects of Trauma on Psychological and Social Well-Being

Secure attachment to caregivers has a profound effect on the healthy development of the brain and on the personality and future health of the individual. Distress in infants affects their future relationships (Bowlby, 1979); and what happens between the child and their primary caregiver is stored as a pattern for future experiences and relationships (Schore, 1994).

Traumatic experiences can break down children's coping skills and defences. This is because of the damage that trauma causes the brain's right hemisphere which is responsible for processing, expressing and regulating emotions, and understanding social interactions (Schore, 1994). Children who have been traumatised may later develop such serious conditions as depression, borderline personality, or post-traumatic stress disorder (PTSD). PTSD is an emotional disorder that may be caused by a one-time traumatic event or by repeated traumatic experiences, such as physical abuse, community violence, or maltreatment. Damage to the right hemisphere occurring through early trauma is associated with later difficulties in establishing love relationships (Mollon, 1993).

In the early months of life, infants establish along with those around them what a normal state of arousal looks like. Babies of depressed mothers adjust to low stimulation and become used to a lack of positive feelings. Babies of agitated mothers may stay overly aroused and have a sense that feelings are explosive and lack control. Well-managed babies come to expect a world that is responsive to feelings and this helps bring intense states back to comfortable levels.

Children react to stress in one of two ways after trauma. They either react in a hyper-responsive mode with uncontrolled anxiety and hyper-reactivity; or in a hypo-responsive mode, withdrawing both socially and emotionally. Traumatised children show a heightened sense of vulnerability and sensitivity to environmental threat; thus, they tend to re-experience the events emotionally from both reminders of the event and from intrusive thoughts of images of the event. Traumatised children have also shown feelings of apathy, withdrawal, and decreased motivation (Armsworth & Holady, 1993).

One response to trauma is dissociation. Dissociation is a process in which external and internal stimuli are stopped as a result of becoming overwhelmed by a traumatic experience. Infants respond to stress with intense crying and screaming, and high levels of hormones are released into the brain (Schore, 2001a; 2001b; 2003). Mothers are ideally able to soothe infants with face-to-face looking and rocking; however, if no emotional comfort or regulation is available, the highly aroused state will eventually cease; and in its place, the infant will quieten, become immobile, avoid contact, become compliant, and restrict output to manage dissociation.

This becomes a familiar sequence: hyperarousal followed by dissociation, accompanied by a rise in pain-numbing endorphins and high hormone levels. This psychic deadening defence is eventually entered into for long periods with its function being to numb the pain and chaos of the body. Repeated experiences of insensitive attachment or abuse cause such distress in infants that they learn to stop feeling. The child can never find a coping strategy when their parent is the abuser, as they need to seek proximity and avoidance at the same time. Input from external stimuli becomes unbearable and prevents emotional learning, reduces development, and makes attachment and understanding impossible.

Traumatised and abused children (Pynoos et al., 1996; Teicher, 2000) can experience the full range of symptoms associated with PTSD. Startling connections have been found between abuses of all kinds and permanent, debilitating changes in the brain leading to psychiatric problems (Teicher, 2000). Attention deficit hyperactivity disorder (ADHD) is often present with PTSD in traumatised children (van der Kolk & McFarlane, 1996).

Infants and toddlers who witness violence in their homes or communities show increased irritability, immature behaviour, sleep disturbances, emotional distress and crying, fears of being alone, and loss of skills (such as regression in toileting and language). Young children who have either witnessed or experienced a traumatic event usually appear very serious, dissociated, or disorganised, and they smile very little (Appleyard & Osofsky, 2003).

When traumatised children are emotionally stimulated, they lose the capacity to make sense of their feelings or to use them as a guide in assessing situations. Instead, they go from stimulus to response, unable to use the thought process in between. This results in aggression or numbing of feelings and becomes a pattern of behaviour (Schore, 2001a; van der Kolk & McFarlane, 1996). Negative outcomes in both children and adolescents can also include disruptiveness, impulsivity, inattentiveness, poor socialisation, and low academic achievement.

Van Der Kolk (2008) argues that childhood trauma violates a child's sense of safety and trust and reduces their sense of worth, increases levels of emotional distress, shame, and grief, and increases destructive behaviours including aggression, adolescent suicide, alcoholism, substance abuse, sexual promiscuity, physical inactivity, smoking, and obesity. Survivors of childhood trauma were shown to be more likely to have difficulty developing and maintaining relationships with caregivers, peers, and partners, and were more likely to develop heart disease, cancer, stroke, and diabetes. Trauma has also been linked to entering and remaining in the criminal justice system. There is a high instance of childhood trauma in the child welfare and juvenile justice systems and later in life in the adult criminal justice system (Atkinson, 2013).

## Effects of Early Trauma on Cognitive Development and Physical Health

Exposure to extreme violence may interfere with a child's developmental processes, affecting memory, cognition, and learning (Pynoos et al., 1996). The years of language acquisition between ages two and ten are especially vulnerable to the effects of early maltreatment.

Normal development enables children to organise a story into a continuous narrative that has a beginning, middle, and end. Alternatively, chaotic narrative construction results from traumatic experiences and adversely impacts reading, writing, and communication skills. Early childhood trauma causes permanent alteration to the development of the left hippocampus, resulting in problems with processing memory and dissociative symptoms that persist into adulthood (Teicher, 2000).

Traumatic experiences may cause physiological damage in vital organs, such as the heart and lungs. People with developmental trauma often have heart disease, diabetes, and asthma, as well as weakened immune systems that can account for early deaths. Infants and toddlers who witness violence in their homes or communities often have physical complaints (Appleyard & Osofsky, 2003).

## TRANSGENERATIONAL TRAUMA

### Colonisation as Trauma for Australian Aboriginals

Aboriginal society pre-colonisation provided optimal conditions for the health and well-being of families and children through its shared nature of caregiving. Multiple mothering was common, men played a significant role in family life, and elders and other extended family members provided important support and nurturing to children. Parents and other caregivers traditionally present in Aboriginal culture provided meaning to infants by leading and responding to play and communication of verbal and non-verbal interactions.

The phenomenon known as the "Stolen Generations" – Aboriginal children who were forcibly removed from their parents – is a specific example of physical and psychological trauma affecting communities, families, and children across several generations. Children of the Stolen Generations were separated from their families, institutionalised, physically and sexually abused, and psychologically mistreated. Anger, substance abuse, ill health, self-harm, suicide, and PTSD are some of the many consequences of this trauma today (Atkinson, 2002). These layers of violence and abuse have created what Atkinson (2002) calls "transgenerational trauma" (p. xi).

Historical or transgenerational trauma was initially conceptualized in the 1980s by First Nations and Aboriginal peoples in Canada to explain the seemingly unending cycle of trauma and despair in their communities. Essentially, the devastating trauma of genocide, loss of culture, and forcible removal from family and communities are all unresolved and become a sort of "psychological baggage...continuously being acted out and recreated in contemporary Aboriginal culture" (Wesley-Esquimaux & Smolewski, 2004, p. 3).

Historical or transgenerational trauma is akin to "cumulative trauma" which is defined as emotional and psychic scarring that accumulates across generations. It passes from parents to children in a cyclic process of wounding (Mu'id, 2004, p. 9). Similarly, Atkinson (2013) says that trauma becomes transgenerational when it is embedded in the collective memory of a people; when it has become a normalised part of life. When this occurs, it is passed on in the same way that culture is transmitted.

Besides suffering the consequences of abuse, Aboriginal Australian children have missed out on the formation or continuation of a traditional "holding" relationship of attachment and bonding, called in the Aboriginal language "Kanyirninpa";

thus further eroding the opportunity for healthy, secure parent-caregiver experiences. Touch and physical holding are important (Kaufman & Zigler, 1993). Young children who are not handled or rocked have a reduced production of thyroid hormones resulting in high levels of stress in the brain. This in turn gives the child an increased feeling of fear and a heightened adrenalin response (Teicher, 2000).

Today, Aboriginal Australians experience higher levels of illness and premature death than non-Aboriginal Australians. Aboriginal life expectancy is up to 20 years less than that of the total population. Non-communicable, largely preventable, diseases account for 70% of this difference. Aboriginal Australians have poorer physical, psychological, and behavioural health, higher stress levels, high incarceration rates, lower socioeconomic status, and higher poverty rates. They have more reported cases of lower birth weights and premature births, more cases of child maltreatment, are more likely to be a perpetrator or victim of violence, have higher rates of PTSD, greater morbidity rates, and higher rates of cardiovascular disease, diabetes, asthma, and sexually transmitted diseases than do non-Aboriginal Australians (Australian Institute of Health and Welfare, 2011).

The current high levels of child abuse and neglect in Aboriginal Communities reflect the deterioration of traditional nurturing practices since colonisation and the impact of transgenerational trauma on caregivers' abilities to successfully nurture children. The traumatic effects of colonisation on the Australian Aboriginal people have made it extremely difficult to maintain their traditional ways of caring for their children. Most Indigenous families have experienced removal of children or displacement of entire families into missions, reserves, or other institutions; and most families have been affected over one or more generations.

Trauma may be experienced by today's Aboriginal children as a one-time event or as an ongoing experience directly or through secondary exposure, such as occurs through transgenerational trauma (Atkinson, 2013). There is also a heightened risk of experiencing complex trauma. Direct experiences of trauma might include abuse, neglect, and exposure to violence. In 2011, Indigenous Aboriginal children were 5.4 times as likely as non-Indigenous children to experience a hospital separation for assault, eight times as likely to be the subject of substantiated child abuse or neglect, and 15 times as likely to be under juvenile justice supervision (Australian Institute of Health and Welfare, 2011).

## Effects of Transgenerational Trauma on Attachment and Bonding

The transgenerational effects of trauma occur through a variety of mechanisms, including the impact on the attachment relationship with caregivers, the impact on parenting and family functioning, the effects of violence across generations, the association with parental physical and mental illness, and the disconnection and alienation from extended family, culture, and society. It is now also being discovered that transgenerational trauma has an impact on people's brain development. The post-colonization fragmenting of Australian Aboriginal people's social, familial, communal, and cultural values is impacting the brain development of Aboriginal children. The effects of transgenerational trauma are posited as literally creating changes in the neural pathways of these children's brains (Perry, 2001).

Attachment is as a bond that provides an enduring emotional relationship with a particular person, providing safety, comfort, soothing, and pleasure (Perry, 2001). The loss of this relationship may cause severe distress. This relationship has been generally viewed as the mother-child relationship. When Aboriginal children were forcibly removed from their homes, this mother-child bond, as well as bonds between the child and other caregivers (which is common in Aboriginal culture), were destroyed. According to attachment theory, the absence of an important primary caregiver relationship can lead to emotional and behavioural problems throughout one's life and can affect the ability to form healthy relationships with others (Ryan, 2011).

Atkinson and Swain (1999) have argued that the removal of generations of Aboriginal children from families and communities in Victoria has denied these separated children the opportunity to bond with parents, to experience their love and acceptance, and has additionally damaged the confidence of Indigenous adults to parent their own children.

Despite the fact that the Stolen Generations children were in close proximity to their community, these children missed out on the continuation of a traditional holding relationship. The values within Kanyirninpa were unable to be exercised, expressed, or experienced as the children grew up, thus eroding the opportunity for a secure attachment and nurturance (Yeo, 2003). The residential experience undermined the social meanings and the creation of a social self in relation to others (e.g. siblings, peers, extended family, elders, larger community) for these children. It separated the children from values and knowledge that were critical for developing social and emotional responsibility, and it destroyed their belief in the safety of their world.

## Effects of Transgenerational Trauma on Aboriginal Culture

For Aboriginal participants in Yeo's (2003) study, the cultural values of interdependence, group cohesion, spiritual connectedness, traditional links to the land, community loyalty, and inter-assistance were common indicators of social and emotional competence. With children being removed from their families and the subsequent negative effects of transgenerational trauma, Aboriginal children and families lost opportunities for practicing these important values. In essence, they lost the very important cultural and family values that were intricately tied to social and emotional competence. It damaged the confidence of Indigenous adults to parent their own children (Atkinson & Swain, 1999), and because it separated children from cultural values, traditions, and knowledge critical for developing social and psychological health, it has undermined their belief in the safety of their world.

## Effects of Transgenerational Trauma on Physical, Mental, and Behavioural Health

Van der Kolk (2008) says that childhood trauma is probably today's single most important public health challenge but one that can be overcome with prevention and intervention. His work shows the links between trauma during childhood and ongoing physical health and behaviour problems and with intra and intergenerational transference of negative attitudes and troubled behaviour from historical trauma across family and communal systems.

Atkinson, Nelson, & Atkinson (2010) argue that normalisation of family violence and the high prevalence of grief, loss, and substance misuse were as much symptoms as causes of traumatic stress. One of the most alarming aspects of Atkinson's study was the consistency of victims who reported severe child sexual abuse from early ages to maturity predicting later acting out behaviours. Atkinson's research also identified a substantial lack of services that effectively supported victims of abuse and interrupted its intergenerational progression.

## ART THERAPY

### How Can Art Therapy Heal Trauma?

In this section, I discuss how art therapy can ameliorate the effects of trauma. I outline the various components and promising practices of art therapy programmes and their role in healing, with a special focus on the neurobiological effects of art therapy. I begin with an overview of how and why art therapy works and conclude with solutions and recommendations to challenges in art therapy programmes with Aboriginal Australians.

## Art Therapy and its Effectiveness

The term "art therapy" was coined in 1942 by an artist, Adrian Hill, but therapy using image-making and art was carried out prior to this time within the context of psychoanalysis. Art therapy is a philosophically conceived, developmentally based, and research-supported approach that helps children cope with and overcome problems (Hogan, 2001).

Art therapy helps give shape and form to human experience, to help express and reflect on experiences, and to expand and deepen personal understanding. It provides a safe space to release stored emotions and foster healthy connections and relationships. Expressive arts therapy places an emphasis on supporting the internal and therapeutic processes of the creation and expression of art making, as opposed to an analysis of the art product (Hogan, 2001).

Expressive arts therapy aids the health, healing, growth, and development of humans through a combination of images, symbols, storytelling, rituals, music, dance, play, drama, poetry, movement, dream work, and visual arts. Art therapy has been demonstrated to be an effective therapeutic approach for a variety of children's problems including, but not limited to, the following: trauma, abuse and neglect, aggression attachment difficulties, autism, and emotional difficulties (Hogan, 2001)

For more than 30 years, art therapists have observed that drawing and painting are useful in the assessment and treatment of traumatic disorders in children and adolescents (Lyshak-Stelzer, Singer, St. John, & Chemtob, 2007). There are many case studies in the literature on the use of art therapy

to reduce trauma symptoms and PTSD in children and adults (Collie, Backos, Malchiodi, & Spiegel, 2006; Gil, 2006; Malchiodi, 2008).

Art therapy has also been shown to modify children's maladaptive behaviours, personality, and social issues. In recent years, advances in neurobiology and psychotherapy have informed the practice of art therapy which has increasingly been utilized when verbal psychotherapy has failed to help clients. In sum, art therapy has a successful history spanning at least six decades; and promising approaches continue to evolve (Hogan, 2001).

Three decades of clinical experience have shown that art therapy processes help regulate and reduce stress and fear-based subcortical right hemispheric, quick stress-survival responses necessary for therapeutic outcomes (Schore, 2003). There is evidence that children receiving art therapy show reduction in acute stress symptoms and that art therapy improves quality of life by emphasizing the mind-body connection (State of the Field Committee, 2009). Through relational verbal experiences and concretized art making, memory, emotion, and cognition are called into bodily action.

Art therapy can be divided into two different forms: art as therapy and art psychotherapy. Art as therapy is the process of creating an object as healing in itself. Rubin (2001) confirms this: "art as therapy... [is seen] as healing through the process" (p. 68); or, as Malchiodi (2007) explains, art as a therapy is "a belief in the inherent healing power of the creative process of making art" (p. 6). Art psychotherapy is more of a triad between client, therapist, and art object. Malchiodi (2007) mentions how "the art image becomes significant in enhancing verbal exchange between the person and the therapist and in achieving insight" (p. 6). Art psychotherapy uses art partly to gain insight and as an analytical tool.

Trauma-focused art therapy (TF-ART) has been shown to reduce symptoms of PTSD in adolescents in an inpatient psychiatric facility.

When compared to a group of adolescents who participated in a standard arts-and-crafts activity protocol, the youth who received the TF-ART group sessions had a greater reduction in PTSD symptoms as measured by a widely used trauma reaction index (Chapman, 2014).

Art therapy can provide distraction and relief from stress and trauma, update memory systems, mediate a compromised immune system, promote positive interpersonal relationships, and facilitate coherent autobiographical narratives. These narratives can be used to inform additional forms of psychosocial therapies, thus leading to an overall improvement in health and well-being (Chapman 2014; Malchiodi, 2008).

## Relation between Expressive Arts and Neurobiology

The brain's right hemisphere is concerned with creativity, art, and imagination. Latto (1995) suggests that art stems from a physiological source rather than an emotional or experiential one. Suspension happens each time the client makes a decision to move from verbal language to visual, sensory language, for example, brush to paint, paint to image.

Expressive arts activate dual processing of the left and right hemispheres of the brain. Observing one's intention and action through the creative process promotes self-perception. Art serves as a means of suspension creating a mirror via the art product so that a person can view the results of their thoughts.

During art therapy, the left hemisphere offers an explanation to the right hemispheric output in the form of a created image. The right hemisphere deals with visual motor activities, intuition, emotions, body, sensory, automatic skills, and the procedures involved in what we call creativity (Bogousslavsky & Boller, 2005). It is directly linked to the subcortical regions of the brain, such as the brain stem. It is the non-verbal, creative aspect that is evoked when clients are asked to draw in an art therapy session.

Children under age three process experiences using the right hemisphere of their brains (Schore, 2001a). Drawing is an activity that also uses right brain activity. Art therapy may activate neurological structures of the brain enabling non-verbal early experiences to become known. Damage to the right hemisphere can be caused by trauma that in turn could be healed, at least in part, using art therapy (O'Brien, 2004). Schore says that traumatic and stressful memories are stored in the right hemisphere of the brain which processes emotions and visual and non-conscious information. Thus, for therapy to be effective it must get into the right brain. Creating art is a fast way to access the right brain and its stored emotions.

Art therapy is a visual-expressive approach in which non-verbal expressions are made easier by creating simple forms, colours, or cut-outs. The approach can provide clients with sensory integrated experiences that facilitate change and safely counterbalance traumatic environmental influences. Verbal discussion of clients' art can further help enlist explicit memory and consolidate verbal autobiographies by bringing the left hemisphere and the hippocampus into play (Siegel, 1999). While making art activates the right brain, talking about it and constructing a coherent story about the traumatic experience activates the left hemisphere as well. Integrating the two leads to healing by expanding the interconnectivity of the brain (Schore, 2003).

Trauma is often kept in one's memory as sensations, symbols, and mental images that can be difficult to access in traditional talk therapy or informal conversation since they may not be part of a person's conscious awareness. Art therapy helps children uncover and manage experiences that are too difficult or painful to assimilate.

## Promising Practices of Art Therapy

This section outlines and discusses ten important reasons why art therapy works.

### 1. Provides an Outlet for Expressing and Processing

Art is a way to express oneself. Art therapy is often an opposition of seeing and saying. The goal of these modalities is to help bring forth emotions and feelings that have been forgotten (Klorer, 2005) or that may be too painful to speak about. In other words, art therapy helps make visible that which cannot be spoken. Art therapists encourage clients to create a tangible, sensory, and visible art expression (Linnell, 2010). The art therapist then provides specific feedback in the form of art therapy directives and interpretation (Hass-Cohen, 2003, 2006).

Expressing oneself (particularly ideas or emotions that may be difficult to express with words) through art can be a safe and very therapeutic method for healing. It is a way to "release" energy related to trauma that may have been repressed for years. Humans often feel the need to tell their story, to "vent" and be heard, upon experiencing something traumatic. Simply having an audience (e.g. a therapist or caregiver) and feeling heard or cared for can go a long way to healing traumatic wounds.

Furthermore, making art can help process difficult feelings. For some urban and displaced Australian Aboriginals, making art creates a space where competing discourses can be worked through and re-considered (Gibson, 2011). These discourses concern the physical and psychological effects of being forcibly removed from their ancestral lands either by displacement or incarceration (Dudgeon, Garvey, & Pickett, 2000).

One reason art works well with Aboriginal Australians is because the entre process of creation is seen as the work of art. Thus, the end product is a ritual giving expression to an actualisation of the way of life (Dudgeon, Garvey, & Pickett, 2000).

### 2. Alters Physiology

Expressive arts heal by altering a person's physiology. When children engage in expressive arts, it alerts the parasympathetic system in their brains (Lane, 2005). Their breathing slows, blood pressure lowers, and they become more relaxed. This helps reduce the fight-or-flight response associated with stress. Creative expression modifies one's biochemistry and improves physical well-being. When children participate in the arts, it actually changes their bodies.

The creative process causes specific areas of the brain to release endorphins and other neurotransmitters that affect brain cells and the immune system by relieving pain and triggering the immune system to function more efficiently. Endorphins are like opiates, creating an experience of expansion, connection, and relaxation. In conjunction with these physiologic changes, art can regularly change people's attitudes, emotional states, and perception of pain (Lane, 2005).

Engaging in the creative process, making decisions, and letting the image emerge with the client activate the mind and body. Neurophysiologists demonstrate that art, meditation, and healing stem from the same source in the body and are associated with similar brainwave patterns and mind-body changes (Lane, 2005). Art therapists encourage simple but novel art activities that are experienced by the amygdala as interpersonally safe and this helps generate coping responses (Lane, 2005).

### 3. Promotes a Common Language

Confirming my belief that art can be the common language for communication if other ways of communications have failed, Cameron (2010) explains that "art not only provides acknowledgment to cultural inclusion, it is a valuable tool for communicating with people from various linguistic, social and educational backgrounds" (p. 407). Joseph (2006) adds, "art therapists should look beyond their roots in classical analysis to understand these differences" (p. 32). Successful art therapy can serve to integrate right- and left-brain functions that, in turn, help integrate experiences on a non-verbal level (Talwar, 2007).

## 4. Utilises Repetition

To counteract the effects of trauma on infants, Aboriginal and Maori healers use traditional healing techniques involving rhythmic drumming, singing, dancing, and touch (Perry, 1997). Atkinson (2013) says that it is the patterned, repetitive stimuli created by these Indigenous-healing rituals that beneficially modify neural systems affected by trauma. Severely traumatised children require interventions that address both low and high brain functions affected by trauma. The use of art helps rebuild the emotional brain as it forms new connections between the prefrontal cortex and other parts of the emotional systems (Perry, 1997).

## 5. Fosters Relationships

Perry emphasises the power of relational health to promote healing and recovery and the need to incorporate social connections into therapeutic work. He reports that "healthy relational interactions with safe and familiar individuals can buffer and heal trauma-related problems" (Perry, 2009, p. 248). Given the relational aspect of Indigenous healing rituals, this finding also points to the capacity of traditional practices to promote healing and recovery.

Many psychologists have found the most important determinant in recovering from trauma is the presence of loving and attentive people (e.g. Werner, 2004), including family and community members, teachers, therapists, elders, and neighbours. This support network provides a relational milieu that has a positive neurological influence on the brain. These relational implications – smile, touch, tone of voice, presence, and literally seeing these people – calm the stress response situation and allow for healing (Perry, 1997).

The therapist-child relationship is also important to healing because it serves as a safe and positive relationship for the child. It creates a safe space for the child to explore his or her emotions. It helps the child build social and relationship skills outside of therapy. It may also help rebuild trust in others, since experiencing trauma at the hands of another person can decrease trust in other people.

The art therapy process is also beneficial because it promotes a positive relationship between the therapist and the child. The child is able to explore his or her personal world through art in a safe environment, thus allowing the therapist to gain insight into the inner dimensions of the child's world. This positive, therapeutic relationship provides growth and healing for the child. Because the experience of trauma leaves one feeling disempowered and disconnected from others, recovery needs to foster the empowerment of the survivor and the creation of new connections and relationships (Herman, 1992).

## 6. Creates a Safe Space

Experiencing trauma can lead to feelings of deep anger or rage. For Aboriginal people growing up in environments where there are multiple violations, this anger likely lacks a safe outlet and is, therefore, stored in the body for expression under duress. This invariably occurs in unstructured and explosive violence (often towards people known by the perpetrator), aided by alcohol.

Art therapy within a therapeutic relationship can create the safe space for anger and rage to be healthfully expressed. During art making, children may open up and express emotions about their traumatic experiences. Positive outcomes through therapeutic setting depend on a secure environment for the child to work through the traumatic event, as children often lose their sense of safety, security, and control, and may feel scared of the world following a traumatic event. Understanding the trauma helps the therapist implement the right therapeutic process (Ogawa, 2004). Often disturbed children need initially to release their repressed feelings regarding the traumatic experience in a cathartic and often formless fashion. Art therapy facilitates this release.

Art therapy provides the opportunity to experience and actively deal with problems or feelings, bringing them to the surface and out in the open, facing them, and either learning to control them or abandon them. A major function of art therapy is the changing of what may be unmanageable in everyday reality to manageable situations. In his research on child trauma, Perry (2009) found that activities like art provide the patterned and repetitive neural input to alter the lower stress-response networks of the brain and help children better cope with the symptoms related to their trauma.

## 7. Fosters Awareness

Art therapy helps children to develop awareness of themselves in context and connection to the outside world; they gain understanding of self and connection with others, the environment and even the spiritual aspect of connection with the divine – so intrinsic to the Indigenous culture (Coholic, Lougheed, & Cadell, 2009). The arts engage the senses in a way that transcends the ordinary and mundane aspects of life. As children connect to their paintings, they become more aware of their thoughts, emotions, and core beliefs. This assists in self-discovery and self-understanding and helps them find meaning (Malchiodi, 2008).

## 8. Promotes Sublimation

Art therapy has long been known as an access to the unconscious; a form of symbolic speech. It, therefore, becomes an excellent tool for both diagnosis and therapy as it gives access to unconscious symbolic content. Art, like dreams, evolves spontaneously and can be understood by free association (Rubin, 2005). Some pioneers of art therapy see it as a means of sublimation

– helping the ego to process conflicting feelings and impulses through the creative process (see Rubin, 2005).

## 9. Engages Limit-Setting

The structure of the therapist-child relationship simulates a real-life relationship. Boundaries provide predictability. Children are not allowed to do anything they want to do; yet it is also not overly restrictive. Messiness is accepted, exploration encouraged, and patience is a guiding principle (Bratton & Ferebee, 1999). These limits have both helpful and practical benefits in that they preserve and promote the patient-therapist relationship, foster responsibility and self-control, and provide a sense of comfort and emotional security. The expressive arts allow for a channelled, controlled "letting go" (Rubin, 2001).

## 10. Minimising Verbal Approaches

Communication during art therapy is multi-layered and complex. Because verbal recollection of the trauma is often difficult or beyond a child's capacity, approaches that do not rely heavily on verbal access to trauma material are important. In trauma treatment it is not the verbal account of the event that is important but the non-verbal memory of the fragmented sensory and emotional elements of the traumatic experience (van der Kolk, 2003).

## Other Factors Influencing the Healing Process

### The Child's Age

The age of the child and the type of trauma experienced will likely impact the therapeutic and healing process. Children and adolescents respond differently to trauma-inducing stressors when compared to adults, particularly in how their behaviour reflects their re-experiencing of the trauma, avoidance of trauma-producing situations, and their symptoms in metaphoric modalities, such as play, drawing, story-telling, and in regard to separation anxiety.

A child's age and stage of development greatly influences how an educational, care-giving, or therapeutic experience will influence the brain (Perry, 2009). Because of the way the brain develops, from the bottom up and from the inside out, different areas of the brain are impacted during trauma depending on the age of the child. The younger a child is during the trauma, the more necessary it is to stimulate specific neuropathways that promote healthy brain development (Perry, 2009).

## Larger Social Network/Environment

Other approaches emerge in the available literature as potential strategies for supporting victims and survivors of trauma. These are an ecological approach to the identification and treatment of trauma, physical activity to promote recovery, and therapeutic residential care. An ecological approach involves taking into consideration the interaction within and between various systems in a child's life in order to identify trauma risk factors. It requires practitioners and service providers to keep a broad rather than narrow view of issues and to recognise that the trauma experienced by children may be the result of a combination of factors related to the child, their parents and carers, and their environment. Therefore, their trauma-specific care needs to seek to tackle issues or problems in all the systems that are negatively affecting the child's situation (Phenice & Griffore, 2003). For example, a child could be experiencing benefits from art therapy; however, if he or she is still living in a stressful or traumatic home situation, where perhaps even the caregivers themselves are suffering from trauma, then more intervention would be needed.

## IMPLEMENTING ART THERAPY IN PRACTICE

Unfortunately, research with Indigenous people in Australia has been met with suspicion. There are perceptions among Indigenous groups that research has neither respected nor benefited Indigenous culture and practices, and as a result, Indigenous people have been rather reticent to participate in research or interventions (Knight, Comino, Harris, & Jackson-Pulver, 2009).

If Aboriginal people are to be adequately supported in their healing journey, four primary principles must be observed. First, a primary focus must be on addressing the causes of community dysfunction, not merely its symptoms. Second, Aboriginal ownership, definition, design, and evaluation of the healing initiative must be incorporated. Third, programme design must be based on Aboriginal worldviews, not Western health understandings alone. Finally, initiatives that utilize positive, strength-based approaches must be strengthened and supported (Healing Foundation, 2013).

When the culture of the tribe (e.g. spirituality, customs, traditions) is incorporated, parent training programmes, including art therapy initiatives, have the most effective outcomes. Principles from modern child development alone are not sufficient (Secretariat of National Aboriginal and Islander Child Care, 2012).

## Include Caregivers, Family, and Community in Healing

As Perry explains, healing rituals provide an intensely relational experience(s) with family and clan participating in the ritual that includes: retelling the story, holding each other, massaging, dancing, singing, creating images of the trauma, sculpture, and drama, reconnecting to loved ones and to community, celebrating, eating, and sharing

(Perry, 2009). This overlap suggests a convergence between modern concepts of neurodevelopment and the traditional healing practices of Indigenous people. However, further research is needed to understand whether and how Indigenous healing rituals support healing and recovery and what factors facilitate or impede the use of such rituals for Indigenous families and communities.

## Foster Open Communication

The single most difficult challenge facing a service provider working with a remote Indigenous community is establishing a space that encourages and supports open communication. It is more difficult when the service provider is not known by community members and/or is unfamiliar with the complex relationships that exist in the community. This problem is further compounded if the visiting service provider is non-Indigenous.

Developing a new relationship between groups, when there has been a history of mistrust or unmet expectations, can be made easier if people are honest and consider one another's viewpoints. Trust develops as a function of the degree of consistency in the nature of interactions (honesty, openness, and dependability), the depth of familiarity between the groups, and time.

Achieving and supporting positive change in Indigenous communities may proceed at a more leisurely pace than in other communities and necessitates a long-term commitment from service providers. Unfortunately, there has been a history of prematurely terminated programmes and failed expectations because of a lack of long-term commitment. An essential component of a successful community programme is having local people support and be active participants in the programme's process.

Service providers should make themselves available to community members upon entering a community, and have informal discussions about the intentions of the visit. It is vital that the service provider is open and honest in these early interactions and also listens to the community members. It is often not the first time a service is being offered and the community may already have witnessed the success or failure of programmes, thus making them a rich resource of information. Being open to the suggestions of community members not only makes this information accessible but also strengthens relationships and builds trust (Atkinson et al., 2010).

## Include Aboriginal Australians in Programme Design and Implementation

Two of my strongest recommendations are to include Aboriginals in the design of art therapy programmes and to consider how to best include or take into account the needs of the carers of children who have experienced trauma. Who better to provide input into healing than the people who have lived the trauma? Rather than take for granted that we are "speaking the same language", this could help ensure we are.

There is increasing evidence indicating that the application of ancient Indigenous wisdom is the most successful factor in facilitating healing and recovery (van der Kolk, 2005). It is critical that communities have responsibility and control for the design, development, and delivery of their own healing.

## Include Carers as Part of Children's Therapy

A young child is highly dependent on the parent for regulation of her emotions. This is especially relevant for children of transgenerational trauma. For example, today Aboriginal children are more likely to be cared for by mothers who are anxious and stressed as the result of transgenerational trauma. Lacking support from the traditional ways of life (e.g. as part of a network of social support providing other caregivers for her children), both she and her children suffer the negative consequences.

## Demonstrate Sensitivity towards Clients and Aboriginal Facilitators

Writers of decolonisation, such as Smith (1999), state that the process of change can instigate violence in a person's mind because they are being asked to change the way they think and that can be difficult because it involves re-evaluating the relationships upon which their reality is based.

Simultaneously, if the facilitators of art therapy are Aboriginal and traumatised themselves, it may double this "violence" in their minds and be a painful setting in which to work. Therapists stepping in to help these facilitators, the families, and the children need to confront and be aware of issues of control and power, as these are central to debate about art therapy and psychotherapy procedures. In making decisions about issues of power and control, the art therapist in assessing what is normal and abnormal behaviour interprets their client's demeanour continuously to guide directions to practice (Hogan, 2001).

The clients' traumatised children often come from vulnerable families. Many of the caregivers of these children have themselves experienced trauma in early childhood and often have not been in therapy or experienced healing. This would mean that much of what they see and feel in the children they work with would also affect them vicariously and possibly trigger a secondary traumatisation process. Therefore, it is important to understand trauma and its impact on individuals, families, and communities, and to approach the therapy process from a more holistic perspective that includes healing at these various levels.

## Respect and Incorporate Culture

Trauma-specific care needs to focus on developing understanding of, and appropriate responses to, the complex psychobiological and social reactions to trauma and less on recounting and categorising the trauma events (van der Kolk, 2008). There is no single way to provide trauma-specific care. Instead, practitioners and service providers, through consultation and feedback with trauma experts and clients, need to identify the strategies and practices best suited to the needs and circumstances (including geographic location and culture) of the individuals, families, and communities they seek to support. That said, care should be taken when determining what an "appropriate response" is when working with populations whose culture is different from one's own. The same care applies when trying to analyse or interpret the artwork.

## Foster Empowerment in Art Therapy Programmes

The core experiences of psychological trauma are disempowerment and disconnection from others. Recovery, therefore, is based upon the empowerment of the survivor and the creation of new connections (Herman, 1992). Recovery can take place only within the context of relationships; it cannot occur in isolation. In renewed connection with other people, the survivor re-creates the psychological facilities that were damaged or deformed by the traumatic experience (Herman, 1992). This represents the therapeutic safe space in which the relationship can grow. It entails the therapist remaining mindful of the past historical traumas and abuses that their clients have experienced cumulatively over time.

## Restore Cultural Identity and Pride

Critical to healing programmes is an emphasis on restoring, reaffirming, and renewing a sense of pride in cultural identity, connection to country, and participation in community. Cultural identity and connection to country are seen as crucial elements of everyday life for Indigenous people. Cultivating a sense of this cultural distinctiveness is inextricably linked with spiritual, emotional, social health, and well-being, and is also an important part of strengthening communities.

## Develop Reflective Listening

Due to the cultural challenges above, it may be beneficial if the therapist takes a more minimal stance. In other words, the therapist can provide a space where the person from the "other side" may come forward and share their story. This would promote a reflective, curious, respectful space that can create a bridge, rather than coming from a more directive (and less connected) space.

## CASE STUDY: ART THERAPY IN PRACTICE

Part of the challenge I faced with creating effective programmes for these preschools and families was the immense emotional need and deprivation the children displayed, together with a lack of basic care.

The key to the success of the programmes that were developed to address the widespread, devastating effects of transgenerational trauma necessitated the collaboration, input, and feedback of the centre staff, and parents or carers, who themselves were living with the effects of trauma. I placed great emphasis on developing these cooperative relationships, which in the process served as healing for the staff themselves. I found the use of art immensely useful in assisting people who were being asked to deal with the trauma of the children in their care to deal with and address their own trauma. Simultaneously, I gained invaluable understanding of their culture, which is very aligned with art and non-verbal communication. For example, before implementing programmes in preschools, I spent a few months prior to the training speaking with directors from the preschools asking what they would want in the programme. What were their school's needs? Would they help me facilitate aspects that they felt positive and comfortable about? The training was a great success as the directors felt ownership of the programme's design and implementation.

I am very fortunate to have created a few precious relationships with Aboriginal people who have made themselves available to support and help me and spend time chatting with me, helping me to understand better my working framework. I have formal discussions with them and informal ones where I can often ask questions or just listen as I am truly learning a new language.

Aboriginal culture is collective; so different from the individualistic nature of white Australian culture. If a child is referred through an agency, I always contact the caregivers and meet with them a few times before seeing the child to create a relationship, to see who is involved with the family, and who is meaningful in the child's life. In preschools we focus on including the families, learning about the communities we work with.

At the back of my mind, I am very aware that I am white, that I am a social worker, and that trust is a huge issue given decades of imperialistic abuse. The families don't know me as an individual but rather have had negative past experiences with someone in the care profession. I always name that. I am aware that trust takes time to develop and will be tested.

Even when invited by a preschool or the Department of Child Services to work with a child, I always include parents and often wider family in the therapy. I have discussions with them before and during the therapy. I introduce myself as a person and as a professional and make a conscious effort to proceed without clichéd presuppositions. Instead, I create a safe space to learn about them as individuals, their influences, way of being, and most importantly their needs. This creates a liminal space (Myerhoff, 1982) that invites the other to enter and in which we sit together in somewhat of a fog until things start to become clear.

With preschools, I also come in as a complete guest, listening actively to learn about their school, the staff, and their families. I listen to their needs and know that it will take time, many conversations, and visits. By listening and asking, a space is created for educators to talk about the link they are forming with the families they work with. The importance of relationships is highlighted. As one Aboriginal director said to me: "I am now standing at the door of the preschool, individually greeting, by name, everyone that enters. That includes the children and whoever brings them" (Ursula Kim, personal communication, June 2012). What a wonderful way to foster relationship, trust and respect – the fundamental values of Aboriginal culture. Sometimes as part of the work, parents who previously would never have entered the school walk in and greet the staff.

From my experiential and theoretical background, combined with staff collaboration or family input, the programmes were to be utilised with the children to help the children celebrate the experience of childhood, play, and imagination, and to meet the challenge of complex phases in their lives. The end result is that the teachers gain an understanding not only of the children and their families but often also of themselves and how their history impacts the way they work. The art therapy used has not only provided a means of expression and, therefore, healing but has also rekindled pride in a culture heavily based on symbology and creativity which, of course, has added its own salve to the healing process.

My goal is not to educate or change primarily but to support and give a chance to express what is going on for the child. Understanding trauma means daring to work with it. Three centres reported supporting staff to go and talk to the parents no one ever talked to. In mixed preschools a real effort to talk with Aboriginal mothers and include a cup of tea was made. One director reported, "It means more work because they trust me now and so they come and talk over difficulties with me!" (Carolyn Leys, personal communication, June 2012).

The programmes have been implemented in 43 Aboriginal childcare centres around rural New South Wales and in the eastern and western suburbs of Sydney. Again and again, what I have witnessed is children and staff finding a means of naming the un-nameable, understanding their trauma, and seeing a new possibility for existence.

## FUTURE RESEARCH DIRECTIONS

### Art Therapy in Early Childhood

There is much evidence supporting the effectiveness of art therapy with older children and adults but there is very little evidence of its use with preschool children (Meyerowitz-katz, 2003). An unpublished research report exploring art therapy with preschool children in the UK revealed that although very few art therapists were working with this age group those who were considered art therapy to be a valuable intervention whose basic principles could be adapted to suit the needs of this group (Meyerowitz-katz, 2003).

### Multimodal Treatment Interventions

Phan, Wager, Taylor, and Liberzon's (2002) research demonstrates the importance of administering higher order (cognitive) interventions during presentation of emotionally charged or traumatic memory activation. It is suggested that multimodal treatment interventions (those which activate multiple brain regions simultaneously) may have benefits in changing the way an individual processes emotional material.

In addition, other neuroimaging studies show that some cognitive-based treatments increase hippocampal functioning for people with major depression (Goldapple et al., 2004). These encouraging results suggest that psychosocial interventions have the capability to affect brain structures and influence their functioning, as well as provide support for the use of brain imaging technology to examine these neurobiological outcomes. The use of neuroscience in both the theoretical development and outcomes measurement of psychosocial interventions is one area where the social work profession can work with other disciplines to advance practice-based research.

## Resiliency and Protective Factors of Trauma

In the face of extreme adversity, the strength and resilience of the Australian Aboriginal culture is to be applauded. This strength comes from solid systems of family and community together with connection to traditional spirituality and the land. Unfortunately, the effects of unresolved transgenerational trauma contribute to many ongoing challenges. Research into protective factors will benefit future healing strategies (Healing Foundation, 2013). Along the same lines, further research is needed to understand whether and how Indigenous healing rituals support healing and recovery and what factors facilitate or impede the use of such rituals for Indigenous families and communities.

## CONCLUSION

While art therapy clearly has a therapeutic role in healing trauma, more research is needed on how to heal transgenerational trauma with Aboriginal Australians, including the identification of risk and protective factors. A key consideration is how to effectively include Aboriginals in the art therapy design process as well as in facilitating art therapy programmes, while being sensitive to how the experience affects them as those who have also experienced trauma. Another important consideration is how to address transgenerational trauma at various levels: individual, familial, and communal. We must find creative ways to move forward and facilitate healing at not only the individual level but also in the larger context in which the individual lives.

## REFERENCES

Appleyard, K., & Osofsky, J. D. (2003). Parenting after trauma: Supporting parents and caregivers in the treatment of children impacted by violence. *Infant Mental Health Journal*, 24(2), 111–125. doi:10.1002/imhj.10050

Armsworth, M. W., & Holaday, M. (1993). The effects of psychological trauma on children and adolescents. *Journal of Counseling and Development*, 72(1), 49–56. doi:10.1002/j.1556-6676.1993.tb02276.x

Atkinson, J. (2002). *Trauma trails, recreating song lines: The transgenerational effects of trauma in Indigenous Australia*. North Melbourne: Spinifex Press.

Atkinson, J. (2013). *Trauma-informed services and trauma-specific care for Indigenous Australian children* (Resource sheet no. 21). Retrieved from Australian Institute of Health and Welfare website: http://www.aihw.gov.au/uploadedFiles/ClosingTheGap/Content/Publications/2013/ctg-rs21.pdf

Atkinson, J., Nelson, J., & Atkinson, C. (2010). Trauma, transgenerational transfer and effects on community wellbeing. In N. Purdie, P. Dudgeon, & R. Walker (Eds.), *Working together: Aboriginal and Torres Strait Islander mental health and wellbeing principles and practice* (pp. 135–144). Canberra: Australian Institute of Health and Welfare.

Atkinson, S., & Swain, S. (1999). A network of support: Mothering across the Koorie community in Victoria, Australia. *Women's History Review*, 8(2), 219–230. doi:10.1080/09612029900200208

Australian Institute of Health and Welfare. (2011). *The health and welfare of Australia's Aboriginal and Torres Strait Islander people: An overview*. Retrieved from http://www.aihw.gov.au/WorkArea/DownloadAsset.aspx?id=10737418955

Bogousslavsky, J., & Boller, F. (Eds.). (2005). *Neurological disorders in famous artists: Part 3* (Frontiers of Neurology and Neuroscience, Vol. 19). Basel, Switzerland: Karger.

Bowlby, J. (1979). *The making and breaking of affectional bonds.* London: Tavistock/Routledge.

Bratton, S. C., & Ferebee, K. W. (1999). The use of structured expressive art activities in group activity therapy with preadolescents. In D. S. Sweeny & L. E. Homeyer (Eds.), *The handbook of group play therapy: How to do it, how it works, whom it's best for* (pp. 192–214). San Francisco: Jossey-Bass.

Cameron, L. (2010). Using the arts as a therapeutic tool for counselling: An Australian Aboriginal perspective. *Procedia: Social and Behavioral Sciences, 5,* 403–407. doi:10.1016/j.sbspro.2010.07.112

Chapman, L. (2014). *Neurobiologically informed trauma therapy with children and adolescents: Understanding mechanisms of change.* New York: Norton.

Coholic, D., Lougheed, S., & Cadell, S. (2009). Exploring the helpfulness of arts-based methods with children living in foster care. *Traumatology, 15*(3), 64–71. doi:10.1177/1534765609341590

Collie, K., Backos, A., Malchiodi, C., & Spiegel, D. (2006). Art therapy for combat-related PTSD: Recommendations for research and practice. *Art Therapy: Journal of the American Art Therapy Association, 23*(4), 157–164. doi:10.1080/07421656.2006.10129335

Colomina, M. T., Albina, M. L., Domingo, J. L., & Corbella, J. (1997). Influence of maternal stress on the effects of prenatal exposure to methylmercury and arsenic on postnatal development and behavior in mice: A preliminary evaluation. *Physiology & Behavior, 61*(3), 455–459. doi:10.1016/S0031-9384(96)00462-3 PMID:9089766

Dissanayake, E. (1992). *Homo aestheticus: Where art comes from and why.* New York: Free Press.

Dudgeon, P., Garvey, D., & Pickett, H. (Eds.). (2000). *Working with Indigenous Australians: A handbook for psychologists.* Perth, WA: Gunada Press.

Felitti, V. J., Anda, R. F., Nordenberg, D., Williamson, D. F., Spitz, A. M., & Edwards, V.,… Marks, J.S. (1998). Relationship of childhood abuse and household dysfunction to many of the leading causes of death in adults: The adverse childhood experiences (ACE) study. *American Journal of Preventive Medicine, 14*(4), 245–258. doi:10.1016/S0749-3797(98)00017-8 PMID:9635069

Gerhardt, S. (2004). *Why love matters: How affection shapes a baby's brain.* Hove, East Sussex: Brunner/Routledge.

Gibson, L. (2011). Politics, pain and pleasure: The art of art-making for "settled" Aboriginal Australians. *Coolibah, 5,* 119–129.

Gil, E. (2006). *Helping abused and traumatized children: Integrating directive and nondirective approaches.* New York: Guilford.

Goldapple, K., Segal, Z., Garson, C., Lau, M., Bieling, P., Kennedy, S., & Mayberg, H. (2004). Modulation of cortical-limbic pathways in major depression: Treatment-specific effects of cognitive behaviour therapy. *Archives of General Psychiatry*, *61*(1), 34–41. doi:10.1001/archpsyc.61.1.34 PMID:14706942

Gunnar, M. R., & Donzella, B. (2002). Social regulation of the cortisol levels in early human development. *Psychoneuroendocrinology*, *27*(1-2), 199–220. doi:10.1016/S0306-4530(01)00045-2 PMID:11750779

Gunnar, M. R., & Nelson, C. A. (1994). Event-related potentials in year-old infants: Relations with emotionality and cortisol. *Child Development*, *65*(1), 80–94. doi:10.2307/1131367 PMID:8131656

Hass-Cohen, N. (2003). Art therapy mind body approaches: Some applications of relational neuroscience to art therapy. *Progress: Family Systems Research and Therapy*, *12*, 24–38.

Hass-Cohen, N. (2006). Art therapy and clinical neuroscience in action. Retrieved from http://www.laiat.com/atcanaction.htm

Healing Foundation. (2013). *Annual Report 2012-2013*. Retrieved from http://healingfoundation.org.au/wordpress/wp-content/files_mf/1388977931HealingFoundationAnnualReport20122013.pdf

Herman, J. L. (1992). *Trauma and recovery*. New York: Basic Books.

Hogan, S. (2001). *Healing arts: The history of art therapy*. London: Jessica Kingsley.

Joseph, C. (2006). Creative alliance: The healing power of art therapy. *Art Therapy: Journal of the American Art Therapy Association*, *23*(1), 30–33. doi:10.1080/07421656.2006.10129531

Kaufman, J., & Zigler, E. (1993). The intergenerational transmission of violence is overstated. In R. J. Gelles & D. R. Loseke (Eds.), *Current controversies on family violence* (pp. 167–196). Newbury Park, CA: Sage.

Klorer, P. G. (2005). Expressive therapy with severely maltreated children: Neuroscience contributions. *Art Therapy: Journal of the American Art Therapy Association*, *22*(4), 213–220. doi:10.1080/07421656.2005.10129523

Knight, J. A., Comino, E. J., Harris, E., & Jackson-Pulver, L. (2009). Indigenous research: A commitment to walking the talk – the Gudaga study – an Australian case study. *Bioethical Inquiry*, *6*(4), 467–476. doi:10.1007/s11673-009-9186-x

Lane, M. R. (2005). Creativity and spirituality in nursing: Implementing art in healing. *Holistic Nursing Practice*, *19*(3), 122–125. doi:10.1097/00004650-200505000-00008 PMID:15923938

Latto, R. (1995). The brain of the beholder. In R. L. Gregory, J. Harris, P. Heard, & D. Rose (Eds.), *The artful eye* (pp. 66–94). Oxford: Oxford University Press.

Levine, S. (2001). Primary social relationships influence the development of the hypothalamic–pituitary–adrenal axis in the rat. *Physiology & Behavior*, *73*(3), 255–260. doi:10.1016/S0031-9384(01)00496-6 PMID:11438350

Linnell, S. (2010). *Art psychotherapy & narrative therapy: An account of practitioner research*. Oak Park, IL: Benthan Science Publishers.

Lyshak-Stelzer, F., Singer, P., St. John, P., & Chemtob, C. M. (2007). Art therapy for adolescents with posttraumatic stress disorder symptoms: A pilot study. *Art Therapy: Journal of the American Art Therapy Association*, *24*(4), 163–169. doi:10.1080/07421656.2007.10129474

Malchiodi, C. A. (2007). *The art therapy sourcebook*. New York: McGraw-Hill.

Malchiodi, C. A. (2008). *Creative interventions with traumatized children*. New York: Guilford Press.

Meyerowitz-katz, J. (2003). Art materials and process: A place of meeting art psychotherapy with a four-year-old boy. *Inscape, 8*(2), 60–69. doi:10.1080/17454830308414055

Mollon, P. (1993). *The fragile self: The structure of narcissistic disturbance*. London: Whurr.

Mu'id, O. (2004). *"...Then I lost my spirit": An analytical essay on transgenerational trauma theory as applied to oppressed people of color nations* (Master's thesis). Retrieved from ProQuest Dissertations and Theses database. (UMI No. 1436180)

Myerhoff, B. (1982). *Number our days: Triumph of continuity and culture among Jewish old people in an urban ghetto*. New York: Simon and Schuster/Touchstone Books.

O'Brien, F. (2004). The making of mess in art therapy: Attachment, trauma and the brain. *International Journal of Art Therapy, 9*, 2–13. doi:10.1080/02647140408405670

Ogawa, Y. (2004). Childhood trauma and play therapy intervention for traumatized children. *Journal of Professional Counseling, 32*, 19–29. Retrieved from http://www.txca.org/tca/TCA_Publications.asp?SnID=2

Pally, R., & Olds, D. (2000). *The mind-brain relationship*. London: Karnac.

Pennebaker, J. W. (1993). Putting stress into words: Health, linguistic and therapeutic implications. *Behaviour Research and Therapy, 31*(6), 539–548. doi:10.1016/0005-7967(93)90105-4 PMID:8347112

Perry, B. (1997). Incubated in terror: Neurodevelopmental factors in the "cycle of violence.". In J. Osofsky (Ed.), *Children in a violent society* (pp. 124–149). New York: Guilford.

Perry, B. D. (2001). The neurodevelopmental impact of violence in childhood. In D. Schetky & E. P. Benedek (Eds.), *Textbook of child and adolescent forensic psychiatry* (pp. 221–238). Washington, DC: American Psychiatric Press.

Perry, B. D. (2009). Examining child maltreatment through a neurodevelopmental lens: Clinical applications of the neurosequential model of therapeutics. *Journal of Loss and Trauma, 14*(4), 240–255. doi:10.1080/15325020903004350

Phan, K. L., Wager, T., Taylor, S. F., & Liberzon, I. (2002). Functional neuroanatomy of emotion: A meta-analysis of emotion activation studies in PET and fMRI. University of Michigan. *NeuroImage, 16*(2), 331–348. doi:10.1006/nimg.2002.1087 PMID:12030820

Phenice, L. A., & Griffore, R. J. (2003). Young children and the natural world. *Contemporary Issues in Early Childhood, 4*(2), 167–178. doi:10.2304/ciec.2003.4.2.6

Pynoos, R. S., Ritzmann, R. F., Steinberg, A. M., Goenjian, A., & Prisecaru, I. (1996). A behavioral animal model of posttraumatic stress disorder featuring repeated exposure to situational reminders. *Biological Psychiatry, 39*, 129-134. doi:10.1016/0006-3223(95)00088-7

Rubin, J. A. (2001). *Approaches to art therapy: Theory and technique*. New York: Routledge.

Rubin, J. A. (2005). *Child art therapy: 25th anniversary edition*. Hoboken, N.J.: John Wiley.

Ryan, F. (2011). Kanyininpa (holding): A way of nurturing children in Aboriginal Australia. *Australian Social Work, 64*(2), 183–197. doi:10.1080/0312407X.2011.581300

Schore, A. N. (1994). *Affect regulation and the origin of the self: The neurobiology of emotional development.* Hillsdale, NJ: Lawrence Erlbaum.

Schore, A. N. (2001a). The effects of a secure attachment relationship on right brain development, affect regulation, and infant mental health. *Infant Mental Health Journal, 22*(1-2), 7–66. doi:10.1002/1097-0355(200101/04)22:1<7::AID-IMHJ2>3.0.CO;2-N

Schore, A. N. (2001b). The effects of relational trauma on right brain development, affect regulation, and infant mental health. *Infant Mental Health Journal, 22*(1-2), 201–269. doi:10.1002/1097-0355(200101/04)22:1<201::AID-IMHJ8>3.0.CO;2-9

Schore, A. N. (2003). *Affect dysregulation and disorders of the self.* New York: Norton.

Schulkin, J., & Rosen, J. (1998). From normal fear to pathological anxiety. In D. M. Hann (Ed.), *Advancing research on developmental plasticity: Integrating the behavioral science and neuroscience of mental health* (pp. 325–350). Washington, DC: National Institutes of Health.

Secretariat of National Aboriginal and Islander Child Care. (2012). *Inquiry into the stronger futures in the Northern Territory bill.* Retrieved from http://www.snaicc.org.au/_uploads/rsfil/02785.pdf

Siegel, D. J. (1999). *The developing mind: Toward a neurobiology of interpersonal experience.* New York, NY: Guilford Press.

Smith, L. T. (1999). *Decolonising methodologies: Research and Indigenous peoples.* London: Zed Books.

State of the Field Committee. (2009). *State of the field report: Arts in healthcare 2009.* Washington, DC: Society for the Arts in Healthcare.

Talwar, S. (2007). Accessing traumatic memory through art making: An art therapy trauma protocol (ATTP). *The Arts in Psychotherapy, 34*(1), 22–35. doi:10.1016/j.aip.2006.09.001

Teicher, M. H. (2000). Wounds that time won't heal: The neurobiology of child abuse. *Cerebrum, 2*(4), 50–67. Retrieved from http://www.dana.org/cerebrum/

van der Kolk, B. A. (2003). The neurobiology of childhood trauma and abuse. *Child and Adolescent Psychiatric Clinics of North America, 12*(2), 293–317. doi:10.1016/S1056-4993(03)00003-8 PMID:12725013

van der Kolk, B. A. (2005). Developmental trauma disorder. *Psychiatric Annals, 35*, 401–408. Retrieved from http://www.healio.com/psychiatry/journals/psycann

van der Kolk, B. A. (2008). Developmental trauma disorder: Towards a rational diagnosis for children with complex trauma histories. In S. Benamer & K. White (Eds.), *Attachment and trauma* (pp. 45–63). London: Karnac.

van der Kolk, B. A., & McFarlane, A. C. (1996). The black hole of trauma. In B. A. van der Kolk, A. C. McFarlane, & L. Weisaeth (Eds.), *Traumatic stress: The effects of overwhelming experience on mind, body, and society* (pp. 5–23). New York: Guilford.

Werner, P. (2004). Reasoned action and planned behavior. In S. J. Peterson & T. S. Bredow (Eds.), *Middle range theories: Application to nursing research* (pp. 125–147). Philadelphia, PA: Lippincott, Williams & Wilkins.

Wesley-Esquimaux, C. C., & Smolewski, M. (2004). *Historical trauma and Aboriginal healing.* Retrieved from the Aboriginal Healing Foundation website: http://www.ahf.ca/downloads/historic-trauma.pdf

Yeo, S. S. (2003). Bonding and attachment of Australian Aboriginal children. *Child Abuse Review*, *12*(5), 292–304. doi:10.1002/car.817

## ADDITIONAL READING

Aldridge, F., & Hastilow, S. (2001). Is it safe to keep a secret? A sibling group in art therapy. In J. Murphy (Ed.), *Art therapy with young survivors of sexual abuse: Lost for words* (pp. 167–183). East Sussex: Brunner-Routledge. doi:10.4324/9780203360927_chapter_9

Alfred, T. (2004). My grandmother, she raised me up again: A tribute, to the memory of Art Tsaqwassupp Thompson. *ĆELÁNEN: A Journal of Indigenous Governance, 1*(1). Retrieved from http://web.uvic.ca/igov/research/journal/contents.htm

Archibald, L., & Dewar, J. (2010). Creative arts, culture and healing: Building an evidence base. *Pimatziwin*, *8*(3), 1–25. Retrieved from http://www.pimatisiwin.com/online/

Asen, E., Dawson, N., & McHugh, B. (2001). *Multiple family therapy: The Marlborough model and its wider implications*. London: Karnac.

Barraket, J. (2005). *Putting people in the picture? The role of the arts in social inclusion* (Social policy working paper no. 4). Melbourne: Brotherhood of St Laurence and University of Melbourne Centre for Public Policy.

Cole, P. (2006). *Coyote and raven go canoeing: Coming home to the village*. Montreal: McGill-Queen's University Press.

Cyrulnik, B. (2005). *The whispering of ghosts: Trauma and resilience*. New York: Other Press.

Dudgeon, P., Wright, M., Paradies, Y., Garvey, D., & Walker, I. (2010). The social, cultural and historical context of Aboriginal and Torres Strait Islander Australians. In N. Purdie, P. Dudgeon, & R. Walker (Eds.), *Working together: Aboriginal and Torres Strait Islander mental health and well-being principles and practice* (pp. 25–42). Canberra: Australian Institute of Health and Welfare.

Dyer, G., & Hunter, E. (2009). Creative recovery: Art for mental health's sake. *Australasian Psychiatry*, *17*(s1Suppl.), S146–S150. doi:10.1080/10398560902948431 PMID:19579130

Ferrara, N. (2004). *Healing through art: Ritualized space and Cree identity*. Montreal: McGill-Queen's University Press.

Fiske, J.-A. (2008). Making the intangible manifest: Healing practices of the Qul-Aun trauma program. In J. B. Waldram (Ed.), *Aboriginal Healing in Canada: Studies in therapeutic meaning and practice* (pp. 31–91). Ottawa, Ontario: Aboriginal Healing Foundation.

Fuery, P., Smith, R., Rae, K., Burgess, R., & Feury, K. (2009). Morality, duty and the arts in health: A project on Aboriginal underage pregnancy. *Arts & Health*, *1*(1), 36–47. doi:10.1080/17533010802528025

Furth, G. M. (2002). *The secret world of drawings: A Jungian approach to healing through art*. Toronto: Inner City Books.

Graveline, F. J. (2004). *Healing wounded hearts*. Halifax, NS: Fernwood.

Herman, J. L. (1992). *Trauma and recovery: The aftermath of violence, from domestic abuse to political terror*. New York: Basic Books.

Kalsched, D. (1996). *The inner world of trauma: Archetypal defenses of the personal spirit.* London: Routledge.

Kunitz, S. J. (1994). *Disease and social diversity: The European impact on the health of non- Europeans.* New York: Oxford University Press.

Langton, M. (1981). Urbanizing Aborigines: The social scientists great deception. *Social Alternatives, 2*(2), 16-22. Retrieved from http://socialalternatives.com/

Levine, S. K. (1997). *Poiesis: The language of psychology and the speech of the soul.* London: Jessica Kingsley.

Libesman, T. (2014). *Decolonising Indigenous child welfare.* Abingdon, Oxon: Routledge.

Little Bear, L. (2000). Jagged worldviews colliding. In M. Battiste (Ed.), *Reclaiming Indigenous voice and vision* (pp. 77–85). Vancouver, BC: UBC.

Malchiodi, C. A. (2003c). Humanistic approaches. In C. A. Malchiodi (Ed.), *Handbook of art therapy* (pp. 58–71). New York: Guilford Press.

Mason, J. W., Wang, S., Yehuda, R., Riney, S., Charney, D. S., & Southwick, S. M. (2001). Psychogenic lowering of urinary cortisol levels linked to increased emotional numbing and a shame-depressive syndrome in combat-related posttraumatic stress disorder. *Psychosomatic Medicine, 63*(3), 387–401. doi:10.1097/00006842-200105000-00008 PMID:11382266

McNiff, S. (2004). *Art heals: How creativity cures the soul.* Boston, MA: Shambhala Publications.

Ogden, P., & Minton, K. (2000). Sensorimotor psychotherapy: One method for processing traumatic memory. *Traumatology, 6*(3), 149–173. doi:10.1177/153476560000600302

Robbins, A. (1998). Introduction to therapeutic presence. In A. Robbins (Ed.), *Therapeutic presence: Bridging expression and form* (pp. 17–35). London: Jessica Kingsley.

Shaw, J. A. (2010). A review of current research on the incidence and prevalence of interpersonal childhood trauma. In E. Gil (Ed.), *Working with children to heal interpersonal trauma: The power of play* (pp. 12–25). New York: Guilford Press.

Siegel, D. J. (2001). Toward an interpersonal neurobiology of the developing mind: Attachment relationships, "mindsight," and neural integration. *Infant Mental Health Journal, 22*(1-2), 67–94. doi:10.1002/1097-0355(200101/04)22:1<67::AID-IMHJ3>3.0.CO;2-G

Stoll, B. (2005). Growing pains: The international development of art therapy. *The Arts in Psychotherapy, 32*(3), 171–191. doi:10.1016/j.aip.2005.03.003

Sweeney, S. (2009). Art therapy: Promoting wellbeing in rural and remote communities. *Australasian Psychiatry, 17*(Suppl.), S151–S154. doi:10.1080/10398560902948498 PMID:19579131

Tarantola, D. (2007). The interface of mental health and human rights in Indigenous peoples: Triple jeopardy and triple opportunity. *Australasian Psychiatry, 15*(Suppl.), S10–S17. doi:10.1080/10398560701701130 PMID:18027129

Tsey, K., Wilson, A., Haswell-Elkins, M., Whiteside, M., McCalman, J., Cadet-James, Y., & Wenitong, M. (2007). Empowerment-based research methods: A 10-year approach to enhancing Indigenous social and emotional wellbeing. *Australasian Psychiatry, 15*(Suppl.), S34–S38. doi:10.1080/10398560701701163 PMID:18027133 van der Kolk, B. A. (2002). Beyond the talking cure: Somatic experience and subcortical imprints in the treatment of trauma. In F. Schapiro (Ed.), *EMDR: Promises for a paradigm shift* (pp. 57–83). New York: APA Press. doi:10.1037/10512-003

van der Kolk, B. A., van der Hart, O., & Marmar, C. R. (1996). Dissociation and information processing in posttraumatic stress disorder. In B. A. van der Kolk, A. C. McFarlane, & L. Weisaeth (Eds.), *Traumatic stress: The effects of overwhelming experience on mind, body, and society* (pp. 303–327). New York: Guilford.

Wilson, S. (2008). *Research is a ceremony: Indigenous Research Methods*. Manitoba, Canada: Fernwood.

Wright, F., & Morphy, F. (1999). *The art & craft centre story: A survey of thirty-nine Aboriginal community art and craft centers in remote Australia undertaken by Desart Inc.* Canberra: Aboriginal and Torres Strait Islander Commission.

## KEY WORDS AND DEFINITIONS

**Aboriginal People:** A term describing the oldest living culture and first peoples of Australia.

**Art Therapy:** Therapy which uses creative modalities, including visual art-making, drama, and dance/movement, within a therapeutic relationship to improve and inform physical, mental, and emotional well-being.

**Attachment:** A term used to describe an emotional bond that typically forms between infant and caregiver(s).

**Early Childhood:** The stage in human development which includes the years from toddlerhood through to school age.

**Neurobiology:** A term referring to the study of the brain and nervous system. It includes study of the effects that therapy has on the brain and how the brain mechanism is directly impacted by life experiences.

**Stress:** A state of high arousal that is difficult to manage and is generated by the unpredictable and uncontrollable. When experiences are too challenging, the body's stress response takes over and produces the stress hormone cortisol. Long-term stress and cortisol production can undermine health. With support, stress may be manageable, particularly with strong social bonds. For example, one study found that children with secure attachments do not release high levels of cortisol under stress whereas insecure children do (Gunnar & Nelson, 1994).

**Transgenerational Trauma:** A kind of trauma that has been transferred from the first generation of survivors, who have experienced or witnessed the trauma directly in the past, to the second and further generations of the survivors' offspring.

**Trauma:** A term describing any experience that threatens a person's life or causes intentional harm and psychologically overwhelms an individual. Experts have found that it is traumatic even to witness trauma toward someone else; also to be the perpetrator of harm or death to another person. Complex trauma results from exposure to multiple or prolonged traumatic events that do not fit psychiatric criteria for PTSD. These events are typically of an interpersonal nature, such as psychological maltreatment, neglect, or physical and sexual abuse.

# Section 3
# Self-Care for Social Workers

*Areas promoting the self-care of social workers are discussed, including responses to critical incident stress management, the use of clinical supervision, and the importance of spirituality in practice.*

# Chapter 14
# Towards an Evidence–Informed Approach to Clinical Social Work Supervision

**Kieran O'Donoghue**
*Massey University, New Zealand*

## ABSTRACT

*This chapter discusses how research evidence may be used to inform clinical social work supervision and explores how an evidence-informed approach may be applied in practice in a scenario. The chapter concludes by encouraging supervisors to be mindful about the evidence that informs their supervisory practice and to ask their supervisees about the evidence that relates to the issues they are presenting in supervision.*

## INTRODUCTION

The aim of this chapter is to discuss the question of what constitutes effective clinical social work supervision. In order to provide an informed background for the discussion, the research evidence related to clinical social work supervision is overviewed before an exploration of how an evidence-informed approach may be applied in clinical supervision practice. The chapter concludes with a scenario and exploratory reflection that considers how evidence-informed practice can inform supervision.

DOI: 10.4018/978-1-4666-6563-7.ch014

## BACKGROUND

The term *clinical social work supervision* was coined by Munson (1983) in order to link social work supervision to the interdisciplinary field of clinical supervision and to also emphasise an interactional approach to social work supervision (O'Donoghue, 2007). In recent years, the term clinical supervision has been used and understood to be synonymous with the term *professional supervision*. What both these terms have in common is that they are concerned with the supervision of client practice and the supervision of the well-being and development of the practitioner (O'Donoghue, 2010). Where these two terms differ is in regard to the frame that is applied to supervision, with clinical supervision applying a focus on the clinical interactions, dynamics, processes, and outcomes, whereas professional supervision is focused on the professional approaches, ethics, and standards. For the purpose of this chapter, clinical social work supervision is supervision that is concerned with the supervisee's practice with clients and the supervisee's development and well-being as a social work practitioner.

The term evidence-based practice entered social work from medicine in the 1990s, with several social work publications (e.g. Gambrill, 2001; Gibbs & Gambrill 2002; McNeece & Thyer, 2004; Webb, 2001) drawing from Sackett, Rosenberg, Gray, Haynes, and Richardson (1996) which stated that "evidence based medicine is the conscientious, explicit, and judicious use of current best evidence in making decisions about the care of individual patients" (p. 71).

Over the course of the last decade there has been debate about what constitutes evidence and evidence-based social work. Witkin and Harrison (2001) asserted that "evidence" is just a word and that its meaning is derived from its use in any particular context. They argue that "evidence is the name given to a culturally preferred reason for an existential claim or the performance of an action" (p. 295). In the first case, evidence functions as factual proof, in the second, evidence functions as an authoritative justification. Factual proof is established through direct evidence derived from the credible reporting of personal experience or the credible observation or recording of an experience. The credibility of the witness or the report is derived from its reliability, the reputation of the witness, and its degree of corroboration with other evidence. In contrast, the function of evidence as an authoritative justification pertains to the role of evidence in authorising and justifying a particular action. This means that the evidence provides the authorisation and rationale for decision-making

and subsequent actions. It is this meaning of evidence that is used in evidence-based practice with evidence from research providing the authorisation for assessment and intervention in practice with clients. Gray, Plath, and Webb (2009) argue that evidence is one form of knowledge used in social work, and they note that there is a range of views within social work about what counts as evidence and knowledge for practice. This range includes, on the one hand, those who adopt the scientific research hierarchy of systematic reviews, random controlled experimental trials, quasi-experimental studies, single-system case-studies designs, surveys, and qualitative research (McNeese & Thyer, 2004). On the other hand, there are those, like Rosen (2003), who acknowledge the limitations of the evidence-based approach and propose that the application of generalist knowledge to a specific client situation needs to be critically weighed against practice wisdom and local knowledge, as well as reflexively evaluated in terms of its contribution to practice outcomes. Overall, there is a consensus that evidence-based social work is best described as a practice model wherein practitioners are informed by research evidence when working with clients.

The notion of being evidence-based within social work has recently been described as misleading by Nevo and Slonim-Nevo (2011) who argue in support of an evidence-informed social work that is more inclusive than evidence-based practice. The essence of this argument is that evidence informs practice, rather than provides the basis for practice. According to Nevo and Slonim-Nevo, in an evidence-informed approach it is the client's needs and the dynamics of interactive social work practice that influence how evidence contributes and enriches practice rather than evidence shaping the practice, as is the case with evidence-based practice. An evidence-informed approach is not constrained by the scientific research hierarchy or the five stage evidence-based model comprising: a) an individual assessment and well-formulated practice question; b) searching for the best evidence, c) critically appraising the evidence, d) application of the evidence, and e) an evaluation of the outcome (Epstein, 2009; Nevo & Slonim-Nevo, 2011; O'Donoghue & Tsui, 2005). Instead, the approach taken is dialogical and reflexive, involving a systematic and interactive conversation about the application of knowledge in practice.

It is the application of an evidence-informed approach in relation to clinical social work supervision that will be the focus of the remainder of this chapter. The next section briefly reviews and discusses the research informing clinical social work supervision.

## RESEARCH INFORMING CLINICAL SOCIAL WORK SUPERVISION

The research pertaining to social work supervision is not well-known and has not been easily accessible until recently. The research literature referred to in this chapter is derived primarily from the search undertaken by O'Donoghue and Tsui (2013) of supervision research from peer-review journal articles between 1970 and 2010 and a more recent search conducted with Google Scholar between 2011 and 2013 using the terms *"social work supervision", research* (302 items); *"professional supervision"*, *"social workers"*, *research* (452 items); *"clinical supervision"*, *"social workers", research* (1450 items). From this recent search, the items were reviewed and 18 research articles were then identified. Seven of the 18 were included in this chapter because the findings contribute to the development of an evidence-informed supervisory approach.

The most recent reviews of social work supervision research have commented upon the dearth of studies and the limited contribution they make to effective supervisory practice (Bogo & McKnight, 2006; Carpenter, Webb, Bostock, & Coomber, 2012; Mor Barak, Travis, Pyun, & Xie, 2009; O'Donoghue & Tsui, 2013). Bogo and McKnight (2006) reviewed 13 North American studies

published between 1994 and 2004. They argued that the studies they reviewed provided evidence to inform supervisory practice in the areas of the supervisory relationship, supervision process, and client outcomes. In regard to the relationship, Bogo and McKnight (2006) stated that

*… supervisors are prized who (a) are available, (b) are knowledgeable about tasks and skills and can relate these techniques to theory, (c) hold practice perspectives and expectations about service delivery similar to the supervisee's, (d) provide support and encourage professional growth, (e) delegate responsibility to supervisees who can do the task, (f) serve as a professional role model, and (g) communicate in a mutual and interactive supervisory style. (p. 59)*

The research pertaining to the supervision process and client outcomes is mainly found in Harkness (1995, 1997) and Harkness and Hensley (1991). These studies were derived from a doctoral dissertation concerned with the link between the supervisor, supervisee, and clients (Harkness, 1987). The research consisted of an experimental design involving 161 clients, four practitioners, and one supervisor across a period of 16 weeks. For the first eight weeks the practitioners received the normal mixed form of supervision, then in the last eight weeks they received supervision that was focused on client issues and the practitioners' interventions as they pertained to client outcomes. The evidence from this study indicated that: a) supervision that was focused on client problems produced improvements in client satisfaction with regard to goal attainment, worker helpfulness, the partnership between worker and client, and small improvements in clients' generalised contentment (Harkness & Hensley, 1991); b) supervisory interactional skills, such as problem solving and empathy, had a positive influence on the supervisory relationship and supervisory helpfulness; c) there was a direct link between supervisory problem solving and client goal attainment; and

d) the supervisory relationship was the medium through which supervisors influence practice outcomes (Harkness, 1995, 1997).

Mor Barak, Travis, Pyun, and Xie (2009) completed a meta-analysis of 27 articles published between 1990 and 2007. This analysis focused on the impact of supervision on worker outcomes. Worker outcomes were defined as either being beneficial or detrimental. Beneficial outcomes were construed as those which contributed to organisational goals and service effectiveness and included job satisfaction, commitment to the organisation, effective job performance, and psychological well-being. Detrimental outcomes, on the other hand, were described as those which organisations wish to limit because of the possibility that they will hinder workers' job performance and the quality of service delivery. These included job stress, burnout, and other forms of mental distress experienced by workers (e.g. anxiety and depression). Mor Barak et al. (2009) concluded that task assistance, high levels of social and emotional support, and constructive supervisory interpersonal interaction were related to beneficial outcomes for social workers, while a lack of social and emotional supervisory support and poor interpersonal interaction contributed to detrimental worker outcomes.

In 2012, a research briefing was published by the British Social Care Institute for Excellence entitled *Effective Supervision in Social Work and Social Care* (Carpenter et al., 2012). This briefing reviewed the research evidence from 50 peer-reviewed journal articles published between 2000 and 2012. The 50 articles were identified from searches that looked for empirical studies on the association between the process of supervision and outcomes for service-users, workers, and organisations. The key messages from this review were that: 1) there is an extensive volume of evidence that supervision is associated with positive outcomes for workers and social service organisations; 2) there is little evidence that the application of formal supervision contributes to the improvement of these outcomes; 3) the evidence regarding the effect that supervision has on worker's practice is weak; and 4) there was no evidence that demonstrated that supervision directly influenced client outcomes. One of the limitations of this review and its findings was that studies that reported supervisors' perspectives were excluded from the review.

## Search Strategy

The most recent review examines empirical research pertaining to the supervision of practising social workers published in peer-reviewed journals between 1970 and 2010 (O'Donoghue & Tsui, 2013). The 86 articles reviewed were selected using the following four criteria: 1) they were published in a refereed journal between 1970 and 2010; 2) the research concerned the supervision of social work practitioners; 3) the study reported first-hand empirical information; and 4) the article was in the English language. The procedures used for selection of the additional articles were also four-fold. First, the reference lists of previous research reviews were scanned (Bogo & McKnight, 2006; Harkness & Poertner, 1989; Tsui, 1997). Second, a search was conducted within the major social work and supervision journals that were cited in the previous research reviews. The third procedure was an electronic database search using PsychInfo and Google Scholar. The search terms included: *research, "social work supervision"; research, "clinical social work supervision"; and research, "professional social work supervision"*. The fourth procedure involved reviewing each article and identifying whether it met the criteria and in the course of that review whether it contained within its reference list any further research articles that had not previously been identified.

## Themes from the Literature on Clinical Supervision

O'Donoghue and Tsui (2013) noted that over 40 years, supervision research has increased in the number of research articles and spread across a wider geographical area with articles being published in journals in the United States, United Kingdom, Europe, Hong Kong, Singapore, Australia, and New Zealand. O'Donoghue and Tsui also identified research evidence derived from reported supervision experiences which specified what supervision involves, how it has evolved, and how it is practiced; and the preferences, satisfaction, and views of supervisees and supervisors regarding the quality of supervision (see Table 1). A second area of evidence concerned supervision

*Table 1. Research evidence derived from reported experiences of supervision*

- Supervision comprises administrative, educative, and support functions.
- There has been a change occurring from: a) a single relationship to a combination of various supervisory relationships; and b) solely an organisational accountability process and responsibility to both an organisational and professional one.
- Practice occurs through meetings or sessions between an individual supervisee and supervisor, lasting between an hour and an hour and a half in duration.
- Group and team supervision models were secondary approaches that are used in settings where the team leader or administrative supervisor was not a social worker.
- Cultural differences affected both the relationship and interactional processes and indicated a need to improve supervisors' cultural competence when working cross-culturally.
- Supervisees preferred supervision that was focused on supervisees' education, support, and practice rather than supervision that was administratively driven.
- Supervisees preferred supervisors who possessed expertise, competence, and skills. Such supervisors were deemed to have more authority, power, and influence upon their supervisees within supervision.
- Practitioners' satisfaction and perceptions of ideal supervision revealed that they were more satisfied with supervision that assisted their practice, developed their professional competence, and occurred within a positive professional relationship.
- There was clear dissatisfaction with supervision that was unstructured in terms of its process, unhelpful with regard to practice problems, and unsupportive of the supervisee's needs.

in child welfare. Here, according to O'Donoghue and Tsui, the evidence showed that supervision was concerned with the oversight of casework to ensure the safety of children, manage risk, and regulate the effects of the emotional nature of the work. Other findings within this field concern the interplay between organisational culture and supervision and the influence of this on client practice, worker support, supervisory training and development, job satisfaction, and retention. The third area concerned supervisory influence upon worker and client outcomes. Regarding worker outcomes, O'Donoghue and Tsui found that the provision of emotional support by supervisors within a trusting relationship mitigates the effects of work stress and is positively related to job satisfaction. However, in regard to the influence supervision has on client outcomes, O'Donoghue and Tsui noted that a small amount of studies showed that where supervisory attention is focused on client issues within supervision there is a greater likelihood of better client outcomes.

There have been several articles published since 2012 that were not included in the research reviews (Chiller & Crisp; 2012; Egan, 2012; Hair, 2013; Manthorpe, Moriarty, Hussein, Stevens, & Sharpe, 2013; O'Donoghue, 2012; O'Donoghue & Tsui, 2012; Pack, 2012). Three of these articles (Egan, 2012; Hair, 2013; Manthorpe et al., 2013) mapped the practice of supervision in each of the author's respective settings. Egan (2012) described how social workers were being supervised in Australia in 2007 and found that 80% were supervised with most being supervised in their workplace; and almost one-third participated in two types of supervision, e.g. internal and/or external, individual and/or group. Egan also identified that 40% of her respondents had difficulty accessing supervision with time being the main reason for this. Other findings from Egan were an increase in the use of organisational supervision policies, a predominance of line managers supervising staff, and limited supervisor training options. Hair (2013) reported the findings from a survey of social workers from Ontario, Canada, about the purpose and duration of supervision and the training and discipline of supervisors. The findings and duration of supervision aligned with those reported in Table 1 in this chapter. However, the findings concerning the training and discipline of supervisors highlight a specific difference related to Ontario, Canada, wherein 36% of the respondents had supervision provided by professionals from other disciplines and the respondents were clear that supervisors needed training and needed to be social workers. Manthorpe et al. (2013) mapped the content and purpose of supervision in social work practice in England with a mixed-methods study which used longitudinal data from: a) three online surveys carried out with newly qualified social workers; b) another online survey of Directors; and c) face to face interviews with social work managers. The results found that 82% of respondents received supervision at least once a month and that supervision was focused on casework and mostly provided by their managers. The over-riding message from these three mapping studies was the variability of supervision and the need for it to be provided regularly by well-trained and competent supervisors.

Regarding the remaining articles which all reported qualitative studies, the first of these, Chiller and Crisp (2012), explored professional supervision as a workforce retention strategy and their findings were that the guidance and support of an effective supervisor can result in the retention of professional social workers. O'Donoghue (2012) explored how supervisees' supervision histories influenced their understanding, participation, and use of supervision, as well as their development and behaviour as supervisees. O'Donoghue found that the participants' understanding, participation, and use of supervision were developed through their foundational experiences and their ongoing professional development, as well as by the changes they experienced in their supervision over time. In addition, it was also found that the participants' histories influenced their develop-

ment and behaviour as supervisees, with positive experiences leading to increased participation, motivation, ownership, and proactivity; whereas negative experiences resulted in participants' disengaging, subverting or managing any perceived threat that supervision posed, or reverting to passively receiving supervision and being instructed by their supervisor. Pack (2012) explored the meaning of clinical supervision amongst ten supervisors and twelve supervisees who had been involved in post-qualifying allied mental health programmes. Fourteen of these participants were social workers (six supervisors and eight supervisees). Pack found both commonalities and differences in the meaning that supervisors and supervisees ascribed to clinical supervision. She noted that among supervisors their primary goal was to ensure that the supervisee's practice was "safe" in terms of risk management on behalf of their employing organisation. For the clinical supervisees priority lay with the relational aspects of having a "safe place" in which to have reflective discussion that was trusting and supportive. The last article, O'Donoghue and Tsui (2012), explored supervisors' views concerning what informed their supervisory practice. O'Donoghue and Tsui found that the supervisors' practice was contextually based, and they were informed through an integrative reflection upon the person, situation, and the interactional process occurring within both the practice discussed and the supervisory interaction. The supervisors also drew from a set of personal, professional, and technical rules derived from their: (a) experiences within supervision; (b) supervisory practice wisdom and approaches; (c) direct practice approaches, style, and assessment checklists; and (d) emotional intelligence. These rules were applied reflexively in response to the practice setting, content and process of supervision, and the person of the supervisee. From these results, O'Donoghue and Tsui developed an emergent knowledge map wherein supervisors were informed by their formative experiences, social work and supervision concepts, ideas, and personal perceptions. This, in turn, contributed to their general understanding of supervision, provided them with working principles and methods to process information and an interpersonal sensitivity to tune into the person and supervision process in action. O'Donoghue and Tsui noted that none of the supervisors in their study specifically identified that they were informed by research, or evidence-based practice, or practice evidence, and that further research is required in regard to use of research within supervisory practice.

Notwithstanding the above findings from O'Donoghue and Tsui (2012), when the conclusions drawn from the four research reviews and the most recent research are taken together, it is apparent that there is evidence that informs the supervision relationship or alliance, the supervision process, the supervision of the practice with clients, and the supervision of the practitioner. The evidence that informs the supervision relationship or alliance signals the centrality of a relationship that is characterised by support, trust, honesty, and openness (O'Donoghue, Munford, & Trlin, 2006; Pack, 2012). The supervisor's ability to demonstrate well-developed personal and professional qualities and attributes (particularly empathy and emotional intelligence) as well as practice expertise and competence, contributes to their standing in the relationship. The evidence that informs the supervision process indicates that it is a purposeful interactive problem-solving process which mirrors the social work interview. Regarding the supervision of the practice with clients, the evidence suggests that focused attention on problem-solving the client's problems is more likely to result in better client goal achievement, whereas the evidence informing the supervision of the worker shows that when supervisors help supervisees with their work and provide them with social and emotional support they are more likely to be satisfied and effective in their work, committed to the organisation, and to be well psychologically.

Having identified and summarised how research evidence informs clinical social work supervision, the next section will explore the application of this evidence in practice through the development of an emergent evidence-informed approach to supervision and its application to a scenario.

## DEVELOPING AN EVIDENCE-INFORMED APPROACH

From the research evidence reviewed above, it is clear that in developing an evidence-informed approach to supervision one needs to be mindful of the evidence pertaining to the supervision relationship or alliance, the supervision process, the supervision of practice, and the supervision of the practitioner. With regard to the supervisory relationship or alliance, this means that the supervisor works to maintain an alliance with the supervisee through the use of empathy, interpersonal and cultural sensitivity, and emotional intelligence, whilst at the same time keeping the focus on the supervisees' needs and learning and what they have brought to supervision. It also involves the supervisor demonstrating supervisory and practice competence. The supervision process is the next aspect of this approach and the evidence suggests that the process is both formal and mirrors the social work interview. This means that supervision sessions have a structure and engage the supervisee in an interactive reflective problem-solving process. The third aspect of this approach is the supervision of the social worker's practice with clients. This involves a focus on the client's situation, issues, and outcomes. In other words, the supervisor and supervisee explore the supervisee's knowing, decision-making, and actions in terms of the content (what), process (how), and rationale (why) in regard to their assessment and intervention. In this exploration process, the supervisor would raise questions with the supervisee about:

a) what research evidence have they considered? b) how might it inform their understanding of the situation? and c) how might it inform and assist their interventions? Attending to the supervision of the practitioner is the final feature of an evidence-informed supervision approach. This involves the application of social and emotional support, practical help, and constructive interpersonal communication in the supervisor's dealings. Clearly, the evidence-informed approach outlined above involves a dynamic inter-relationship between all of the four areas that is contingent upon the supervisee, supervisor, and issues present in the supervision session. Figure 1 illustrates the inter-relationship between the four areas of evidence and an evidence-informed approach.

## SCENARIO AND REFLECTION

The following scenario and exploration of it are offered to the reader as a means of exploring how one might use an evidence-informed supervision approach in practice:

*Charlotte is a recent graduate who has been employed as a school social worker in a Non-Government Organisation. Her role involves working with difficult students who have behavioural and emotional issues. Charlotte usually finds the work with the students to be both challenging and rewarding and has been able to engage well with students and work with them towards agreed goals. She has been referred (by the Year 13 Dean) a*

*Figure 1. Evidence-informed approach to supervision*

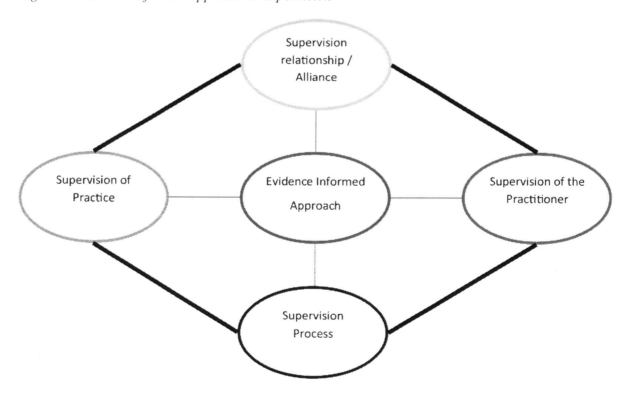

*17 year old student who has recently been before the School Board for using drugs on the school grounds and for bullying and intimating younger students. The referral has come about because of the requirement made by the Board in relation to the student remaining at school. The student is reluctant to meet with Charlotte and when he does she feels that the student is playing mind games with her and trying to intimidate her. Charlotte arrives late to a supervision session with you and starts to talk about the situation.*

## Exploring the Scenario

Using an evidence-informed approach, as Charlotte's supervisor, you would be mindful of ensuring that you were attuned to Charlotte's needs and priorities within the supervision relationship. From the research discussed above, you would be aware of the findings from O'Donoghue (2012) regarding the need with beginning practitioners to provide the safe secure base for her to construct a positive mental map of supervision and supervisory relationships. In the same vein, you would also note the findings from Pack (2012) regarding supervisees needing a safe place of trust and support. As a supervisor, you would also think about how you can demonstrate this through an interpersonal sensitivity that tunes into where Charlotte is, as well as the supervision dynamic between the two of you, through the use of empathy, interpersonal skills, and emotional intelligence (Bogo & McKnight, 2006; O'Donoghue & Tsui, 2012, 2013).

In terms of the supervision process, this would be based upon the social work interview which means that the session is structured in terms of engaging and orientating Charlotte to supervision, establishing the agenda for the meeting, then interactively processing the issues through a reflective dialogue that assists Charlotte with her practice

issues concerning engaging and working with this young person. The session would conclude with a review that identified the actions and learnings and the practicalities of setting another session and finishing the notes (Bogo & McKnight, 2006; O'Donoghue & Tsui, 2013).

Applying an evidence-informed approach to the supervision of Charlotte's practice with the young person involves, firstly, keeping the focus on the client, their issues, and outcomes (Harkness, 1995, 1997; Harkness & Hensley, 1991; O'Donoghue & Tsui, 2013). In regard to the situation Charlotte brings to supervision, this involves exploring her awareness, understanding, and consideration of evidence-based interventions related to the two main issues of youth substance use and bullying and intimidating behaviour. This may include searching with Charlotte, for example, using Google Scholar to search evidence-based social work interventions with youth substance users. An alternative search strategy might involve a search of specialist journals, for example, the *Journal of Social Work Practice in the Addictions*, or *Children in Schools* using the terms "effective interventions" and "substances". A discussion could then follow on the selection and how the selected research evidence could inform Charlotte's practice with the presenting situation.

The fourth dimension of an evidence-informed approach concerns the supervision of the practitioner and pertains to attending to Charlotte's well-being and development as practitioner (O'Donoghue & Tsui, 2013). This involves the provision of practical help, emotional support, and positive interpersonal interaction by the supervisor (Mor Barak et al., 2009). In Charlotte's situation this involves providing a safe space for Charlotte to process and learn from her emotions, particularly those pertaining to her safety, vulnerabilities, and fears (O'Donoghue, 2012; Pack, 2012). It also involves assisting Charlotte to further develop her professional competence through reinforcing her learning and by role modelling ethical professional standards.

## CONCLUSION

This chapter has made the case for an evidence-informed approach to clinical social work supervision through a review of the research evidence found in recent reviews and research articles. The evidence-informed approach to supervision proposed has highlighted the importance and inter-relationship between the evidence informing the supervision relationship and alliance, the supervision process, the supervision of practice, and the supervision of the practitioner, as well as the contingent and dynamic nature of supervision. In conclusion, perhaps the most important message of this chapter is for supervisors to be mindful about the evidence that informs their supervisory practice and to ask their supervisees about the evidence that relates to the issues they are presenting in supervision.

## REFERENCES

Bogo, M., & McKnight, K. (2006). Clinical supervision in social work: A review of the research literature. *The Clinical Supervisor*, *24*(1-2), 49–67. doi:10.1300/J001v24n01_04

Carpenter, J., Webb, C., Bostock, L., & Coomber, C. (2012). *Effective supervision in social work and social care* (SCIE Research Briefing 43). London: Social Care Institute for Excellence; Retrieved from http://www.scie.org.uk/publications/briefings/files/briefing43.pdf

Chiller, P., & Crisp, B. (2012). Professional supervision: A workforce retention strategy for social work? *Australian Social Work*, *65*(2), 232–242. doi:10.1080/0312407X.2011.625036

Egan, R. (2012). Australian social work supervision practice in 2007. *Australian Social Work*, *65*(2), 171–184. doi:10.1080/0312407X.2011.653575

Epstein, I. (2009). Promoting harmony where there is commonly conflict: Evidence-informed practice as an integrative strategy. *Social Work in Health Care*, *48*(3), 216–231. doi:10.1080/00981380802589845 PMID:19360527

Gambrill, E. (2001). Social work: An authority-based profession. *Research on Social Work Practice*, *11*(2), 166–175. doi:10.1177/104973150101100203

Gibbs, L., & Gambrill, E. (2002). Evidence-based practice: Counterarguments to objections. *Research on Social Work Practice*, *12*(3), 452–476. doi:10.1177/1049731502012003007

Gray, M., Plath, D., & Webb, S. A. (2009). *Evidence-based social work: A critical stance*. New York, NY: Routledge.

Hair, H. J. (2013). The purpose and duration of supervision, and the training and discipline of supervisors: What social workers say they need to provide effective services. *British Journal of Social Work*, *43*(8), 1562–1588. doi:10.1093/bjsw/bcs071

Harkness, D. R. (1987). *Social work supervision in community mental health: Effects of normal and client-focused supervision on client satisfaction and generalized contentment* (Doctoral dissertation). Retrieved from Proquest Dissertations and Theses Global database. (UMI No. 8813410)

Harkness, D. (1995). The art of helping in supervised practice: Skills, relationships, and outcomes. *The Clinical Supervisor*, *13*(1), 63–76. doi:10.1300/J001v13n01_05

Harkness, D. (1997). Testing interactional social work theory: A panel analysis of supervised practice and outcomes. *The Clinical Supervisor*, *15*(1), 33–50. doi:10.1300/J001v15n01_03

Harkness, D., & Hensley, H. (1991). Changing the focus of social work supervision: Effects on client satisfaction and generalized contentment. *Social Work, 36,* 506–512. doi:10.1093/sw/36.6.506 PMID:1754927

Harkness, D., & Poertner, J. (1989). Research and social work supervision: A conceptual review. *Social Work, 34,* 115–119.

Manthorpe, J., Moriarty, J., Hussein, S., Stevens, M., & Sharpe, E. (2013). Content and purpose of supervision in social work practice in England: Views of newly qualified social workers, managers and directors. *British Journal of Social Work.* Advance online publication. doi:10.1093/bjsw/bct102

McNeece, C. A., & Thyer, B. A. (2004). Evidence-based practice and social work. *Journal of Evidence-Based Social Work, 1*(1), 7–25. doi:10.1300/J394v01n01_02

Mor Barak, M. E., Travis, D. J., Pyun, H., & Xie, B. (2009). The impact of supervision on worker outcomes: A meta-analysis. *The Social Service Review, 83*(1), 3–32. doi:10.1086/599028

Munson, C. (1983). *An introduction to clinical social work supervision.* New York: Haworth Press.

Nevo, I., & Slonim-Nevo, V. (2011). The myth of evidence-based practice: Towards evidence-informed practice. *British Journal of Social Work, 41*(6), 1176–1197. doi:10.1093/bjsw/bcq149

O'Donoghue, K. (2007). Clinical supervision within the social work profession in Aotearoa New Zealand. In D. Wepa (Ed.), *Clinical supervision in Aotearoa New Zealand: A health perspective* (pp. 12–25). Auckland: Pearson Education.

O'Donoghue, K. (2010). *Towards the construction of social work supervision in Aotearoa New Zealand: A study of the perspectives of social work practitioners and supervisors* (Doctoral thesis, Massey University, Palmerston North, New Zealand). Retrieved from http://mro.massey.ac.nz/handle/10179/1535

O'Donoghue, K. (2012). Windows on the supervisee experience: An exploration of supervisees' supervision histories. *Australian Social Work, 65*(2), 214–231. doi:10.1080/0312407X.2012.667816

O'Donoghue, K., Munford, R., & Trlin, A. (2006). What's best about social work supervision according to Association members. *Social Work Review, 18,* 79-91. Retrieved from http://anzasw.org.nz/about/topics/show/207-aotearoa-nz-social-work-review

O'Donoghue, K., & Tsui, M.-S. (2005). Towards informed supervisory practice: Knowledge, theory, and methods. In L. Beddoe, J. Worrall, & F. Howard (Eds.), *Supervision Conference 2004: "Weaving together the strands of supervision"* (pp.131-137). Auckland, NZ: University of Auckland.

O'Donoghue, K. B., & Tsui, M.-S. (2012). In search of an informed supervisory practice: An exploratory study. *Practice: Social Work in Action, 24*(1), 3–20. doi:10.1080/09503153.2011.632678

O'Donoghue, K., & Tsui, M.-S. (2013). Social work supervision research (1970-2010): The way we were and the way ahead. *British Journal of Social Work.* Advance online publication. doi:10.1093/bjsw/bct115

Pack, M. (2012). Two sides to every story: A phenomenological exploration of the meaning of clinical supervision from supervisee and supervisor perspectives. *Journal of Social Work Practice, 26*(2), 163–179. doi:10.1080/02650533.2011.611302

Rosen, A. (2003). Evidence-based social work practice: Challenges and promise. *Social Work Research, 27*(4), 197–208. doi:10.1093/swr/27.4.197

Sackett, D. L., Rosenberg, W. M. C., Gray, J. A. M., Haynes, R. B., & Richardson, W. S. (1996). Evidence-based medicine: What it is and what it isn't. *British Medical Journal, 312*(7023), 71–72. doi:10.1136/bmj.312.7023.71 PMID:8555924

Tsui, M. S. (1997). Empirical research on social work supervision: The state of the art (1970-1995). *Journal of Social Service Research, 23*(2), 39–54. doi:10.1300/J079v23n02_03

Webb, S. (2001). Some considerations on the validity of evidence based practice in social work. *British Journal of Social Work, 31*(1), 57–79. doi:10.1093/bjsw/31.1.57

Witkin, S. L., & Harrison, W. D. (2001). Whose evidence and for what purpose? *Social Work, 46*(4), 293–296. doi:10.1093/sw/46.4.293 PMID:11682970

## ADDITIONAL READING

Barnett, J. E., Youngstrom, J. K., & Smook, R. G. (2002). Clinical supervision, teaching and mentoring: Personal perspectives and guiding principles. *The Clinical Supervisor, 20*(2), 217–230. doi:10.1300/J001v20n02_16

Bedford, C., & Gehlert, K. M. (2013). Situational supervision: Applying situational leadership to clinical supervision. *The Clinical Supervisor, 32*(1), 56–69. doi:10.1080/07325223.2013.778727

Bernard, J. M. (2006). Tracing the development of clinical supervision. *The Clinical Supervisor, 24*(1-2), 3–21. doi:10.1300/J001v24n01_02

Borders, L. D. (2006). Snapshot of clinical supervision in counseling and counsellor education: A five-year review. *The Clinical Supervisor, 24*(1-2), 69–113. doi:10.1300/J001v24n01_05

Borders, L. D. (2009). Subtle messages in clinical supervision. *The Clinical Supervisor, 28*(2), 200–209. doi:10.1080/07325220903324694

Britt, E., & Gleaves, D. H. (2011). Measurement and prediction of clinical psychology students' satisfaction with clinical supervision. *The Clinical Supervisor, 30*(2), 172–182. doi:10.1080/07325223.2011.604274

Clarke, P. B., & Giordano, A. L. (2013). The motivational supervisor: Motivational interviewing as a clinical supervision approach. *The Clinical Supervisor, 32*(2), 244–259. doi:10.1080/07325223.2013.851633

Cramer, K., & Rosenfield, S. (2004). Clinical Supervision of Consultation. *The Clinical Supervisor, 22*(1), 111–124. doi:10.1300/J001v22n01_08

Deal, K. H. (2004). The relationship between critical thinking and interpersonal skills: Guidelines for clinical supervision. *The Clinical Supervisor, 22*(2), 3–19. doi:10.1300/J001v22n02_02

Ellis, M. V. (2010). Bridging the science and practice of clinical supervision: Some discoveries, some misconceptions. *The Clinical Supervisor, 29*(1), 95–116. doi:10.1080/07325221003741910

Falender, C. A., & Shafranske, E. P. (2004). *Clinical supervision: A competency-based approach*. Washington, DC: American Psychological Association.

Falvey, J. E., & Cohen, C. R. (2004). The buck stops here: Documenting clinical supervision. *The Clinical Supervisor, 22*(2), 63–80. doi:10.1300/J001v22n02_05

Gallant, J. P., Thyer, B. A., & Bailey, J. S. (1991). Using bug-in-the-ear feedback in clinical supervision: Preliminary evaluations. *Research on Social Work Practice, 1*(2), 175–187. doi:10.1177/104973159100100205

Ganzer, C., & Ornstein, E. D. (2004). Regression, self-disclosure, and the teach or treat dilemma: Implications of a relational approach for social work supervision. *Clinical Social Work Journal, 32*(4), 431–449. doi:10.1007/s10615-004-0541-4

Giddings, M. M., Cleveland, P., Smith, C. H., Collins-Camargo, C., & Russell, R. G. (2008). Clinical supervision for MSWs in child welfare: A professional development model. *Journal of Public Child Welfare, 2*(3), 339–365. doi:10.1080/15548730802463587

Heckman-Stone, C. (2004). Trainee preferences for feedback and evaluation in clinical supervision. *The Clinical Supervisor, 22*(1), 21–33. doi:10.1300/J001v22n01_03

Keller, J. F., Protinsky, H. O., Lichtman, M., & Allen, K. (1996). The process of clinical supervision: Direct observation research. *The Clinical Supervisor, 14*(1), 51–63. doi:10.1300/J001v14n01_04

Kitzrow, M. A. (2001). Applications of psychological type in clinical supervision. *The Clinical Supervisor, 20*(2), 133–146. doi:10.1300/J001v20n02_11

Lenz, A. S., & Smith, R. L. (2010). Integrating wellness concepts within a clinical supervision model. *The Clinical Supervisor, 29*(2), 228–245. doi:10.1080/07325223.2010.518511

MacDonald, J. (2002). Clinical supervision: A review of underlying concepts and developments. *The Australian and New Zealand Journal of Psychiatry, 36*(1), 92–98. doi:10.1046/j.1440-1614.2002.00974.x PMID:11929444

McTighe, J. P. (2011). Teaching the use of self through the process of clinical supervision. *Clinical Social Work Journal, 39*(3), 301–307. doi:10.1007/s10615-010-0304-3

Nelson, M. L., Barnes, K. L., Evans, A. L., & Triggiano, P. J. (2008). Working with conflict in clinical supervision: Wise supervisors' perspectives. *Journal of Counseling Psychology, 55*(2), 172–184. doi:10.1037/0022-0167.55.2.172

Pack, M. (2009). Clinical supervision: An interdisciplinary review of literature with implications for reflective practice in social work. *Reflective Practice Journal: International and Multi-disciplinary Perspectives, 10*(5), 657–668. doi:10.1080/14623940903290729

Ross, J. W. (1992). Clinical supervision: Key to effective social work. *Health & Social Work, 17*, 83–85. Retrieved from http://hsw.oxfordjournals.org/ PMID:1482436

Schroffel, A. (1999). How does clinical supervision affect job satisfaction? *The Clinical Supervisor, 18*(2), 91–105. doi:10.1300/J001v18n02_07

Shulman, L. (2006). The clinical supervisor-practitioner working alliance: A parallel process. *The Clinical Supervisor, 24*(1-2), 23–47. doi:10.1300/J001v24n01_03

## KEY TERMS AND DEFINITIONS

**Clinical Supervision:** Supervision with a focus on the interactions between the social worker and client, which includes the interpersonal dynamics of the therapeutic relationship, transference, and countertransference.

**Emotional Intelligence:** A person's ability to creatively stand in the shoes of another and empathise in any interpersonal situation to recognise emotions and respond appropriately towards the other in a line of action that is congruent with clients.

**Evidence-Based Practice:** A practice model by which social work practice is based upon research evidence when working with clients.

**Evidence-Informed Practice:** A dialogical and reflexive process involving both a systemic and interactive conversation about the application of knowledge in practice.

**Professional Supervision:** Supervision with a focus on professional ethics, approaches, and standards of practice.

# Chapter 15

# Best Practice in Responding to Critical Incidents and Potentially Traumatic Experience within an Organisational Setting

**Carole Adamson**
*University of Auckland, New Zealand*

## ABSTRACT

*This chapter addresses best practice for organisational support after critical incidents and traumatic events within social work. Critical incidents are situations and incidents within workplace settings or roles, which, whilst able to be anticipated and planned for, have the potential to create a sense of emergency, crisis, and extreme stress, or have a traumatic impact on those directly or indirectly affected. Alongside the notion of critical incidents are concepts of debriefing, psychological debriefing, critical incident stress debriefing (CISD), and critical incident stress management (CISM). Debate about debriefing models has concerned their effectiveness and safety; the terms being loaded with meaning and tensions between scientific and holistic paradigms and between academic and practitioner perspectives. The chapter suggests areas of research and exploration for agency managers and senior practitioners wishing to make sense of the debates and enables the reader to consider best practice for critical incident response within organisational settings.*

## INTRODUCTION

### Planning for Critical Incidents within an Organisational Setting

Social work is a professional activity long recognised for its complex and at times stressful engagement with challenging human problems. A growing awareness of the impact of stress, trauma, and critical incidents has seen a concomitant rise in organisational attention to staff support, with burgeoning research and practice activity in fields such as supervision, resilience, and response to critical incidents (Adamson, Beddoe, & Davys, 2012; Pack, 2013; Storey & Billingham, 2001; Wendt, Tuckey, & Prosser, 2011). For this chapter, a broad working definition of a critical incident is an event or situation within workplace settings or roles which have the potential to create a sense of emergency, crisis, and extreme stress, or have a

DOI: 10.4018/978-1-4666-6563-7.ch015

traumatic impact on those directly or indirectly affected. Attention to the impact of critical incidents within the workplace, such as violence against social workers (Koritsas, Coles, & Boyle, 2010) and the risks of secondary or vicarious trauma (Bride, 2007; Cox & Steiner, 2013), has led to the embedding of workplace strategies aimed at mitigating the effects of sudden, potentially traumatic events. Evaluations of these strategies has resulted in debate over the most effective means of protecting social workers from critical incident stress and vicarious traumatisation. The focus of this chapter is a search for best practice evidence regarding the most effective means of establishing a robust system of critical incident support within an agency, of planning for the unpredictable, and of sustaining social workers in their desire to remain committed professionals with job satisfaction and healthy engagement with service-user communities.

## ESTABLISHING A SYSTEM OF CRITICAL INCIDENT SUPPORT

The outline of the chapter is as follows: using the case example of Jo, a manager of a community social work agency, objectives are established for a literature search of current research knowledge regarding the provision of critical incident support. A search strategy is outlined and principles from current research extracted, with attention paid to the strands of the debate about critical incident stress debriefing (CISD) playing a role in highlighting the key factors for the design and embedding of critical incident response within a social work setting. The chapter now introduces Jo.

### Case Study

Jo is an experienced social worker with ten years' child protection practice in a large, statutory organisation. Having commenced her career in front-line risk assessment and intervention, she

has progressed to being a practice supervisor for both practitioners and social work practicum students, and for the last three years she has been team leader in a multi-cultural, suburban, and semi-rural area on the fringes of a large city. She has recently been appointed as the manager of a small, non-government organisation (NGO) family support service in the same locality. Within the statutory setting, Jo encountered service-user histories of severe abuse and neglect, families struggling to stay together in the face of extreme poverty and housing crises, the threat of violence to herself and her colleagues, and the impact of sudden death by suicide of teenage clients and on one occasion, a much-loved colleague.

Jo's experience and awareness of the potential for workplace crises, which she broadly defines as "critical incidents", and the potential for trauma exposure when working with families in distress and transition are now a challenge for her in her new role. Team members in this NGO setting have a wide range of education and training backgrounds, largely from social work but also from nursing, and some have achieved their positions as a result of cultural expertise not determined by formal educational achievement. Mindful that the service-users of a family support service are families with vast experience of disruption, struggle, and crisis, Jo is now asking key questions of herself as manager and of the service as a whole about the most appropriate means of providing support for the team members for when the inevitable critical incident or traumatic event occurs. As they are a small and close-knit team, she is focusing her search on interventions that will take into account an incident's impact on all team members. "Planning for the unpredictable" begins with her review of what she already knows.

Her statutory child protection background and her own student placement experience within a health service setting have given her knowledge that formal organisational supports known as CISD exist. Indeed, in her first year of child protection practice, Jo was part of a group debriefing process after a particularly distressing "uplift", or removal of a child, from an abusive gang-related environment in which she was intimidated and threatened with violence. "I know where you live" was not, she still feels, an empty threat, as she both lives and works in the same area and has two children at the local school. She recalls the benefits of having been able to have her emotional reactions of fear and anger validated by others who had been involved, and the team support that resulted, she considers, enabled her to discover strengths both within herself and the work environment with which to face similar events during her career. However, the statutory organisation's response to critical incidents has vacillated over the years, and Jo's team leader position gave her access to some of the policy papers that seemed to suggest that CISD was no longer the preferred organisational response, and that it may in fact, as the research reports indicated, make a situation worse. Instead, an individualised system of support was mandated by Head Office, with team leaders and managers being enabled to refer stressed staff to Employee Assistance Programmes (EAP). Curious as to the recommended best practice in critical incident support that she can apply to her new position, Jo takes some time to research her key question, "what is the best means of providing organisational support to staff following a critical incident in the workplace?"

Her aims and objectives are clear. As a manager, she wants to have a system of staff support and response that can provide the best means of managing critical incidents whenever (rather than whether) they occur. This, she knows, will require preparation of any new staff members for the realities of the work that the agency does, as well as ongoing awareness for the team about the impact on them of the work with families in stress. Immediate support for those directly affected will need to be provided. As the team is small and most live within the locality, Jo is aware that the effects of any incident are also likely to reverberate throughout the agency and into their

families and communities within their area. Jo recalls from her own experience that reminders of the critical incident reoccurred throughout many months and even years afterwards and so is mindful of the need for designing adequate follow-up in her critical incident planning. Into this planning, she carries her own social work identity that is formulated within a systems and ecological framework of understanding. This perspective, she implicitly accepts, assumes a multi-level response to the complex challenge of critical incident stress management (CISM). The development of any organisational response to critical incidents should, in her worldview as a social work practitioner, reflect a person-in-environment perspective.

She constructs the following objectives:

1. to define and understand current best practice in critical incident response;
2. to critically assess models of critical incident support;
3. to use this knowledge to construct a critical incident management plan that fits the needs of a social work agency.

## The Process of Searching for Literature: Foundation, Contributory, and Focused Knowledge

Removing ourselves from the immediacy of Jo's practice context, the challenge faced by social workers in practice is that of determining the best practice response in the provision of staff support systems after critical incidents and traumatic events. A scoping exercise now occurs, critically appraising the available literature that will inform agency environments like Jo's about best practice in the management of critical incidents and potentially traumatic events.

The starting point for any best practice inquiry is what is already known. Professional environments, such as social work organisations, have an underpinning of educated, and in some jurisdictions, professionally registered, competent practice with a recognised knowledge base from social work and social, cultural, and health sciences (International Federation of Social Workers, 2012).

The knowledge bases that inform an understanding of critical incident response are demonstrated in Figure 1. Underpinning any consideration of organisationally-located stress or incident response lays a foundational social work knowledge base that constructs a person-in-environment, interactive, and dynamic relationship between the persons involved, their workplace context, and the relational components that mediate the quality and intensity of their stress and resilience responses (Adamson, Beddoe, & Davys, 2012). This includes perspectives such as ecological systems and structural analysis; theories of human behaviour and social systems; methods such as group work; the management of cultural relationships; narrative approaches; and reflective processes, such as clinical supervision. It carries with it attention to social work ethics and

values that emphasise social work commitment to human rights, social justice, and empowerment principles, as well as a working understanding of the interpretation of research, evaluation, and best practice guidelines. This chapter assumes a familiarity with this knowledge base which underpins the next level, the contributory knowledge base for the understanding of crisis, stress, and trauma within a workplace setting.

The relationship between these two levels is not clear-cut. Most social work education will have addressed, whether to any great degree, the contributing knowledge of stress, resilience and trauma, the nature of crises and crisis intervention theories, and the organisational context that involves concepts of leadership and management. Whether these knowledge bases will have been brought together in order to frame up sufficient understanding in which to assess appropriate critical incident response cannot be assumed. Crisis theory, for instance, may have been taught with an "other" focus in relation only to service-users

*Figure 1. Knowledge bases for critical incidents*

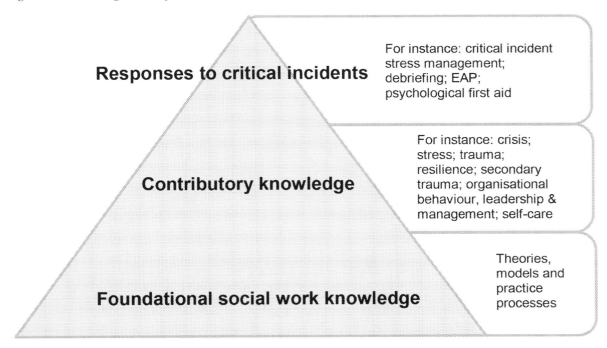

and social work engagement rather than with a spotlight on the impact on the worker. Effective use of supervision may have been taught without consideration of the role of supervision and supervisor in the event of a critical incident or traumatic event. Organisational and management theory may have been taught as a static concept without including change management and crisis response.

The challenge for our manager, Jo, and others looking to understand best practice approaches to critical incident response, is to bring their awareness of knowledge bases such as these into direct relationship with each other and to look at them through the lens of critical incidents. Adding, therefore, to our core question of "what is the best means of providing organisational support to staff following a critical incident in the workplace?", we now have subsidiary lines of inquiry that may shape our literature search. We may ask questions about the relationship between our core social work knowledge and crisis in the workplace; about organisational systems and structures and their preparedness for critical incidents; about how we interpret and view critical incidents themselves; and we may query the depth of the understanding we have about the relationship between trauma, stress, and resilience. Whilst serving as an underpinning for the following focused inquiry about critical incident support, we may also need to return to and update this knowledge to strengthen our understanding of some of the issues arising within a critical incident literature search.

The third tier of our knowledge base, and the focal point of this literature review, is that of critical incidents and critical incident response. For this purpose, and to aid with definitional attention to the key concepts, a library database search was conducted, instituted through access to a university library. For practitioners, of course, access to tertiary libraries with subscriptions to a variety of academic journals is not a given and may be a resourcing, partnership, and/or structural issue; for example, publicly available search engines such

as Google Scholar allow for access to abstracts only. Some large, usually national organisations within child protection, justice, and health, have central library access, with library staff available to do key word searches. The key word search was conducted using combinations of *"social work"*, *"critical incident"*, *"critical incident stress"*, *"debriefing"*, *"psychological debriefing"*, *"critical incident debriefing"*, and *"critical incident stress management"*. Further key word searches, as a result of the initial scoping exercise, were conducted using *"psychological first aid"* and *"employee assistance programme"*.

Even with a database search from within a university setting, many variables come into play in the selection of relevant material. It is possible to do general searches for key words, using terms such as "social work" and "critical incident" (the "and" enabling an inclusive search for both terms, with "or" being used to search for either one of the terms). Library searches also allow for selected databases to be searched, either by category (for instance, "social science" or "psychology") or individually through databases identified by the searcher as relevant, such as PsychInfo. What you look for is what you get, so the choice of key word search for this literature review was crucial. For the search about critical incidents, whilst social work is the context for this to be explored, much of the research occurs outside a social work setting and from a psychological or psychiatric perspective.

Within academic searches, specific inclusion and exclusion criteria are often employed to manage the acquisition of relevant references and to rule out irrelevant material. Most search engines (Google Scholar or specific academic databases) use Boolean search methodology, that is, they use "and", "or" and "not" to link words and phrases together. This is particularly useful when exploring a wide field of literature, so that, for instance, searching for *"critical incident"* and *"social work"* produced a focused list of potentially useful research articles. Given the inter-disciplinary and commercial and scientific nature of the critical incident field, however, manual culling of relevant articles was still required, as both relevance and definitional accuracy needed to be assessed. Critical incidents, of course, can also refer to a means of focused reflective practice (Fook & Askeland, 2007) and debriefing is often used to describe processes outside of crisis and trauma. Some search selections can be quickly discarded, others require closer reading. Perhaps some thirty articles were deemed relevant for this review, benefitting from some previous literature reviews, such as Adamson (2006), Everly, Flannery, & Mitchell (2000), and Pack (2013).

In determining the best time period within which to search for publications, an open period of publication dates was used initially to enable an overview of when the peak of critical incident research was conducted. A useful, if somewhat general, tool for this is the Google Ngram viewer which enables the capture and illustration of key words in book titles published over given time periods. Searching for *critical incidents* (without being able to define this term further) within this tool reveals three periods of time where books were published on the subject, peaking in 1971, 1986, and 2002. Relevant literature was privileged from the two main periods in the mid- to late 1980s (the time period, as explained below, when organisational critical incident supports

were developed and promoted) and around the turn of the century (when scientific critique and debate was at its height). Given the inevitable time lapse between research and its implication in mainstream practice, exclusion of pre-2000 literature, a preferred option for locating only current research and debates, for example, was not deemed necessary.

## Critical Incidents and their Management: Definitions and their Knowledge Bases

The key objectives for this literature review were to define critical incident support, response, and intervention, to critically review what the literature says about these models, and to use this knowledge to construct a critical incident management plan that fits the needs of a social work agency (these key terms are defined both within the following text and in the glossary at the end of the chapter). The chapter now surveys current understanding of critical incident response within social work and related environments, prior to articulating the strands of the debate which has raged concerning the efficacy of CISD, and from this critical appraisal, suggests best practice guidelines for CISM within social work settings. This inquiry process is illustrated by Figure 2.

*Figure 2. The process of inquiry*

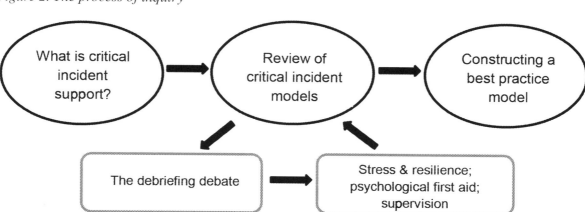

As described above, the term critical incident is applied to situations and incidents within workplace settings or roles which, whilst potentially able to be anticipated and therefore planned for, have the potential to create a sense of emergency, crisis, and extreme stress, or have a traumatic impact on those directly or indirectly affected. As an experience with some degree of a beginning and an endpoint (as opposed to "ambient", background, or environmental stress which may be constant but diffuse and undifferentiated in nature), a critical incident has focal points of increased stress and potential trauma and challenges to homeostasis, to coping within existing resources, and to resilience. Models of stress-vulnerability offer some contributory frameworks of understanding regarding the interaction of individual and contextual factors in the appraisal of an event (Belsky & Pluess, 2009). For social work organisational settings, as with many of the occupational groups around which critical incident processes have been constructed, the impact may result either from a direct stressor, such as an assault, or from a secondary source, such as the sudden death of a service-user. Stress and trauma literature confirms that secondary or vicarious impact has the same potential for harm as does a direct threat (Adams, Boscarino, & Figley, 2006; Baird & Kracen, 2006). The current crisis, stress, trauma, and resilience knowledge bases with which we view this definition provide us with a theoretical assumption that the impact of events upon any given individual will have a considerable variability, resulting from an interplay of genetic, epigenetic, experiential, and contextual factors (Bonanno, Galea, Bucciarelli, & Vlahov, 2007; Davis, 2013; McCann et al., 2013; Thoits, 2010; van Breda, 2011). Research into bi-directional processes within the stress experience highlights the interconnectedness between the physiological and the socio-cultural experience of stress (McEwen & Gianaros, 2010; Thoits, 2010). With this knowledge, a critical incident becomes a subjective (individually-defined) and constructed experience, dependent upon the preparation, interpretation, and processing of an event within the environments in which it plays out, suggesting too that intervention can (or perhaps, should) occur at the many levels that connect the individual to their environment. The literature regarding critical incident response should, therefore, be assessed in this light.

From the previous discussion about the application of interacting contributory knowledge bases, it is important to recognise that the term critical incident is a contextual definition, referring to events that occur within a workplace context. The origins and causation of the incidents, their impact, and the responses made, all are determined by organisational and professional factors. A set of contributory knowledge comes from the occupational health literature (for a New Zealand example, see Department of Labour, 2003, which identifies key professional and occupational groupings most at risk). Social work is recognised as an inherently stressful occupation due to its complex interactions with potentially conflictive and distressing situations. Knowledge of this literature (with which many management level social workers will interact) provides models of support and intervention along principles of elimination, isolation, and minimisation of hazards, a harm reduction strategy that suggests that if the removal of stressors in the work environment is not possible, then these should be contained or, at least, their impact minimised. Research emphasises the role that management strategies and support have in increasing the resilience of employees (Devilly, Gist, & Cotton, 2006; Regel, 2007). Health and safety legislation in many Western jurisdictions now also describes a shared responsibility between the worker and the organisation for the management of stressors and their impact. It is with this knowledge base that a review of interventions for critical incident stress is now considered.

Aligned with the notion of critical incidents are the concepts of debriefing, psychological debriefing, CISD, and CISM, organisationally-located processes developed in the 1980s and designed to provide structured and peer-led support for those affected by critical incidents (see, for instance, Everly, Flannery, & Mitchell, 2000; Mitchell & Everly, 2000). For the purposes of this chapter, the term critical incident stress debriefing (or CISD) rather than psychological debriefing is employed in order to emphasise the workplace-specific context of responses to extreme events. (The debate that has occurred over CISD and psychological debriefing has in part mudded these definitional waters by including debriefing procedures that took place in service-user as well as worker settings.)

Debriefing has been vaunted as a considerable – and sometimes first – contribution towards validating and responding to the potential stressors within an employment environment. Previously, the impact of incidents such as assaults and sudden deaths had, proponents argued, often been overlooked or underplayed, and the potential for traumatic stress reactions led to individualised and reactive support systems and a general sense of organisational denial about the emotional and psychological impact of the work role (Mitchell & Everly, 2000). CISD and CISM processes have functional roots within emergency services, within whose para-military composition was identified a need for psychological and emotional support following critical incidents and other potentially traumatising events (Everly, Flannery, & Mitchell, 2000). CISD and CISM have conceptual origins in crisis intervention theory (Mitchell & Everly, 2000). These grass-roots initiatives were rapidly adopted from the 1980s to the early 2000s by a variety of health and welfare organisations, and the CISD model (with its orthodox form termed the "Mitchell model" after the United States paramedic responsible for its early development) was promoted widely, mostly in the English-speaking world and in Western Europe, through training and implementation within organisations. Early descriptions of these workplace interventions focus on CISD as a univariate, standalone intervention and suggest that it could be effective as trauma prevention (Mitchell, 1983; Mitchell, & Everly,

1995). Later accounts moderate these claims and embed CISD within a CISM framework which spans planning and preparation, intervention, and follow-up phases within organisational life (Everly, Flannery, & Mitchell, 2000).

CISM, as conceptualised by Mitchell and Everly (2000), is a framework of interdependent responses spanning primary, secondary, and tertiary interventions. These manifest in organisational settings as prevention (for instance, pre- and post-employment education and training, and "stress inoculation" processes), early intervention (described in military language as demobilisation, defusing, and debriefing), and follow-up strategies on group and individual levels as required. The literature describes such organisationally-based initiatives in a manner compatible with the psychosocial and systems perspective of social work (Defraia, 2013), and the CISM approach appears to reflect the contextually-sensitive, variable impact, and differential outcomes informed by the stress, resilience, and trauma literature that underpins this review. There is, however, a dearth of research regarding the effectiveness of a CISM approach to critical incident stress response, possibly due to context-dependent development. Most investigation has been directed specifically at its single component of CISD and specifically upon traumatic impact and prevalence; vulnerability, risk, and resilience; and the model's risk factors for re-traumatisation (Defraia, 2013). The clinical, methodological, and sometimes political and commercial elements of the debate explored in this literature search highlight the reasons for this lack of evidence and suggest a way forward for those seeking to develop critical incident support within the social work workplace.

CISD is described as a structured, seven phase peer-driven, clinician-supported process for those involved in the immediate days following a serious event within a workplace setting (Mitchell & Everly, 1995). The seven phases are designed to introduce the purpose of the session and to establish safety, and then to follow a hierarchy of factual, cognitive, emotional, and behavioural descriptions of the event, with following stages of psycho-education and practical support before the closure of the session. Debriefing, as outlined in this model, is far more of a structured process than the demobilisation and defusing stages of a CISM framework that have conceptual similarity to the concept of psychological first aid, considered later in this chapter. It contains a greater emphasis on the ventilation of emotional responses than do other interventions, and it is this factor that has been a linkage into the trauma literature and the focal point for research evaluation and critique.

The rationale for debriefing connects us to two important contributory knowledge bases to which social work has affinity. From a social constructivist knowledge base, it is understood that extreme events challenge our cognitive schemas and that meaning making and narrative construction enable us to make sense and construct and develop effective coping strategies that frame up and serve to remove ourselves from being emotionally overwhelmed (Pennebaker, 1997). From a trauma standpoint, however, we also receive guidance that unleashing emotion-based memory of experiences can potentially re-traumatise without sufficient cognitive and practical preparation for its processing and support (Herman, 1997). The tensions between these two arguments inform the following discussion about the appropriateness of CISD as a post-incident intervention.

## The Debate Over CISD

The literature search reveals that the "debriefing debate" has spanned some fifteen years of research and evaluation, during which CISD has been adopted, adapted to context, and in some cases, abandoned as the primary form of post-incident workplace intervention (Adamson, 2006; Avery & Ørner, 1998: Bisson, McFarlane, & Rose, 2000; Deahl, 2000; Pack, 2013; Raphael & Wilson, 2000; Regel, 2007). Deconstruction of this debate allows a social work voice to be developed alongside other

evidence-based arguments about the provision of critical incident support in organisational settings, highlighting the tensions between some of the psychological literature that can be critiqued for its lack of attention to context and a social work appreciation of the importance of context and relationship when responding to crisis (Adamson, 2006; Defraia, 2013; Miller, 2003; Pack, 2013). The debate centres on the following inter-related elements: clinical concerns about efficacy and re-traumatisation; perceived purpose, "ownership", and structure of CISD; and methodological issues in the evaluation studies.

## Does CISD Re-Traumatise?

The rapid take-up of debriefing, usually but not exclusively with a wider system of some form of CISM, began to be challenged within psychological research. Within the first five years of this century, a significant number of organisations had abandoned this peer-initiated, clinician-led group process on the basis of a concern that the emotional component of the debriefing process (where participants were encouraged to recall their involvement in an incident) was deemed to heighten risk of re-traumatisation and further vulnerability to traumatic impact and that there was no proven efficacy in terms of the reduction of post-traumatic symptoms. The evidence for this comes from psychologically-informed research related to trauma symptomatology and tended to define CISD as a trauma intervention (Deahl, 2000; Kenardy, 2000; McNally, Bryant, & Ehlers, 2003; Rose, Bisson, & Wessely, 2003), as its early iterations had confusingly claimed. Analysis of the debate suggests that those who were arguing for the effectiveness of CISD within a framework of organisational CISM were doing so from the standpoint of debriefing as a contextually located, organisationally sanctioned initiative that fulfilled moral obligations for workplace support, arguments that may resonate with social work's systemic and constructivist stance. Ormerod (2002) suggested that factors such as participant satisfaction and organisational functioning be taken into account, elements that reflect both a constructivist and an ecological perspective missing from a systematic review conducted by Rose, Bisson, and Wessely (2003) and similar psychologically-based evaluations that focused on the potential for CISD to reduce traumatic impact and its risk for further harm. Cessation of compulsory psychological debriefing was recommended by this review. In risk-averse environments, such as health and social services, it has been the psychological rather than the ecological arguments that have held sway and, indeed, any social work agency considering the adoption of CISD processes must, as a result of this evidence, scrutinise the requirements for emotional content and disclosure.

## Who Determines the Shape and Function of CISD?

The second element of the debate addresses the confusion in regards to the perceived purpose, form, and ownership of CISD. This is a great example of how organisational context must be taken into account for any intervention to be implemented and evaluated. The articles by Mitchell, Everly, and Flannery, in various combinations of authorship, strongly argue for CISD and for CISM as "grassroots" initiatives, originating as effectively the first workplace support systems within emergency services and imposing a strict formula on their delivery (see, for instance, Flannery & Everly, 2004). CISD's promotion, often by commercial as well as welfare interests, located the model outside of the traditional scientific research community and within a more entrepreneurial (and potentially less rigorously evidence-based) training and delivery mode. Once the "Mitchell model" gained traction within the emergency services for which it was designed, its extension to health, welfare, commercial, and industrial settings led to a context-dependent morphing that may have

provided the ecological competence required for its acceptance within workplaces but also let loose a multiplicity of unstandardised models applied in organisations outside of its original emergency service terrain. Debriefings also gained traction within service-user settings, such as in the aftermath of road traffic accidents (Mayou, Ehlers, & Hobbs, 2000), victims of violent crime (Rose, Brewin, Andrews, & Kirk, 1999), or traumatic childbirth (Small, Lumley, Donohue, Potter, & Walderström, 2000).

The rationales for, and process of, debriefing were also critiqued, with Devilly and Cotton (2004) querying whether workplace disputes could have the same traumatic quality as other incidents where physical violence or sudden death occurred. Debriefings were conducted with individuals as opposed to pre-established groups with internally recognised roles and processes, reflecting Yule's (2001) concern of definitional creep whereby any brief intervention acquired the label of a "debriefing". Some debriefings occurred within existing workplace support systems recognisable as CISM (but without this inter-connection being recognised within the research), and some CISD processes stood alone without a CISM structure. This latter finding in the literature is crucial, for agencies wishing to establish an effective means of managing critical incidents, what the research literature actually considered as debriefing and its relationship with other organisational initiatives needs to be clear. Devilly and Cotton (2006) go as far as to term interventions as "CISD/M", arguing that there is no robust and universally accepted articulation of a stress management approach and that debriefings may or may not occur as standalone and single session interventions. Further critique can be found in the literature in regard to the quality and process of the debriefings themselves, including training and skills of the clinicians, adherence to the CISD formulation, location, and span of time between incident and intervention (Dyregrov, 1997).

## How is the Effectiveness of CISD Evaluated?

The third strand of the debriefing debate that the literature reveals is that of methodological issues with the research and evaluation studies. The systematic review by Rose et al. (2003) concerned single session debriefing with a range of groups, not all within employment settings. Its focus was on the post-traumatic symptoms experienced by those taking part. Crucially, the research (and the subsequent abandonment of the model) did not evaluate the context of the debriefing and so did not consider the systemic or structural factors embedded in a framework of CISM that included, for instance, preparation and planning, other organisationally based processes, or post-debriefing follow-up. This chapter suggests a line of literature inquiry that raises fundamental concerns over a too-narrow interpretation of traumatic impact and recovery (Marlowe & Adamson, 2011). Psychologically-based research is indicative of the restrictions potentially imposed by frameworks of evidence-based practice which have as their intellectual basis a requirement to implement positivist methods of inquiry (Adamson, 2001; Webb, 2001). Whilst the model's potential for re-traumatisation as a result of its encouragement to participants to re-visit the emotional aspects of their experience is a crucial element in any consideration of the use of debriefing, there is also a risk of the exclusion of other, more complex, environmental factors that determine resilience and recovery. This may in some way contribute to the apparent conundrum that social workers stressed by experiences in the workplace may often retain high levels of job satisfaction and passion for the work. The focus on the "other" appears to contribute to resilience in the face of high stress levels (Collins, 2008; Mandell, Stalker, de Zeeuw Wright, Frensch, & Harvey, 2013; Stalker, Mandell, Frensch, Harvey, & Wright, 2007). Complex relational and interactive contexts, such as the well-being of social

workers after the experience of critical incidents, stretch the ability of some scientific methods of inquiry and perhaps suggest that different forms of intervention as well as evaluation (ones that incorporate multi-systemic perspectives) be employed.

## Learning from the Debriefing Debate: A Contemporary Perspective on CISM

For someone in a position such as Jo, where a literature search has revealed such a plethora of arguments, it is important to see how the strands of this debate have been resolved, so that effective, contemporary, and contextually-relevant models of support can be developed.

Some settling of the "debriefing debate" within the literature appears to have occurred by about 2005. Whilst research studies are periodically published in support of CISD, most appear to have acknowledged the risks of emotional harm and models appear to have had this component of a debriefing muted. There is a sense in the literature that now that the initial enthusiasm for debriefing has subsided in the face of scientific criticism, there is a synthesis of knowledge bases occurring, albeit in resource-constrained environments where organisational support for critical incident response is not universally developed or applied. The current status of research concerning stress and resilience, such as the importance of bi-directional influences within the human stress experience that link social and cultural stress to the body experience (McEwen & Gianaros, 2010; Thoits, 2010) and the incorporation of contextual and cultural elements in the definition of resilience (Bonanno, Westphal & Mancini, 2011; Bottrell, 2009; Powley, 2009; Ungar, 2004), serve to update and strengthen a social work perspective on the evidence for critical incident response. Both knowledge bases represent a move towards a more holistic appreciation of human experience – multi-layered, multi-levelled, and culturally sensitive –

and a lessening of the influence of a bio-medical perspective that tends to privilege attention to the part rather than to the whole.

On an organisational basis, risk averse environments have tended to abandon a debriefing process in favour of what Dyregrov and Regel (2011) term "watchful waiting"; Ørner and Schnyder (2003) describe organisational responses of management vigilance in case those affected do not display recovery and restored resilience. From a systems and a human rights perspective and given that CISD came into vogue as a grassroots initiative because organisational systems had not provided adequate care after an incident, this reluctance to engage actively in support for staff or to individualise response to those displaying need is potentially a risk in itself. Recovery from the impact of a highly stressful incident can be facilitated through the perception of organisational support (Devilly, Gist, & Cotton, 2006; Regel, 2007). Visible impact of an event may manifest and be interpreted as under-performance in the work role, and the tension between supportive intervention and disciplinary action may be revealed (Defraia, 2013). Adoption of alternate means of staff support, such as Employee Assistance Programmes (EAP), appears common in large organisations. These programmes provide individualised support to employees by external providers contracted at agency level. EAP has frequently been instituted as a substitute for internally-provided CISD. The focus is largely supportive counselling but group or individual debriefing can also be provided. From a perspective of ecologically-informed stress and resilience, EAP schemes, whilst potentially meeting a need, do not provide the multi-systemic engagement that conceptually may provide greater effectiveness and the ability to initiate preventive measures on the basis of learning from each incident (Adamson, 2006). Sited outside of the organisation, their focus is inevitably on the stress-reduction and resilience building of the individual, devoid of a full acknowledgement of their context and of the opportunities for organisational initia-tives that may address the bi-directional flow of energy. Without opportunity to create environment change (to reduce systemic stressors and barriers to resilience, for instance) their use is reactive rather than proactive and potentially pathologising rather than salutogenic. Good work may be done, but a social work reading of stress and resilience theory suggests that other models may have greater sustainable effect. Resilience in itself is, of course, not a politically neutral concept, for strategies to increase worker resilience may be cited by an organisation as a response to what may, in fact, be structural issues such as workload or poor management practices (Adamson, 2011).

Responding to concerns about a "watchful waiting" approach following a critical incident, alternate strategies are now arising in the literature. The evidence review revealed an important development in terms of critical incident response in the form of psychological first aid (PFA). As a concept, PFA can be described as an intervention similar to the demobilisation and defusing processes within a CISM framework, designed to remove a person from ongoing harm, stablise their functioning, and re-connect them with practical and social supports that will encourage use of coping strategies and foster resilience (Everly & Flynn, 2006; Mansdorf, 2008; Ruzek et al., 2007; Vernberg et al., 2008). Importantly, it focusses on those immediately involved in an incident, potentially individuals rather than teams, and similar to CISD processes, it is predicated upon crisis intervention theory that emphasises the importance of early intervention and natural recovery processes. Ruzek et al. (2007) describe its principles as establishing safety and comfort, offering practical support and social connection, information gathering and giving, and linking to other sources of support. Psychological first aid has many conceptual links to a debriefing process, without a focus on the re-telling of the story and the emphasis on team functioning. It is less explicitly a workplace process than it is a crisis intervention strategy, and database searches reveal its application within primary mental health contexts and the broader community. Removal of the encouragement for emotional reiteration of experience appears to have facilitated a focus toward resilience and coping, and whilst evidence-based evaluation of PFA is still continuing, it appears less likely to be contested by psychological research and has not attracted the levels of attention and acrimony as did CISD (in part due to the removal of the emotional re-processing component, but also perhaps because, like a CISM process, it is context-dependent and structurally less prescribed). Without claims of reducing traumatic impact, psychological first aid appears to be constructed as an acute intervention strategy that can be embedded within organisational functioning but which in itself does not mandate training, preparation, or follow-up within the context in which it is applied. It is, therefore, considered safe when viewed from within a psychological lens but perhaps not comprehensive and context-informed when viewed as an organisationally-based intervention. It can best be described as the crisis component of an integrated staff support system, and its efficacy will in part be dependent upon the overall organisational functioning and well-being of any agency environment.

## Linking Debriefing to Resilience and Clinical Supervision

A crucial factor for the design of any workplace intervention is the synergy between critical incident response and other pre-existing supports. Within a social work setting, this will include the professional social work commitment to supervision, a process that contributes to reflective practice and resilience (Howard, 2008; Miehls, 2010). Supervision within an organisational setting appears to have traction as an ecological sound model of stress and resilience support, dependent, of course, on the organisational willingness to fund and maintain a commitment to it. The models of CISD, EAP,

and supervision are not, of course, designed for the same specific purposes: CISD (without a complete CISM framework) follows critical incidents; EAP spans incident support and counselling as well as other functions; professional supervision has elements of accountability and professional development as well as stress management and the provision of reflective space but is not constructed as a crisis management tool. In terms of ecological viability, however, supervision appears to have some sound conceptual arguments for its construction as a process for resilience within the workplace and current research supports this.

Studies of resilience in social workers are now frequently citing supervision as a key protective factor that contributes to stress management, job satisfaction, and potentially to competency and job retention (Ellett, Ellis, Westbrook, & Dews, 2007; Guerin, Devitt, & Redmond, 2010). A meta-analysis on the impact of supervision by Mor Barak, Travis, Pyun, and Xie (2009) suggests that supervision can combat adversity and assist positive outcomes within social service organisations. Supervision is now often constructed as a mediating factor that can support and sustain resilience within organisational settings (Beddoe, Davys, & Adamson, 2011) and, as an extension, it can be posited that effective supervision can be a site of reflection for responding to the aftermath of a critical incident, with the previously acknowledged caveat that supervision has to be accepted and sustained as an integral element in workforce support and professional development.

Several factors associated with supervision are worthy of note here. Firstly, it is a process that is embedded within an organisation and usually provided by colleagues as opposed to external providers. Evidence suggests that its provision and effectiveness will be linked to the organisational culture in which it occurs, with the concept of organisational resilience (Russ, Lonne, & Darlington, 2009) employed to describe conditions in which employees can provide and receive support, learn, reflect, and engage in professional development. This is synergistic with what we have learned about critical incident support. The construction of the supervision process as a mediating space in which to link workplace experiences from many different levels (personal and emotional impact; organisational structures, policies, and processes; relational dynamics; service-user needs and narratives) suggests that supervision can incorporate our understanding of the systemic, structural, and constructivist components of stress and resilience within a contextual setting. Systems perspectives on supervision suggest, too, that the balance between these different perspectives will be determined by the developmental stage attained by the social worker, so that new graduates or those affected by major stressors that inhibit the integration of multiple elements of experience may be utilising different facets of the supervision experience at different times (Brown & Bourne, 1996).

What is clear from this brief summary of the debriefing debate is that there are some fundamental assumptive positions to be challenged in the provision of critical incident support which need to be taken into account in any organisational planning. Whilst organisational support systems after critical incidents and potentially traumatic events clearly have an ethical obligation to do no more harm, they are also required to apply research evidence to their own environmental conditions. The challenge for Jo, and others in her position, is to construct critical incident responses within a social work organisation that combine the research evidence from different perspectives and knowledge bases. What follows is a statement of principles for the construction of critical incident stress response, based on the literature review, which aims to resolve the dilemma facing social work organisations seeking to establish best practice interventions.

## The Design of Best Practice Responses to Critical Incidents in the Workplace

The case study cited in this chapter posed the question "what is the best means of providing organisational support to staff following a critical incident in the workplace?" and the subsequent literature review had the objectives of exploring the research base for critical incident response and critically assessing the models identified. Reconciling the issues emerging from the debate enables construction of an appropriate critical incident management plan, responsive both to the needs of the social workers within the agency and to the best practice guidelines emerging from the literature. Jo's initial question launched the literature review into a consideration of the evidence regarding CISD as a model for intervention. Foundational and contributory knowledge bases may need to be re-visited; as above, the stress and trauma literature has taken on a newly enhanced resilience perspective, and new questions about how support services within an organisation may be asked.

Linking the social work and contributing knowledge bases, such as stress, trauma, and resilience, to that of critical incident stress response enables an ecological lens to be applied to the question of best practice. The stress and resilience literature has a synergy with social work's systems perspective on the need for a whole-of-organisation response to critical incidents. Combined with a health promotion approach that mandates prevention, early intervention, and follow-up for those affected by an incident, a comprehensive stress response framework responsive to the needs of the organisation can be mapped out. Within our case example, Jo's question is not asked in a vacuum. Her team is already established, the demands of the work known, and existing micro- and meso-system connections already engaged. She knows, for example, that her multi-cultural staff may utilise practices such as *whanaungatanga* (a Māori value-based process of establishing and maintaining inter-relationship), *karakia* (prayer), food, and singing, in order to create and maintain harmony in the workplace. Ethnic sensitive cultural practices, but also the micro-culture of how organisations manage relational processes, are mandated here (the writer's own workplace uses cake for this purpose). Such environmental scoping is crucial if the model of CISD and CISM, created within Western emergency service contexts, is to be updated and adapted to suit, perhaps, multi-cultural or collective cultures, different political philosophies, and health and welfare resource bases. This chapter suggests that it is not only the critical incident knowledge bases that need to be scrutinised but the contributory and foundational knowledge bases and their assumptions that will produce the most integrated and potentially more effective models for intervention.

From this review, key principles emerge that assist in the creation of best practice guidelines. Utilising the knowledge framework from Figure 1, best practice principles from the literature review are suggested in Table 1. For our manager, Jo, and others in her situation, a whole-of-organisation approach is suggested by the knowledge gained from this inquiry. Whilst context-dependent in terms of agency capacity and expertise, management of an incident needs to be safe, responsive, and integrated with other processes within the functioning of an agency.

On a primary level, prevention and population-based interventions for critical incidents clearly lie at the level of whole-of-organisation responsibility. They include recruitment and selection

*Table 1. Key principles for best practice*

| Knowledge Base | Examples of Content | Principles for Best Practice |
|---|---|---|
| **Critical incident knowledge bases** | Critical incident stress management<br>Debriefing<br>EAP<br>Psychological first aid | Intervention strategies should contain elements of prevention, planning, and preparation, response, and follow-up within a framework of CISM appropriate to each environment.<br>Critical incident responses should be aligned with other forms and traditions of support within the organisation.<br>Intervention after an event should be practical and aimed at reconnecting/re-establishing coping.<br>Re-traumatisation should be avoided by reducing a focus on emotional re-telling of events.<br>Planning for individual and team processes is needed.<br>Reciprocal alliances with other organisations may be necessary. |
| **Contributory knowledge bases** | Crisis intervention theories<br>Stress and trauma<br>Resilience and self-care<br>Organisational theories | All staff should have a working knowledge of what makes them resilient, have a wellness plan, and understand stress and trauma principles.<br>Meaning making opportunities are necessary.<br>People are resilient and can recover from adversity with support.<br>Organisational knowledge of resources for support is important. |
| **Foundational knowledge from social work** | Systems and ecological approaches<br>Constructivism<br>Strengths and recovery based practice<br>Social science knowledge (e.g. human development, attachment theory)<br>Practice knowledge (e.g. supervision)<br>Cultural knowledge | Interventions should be ecologically competent and compatible with organisational contexts.<br>Cultural processes should be incorporated into interventions.<br>People in the environment will be affected too.<br>Intervention strategies should have functional relationship with other processes, such as supervision. |

strategies that acknowledge the realities of social work and related disciplines and the potential for stressful engagement with service-user needs, issues, and crises; organisational awareness of risk, of safety, and of skills in responding to conflict, such as inclusive engagement at the start of an encounter and de-escalation should tensions rise; organisational processes that affirm relational resilience and caring within team members; and specific stress inoculation strategies, such as professional development opportunities that educate about stress management, resilience, and trauma. Cultural identities and relationships are active factors here. Organisational audits (playing the "what if" game of asking how people may cope in a critical incident) may raise awareness that planning may be necessary for the unpredictable, and a context-appropriate CISM framework can be developed that incorporates educational, relational, and structured responses.

Specific secondary strategies focused around critical incident response need to be designed cognisant of the research caveat about emotional re-traumatisation. Psychological first aid processes appear to be solid interventions that satisfy a resilience-informed and strengths-based understanding of coping that emphasises practical assistance during the immediate period of a crisis, whilst producing therapeutic results that satisfy our human need to exercise empathetic compassion. Organisationally significant other processes, such as supervision, can re-visit their purpose, function, and process from a trauma-informed perspective. Small agencies, such as Jo's, may need to have established and to sustain reciprocal arrangements with co-working agencies in the event of an incident overwhelming their capacity to respond.

On a tertiary or follow-up basis, the period after an incident is crucial. Research indicates that (from a trauma knowledge base) consolidation of psychological schema occurs in the hours and days following exposure. This was a rationale for the establishment of CISD. However, assumption of a "watchful waiting" approach to the potential development of traumatic symptoms does not necessarily sit comfortably with current understandings of resilience being contextually and relationally constructed. This provides an imperative for trauma-informed supervision, as well as, for example, organisationally-unique processes that honour both pre-existing relationships and the intrusive impact of a critical incident.

## CONCLUSION

Resolution of the initial question "what is the best means of providing organisational support to staff following a critical incident in the workplace?" has traversed an inquiry inclusive of professional social work knowledge, contributory knowledge from fields such as stress, trauma, and resilience, and it has considered specific and contested research evidence in regard to CISD. What emerges from this inquiry is a complex matrix of organisationally-aware, context-sensitive, and stress, resilience, and trauma-informed knowledge bases which, it is hoped, can support the development of an effective and compassionate workplace response to critical incidents.

## REFERENCES

Adams, R. E., Boscarino, J. A., & Figley, C. R. (2006). Compassion fatigue and psychological distress among social workers: A validation study. *The American Journal of Orthopsychiatry*, *76*(1), 103–108. doi:10.1037/0002-9432.76.1.103 PMID:16569133

Adamson, C. E. (2001). Social work and the call for evidence-based practice in mental health: Where do we stand? *Social Work Review, 13*(2), 8-12. Retrieved from http://anzasw.org.nz/about/topics/show/207-aotearoa-nz-social-work-review

Adamson, C. E. (2006). *Complexity and context: Staff support systems in mental health after critical incidents and traumatic events* (Doctoral thesis, Massey University, Wellington, New Zealand). Retrieved from http://hdl.handle.net/2292/10318

Adamson, C. (2011). Supervision is not politically innocent. *Australian Social Work, 65*(2), 185–196. doi:10.1080/0312407X.2011.618544

Adamson, C., Beddoe, L., & Davys, A. (2012). Building resilient practitioners: Definitions and practitioner understandings. *British Journal of Social Work, 32*, 100–117. doi:10.1093/bjsw/bcs142

American Psychiatric Association. (2013). *Diagnostic and statistical manual of mental disorders* (5th ed.). Washington, D.C.: Author.

Avery, A., & Ørner, R. (1998). First report of psychological debriefing abandoned: The end of an era? *Traumatic Stress Points, 12*(3). doi:10.1037/e519832011-004

Baird, K., & Kracen, A. C. (2006). Vicarious traumatization and secondary traumatic stress: A research synthesis. *Counselling Psychology Quarterly, 19*(2), 181–188. doi:10.1080/09515070600811899

Beddoe, L., Davys, A., & Adamson, C. (2011). Educating resilient practitioners. *Social Work Education, 32*(1), 100–117. doi:10.1080/02615479.2011.644532

Belsky, J., & Pluess, M. (2009). Beyond diathesis stress: Differential susceptibility to environmental influences. *Psychological Bulletin, 135*(6), 885–908. doi:10.1037/a0017376 PMID:19883141

Bisson, J. I., McFarlane, A. C., & Rose, S. (2000). Psychological debriefing. In E. B. Foa, T. M. Keane, & M. J. Friedman (Eds.), *Effective treatments for PTSD: Practice guidelines from the International Society for Traumatic Stress Studies* (pp. 39–59). New York: Guilford.

Bonanno, G. A., Galea, S., Bucciarelli, A., & Vlahov, D. (2007). What predicts psychological resilience after disaster? The role of demographics, resources, and life stress. *Journal of Consulting and Clinical Psychology, 75*(5), 671–682. doi:10.1037/0022-006X.75.5.671 PMID:17907849

Bonanno, G. A., Westphal, M., & Mancini, A. D. (2011). Resilience to loss and potential trauma. *Annual Review of Clinical Psychology, 7*(1), 511–535. doi:10.1146/annurev-clinpsy-032210-104526 PMID:21091190

Bottrell, D. (2009). Understanding "marginal" perspectives: Towards a social theory of resilience. *Qualitative Social Work: Research and Practice, 8*(3), 321–339. doi:10.1177/1473325009337840

Bride, B. E. (2007). Prevalence of secondary traumatic stress among social workers. *Social Work, 52*(1), 63–70. doi:10.1093/sw/52.1.63 PMID:17388084

Brown, A., & Bourne, I. (1996). *The social work supervisor.* Buckingham: Open University Press.

Collins, S. (2008). Statutory social workers: Stress, job satisfaction, coping, social support and individual differences. *British Journal of Social Work, 38*(6), 1173–1193. doi:10.1093/bjsw/bcm047

Cox, K., & Steiner, S. (2013). Preserving commitment to social work service through the prevention of vicarious trauma. *Journal of Social Work Values and Ethics, 10*(1), 52–60. Retrieved from http://www.jswve.org/

Davis, H. (2013). Contextual challenges for crisis support in the immediate aftermath of major incidents in the UK. *British Journal of Social Work, 43*(3), 504–521. doi:10.1093/bjsw/bcr197

Deahl, M. (2000). Psychological debriefing: Controversy and challenge. *The Australian and New Zealand Journal of Psychiatry, 34*(6), 929–939. doi:10.1080/000486700267 PMID:11127623

Defraia, G. S. (2013). Organizational outcomes following traumatic workplace incidents: A practice-based exploration of impact of incident severity level. *Social Work in Mental Health, 11*(5), 404–433. doi:10.1080/15332985.2013.784224

Department of Labour. (2003). *Managing stress in the workplace*. Retrieved from http://www.business.govt.nz/worksafe/information-guidance/all-guidance-items/healthy-work-managing-stress-and-fatigue-in-the-workplace/stressfatigue.pdf

Devilly, G. J., & Cotton, P. (2004). Caveat emptor, caveat venditor, and critical incident stress debriefing/management (CISD/M). *Australian Psychologist, 39*(1), 35–40. doi:10.1080/00050060410001660317

Devilly, G. J., Gist, R., & Cotton, P. (2006). Ready! Fire! Aim!: The status of psychological debriefing and therapeutic interventions – In the work place and after disasters. *Review of General Psychology, 10*(4), 318–345. doi:10.1037/1089-2680.10.4.318

Dyregrov, A. (1997). The process in psychological debriefings. *Journal of Traumatic Stress, 10*(4), 589–605. doi:10.1002/jts.2490100406 PMID:9391943

Dyregrov, A., & Regel, S. (2011). Early interventions following exposure to traumatic events: Implications for practice from recent research. *Journal of Loss and Trauma, 17*(3), 271–291. doi:10.1080/15325024.2011.616832

Ellett, A. J., Ellis, J. I., Westbrook, T. M., & Dews, D. (2007). A qualitative study of 369 child welfare professionals' perspectives about factors contributing to employee retention and turnover. *Children and Youth Services Review, 29*(2), 264–281. doi:10.1016/j.childyouth.2006.07.005

Everly, G. S. Jr., Flannery, R. B. Jr., & Mitchell, J. T. (2000). Critical incident stress management (CISM): A review of the literature. *Aggression and Violent Behavior, 5*(1), 23–40. doi:10.1016/S1359-1789(98)00026-3

Everly, G. S., & Flynn, B. W. (2006). Principles and practical procedures for acute psychological first aid training for personnel without mental health experience. *International Journal of Emergency Mental Health, 8*(2), 93–100. Retrieved from http://www.omicsonline.com/open-access/international-journal-of-emergency-mental-health-and-human-resilience.php PMID:16703847

Flannery, R. B. Jr., & Everly, G. S. Jr. (2004). Critical incident stress management (CISM): Updated review of findings, 1998-2002. *Aggression and Violent Behavior, 9*(4), 319–329. doi:10.1016/S1359-1789(03)00030-2

Fook, J., & Askeland, G. A. (2007). Challenges of critical reflection: "Nothing ventured, nothing gained. *Social Work Education, 26*(5), 520–533. doi:10.1080/02615470601118662

Guerin, S., Devitt, C., & Redmond, B. (2010). Experiences of early-career social workers in Ireland. *British Journal of Social Work, 40*(8), 2467–2484. doi:10.1093/bjsw/bcq020

Herman, J. L. (1997). *Trauma and recovery* (Revised reprint). New York: Basic Books.

Howard, F. (2008). Managing stress or enhancing wellbeing?: Positive psychology's contributions to clinical supervision. *Australian Psychologist, 43*(2), 105–113. doi:10.1080/00050060801978647

International Federation of Social Workers. (2012). Definition of social work. Retrieved November 28, 2013, from http://ifsw.org/policies/definition-of-social-work/

Kenardy, J. (2000). The current status of psychological debriefing. *British Medical Journal, 321*(7268), 1032–1033. doi:10.1136/bmj.321.7268.1032 PMID:11053152

Koritsas, S., Coles, J., & Boyle, M. (2010). Workplace violence towards social workers: The Australian experience. *British Journal of Social Work, 40*(1), 257–271. doi:10.1093/bjsw/bcn134

Mandell, D., Stalker, C., de Zeeuw Wright, M., Frensch, K., & Harvey, C. (2013). Sinking, swimming and sailing: Experiences of job satisfaction and emotional exhaustion in child welfare employees. *Child & Family Social Work, 18*(4), 383–393. doi:10.1111/j.1365-2206.2012.00857.x

Mansdorf, I. J. (2008). Psychological interventions following terrorist attacks. *British Medical Bulletin, 88*(1), 7–22. doi:10.1093/bmb/ldn041 PMID:19011264

Marlowe, J. M., & Adamson, C. E. (2011). Teaching trauma: Critically engaging a troublesome term. *Social Work Education, 30*(6), 623–634. doi:10.1080/02615479.2011.586559

Mayou, R. A., Ehlers, A., & Hobbs, M. (2000). Psychological debriefing for road traffic accident victims: Three-year follow-up of a randomised controlled trial. *The British Journal of Psychiatry, 176*(6), 589–593. doi:10.1192/bjp.176.6.589 PMID:10974967

McCann, C. M., Beddoe, E., McCormick, K., Huggard, P., Kedge, S., Adamson, C., & Huggard, J. (2013). Resilience in the health professions: A review of recent literature. *International Journal of Wellbeing, 3*(1), 60–81. doi:10.5502/ijw.v3i1.4

McEwen, B. S., & Gianaros, P. J. (2010). Central role of the brain in stress and adaptation: Links to socioeconomic status, health, and disease. *Annals of the New York Academy of Sciences, 1186*(1), 190–222. doi:10.1111/j.1749-6632.2009.05331.x PMID:20201874

McNally, R. J., Bryant, R. A., & Ehlers, A. (2003). Does early psychological intervention promote recovery from posttraumatic stress? *Psychological Science in the Public Interest, 4*, 45–79. doi:10.1111/1529-1006.01421

Miehls, D. (2010). Contemporary trends in supervision theory: A shift from parallel process to relational and trauma theory. *Clinical Social Work Journal, 38*(4), 370–378. doi:10.1007/s10615-009-0247-8

Miller, J. (2003). Critical incident debriefing and social work: Expanding the frame. *Journal of Social Service Research, 30*(2), 7–25. doi:10.1300/J079v30n02_02

Mitchell, J. T. (1983). When disaster strikes: The critical incident stress debriefing process. *Journal of Emergency Medical Services, 8*, 36–39. Retrieved from http://www.jems.com/ PMID:10258348

Mitchell, J. T., & Everly, G. S. (1995). Critical incident stress debriefing (CISD) and the prevention of work related traumatic stress among high risk occupational groups. In G. S. Everly & J. M. Lating (Eds.), *Psychotraumatology: Key papers and core concepts in post-traumatic stress* (pp. 267-280). New York: Plenum Press.

Mitchell, J. T., & Everly, G. S. (2000). Critical incident stress management and critical incident stress debriefings: Evolutions, effects and outcomes. In B. Raphael & J. P. Wilson (Eds.), *Psychological debriefing: Theory, practice and evidence*. Cambridge, UK: Cambridge University Press. doi:10.1017/CBO9780511570148.006

Mor Barak, M., Travis, D. J., Pyun, H., & Xie, B. (2009). The impact of supervision on worker outcomes: A meta-analysis. *The Social Service Review, 83*(1), 3–32. doi:10.1086/599028

Ormerod, J. (2002). Current research into the effectiveness of debriefing. In N. Tehrani, S. Rose, & J. Omerod (Eds.), *Psychological debriefing: Professional Practice Board Working Party* (pp. 8–17). Leicester: British Psychological Society.

Ørner, R., & Schnyder, U. (Eds.). (2003). *Reconstructing early intervention after trauma*. Oxford: Oxford University Press.

Pack, M. J. (2013). Critical incident stress management: A review of the literature with implications for social work. *International Social Work, 56*(5), 608–627. doi:10.1177/0020872811435371

Pennebaker, J. W. (1997). *Opening up: The healing power of expressing emotion*. New York: Guilford Press.

Powley, E. H. (2009). Reclaiming resilience and safety: Resilience activation in the critical period of crisis. *Human Relations, 62*(9), 1289–1326. doi:10.1177/0018726709334881

Raphael, B., & Wilson, J. P. (2000). *Psychological debriefing: Theory, practice and evidence*. Cambridge: Cambridge University Press. doi:10.1017/CBO9780511570148

Regel, S. (2007). Post-trauma support in the workplace: The current status and practice of critical incident stress management (CISM) and psychological debriefing (PD) within organizations in the UK. *Occupational Medicine, 57*(6), 411–416. doi:10.1093/occmed/kqm071 PMID:17728314

Rose, S., Bisson, J., & Wessely, S. (2003). A systematic review of single-session psychological interventions ("debriefing") following trauma. *Psychotherapy and Psychosomatics, 72*(4), 176–184. doi:10.1159/000070781 PMID:12792122

Rose, S., Brewin, C. R., Andrews, B., & Kirk, M. (1999). A randomized controlled trial of individual psychological debriefing for victims of violent crime. *Psychological Medicine, 29*(4), 793–799. doi:10.1017/S0033291799008624 PMID:10473306

Russ, E., Lonne, B., & Darlington, Y. (2009). Using resilience to reconceptualise child protection workforce capacity. *Australian Social Work, 62*(3), 324–338. doi:10.1080/03124070903060042

Ruzek, J. I., Brymer, M. J., Jacobs, A. K., Layne, C. M., Vernberg, E. M., & Watson, P. J. (2007). Psychological first aid. *Journal of Mental Health Counseling, 29*, 17–49. Retrieved from http://www.amhca.org/news/journal.aspx

Small, R., Lumley, J., Donohue, L., Potter, A., & Walderström, U. (2000). Randomised controlled trial of midwife led debriefing to reduce maternal depression after operative childbirth. *British Medical Journal, 321*(7268), 1043–1047. doi:10.1136/bmj.321.7268.1043 PMID:11053173

Stalker, C. A., Mandell, D., Frensch, K. M., Harvey, C., & Wright, M. (2007). Child welfare workers who are exhausted yet satisfied with their jobs: How do they do it? *Child & Family Social Work, 12*(2), 182–191. doi:10.1111/j.1365-2206.2006.00472.x

Storey, J., & Billingham, J. (2001). Occupational stress and social work. *Social Work Education, 20*(6), 659–670. doi:10.1080/02615470120089843a

Thoits, P. A. (2010). Stress and health. *Journal of Health and Social Behavior, 51*(1suppl), S41–S53. doi:10.1177/0022146510383499 PMID:20943582

Ungar, M. (2004). A constructionist discourse on resilience: Multiple contexts, multiple realities among at-risk children and youth. *Youth & Society, 35*(3), 341–365. doi:10.1177/0044118X03257030

van Breda, A. (2011). Resilient workplaces: An initial conceptualization. *Families in Society, 92*(1), 33–40. doi:10.1606/1044-3894.4059

Vernberg, E. M., Steinberg, A. M., Jacobs, A. K., Brymer, M. J., Watson, P. J., & Osofsky, J. D., … Ruzek, J.I. (2008). Innovations in disaster mental health: Psychological first aid. *Professional Psychology: Research and Practice, 39*(4), 381–388. doi:10.1037/a0012663

Webb, S. A. (2001). Some considerations on the validity of evidence-based practice in social work. *British Journal of Social Work, 31*(1), 57–79. doi:10.1093/bjsw/31.1.57

Wendt, S., Tuckey, M. R., & Prosser, B. (2011). Thriving, not just surviving, in emotionally demanding fields of practice. *Health & Social Care in the Community, 19*(3), 317–325. doi:10.1111/j.1365-2524.2010.00983.x PMID:21276106

Yule, W. (2001). When disaster strikes: The need to be "wise before the event" – Crisis intervention with children and adolescents. *Advances in Mind-Body Medicine, 17*(3), 191–196. doi:10.1054/ambm.2000.0313 PMID:11572847

## ADDITIONAL READING

Bonanno, G. A. (2004). Loss, trauma, and human resilience: Have we underestimated the human capacity to thrive after extremely aversive events? *The American Psychologist, 59*(1), 20–28. doi:10.1037/0003-066X.59.1.20 PMID:14736317

Bonanno, G. A., Westphal, M., & Mancini, A. D. (2011). Resilience to loss and potential trauma. *Annual Review of Clinical Psychology, 7*(1), 511–535. doi:10.1146/annurev-clinpsy-032210-104526 PMID:21091190

Bowman, P. J. (2013). A strengths-based social psychological approach to resiliency: Cultural diversity, ecological, and life span issues. In S. Prince-Embury & D. H. Saklofske (Eds.), *Resilience in children, adolescents, and adults: Translating research into practice* (pp. 299–324). New York: Springer. doi:10.1007/978-1-4614-4939-3_21

Carson, E., King, S., & Papatraianou, L. H. (2011). Resilience among social workers: The role of informal learning in the workplace. *Practice, 23*(5), 267–278. doi:10.1080/09503153.2011.581361

Cicchetti, D. (2010). Resilience under conditions of extreme stress: A multilevel perspective. *World Psychiatry: Official Journal of the World Psychiatric Association (WPA), 9,* 145–154. doi:10.1002/j.2051-5545.2010.tb00297.x PMID:20975856

Collins, S. (2007). Social workers, resilience, positive emotions and optimism. *Practice, 19*(4), 255–269. doi:10.1080/09503150701728186

Folke, C. (2006). Resilience: The emergence of a perspective for social-ecological systems analyses. *Global Environmental Change, 16*(3), 253–267. doi:10.1016/j.gloenvcha.2006.04.002

Harney, P. A. (2007). Resilience processes in context: Contributions and implications of Bronfenbrenner's person-process-context model. *Journal of Aggression, Maltreatment & Trauma, 14*(3), 73–87. doi:10.1300/J146v14n03_05

Levine, S. Z., Laufer, A., Stein, E., Hamama-Raz, Y., & Solomon, Z. (2009). Examining the relationship between resilience and posttraumatic growth. *Journal of Traumatic Stress, 22*(4), 282–286. doi:10.1002/jts.20409 PMID:19593805

Norris, F. H., Tracy, M., & Galea, S. (2009). Looking for resilience: Understanding the longitudinal trajectories of responses to stress. *Social Science & Medicine, 68*(12), 2190–2198. doi:10.1016/j.socscimed.2009.03.043 PMID:19403217

Sanders, S., Jacobson, J. M., & Ting, L. (2008). Preparing for the inevitable: Training social workers to cope with client suicide. *Journal of Teaching in Social Work*, 28(1-2), 1–18. doi:10.1080/08841230802178821

## KEY TERMS AND DEFINITIONS

**Critical Incident:** Situations and incidents within workplace settings or roles which have the potential to create a sense of emergency, crisis, extreme stress, or have a traumatic impact on those directly or indirectly affected.

**Critical Incident Stress:** The stress which follows exposure to a critical incident within the workplace and which may affect an employee's well-being, social or employment functioning.

**Critical Incident Stress Debriefing (CISD):** Also called psychological debriefing, this is part of a critical incident stress management (CISM) approach to workplace incidents involving a planned, group intervention using crisis theory and psycho-educational principles.

**Critical Incident Stress Management (CISM):** An organisationally-based process or set of processes that support staff through the preparation for, experience of, and recovery from critical incidents within the workplace.

**Employee Assistance Programme (EAP):** A workplace-based (internal or external to the organisation) programme that provides support, advice, and counselling for staff welfare, job satisfaction, and organisational benefits.

**Psychological First Aid:** Practical, informational, and emotional support provided immediately after an incident with the intention of re-stabilising and containing emotional distress.

**Traumatic Event:** An event that may create a severe psychological response with symptoms connected to the descriptions of acute and post-traumatic stress disorders in the American Psychiatric Association's *Diagnostic and statistical manual of mental disorders.*

# Chapter 16

# Post–Qualifying Practice:
## Implications for Social Workers with a Spiritual Approach to Practice

**Mary Nash**
*Massey University, New Zealand*

## ABSTRACT

*A spiritual approach to social work practice is gaining recognition. This chapter considers the implications for practitioners who draw on spirituality in their work and the requirements for post-qualifying practice or Continuous Professional Development (CPD). Key terms are defined drawing on research and publications relating to CPD, and spiritual worldviews and their influence on social work are discussed. A case study illustrates how practitioners may choose to reflect on their own spiritual worldview in order to be better equipped when working with clients for whom the spiritual or religious dimension is important. It is suggested that this helps the practitioner to establish good working relationships across cultures and beliefs, and it consequently increases the chances of successful interventions. A second case study provides an example of how the social work practitioner, through involvement in a creative project, drew on spirituality in order to promote her own self-care.*

## INTRODUCTION

There are many expressions of spirituality and I consider that it is now widely accepted that a spiritual approach to practice can be an appropriate, sustaining, and creative dimension for social workers and service-users. Accordingly, this chapter addresses spirituality as potentially a sustaining and creative dimension for social workers with their need for self-care and reflects on its implications for those who use their services. Writing about spirituality and social work in a Continuous Professional Development (CPD) environment means taking the discussion beyond the, by now familiar, introductory level. I will, therefore, be considering how social workers with a spiritual stance may respond to the task of "maintaining and developing the professional identity of social work, be it [their] own or a colleagues [which] is an important part of [their] professional development as a Social Worker" (Australian Association of Social Workers [AASW], 2012/13, p. 7). In

DOI: 10.4018/978-1-4666-6563-7.ch016

order to contextualise this discussion, key terms are defined and relevant research and publications are covered.

## The Search Strategy

The literature search has been guided by several criteria, with most sources being published within the last ten years. Key words and phrases were *spirituality, social work*, *"community gardening"*, *"environmental social work"*, *"accreditation standards"*, and *"continuing professional development"*. A deliberate policy of using free access literature where possible was adopted. Recent literature spanning books, journal articles, and websites suggests that authors and researchers have increasing confidence in asserting a place for a spiritual dimension in social work theory and practice (Canda & Furman, 2010; Crisp, 2010; Gale & Dudley, 2013; Gardner, 2011; Holloway & Moss, 2010; Nash & Stewart, 2002; Walsh, 2011; Wong & Vinsky, 2009). Practical applications and the cultural significance of spirituality derived from research and practice show how practitioners and clients may work together, drawing on their diverse spiritual strengths and insights to achieve mutually agreed goals. It is acknowledged that there is ongoing, probably endemic, diversity in how spirituality is defined in the context of social work.

## THE ROLE OF SPIRITUALITY

In the USA, social workers must recognise the importance of service-users' religious beliefs and they also have a duty to "advance human rights and social and economic justice" (Council on Social Work Education, 2008, Educational Policy 2.1.5). Freedom of religious belief is one of those human rights (International Covenant on Civil and Political Rights, 1966, Article 18). The first case study illustrates the importance of recognising when the spiritual (and cultural)

world view of a client must be taken into account in order to achieve a good working relationship and consequently successful intervention. The second case study discusses how the practitioner can draw on their personal spirituality to sustain themselves at a transformative level through a shared garden project. When presenting the case studies, the author refers to the reflective, critical, and transformative practice framework for continuing professional development (Adams, 2007).

## Definitions

### Social Work

According to the International Federation of Social Workers (IFSW, 2012a),

*... the social work profession promotes social change, problem solving in human relationships and the empowerment and liberation of people to enhance well-being. Utilising theories of human behaviour and social systems, social work intervenes at the points where people interact with their environments. Principles of human rights and social justice are fundamental to social work. (Definition)*

The principle of human rights and human dignity recognises the link between social justice, human rights, and respect for people's spiritual and religious beliefs, stating that "social work is based on respect for the inherent worth and dignity of all people, and the rights that follow from this. Social workers should uphold and defend each person's physical, psychological, emotional and spiritual integrity and well-being" (IFSW, 2012b, 4.1. Human Rights and Human Dignity).

Respect is being paid here to spiritual integrity but exactly what this means is not spelled out. In each cultural environment, practitioners must take time to sensitively discern it. In this chapter, social work is inclusively defined to recognise that within the conventional definition there is room for community development, described as "the saving grace of social work" (Napan, 2010, n.p.). Our environments in social work are extensive and it is widely accepted that the environment we interact with is not just structural or political but also physical and ecological.

## Spirituality and Social Work

National social work standards and codes of ethics call for recognition of, and competence in, working with a service-user's spiritual stance (AASW, 2010; Aotearoa New Zealand Association of Social Workers, 2008) and in doing so also recognise and legitimise the place of spirituality in social work practice.

Sermabeikian (1994) makes a case for including spirituality in the field of social work, describing it as a human need which

*… is too important to be misunderstood; avoided; or viewed as regressive, neurotic, or pathological in nature. Social workers must recognise that a person's spiritual beliefs, values, perceptions, feelings, and ideals are intrinsically connected to religious, philosophical, cultural, ethnic, and life experiences. It is important that the practitioner acknowledge that spirituality in a person's life can be a constructive way of facing life's difficulties. (p. 181)*

If a social worker practices from a spiritual or religious stance, then they need to be critically mindful of this and constantly alert to what it means, both as it informs their client assessments and interventions and as it supports (or possibly interferes with) their work. If neither spirituality nor religion have meaning for the practitioner, that person, nevertheless, needs to be aware that whoever they are working with may consider either or both to be of central importance. This is especially relevant in working with asylum seekers, refugees, and immigrants. For this reason, the practitioner

needs to work at maintaining and developing their awareness and understanding, either as an insider or as an outsider, of spirituality and religion. Some people perceive a connection between the natural, or earth-centred, world (the mountains, rivers, flora, and fauna of which humans are only a small part) and the spiritual dimension. In this context, Puketapu-Hetet (Erenora Puketapu-Hetet, Te Atiawa: Interview by Darcy Nicholas, 1986), a traditional Maori weaver, has talked and written about the need to respect the environment and natural materials (often flax plants) used in weaving:

*It is important to me as a weaver that I respect the mauri (life force) of what I am working with. Once I have taken it from where it belongs, I must give another dimension to its life force so that it is still a thing of beauty. I am talking about a whole way of living in harmony with natural things – nature itself, natural lines, natural movements and being at one with these things. (p. 40)*

What are the connections between this approach to living in the world and how social workers or their clients aspire to live? It is imbued with respect for the other in one's life, be that material, human, spiritual, and familial, or all of these together. It is, I believe, profound in its simplicity and capable of transforming the person who implements what it means. Whether or not one's imagination is caught by spirituality as an appropriate area for social workers to be involved with, the notion of respect for all around one is accessible in a secular context. How one understands mauri or life force is up to each person. It is a concept indigenous to Aotearoa New Zealand, where it has animistic connotations, reminding people of the need to respect Papatuanuku (mother earth) and the environment just as we should respect one another. Van Wormer and Besthorne (2010) link such ideas to social work when they propose

*... a way of understanding ourselves with nature that can carry social work deeper into the next millennium with a sober sense of responsibility, a heartfelt sense of compassion, and a joyful sense of celebration for our connection with all people in this complex and amazing world. (p. 308)*

Spirituality is generally recognised to be an elusive, subtle, and complex concept, and personal definitions vary and will need to be respected (Nash & Stewart, 2002). Based on their comprehensive research of the literature and their international surveys of social work practitioners, Canda & Furman (2010) argue that

*... spirituality is: A process of human life and development focusing on the search for a sense of meaning, purpose, morality, and well-being; in relationship with oneself, other people, other beings, the universe, and ultimate reality however understood (e.g. animistic, atheistic, nontheistic, polytheistic, theistic, or other ways); orienting around centrally significant priorities; and engaging a sense of transcendence (experienced as deeply profound, sacred, or transpersonal). (p. 75)*

Spiritually has been defined as "a search for meaning, and purpose and connection with self, others, the encompassing universe and ultimate reality" (Gilligan, 2010, p. 60). This uncomplicated definition is attractive in that it provides enough to go on for most people without proceeding into difficult territory.

Canda & Furman (2010) have described religion as subsumed within this all-encompassing conceptualisation, writing that religion is

*... an institutionalised (i.e. systematic and organized) pattern of values, beliefs, symbols, behaviors, and experiences that involves*

- *spirituality*
- *a community of adherents*
- *transmission of traditions over time and*
- *community support functions (e.g. organizational structure, material assistance, emotional support, or political advocacy) that are directly or indirectly related to spirituality. (p. 76)*

It is common to find spirituality distinguished from religion (Canda & Furman, 2010; Gale & Dudley, 2013). However, not everyone feels entirely comfortable with such a position (Eastham, 2002; Wong & Vinsky, 2009). Wong & Vinsky (2009), for example, position themselves as speaking from the margins and critique the social work discourse which divides spirituality and religion. They question the othering of religion, arguing that

*... such a tentative and humble posturing can work to reduce the risk of taking away the client's authority of meanings, to prevent a further marginalization and othering of non-dominant spiritual knowing such as labelling "religious" clients as traditional, conservative or bounded by culture, and to support us in working towards social justice in spirituality and social work. (p. 1355)*

This critical point signals the need to avoid thinking of social workers as scientific professionals with little interest in spirituality or religion and service-users as vulnerable people who amongst other characteristics are likely to have religious or spiritual leanings. Crisp (2010) is careful to acknowledge complexities in discussing the interplay between spirituality and religion, as are Holloway and Moss (2010). Spirituality is usually conceptualised as being benign but it does also have a dark side. Space does not allow for coverage of this here but interested readers could begin with de Souza's (2012) article: "Connectedness and *Connectedness*: The Dark Side of Spirituality: Implications for Education".

## Continuing Professional Development

Members of the AASW are required to develop their practice standards through CPD. The AASW (2012) describes CPD as

*... how AASW members maintain, improve and broaden their skills, knowledge and expertise, and develop the qualities required for professional practice. CPD is an ongoing process throughout a career informed by the changing practice environment, professional domains, new information and community need. (p. 3)*

CPD is also referred to as post-qualifying practice, and Adams (2007) has developed three lenses through which practitioners can assess their practice in order to ensure they keep adding to their understanding, skills, and knowledge as social workers. He describes the three practice levels as reflective, critical, and transformative. Reflective practice involves working methodically within the system and being mindful about what one does. Critical practitioners locate themselves in their social and political context, act in a self-reflexive manner, and consistently review their actions in order to improve practice. Transformative practitioners work for social change and seek to empower the people they work with and for. At the same time, such practitioners will take an analytical approach to practice in context, interrogating what may otherwise be taken for granted.

## The Implications of Spiritual Approaches for Social Work

Four spiritual needs were identified by McGilloway and Myco (1985). These continue to resonate with practitioners and help to bridge the space between the abstract activity of defining spirituality and integrating it into practice. They suggested that human beings want to find meaning and purpose in life, to love and be loved, to have good self-esteem, and to have hope for the future. McGilloway and Myco wrote in a nursing context for people facing life-threatening conditions but their words apply equally well in the broader context of social work.

Practitioners and clients may work together drawing on their spiritual strengths and insights to achieve mutually agreed goals. They may, however, find themselves facing difficult and even intractable dilemmas. If working with people facing life and death choices, such as abortion, suicide, or even mercy killing, then where a spiritual or religious approach is paramount for either the client or the worker and their views differ there will be dilemmas. Should the social worker really broach the subject of spiritual belief with a client or might this be trespassing on territory belonging to their spiritual advisor? What should social workers do when working with clients whose beliefs about the purpose of life differ from theirs, resulting in disputes over, say, child discipline ("spare the rod and spoil the child") or where the parents refuse medical treatment (e.g. a blood transfusion)? What are the practice boundaries between a spiritually informed approach to social work practice and the kind of pastoral counselling normally expected from, say, a vicar, rabbi, or muslim advisor? These are just a few of the dilemmas which will from time to time occur to the spiritually informed social worker.

It is, nevertheless, argued here that spirituality, when integrated in social work practice, supports all aspects of human development and deepens the therapeutic effect of professional helping (Nash & Stewart, 2002). Integration entails being fully aware of the contribution spirituality makes to client well-being and putting one's spiritual wisdom (the knowledge of the heart) into practice. In their editorial for the *International Social Work* special issue on spirituality and social work, Furness &

Gilligan (2013) endorse this point when they call on social workers to recognise that they need to be able to work in knowledgeable and respectful ways with clients for whom diverse forms of spiritual beliefs are important. They argue that to do this, social workers need "to be self-aware and reflexive about their own beliefs and their responses to beliefs of others; to recognise service-users' expertise about their own needs and beliefs and to listen to what they say about these" (p. 273).

According to Gilligan & Furness (2006),

*… findings from surveys of qualified social work practitioners and students indicate a need for social work education and practice to focus attention both on the importance of religious and spiritual beliefs in the lives of many service-users and on the potential usefulness of religious and spiritual interventions. (p. 617)*

As mentioned earlier, references to the rights of service-users to have their religious and/or spiritual beliefs and attitudes recognised and treated with respect can increasingly be found in standard-setting bodies for professionals, including social work professionals. Social workers, therefore, have a responsibility to develop their professional knowledge and skills in this area in order to meet CPD standards and, where necessary, to be able to assert that they are using evidence-based practice (EBP) or, alternatively, evidence-informed practice (EIP). "Under the EIP model, [the main requirement is] that practitioners will become knowledgeable of a wide range of sources – empirical studies, case studies and clinical insights – and use them in creative ways throughout the intervention process" (Nevo & Slonim-Nevo, 2011, p. 1176).

Frameworks with models and tools for practice are becoming increasingly available as a result of research and consultation around spirituality and social work. One of these is the spiritual genogram, of which there are several versions, based on the conventional three generational genogram but focusing on looking at a person's spiritual heritage or history and seeking to illustrate what part, if any, spirituality and/or religion play in their life (Bullis, 1996; Canda & Furman, 2010; Frame, 2001; Hodge, 2011). The spiritual genogram may be used in clinical supervision or it may be used as part of a client assessment process. Frame (2001) uses a clinically tested spiritual genogram to invite "clients to gain fresh perspectives on how their religious or spiritual history continues to affect their current family functioning" (p. 109). She also discusses its use in clinical supervision, where it facilitates supervisor and supervisee in working out how the practitioner's faith system (or lack thereof) may be impacting on their work with clients.

Furness and Gilligan (2010) developed a framework with nine interconnected principles which combine reflexive qualities with tools for assessment. The authors describe how the majority of a sample of MA student respondents found the framework helpful and argue that it provides a useful context for practice. Social work students used a set of reflective questions about spiritual and religious knowledge aimed at developing self-examination, self-awareness, reflexivity, and the ability to take service-user's views explicitly into account. This was helpful in assessing the significance for social work practitioners of their own religion and beliefs and that of their clients. It seems that this framework would provide a safe context for working with a client on drawing up a spiritual genogram while meeting the criteria for EBP.

Two examples of these principles relate to the case studies below: "Recognition of individuals' expertise about their own needs and beliefs" and "self-awareness and reflexivity about [one's] own religious and spiritual beliefs and responses to the beliefs of others" (Furness & Gilligan, 2010, p. 2189).

The following case study illustrates how important it is to recognise the spiritual (and cultural) world-view of a client which when taken into account may serve to achieve a good working relationship and consequently successful intervention.

## Case Study One: The Spiritual Genogram as a Practice Tool

A successful business man (James), approaching retirement, was referred for depression to a social worker (Jenny) with a known reputation for her wisdom and spiritual approach to practice. His medical practitioner had already referred him to a series of mental health practitioners and now as a last resort to Jenny, as nothing seemed to shift his deep unhappiness with life and previous practitioners were at a loss as to how to proceed. James told Jenny that his GP was losing patience with him because none of the earlier interventions had made any difference and he felt like giving up. While establishing a good working relationship, Jenny asked James to tell her about his childhood and the values he grew up with. James had grown up in a loving and religious environment where unselfishness and generosity were praised but success at the expense of others was unacceptable. After leaving home, James discovered he had a talent for making money and at first his parents were full of praise and admiration. After their deaths, he became a well-known and respected figure in the business world. Now, as he was facing retirement, he felt his success was empty and had become depressed.

Jenny showed self-awareness and reflexivity about her own religious and spiritual beliefs and sensed a deep malaise relating to James' abandonment of his early religious beliefs. They worked together on his spiritual genogram and James began to see how his material success had been at the expense of the values that were embedded in his psyche in childhood. He was now enduring a deep inner conflict which neither he nor his therapists had recognised. This insight made it possible for James to understand what was going on and with Jenny's encouragement he was able

to find a meaningful way to make reparation for what he felt he had done and which was causing his depression. None of the previous practitioners had tuned into this spiritual or religious aspect of James's distress. His apparently unresolvable dis-ease was, once understood, both reasonable and manageable.

The case study illustrates how the social worker acted on her understanding that "in each of us there is an interior life, intimate, emotional, spiritual" (de Hennezel, 1997, p. 160), and she was fully aware of the contribution spirituality makes to client well-being. Her sensitivity with someone who had presented with no apparent spiritual inclination differentiated her from previous practitioners. This intervention is consistent with that of critical practitioners who, according to Adams (2007), locate themselves in their social and political context, act in a self-reflexive manner, and consistently review their actions in order to improve practice. She knew that her spiritual stance in relation to the person she was working with was unusual in the social and political context of her practice; she was a conscientious practitioner used to self-critique and studying to develop and improve her practice.

It can be argued that recognition of the spiritual dimension in social work serves to unite concern for the personal with concern about social and political inequity. "An integrated spirituality is a spirituality in which who we are and what we do are intimately related" (Masango, 2006, p. 930). If spiritual awareness strengthens the connections between social work and social justice, providing hope and a sustainable approach to work (Nash & Stewart, 2005), then it also has a place alongside the radical in social work in so far as radical social work "insists on a truly human response to suffering" (Leonard & Corrigan, 1978, p. 157). It is about recognising the social justice component in the spiritual dimensions of our practice (Consedine, 2002).

Earlier in this chapter, community development was described as "the saving grace of social work" (Napan, 2010, n.p.). Heavy caseloads, increasingly complex cases, and contract conditions which impose political discretion upon agencies mean that today's social workers are hard pressed to uphold the profession's principle of social justice. Under these circumstances, the social work helping relationship is also inevitably jeopardised. In this context, the "relational quality of spirituality as it can engage empathetic connection, understanding of others' perspectives, partnership, connection across diversities, and striving for justice for individuals and communities" (Canda & Furman, 2010, pp. 66-67) is put at risk. The need for social workers to look after themselves is accepted but self-care can too easily be postponed or neglected. Bloemhard's (2008) argument that "looking after one's own spiritual needs has to be the first and most important step

in the direction of encouraging clients to finding their own spiritual strength and purpose" (p. 60) reminds us of this need for self-care in all aspects of our lives when practising social work.

## Case Study Two: Self-Care and a Shared Garden for Body and Soul

This second case study could have been presented as an example of volunteering within the community, since volunteering meets a CPD criteria suggested by the AASW (2012), but in fact it is an example of practitioner self-care, in that the practitioner (in this case the author) was sustained by involvement in a project which gave expression to her creativity. It is the story of the establishment of a shared garden which drew together a diverse group of people, all of whom wanted to

*Figure 1. Garden project (Nash, W., 2009)*

engage in an intentional community, growing and sharing food in supportive, sustainable, and environmentally friendly ways. Many of the people involved are working towards forming a small Catholic Worker group. The aims and means of the Catholic Worker movement are described on their website ("The aims and means", n.d.). The group met (and still meets) on Friday evenings for liturgy followed by a pot-luck meal. This case study is presented, drawing on recordings in which people talked about their experience of the garden project and what it meant to them. The self-care theme is embedded in the text.

The photo shows a spiral planting of maize and sweet corn being blessed as the gardeners gather around. The group includes three generations with various degrees of gardening knowledge and experience. The gardeners were attracted by a shared philosophy of life, drawing on Rudolf Steiner as well as Christian and pagan insights, all placing value in the environment. The group consisted of a family with four young daughters, a widow, a university veterinary technician, several unemployed people, a young couple with two young children, and several people marginalised from society as a result of being autistic, alcoholic, or homeless.

Planting in spirals appealed to most of the group, for as Buzz (personal communication, April 9, 2010) said

*I was really happy to see we were planting in circles, though Will said that was not very efficient. It says a lot about the way it attracted me. It's not entirely about the production of food; it's also about trying to rediscover our agricultural and common history of living off the land, connection with the earth, and where our food comes from.*

For Krista (personal communication, April 16, 2010), the process of sharing was important:

*The biggest thing is that it is a shared garden, not a divided area with individual plots. We got in and put some potatoes in the ground and some onions in the ground, and all of it was shared, and then people came and took what they needed or some people got more than others. I think all things were shared, the weeding was shared, everything was shared without having to equally divide it up and count, and that was probably one of the most precious experiences because that doesn't often happen in life that a group of people can get together and say "lets share but we are not going to count the cost and count the pennies and the potatoes", and that was all unsaid. It must be almost a record of community working together and there was no quarrelling.*

Krista and Buzz, mothers of young children, both observed how valuable this experience was for their children. Krista (personal communication, April 16, 2010) observed that "our children benefitted from it too – community, giving, companionship, weeding, sunflowers, scarecrow, fun; and they saw what came out of the ground and was now on our plates. We talk to them about that."

Buzz (personal communication, April 9, 2010) also commented that

*… sharing food in the garden has provided moments for us to come together and connect – organised and spontaneous. The children have loved it, having honey; the blessing of our plants or the garden before we started; and the games have been fun too.*

The garden in this case study is an expression of a wider project which has grown and changed over time. A house, which is attached to the garden, provides sheltered accommodation; beehives give honey with shared activities around its production; and chickens and a few sheep reward the care given them. The pot luck meal, preceded by liturgy and prayers every Friday evening, is the heart of the group, not all of whom are gardeners. As Krista pointed out, "whether on Fridays with prayer or in the garden under the big sky without the prayers, the food has been a great connection". For Mike, the gathering together and sharing of a meal had great importance and the Friday evening liturgy was, for him, more sustainable than anything else.

The shared garden and associated activities have been a place where life is lived at a slower pace and where people can be at peace with humanity in an accepting environment, and in this way it makes a valuable contribution to self-care. It is founded upon common aims, such as sustainability, interdependence, and fellowship with people who are in some way isolated, lonely, or vulnerable. For those on a benefit, it has been a source of fresh vegetables, honey, and meat; for the lonely of companionship; and for people concerned about the environment, it is a small step in caring for mother earth.

Crisp (2010) notes the importance of creativity for human beings, linking it to an expression of spirituality and a way of meaning-making. She observes the way in which a garden can help to shape its creator's identity while also providing opportunities for connecting with communities. Hawkins stresses the importance of recognising the "connections between social work, sustainability, human rights, and environmental justice in our contemporary world" (Hawkins, 2010, Abstract), and the shared garden project has been a step in this direction. Regarding Adams' (2007) three practice levels for CPD, I would assess my involvement in the project as being consistent with the transformative level, for we could be seen to be using our creativity to empower ourselves as well as the people to whom we reach out. We take an analytical approach to what we are doing and experiencing and we are prepared to get involved in social and political action.

## CONCLUSION

This chapter has argued that the spiritual dimension has an assured place in the field of social work. There is nothing prescriptive about this. It is simply a matter of awareness and sensitivity, both to one's inner self and to the people one works with. In the last ten years, the growth of literature on this topic has expanded and there are now good resources available for the beginning practitioner. Some of the core themes in the literature have been briefly covered and the two case studies are presented with CPD in mind.

Clinical practice supervision is one of the most important resources for the professional social worker and certainly for the reflective practitioner who may be keen to draw on their own sense of spirituality when working with clients or who needs to acknowledge their client's spiritual world despite finding this to be new territory. Ongoing research into most aspects of the implications of a spiritual dimension for practice is required. I believe there is a place for research to explore how social workers see themselves as a resource for the migrant or refugee for whom religion and spirituality are often important factors in managing their lives. In addition, we need more information about how we can best inform and educate social workers in this aspect of social work which is at once intensely personal and also a human rights requirement. It is an area where practitioners and service-users need, above all, to feel safe and secure and in no way open to coercion or any kind of prescriptive practice.

## REFERENCES

Adams, R. (2007). Reflective, critical and transformative practice. In W. Tovey (Ed.), *The post-qualifying handbook for social workers* (pp. 28–42). London: Jessica Kingsley.

The aims and means of the Catholic worker. (n.d.). Catholic Worker Movement. Retrieved from http://www.catholicworker.org/aimsand-meanstext.cfm?Number=5

Aotearoa New Zealand Association of Social Workers. (2008). *Code of ethics*. Christchurch, New Zealand: Author.

Australian Association of Social Workers. (2010). *Code of Ethics*. Retrieved from www.aasw.asn.au/practitioner-resources/code-of-ethics

Australian Association of Social Workers. (2012). *Education and Accreditation Standards*. Retrieved from http://www.aasw.asn.au/careers-study/education-standards-accreditation

Australian Association of Social Workers. (2012/13). *Continuing Professional Development for members*. Retrieved from http://www.aasw.asn.au/document/item/3374

Bloemhard, A. (2008). *Spiritual care for self and others*. Coffs Harbour: The Mid North Coast Division of General Practice/Australian Department of Health and Ageing.

Bullis, R. K. (1996). *Spirituality in social work practice*. Washington, DC: Taylor & Francis.

Canda, E. R., & Furman, L. D. (2010). *Spiritual diversity in social work practice: The heart of helping* (2nd ed.). New York: Oxford University Press.

Consedine, J. (2002). Spirituality and social justice. In M. Nash & B. Stewart (Eds.), *Spirituality and social care: Contributing to personal and community well-being* (pp. 31–48). London: Jessica Kingsley.

Council on Social Work Education. (2008). *Educational policy and accreditation standards*. Retrieved from http://www.cswe.org/Accreditation/2008EPASDescription.aspx

Crisp, B. R. (2010). *Spirituality and social work*. Southampton: Ashgate.

de Hennezel, M. (1997). *Intimate death: How the dying teach us how to live*. New York: Alfred A. Knopf.

de Souza, M. (2012). Connectedness and *connectedness*: The dark side of spirituality – Implications for education. *International Journal of Children's Spirituality*, *17*(4), 291–303. doi:10.1080/1364436X.2012.752346

Eastham, M. (2002). Vocation and social care. In M. Nash & B. Stewart (Eds.), *Spirituality and social care: Contributing to personal and community well-being* (pp. 71–91). London: Jessica Kingsley.

Erenora Puketapu-Hetet. (1986). Te Atiawa: Interview by Darcy Nicholas. In *Seven Maori artists: Interviews by Darcy Nicholas and Keri Kaa* (pp. 38–42). Wellington, New Zealand: Government Printer.

Frame, M. W. (2001). The spiritual genogram in training and supervision. *The Family Journal*, *9*(2), 109–115. doi:10.1177/1066480701092004

Furness, S., & Gilligan, P. (2010). Social work, religion and belief: Developing a framework for practice. *British Journal of Social Work*, *40*(7), 2185–2202. doi:10.1093/bjsw/bcp159

Furness, S., & Gilligan, P. (2013). Editorial. *International Social Work*, *56*(3), 271–275. doi:10.1177/0020872813476447

Gale, F., & Dudley, M. (2013). Spirituality in social work. In M. Connolly & L. Harms (Eds.), *Social work: Contexts and practice* (3rd ed., pp. 60–73). Melbourne: Oxford University Press.

Gardner, F. (2011). *Critical spirituality: A holistic approach to contemporary practice*. Farnham, UK: Ashgate.

Gilligan, P. (2010). Faith-based approaches. In M. Gray & S. Webb (Eds.), *Ethics and value perspectives in social work* (pp. 60–70). Basingstoke, UK: Palgrave Macmillan.

Gilligan, P., & Furness, S. (2006). The role of religion and spirituality in social work practice: Views and experiences of social workers and students. *British Journal of Social Work, 36*(4), 617–637. doi:10.1093/bjsw/bch252

Hawkins, C. A. (2010). Sustainability, human rights, and environmental justice: Critical connections for social work. *Critical Social Work, 11*(3). Retrieved from http://www1.uwindsor.ca/criticalsocialwork/the-nexus-of-sustainability-human-rights-and-environmental-justice-a-critical-connection-for-contemp

Hodge, D. R. (2011). Evidence-based spiritual practice: Using research to inform the selection of spiritual interventions. *Journal of Religion & Spirituality in Social Work: Social Thought, 30*(4), 325–339. doi:10.1080/15426432.2011.619896

Holloway, M., & Moss, B. (2010). *Spirituality and social work*. Basingstoke, UK: Palgrave Macmillan.

International Covenant on Civil and Political Rights, Dec .19, 1966, 999 U.N.T.S. 171.

International Federation of Social Workers. (2012a). Definition of social work. Retrieved from http://ifsw.org/policies/definition-of-social-work/

International Federation of Social Workers. (2012b). Statement of ethical principles. Retrieved from http://ifsw.org/policies/statement-of-ethical-principles/

Leonard, P., & Corrigan, P. (1978). *Social work practice under capitalism: A Marxist approach*. London: Macmillan.

Masango, M. J. S. (2006). African spirituality that shapes the concept of Ubunten. *Verbum et Ecclesia JRG, 27*, 930–943. doi:10.4102/ve.v27i3.195

McGilloway, O., & Myco, F. (1985). *Nursing and spiritual care*. Harper & Row.

Napan, K. (2010). *Co-creative enquiry*. Paper presented at the Symposium on Spirituality and Social Work. Inter-University Centre, Dubrovnik.

Nash, M., & Stewart, B. (Eds.). (2002). *Spirituality and social care*. London: Jessica Kingsley.

Nash, M., & Stewart, B. (2005). Spirituality and hope in social work for social justice. *Currents: New Scholarship in the Human Services, 4*(1), 1-10. Retrieved from http://www.ucalgary.ca/currents/files/currents/v4n1_nash.pdf

Nevo, I., & Slonim-Nevo, V. (2011). The myth of evidence-based practice: Towards evidence-informed practice. *British Journal of Social Work, 41*(6), 1176–1197. doi:10.1093/bjsw/bcq149

Sermabeikian, P. (1994). Our clients, ourselves: The spiritual perspective and social work practice. *Social Work, 39*, 178–183. Retrieved from https://www.naswpress.org/publications/journals/sw.html

Van Wormer, K., & Besthorn, F. H. (2010). *Human behaviour and the social environment, macro level: Groups, communities, and organizations* (2nd ed.). New York: Oxford University Press.

Walsh, N. M. (2011). Jean Vanier: An alternative voice for the social work profession. *Journal of Religion & Spirituality in Social Work: Social Thought, 30*(4), 340–357. doi:10.1080/15426432.2011.619898

Wong, Y. R., & Vinsky, J. (2009). Speaking from the margins: A critical reflection on the "spiritual-but-not-religious" discourse in social work. *British Journal of Social Work, 39*(7), 1343–1359. doi:10.1093/bjsw/bcn032

## ADDITIONAL READING

Besthorn, F. H., & Saleebey, D. (2003). Nature, genetics and the biophilia connection: Exploring linkages with social work values and practice. *Advances in Social Work, 4*, 1-18. Retrieved from https://journals.iupui.edu/index.php/advancesinsocialwork

Carrington, A. M. (2010). Spiritual paradigms: A response to concerns within social work in relation to the inclusion of spirituality. *Journal of Religion & Spirituality in Social Work, 29*(4), 300–320. doi:10.1080/15426432.2010.518869

Cowlishaw, S., Niele, S., Teshuva, K., Browning, C., & Kendig, H. (2013). Older adults' spirituality and life satisfaction: A longitudinal test of social support and sense of coherence as mediating mechanisms. *Ageing and Society, 33*(07), 1243–1262. doi:10.1017/S0144686X12000633

Crisp, B. R. (2008). Social work and spirituality in a secular society. *Journal of Social Work, 8*(4), 363–375. doi:10.1177/1468017308094990

Edwards, P. B. (2002). Spiritual themes in social work counselling: Facilitating the search for meaning. *Australian Social Work, 55*(1), 78–87. doi:10.1080/03124070208411674

Edwards, P. (2003). Aging, spirituality and pastoral care: A multi-national perspective. *Australian Social Work, 56*(4), 371–372. doi:10.1111/j.1447-0748.2003.00101.x

Evans, C. (2009). Spirited practices: Spirituality and the helping professions. *Australian Social Work, 62*(3), 425–427. doi:10.1080/03124070903092730

Furness, S., & Gilligan, P. (2010). *Religion, belief and social work: Making a difference*. Bristol, U.K.: Policy Press.

Furness, S., & Gilligan, P. (2014). "It never came up": Encouragements and discouragements to addressing religion and belief in professional practice – What do social work students have to say? *British Journal of Social Work, 44*(3), 763–781. doi:10.1093/bjsw/bcs140

Galloway, G., Wilkinson, P., & Bissell, G. (2008). Empty space or sacred place? Place and belief in social work training. *The Journal of Practice Teaching & Learning, 8*(3), 28–47. doi:10.1921/146066909X478262

Gilbert, M. C. (2000). Spirituality in social work groups: Practitioners speak out. *Social Work with Groups, 22*(4), 67–84. doi:10.1300/J009v22n04_06

Gilligan, P. (2003). "It isn't discussed": Religion, belief and practice teaching – Missing components of cultural competence in social work education. *Journal of Practice Teaching in Health and Social Care, 5*(1), 75–95. doi:10.1921/17466105.5.1.75

Gray, M. (2008). Viewing spirituality in social work through the lens of contemporary social theory. *British Journal of Social Work, 38*(1), 175–196. doi:10.1093/bjsw/bcl078

Gray, M., Coates, J., & Hetherington, T. (2007). Hearing indigenous voices in mainstream social work. *Families in Society, 88*(1), 55–66. doi:10.1606/1044-3894.3592

Henery, N. (2003). Critical commentary: The reality of visions: Contemporary theories of spirituality in social work. *British Journal of Social Work, 33*(8), 1105–1113. doi:10.1093/bjsw/33.8.1105

Hodge, D. R. (2001). Spiritual assessment: A review of major qualitative methods and a new framework for assessing spirituality. *Social Work, 46*(3), 203–214. doi:10.1093/sw/46.3.203 PMID:11495366

Holloway, M. (2007). Spiritual need and the core business of social work. *British Journal of Social Work, 37*(2), 265–280. doi:10.1093/bjsw/bcl014

Lindsay, R. (2002). *Recognizing spirituality: The interface between faith and social work.* Crawley: University of Western Australia Press.

Mark, G. T., & Lyons, A. C. (2010). Maori healers' views on wellbeing: The importance of mind, body, spirit, family and land. *Social Science & Medicine, 70*(11), 1756–1764. doi:10.1016/j.socscimed.2010.02.001 PMID:20338680

McFadden, S. H. (2008). Healing, health care, and spirituality. *The Gerontologist, 48*(1), 126–130. doi:10.1093/geront/48.1.126

Nash, M. (2010). *Change and continuity in what inspires and sustains work: A personal account with a community voice.* Paper presented at the Symposium on Spirituality and Social Work. Inter-University Centre, Dubrovnik.

Pattel-Gray, A. (1996). *Aboriginal spirituality: Past, present, future.* Australia: Harper Collins Religious.

Rice, S. (2002). Magic happens: Revisiting the spirituality and social work debate. *Australian Social Work, 55*(4), 303–312. doi:10.1080/03124070208410988

Rice, S. (2003). Recognizing spirituality: The interface between faith and social work. *Australian Social Work, 56*(4), 380–383. doi:10.1111/j.1447-0748.2003.00105.x

Rice, S., & McAuliffe, D. (2009). Ethics of the spirit: Comparing ethical views and usages of spiritually influenced interventions. *Australian Social Work, 62*(3), 403–420. doi:10.1080/03124070902964640

Senreich, E. (2013). An inclusive definition of spirituality for social work education and practice. *Journal of Social Work Education, 49*, 548–563. doi:10.1080/10437797.2013.812460

Sheridan, M. J. (2004). Predicting the use of spiritually-derived interventions in social work practice: A survey of practitioners. *Journal of Religion & Spirituality in Social Work, 23*(4), 5–25. doi:10.1300/J377v23n04_02

Sheridan, M. (2009). Ethical issues in the use of spiritually based interventions in social work practice: What are we doing and why? *Journal of Religion and Spirituality in Social Work: Social Thought, 28*(1-2), 99–126. doi:10.1080/15426430802643687

Stirling, B., Furman, L. D., Benson, P. W., Canda, E. R., & Grimwood, C. (2010). A comparative survey of Aotearoa New Zealand and UK social workers on the role of religion and spirituality in practice. *British Journal of Social Work, 40*(2), 602–621. doi:10.1093/bjsw/bcp008

Streets, F. (2009). Overcoming a fear of religion in social work education and practice. *Journal of Religion and Spirituality in Social Work: Social Thought, 28*(1-2), 185–199. doi:10.1080/15426430802644214

Yunupingu, G. (1996). Concepts of land and spirituality. In *A. Pattel-Gray. Aboriginal spirituality: Past, present and future* (pp. 4–10). Australia: Harper Collins Religious.

## KEY TERMS AND DEFINITIONS

**Accreditation Standards:** The standards of practice required by the professional association of its individual members.

**Continuing Professional Development:** Members of the Australian Association of Social Workers (AASW) are required to develop their practice standards through Continuing Professional Development (CPD). This involves description of how members maintain, improve, and broaden their skills, knowledge, and expertise, and how they develop the qualities required for professional practice.

**Environment:** A term which in social work embraces not only the structural or political with which humans interact but also the physical and ecological.

**Religion:** An institutionalised (i.e. systematic and organised) pattern of values, beliefs, symbols, behaviours, and experiences that invokes spirituality and a community of adherents.

**Social Work:** A profession based in the unique person-in-environment perspective focusing on individuals and the networks and systems that surround them.

**Spirituality:** Generally recognised to be elusive, subtle, and complex, this concept relates to the intangible aspects of everyday life. Personal definitions will vary and need to be respected.

# Chapter 17
# Conclusion:
## Beyond Binary Oppositions in Evidence-Based Practice in Social Work

**Margaret Pack**
*Australian Catholic University, Australia*

## ABSTRACT

*This chapter gathers together and synthesises the concepts used and developed throughout this book. These themes include the challenges posed for social work as a profession in relation to notions of rationality and scientific research methods when considering what constitutes "evidence" for social work practice. This critique challenges the definition and application of evidence to complex scenarios where there are no easy answers, yet the agency and systems seem to demand them from social workers. In response to these challenges, social work has developed expertise in the use of case study and action research methods, drawing from interpretive and participative epistemologies. Such research studies aim to give resonance to voices hitherto missed, marginalised, or ignored. To redress this marginalisation and to provide much needed balance in what constitutes "evidence," narratives of service-users and their caregivers have become primary sources of evidence, which are used to guide social work practice.*

## INTRODUCTION

The range of individual therapeutic, social, and organisational policy and legal factors identified by the authors throughout this book constitute an evidence-base for practice that differs qualitatively from the evidence searching process in other helping professions. Whilst social workers draw also from empirical research derived from positivistic and scientific traditions to guide their practice, social work through its critique of itself and the socio-political and cultural contexts and structures that surround it reformulates the practice questions being raised. Social workers review the available sources to inform practice and synthesise these into an investigation of the manifold issues, systems, processes, policies, and experiences that inform practice. Evidence conceptualised in this way has a much broader focus, with the search for evidence for practice needing to be approached as a pervading "need to know" that arises from the experience of the work and is underpinned by the social worker's use of self in the practitioner's role, as well as personal and professional values

DOI: 10.4018/978-1-4666-6563-7.ch017

and ethical principles. As a consequence, evidence-informed practice needs to be approached whenever the practitioner experiences a pervading sense of dissonance about "not knowing". This experience of "not knowing" brings the practitioner into proximity with the ambiguity of gaps in existing knowledge and a failure to find a coherent base for practice. Such deficits in the state of the existing knowledge occurs across a range of fields and contexts for practice. These situations in practice include scenarios where clients fail to improve; where systems exist in tension; when information is compartmentalised and not shared across sectors; where injustice, oppression, poverty and marginalisation exist unaddressed; and where organisations fail to work to provide the baseline needs of workers and their clients. This dissonance of "not knowing" and of wanting to have the answers to practice questions exists at the interface of all these concerns across different fields of social work practice. Dissonance also predominates where an evidence-base does not yet exist, or alternatively what does exist does not fit, or is deemed to be inappropriate by the social worker. There may be some knowledge in the field of practice but the understanding is fragmented and the knowledge may not yet be synthesised in a coherent, clear, and integrated form to be applied to the practice issue under review. This dissonance is experienced by the social worker searching for evidence for practice on a number of levels that are interrelated, with each level simultaneously impacting upon the others.

Whenever this dissonance is present for social workers, liminal spaces (Myerhoff, 1982) are created to process and deal with the experience. Liminal spaces are actively created by social workers and other helping practitioners, such as counsellors and therapists, when there is a jarring sense of disjuncture between what is known and an actual situation encountered in practice. Within such spaces, social workers choose from and integrate a diverse range of evidence and searching techniques, including reference to personal and

professional philosophies and theoretical frameworks, to inform their practice. I have described this process of social workers entering liminal spaces in my chapter about navigating evidence and elsewhere (Pack, 2013a). Barbara Myerhoff (1982, 1992) describes how people search for meaning in new situations guided by what is already known. Myerhoff found that those Jewish elders who lived through the Holocaust to come to settle in a new land (Florida, USA) were jettisoned into an unknown zone. In this unknown zone, there is a testing out and comparisons are made between the old ways in the new environment to see if there is relevance. In a similar way, so also social workers are able to effectively create new meanings to be applied in a new context through narrative and relationship.

Whilst encountering situations in which new meanings need to be brought to bear, a process of reviewing past meanings and experiences in practice is entered. I now propose a model to bring together what is suggested by this framework to inform an understanding of how social workers search for and apply evidence to their practice.

## PART ONE: A MULTI-DIMENSIONAL MODEL OF EVIDENCE SEARCHING AND APPLICATION

Evidence-searching occurs on several levels that interact, hence the complexity of the notion of "evidence" for social work and the difficulty of promoting awareness of it through the identification of a linear step-by-step approach to guide this search and assessment of relevance to practice. Adding to this complexity is the eclectic nature of social work theory and its relationship to practice and the ambiguous position social work holds as a consequence of its development as a profession. Social work is a bricolage of ideas drawn from several different disciplines within the social sciences including sociology, law, psychology, cultural studies, and human development among others.

The eclectic nature of "evidence" for social work practice reflects all these disciplines and develops its own unique perspectives and approaches. For example, social workers espouse a dual perspective due to the unique person-in-environment perspective which incorporates ideals of individual social rights and collective social justice for all. Secondly, social work seeks to redress inequities on the individual level as well as addressing wider social change. Evidence-based searching, therefore, is conceived of as a spiralling recursive process rather than a linear one, with social workers simultaneously critiquing the medico-legal processes within which they are working. Social workers thus strive to develop evidence for their practice outside the existing predominant medico-legal discourses within which they work whilst paradoxically attempting to work within them and transcend them. Part of the practice wisdom and intuition referred to in each of the chapters relates to the social worker's ability to do precisely this by balancing the demands of the individual client, the employing agency, the practice team, and surrounding organisations in which they work. This holistic focus on the individual, the team, and the agency within which they work is ecological systems theory in action. At the same time, social workers develop their own evidence-base for practice that is positioned both within and without the structures and institutions in which the social worker's practice is derived.

This dynamic interplay between working to find, source, and apply evidence for practice, therefore, involves a search within frameworks that better fit with social work needs and the epistemologies that underlie the eclectic nature of the profession. The therapeutic relationship with the individual service-user or client often fuels or inspires this search for evidence as well as sustains the social worker's journey of discovery of a knowledge-base for practice. This search both works within and transcends the organisational framework to explore the wider legal and bureaucratic structures that surround the worker and client, handed down from social worker to social worker in peer supervision, team meetings, and case reviews. Therefore, this knowledge forms part of the legitimate evidence-base for social work practice.

The term "evidence-informed practice" seems to suit the way that social workers search for evidence and their information-seeking needs. I have described this search for evidence in chapter four as being akin to an act of "foraging" in which social workers are engaged on a daily basis. Social workers glean information on their feet to inform their practice in busy jobs with complex workloads, working across agencies and systems in order to support and advocate for service-users and their families.

In my chapter on navigating different modes and discourses within evidence-based practice, I draw on the findings of the evidence-searching techniques of general practitioners. This metaphor of the seabird scavenging food from multiple sources has been discovered as a theme describing self-reports of general practitioners' information-seeking behaviour (Dwairy, Dowell, & Stahl, 2011). Like social workers, general practitioners are daily confronted with a diverse range of complex client presentations that have no simple answers, yet their role requires them to think quickly in the moment. To do this, general practitioners have been found to less frequently engage in systematic reviews of the online database sources, preferring to consult with colleagues to ask what to do next (Dwairy et al., 2011). Likewise, social workers in a time-poor, resource-strapped environment, share narratives of "what worked" with clients who have similar needs and presenting issues. Although seemingly haphazard, this evidence-searching approach works, not as one method but as a mosaic of many, in which the practitioner weaves differing threads of information forming a coherent fabric, constituting an integrated knowledge-base for practice. Social workers take together disparate sources of evidence which are continuously and reflectively investigated for directions for practice both now and into the future. Therefore, this act of foraging and the process of triangulating insights, findings from research, and decisions from case meetings and peer review represent a dynamic rather than static process. This knowledge-base once formed dynamically is then used to operationalise policy and to identify gaps in knowledge in order to supplement existing evidence, such as practice guidelines and the use of decision-making trees. Abstract descriptions based in theory and described in practice in agency and policy manuals are enacted through active knowledge generation by the social worker.

This act of "foraging" is similar to the "unsettling practices" referred to by Rossiter (2011) and Fook and Askeland (2007) who see the role of social workers as seeking to understand the implicit ideas and concepts and to enact these in practice in new ways that transcend the traditional meanings. For Rossiter, there is a need for social workers to question the assumed or taken-for-granted meanings of policies and prescribed practices to put ethics first and foremost in their search for knowledge. Nettie Flaherty's application of the sociological notion of "dirty work", building on Hughes' (1951, 1962) foundational work, is but one example of the many "unsettling practices" that form part of the evidence-informed practice described throughout this book. This reflective and reflexive critique of the overarching conditions that impact upon one's practice as a social worker, therefore, forms an important part of the evidence-base informing practice.

## PART TWO: THE CONTEXTS OF SOCIAL WORK PRACTICE

There are three levels discussed by the chapter authors as being related to the notion of dissonance indicating a need to search for evidence. Each level is interrelated with each impacting upon the other levels. This "ripple effect" is not referred

to in other literature on evidence-based practice in more medically-based models of literature searching. The processes of searching, discovering, assessing, and then applying evidence relates to the following dimensions of practice:

1. The individual practitioner working with an individual service-user, group, or family.
2. The therapeutic relationship established with the worker, client, group, or family as a co-created space in which each engage on a mutual search for "what works".
3. The organisation that employs the social worker and offers services to the client and the associated social structures that surround their work together.

## The Individual Practitioner and Service-User/Group/Family

An example of this diversity of evidence sources is apparent in relation to the debates about what constitutes "evidence" in social work practice. The dilemmas and contradictions in the existing evidence-base are illustrated by the powerful account of the re-settlement of refugee women in a new country recounted by Mary Nash and Antoinette Umugwaneza. In the chapter dealing with women refugees as "resilient yet reluctant users of social work services", Antoinette Umugwaneza discusses her own experiences as a refugee woman, wife, mother, and daughter, settling in New Zealand with her extended family. In her role with the Red Cross as a social worker, she explores considerations and recommendations for working with other refugee women in resettlement in chapter five of this book.

In the process of hearing these kinds of narratives, representing alternative knowledge sources, social workers bear witness to a new kind of evidence discovery. Direct accounts of experience from service-users and their families, therefore, need to inform social work practice in direct and often confronting ways. This "evidence" begins as a conversation and dialogue with the narrative constituting new ways of knowing from which practice directions can be actively constructed. The service-user feedback needs to be asked for and reviewed for relevance in an ongoing way by social workers to provide guidance and direction for practice, as well as to refine the ongoing contact between worker and service-user.

## The Therapeutic Relationship as a Co-Created Space

The changing nature of our society and its social mores also shifts the focus of attention for social workers. Often the shifting and changing attitudes in society means it is necessary for social workers to build the evidence-base where there is little empirical research but much theorising. The changing definition of what a family looks like in the 21st century, with the availability of new reproductive technologies, blended or reconstituted, same gender, and single parent families now common in many parts of the world, alters the state of the existing knowledge-base for practice. These reformulated definitions of "family" put the onus on social workers to develop new theory for practising collaboratively with "family" in all its diverse modern day forms. This diversity heralds new specialisms and fields of practice in relation to the role of fathers in society and their role in the family. One example is the recent theorising on how to effectively engage with fathers which is under-reported in the research literature. As the authors of the penultimate chapter of Part Two of this book review the research literature, they add their own research to this, in order to evolve new and innovative approaches and strategies for engaging and working with fathers. The evidence-base for working with fathers as parents is in a state of development where hitherto there has been a focus on women as the primary parent and caregiver, so this field is a new direction in social work practice and, therefore, represents a work in progress.

## The Organisational Frameworks and Systems that Surround Practice

In the process of hearing these kinds of narratives, representing alternative knowledge sources and bringing them together into a synthesis, social workers bear witness to multiple shifting accounts of experience and integrate these to construct the "big picture" view of the whole person-in environment. Another example of this kind of discovery is outlined in the social worker in school's project evaluation reported by Colin Pritchard. The study, using a mixed methods research design and methodology, draws evidence from many sources. The author's evaluation of existing services of social workers in schools used qualitative in-depth interviews with teachers, parents, and children, and secondly, quantitative methods, guided by the content analysis of case records, as well as education, police, and social services data, to effectively triangulate differing types and sources of information about the effectiveness of service provision. This mixed methods research design strengthens and adds methodological rigour to the evaluation's finding that providing social workers in schools adds value to children's lives when they are raised in geographical areas which are economically impoverished and under-resourced. The same mixed methods research approach in neurosurgery described in Colin Pritchard's and Richard William's chapter similarly makes a case for social work services across practice contexts.

Since gaps in knowledge and systemic failures pose a social cost, policy analysis and critique leading to recommendation and development of new policy is and should be within the social worker's brief, motivating a search for systemic solutions as well as individual interventions in practice. In a similar way, Sebastian Rosenberg and Fiona McDermott make a convincing case for refocusing attention on the quality of inpatient care away from the "quick fix" approach, based in monetarist policies within a climate of cost cutting, to suggest the need for challenging the organisational push in mental health for "more pills than beds". To do this, the authors challenge the narratives of failure surrounding service-users who become known as "bed blockers" to reframe these narratives of long-term care differently. The alternative narratives evolved coalesce around the process of recovery from service-users and their families' perspectives (Pack, 2013c).

## Illustrating the Model of Evidence Searching In Action

Liminal sites or spaces as well as being places of possibility are places of the unknown and the unexplored (Myerhoff, 1982). A process of testing if the existing knowledge can be applied in a new situation is entered in this site. These directions in practice lead on to one of the most important contributions of this book to the debates about evidence-based practice and evidence-informed approaches more generally. This book has extended understanding of evidence-based practice beyond binary oppositions to a more nuanced understanding of the concepts and approaches, such as "knowledge aware practice" discussed by Ian Dore in his chapter. Knowledge-aware is a term that sees the research literature being shaped and mediated by the practitioner's self-awareness and the use of self in practice.

Many proponents of evidence-based practice in social work do see the traditional act of ranking the quality of evidence methodologically to reveal directions in the research literature as being useful but an insufficient base for social work practice (Gambrill, 2006; Thyer, 2010, 2012). However, a stronger view of evidence-based practice, one more firmly grounded in a risk-averse society, needs to have answers to complex questions. But there may not yet be any answers or, alternatively, only a partial understanding. This latter view of evidence-based practice whilst well-intentioned is seen as elevating the scientific paradigm akin to an imperialist form of Western colonisation where individual narratives can become subsumed

and in many cases are relegated to the sidelines to exist on the fringes of what is known to exist as subjugated knowledge within the predominant scientific discourse (Smith, 1999). Such scientific or positivistic ways of knowing are potentially a means of misrepresenting disparate views. As an example, if randomised controlled trials (RCTs) are seen as the sole source of evidence for social work practice, they can miss the experiences and views of marginalised individuals and groups which are of central importance to social workers' practice from within an anti-oppressive and strengths-based theoretical stance.

There is, in fact, a place for evidence in both senses for social work, for the practitioner-researcher concerned with systematically reviewing literature and for the social worker who uses psychodynamic and relational understandings, including decolonising approaches to working with First Nations' people (Smith, 1999). In using art therapy to address intergenerational trauma in remote Aboriginal communities in Australia, Sheri Hergass, in concluding our practice section, enters a liminal space or unknown zone in her practice. Searching the evidence on Western art therapy practices assists in the theoretical grounding for her work, however, she concludes that this approach itself needs to be reflectively adapted with the Aboriginal artists and community workers in a community development model, so that they might translate Western art therapy and trauma-informed therapy into the language and symbology which is culturally and contextually appropriate to working with remote Aboriginal communities. In the collectivistic culture of the Aboriginal clan-based system, she is faced with the need to enter into a partnership with the communities she works with to evolve new understandings of what it means to have had one's culture and children stolen through policies of assimilation. The use of decolonising methodologies (Smith, 1999), narrative, and of "yarning" in Aboriginal and other indigenous cultures is a primary means of discovering new directions in practice (Bennett, Green, Gilbert, &

Bessarab, 2013). As discussed in the chapter on the recovery process for adult women recovering from sexual abuse trauma, Western trauma theory needs to be triangulated with the findings from indigenous theoreticians about how to work responsively, creatively, and respectfully with cultural differences. Social workers, therefore, need to tolerate complexity and ambiguity to forge such partnerships in practice whilst they actively "decolonise" (Smith, 1999) their own practices to evolve culturally appropriate ways of working with the individual service-users and their families within the communities in which they practise.

## PART THREE: THE SELF CARE OF SOCIAL WORKERS

Social work exists on the boundary between art and science with elements of both. As an artistic endeavour, social work relies on ethical decision-making which is mediated by the totality of the social worker's experiences, personal and professional, and their use of self in the practitioner's role. Values, both personal and professional, influence the way in which the particular strand of theory or intervention is chosen and implemented in negotiation with the client, caregiver, and family in an agency context. In this creative process, the social worker's past experiences, the knowledge of what has worked in the past with similar client presentations, is combed continuously for directions to guide practice. How integrated these values and experiences are in turn influences the outcome of the intervention or theory in practice. Therefore, the need for opportunities for social workers to reflect in an ongoing way on themselves, their practices, values, and ethical standards is an essential part of professional development. Self-awareness as well as awareness of oneself in the practitioner's role is, therefore, central to the understanding of the concept of the practitioner using critical-reflection for being

"knowledge aware" in social work practice, as Ian Dore demonstrates in his chapter.

One of the primary means of creating a reflective space in which to process these knowledge sources is in clinical supervision, which is described by Kieran O'Donoghue. In the clinical supervisory relationship, a space is created in which current themes in the social worker's practice and caseload can be critically reflected and evaluated. Elsewhere, I have conceptualised the clinical supervisory relationship as needing to be distinguished clearly from line management and to enable trust to be developed (Pack, 2009a, 2009b). In such relationships within the supervision of practice a liminal space for reflection is created (Pack, 2013a).

In this place of betwixt and between, being neither one nor the other, social work practitioners similarly enter a place of being tested and of not having the answers. In this liminal space within clinical supervision, social workers with their clinical supervisors deliberate freely on which past situations and meanings are relevant and can be applied, based on past experience and practices (Pack, 2009a, 2009b). Theories of practice developed in parts may be revised, discarded, or considered as no longer appropriate in this testing of their relevance in a new practice situation. One aspect of this exploration involves what Mary Nash conceptualises in her chapter about social work and spirituality as developing post-qualifying competencies for social workers. Through ritual and involvement with like-minded others in community, whether this be in a community garden or church, a liminal space is created for exploring and attaching new meaning from, and to, experience to enrich and develop one's practice as a social worker. These reformulated meanings are then available for use by social workers in their practice in a continuous cycle of review and refinement.

Entering into liminal zones occurs routinely when practitioners engage with traumatic situations and disclosures. For social workers, these kinds of situations are a regular feature of their everyday work. In her chapter about critical incidents in the workplace, Carol Adamson suggests how and where these liminal spaces can be created as a safe haven within social workers' employing agencies. Responsibility for ensuring access to such reflective spaces within the provision of a critical incident stress management programme is recommended (Pack, 2014). Whether these spaces are in individual counselling sessions for social workers who have had involvement in critical events or traumas or in formal debriefings within the team, a comprehensive stress management policy is needed for positive resolution and moving onwards (Pack, 2014). In critical events, opportunities are created for re-authoring personal and professional narratives of social workers to evolve new definitions of the social worker's identity. Critical incident stress management policies are needed also to enable social workers to find a way of integrating what has happened in their repertoire of coping strategies for the future (Pack, 2014). Such an ongoing analysis of one's practice builds resilience and ensures workforce retention for the future, for which employers of social workers have a primary responsibility (Pack, 2013b, 2014).

To summarise, reflecting on the issues emerging from the debates in the research literature enables construction of an appropriate response to critical events, both to the needs of the social workers within the agency and to add to and refine the best practice guidelines emerging from an ongoing engagement and critique of the practice research literature. Ecological systems thinking is referred to as connecting social work and contributing knowledge-bases, such as stress, trauma, and resilience, to that of the specific critical incident stress response to any practice situation, as Adamson explores. This approach enables an ecological lens to be applied to the question of best practice in the development of services for employees who are social workers operating day to day in an organisational framework.

## SOLUTIONS AND RECOMMENDATIONS

### The Future: Beyond Binary Oppositions in Evidence-based Practice in Social Work

So what have we learned about evidence and its relationship to social work practice across different fields of practice? The first learning relates to the meanings that service-users give to their experiences and the implications of these meanings for social workers in delivering effective services to their clients (Stanhope & Solomon, 2008). The recovery paradigm poses a challenge to the conventional ideas about the positioning of service-users and their families and their relationship with social workers. The power dynamics within this relationship is reformulated as service-users, their caregivers, and families have primary and constitutive input into shaping the knowledge-base for social workers in their practice. Service-user feedback features in a cycle of continuous improvement when social workers ask clients and caregivers about what brings them to seek social work services and how they think social work can assist them in their healing journey (Pack, 2013c).

In assessing the relevance to practice, social workers choose from an eclectic mix of sources to inform their clinical reasoning. These sources include service-user and their families' preferences and feedback, ethical principles, the field of practice, and empirical research findings, a point which Justin Cargill also reinforces in chapter 1. These sources are all considered as legitimate "evidence" for practice. The terms used more recently by social work theorists, such as "evidence-informed" and "knowledge-aware", seem to fit social work's eclecticism and the preference for multi-theoretical approaches to practice. The identification of gaps in research literature, legal frameworks, and policy are used to highlight where to focus the search for evidence. A critical reflective approach involving the use of self, professional and personal experience, and other contextual factors, as well as the state of the research evidence, then, is the way forward for social work practitioners. Taken together, these sources are combed for directions to practice and form a unique, integrated framework for practice. This framework is then available to be applied to the field of practice to address the practice scenario. There is a need for social workers to question the assumed or taken-for-granted meanings of policies and prescribed practices to put ethics first and foremost in their search for knowledge (Rossiter, 2011).

## CONCLUSION

### Weaving the Strands Together

In looking towards the future, this book adds to the body of knowledge about the ways that social workers approach, search, assess, and apply evidence to and for practice. It suggests that social workers develop a multi-layered and multi-dimensional awareness and understanding of evidence-based and informed practice. It also underlines the need to expand the range of research designs and methodologies and sources constituting "evidence" for practice.

In relation to the research approaches informing social work practice, there is clearly a need to expand the range of research designs to increase the diversity of evidence for social work as a profession. When social workers consider studies drawn from a variety of designs and methodologies, this diversity facilitates the establishment of, and evidence base for, guiding practice. For, example, an expanded definition of "evidence" encompasses the kinds of psychosocial interventions envisaged in an ecological systems and strengths-based approach to social work practice (Pack, 2013a). This approach aligns more closely with a broader epistemology drawing from recovery principles and the experiences of service-users and their

families. The adoption of constructivist as well as critical-reflective approaches, drawing from emancipatory and participatory epistemologies, rely on interpretive, participatory designs using a mix of quantitative and qualitative methods. This expanded range of research methods, in turn, is guided by social work's practice priorities which include the use of self, personal and professional ethics, and values in social work practice, as Pritchard and Williams have shown in their chapter (see also, McDermott, 1996).

The conclusion from the authors in this book is that these meanings, preferences, and guidance about the healing trajectory from the perspective of service-users and their families need to be considered as a legitimate knowledge source to be used to inform practice across a range of contexts, including mental health and child protection, youth justice, and sexual abuse recovery. The recovery paradigm given voice by the chapter authors contests the dominant knowledge-base of professional "expert-knows-best". From this perspective critical inquiry is needed when considering the nature of "evidence" and in assessing its value. From such deliberations and questioning it is then a matter for each social worker to decide from within a framework of ethical standards and personal judgement which sources constitute legitimate knowledge for social work practice. For example, in the empirical research evidence presented by Colin Pritchard and Richard Williams in their outcome evaluations of the effectiveness of social work practice across the fields of neurosurgery, youth justice, and school social work, the predominant narratives involving economic retrenchment subsumes the value added potential of social work to service delivery in these fields. Social work's role in humanising medical and hospital contexts, in which social workers assess the needs of people holistically, enables a smoother transition from hospital to community, as the involvement of social workers assists in facilitating constructive dialogue between service-users, their families, and their healthcare professionals. The relative power positioning of consumers vis a vis their healthcare and welfare providers is discussed as influencing who defines "effectiveness" within the organisational policies and the social structures that surround social work practice.

The benefits of having dedicated social workers or those who work within a holistic, strengths-based, ecological systems approach associated with health and welfare teams are acknowledged as a knowledge source brought to life by such evaluative research studies. The legitimacy of social work as a profession to offer a valuable contribution to care is demonstrated both quantitatively and qualitatively drawing upon Pritchard and Williams' own and others' research. Pritchard and Williams triangulate differing sources of evidence to demonstrate social work's true potential to "make a difference". Such empirical research moves beyond opinion or conjecture based on anecdotal accounts to establish empirically social work's value as a profession in the eyes of the general public and the multi-disciplinary team across those fields of practice.

A further conclusion is that social work's unique person-in environment approach, based in ecological systems thinking, brings with it a consideration of the individual, family, and community, and the overarching systems of which they are a part. This approach is illustrated in the focus of the various authors in reviewing evidence for directions with the aim of addressing individual issues and presenting problems as a starting point to influence existing social structures to effect social change. The authors then analyse and critique reflectively the legislation and policies to address gaps in service provision and contradictions across social service agencies in the provision of services to suggest new frameworks in different contexts of practice. Bill Whyte's chapter is a good example of how the divide between the adult and youth justice systems fails operationally to effectively rehabilitate when young men fall between the adult and youth justice systems leading to their becoming enmeshed in the stigma of having offended. Once defined in this way, a young person's identity can be labelled negatively across the life course, thus influencing the attainment of developmental milestones in education and relationship building in pro-social ways.

Social workers are in a unique position to be well-prepared to argue from a strengths-based and person-in-environment perspective that entering the criminal justice system may itself be grounds for social work and child protection activity, even if alongside rather than as an alternative to criminal processes for young people up to the age of 18. Social work in the field of youth offending, therefore, raises questions and dilemmas for social work practice for which there are few clear answers. In the absence of a clear evidence-base for practice, this gap in knowledge challenges those responsible for child welfare and child protection and, in particular, social workers to consider how social work as a profession should respond when young people under 18 are enmeshed in criminal processes. Whyte in his chapter demonstrates through an analysis of policy and human rights legislation that such an approach can synthesise what is known and in this process create guidance for social work practitioners grappling with these practice dilemmas.

In making effective practice decisions the social work practitioner is asked to consider all sources of evidence including empirical research evidence. Secondly through a process of critical reflection, both individually and collaboratively with clinical supervisors, colleagues, and service-users and their families, social workers need to examine and adapt both personal and professional assumptions and actions, informed by the research evidence and their own responses. If social workers are to embrace the ethical principles of their profession, values above all else need to be the starting point to applying evidence to practice.

# REFERENCES

Bennett, B., Green, S., Gilbert, S., & Bessarab, D. (Eds.). (2013). *Our voices: Aboriginal and Torres Strait Islander social work*. South Yarra, Australia: Palgrave Macmillan.

Dwairy, M., Dowell, A. C., & Stahl, J.-C. (2011). The application of foraging theory to the information searching behaviour of general practitioners. *BMC Family Practice*, *12*(1), 90. doi:10.1186/1471-2296-12-90 PMID:21861880

Fook, J., & Askeland, G. A. (2007). Challenges of critical reflection: "Nothing ventured, nothing gained. *Social Work Education*, *26*(5), 520–533. doi:10.1080/02615470601118662

Gambrill, E. (2006). Evidence-based practice and policy: Choices ahead. *Research on Social Work Practice*, *16*(3), 338–357. doi:10.1177/1049731505284205

Hughes, E. (1951). Work and the self. In J. Roher & M. Sherif (Eds.), *Social psychology at the crossroads* (pp. 313–323). New York: Harper and Brothers.

Hughes, E. C. (1962). Good people and dirty work. *Social Problems*, *10*(1), 3–11. doi:10.2307/799402

McDermott, F. (1996). Social work research: Debating the boundaries. *Australian Social Work*, *49*(1), 5–10. doi:10.1080/03124079608411156

Myerhoff, B. (1982). *Number our days: Triumph of continuity and culture among Jewish old people in an urban ghetto*. New York: Simon and Schuster/ Touchstone Books.

Myerhoff, B. (1992). *Remembered lives: The work of ritual, storytelling, and growing older*. Ann Arbor, MI: University of Michigan Press.

Pack, M. (2009a). Clinical supervision: An interdisciplinary review of literature with implications for reflective practice in social work. *Reflective Practice*, *10*(5), 657–668. doi:10.1080/14623940903290729

Pack, M. (2009b). Supervision as a liminal space: Towards a dialogic relationship. *Gestalt Journal of Australia and New Zealand*, *5*(2), 60-78. Retrieved from http://ganzwebsite.wordpress.com/journal/

Pack, M. (2013a). Vicarious traumatisation and resilience: An ecological systems approach to sexual abuse counsellors' trauma and stress. *Sexual Abuse in Australia and New Zealand*, *5*, 69-76. Retrieved from http://www.anzatsa.org/

Pack, M. J. (2013b). Critical incident stress management: A review of the literature with implications for social work. *International Social Work*, *56*(5), 608–627. doi:10.1177/0020872811435371

Pack, M. J. (2013c). An evaluation of critical-reflection on service-users and their families' narratives as a teaching resource in a post-graduate allied mental health program: An integrative approach. *Social Work in Mental Health*, *11*(2), 154–166. doi:10.1080/15332985.2012.748003

Pack, M. J. (2014). The role of managers in critical incident stress management programmes: A qualitative study of New Zealand social workers. *Journal of Social Work Practice*, *28*(1), 43–57. doi:10.1080/02650533.2013.828279

Rossiter, A. (2011). Unsettled social work: The challenge of Levinas's Ethics. *British Journal of Social Work*, *41*(5), 980–995. doi:10.1093/bjsw/bcr004

Smith, L. T. (1999). *Decolonising methodologies: Research and Indigenous peoples*. London: Zed Books.

Stanhope, V., & Solomon, P. (2008). Getting to the heart of recovery: Methods for studying recovery and their implications for evidence-based practice. *British Journal of Social Work*, *38*(5), 885–899. doi:10.1093/bjsw/bcl377

Thyer, B. A. (2010). Introductory principles of social work research. In B. A. Thyer (Ed.), *The handbook of social work research methods* (2nd ed., pp. 1–24). Thousand Oaks, CA: SAGE.

Thyer, B. A. (2012). The scientific value of qualitative research for social work. *Qualitative Social Work: Research and Practice*, *11*, 115–125. doi:10.1177/1473325011433928

## KEY TERMS AND DEFINITIONS

**Critical-Reflective Practice:** A form of practice which challenges cultures, that is, the preconceived ideas which are embedded in practices, in order to examine and change them.

**Decolonising Methodologies:** Contextual histories, politics, and cultural considerations reveal how Indigenous people are disenfranchised by the imposition of Western models of research and practice. Thus research is viewed as a form of imperialism.

**Evidence-Based Practice:** A systematic process integrating available best evidence with client preferences and values (wherever possible), client's circumstances, and professional expertise, resulting in services that are individualised to the client.

**Knowledge-Aware Practice:** An approach which emphasises a knowledge base that includes a broad range of evidence, use of self and professional judgement based on experience and intuition, and knowledge of the individual client.

**Liminal Space:** A concept developed by Myerhoff (1982) to describe a place of reflection where the practitioner deliberates on an unknown situation from what is already known or familiar.

**Person-in-Environment:** A practice orienting perspective which affirms that an individual and his or her behavior can only be understood adequately when that individual's physical, social, political, familial, economic, and spiritual environment is considered.

**Recovery Paradigm:** Service-users' accounts of their healing journey from trauma, health, and mental health issues which is a source of evidence for social work practice.

# Compilation of References

Adams, K. B., Matto, H. C., & LeCroy, C. W. (2009). Limitations of evidence-based practice for social work education: Unpacking the complexity. *Journal of Social Work Education, 45*(2), 165–186. doi:10.5175/JSWE.2009.200700105

Adamson, C. E. (2001). Social work and the call for evidence-based practice in mental health: Where do we stand? *Social Work Review, 13*(2), 8-12. Retrieved from http://anzasw.org.nz/about/topics/show/207-aotearoa-nz-social-work-review

Adamson, C. E. (2006). *Complexity and context: Staff support systems in mental health after critical incidents and traumatic events* (Doctoral thesis, Massey University, Wellington, New Zealand). Retrieved from http://hdl.handle.net/2292/10318

Adamson, C. (2011). Supervision is not politically innocent. *Australian Social Work, 65*(2), 185–196. doi:10.1080/0312407X.2011.618544

Adamson, C., Beddoe, L., & Davys, A. (2012). Building resilient practitioners: Definitions and practitioner understandings. *British Journal of Social Work, 32*, 100–117. doi:10.1093/bjsw/bcs142

Adams, R. (2007). Reflective, critical and transformative practice. In W. Tovey (Ed.), *The post-qualifying handbook for social workers* (pp. 28–42). London: Jessica Kingsley.

Adams, R. E., Boscarino, J. A., & Figley, C. R. (2006). Compassion fatigue and psychological distress among social workers: A validation study. *The American Journal of Orthopsychiatry, 76*(1), 103–108. doi:10.1037/0002-9432.76.1.103 PMID:16569133

Age Round Table on child protection. (2009, November 25). *The Age*. Retrieved from http://www.theage.com.au/national/

Ager, A., & Strang, A. (2004). *Indicators of refugee integration: Final report – Report to the Home Office Immigration Research and Statistics Service*. Retrieved from Home Office website: http://www.homeoffice.gov.uk/rds/pdfs04/dpr28.pdf

The aims and means of the Catholic worker. (n.d.). Catholic Worker Movement. Retrieved from http://www.catholicworker.org/aimsandmeanstext.cfm?Number=5

Aisenberg, E. (2008). Evidence-based practice in mental health care to ethnic minority communities: Has its practice fallen short of its evidence? *Social Work, 53*(4), 297–306. doi:10.1093/sw/53.4.297 PMID:18853666

Al-Qdah, T., & Lacroix, M. (2010). Iraqi refugees in Jordan: Lessons for practice with refugees globally. *International Journal of Social Work, 54*(4), 521–534. doi:10.1177/0020872810383449

Alvesson, M., & Sköldberg, K. (2009). *Reflexive methodology: New vistas for qualitative research* (2nd ed.). London: SAGE.

American Psychiatric Association. (2013). *Diagnostic and statistical manual of mental disorders* (5th ed.). Washington, D.C.: Author.

Anderson, K. M., & Hiersteiner, C. (2007). Listening to the stories of adults in treatment who were sexually abused as children. *Families in Society, 88*(4), 637–644. doi:10.1606/1044-3894.3686

Andrews, D. A., Zinger, I., Hoge, R. D., Bonta, J., Gendreau, P., & Cullen, F. T. (1990). Does correctional treatment work? A clinically relevant and psychologically informed meta-analysis. *Criminology, 28*(3), 369–404. doi:10.1111/j.1745-9125.1990.tb01330.x

Aotearoa New Zealand Association of Social Workers. (2008). *Code of ethics.* Christchurch, New Zealand: Author.

Aotearoa New Zealand Association of Social Workers. (2013). *The code of ethics of the Aotearoa New Zealand Association of Social Workers.* Retrieved from http://anzasw.org.nz/social_work_practice/topics/show/158-summary-of-the-code-of-ethics

Appleyard, K., & Osofsky, J. D. (2003). Parenting after trauma: Supporting parents and caregivers in the treatment of children impacted by violence. *Infant Mental Health Journal, 24*(2), 111–125. doi:10.1002/imhj.10050

Armsworth, M. W., & Holaday, M. (1993). The effects of psychological trauma on children and adolescents. *Journal of Counseling and Development, 72*(1), 49–56. doi:10.1002/j.1556-6676.1993.tb02276.x

Arnd-Caddigan, M., & Pozzuto, R. (2010). Evidence-based practice and the purpose of clinical social work. *Smith College Studies in Social Work, 80*(1), 35–52. doi:10.1080/00377310903504965

Ashforth, B. E., & Kreiner, G. E. (1999). "How can you do it?" Dirty work and the challenge of constructing a positive identity. *Academy of Management Review, 24*, 413–434. doi:10.5465/AMR.1999.2202129

Ashforth, B. E., & Kreiner, G. E. (2013). Dirty work and dirtier work: Differences in countering physical, social and moral stigma. *Management and Organization Review, 10*(1), 81–108. doi:10.1111/more.12044

Ashley, C., Featherstone, B., Roskill, C., Ryan, M., & White, S. (2006). *Fathers matter: Research findings on fathers and their involvement with social care services.* London: Family Rights Group.

Atkinson, J. (2002). *Trauma trails, recreating song lines: The transgenerational effects of trauma in Indigenous Australia.* North Melbourne: Spinifex Press.

Atkinson, J. (2013). *Trauma-informed services and trauma-specific care for Indigenous Australian children* (Resource sheet no. 21). Retrieved from Australian Institute of Health and Welfare website: http://www.aihw.gov.au/uploadedFiles/ClosingTheGap/Content/Publications/2013/ctg-rs21.pdf

Atkinson, J., Nelson, J., & Atkinson, C. (2010). Trauma, transgenerational transfer and effects on community wellbeing. In N. Purdie, P. Dudgeon, & R. Walker (Eds.), *Working together: Aboriginal and Torres Strait Islander mental health and wellbeing principles and practice* (pp. 135–144). Canberra: Australian Institute of Health and Welfare.

Atkinson, S., & Swain, S. (1999). A network of support: Mothering across the Koorie community in Victoria, Australia. *Women's History Review, 8*(2), 219–230. doi:10.1080/09612029900200208

Australian Association of Social Workers. (2003). *Practice standards for social workers: Achieving outcomes.* Retrieved November 17, 2013, from http://svc037.bne242p.server-web.com/adobe/publications/Practice_Standards_Final_Oct_2003.pdf

Australian Association of Social Workers. (2010). *Code of Ethics.* Retrieved from www.aasw.asn.au/practitioner-resources/code-of-ethics

Australian Association of Social Workers. (2011). *Submission to the Senate Community Affairs Committee into commonwealth funding and administration of mental health services.* August. Retrieved from http://www.aasw.asn.au/document/item/2265

Australian Association of Social Workers. (2012). *Education and Accreditation Standards.* Retrieved from http://www.aasw.asn.au/careers-study/education-standards-accreditation

Australian Association of Social Workers. (2012/13). *Continuing Professional Development for members.* Retrieved from http://www.aasw.asn.au/document/item/3374

Australian Association of Social Workers. (2013). *Practice standards 2013.* Retrieved from http://www.aasw.asn.au/document/item/4551

Australian Bureau of Statistics. (1998). *National survey of mental health and wellbeing 1997*. Canberra: Author.

Australian Bureau of Statistics. (2008). *National survey of mental health and wellbeing 2007*. Canberra: Author.

Australian Bureau of Statistics. (2011). *Regional statistics, NT*. Canberra, Australia: Author.

Australian Government, Department of Immigration and Border Protection. (2013). *Fact Sheet 60: Australia's refugee and humanitarian programme*. Retrieved from http://www.immi.gov.au/media/fact-sheets/60refugee.htm

Australian Government, Department of Social Services. (2013). *Getting settled: Women refugees in Australia*. Retrieved from http://www.dss.gov.au/sites/default/files/documents/01_2014/sc_update_women_at_risk.pdf

Australian Health Ministers' Advisory Council. (2013). *A national framework for recovery-oriented mental health services: Policy and theory*. Retrieved from Commonwealth of Australia Department of Health website: http://www.health.gov.au/internet/main/publishing.nsf/Content/ B2CA4C28D59C74EBCA257C1D0004A79D/$File/recovpol.pdf

Australian Institute of Health and Welfare. (2011). *The health and welfare of Australia's Aboriginal and Torres Strait Islander people: An overview*. Retrieved from http://www.aihw.gov.au/WorkArea/DownloadAsset.aspx?id=10737418955

Australian Institute of Health and Welfare. (2012). *Australia's health 2012*. Canberra: Author.

Australian National Committee on Refugee Women. (n.d.). ANCORW Mission Statement. Retrieved May 10, 2014, from http://www.ancorw.org/mission.htm

Avby, G., Nilsen, P., & Dahlgren, M. A. (2013). Ways of understanding evidence-based practice in social work: A qualitative study. *British Journal of Social Work*, 1–18. doi:10.1093/bjsw/bcs198

Avery, A., & Ørner, R. (1998). First report of psychological debriefing abandoned: The end of an era? *Traumatic Stress Points*, *12*(3). doi:10.1037/e519832011-004

Ayre, P. (2001). Child protection and the media: Lessons from three decades. *British Journal of Social Work*, *31*(6), 887–901. doi:10.1093/bjsw/31.6.887

Baird, K., & Kracen, A. C. (2006). Vicarious traumatization and secondary traumatic stress: A research synthesis. *Counselling Psychology Quarterly*, *19*(2), 181–188. doi:10.1080/09515070600811899

Baisch, S. B., Schenk, T., & Noble, A. J. (2011). What is the cause of post-traumatic stress disorder following subarachnoid haemorrhage? Post-ictal events are key. *Acta Neurochirurgica*, *153*(4), 913–922. doi:10.1007/s00701-010-0843-y PMID:20963450

Bamblett, M., Bath, H., & Roseby, R. (2010). *Growing them strong together: Promoting the safety and wellbeing of the Northern Territory's children. Report of the Board of Inquiry into the Child Protection System in the Northern Territory*. Darwin: Northern Territory Government.

Banks, S. (2012). *Ethics and values in social work* (4th ed.). Basingstoke, UK: Palgrave Macmillan.

Bantry White, E. (2010). Review: H. U. Otto, A. Polutta, and H. Zieglar (eds): Evidence-based practice: Modernising the knowledge base of social work? Voluntas, *21*(1), 132-134. doi:10.1007/s11266-009-9114-z

Barber, J. G. (2012). Putting evidence-based practice into practice. In C. N. Dulmus & K. M. Sowers (Eds.), *The profession of social work: Guided by history, led by evidence* (pp. 191–202). Hoboken, NJ: John Wiley.

Baron-Cohen, S. (2011). *Zero degrees of empathy: A new theory of human cruelty*. London: Allen Lane.

Batista, T. (2010). A case for evidence based practice. *Columbia Social Work Review*, *1*, 45–53.

Baum, N., & Negbi, I. (2013). Children removed from home by court order: Fathers' disenfranchised grief and reclamation of paternal functions. *Children and Youth Services Review*, *35*(10), 1679–1686. doi:10.1016/j.childyouth.2013.07.003

Baxter, J., & Smart, D. (2011). *Fathering in Australia among couple families with young children* (Occasional Paper Series No. 37). Canberra: Department of Families, Housing, Community Services and Indigenous Affairs.

Beddoe, L. (2011). Investing in the future: Social workers talk about research. *British Journal of Social Work, 41*(3), 557–575. doi:10.1093/bjsw/bcq138

Beddoe, L., Davys, A., & Adamson, C. (2011). Educating resilient practitioners. *Social Work Education, 32*(1), 100–117. doi:10.1080/02615479.2011.644532

Bellamy, J. L., Bledsoe, S. E., & Mullen, E. J. (2009). The cycle of evidence-based practice. In H.-U. Otto, A. Polutta, & H. Ziegler (Eds.), *Evidence-based practice: Modernising the knowledge base of social work?* (pp. 21–29). Opladen, Germany: Barbara Budrich.

Belling, R., Whittock, M., McLaren, S., Burns, T., Catty, J., Rees Jones, I., & Wykes, T. (2011). Achieving continuity of care: Facilitators and barriers in community mental health teams. *Implementation Science, 6*(1), 23. doi:10.1186/1748-5908-6-23 PMID:21418579

Belsky, J., & Pluess, M. (2009). Beyond diathesis stress: Differential susceptibility to environmental influences. *Psychological Bulletin, 135*(6), 885–908. doi:10.1037/a0017376 PMID:19883141

Bennett, B., Green, S., Gilbert, S., & Bessarab, D. (Eds.). (2013). *Our voices: Aboriginal and Torres Strait Islander social work*. South Yarra, Australia: Palgrave Macmillan.

Bergeron, M., & Hebert, M. (2006). Evaluation of a group intervention using a feminist approach for victims of sexual abuse. *Child Abuse & Neglect, 30*, 1143–1159. doi:10.1016/j.chiabu.2006.04.007 PMID:17034852

Berger, R. (2010). EBP: Practitioners in search of evidence. *Journal of Social Work, 10*(2), 175–191. doi:10.1177/1468017310363640

Bergmark, A., Bergmark, Å., & Lundstrom, T. (2012). The mismatch between the map and the terrain: Evidence-based social work in Sweden. *European Journal of Social Work, 15*(4), 598–609. doi:10.1080/13691457.2012.706215

Berk, L. (2006). *Child development* (7th ed.). Boston: Pearson Publishing.

Berlyn, C., Wise, S., & Soriano, G. (2008). *Engaging fathers in child and family services: Participation, perceptions and good practice* (Occasional Paper No. 22). Sydney: National Evaluation Consortium.

Bessarab, D., & Crawford, F. R. (2013). Trauma, grief and loss: The vulnerability of Aboriginal families in the child protection system. In B. Bennett, S. Green, S. Gilbert, & D. Bessarab (Eds.), *Our voices: Aboriginal and Torres Strait Islander social work* (pp. 93–113). South Yarra: Palgrave MacMillan.

Bianchi, S. (2000). Maternal employment and time with children: Dramatic change or surprising continuity. *Demography, 37*(4), 401–414. doi:10.1353/dem.2000.0001 PMID:11086567

Biehal, N., Clayden, J., & Stein, M. (1995). *Moving on: Young people and leaving care schemes*. London: HMSO.

Bisson, J. I., McFarlane, A. C., & Rose, S. (2000). Psychological debriefing. In E. B. Foa, T. M. Keane, & M. J. Friedman (Eds.), *Effective treatments for PTSD: Practice guidelines from the International Society for Traumatic Stress Studies* (pp. 39–59). New York: Guilford.

Bland, R., Renouf, N., & Tullgren, A. (2009). *Social work practice in mental health: An introduction*. Crows Nest, NSW: Allen & Unwin.

Bloemhard, A. (2008). *Spiritual care for self and others*. *Coffs Harbour*: The Mid North Coast Division of General Practice/Australian Department of Health and Ageing.

Bloomer, K. (2008). Modernising Scotland's teaching workforce. In K. Bloomer (Ed.), *Working it out: Developing the children's sector workforce* (pp. 32–35). Edinburgh, UK: Children in Scotland.

Blyth, E., & Milner, J. (1990). The process of inter-agency work. In M. Langan (Ed.), *Taking child abuse seriously: Contemporary issues in child protection theory and practice* (pp. 194–211). London: Unwin Hyman.

Boeker, M., Vach, W., & Motschall, E. (2013). Google Scholar as replacement for systematic literature searches: Good relative recall and precision are not enough. *BMC Medical Research Methodology*, *13*(1), 131. doi:10.1186/1471-2288-13-131 PMID:24160679

Bogels, S., & Phares, V. (2008). Fathers' role in the etiology, prevention and treatment of child anxiety: A review and new model. *Clinical Psychology Review*, *28*(4), 539–558. doi:10.1016/j.cpr.2007.07.011 PMID:17854963

Bogo, M., & McKnight, K. (2006). Clinical supervision in social work: A review of the research literature. *The Clinical Supervisor*, *24*(1-2), 49–67. doi:10.1300/J001v24n01_04

Bogousslavsky, J., & Boller, F. (Eds.). (2005). Neurological disorders in famous artists: Part 3 (Frontiers of Neurology and Neuroscience, Vol. 19). Basel, Switzerland: Karger.

Bologna, M. J., & Pulice, R. T. (2011). Evaluation of a peer-run hospital diversion program: A descriptive study. *American Journal of Psychiatric Rehabilitation*, *14*(4), 272–286. doi:10.1080/15487768.2011.622147

Bolton, S. C. (2005). Women's work, dirty work: The gynaecology nurse as "other". *Gender, Work and Organization*, *12*(2), 169–186. doi:10.1111/j.1468-0432.2005.00268.x

Bonanno, G. A., Galea, S., Bucciarelli, A., & Vlahov, D. (2007). What predicts psychological resilience after disaster? The role of demographics, resources, and life stress. *Journal of Consulting and Clinical Psychology*, *75*(5), 671–682. doi:10.1037/0022-006X.75.5.671 PMID:17907849

Bonanno, G. A., Westphal, M., & Mancini, A. D. (2011). Resilience to loss and potential trauma. *Annual Review of Clinical Psychology*, *7*(1), 511–535. doi:10.1146/annurev-clinpsy-032210-104526 PMID:21091190

Bottoms, A. E., & McWilliams, W. (1979). A nontreatment paradigm for probation practice. *British Journal of Social Work*, *9*, 159–202. Retrieved from http://bjsw.oxfordjournals.org/

Bottrell, D. (2009). Understanding "marginal" perspectives: Towards a social theory of resilience. *Qualitative Social Work: Research and Practice*, *8*(3), 321–339. doi:10.1177/1473325009337840

Bouffard, M., & Reid, G. (2012). The good, the bad, and the ugly of evidence-based practice. *Adapted Physical Activity Quarterly*, *29*, 1-24. Retrieved from http://journals.humankinetics.com/apaq

Bowlby, J. (1979). *The making and breaking of affectional bonds*. London: Tavistock/Routledge.

Bowlby, J. (1988). *A secure base: Clinical applications of attachment theory*. London: Routledge.

Bramer, W. M., Giustini, D., Kramer, B. M. R., & Anderson, P. F. (2013). The comparative recall of Google Scholar versus PubMed in identical searches for biomedical systematic reviews: A review of searches used in systematic reviews. *Systematic Reviews*, *2*(1), 115. doi:10.1186/2046-4053-2-115 PMID:24360284

Brandon, M., Belderson, P., Warren, C., Howe, D., Gardner, R., Dodsworth, J., & Black, J. (2008). *Analysing child deaths and serious injury through abuse and neglect: What can we learn? A biennial analysis of serious case reviews 2003-2005* (Research Report DCSF-RR023). London: Department for Children, Schools and Families.

Bratton, S. C., & Ferebee, K. W. (1999). The use of structured expressive art activities in group activity therapy with preadolescents. In D. S. Sweeny & L. E. Homeyer (Eds.), *The handbook of group play therapy: How to do it, how it works, whom it's best for* (pp. 192–214). San Francisco: Jossey-Bass.

Braun, V., & Clarke, V. (2006). Using thematic analysis in psychology. *Qualitative Research in Psychology*, *3*(2), 77–101. doi:10.1191/1478088706qp063oa

Bride, B. E. (2007). Prevalence of secondary traumatic stress among social workers. *Social Work*, *52*(1), 63–70. doi:10.1093/sw/52.1.63 PMID:17388084

Briere, J. (1992). *Child abuse trauma theory and treatment of the lasting effects*. Newbury Park, C.A.: Sage Publications.

Briere, J. (Ed.). (2004). *Psychological assessment of adult post-traumatic states: Phenomenology, diagnosis and measurement.* Washington, DC: American Psychological Association.

Broadhurst, K., White, S., Fish, S., Munro, E., Fletcher, K., & Lincoln, H. (2010). *Ten pitfalls and how to avoid them: What research tells us.* Retrieved from National Society for the Prevention of Cruelty to Children website: http://www.nspcc.org.uk/Inform/publications/downloads/tenpitfalls_wdf48122.pdf

Broadhurst, K., Wastell, D., White, S., Hall, C., Peckover, S., & Thompson, K. et al. (2010). Performing "initial assessment": Identifying the latent conditons for error at the front-door of local authority children's services. *British Journal of Social Work, 40*(2), 352–370. doi:10.1093/bjsw/bcn162

Bronson, D. E., & Davis, T. S. (2011). *Finding and evaluating evidence: Systematic reviews and evidence-based practice.* Oxford, UK: Oxford University Press. doi:10.1093/acprof:oso/9780195337365.001.0001

Brown, A., & Bourne, I. (1996). *The social work supervisor.* Buckingham: Open University Press.

Brown, D., Reyes, S., Brown, B., & Gonzenbach, M. (2013). The effectiveness of group treatment for female adult incest survivors. *Journal of Child Sexual Abuse, 22*(2), 143–152. doi:10.1080/10538712.2013.737442 PMID:23428148

Brown, L., Callahan, M., Strega, S., Walmsley, C., & Dominelli, L. (2009). Manufacturing ghost fathers: The paradox of father presence and absence in child welfare. *Child & Family Social Work, 14*(1), 25–34. doi:10.1111/j.1365-2206.2008.00578.x

Brown, S. (2005). *Understanding youth and crime: Listening to youth?* Maidenhead, UK: Open University Press.

Brown, T., & Tyson, D. (2012). An abominable crime: Filicide in the context of parental separation and divorce. *Children Australia, 37*(04), 151–160. doi:10.1017/cha.2012.36

Bruce, N. (1985, April). *Juvenile justice in Scotland: A historical perspective?* Paper presented at a Franco-British workshop, The Best Interests of the Child. Edinburgh, UK.

Bryson, J. M., Crosby, B. C., & Stone, M. M. (2006). The design and implementation of cross-sector collaborations: Propositions from the literature. *Public Administration Review, 66*(s1), 44–55. doi:10.1111/j.1540-6210.2006.00665.x

Buchanan, K. M., Elias, L. J., & Goplen, G. B. (2000). Differing perspectives on outcome after subarachnoid hemorrhage: The patient, the relative, the neurosurgeon. *Neurosurgery, 46*, 831–838. Retrieved from http://journals.lww.com/neurosurgery/pages/default.aspx PMID:10764256

Buckley, H. (2003). *Child protection workforce: Beyond the rhetoric.* London: Jessica Kingsley.

Bullis, R. K. (1996). *Spirituality in social work practice.* Washington, DC: Taylor & Francis.

Bunston, W. (2013). What about the fathers? Bringing "dads on board" with their infants and toddlers following violence. *Journal of Family Studies, 19*(1), 70–79. doi:10.5172/jfs.2013.19.1.70

Butler, S. (1996). Child protection or professional self-preservation by the baby nurses? Public health nurses and child protection in Ireland.[PubMed]. *Social Science & Medicine, 43*(3), 303–314. doi:10.1016/0277-9536(95)00378-9

Cabot, W., & Cronin, B. (2013, April). *Recovery: The journey within three rural communities in NSW.* Paper presented at the 12th National Rural Health Conference, South Australia.

Cabrera, N., Tamis-LeMonda, C. S., Bradley, R. H., Hofferth, S., & Lamb, M. E. (2000). Fatherhood in the 21st century. *Child Development, 71*(1), 127–136. doi:10.1111/1467-8624.00126 PMID:10836566

Callaghan, B., Feldman, D., Gruis, K., & Feldman, E. (2011). The association of exposure to lead, mercury, and selenium and the development of amyotrophic lateral sclerosis and the epigenetic implications. *Neurodegenerative Diseases*, *8*(1-2), 1–8. doi:10.1159/000315405 PMID:20689252

Cameron, A., Macdonald, G., Turner, W., & Lloyd, L. (2007). The challenges of joint working: Lessons from the supporting People Health Pilot evaluation.[PubMed]. *International Journal of Integrated Care*, *7*, 1–10. Retrieved from https://www.ijic.org/index.php/ijic

Cameron, C. (2004). Social pedagogy and care: Danish and German practice in young people's residential care. *Journal of Social Work*, *4*(2), 133–151. doi:10.1177/1468017304044858

Cameron, L. (2010). Using the arts as a therapeutic tool for counselling: An Australian Aboriginal perspective. *Procedia: Social and Behavioral Sciences*, *5*, 403–407. doi:10.1016/j.sbspro.2010.07.112

Canda, E. R., & Furman, L. D. (2010). *Spiritual diversity in social work practice: The heart of helping* (2nd ed.). New York: Oxford University Press.

Cantor, C. H., Leenaars, A. A., & Lester, D. (1997). Underreporting of suicide in Ireland 1960-1989. *Archives of Suicide Research*, *3*(1), 5–12. doi:10.1080/13811119708258251

Carpenter, J. (2002). Mental health recovery paradigm: Implications for social work. *Health & Social Work*, *27*(2), 86–94. doi:10.1093/hsw/27.2.86 PMID:12079172

Carpenter, J., Webb, C., Bostock, L., & Coomber, C. (2012). *Effective supervision in social work and social care* (Research Briefing 43). Retrieved from Social Care Institute for Excellence website: http://www.scie.org.uk/publications/briefings/files/briefing43.pdf

Carroll, R. (2007, October 8). Killer law. *Guardian*. Retrieved from http://www.theguardian.com/society/2007/oct/08/health.lifeandhealth

Catalano, R. F., Hill, K. G., Haggerty, K. P., Fleming, C. B., & Hawkins, J. D. (2010). Social development interventions have extensive, long-lasting effects. In A. E. Fortune, P. McCallion, & K. Briar-Lawson (Eds.), *Social work practice research for the twenty-first century* (pp. 72–80). New York: Columbia University Press.

Chalmers, I. (2005). If evidence-informed policy works in practice, does it matter if it doesn't work in theory? *Evidence & Policy: A Journal of Research, Debate and Practice*, *1*(2), 227–242. doi:10.1332/1744264053730806

Chapman, L. (2014). *Neurobiologically informed trauma therapy with children and adolescents: Understanding mechanisms of change*. New York: Norton.

Chief Medical Officer. (2007). *Towards a safer surgery*. London: HMSO.

Chiller, P., & Crisp, B. (2012). Professional supervision: A workforce retention strategy for social work? *Australian Social Work*, *65*(2), 232–242. doi:10.1080/0312407X.2011.625036

Chio, A., Magnani, C., & Schiffer, D. (1995). Gompertzian analysis of amyotrophic lateral sclerosis mortality in Italy, 1957-1987: Application to birth cohorts. *Neuroepidemiology*, *14*(6), 269–277. doi:10.1159/000109802 PMID:8569998

Chouliara, Z., Karatzias, T., Scott-Brien, G., Macdonald, A., MacArthur, J., & Frazer, N. (2011). Talking therapy services for adult survivors of childhood sexual abuse (CSA) in Scotland: Perspectives of service users and professionals. *Journal of Child Sexual Abuse*, *20*(2), 128–156. doi:10.1080/10538712.2011.554340 PMID:21442530

Christie, A. (Ed.). (2001). *Men and social work: Theories and practices*. Basingstoke: Palgrave.

Clapton, G. (2009). How and why social work fails fathers: Redressing an imbalance, social work's role and responsibility. *Practice*, *21*(1), 17–34. doi:10.1080/09503150902745989

Clark, C. (2006). Moral character in social work. *British Journal of Social Work, 36*(1), 75–89. doi:10.1093/bjsw/bch364

Clark, M. D. (2013). The strengths perspective in criminal justice. In T. D. Saleebey (Ed.), *The strengths perspective in social work practice* (6th rev. ed., pp. 129–148). Pearson Education.

Cleverley, K., & Boyle, M. H. (2010). The individual as a moderating agent of the long-term impact of sexual abuse. *Journal of Interpersonal Violence, 25*(2), 274–290. doi:10.1177/0886260509334284 PMID:19423747

Coady, N., Hoy, S. L., Cameron, G., & Hallman, L. S. (2013). Fathers' experiences with child welfare services. *Child & Family Social Work, 18*(3), 275–284. doi:10.1111/j.1365-2206.2012.00842.x

Coakley, T. M. (2013). The influence of father involvement on child welfare permanency outcomes: A secondary data analysis. *Children and Youth Services Review, 35*(1), 174–182. doi:10.1016/j.childyouth.2012.09.023

The Cochrane Collaboration. (2002). Publication bias: What is publication bias? Retrieved from http://www.cochrane-net.org/openlearning/html/mod15-2.htm

Coholic, D., Lougheed, S., & Cadell, S. (2009). Exploring the helpfulness of arts-based methods with children living in foster care. *Traumatology, 15*(3), 64–71. doi:10.1177/1534765609341590

Collie, K., Backos, A., Malchiodi, C., & Spiegel, D. (2006). Art therapy for combat-related PTSD: Recommendations for research and practice. *Art Therapy: Journal of the American Art Therapy Association, 23*(4), 157–164. doi:10.1080/07421656.2006.10129335

Collier, R. (2009). *Men, law and gender: Essays on the "man" of law*. Abingdon: Routledge.

Collier, S., & Sheldon, S. (2008). *Fragmenting fatherhood: A socio-legal study*. Oxford: Hart.

Collins, S. (2008). Statutory social workers: Stress, job satisfaction, coping, social support and individual differences. *British Journal of Social Work, 38*(6), 1173–1193. doi:10.1093/bjsw/bcm047

Collishaw, S., Pickles, A., Messer, J., Rutter, M., Shearer, C., & Maughan, B. (2007). Resilience to adult psychopathology following childhood maltreatment: Evidence from a community sample. *Child Abuse & Neglect, 31*(3), 211–229. doi:10.1016/j.chiabu.2007.02.004 PMID:17399786

Colomina, M. T., Albina, M. L., Domingo, J. L., & Corbella, J. (1997). Influence of maternal stress on the effects of prenatal exposure to methylmercury and arsenic on postnatal development and behavior in mice: A preliminary evaluation. *Physiology & Behavior, 61*(3), 455–459. doi:10.1016/S0031-9384(96)00462-3 PMID:9089766

Coltrane, S. (1996). *Family man: Fatherhood, housework, and gender equity*. New York: Oxford Press.

Combs-Orme, T. (1988). Infant mortality and social work: Legacy of success. *The Social Service Review, 62*(1), 83–102. doi:10.1086/603662

Comm. of Ministers, *Recommendation*, 1040th Meeting, Doc. No. CM/Rec(2008)11 (2008).

Committee on Children and Young Persons. (1964). *The Kilbrandon report: Children and young persons: Scotland*. Edinburgh, Scotland: Scottish Home and Health Department, Scottish Education Department. Retrieved from http://www.scotland.gov.uk/Publications/2003/10/18259/26879

Consedine, J. (2002). Spirituality and social justice. In M. Nash & B. Stewart (Eds.), *Spirituality and social care: Contributing to personal and community well-being* (pp. 31–48). London: Jessica Kingsley.

Convention Relating to the Status of Refugees, July 28, 1951, 189 U.N.T.S. 137.

Cook, J. A., Copeland, M. E., Corey, L., Buffington, E., Jonikas, J. A., & Curtis, L. C. et al. (2010). Developing the evidence base for peer-led services: Changes among participants following Wellness Recovery Action Planning (WRAP) education in two statewide initiatives. *Psychiatric Rehabilitation Journal*, *34*(2), 113–120. doi:10.2975/34.2.2010.113.120 PMID:20952364

Cosson, B., & Graham, E. (2012). "I felt like a third wheel": Fathers' stories of exclusion from the "parenting team". *Journal of Family Studies*, *18*(2-3), 121–129. doi:10.5172/jfs.2012.18.2-3.121

Council on Social Work Education. (2008). *Educational policy and accreditation standards*. Retrieved from http://www.cswe.org/Accreditation/2008EPASDescription.aspx

Cowan, P. A., Cowan, C. P., Pruett, M. K., Pruett, K., & Wong, J. J. (2009). Promoting fathers' engagement with children: Preventive interventions for low-income families. *Journal of Marriage and the Family*, *71*(3), 663–679. doi:10.1111/j.1741-3737.2009.00625.x

Cox, K., & Steiner, S. (2013). Preserving commitment to social work service through the prevention of vicarious trauma. *Journal of Social Work Values and Ethics*, *10*(1), 52–60. Retrieved from http://www.jswve.org/

Crawford, K. (2011). Conclusion: Why is it necessary to consider the evidence and knowledge that underpins practice? In I. Mathews & K. Crawford (Eds.), *Evidence-based practice in social work* (pp. 115–130). Exeter, UK: Learning Matters.

Crawford, K. (2011). What underpins social work practice? In I. Mathews & K. Crawford (Eds.), *Evidence-based practice in social work* (pp. 3–21). Exeter, UK: Learning Matters.

Creighton, S. J. (1993). Children's homicide: An exchange[Letter to the editors]. *British Journal of Social Work*, *23*, 643–644. Retrieved from http://bjsw.oxfordjournals.org/

Crisp, B. R. (2004). Evidence-based practice and the borders of data in the global information era. *Journal of Social Work Education*, *40*, 73–86. doi:10.1080/10437797.2004.10778480

Crisp, B. R. (2010). *Spirituality and social work*. Southampton: Ashgate.

Crisp, B. R., Anderson, M. R., Orme, J., & Lister, P. G. (2003). *Knowledge review 1: Learning and teaching in social work education: Assessment*. Retrieved from Social Care Institute for Excellence website: http://www.scie.org.uk/publications/knowledgereviews/kr01.pdf

Crisp, B. R., Anderson, M. R., Orme, J., & Lister, P. G. (2005). *Knowledge review 9: Learning and teaching in social work education: Textbooks and frameworks on assessment*. Retrieved from Social Care Institute for Excellence website: http://www.scie.org.uk/publications/knowledgereviews/kr09.asp

Crocket, K., Drewery, W., McKenzie, W., Smith, L., & Winslade, J. (2004). Working for ethical research in practice. *International Journal of Narrative Therapy and Community Work*, *3*, 61–66. Retrieved from http://www.dulwichcentre.com.au/e-journal.html

Cullen, S. M., Cullen, M. A., Band, S., Davis, L., & Lindsay, G. (2011). Supporting fathers to engage with their children's learning and education: An under-developed aspect of the parent support adviser pilot. *British Educational Research Journal*, *37*(3), 485–500. doi:10.1080/01411921003786579

Curlin, F. A., Nwodim, C., Vance, J. L., Chin, M. H., & Lantos, J. D. (2008). To die, to sleep: US physicians' religious and other objections to physician-assisted suicide, terminal sedation, and withdrawal of life support. *The American Journal of Hospice & Palliative Medicine*, *25*(2), 112–120. doi:10.1177/1049909107310141 PMID:18198363

Curran, A., & Gilbert, I. (2008). *The little book of big stuff about the brain: The true story of your amazing brain.* Carmarthen: Crown House.

Curran, L. (2003). Social work and fathers: Child support and fathering programs. *Social Work, 48*(2), 219–227. doi:10.1093/sw/48.2.219 PMID:12718417

Curtis, C. (2006). Sexual abuse and subsequent suicidal behaviour: Exacerbating factors and implications for recovery. *Journal of Child Sexual Abuse, 15*(2), 1–21. doi:10.1300/J070v15n02_01 PMID:16702144

D'Cruz, H., & Jones, M. (2014). *Social work research in practice: Ethical and political contexts* (2nd ed.). London: SAGE.

Daigneault, I., Hebert, M., & McDuff, P. (2009). Men's and women's childhood sexual abuse and victimization in adult partner relationships: A study of risk factors. *Child Abuse & Neglect, 33*(9), 638–647. doi:10.1016/j.chiabu.2009.04.003 PMID:19811827

Daniel, B., & Taylor, J. (2001). *Engaging with fathers: Practice issues for health and social care.* London: Jessica Kingsley.

Darlington, Y., Feeney, J. A., & Rixon, K. (2005). Interagency collaboration between child protection and mental health services: Practices, attitudes and barriers. [PubMed]. *Child Abuse & Neglect, 29*(10), 1085–1098. doi:10.1016/j.chiabu.2005.04.005

Davidson, L., Belamy, C., Guy, K., & Miller, R. (2012). Peer support among persons with severe mental illnesses: A review of evidence and experience. *World Psychiatry: Official Journal of the World Psychiatric Association (WPA), 11*(2), 123–128. doi:10.1016/j.wpsyc.2012.05.009 PMID:22654945

Davis, H. (2013). Contextual challenges for crisis support in the immediate aftermath of major incidents in the UK. *British Journal of Social Work, 43*(3), 504–521. doi:10.1093/bjsw/bcr197

Davys, A. M., & Beddoe, L. (2009). The reflective learning model: Supervision of social work students. *Social Work Education, 28*(8), 919–933. doi:10.1080/02615470902748662

De Brun, C., & Pearce-Smith, N. (2009). *Searching skills toolkit: Finding the evidence.* Chichester, UK: Wiley Blackwell. doi:10.1002/9781444303599

de Hennezel, M. (1997). *Intimate death: How the dying teach us how to live.* New York: Alfred A. Knopf.

de Souza, M. (2012). Connectedness and *connectedness*: The dark side of spirituality – Implications for education. *International Journal of Children's Spirituality, 17*(4), 291–303. doi:10.1080/1364436X.2012.752346

de Vries, E. N., Ramrattan, M. A., Smorenburg, S. M., Gouma, D. J., & Boermeester, M. A. (2008). The incidence and nature of in-hospital adverse events: A systematic review. *Quality & Safety in Health Care, 17*(3), 216–223. doi:10.1136/qshc.2007.023622 PMID:18519629

Deahl, M. (2000). Psychological debriefing: Controversy and challenge. *The Australian and New Zealand Journal of Psychiatry, 34*(6), 929–939. doi:10.1080/000486700267 PMID:11127623

Defraia, G. S. (2013). Organizational outcomes following traumatic workplace incidents: A practice-based exploration of impact of incident severity level. *Social Work in Mental Health, 11*(5), 404–433. doi:10.1080/15332985.2013.784224

Department for Education. (2013). *Working together to safeguard children: A guide to inter-agency working to safeguard and promote the welfare of children.* Retrieved from http://media.education.gov.uk/assets/files/pdf/w/working%20together.pdf

Department of Health and Ageing. (2013). *National mental health report 2013: Tracking progress of mental health reform in Australia 1993-2011.* Retrieved from Commonwealth of Australia Department of Health website: http://www.health.gov.au/internet/main/publishing.nsf/Content/B090F03865A7FAB9CA257C1B0079E198/$File/rep13.pdf

Department of Labour. (2003). *Managing stress in the workplace.* Retrieved from http://www.business.govt.nz/worksafe/information-guidance/all-guidance-items/healthy-work-managing-stress-and-fatigue-in-the-workplace/stressfatigue.pdf

Devaney, J., & Spratt, T. (2009). Child abuse as a complex and wicked problem: Reflecting on policy developments in the United Kingdom in working with children and families with multiple problems. *Children and Youth Services Review, 31*(6), 635–641. doi:10.1016/j.childyouth.2008.12.003

Devilly, G. J., & Cotton, P. (2004). Caveat emptor, caveat venditor, and critical incident stress debriefing/management (CISD/M). *Australian Psychologist, 39*(1), 35–40. doi:10.1080/00050060410001660317

Devilly, G. J., Gist, R., & Cotton, P. (2006). Ready! Fire! Aim!: The status of psychological debriefing and therapeutic interventions – In the work place and after disasters. *Review of General Psychology, 10*(4), 318–345. doi:10.1037/1089-2680.10.4.318

Dickersin, K., Scherer, R., & Lefebvre, C. (1995). Identifying relevant studies for systematic reviews. In I. Chalmers & D. G. Altman (Eds.), *Systematic Reviews* (pp. 17–36). London: BMJ.

Dissanayake, E. (1992). *Homo aestheticus: Where art comes from and why*. New York: Free Press.

Dore, I. J. (2006). Evidence-focused social care: On target or off-side? *Social Work & Society, 4*, 232-255. Retrieved from http://www.socwork.net/sws

Draucker, C. B., Martsolf, D. S., Roller, C., Knapik, G., Ross, R., & Stidham, A. W. (2011). Healing from childhood sexual abuse: A theoretical model. *Journal of Child Sexual Abuse, 20*(4), 435–466. doi:10.1080/10538712.2011.588188 PMID:21812546

Drew, S. K., Mills, M., & Gassaway, B. M. (2007). *Dirty work: The social construction of taint*. Waco, TX: Baylor University Press.

Drisko, J. (2014). Research evidence and social work practice: The place of evidence-based practice. *Clinical Social Work Journal, 42*(2), 123–133. doi:10.1007/s10615-013-0459-9

Drisko, J. W., & Grady, M. D. (2012). *Evidence-based practice in clinical social work*. New York: Springer. doi:10.1007/978-1-4614-3470-2

Dudgeon, P., Garvey, D., & Pickett, H. (Eds.). (2000). *Working with Indigenous Australians: A handbook for psychologists*. Perth, WA: Gunada Press.

Dulmus, C., & Sowers, K. (Eds.). (2012). *Social work fields of practice: Historical trends, professional issues, and future opportunities*. New Jersey: Wiley.

Dulwich Centre Publications. (2004). Narrative therapy and research. *International Journal of Narrative Therapy and Community Work, 2*, 29–36. Retrieved from http://www.dulwichcentre.com.au/e-journal.html

Durkheim, E. (1897). *Suicide: A study in sociology* (J. A. Spaulding & G. George Simpson, Trans.). New York: Free Press.

Dwairy, M., Dowell, A. C., & Stahl, J.-C. (2011). The application of foraging theory to the information searching behaviour of general practitioners. *BMC Family Practice, 12*(1), 90. doi:10.1186/1471-2296-12-90 PMID:21861880

Dyregrov, A. (1997). The process in psychological debriefings. *Journal of Traumatic Stress, 10*(4), 589–605. doi:10.1002/jts.2490100406 PMID:9391943

Dyregrov, A., & Regel, S. (2011). Early interventions following exposure to traumatic events: Implications for practice from recent research. *Journal of Loss and Trauma, 17*(3), 271–291. doi:10.1080/15325024.2011.616832

E.S.C. Res. 1997/30, U.N. Doc. E/RES/1997/30 (July 21, 1997).

Eastham, M. (2002). Vocation and social care. In M. Nash & B. Stewart (Eds.), *Spirituality and social care: Contributing to personal and community well-being* (pp. 71–91). London: Jessica Kingsley.

Easton, S. D., Coohey, C., O'Leary, P., Zhang, Y., & Hua, L. (2011). The effect of childhood sexual abuse on psychosexual functioning during adulthood. *Journal of Family Violence, 26*(1), 41–50. doi:10.1007/s10896-010-9340-6

Edmond, T., Megivern, D., Williams, C., Rochman, E., & Howard, M. (2006). Integrating evidence based practice and social work field education. *Journal of Social Work Education, 42*(2), 377–396. doi:10.5175/JSWE.2006.200404115

Egan, R. (2012). Australian social work supervision practice in 2007. *Australian Social Work, 65*(2), 171–184. doi:10.1080/0312407X.2011.653575

Eketone, A. (2012). The purposes of cultural supervision. *Aotearoa New Zealand Social Work, 24*(3-4), 20-30. Retrieved from http://anzasw.org.nz/en/about/topics/show/207-professional-journal-aotearoa-new-zealand-social-work

Ellett, A. J., Ellis, J. I., Westbrook, T. M., & Dews, D. (2007). A qualitative study of 369 child welfare professionals' perspectives about factors contributing to employee retention and turnover. *Children and Youth Services Review, 29*(2), 264–281. doi:10.1016/j.childyouth.2006.07.005

England, H. (1986). *Social work as art: Making sense for good practice.* London: Allen and Unwin.

Epstein, I. (2009). Promoting harmony where there is commonly conflict: Evidence-informed practice as an integrative strategy. *Social Work in Health Care, 48*(3), 216–231. doi:10.1080/00981380802589845 PMID:19360527

Erenora Puketapu-Hetet. (1986). Te Atiawa: Interview by Darcy Nicholas. In *Seven Maori artists: Interviews by Darcy Nicholas and Keri Kaa* (pp. 38–42). Wellington, New Zealand: Government Printer.

Erikson, E. H. (1964). *Insight and responsibility.* New York: Norton.

Evans, S., Huxley, P., Baker, C., White, J., Madge, S., Onyett, S., & Gould, N. (2012). The social care component of multidisciplinary mental health teams: A review and national survey. *Journal of Health Services Research & Policy, 17*(Suppl. 2), 23–29. doi:10.1258/jhsrp.2012.011117 PMID:22572713

Everly, G. S. Jr., Flannery, R. B. Jr., & Mitchell, J. T. (2000). Critical incident stress management (CISM): A review of the literature. *Aggression and Violent Behavior, 5*(1), 23–40. doi:10.1016/S1359-1789(98)00026-3

Everly, G. S., & Flynn, B. W. (2006). Principles and practical procedures for acute psychological first aid training for personnel without mental health experience. *International Journal of Emergency Mental Health, 8*(2), 93–100. Retrieved from http://www.omicsonline.com/open-access/international-journal-of-emergency-mental-health-and-human-resilience.php PMID:16703847

Fadiman, J., & Frager, R. (1997). *Essential Sufism.* San Francisco: Harper Collins.

Falkov, A. (1996). *Study of working together "Part 8" reports: Fatal child abuse and parental psychiatric disorders: An analysis of 100 area child protection committee case reviews conducted under the terms of part 8 of Working Together Under the Childrens Act 1989 (ACPC Series, Report No.1).* London: Department of Health.

Fallot, R. D. (2007). Spirituality and religion in recovery: Some current issues. *Psychiatric Rehabilitation Journal, 30*(4), 261–270. doi:10.2975/30.4.2007.261.270 PMID:17458450

Farace, D. J. (1998). Foreword. In *Perspectives on the design and transfer of scientific and technical information. Third international conference on grey literature, 13-14 November 1997. Luxembourg. GL'97 proceedings* (p. iii). Amsterdam: TransAtlantic GreyNet.

Fargo, J. D. (2009). Pathways to adult sexual revictimization: Direct and indirect behavioral risk factors across the lifespan. *Journal of Interpersonal Violence, 24*(11), 1771–1791. doi:10.1177/0886260508325489 PMID:18931368

Featherstone, B. (2006). Why gender matters in child welfare and protection. *Critical Social Policy, 26*(2), 94–314. doi:10.1177/0261018306062587

Featherstone, B. (2009). *Contemporary fathers: Theory, policy and practice.* Bristol: Policy Press.

Featherstone, B. (2010). Writing fathers in but mothers out!!! *Critical Social Policy, 30*(2), 208–224. doi:10.1177/0261018309358290

Featherstone, B., & Fraser, C. (2012). Working with fathers around domestic violence: Contemporary debates. *Child Abuse Review, 21*(4), 255–263. doi:10.1002/car.2221

Featherstone, B., Rivett, M., & Scourfield, J. (2007). *Working with men: Theory and practice in health and social welfare.* London: Sage.

Feerick, M. M., & Snow, K. L. (2005). The relationships between childhood sexual abuse, social anxiety, and symptoms of posttraumatic stress disorder in women. *Journal of Family Violence, 20*(6), 409–419. doi:10.1007/s10896-005-7802-z

Felitti, V. J., Anda, R. F., Nordenberg, D., Williamson, D. F., Spitz, A. M., & Edwards, V.,...Marks, J.S. (1998). Relationship of childhood abuse and household dysfunction to many of the leading causes of death in adults: The adverse childhood experiences (ACE) study. *American Journal of Preventive Medicine, 14*(4), 245–258. doi:10.1016/S0749-3797(98)00017-8 PMID:9635069

Fenwick, T. (2012). Complexity science and professional learning for collaboration: A critical reconsideration of possibilities and limitations. *Journal of Education and Work, 25*(1), 141–162. doi:10.1080/13639080.2012.644911

Ferguson, H. (2003). Outline of a critical best practice perspective on social work and social care. *British Journal of Social Work, 33*(8), 1005–1024. doi:10.1093/bjsw/33.8.1005

Ferguson, H. (2011). *Child protection practice.* Basingstoke: Palgrave Macmillan.

Ferguson, H. (2013). Critical best practice. In M. Gray & S. Webb (Eds.), *The new politics of social work* (pp. 116–127). Basingstoke, UK: Palgrave MacMillan.

Ferguson, H., & Hogan, F. (2004). *Strengthening families through fathers: Issues for policy and practice in working with vulnerable fathers and their families.* Dublin: Department of Social, Community and Family Affairs.

Fineout-Overholt, E., & Johnston, L. (2005). Teaching EBP: Asking searchable, answerable clinical questions. *Worldviews on Evidence-Based Nursing, 2*(3), 157–160. doi:10.1111/j.1741-6787.2005.00032.x PMID:17040536

Fisher, T., & Somerton, J. (2000). Reflection on action: The process of helping social work students to develop their use of theory in practice. *Social Work Education, 19*(4), 387–401. doi:10.1080/02615470050078384

Flannery, R. B. Jr., & Everly, G. S. Jr. (2004). Critical incident stress management (CISM): Updated review of findings, 1998-2002. *Aggression and Violent Behavior, 9*(4), 319–329. doi:10.1016/S1359-1789(03)00030-2

Fleming, J. (1998). Valuing families in statutory practice. *Child Abuse Prevention, 6*, 1-4. Retrieved from http://www.aifs.org.au

Fleming, J. (2010). *The absence of fathers in child and family welfare practice* (Doctoral dissertation). Retrieved from http://arrow.monash.edu.au/vital/access/manager/Repository/monash:80105

Fleming, J., & King, A. (2010). A road less travelled: Working with men as fathers in family based services. *Developing Practice, 26*, 40-51. Retrieved from: http://www.acwa.asn.au/developing_practice11.html

Fletcher, R. (2011). *The dad factor: How the father-baby bond helps a child for life.* Warriewood, Australia: Finch Publishing.

Fletcher, R., Fairbairn, H., & Pascoe, S. (2003). *Fatherhood research in Australia.* Newcastle, Australia: The Family Action Centre.

Fletcher, R., Morgan, P. J., May, C., Lubans, D. R., & St George, J. (2011). Fathers' perceptions of rough-and-tumble play: Implications for early childhood services. *Australian Journal of Early Childhood, 36*, 131–138. Retrieved from http://www.earlychildhoodaustralia.org.au/australian_journal_of_early_childhood/

Fletcher, R., Silberberg, S., & Baxter, R. (2001). *Fathers' access to family-related service.* Newcastle, Australia: The Family Action Centre.

Fletcher, R. J., & Visser, A. L. (2008). Facilitating father engagement: The role of family relationship centres. *Journal of Family Studies, 14*(1), 53–64. doi:10.5172/jfs.327.14.1.53

Fontes, L. A., & Plummer, C. (2010). Cultural issues in disclosures of child sexual abuse. *Journal of Child Sexual Abuse, 19*(5), 491–518. doi:10.1080/10538712.2010.512520 PMID:20924908

Fook, J. (2004). What professionals need from research: Beyond evidence-based practice. In D. Smith (Ed.), *Social work and evidence-based practice* (pp. 29–46). London: Jessica Kingsley.

Fook, J. (2012). *Social work: A critical approach to practice* (2nd ed.). London: Sage.

Fook, J., & Askeland, G. A. (2007). Challenges of critical reflection: "Nothing ventured, nothing gained. *Social Work Education, 26*(5), 520–533. doi:10.1080/02615470601118662

Fortune, A. E. (2010). Empirical practice in social work. In A. E. Fortune, P. McCallion, & K. Briar-Lawson (Eds.), Social work practice research for the twenty-first century (pp. 23-30). New York: Columbia University Press.

Fortune, A. E., McCallion, P., & Briar-Lawson, K. (2010). Building evidence-based intervention models. In A. E. Fortune, P. McCallion, & K. Briar-Lawson (Eds.), Social work practice research for the twenty-first century (pp. 279–295). New York: Columbia University Press.

Fossey, E., Cuff, R., Ennals, P., Grey, F., McKenzie, P., & Meadows, G. ... Zimmerman, A. (2012). Supporting recovery and living well. In G. Meadows, J. Farhall, E. Fossey, M. Grigg, F. McDermott, & B. Singh. (Eds.), Mental health in Australia: Collaborative community practice (3rd ed.. pp. 502-528). Sydney, Australia: Oxford University Press.

*Fourth national mental health plan: An agenda for collaborative government action in mental health 2009-2014.* (2009). Retrieved from Commonwealth of Australia Department of Health website: http://www.health.gov.au/internet/main/publishing.nsf/Content/9A5A0E8BDFC55D3BCA257BF0001C1B1C/$File/plan09v2.pdf

Frambach, R. T., & Schillewaert, N. (2002). Organisational innovation adoption: A multi-level framework of determinants and opportunities for future research. *Journal of Business Research*, 55(2), 163–176. doi:10.1016/S0148-2963(00)00152-1

Frame, M. W. (2001). The spiritual genogram in training and supervision. *The Family Journal*, 9(2), 109–115. doi:10.1177/1066480701092004

Franklin, B. (1999). *Social policy, the media and misrepresentation*. London: Routledge.

Fraser, M. W. (2003). Intervention research in social work: A basis for evidence-based practice and practice guidelines. In A. Rosen & E. K. Proctor (Eds.). *Developing practice guidelines for social work intervention: Issues, methods, and research agenda* (pp. 17–36). New York: Columbia University Press.

Frazer, D., Ahuja, A., Watkins, L., & Cipolitti, L. (2007). Coiling versus clipping for the treatment of aneurysmal subarachnoid hemorrhage: A longitudinal investigation into cognitive outcome. *Neurosurgery*, 60(3), 434–441. doi:10.1227/01.NEU.0000255335.72662.25 PMID:17327787

Freeth, D., & Reeves, S. (2004). Learning to work together: Using the presage, process, product (3P) model to highlight decisions and possibilities.[PubMed]. *Journal of Interprofessional Care*, 18(1), 43–56. doi:10.1080/13561820310001608221

Fritch, A. M., & Lynch, S. M. (2008). Group treatment for adult survivors of interpersonal trauma. *Journal of Psychological Trauma*, 7(3), 145–169. doi:10.1080/19322880802266797

Fronek, P. (Host). (2013a, February 2). Involving fathers: In conversation with Joseph Fleming [Episode 42]. Podsocs. Podcast retrieved November 18, 2013, from http://www.podsocs.com/podcast/involving-fathers/

Fronek, P. (Host). (2013b, March 16). *Working with fathers from a strengths perspective: In conversation with Andrew King* [Episode 46]. Podsocs. Podcast retrieved November 24, 2013, from http://www.podsocs.com/podcast/working-with-fathers-from-a-strengths-perspective/

Furness, S., & Gilligan, P. (2010). Social work, religion and belief: Developing a framework for practice. *British Journal of Social Work*, 40(7), 2185–2202. doi:10.1093/bjsw/bcp159

Furness, S., & Gilligan, P. (2013). Editorial. *International Social Work*, 56(3), 271–275. doi:10.1177/0020872813476447

G.A. Res 44/25, U.N. Doc. A/RES/44/25 (Nov. 20, 1989).

G.A. Res. 40/33. U.N. Doc. A/RES/40/33 (Nov 29, 1985).

G.A. Res. 45/110. U.N. Doc. A/RES/45/110 (Dec. 14, 1990).

G.A. Res. 45/112. U.N. Doc. A/RES/45/112 (Dec. 14, 1990).

G.A. Res. 45/113, U.N. Doc. A/RES/45/113 (Dec. 14, 1990).

Gale, F., & Dudley, M. (2013). Spirituality in social work. In M. Connolly & L. Harms (Eds.), *Social work: Contexts and practice* (3rd ed., pp. 60–73). Melbourne: Oxford University Press.

Gallegos, D. (2006). *Fly-in fly-out employment: Managing the parenting transitions*. Perth, Australia: Centre for Social and Community Research.

Gambrill, E. (2001). Social work: An authority-based profession. *Research on Social Work Practice, 11*(2), 166–175. doi:10.1177/104973150101100203

Gambrill, E. (2003). Evidence-based practice: Implications for knowledge development and use in social work. In A. Rosen & E. K. Proctor (Eds.), *Developing practice guidelines for social work intervention: Issues, methods, and research agenda* (pp. 37–58). New York: Columbia University Press.

Gambrill, E. (2006). Evidence-based practice and policy: Choices ahead. *Research on Social Work Practice, 16*(3), 338–357. doi:10.1177/1049731505284205

Gambrill, E. (2007). Views of evidence-based practice: Social workers' code of ethics and accreditation standards as guides of choice. *Journal of Social Work Education, 43*(3), 447–462. doi:10.5175/JSWE.2007.200600639

Gambrill, E. (2008). Evidence-based (informed) macro practice: Process and philosophy. *Journal of Evidence-Based Social Work, 5*(3-4), 423–452. doi:10.1080/15433710802083971 PMID:19042875

Gambrill, E. (2010). Evidence-informed practice: Antidote to propaganda in the helping professions? *Research on Social Work Practice, 20*(3), 302–320. doi:10.1177/1049731509347879

Gambrill, E. (2011). Evidence-based practice and the ethics of discretion. *Journal of Social Work, 11*(1), 26–48. doi:10.1177/1468017310381306

Gambrill, E. (2013). Evidence-informed practice. In B. A. Thyer, C. N. Dulmus, & K. M. Sowers (Eds.), *Developing evidence-based generalist practice skills* (pp. 1–24). Hoboken, NJ: John Wiley.

Gardner, F. (2009). Affirming values: Using critical reflection to explore meaning and professional practice. *Reflective Practice, 10*(2), 179–190. doi:10.1080/14623940902786198

Gardner, F. (2011). *Critical spirituality: A holistic approach to contemporary practice*. Farnham, UK: Ashgate.

Garfield, C. F., & Isacco, A. (2006). Fathers and the well-child visit. *Pediatrics, 117*(4), 637–645. doi:10.1542/peds.2005-1612 PMID:16585280

Gask, L. (2005). Overt and covert barriers to the integration of primary and specialist mental health care. [PubMed]. *Social Science & Medicine, 61*(8), 1785–1794. doi:10.1016/j.socscimed.2005.03.038

Gellis, Z., & Reid, W. J. (2004). Strengthening evidence-based practice. *Brief Treatment and Crisis Intervention, 4*(2), 155–165. doi:10.1093/brief-treatment/mhh012

George, U. (2002). A needs-based model for settlement service delivery for newcomers to Canada. *International Social Work, 45*(4), 465–480. doi:10.1177/00208728020450040501

Gerhardt, S. (2004). *Why love matters: How affection shapes a baby's brain*. Hove, East Sussex: Brunner/Routledge.

Germain, C., & Gitterman, A. (1980). *Life model of social work practice*. New York: Columbia University Press.

Ghate, D., Shaw, C., & Hazel, N. (2000). *Fathers and family centres: Engaging fathers in preventive services*. York, UK: York Publishing Services.

Gibbons, J. (2001). Effective practice: Social work's long history of concern about outcomes. *Australian Social Work, 54*(3), 3–13. doi:10.1080/03124070108414328

Gibbs, L. E. (2003). *Evidence-based practice for the helping professions: A practical guide with integrated multimedia*. Pacific Grove, CA: Brooks/Cole-Thomson Learning.

Gibbs, L., & Gambrill, E. (2002). Evidence-based practice: Counterarguments to objections. *Research on Social Work Practice, 12*(3), 452–476. doi:10.1177/1049731502012003007

Gibson, F., & Glenny, A.-M. (2007). Critical apprisal of quantitative studies 1: Is the quality of the study good enough for you to use the findings? In J. V. Craig & R. L. Smyth (Eds.), *The evidence based practice manual for nurses* (2nd ed., pp. 95–126). Edinburgh, UK: Churchill Livingstone.

Gibson, L. (2011). Politics, pain and pleasure: The art of art-making for "settled" Aboriginal Australians. *Coolibah*, 5, 119–129.

Gil, E. (2006). *Helping abused and traumatized children: Integrating directive and nondirective approaches*. New York: Guilford.

Gilgun, J. F. (2005). The four cornerstones of evidence-based practice in social work. *Research on Social Work Practice*, 15(1), 52–61. doi:10.1177/1049731504269581

Gilligan, P. (2010). Faith-based approaches. In M. Gray & S. Webb (Eds.), *Ethics and value perspectives in social work* (pp. 60–70). Basingstoke, UK: Palgrave Macmillan.

Gilligan, P., & Furness, S. (2006). The role of religion and spirituality in social work practice: Views and experiences of social workers and students. *British Journal of Social Work*, 36(4), 617–637. doi:10.1093/bjsw/bch252

Gitterman, A., & Germain, C. B. (2008). *The life model of social work practice: Advances in theory and practice* (3rd ed.). Chichester, UK: Columbia University.

Gladstone, B. M., McKeever, P., Seeman, M., & Boydell, K. M. (2014). Analysis of a support group for children of parents with mental illnesses: Managing stressful situations. *Qualitative Health Research*, 24(9), 1171–1182. doi:10.1177/1049732314528068 PMID:24659228

Glanville, J. M., Lefebvre, C., Miles, J. N. V., & Camosso-Stefinovic, J. (2006). How to identify randomized controlled trials in MEDLINE: Ten years on. *Journal of the Medical Library Association: JMLA*, 94, 130–136. Retrieved from http://www.mlanet.org/publications/jmla/ PMID:16636704

Gleeson, J. F., Cotton, S. M., Alvarez-Jimenez, M., Wade, D., Crisp, K., & Newman, B. et al. (2010). Family outcomes from a randomized control trial of relapse prevention therapy in first-episode psychosis. *The Journal of Clinical Psychiatry*, 71(04), 475–483. doi:10.4088/JCP.08m04672yel PMID:20021994

Goddard, C., & Saunders, B. (2001). *Child abuse and the media*. Canberra: Australian Insitute of Family Studies.

Godin, P. (2000). A dirty business: Caring for people who are a nuisance or a danger.[PubMed]. *Journal of Advanced Nursing*, 32(6), 1396–1402. doi:10.1046/j.1365-2648.2000.01623.x

Goldapple, K., Segal, Z., Garson, C., Lau, M., Bieling, P., Kennedy, S., & Mayberg, H. (2004). Modulation of cortical-limbic pathways in major depression: Treatment-specific effects of cognitive behaviour therapy. *Archives of General Psychiatry*, 61(1), 34–41. doi:10.1001/archpsyc.61.1.34 PMID:14706942

Goldson, B. (2009). Counterblast: "Difficult to understand or defend" – A reasoned case for raising the age of criminal responsibility. *Howard Journal of Criminal Justice*, 48(5), 514–521. doi:10.1111/j.1468-2311.2009.00592.x

Goldson, B., & Muncie, J. (2012). Towards a global "child friendly" juvenile justice? *International Journal of Law, Crime and Justice*, 40(1), 47–64. doi:10.1016/j.ijlcj.2011.09.004

Gordon, D. M., Oliveros, A., Hawes, S. W., Iwamoto, D. K., & Rayford, B. S. (2012). Engaging fathers in child protection services: A review of factors and strategies across ecological systems. *Children and Youth Services Review*, 34(8), 1399–1417. doi:10.1016/j.childyouth.2012.03.021 PMID:25232202

Gordon, D. M., Watkins, N. D., Walling, S. M., Wilhelm, S., & Rayford, B. S. (2011). Adolescent fathers involved with child protection: Social workers speak! *Child Welfare*, 90, 95–114. Retrieved from http://www.cwla.org/ PMID:22533056

Gordon, S. E., & Ellis, P. M. (2013). Recovery of evidence-based practice. *International Journal of Mental Health Nursing*, 22(1), 3–14. doi:10.1111/j.1447-0349.2012.00835.x PMID:22830603

Grady, M. D. (2010). The missing link: The role of social work schools and evidence-based practice. *Journal of Evidence-Based Social Work*, 7(5), 400–411. doi:10.1080/15433711003591101 PMID:21082470

Grady, M., & Drisko, J. W. (2014). Thorough clinical assessment: The hidden foundation of evidence-based practice. *Families in Society*, 95(1), 5–14. doi:10.1606/1044-3894.2014.95.2

Gray, B. (1989). *Collaborating: Finding common ground for multi-party problems*. San Francisco: Jossey-Bass.

Gray, M., Joy, E., Plath, D., & Webb, S. A. (2013). Implementing evidence-based practice: A review of the empirical research literature. *Research on Social Work Practice*, 23(2), 157–166. doi:10.1177/1049731512467072

Gray, M., Joy, E., Plath, D., & Webb, S. A. (2014). Opinions about evidence: A study of social workers' attitudes towards evidence-based practice. *Journal of Social Work*, 14(1), 23–40. doi:10.1177/1468017313475555

Gray, M., & Mcdonald, C. (2006). Pursuing good practice?: The limits of evidence-based practice. *Journal of Social Work*, 6(1), 7–20. doi:10.1177/1468017306062209

Gray, M., Plath, D., & Webb, S. A. (2009). *Evidence-based social work: A critical stance*. New York, NY: Routledge.

Gray, M., & Webb, S. A. (2008). Social work as art revisited. *International Journal of Social Welfare*, 17(2), 182–193. doi:10.1111/j.1468-2397.2008.00548.x

Gray, M., & Webb, S. A. (2013). Critical social work. In M. Gray & S. A. Webb (Eds.), *Social work theories and methods* (2nd ed., pp. 99–109). London: Sage.

Gray, M., & Webb, S. A. (2013). Introduction. In M. Gray & S. A. Webb (Eds.), *Social work theories and methods* (2nd ed., pp. 1–10). London: Sage.

Grimmer-Somers, K. (Ed.). (2009). *Practical tips in finding the evidence: An allied health primer. España*. Manila: UST.

Group of Specialists on Child-Friendly Justice (CJ-S-CH). (2010). *4th draft of the Council of Europe guidelines on child-friendly justice*. Strasbourg, France: Council of Europe.

Guerin, S., Devitt, C., & Redmond, B. (2010). Experiences of early-career social workers in Ireland. *British Journal of Social Work*, 40(8), 2467–2484. doi:10.1093/bjsw/bcq020

Gunnar, M. R., & Donzella, B. (2002). Social regulation of the cortisol levels in early human development. *Psychoneuroendocrinology*, 27(1-2), 199–220. doi:10.1016/S0306-4530(01)00045-2 PMID:11750779

Gunnar, M. R., & Nelson, C. A. (1994). Event-related potentials in year-old infants: Relations with emotionality and cortisol. *Child Development*, 65(1), 80–94. doi:10.2307/1131367 PMID:8131656

Hadorn, G. H., Pohl, C., & Bammer, G. (2010). Solving problems through transdisciplinary research. In R. Frodeman, J. T. Klein, & C. Mitcham (Eds.), *The Oxford handbook of interdisciplinarity* (pp. 431–452). New York, NY: Oxford University Press.

Hair, H. J. (2013). The purpose and duration of supervision, and the training and discipline of supervisors: What social workers say they need to provide effective services. *British Journal of Social Work*, 43(8), 1562–1588. doi:10.1093/bjsw/bcs071

Halliday, S., Burns, N., Hutton, N., McNeill, F., & Tata, C. (2009). Street-level bureaucracy, interprofessional relations, and coping mechanisms: A study of criminal justice social workers in the sentencing process. *Law & Policy*, 31(4), 405–428. doi:10.1111/j.1467-9930.2009.00306.x

Hämäläinen, J. (2003). The concept of social pedagogy in the field of social work. *Journal of Social Work*, 3(1), 69–80. doi:10.1177/1468017303003001005

Hannes, K. (2011). Critical appraisal of qualitative research. In J. Noyes, A. Booth, K. Hannes, A. Harden, J. Harris, S. Lewin, & C. Lockwood (Eds.), *Supplementary guidance for inclusion of qualitative research in Cochrane systematic reviews of interventions: Version 1*. Cochrane Collaboration Qualitative Methods Group. Retrieved from http://cqrmg.cochrane.org/supplemental-handbook-guidance

Hansen, L., & Pritchard, C. (2008). Consistency in suicide rates in twenty-two developed countries by gender over time 1874-78, 1974-76, and 1998-2000. *Archives of Suicide Research, 12*(3), 251–262. doi:10.1080/13811110802101153 PMID:18576206

Harkness, D. R. (1987). *Social work supervision in community mental health: Effects of normal and client-focused supervision on client satisfaction and generalized contentment* (Doctoral dissertation). Retrieved from Proquest Dissertations and Theses Global database. (UMI No. 8813410)

Harkness, D. (1995). The art of helping in supervised practice: Skills, relationships, and outcomes. *The Clinical Supervisor, 13*(1), 63–76. doi:10.1300/J001v13n01_05

Harkness, D. (1997). Testing interactional social work theory: A panel analysis of supervised practice and outcomes. *The Clinical Supervisor, 15*(1), 33–50. doi:10.1300/J001v15n01_03

Harkness, D., & Hensley, H. (1991). Changing the focus of social work supervision: Effects on client satisfaction and generalized contentment. *Social Work, 36*, 506–512. doi:10.1093/sw/36.6.506 PMID:1754927

Harkness, D., & Poertner, J. (1989). Research and social work supervision: A conceptual review. *Social Work, 34*, 115–119.

Harvey, R. (2002). The UK before the UN Committee on the Rights of the Child. *ChildRIGHT, 10*(190), 9-11. Retrieved from http://www.childrenslegalcentre.com/index.php?page=childright_archive

Haskett, M. E., Marziano, B., & Dover, E. R. (1996). Absence of males in maltreatment research: A survey of recent literature. *Child Abuse & Neglect, 20*(12), 1175–1182. doi:10.1016/S0145-2134(96)00113-5 PMID:8985608

Hass-Cohen, N. (2003). Art therapy mind body approaches: Some applications of relational neuroscience to art therapy. *Progress: Family Systems Research and Therapy, 12*, 24–38.

Hass-Cohen, N. (2006). Art therapy and clinical neuroscience in action. Retrieved from http://www.laiat.com/atcanaction.htm

Hawkins, C. A. (2010). Sustainability, human rights, and environmental justice: Critical connections for social work. *Critical Social Work, 11*(3). Retrieved from http://www1.uwindsor.ca/criticalsocialwork/the-nexus-of-sustainability-human-rights-and-environmental-justice-a-critical-connection-for-contemp

Hawkins, A. J., & Dollahite, D. C. (1997). *Generative fathering: Beyond deficit perspectives.* Thousand Oaks, CA: Sage.

Hayes, D., & Spratt, T. (2009). Child welfare interventions: Patterns of social work practice. *British Journal of Social Work, 39*(8), 1575–1597. doi:10.1093/bjsw/bcn098

Headspace. (2010, May 17). *Headspace concern over exclusion of key workers from mental healthcare* [Press release]. Retrieved from http://www.headspace.org.au/about-headspace/media-centre/media-release-archive/headspace-concern-over-exclusion-of-key-workers-from-mental-health-care

Healing Foundation. (2013). *Annual Report 2012-2013.* Retrieved from http://healingfoundation.org.au/wordpress/wp-content/files_mf/1388977931HealingFoundationAnnualReport20122013.pdf

Health and Care Professions Council. (2012). *Standards of conduct, performance and ethics.* Retrieved from http://www.hcpc-uk.org/assets/documents/10003B6EStandardsofconduct,performanceandethics.pdf

Healy, K., & Lonne, B. (2010). *The social work and human services workforce: Report from a national study of education, training and workforce needs.* Strawberry Hills, Australia: Australian Learning and Teaching Council.

Helm, D. (2011). Judgements or assumptions? The role of analysis in assessing children and young people's needs. *British Journal of Social Work, 41*(5), 894–911. doi:10.1093/bjsw/bcr096

Herman, J. (1992). *Trauma and recovery: The aftermath of violence from domestic abuse to political terror.* New York: Basic Books.

Herman, J. L. (1997). *Trauma and recovery (Revised reprint).* New York: Basic Books.

Hickie, I. B., Rosenberg, S., & Davenport, T. A. (2011). Australia's Better Access initiative: Still awaiting serious evaluation? *The Australian and New Zealand Journal of Psychiatry*, *45*(10), 814–823. doi:10.3109/00048674.2011.610744 PMID:21980930

Higgins, J. P. T., & Green, S. (Eds.). (2011). *Cochrane handbook for systematic reviews of interventions: Version 5.1.0*. Retrieved from http://handbook.cochrane.org/

Hodge, D. R. (2011). Evidence-based spiritual practice: Using research to inform the selection of spiritual interventions. *Journal of Religion & Spirituality in Social Work: Social Thought*, *30*(4), 325–339. doi:10.1080/15426432.2011.619896

Hogan, S. (2001). *Healing arts: The history of art therapy*. London: Jessica Kingsley.

Holden, G., Barker, K., Rosenberg, G., & Cohen, J. (2012). Information for clinical social work practice: A potential solution. *Clinical Social Work Journal*, *40*(2), 166–174. doi:10.1007/s10615-011-0336-3

Holden, G., Tuchman, E., Barker, K., Rosenberg, G., Thazin, M., Kuppens, S., & Watson, K. (2012). A few thoughts on evidence in social work. *Social Work in Health Care*, *51*(6), 483–505. doi:10.1080/00981389.2012.671649 PMID:22780700

Holland, S. (2011). *Child and family assessment in social work practice* (2nd ed.). London: Sage. doi:10.4135/9781446288580

Holmes, E. K., Galovan, A. M., Yoshida, K., & Hawkins, A. J. (2010). Meta-analysis of the effectiveness of resident fathering programs: Are family life educators interested in fathers? *Family Relations*, *59*(3), 240–252. doi:10.1111/j.1741-3729.2010.00599.x

Hopewell, S., McDonald, S., Clarke, M. J., & Egger, M. (2008). Grey literature in meta-analyses of randomized trials of health care interventions. *Cochrane Database of Systematic Reviews*, (2). doi:10.1002/14651858.MR000010.pub3 PMID:17443631

Hopps, J. G., Lowe, T. B., & Rollins, L. S. (2010). Evidence-based services to children in a conservative environment. In A. E. Fortune, P. McCallion, & K. Briar-Lawson (Eds.), *Social work practice research for the twenty-first century* (pp. 108–127). New York: Columbia University Press.

Horwath, J., & Morrison, T. (2007). Collaboration, integration and change in children's services: Critical issues and key ingredients.[PubMed]. *Child Abuse & Neglect*, *31*(1), 55–69. doi:10.1016/j.chiabu.2006.01.007

Howard League for Penal Reform. (2007, July 26). *Press release: Howard League hails Court of Appeal victory*. London: Author.

Howard, J. (2006, May 9). *Better mental health services for Australia* [Press release]. Retrieved from http://pandora.nla.gov.au/pan/10052/20061221-0000/www.pm.gov.au/news/media_releases/media_Release1858.html

Howard, F. (2008). Managing stress or enhancing well-being?: Positive psychology's contributions to clinical supervision. *Australian Psychologist*, *43*(2), 105–113. doi:10.1080/00050060801978647

Howard, M. O., & Jenson, J. M. (1999). Clinical practice guidelines: Should social work develop them? *Research on Social Work Practice*, *9*(3), 283–301. doi:10.1177/104973159900900302

Howard, M. O., McMillen, C. J., & Pollio, D. E. (2003). Teaching evidence-based practice: Toward a new paradigm for social work education. *Research on Social Work Practice*, *13*(2), 234–259. doi:10.1177/1049731502250404

Howe, D. (1996). Surface and depth in social-work practice. In N. Parton (Ed.), *Social theory, social change and social work* (pp. 77–97). London: Routledge.

Huebner, R. A., Werner, M., Hartwig, S., White, S., & Shewa, D. (2008). Engaging fathers: Needs and satisfaction in child protective services. *Administration in Social Work*, *32*(2), 87–103. doi:10.1300/J147v32n02_06

Hughes, E. C. (1951). Work and the self. In J. H. Rohrer & M. Sherif (Eds.), *Social psychology at the crossroads* (pp. 313–323). New York: Harper and Brothers.

Hughes, E. C. (1962). Good people and dirty work. *Social Problems*, *10*(1), 3–11. doi:10.2307/799402

Human Rights and Equal Opportunity Commission. (1997). Bringing them home: Report of the National Inquiry into the Separation of Aboriginal and Torres Strait Islander Children from their Families. Sydney, Australia: Author.

Hunter, S. V. (2011). Disclosure of child sexual abuse as a life-long process: Implications for health professionals. *The Australian and New Zealand Journal of Family Therapy*, *32*(2), 159–172. doi:10.1375/anft.32.2.159

Hutchinson, M., & Dorsett, P. (2012). What does the literature say about resilience in refugee people? Implications for practice. *Journal of Social Inclusion*, *3*(2), 55–78. Retrieved from https://www104.griffith.edu.au/index.php/inclusion/index

Hutchison, K. J., & Rogers, W. A. (2012). Challenging the epistemological foundations of EBM: What kind of knowledge does clinical practice require? *Journal of Evaluation in Clinical Practice*, *18*(5), 984–991. doi:10.1111/j.1365-2753.2012.01905.x PMID:22994996

Huxham, C., & Vangen, S. (2000). Ambiguity, complexity and dynamics in the membership of collaboration. *Human Relations*, *53*(6), 771–806. doi:10.1177/0018726700536002

International Association of Schools of Social Work. (n.d.). Global definition of the social work profession. Retrieved March 14, 2014, from http://www.iassw-aiets.org/uploads/file/20140303_IASSW%20Website-SW%20DEFINITION%20approved%20IASSW%20Board%2021%20Jan%202014.pdf

International Covenant on Civil and Political Rights, Dec. 19, 1966, 999 U.N.T.S. 171.

International Federation of Social Workers. (2012). Definition of social work. Retrieved from

http://ifsw.org/policies/definition-of-social-work/

International Federation of Social Workers. (2012). Refugees. Retrieved from http://ifsw.org/policies/refugees/

International Federation of Social Workers. (2012). Statement of ethical principles. Retrieved from http://ifsw.org/policies/statement-of-ethical-principles/

Janes, F., Gigli, G. L., D'Anna, L., Cancelli, I., Perelli, A., Canal, G.,...& Valente M. (2013). Stroke incidence and 30-day and six-month case fatality rates in Udine, Italy: A population-based prospective study. *International Journal of Stroke*, *8*(Suppl. A100), 100-105. doi:10.1111/ijs.12000

Jenkins, B., Bebbington, P., Brugha, T. S., Farrell, M., Lewis, G., & Meltzer, H. (1998). British psychiatric morbidity survey. *The British Journal of Psychiatry*, *173*(1), 4–7. doi:10.1192/bjp.173.1.4 PMID:9850201

Johansen, C. (2004). Electromagnetic fields and health effects: Epidemiological studies of cancer, diseases of the central nervous system and arrhythmia-related heart disease. *Scandinavian Journal of Work, Environment & Health*, *30*(Suppl. 1), 1–30. Retrieved from http://www.sjweh.fi/ PMID:15255560

John Hopkins University. (2001). *Report of internal investigation into the death of a volunteer research subject*. Retrieved from http://www.hopkinsmedicine.org/press/2001/july/report_of_internal_investigation.htm

Jones, J. M., & Sherr, M. E. (2014). The role of relationships in connecting social work research and evidence-based practice. *Journal of Evidence-Based Social Work*, *11*(1-2), 139–147. doi:10.1080/15433714.2013.845028 PMID:24405138

Jonzon, E., & Lindblad, F. (2006). Risk factors and protective factors in relation to subjective health among adult female victims of child sexual abuse. *Child Abuse & Neglect*, *30*(2), 127–143. doi:10.1016/j.chiabu.2005.08.014 PMID:16466788

Joseph, C. (2006). Creative alliance: The healing power of art therapy. *Art Therapy: Journal of the American Art Therapy Association*, *23*(1), 30–33. doi:10.1080/07421656.2006.10129531

Kadushin, A. (1957). The effect on the client of interview observation at intake. *The Social Service Review, 31*(1), 22–38. doi:10.1086/640166

Kadushin, A. (1968). Games people play in supervision. *Social Work, 3*(3), 23–32. doi:10.1093/sw/13.3.23

Kadushin, A. (1999). The past, the present, and the future of professional social work. *Arete, 23*(3), 76–84.

Kanter, R. (1977). *Work and family in the United States: A critical review and agenda for research and policy.* New York, NY: Russell Sage Foundation.

Karpetis, G. (2010). Psychodynamic clinical social work practice with parents in child and adolescent mental health services: A case study on the role of the father. *Journal of Social Work Practice, 24*(2), 155–170. doi:10.1080/02650531003741629

Kaufman, J., & Zigler, E. (1993). The intergenerational transmission of violence is overstated. In R. J. Gelles & D. R. Loseke (Eds.), *Current controversies on family violence* (pp. 167–196). Newbury Park, CA: Sage.

Keiser, L. R. (2010). Understanding street-level bureaucrats' decision making: Determining eligibility in the social security disability program. *Public Administration Review, 70*(2), 247–257. doi:10.1111/j.1540-6210.2010.02131.x

Kelleher, M. J., Chambers, D., Corcoran, P., Williamson, E., & Keeley, H. S. (1998). Religious sanctions and rates of suicide worldwide. *Crisis, 19*(2), 78–86. doi:10.1027/0227-5910.19.2.78 PMID:9785649

Kelly, B. L., & Gates, T. G. (2010). Using the strengths perspective in the social work interview with young adults who have experienced childhood sexual abuse. *Social Work in Mental Health, 8*(5), 421–437. doi:10.1080/15332981003744438

Kempe, C. H., Silverman, F. N., Steele, B. F., Droegemueller, W., & Silver, H. K. (1962). The battered-child syndrome. *Journal of the American Medical Association, 181*(1), 17–24. doi:10.1001/jama.1962.03050270019004 PMID:14455086

Kenardy, J. (2000). The current status of psychological debriefing. *British Medical Journal, 321*(7268), 1032–1033. doi:10.1136/bmj.321.7268.1032 PMID:11053152

Kessler, R. C., Berglund, P., Demler, O., Jin, R., Merikangas, K. R., & Walters, E. E. (2005). Lifetime prevalence and age-of-onset distributions of DSM-IV disorders in the National Comorbidity Survey Replication. *Archives of General Psychiatry, 62*, 593-602. doi:10.1001/archpsyc.62.6.593

Khan, M. M., & Hyder, A. A. (2006). Suicides in the developing world: Case study from Pakistan. *Suicide & Life-Threatening Behavior, 36*(1), 76–81. doi:10.1521/suli.2006.36.1.76 PMID:16676628

Khoo, E. G., Hyvonen, U., & Nygren, L. (2003). Gate keeping decisions in child welfare: A comparative study of intake decision making in Canada and Sweden. [PubMed]. *Child Welfare, 82*, 507–525. Retrieved from http://www.ncbi.nlm.nih.gov/pubmed/14524423

King, A. (2000). Working with fathers: The non-deficit perspective. *Children Australia, 25*(3), 23-27. Retrieved from

http://journals.cambridge.org/action/displayJournal?jid=CHA

King, A. (2005). The quiet revolution amongst men: Developing the practice of working with men in family relationships. *Children Australia, 30*(2), 33-37. Retrieved from

http://journals.cambridge.org/action/displayJournal?jid=CHA

King, A., Sweeney, S., & Fletcher, R. (2004). A checklist for organisations working with men. *Developing Practice, 11,* 55-66. Retrieved from

http://www.acwa.asn.au/developing_practice11.html

Kirkman, E., & Melrose, K. (2014). *Clinical judgement and decision-making in children's social work: An analysis of the "front door" system.* Retrieved from Department for Education website:

https://www.gov.uk/government/uploads/system/uploads/attachment_data/file/305516/R337_-_Clinical_Judgement_and_Decision-Making_in_Childrens_Social_Work.pdf

Kjorstad, M. (2008). Opening the back box: Mobilising practical knowledge in social research – Methodological reflections based on a study of social work practice. *Qualitative Social Work: Research and Practice*, 7(2), 143–161. doi:10.1177/1473325008089627

Klorer, P. G. (2005). Expressive therapy with severely maltreated children: Neuroscience contributions. *Art Therapy: Journal of the American Art Therapy Association*, 22(4), 213–220. doi:10.1080/07421656.2005.10129523

Knight, J. A., Comino, E. J., Harris, E., & Jackson-Pulver, L. (2009). Indigenous research: A commitment to walking the talk – the Gudaga study – an Australian case study. *Bioethical Inquiry*, 6(4), 467–476. doi:10.1007/s11673-009-9186-x

Knox, V., Cowan, P., Cowan, C. P., & Bildner, E. (2011). Policies that strengthen fatherhood and family relationships: What do we know and what do we need to know? *The Annals of the American Academy of Political and Social Science*, 635(1), 216–239. doi:10.1177/0002716210394769

Koritsas, S., Coles, J., & Boyle, M. (2010). Workplace violence towards social workers: The Australian experience. *British Journal of Social Work*, 40(1), 257–271. doi:10.1093/bjsw/bcn134

Kreiner, G. E., Ashforth, B. E., & Sluss, D. M. (2006). Identity dynamics in occupational dirty work: Integrating social identity and system justification perspectives. *Organization Science*, 17(5), 619–636. doi:10.1287/orsc.1060.0208

Kreitzer, L. (2002). Liberian refugee women: A qualitative study of their participation in planning camp programmes. *International Social Work*, 45(1), 45–58. doi:10.1177/0020872802045001319

Kwek, G. (2013, December 30). Miner dies at Fortescue's Christmas Creek Mine in WA. *Sydney Morning Herald*. Retrieved January 28, 2014, from http://www.smh.com.au/business/mining-and-resources/miner-dies-at-fortescues-christmas-creek-mine-in-wa-20131230-302bo.html#ixzz2rg1Bq900

Ladbrook, D. (2003). *Being dad to a child under two: Exploring images and visions of fatherhood, evolving expectations in a changing society*. Perth, W.A.: Ngala Family Resource Centre. Retrieved from http://www.ngala.com.au/For-Professionals/Being-Dad-to-a-Child-Under-Two

Lagattuta, K. H., & Sayfan, L. (2013). Not all past events are equal: Biased attention and emerging heuristics in children's past-to-future forecasting. *Child Development*, 84(6), 2094–2111. doi:10.1111/cdev.12082 PMID:23480128

Lalor, K., & McElvaney, R. (2010). Child sexual abuse, links to later sexual exploitation/high-risk sexual behavior, and prevention/treatment programs. *Trauma, Violence, & Abuse: A Review Journal*, 11, 159-177. doi:10.1177/1524838010378299

Lamb, M., & Tamis-LeMonda, C. (2004). The role of the father. In M. E. Lamb (Ed.), *The role of the father in child development* (4th ed., pp. 222–271). Hoboken, NJ: Wiley.

Lane, M. R. (2005). Creativity and spirituality in nursing: Implementing art in healing. *Holistic Nursing Practice*, 19(3), 122–125. doi:10.1097/00004650-200505000-00008 PMID:15923938

Langer, A. (2002). El embarazo no deseado: Impacto sobre la salud y la sociedad en América Latina y el Caribe[Unwanted pregnancy: Impact on health and society in Latin America and the Caribbean]. *Revista Panamericana de Salud Pública*, 11(3), 192–205. doi:10.1590/S1020-49892002000300013 PMID:11998185

Latto, R. (1995). The brain of the beholder. In R. L. Gregory, J. Harris, P. Heard, & D. Rose (Eds.), *The artful eye* (pp. 66–94). Oxford: Oxford University Press.

Leech, N., & Trotter, J. (2006). Alone and together: Some thoughts on reflective learning for work with adult survivors of child sexual abuse. *Journal of Social Work Practice*, *20*(2), 175–187. doi:10.1080/02650530600776889

Leighninger, L. (2012). The history of social work and social welfare. In C. N. Dulmus & K. M. Sowers (Eds.), *The profession of social work: Guided by history, led by evidence* (pp. 1–34). Hoboken, NJ: John Wiley.

Lenette, C., Brough, M., & Cox, L. (2013). Everyday resilience: Narratives of single refugee women with children. *Qualitative Social Work: Research and Practice*, *12*(5), 637–653. doi:10.1177/1473325012449684

Leonard, P., & Corrigan, P. (1978). *Social work practice under capitalism: A Marxist approach*. London: Macmillan.

Levine, S. (2001). Primary social relationships influence the development of the hypothalamic–pituitary–adrenal axis in the rat. *Physiology & Behavior*, *73*(3), 255–260. doi:10.1016/S0031-9384(01)00496-6 PMID:11438350

Lev-Wiesel, R. (2008). Child sexual abuse: A critical review of intervention and treatment modalities. *Children and Youth Services Review*, *30*(6), 665–673. doi:10.1016/j.childyouth.2008.01.008

Liang, B., Williams, L. M., & Siegel, J. A. (2006). Relational outcomes of childhood sexual trauma in female survivors: A longitudinal study. *Journal of Interpersonal Violence*, *21*(1), 42–57. doi:10.1177/0886260505281603 PMID:16399923

Lifelong Learning UK. (2011). *Work with parents: National occupational standards*. Retrieved from https://www.gov.uk/government/uploads/system/uploads/attachment_data/file/175555/NOS-PARENTS.pdf

Lim, D., Sanderson, K., & Andrews, G. (2000). Lost productivity among full-time workers with mental disorders. *The Journal of Mental Health Policy and Economics*, *3*(3), 139–146. doi:10.1002/mhp.93 PMID:11967449

Lincoln, Y. S., & Guba, E. G. (1985). *Naturalistic inquiry*. Newbury Park, CA: SAGE.

Lindsay, K. W., Bone, I., & Fuller, G. (2010). *Neurology & neurosurgery illustrated*. Edinburgh: Churchill Livingstone.

Ling, T. (2012). Evaluating complex and unfolding interventions in real time. *Evaluation*, *18*(1), 79–91. doi:10.1177/1356389011429629

Linnell, S. (2010). *Art psychotherapy & narrative therapy: An account of practitioner research*. Oak Park, IL: Benthan Science Publishers.

Lipsky, M. (2010). Street-level democracy: Dilemmas of the individual in public services (Updated Edition). New York: Russell Sage Foundation.

Littell, J. H. (2010). Pulling together research studies to inform social work practice: The science of research synthesis. In A. E. Fortune, P. McCallion, & K. Briar-Lawson (Eds.), *Social work practice research for the twenty-first century* (pp. 162–180). New York: Columbia University Press.

Litva, A., & Jacoby, A. (2007). Qualitative research: Critical appraisal. In J. V. Craig & R. L. Smyth (Eds.), *The evidence based practice manual for nurses* (2nd ed., pp. 153–183). Edinburgh, UK: Churchill Livingstone.

Lonne, B., Parton, N., Thomson, J., & Harries, M. (2008). *Reforming child protection*. London: Routledge.

Loughlin, M. (2006). The future for medical epistemology? Commentary on Tonelli (2006), Integrating evidence into clinical practice: An alternative to evidence-based approaches. *Journal of Evaluation in Clinical Practice*, *12*(3), 289–291. doi:10.1111/j.1365-2753.2006.00589.x PMID:16722910

Luzi, D. (2000). Trends and evolution in the development of grey literature: A review. *International Journal on Grey Literature*, *1*(3), 106–116. doi:10.1108/14666180010345537

Lyshak-Stelzer, F., Singer, P., St. John, P., & Chemtob, C. M. (2007). Art therapy for adolescents with posttraumatic stress disorder symptoms: A pilot study. *Art Therapy: Journal of the American Art Therapy Association*, *24*(4), 163–169. doi:10.1080/07421656.2007.10129474

Macdonald, E., Herrman, H., Hinds, P., Crowe, J., & McDonald, P. (2002). Beyond interdisciplinary boundaries: Views of consumers, carers and non-government organizations on teamwork. *Australasian Psychiatry*, *10*(2), 125–129. doi:10.1046/j.1440-1665.2002.00420.x

Malchiodi, C. A. (2007). *The art therapy sourcebook*. New York: McGraw-Hill.

Malchiodi, C. A. (2008). *Creative interventions with traumatized children*. New York: Guilford Press.

Mandell, D., Stalker, C., de Zeeuw Wright, M., Frensch, K., & Harvey, C. (2013). Sinking, swimming and sailing: Experiences of job satisfaction and emotional exhaustion in child welfare employees. *Child & Family Social Work*, *18*(4), 383–393. doi:10.1111/j.1365-2206.2012.00857.x

Mansdorf. I. J. (2008). Psychological interventions following terrorist attacks. *British Medical Bulletin*, *88*(1), 7–22. doi:10.1093/bmb/ldn041 PMID:19011264

Manthorpe, J., Moriarty, J., Hussein, S., Stevens, M., & Sharpe, E. (2013). Content and purpose of supervision in social work practice in England: Views of newly qualified social workers, managers and directors. *British Journal of Social Work*. Advance online publication. doi:10.1093/bjsw/bct102

Margolis, J. D., & Molinsky, A. (2008). Navigating the bind of necessary evils: Psychological engagement and the production of interpersonally sensitive behaviour. *Academy of Management Journal*, *51*(5), 847–872. doi:10.5465/AMJ.2008.34789639

Marlowe, J. M., & Adamson, C. E. (2011). Teaching trauma: Critically engaging a troublesome term. *Social Work Education*, *30*(6), 623–634. doi:10.1080/02615479.2011.586559

Marsh, P., Fisher, M., Mathers, N., & Fish, S. (2005). *Developing the evidence base for social work and social care practice*. Retrieved from Social Care Institute for Excellence website:
http://www.scie.org.uk/publications/reports/report10.pdf

Marshall, K. (2007). The present state of youth justice in Scotland. *The Scottish Journal of Criminal Justice Studies: The Journal of the Scottish Association for the Study of Delinquency*, *13*, 4–19. Retrieved from http://www.sastudyoffending.org.uk/journal

Marsiglio, W., Day, R. D., & Lamb, M. E. (2000). Exploring fatherhood diversity: Implications for conceptualizing father Involvement. *Marriage & Family Review*, *29*(4), 269–293. doi:10.1300/J002v29n04_03

Martin, B., & Healey, J. (2010). *Who works in community services: A profile of Australian workforces in child protection, juvenile justice, disability services and general community services*. Adelaide: National Institute of Labour Studies, Flinders University.

Masango, M. J. S. (2006). African spirituality that shapes the concept of Ubunten. *Verbum et Ecclesia JRG*, *27*, 930–943. doi:10.4102/ve.v27i3.195

Mathers, C., Vos, T., & Stevenson, C. (1999). *The burden of disease and injury in Australia*. Canberra: Australian Institute of Health and Welfare.

Mattejat, F., & Remschmidt, H. (2008). The children of mentally ill parents. *Deutsches Ärzteblatt International*, *105*, 413–418.
doi:10.3238/arztebl.2008.0413 PMID:19626164

Maxwell, N., Scourfield, J., Featherstone, B., Holland, S., & Tolman, R. (2012). Engaging fathers in child welfare services: A narrative review of recent research evidence. *Child & Family Social Work*, *17*(2), 160–169. doi:10.1111/j.1365-2206.2012.00827.x

Maynard-Moody, S. W., & Musheno, M. C. (2003). *Cops, teachers, counselors: Stories from the front lines of public service*. University of Michigan Press.

Mayou, R. A., Ehlers, A., & Hobbs, M. (2000). Psychological debriefing for road traffic accident victims: Three-year follow-up of a randomised controlled trial. *The British Journal of Psychiatry*, *176*(6), 589–593. doi:10.1192/bjp.176.6.589 PMID:10974967

May, P. J., & Winter, S. C. (2009). Politicians, managers, and street-level bureaucrats: Influences on policy implementation. *Journal of Public Administration Research and Theory, 19*(3), 453–476. doi:10.1093/jopart/mum030

McBeath, G., & Webb, S. A. (2002). Virtue ethics and social work: Being lucky, realistic, and not doing ones duty. *British Journal of Social Work, 32*(8), 1015–1036. doi:10.1093/bjsw/32.8.1015

McCann, C. M., Beddoe, E., McCormick, K., Huggard, P., Kedge, S., Adamson, C., & Huggard, J. (2013). Resilience in the health professions: A review of recent literature. *International Journal of Wellbeing, 3*(1), 60–81. doi:10.5502/ijw.v3i1.4

McCann, I. L., & Pearlman, L. A. (1990). Vicarious traumatization: A framework for understanding the psychological effects of working with victims. *Journal of Traumatic Stress, 3*(1), 131–149. doi:10.1007/BF00975140

McDermott, F. (1996). Social work research: Debating the Boundaries. *Australian Social Work, 49*(1), 5–10. doi:10.1080/03124079608411156

McEwen, B. S., & Gianaros, P. J. (2010). Central role of the brain in stress and adaptation: Links to socioeconomic status, health, and disease. *Annals of the New York Academy of Sciences, 1186*(1), 190–222. doi:10.1111/j.1749-6632.2009.05331.x PMID:20201874

McGeorge, P. (2012). Lessons learned in developing community mental healthcare in Australasia and the South Pacific. *World Psychiatry: Official Journal of the World Psychiatric Association (WPA), 11*(2), 129–132. doi:10.1016/j.wpsyc.2012.05.010 PMID:22654946

McGilloway, O., & Myco, F. (1985). *Nursing and spiritual care.* Harper & Row.

McKeering, H., & Pakenham, K. I. (2000). Gender and generativity issues in parenting: Do fathers benefit more than mothers from involvement in child care activities? *Sex Roles, 43*(7/8), 459–480. doi:10.1023/A:1007115415819

McNally, R. J., Bryant, R. A., & Ehlers, A. (2003). Does early psychological intervention promote recovery from posttraumatic stress? *Psychological Science in the Public Interest, 4*, 45–79. doi:10.1111/1529-1006.01421

McNeece, C. A., & Thyer, B. A. (2004). Evidence-based practice and social work. *Journal of Evidence-Based Social Work, 1*(1), 7–25. doi:10.1300/J394v01n01_02

McNeill, F. (2006). A desistance paradigm for offender management. *Criminology & Criminal Justice, 6*(1), 39–62. doi:10.1177/1748895806060666

McPhail, B. A. (2004). Setting the record straight: Social work is not a female-dominated profession. *Social Work, 49*(2), 323–326. doi:10.1093/sw/49.2.323 PMID:15124974

Mechling, B. M. (2011). The experiences of youth serving as caregivers for mentally ill parents: A background review of the literature. *Journal of Psychosocial Nursing and Mental Health Services, 49*, 28–33. doi:10.3928/02793695-20110201-01 PMID:21323266

Medibank Private and Nous Group. (2013). *The case for mental health reform in Australia: A review of expenditure and system design.* Retrieved from https://www.medibankhealth.com.au/files/editor_upload/File/Mental%20Health%20Full%20Report.pdf

Medicare Australia Statistics. (2014). Medicare item reports. Retrieved April 5, 2014, from https://www.medicareaustralia.gov.au/statistics/mbs_item.shtml

Mendes, P. (2001). Blaming the messenger: The media, social workers and child abuse. *Australian Social Work, 54*(2), 27–36. doi:10.1080/03124070108414321

Mendoza, J., Bresnan, A., Rosenberg, S., Elson, A., Gilbert, Y., Long, P.,…Hopkins, J. (2013). *Obsessive hope disorder: Reflections on 30 years of mental health reform in Australia and visions for the future.* Sippy Downs, Australia: ConNetica.

Mental Health Commission of New South Wales. (2013). *Living well in our community: Towards a strategic plan for mental health in NSW*. Sydney, Australia: Author.

Mental Health Council of Australia. (2005). *Not for service: Experiences of injustice and despair in mental healthcare in Australia*. Canberra: Author.

Mental Health Council of Australia. (2013). *Mental health and the National Disability Insurance Scheme, position paper, November 2013*. Canberra: Author.

Metzler, H., Gill, B., Pettigrew, M., & Hinds, K. (1995). *The prevalence of psychiatric morbidity among adults living in private households*. London: The Stationery Office.

Meyerowitz-katz, J. (2003). Art materials and process: A place of meeting art psychotherapy with a four-year-old boy. *Inscape, 8*(2), 60–69. doi:10.1080/17454830308414055

Mezue, W., Matthew, B., Draper, P., & Watson, R. (2004). The impact of care on carers of patients treated for aneurysmal subarachnoid haemorrhage. *British Journal of Neurosurgery, 18*(2), 135–137. doi:10.1080/02688690410001680984 PMID:15176554

Miehls, D. (2010). Contemporary trends in supervision theory: A shift from parallel process to relational and trauma theory. *Clinical Social Work Journal, 38*(4), 370–378. doi:10.1007/s10615-009-0247-8

Milbourne, L., Macrea, S., & Maguire, M. (2003). Collaborative solutions or new policy problems: Exploring multiagency partnerships in education and health work. *Journal of Education Policy, 18*(1), 19–35. doi:10.1080/268093032000042182

Miller, J. (2003). Critical incident debriefing and social work: Expanding the frame. *Journal of Social Service Research, 30*(2), 7–25. doi:10.1300/J079v30n02_02

Milner, J. (1993). A disappearing act: The differing career paths of fathers and mothers in child protection investigations. *Critical Social Policy, 38*(38), 48–63. doi:10.1177/026101839301303803

Milner, J. (2004). From "disappearing" to "demonised": The effects on men and women of professional interventions based on challenging men who are violent. *Critical Social Policy, 24*(1), 79–101. doi:10.1177/0261018304241004

Mitchell, J. T., & Everly, G. S. (1995). Critical incident stress debriefing (CISD) and the prevention of work related traumatic stress among high risk occupational groups. In G. S. Everly & J. M. Lating (Eds.), *Psychotraumatology: Key papers and core concepts in post-traumatic stress* (pp. 267-280). New York: Plenum Press.

Mitchell, J. T. (1983). When disaster strikes: The critical incident stress debriefing process. *Journal of Emergency Medical Services, 8*, 36–39. Retrieved from http://www.jems.com/ PMID:10258348

Mitchell, J. T., & Everly, G. S. (2000). Critical incident stress management and critical incident stress debriefings: Evolutions, effects and outcomes. In B. Raphael & J. P. Wilson (Eds.), *Psychological debriefing: Theory, practice and evidence*. Cambridge, UK: Cambridge University Press. doi:10.1017/CBO9780511570148.006

Mollon, P. (1993). *The fragile self: The structure of narcissistic disturbance*. London: Whurr.

Molyneux, A. J., Kerr, R. S., Birks, J., Ramzi, N., Yarnold, J., Sneade, M., & Rischmiller, J. (2009). Risk of recurrent subarachnoid haemorrhage, death, or dependence and standardised mortality ratios after clipping or coiling for intracranial aneurysm in the international subarachnoid aneurysm trial (ISAT): Long-term follow-up. *Lancet Neurology, 8*(5), 427–433. doi:10.1016/S1474-4422(09)70080-8 PMID:19329361

Monahan, K. (2010). Themes of adult sibling sexual abuse survivors in later life: An initial exploration. *Clinical Social Work Journal, 38*(4), 361–369. doi:10.1007/s10615-010-0286-1

Mor Barak, M. E., Travis, D. J., Pyun, H., & Xie, B. (2009). The impact of supervision on worker outcomes: A meta-analysis. *The Social Service Review, 83*(1), 3–32. doi:10.1086/599028

Morago, P. (2006). Evidence-based practice: From medicine to social work. *European Journal of Social Work, 9*(4), 461–477. doi:10.1080/13691450600958510

Morago, P. (2010). Dissemination and implementation of evidence-based practice in the social services: A UK survey. *Journal of Evidence-Based Social Work, 7*(5), 452–465. doi:10.1080/15433714.2010.494973 PMID:21082474

Morris, J. (2005). For the children: Accounting for careers in child protective services. *Journal of Sociology and Social Welfare, 32,* 131–140. Retrieved from http://www.wmich.edu/socialwork/journal/

Morris, T. (2006). *Social work research methods: Four alternative paradigms.* Thousand Oaks, CA: Sage.

Morseu-Diop, N. (2010). *Healing in justice: An international study of Indigenous peoples' custodial experiences of prison programs and the impact on their journey from prison to community.* Brisbane, Australia: University of Queensland Press.

Moss, P., & Petrie, P. (2002). *From children's services to children's spaces: Public policy, children and childhood.* London. Falmer Routledge.

Mu'id, O. (2004). *"…Then I lost my spirit": An analytical essay on transgenerational trauma theory as applied to oppressed people of color nations* (Master's thesis). Retrieved from ProQuest Dissertations and Theses database. (UMI No. 1436180)

Mullen, E. J. (2006). Choosing outcome measures in systematic reviews: Critical challenges. *Research on Social Work Practice, 16*(1), 84–90. doi:10.1177/1049731505280950

Mullen, E. J., & Bacon, W. F. (2003). Practitioner adoption and implementation of practice guidelines and issues of quality control. In A. Rosen & E. K. Proctor (Eds.), *Developing practice guidelines for social work intervention: Issues, methods, and research agenda* (pp. 223–235). New York: Columbia University Press.

Mullen, E. J., Bledsoe, S. E., & Bellamy, J. L. (2008). Implementing evidence-based social work practice. *Research on Social Work Practice, 18*(4), 325–338. doi:10.1177/1049731506297827

Mullen, E. J., Shlonsky, A., Bledsoe, S. E., & Bellamy, J. L. (2005). From concept to implementation: Challenges facing evidence-based social work. *Evidence & Policy: A Journal of Research. Debate and Practice, 1*(1), 61–84. doi:10.1332/1744264052703159

Mullen, E. J., & Streiner, D. L. (2004). The evidence for and against evidence-based practice. *Brief Treatment and Crisis Intervention, 4*(2), 111–121. doi:10.1093/brief-treatment/mhh009

Mulrow, C. D. (1995). Rationale for systematic reviews. In I. Chalmers & D. G. Altman (Eds.), *Systematic Reviews* (pp. 1–8). London: BMJ.

Muncie, J. (2008). The "punitive" turn in juvenile justice: Cultures of control and rights compliance in Western Europe and the USA. *Youth Justice, 8*(2), 107–121. doi:10.1177/1473225408091372

Munro, E. (2011). *The Munro review of child protection: Final report – A child-centred system.* London: TSO. Retrieved from Department for Education website: https://www.gov.uk/government/uploads/system/uploads/attachment_data/file/175391/Munro-Review.pdf

Munro, E. (1999). Common errors of reasoning in child protection work. *Child Abuse & Neglect, 23*(8), 745–758. doi:10.1016/S0145-2134(99)00053-8 PMID:10477235

Munro, E. (2011). *The Munro review of child protection: Final report – A child-centred system. CM, 8062.* London: The Stationery Office.

Munson, C. (1983). *An introduction to clinical social work supervision.* New York: Haworth Press.

Murdach, A. D. (2010). What good is soft evidence? *Social Work, 55*(4), 309–316. doi:10.1093/sw/55.4.309 PMID:20977054

Myerhoff, B. (1982). *Number our days: A triumph of continuity and culture among Jewish old people in an urban ghetto.* New York: Simon and Schuster/Touchstone Books.

Myerhoff, B. (1992). *Remembered lives: The work of ritual, storytelling, and growing older.* Ann Arbor, MI: University of Michigan Press.

Napan, K. (2010). *Co-creative enquiry.* Paper presented at the Symposium on Spirituality and Social Work. Inter-University Centre, Dubrovnik.

Nash, M., & Stewart, B. (2005). Spirituality and hope in social work for social justice. *Currents: New Scholarship in the Human Services, 4*(1), 1-10. Retrieved from http://www.ucalgary.ca/currents/files/currents/v4n1_nash.pdf

Nash, M., & Stewart, B. (Eds.). (2002). *Spirituality and social care.* London: Jessica Kingsley.

Nash, M., & Trlin, A. (2001). *Research into non-government/not for profit agencies and organizations providing services to immigrants and refugees in New Zealand.* Palmerston North, NZ: New Settlers Programme, Massey University.

Nash, M., Wong, J., & Trlin, A. (2006). Civic and social integration: A new field of social work practice with immigrants, refugees and asylum seekers. *International Social Work, 49*(3), 345–363. doi:10.1177/0020872806063407

*National standards for mental health services 2010.* (2010). Retrieved from Commonwealth of Australia Department of Health website: http://www.health.gov.au/internet/main/publishing.nsf/Content/CFA833CB8C1AA178CA257BF0001E7520/$File/servst10v2.pdf

Nevo, I., & Slonim-Nevo, V. (2011). The myth of evidence-based practice: Towards evidence-informed practice. *British Journal of Social Work, 41*(6), 1176–1197. doi:10.1093/bjsw/bcq149

Newell, S., & Swan, J. (2000). Trust and inter-organisational working. *Human Relations, 53,* 1287–1328. Retrieved from http://hum.sagepub.com/

Newhouse, R. P., & Spring, B. (2010). Interdisciplinary evidence-based practice: Moving from silos to synergy. *Nursing Outlook, 58*(6), 309–317. doi:10.1016/j.outlook.2010.09.001 PMID:21074648

Newton, A. W., & Vandeven, A. M. (2006). Unexplained infant and child death: A review of sudden infant death syndrome, sudden unexplained infant death, and child maltreatment fatalities including shaken baby syndrome. *Current Opinion in Pediatrics, 18*(2), 196–200. doi:10.1097/01.mop.0000193296.32764.1e PMID:16601503

Ng, C., Herrman, H., Chiu, E., & Singh, B. (2009). Community mental healthcare in the Asia-Pacific region: Using current best-practice models to inform future policy. *World Psychiatry: Official Journal of the World Psychiatric Association (WPA), 8*(1), 49–55. Retrieved from http://www.world-psychiatry.com/ PMID:19293961

Noble, A. J., Baisch, S., Covey, J., Mukerji, N., Nath, F., & Schenk, T. (2011). Subarachnoid hemorrhage patients' fears of recurrence are related to the presence of post-traumatic stress disorder. *Neurosurgery, 69*(2), 323–332. doi:10.1227/NEU.0b013e318216047e PMID:21415779

Nomaguchi, K. (2009). Change in work-family conflict among employed parents between 1977 and 1997. *Journal of Marriage and the Family, 71*(1), 15–32. doi:10.1111/j.1741-3737.2008.00577.x

Non-Government Working Group on Women. Peace and Security. (n.d.). About us. Retrieved from http://www.womenpeacesecurity.org/about/

Nothdurfter, U., & Lorenz, W. (2010). Beyond the pro and contra of evidence-based practice: Reflections on a recurring dilemma at the core of social work. *Social Work & Society, 8.* Retrieved from http://www.socwork.net/sws/article/view/22/62

O'Brien, F. (2004). The making of mess in art therapy: Attachment, trauma and the brain. *International Journal of Art Therapy, 9,* 2–13. doi:10.1080/02647140408405670

O'Donnell, J. M., Johnson, W. E. Jr., D'Aunno, L. E., & Thornton, H. L. (2005). Fathers in child welfare: Caseworkers' perspectives. *Child Welfare, 84*, 387–414. Retrieved from http://www.questia.com/library/p435256/child-welfare PMID:15984170

O'Donoghue, K. (2007). Clinical supervision within the social work profession in Aotearoa New Zealand. In D. Wepa (Ed.), *Clinical supervision in Aotearoa New Zealand: A health perspective* (pp. 12–25). Auckland: Pearson Education.

O'Donoghue, K. (2010). *Towards the construction of social work supervision in Aotearoa New Zealand: A study of the perspectives of social work practitioners and supervisors* (Doctoral thesis, Massey University, Palmerston North, New Zealand). Retrieved from http://mro.massey.ac.nz/handle/10179/1535

O'Donoghue, K. (2012). Windows on the supervisee experience: An exploration of supervisees' supervision histories. *Australian Social Work, 65*(2), 214–231. doi:10.1080/0312407X.2012.667816

O'Donoghue, K., Munford, R., & Trlin, A. (2006). What's best about social work supervision according to Association members. *Social Work Review, 18*, 79-91. Retrieved from http://anzasw.org.nz/about/topics/show/207-aotearoa-nz-social-work-review

O'Donoghue, K., & Tsui, M.-S. (2005). Towards informed supervisory practice: Knowledge, theory, and methods. In L. Beddoe, J. Worrall & F. Howard (Eds.), *Supervision Conference 2004: "Weaving together the strands of supervision"* (pp.131-137). Auckland, NZ: University of Auckland.

O'Donoghue, K. B., & Tsui, M.-S. (2012). In search of an informed supervisory practice: An exploratory study. *Practice: Social Work in Action, 24*(1), 3–20. doi:10.1080/09503153.2011.632678

O'Donoghue, K., & Tsui, M.-S. (2013). Social work supervision research (1970-2010): The way we were and the way ahead. *British Journal of Social Work*. Advance online publication. doi:10.1093/bjsw/bct115

O'Hagan, K. (1997). The problem of engaging men in child protection work. *British Journal of Social Work, 27*(1), 25–42. doi:10.1093/oxfordjournals.bjsw.a011194

O'Hagan, K., & Dillenberger, K. (1995). *The abuse of women within child care work*. Buckingham, UK: Open University Press.

O'Leary, P., Coohey, C., & Easton, S. D. (2010). The effect of severe child sexual abuse and disclosure on mental health during adulthood. *Journal of Child Sexual Abuse, 19*(3), 275–289. doi:10.1080/10538711003781251 PMID:20509077

Oades, L. G., & Anderson, J. (2012). Recovery in Australia: Marshalling strengths and living values. *International Review of Psychiatry, 24*(1), 5–10. doi:10.3109/09540261.2012.660623 PMID:22385421

Ogawa, Y. (2004). Childhood trauma and play therapy intervention for traumatized children. *Journal of Professional Counseling, 32*, 19–29. Retrieved from http://www.txca.org/tca/TCA_Publications.asp?SnID=2

Orcutt, B. A. (1990). *Science and inquiry in social work practice*. New York: Columbia University Press.

Ormerod, J. (2002). Current research into the effectiveness of debriefing. In N. Tehrani, S. Rose, & J. Omerod (Eds.), *Psychological debriefing: Professional Practice Board Working Party* (pp. 8–17). Leicester: British Psychological Society.

Ørner, R., & Schnyder, U. (Eds.). (2003). *Reconstructing early intervention after trauma*. Oxford: Oxford University Press.

Osmond, J., & O'Connor, I. (2006). Use of theory and research in social work practice: Implications for knowledge-based practice. *Australian Social Work, 59*(1), 5–19. doi:10.1080/03124070500449747

Ostman, M., & Afzelius, M. (2011). Children's representatives in psychiatric services: What is the outcome? *The International Journal of Social Psychiatry, 57*(2), 144–152. doi:10.1177/0020764008100605 PMID:19875625

Otto, H.-U., Polutta, A., & Ziegler, H. (2009). Struggling through to find what works: Evidence-based practice as a challenge for social work. In H.-U. Otto, A. Polutta, & H. Ziegler (Eds.), *Evidence-based practice: Modernising the knowledge base of social work?* (pp. 9–16). Opladen, Germany: Barbara Budrich.

Oxman, A. D. (1995). Checklists for review articles. In I. Chalmers & D. G. Altman (Eds.), *Systematic Reviews* (pp. 75–85). London: BMJ.

Pack, M. (2004). Sexual abuse counsellors' responses to stress and trauma: A social work perspective. *Aotearoa New Zealand Social Work Review, 16*, 19-25. Retrieved from http://anzasw.org.nz/about/topics/show/207-aotearoa-nz-social-work-review

Pack, M. J. (2004). Sexual abuse counsellors' responses to stress and trauma: A social work perspective. *New Zealand Journal of Counselling, 25*(2), 1–17. Retrieved from http://www.nzac.org.nz/new_zealand_journal_of_counselling.cfm

Pack, M. J. (2008). Back from the edge of the world: Re-authoring a story of practice with stress and trauma using Gestalt theory and narrative approaches. *Journal of Systemic Therapies, 27*(3), 30–44. doi:10.1521/jsyt.2008.27.3.30

Pack, M. J. (2009). The body as a site of knowing: Sexual abuse counsellors' responses to traumatic disclosures. *Women's Studies Journal, 23*, 46-56. Retrieved from http://www.wsanz.org.nz/journal.htm

Pack, M. (2009). Clinical supervision: An interdisciplinary review of literature with implications for reflective practice in social work. *Reflective Practice, 10*(5), 657–668. doi:10.1080/14623940903290729

Pack, M. (2009). Social work (adult). In K. Grimmer-Somers & G. Nehrenz (Eds.), *Practical tips in finding the evidence: An allied health primer* (pp. 176–199). Manila, Philippines: UST.

Pack, M. (2009). Supervision as a liminal space: Towards a dialogic relationship. *Gestalt Journal of Australia and New Zealand, 5*(2), 60-78. Retrieved from

http://ganzwebsite.wordpress.com/journal/

Pack, M. (2010). Allies in learning: Critical-reflective practice on-line with allied mental health practitioners. *Social Work Education, 29*(1), 67–79. doi:10.1080/02615470902810876

Pack, M. (2010). Career themes in the lives of sexual abuse counsellors. *New Zealand Journal of Counselling, 30*(2), 75–92. Retrieved from http://www.nzac.org.nz/new_zealand_journal_of_counselling.cfm

Pack, M. J. (2010). Revisions to the therapeutic relationship: A qualitative inquiry into sexual abuse therapists' theories for practice as a mitigating factor in VT. *Social Work Review. Journal of New Zealand Association of Social Workers, 12*, 73–82. Retrieved from http://anzasw.org.nz/about/topics/show/207-aotearoa-nz-social-work-review

Pack, M. J. (2010). Transformation in progress: The effects of trauma on the significant others of sexual abuse therapists. *Qualitative Social Work: Research and Practice, 9*(2), 249–265. doi:10.1177/1473325009361008

Pack, M. (2011). Discovering an integrated framework for practice: A qualitative investigation of theories used by social workers working as sexual abuse therapists. *Journal of Social Work Practice, 25*(1), 79–93. doi:10.1080/02650533.2010.530646

Pack, M. (2012). Two sides to every story: A phenomenological exploration of the meaning of clinical supervision from supervisee and supervisor perspectives. *Journal of Social Work Practice, 26*(2), 163–179. doi:10.1080/02650533.2011.611302

Pack, M. J. (2012). Vicarious traumatisation: An organisational perspective. *Social Work Now, 50*, 14-23. Retrieved from http://www.cyf.govt.nz/about-us/publications/social-work-now.html

Pack, M. J. (2013). An evaluation of critical-reflection on service-users and their families' narratives as a teaching resource in a post-graduate allied mental health program: An integrative approach. *Social Work in Mental Health, 11*(2), 154–166. doi:10.1080/15332985.2012.748003

Pack, M. J. (2013). Critical incident stress management: A review of the literature with implications for social work. *International Social Work*, 56(5), 608–627. doi:10.1177/0020872811435371

Pack, M. (2013). Vicarious traumatisation and resilience: An ecological systems approach to sexual abuse counsellors' trauma and stress. *Sexual Abuse in Australia and New Zealand,* 5(2), 69-76. Retrieved from http://www.anzatsa.org/index.php?page=SAANZ&PHPSESSID=NXlr8FauuICTIxqV%2CK2Wu2

Pack, M. (2013). What brings me here? Integrating evidence-based and critical-reflective approaches in social work education. *Journal of Systemic Therapies*, 32(4), 65–78. doi:10.1521/jsyt.2013.32.4.65

Pack, M. J. (2014). The role of managers in critical incident stress management programmes: A qualitative study of New Zealand social workers. *Journal of Social Work Practice*, 28(1), 43–57. doi:10.1080/02650533.2013.828279

Pack, M. (2014). Vicarious resilience: A multilayered model of stress and trauma. *Affilia: Journal of Women & Social Work*, 29(1), 18–29. doi:10.1177/0886109913510088

Paetzold, R. L., Dipboye, R. L., & Elsbach, K. D. (2008). A new look at stigmatization in and of organizations. *Academy of Management Review*, 33(1), 186–193. doi:10.5465/AMR.2008.27752576

Palkovitz, R. (2002). *Involved fathering and men's adult development*. New Jersey: Erlbaum.

Pally, R., & Olds, D. (2000). *The mind-brain relationship*. London: Karnac.

Paquette, D. (2004). Theorizing the father–child relationship: Mechanisms and developmental outcomes. *Human Development*, 47(4), 193–219. doi:10.1159/000078723

Paquette, D., & Dumont, C. (2013). Is father-child rough-and-tumble play associated with attachment or activation relationships? *Early Child Development and Care*, 183(6), 760–773. doi:10.1080/03004430.2012.723440

Parent, C., Saint-Jacques, M.-C., Beaudry, M., & Robitalle, C. (2007). Stepfather involvement in social interventions made by youth protection services in step-families. *Child & Family Social Work*, 12(3), 229–238. doi:10.1111/j.1365-2206.2007.00494.x

Parke, R. D., McDowell, D. J., Kim, M., Killian, C., Dennis, J., Flyr, M. L., & Wild, M. N. (2002). Fathers' contributions to children's peer relationships. In C. S. Tamis-LeMonda & N. J. Cabrera (Eds.), *Handbook of father involvement: Multidisciplinary perspectives* (pp. 141–167). New Jersey: LEA.

Parker, J., & Ashencaen Crabtree, S. (2014). Fish need bicycles: An exploration of the perceptions of male social work students on a qualifying course. *British Journal of Social Work*, 44(2), 310–327. doi:10.1093/bjsw/bcs117

Parrish, D. E., & Rubin, A. (2012). Social workers' orientations toward the evidence-based practice process: A comparison with psychologists and licensed marriage and family therapists. *Social Work*, 57(3), 201–210. doi:10.1093/sw/sws016 PMID:23252312

Parton, N. (2010). Child protection and safeguarding in England: Changing and competing conceptions of risk and their implications for social work. *British Journal of Social Work*, 41(5), 854–875. doi:10.1093/bjsw/bcq119

Paterson, L. (2000). Scottish democracy and Scottish utopias: The first year of the Scottish Parliament. *Scottish Affairs,* 33, 45-61. Retrieved from http://www.euppublishing.com/journal/scot

Pavlish, C. (2005). Refugee women's health: Collaborative inquiry with refugee women in Rwanda. *Health Care for Women International*, 26(10), 880–896. doi:10.1080/07399330500301697 PMID:16263661

Pawson, R., Boaz, A., Grayson, L., Long, A., & Barnes, C. (2003). *Knowledge review 3: Types and quality of knowledge in social care*. Retrieved from Social Care Institute for Excellence website: http://www.scie.org.uk/publications/knowledgereviews/kr03.pdf

Payne, M. (2009). Understanding social work process. In R. Adams, L. Dominelli, & M. Payne (Eds.), *Social work: Themes, issues and critical debates* (3rd ed., pp. 159–174). Basingstoke, UK: Palgrave Macmillan.

Payne, M. (2009). *Social care practice in context*. Basingstoke, UK: Palgrave Macmillan.

Pearlman, L. A., & Saakvitne, K. W. (1995). *Trauma and the therapist: Countertransference and VT in psychotherapy with incest survivors*. New York: Norton.

Pearson, A., & Hannes, K. (2013). Evidence about patients' experiences and concerns. In T. Hoffmann, S. Bennett, & C. Del Mar (Eds.), *Evidence-based practice across the health professions* (2nd ed., pp. 221–239). Sydney: Churchill Livingstone.

Peebles-Wilkins, W., & Amodeo, M. (2003). Performance standards and quality control: Application of practice guidelines to service delivery. In A. Rosen & E. K. Proctor (Eds.), *Developing practice guidelines for social work intervention: Issues, methods, and research agenda* (pp. 207–220). New York: Columbia University Press.

Pellegrini, A. D., & Smith, P. K. (1998). Physical activity play: The nature and function of a neglected aspect of play. *Child Development*, *69*(3), 577–598. doi:10.1111/j.1467-8624.1998.tb06226.x PMID:9680672

Pellis, S. M., & Pellis, V. C. (2007). Rough-and-tumble play and the development of the social brain. *Current Directions in Psychological Science*, *16*(2), 95–98. doi:10.1111/j.1467-8721.2007.00483.x

Pennebaker, J. W. (1993). Putting stress into words: Health, linguistic and therapeutic implications. *Behaviour Research and Therapy*, *31*(6), 539–548. doi:10.1016/0005-7967(93)90105-4 PMID:8347112

Pennebaker, J. W. (1997). *Opening up: The healing power of expressing emotion*. New York: Guilford Press.

Perkins, E. (2001). Johns Hopkins' tragedy: Could librarians have prevented a death? Retrieved from http://newsbreaks.infotoday.com/nbreader.asp?ArticleID=17534

Perry, B. (1997). Incubated in terror: Neurodevelopmental factors in the "cycle of violence.". In J. Osofsky (Ed.), *Children in a violent society* (pp. 124–149). New York: Guilford.

Perry, B. D. (2001). The neurodevelopmental impact of violence in childhood. In D. Schetky & E. P. Benedek (Eds.), *Textbook of child and adolescent forensic psychiatry* (pp. 221–238). Washington, DC: American Psychiatric Press.

Perry, B. D. (2009). Examining child maltreatment through a neurodevelopmental lens: Clinical applications of the neurosequential model of therapeutics. *Journal of Loss and Trauma*, *14*(4), 240–255. doi:10.1080/15325020903004350

Peterson, G. W., & Steinmetz, S. K. (2000). The diversity of fatherhood. *Marriage & Family Review*, *29*(4), 315–322. doi:10.1300/J002v29n04_05

Phanichrat, T., & Townshend, J. M. (2010). Coping strategies used by survivors of childhood sexual abuse on the journey to recovery. *Journal of Child Sexual Abuse*, *19*(1), 62–78. doi:10.1080/10538710903485617 PMID:20390779

Phan, K. L., Wager, T., Taylor, S. F., & Liberzon, I. (2002). Functional neuroanatomy of emotion: A meta-analysis of emotion activation studies in PET and fMRI. University of Michigan. *NeuroImage*, *16*(2), 331–348. doi:10.1006/nimg.2002.1087 PMID:12030820

Phenice, L. A., & Griffore, R. J. (2003). Young children and the natural world. *Contemporary Issues in Early Childhood*, *4*(2), 167–178. doi:10.2304/ciec.2003.4.2.6

Pirkis, J., Ftanou, M., Williamson, M., Machlin, A., Spittal, M. J., Bassilios, B., & Harris, M. (2011). Australia's Better Access initiative: An evaluation. *The Australian and New Zealand Journal of Psychiatry*, *45*(9), 726–739. doi:10.3109/00048674.2011.594948 PMID:21888609

Pithouse, A. (1998). *Social work: The social organisation of an invisible trade* (2nd ed.). Aldershot, England: Ashgate.

Pittaway, E., & Van Genderen Stort, A. (2011). *Protectors, providers, survivors: A dialogue with refugee women in Finland*. Retrieved from United Nations High Commissioner for Refugees website: http://www.unhcr.org/4ec3d7606.pdf

Plath, D. (2006). Evidence-based practice: Current issues and future directions. *Australian Social Work*, *59*(1), 56–72. doi:10.1080/03124070500449788

Plath, D. (2013). Evidence-based practice. In M. Gray & S. A. Webb (Eds.), *Social work theories and methods* (2nd ed., pp. 229–240). London: Sage.

Pope, N. D., Rollins, L., Chaumba, J., & Risler, E. (2011). Evidence-based practice knowledge and utilization among social workers. *Journal of Evidence-Based Social Work*, *8*(4), 349–368. doi:10.1080/15433710903269149 PMID:21827303

Potocky-Tripodi, M. (2002). *Best practices for social work with refugees and immigrants*. New York: Columbia University Press.

Power, J. J., Perlesz, A., Brown, R., Schofield, M. J., Pitts, M. K., McNair, R., & Bikerdike, A. (2012). Bisexual parents and family diversity: Findings from the work, love, play study. *Journal of Bisexuality*, *12*(4), 519–538. doi:10.1080/15299716.2012.729432

Powley, E. H. (2009). Reclaiming resilience and safety: Resilience activation in the critical period of crisis. *Human Relations*, *62*(9), 1289–1326. doi:10.1177/0018726709334881

Pritchard, C. (2001). *A family-teacher-social work alliance to reduce truancy and delinquency: The Dorset Healthy Alliance project* (RDS Occasional Paper No 78). London: Home Office, Research, Development and Statistics Directorate.

Pritchard, C. (1992). Changes in children's homicide in England and Wales and Scotland 1973-1988 as an indicator of effective child protection: A comparative study of Western European statistics. *British Journal of Social Work*, *22*, 663–684.

Pritchard, C. (1995). *Suicide: The ultimate rejection? – A psycho-social study*. Buckingham: Open University Press.

Pritchard, C. (2002). Children's homicide and road deaths in England and Wales and the USA: An international comparison 1974-1997. *British Journal of Social Work*, *32*(4), 495–502. doi:10.1093/bjsw/32.4.495

Pritchard, C. (2004). *The child abusers: Research & controversy*. Maidenhead: Open University Press.

Pritchard, C. (2004). Effective social work: A micro approach – Reducing truancy, delinquency and school exclusions. In D. Smith (Ed.), *Social work and evidence-based practice* (pp. 61–86). London: Jessica Kingsley.

Pritchard, C. (2004). The extremes of child abuse: A macro approach to measuring effective prevention. In D. Smith (Ed.), *Social work and evidence-based practice* (pp. 47–60). London: Jessica Kingsley.

Pritchard, C. (2006). *Mental health social work: Evidence-based practice*. Abingdon: Routledge.

Pritchard, C., & Amanullah, S. (2007). An analysis of suicide and undetermined deaths in 17 predominately Islamic countries contrasted with the UK. *Psychological Medicine*, *37*(3), 421–430. doi:10.1017/S0033291706009159 PMID:17176500

Pritchard, C., & Bagley, C. (2001). Suicide and murder in child murderers and child sexual abusers. *Journal of Forensic Psychiatry*, *12*(2), 269–286. doi:10.1080/09585180110057208

Pritchard, C., & Brackstone, J. (2009). "The voice of the surgeon" on patient safety: The ASGBI survey. *Newsletter (Association of Surgeons of Great Britain & Ireland)*, *28*, 34-36.

Pritchard, C., Brackstone, J., & MacFie, J. (2010). Adverse events and patient safety in the operating theatre: Perspectives of 549 surgeons. *Bulletin of the Royal College of Surgeons of England*, *92*(6), 1–4. doi:10.1308/147363510X507972

Pritchard, C., Clapham, L., Davis, A., Lang, D. A., & Neil-Dwyer, G. (2004). Psycho-socio-economic outcomes in acoustic neuroma patients and their carers related to tumour size. *Clinical Otolaryngology and Allied Sciences*, *29*(4), 324–330. doi:10.1111/j.1365-2273.2004.00822.x PMID:15270817

Pritchard, C., Clapham, L., Foulkes, L., Lang, D. A., & Neil-Dwyer, G. (2004). Comparison of cohorts of elective and emergency neurosurgical patients: Psychosocial outcomes of acoustic neuroma and aneurysmal sub arachnoid hemorrhage patients and carers. *Surgical Neurology*, *62*(1), 7–16. doi:10.1016/j.surneu.2004.01.018 PMID:15226061

Pritchard, C., Cotton, A., Bowen, D., & Williams, R. (1998). A consumer study of young people's views on their educational social worker: Engagement as a measure of an effective relationship. *British Journal of Social Work*, *28*(6), 915–938. doi:10.1093/oxfordjournals.bjsw.a011408

Pritchard, C., Davey, J., & Williams, R. (2013). Who kills children?: Re-examining the evidence. *British Journal of Social Work*, *43*(7), 1403–1438. doi:10.1093/bjsw/bcs051

Pritchard, C., Foulkes, L., Lang, D. A., & Neil-Dwyer, G. (2001). Psychosocial outcomes for patients and carers after aneurysmal subarachnoid haemorrhage. *British Journal of Neurosurgery*, *15*(6), 456–463. doi:10.1080/02688690120097679 PMID:11813996

Pritchard, C., Foulkes, L., Lang, D. A., & Neil-Dwyer, G. (2004). Two year prospective study of psychosocial outcomes and a cost-analysis of "treatment-as-usual" versus an "enhanced" (specialist liaison nurse) service for aneurysmal sub arachnoid haemorrhage (ASAH) patients and families. *British Journal of Neurosurgery*, *18*(4), 347–356. doi:10.1080/02688690400004993 PMID:15702833

Pritchard, C., & Hean, S. (2008). Suicide and undetermined deaths among youths and young adults in Latin America: Comparison with the 10 major developed countries – A source of hidden suicides? *Crisis*, *29*(3), 145–153. doi:10.1027/0227-5910.29.3.145 PMID:18714911

Pritchard, C., & Hickish, T. (2011). Comparing cancer mortality and GDP health expenditure in England and Wales with other major developed countries from 1979 to 2006. *British Journal of Cancer*, *105*(11), 1788–1794. doi:10.1038/bjc.2011.393 PMID:21970877

Pritchard, C., Lindsay, K., Cox, M., & Foulkes, L. (2011). Re-evaluating the national subarachnoid haemorrhage study (2006) from a patient-related-outcome-measure perspective: Comparing fiscal outcomes of treatment-as-usual with an enhanced service. *British Journal of Neurosurgery*, *25*(3), 376–383. doi:10.3109/02688697.2011.566379 PMID:21513445

Pritchard, C., Mayers, A., & Baldwin, D. (2013). Changing patterns of neurological mortality in the 10 developed countries: 1979-2010. *Public Health*, *127*(4), 357–368. doi:10.1016/j.puhe.2012.12.018 PMID:23601790

Pritchard, C., Roberts, S., & Pritchard, C. E. (2013). "Giving a voice to the unheard"? Is female youth (15-24 years) suicide linked to restricted access to family planning? Comparing two Catholic continents. *International Social Work*, *56*(6), 798–815. doi:10.1177/0020872812441645

Pritchard, C., & Sayer, T. (2006). Exploring potential "extra-familial" child homicide assailants in the UK and estimating their homicide rate: Perception of risk — The need for debate. *British Journal of Social Work*, *38*(2), 290–307. doi:10.1093/bjsw/bcl333

Pritchard, C., & Sharples, A. (2008). "Violent" deaths of children in England and Wales and the major developed countries 1974-2002: Possible evidence for improving child protection? *Child Abuse Review*, *17*(5), 297–312. doi:10.1002/car.1016

Pritchard, C., & Silk, A. (2014). A case-study survey of an eight-year cluster of motor neurone disease (MND) referrals in a rural English village: Exploring possible aetiological influences in a hypothesis stimulating study. *Journal of Neurological Disorders*, *2*, 147. doi:10.4172/2329-6895.1000147

Pritchard, C., & Wallace, M. S. (2011). Comparing the USA, UK and 17 Western countries' efficiency and effectiveness in reducing mortality. *Journal of the Royal Society of Medicine Short Reports*, 2(60), 1–10. doi:10.1258/shorts.2011.011076 PMID:21847442

Pritchard, C., & Wallace, M. S. (2014). Comparing UK and other Western countries' health expenditure, relative poverty and child mortality: Are British children doubly disadvantaged? *Children and Society*. Advance online publication. doi:10:1111/ CHSO12079

Pritchard, C., & Williams, R. (2001). A three-year comparative longitudinal study of a school-based social work family service to reduce truancy, delinquency and school exclusions. *Journal of Social Welfare and Family Law*, 23(1), 23–43. doi:10.1080/01418030121650

Pritchard, C., & Williams, R. (2011). Poverty and child (0-14 years) mortality in the USA and other Western countries as an indicator of "how well a country meets the needs of its children" (UNICEF). *International Journal of Adolescent Medicine and Health*, 23(3), 251–255. doi:10.1515/ijamh.2011.052 PMID:22191192

Pugh, R. (2007). Dual relationships: Personal and professional boundaries in rural social work. *British Journal of Social Work*, 37(8), 1405–1423. doi:10.1093/bjsw/bcl088

Pynoos, R. S., Ritzmann, R. F., Steinberg, A. M., Goenjian, A., & Prisecaru, I. (1996). A behavioral animal model of posttraumatic stress disorder featuring repeated exposure to situational reminders. *Biological Psychiatry, 39*, 129-134. doi: (95)00088-710.1016/0006-3223

R (on the application of HC) v. Secretary of State for the Home Department, [2013] EWHC (Admin) 982, [2013] W.L.R. (D) 157 (Eng).

R (on the application of K) v. Manchester City Council, [2006] EWHC (Admin) 3164.

R (on the application of the Howard League for Penal Reform) v. Secretary of State for the Home Department, [2002] EWHC (Admin) 2497, [2003] 1 F.L.R. 484 (Eng).

Raphael, B., & Wilson, J. P. (2000). *Psychological debriefing: Theory, practice and evidence*. Cambridge: Cambridge University Press. doi:10.1017/CBO9780511570148

Rapp, C. A., & Goscha, R. J. (2006). *The strengths-model: Case management with people with psychiatric disabilities* (2nd ed.). New York, NY: Oxford University Press.

Raynor, P. (1985). *Social work, justice and control*. Oxford, UK: Blackwell.

Raynor, P., & Vanstone, M. (1994). Probation practice, effectiveness and the non- treatment paradigm. *British Journal of Social Work, 24*, 387–404. Retrieved from http://bjsw.oxfordjournals.org/

Razzano, L., Jonikas, J., Goelitz, M., Hamilton, M., Marvin, R., & Jones-Martinex, N. et al. (2010). The recovery education in the academy program: Transforming academic curricula with the principles of recovery and self-determination. *Psychiatric Rehabilitation Journal, 34*(2), 130–136. doi:10.2975/34.2.2010.130.136 PMID:20952366

Reavey, P., & Brown, S. D. (2007). Rethinking agency in memory: Space and embodiment in memories of child sexual abuse. *Journal of Social Work Practice, 21*(1), 5–21. doi:10.1080/02650530601173508

Reder, P., & Duncan, S. (2003). Understanding communication in child protection networks. *Child Abuse Review, 12*(2), 82–100. doi:10.1002/car.787

Reder, P., Duncan, S., & Gray, M. (1993). *Beyond blame: Child abuse tragedies revisited*. London: Routledge.

Regel, S. (2007). Post-trauma support in the workplace: The current status and practice of critical incident stress management (CISM) and psychological debriefing (PD) within organizations in the UK. *Occupational Medicine, 57*(6), 411–416. doi:10.1093/occmed/kqm071 PMID:17728314

Regina v. G, [2003] UKHL 50, [2004] 1 A.C. 1034 (appeal taken from Eng.).

Reid, J. A., & Sullivan, C. J. (2009). A model of vulnerability for adult sexual victimization: The impact of attachment, child maltreatment, and scarred sexuality. *Violence and Victims*, 24(4), 485–501. doi:10.1891/0886-6708.24.4.485 PMID:19694353

Reid, W. J., & Fortune, A. E. (2003). Empirical foundations for practice guidelines in current social work knowledge. In A. Rosen & E. K. Proctor (Eds.), *Developing practice guidelines for social work intervention: Issues, methods, and research agenda* (pp. 59–79). New York: Columbia University Press.

Reid, W. J., Kenaley, B. D., & Colvin, J. (2004). Do some interventions work better than others? A review of comparative social work experiments. *Social Work Research*, 28(2), 71–81. doi:10.1093/swr/28.2.71

Retsky, M. W., Swartzendruber, D. E., Bame, P. D., & Wardwell, R. H. (1994). Computer model challenges breast cancer treatment strategy. *Cancer Investigation*, 12(6), 559–567. doi:10.3109/07357909409023040 PMID:7994590

Reynolds, S. (2000). The anatomy of evidence-based practice: Principles and methods. In L. Trinder (with S. Reynolds) (Eds.), *Evidence-based practice: A critical appraisal* (pp. 17-34). Oxford, UK: Blackwell.

Rice, K., Hwang, J., Abrefa-Gyan, T., & Powell, K. (2010). Evidence-based practice questionnaire: A confirmatory factor analysis in a social work sample. *Advances in Social Work, 11*, 158-173. Retrieved from http://advancesinsocialwork.iupui.edu/

Richman, J. M. (2010). Building capacity for intervention research. In A. E. Fortune, P. McCallion, & K. Briar-Lawson (Eds.), *Social work practice research for the twenty-first century* (pp. 269–278). New York: Columbia University Press.

Riggs, J. E., Schochet, S. S., Jr. (1992). Rising mortality due to Parkinson's disease and amyotrophic lateral sclerosis: A manifestation of the competitive nature of human mortality. *Journal of Clinical Epidemiology, 45,* 1007-1012. doi: 10.1016/0895-4356(92)90116-5

Roberts, A. R., Yeager, K., & Regehr, C. (2006). Bridging evidence-based health care and social work: How to search for, develop, and use evidence-based studies. In A. R. Roberts & K. R. Yeager (Eds.), *Foundations of evidence-based social work practice* (pp. 3–20). New York: Oxford University Press.

Rojas, A., & Kinder, B. N. (2009). Are males and females sexually abused as children socially anxious adults? *Journal of Child Sexual Abuse*, 18(4), 355–366. doi:10.1080/10538710903051112 PMID:19842534

Rosen, A. (2003). Evidence-based social work practice: Challenges and promise. *Social Work Research*, 27(4), 197–208. doi:10.1093/swr/27.4.197

Rosen, A., & Proctor, E. K. (2003). Practice guidelines and the challenge of effective practice. In A. Rosen & E. K. Proctor (Eds.), *Developing practice guidelines for social work intervention: Issues, methods, and research agenda* (pp. 1–14). New York: Columbia University Press.

Rosenberg, S. P., & Hickie, I. B. (2013). Making activity-based funding work for mental health. *Australian Health Review*, 37(3), 277–280. doi:10.1071/AH13002 PMID:23731959

Rosenthal, P., & Peccei, R. (2006). The social construction of clients by service agents in reformed welfare administration. *Human Relations*, 59(12), 1633–1658. doi:10.1177/0018726706073194

Rose, S., Bisson, J., & Wessely, S. (2003). A systematic review of single-session psychological interventions ("debriefing") following trauma. *Psychotherapy and Psychosomatics*, 72(4), 176–184. doi:10.1159/000070781 PMID:12792122

Rose, S., Brewin, C. R., Andrews, B., & Kirk, M. (1999). A randomized controlled trial of individual psychological debriefing for victims of violent crime. *Psychological Medicine*, 29(4), 793–799. doi:10.1017/S0033291799008624 PMID:10473306

Rossiter, A. (2011). Unsettled social work: The challenge of Levinas's ethics. *British Journal of Social Work*, 41(5), 980–995. doi:10.1093/bjsw/bcr004

Rothschild, B. (2003). *The body remembers: Unifying methods and models in the treatment of trauma and PTSD.* New York: Norton.

Royal College of Surgeons of England. (2006). *The national subarachnoid haemorrhage evaluation study: Final report of an audit carried out in 34 neurosurgical units in the UK and Ireland between 14 September 2001 to 13 September 2002.* London: British Society of Neurological Surgeons, Royal College of Surgeons. Retrieved from http://www.rcseng.ac.uk/publications/docs/nat_study_subarachnoid_haem_feb2006.html

Rubin, A. (2011). Teaching EBP in social work: Retrospective and prospective. *Journal of Social Work, 11*(1), 64–79. doi:10.1177/1468017310381311

Rubin, A., & Parrish, D. (2007). Challenges to the future of evidence-based practice in social work education. *Journal of Social Work Education, 43*(3), 405–428. doi:10.5175/JSWE.2007.200600612

Rubin, A., & Parrish, D. E. (2012). Improving the scientific base of social work practice. In C. N. Dulmus & K. M. Sowers (Eds.), *The profession of social work: Guided by history, led by evidence* (pp. 203–223). Hoboken, NJ: John Wiley.

Rubin, J. A. (2001). *Approaches to art therapy: Theory and technique.* New York: Routledge.

Rubin, J. A. (2005). *Child art therapy: 25th anniversary edition.* Hoboken, N.J.: John Wiley.

Ruch, G. (2007). Reflective practice in contemporary child-care social work: The role of containment. *British Journal of Social Work, 37*(4), 659–680. doi:10.1093/bjsw/bch277

Ruch, G. (2010). The contemporary context of relationship-based practice. In G. Ruch, D. Turney, & A. Ward (Eds.), *Relationship-based social work: Getting to the heart of practice* (pp. 13–28). London: Jessica Kingsley.

Ruch, G. (2012). Two halves make a whole: Developing integrated critical, analytic and reflective thinking in social work practice and education. In J. Lishman (Ed.), *Social work education and training* (pp. 69–83). London: Jessica Kingsley.

Russ, E., Lonne, B., & Darlington, Y. (2009). Using resilience to reconceptualise child protection workforce capacity. *Australian Social Work, 62*(3), 324–338. doi:10.1080/03124070903060042

Russell, G., & Hwang, C. (2004). The impact of workplace practices on father involvement. In M. Lamb (Ed.), *The role of the father in child development* (4th ed., pp. 476–501). New York: John Wiley & Sons.

Russinova, Z., Rogers, E. S., Ellison, M. L., & Lyass, A. (2011). Recovery-promoting professional competencies: Perspectives of mental health consumers, consumer-providers and providers. *Psychiatric Rehabilitation Journal, 34*(3), 177–185. doi:10.2975/34.3.2011.177.185 PMID:21208856

Ruzek, J. I., Brymer, M. J., Jacobs, A. K., Layne, C. M., Vernberg, E. M., & Watson, P. J. (2007). Psychological first aid. *Journal of Mental Health Counseling, 29,* 17–49. Retrieved from http://www.amhca.org/news/journal.aspx

Ryan, F. (2011). Kanyininpa (holding): A way of nurturing children in Aboriginal Australia. *Australian Social Work, 64*(2), 183–197. doi:10.1080/0312407X.2011.581300

S.C. Res. 1325, U.N. Doc. S/RES/1325 (Oct. 31. 2000).

Sabla, K.-P. (2009). *Fatherhood and parenting support: Lifeworld perspectives and aspects of a successful cooperation.* Munich: Juventa-Verl.

Sackett, D. L., Richardson, W. S., Rosenberg, W., & Haynes, R. B. (1997). *Evidence-based medicine: How to practice and teach EBM.* Edinburgh, UK: Churchill Livingstone.

Sackett, D. L., Rosenberg, W. M. C., Muir Gray, J. A., Haynes, R. B., & Richardson, W. S. (1996). Evidence based medicine: What it is and what it isn't: It's about integrating individual clinical expertise and the best external evidence. *BMJ (Clinical Research Ed.), 312*(7023), 71–72. doi:10.1136/bmj.312.7023.71 PMID:8555924

Sackett, D. L., Straus, S. E., Richardson, W. S., Rosenberg, W., & Haynes, R. B. (2000). *Evidence- based medicine: How to practice and teach EBM* (2nd ed.). Edinburgh, UK: Churchill Livingstone.

Saleebey, D. (2005). *The strengths perspective in social work practice* (4th ed.). Boston: Pearson/Allyn & Bacon.

Salyers, M. P., & Tsemberis, S. (2007). ACT and recovery: Integrating evidence-based practice and recovery orientation on assertive community treatment teams. *Community Mental Health Journal*, *43*(6), 619–641. doi:10.1007/s10597-007-9088-5 PMID:17514503

Savulescu, J., & Spriggs, M. (2002). The hexamethonium asthma study and the death of a normal volunteer in research. *Journal of Medical Ethics*, *28*(1), 3–4. doi:10.1136/jme.28.1.3 PMID:11834748

Schardt, C., Adams, M. B., Owens, T., Keitz, S., & Fontelo, P. (2007). Utilization of the PICO framework to improve searching PubMed for clinical questions. *BMC Medical Informatics and Decision Making*, *7*(16). doi:10.1186/1472-6947-7-16 PMID:17573961

Schofield, G. (1998). Inner and outer worlds: A psychosocial framework for child and family social work. *Child & Family Social Work*, *3*(1), 57–67. doi:10.1046/j.1365-2206.1998.00062.x

Schore, A. N. (1994). *Affect regulation and the origin of the self: The neurobiology of emotional development*. Hillsdale, NJ: Lawrence Erlbaum.

Schore, A. N. (2001). The effects of a secure attachment relationship on right brain development, affect regulation, and infant mental health. *Infant Mental Health Journal*, *22*(1-2), 7–66. doi:10.1002/1097-0355(200101/04)22:1<7::AID-IMHJ2>3.0.CO;2-N

Schore, A. N. (2001). The effects of relational trauma on right brain development, affect regulation, and infant mental health. *Infant Mental Health Journal*, *22*(1-2), 201–269. doi:10.1002/1097-0355(200101/04)22:1<201::AID-IMHJ8>3.0.CO;2-9

Schore, A. N. (2003). *Affect dysregulation and disorders of the self*. New York: Norton.

Schulkin, J., & Rosen, J. (1998). From normal fear to pathological anxiety. In D. M. Hann (Ed.), *Advancing research on developmental plasticity: Integrating the behavioral science and neuroscience of mental health* (pp. 325–350). Washington, DC: National Institutes of Health.

Scott, D., & Arney, F. (Eds.). (2010). *Working with vulnerable families: A partnership approach*. New York: Cambridge.

Scott, D. (2005). Inter-organisational collaboration in family-centred practice: A framework for analysis and action. *Australian Social Work*, *58*(2), 132–141. doi:10.1111/j.1447-0748.2005.00198.x

Scott, D., & Swain, S. (2002). *Confronting cruelty, historical perspectives on child protection*. Melbourne: Melbourne University Press.

Scott, E., Naismith, S., Whitwell, B., Hamilton, B., Chudleigh, C., & Hickie, I. (2009). Delivering youth-specific mental health services: The advantages of a collaborative, multi-disciplinary system. *Australasian Psychiatry*, *17*(3), 189–194. doi:10.1080/10398560802657322 PMID:19296265

Scott, E., & Panksepp, J. (2003). Rough and tumble play in human children. *Aggressive Behavior*, *29*(6), 539–551. doi:10.1002/ab.10062

Scott, K. L., & Crooks, C. V. (2004). Effecting change in maltreating fathers: Critical principles for intervention planning. *Clinical Psychology: Science and Practice*, *10*(1), 95–111. doi:10.1093/clipsy.bph058

Scourfield, J. (2001). Constructing men in child protection work. *Men and Masculinities*, *4*(1), 70–89. doi:10.1177/1097184X01004001004

Scourfield, J. (2003). *Gender and child protection*. London: Palgrave MacMillan.

Scourfield, J. (2006). The challenge of engaging fathers in the child protection process. *Critical Social Policy*, *26*(2), 440–449. doi:10.1177/0261018306062594

Scourfield, J. B., & Drakeford, M. (2002). New labour and the "problem of men". *Critical Social Policy*, *22*(4), 619–640. doi:10.1177/02610183020220040401

Secretariat of National Aboriginal and Islander Child Care. (2012). *Inquiry into the stronger futures in the Northern Territory bill*. Retrieved from http://www.snaicc.org.au/_uploads/rsfil/02785.pdf

Sedgh, G., Henshaw, S., Singh, S., Ahman, E., & Shah, I. H. (2007). Induced abortion: Estimated rates and trends worldwide. *Lancet, 370*(9595), 1338–1345. doi:10.1016/S0140-6736(07)61575-X PMID:17933648

Séguin, J. R., Parent, S., Tremblay, R. E., & Zelazo, P. D. (2009). Different neurocognitive functions regulating physical aggression and hyperactivity in early childhood. *Journal of Child Psychology and Psychiatry, and Allied Disciplines, 50*(6), 679–687. doi:10.1111/j.1469-7610.2008.02030.x PMID:19298475

Senate Community Affairs Reference Committee. (2010). *The hidden toll: Suicide in Australia.* Canberra: Commonwealth of Australia.

Senate Select Committee on Mental Health. (2006). *A national approach to mental health: From crisis to community.* Canberra: Commonwealth of Australia.

Sermabeikian, P. (1994). Our clients, ourselves: The spiritual perspective and social work practice. *Social Work, 39*, 178–183. Retrieved from https://www.naswpress.org/publications/journals/sw.html

Sheldon, B. (2001). The validity of evidence-based practice in social work: A reply to Stephen Webb. *British Journal of Social Work, 31*(5), 801–809. doi:10.1093/bjsw/31.5.801

Shlonsky, A., Baker, T. M., & Fuller-Thomson, E. (2011). Using methodological search filters to facilitate evidence-based social work practice. *Clinical Social Work Journal, 39*(4), 390–399. doi:10.1007/s10615-010-0312-3

Shlonsky, A., & Gibbs, L. (2004). Will the real evidence-based practice please stand up? Teaching the process of evidence-based practice to the helping professions. *Brief Treatment and Crisis Intervention, 4*(2), 137–153. doi:10.1093/brief-treatment/mhh011

Shlonsky, A., Noonan, E., Littell, J., & Montgomery, P. (2011). The role of systematic reviews and the Campbell Collaboration in the realization of evidence-informed practice. *Clinical Social Work Journal, 39*(4), 362–368. doi:10.1007/s10615-010-0307-0

Shultz, M. (2007). Comparing test searches in PubMed and Google Scholar. *Journal of the Medical Library Association: JMLA, 95*(4), 442–445. doi:10.3163/1536-5050.95.4.442 PMID:17971893

Siegel, D. J. (1999). *The developing mind: Toward a neurobiology of interpersonal experience.* New York, NY: Guilford Press.

Siegel, D. J. (2012). *The developing mind: How relationships and the brain interact to shape who we are* (2nd ed.). New York: The Guildford Press.

Siegenthaler, E., Munder, T., & Egger, M. (2012). Effect of preventative interventions in mentally ill parents on the mental health of the offspring: Systematic review and meta-analysis. *Journal of the American Academy of Child and Adolescent Psychiatry, 51*(1), 8–17. doi:10.1016/j.jaac.2011.10.018 PMID:22176935

Simmons, B. M. (2011). The complexity of evidence-based practice: A case study. *Smith College Studies in Social Work, 81*(2-3), 252–267. doi:10.1080/00377317.2011.589352

Simmons, B. M. (2012). Evidence-based practice, person-in-environment, and clinical social work: Issues of practical concern. *Smith College Studies in Social Work, 82*(1), 3–18. doi:10.1080/00377317.2011.638889

Slade, M., Adams, N., & O'Hagan, M. (2012). Recovery: Past progress and future challenges. *International Review of Psychiatry, 24*(1), 1–4. doi:10.3109/09540261.2011.644847 PMID:22385420

Sledge, W. H., Lawless, M., Sells, D., Wieland, M., O'Connell, M. J., & Davidson, L. (2011). Effectiveness of peer support in reducing readmissions of persons with multiple psychiatric hospitalizations. *Psychiatric Services, 62*(5), 541–544. doi:10.1176/appi.ps.62.5.541 PMID:21532082

Small, R., Lumley, J., Donohue, L., Potter, A., & Walderström, U. (2000). Randomised controlled trial of midwife led debriefing to reduce maternal depression after operative childbirth. *British Medical Journal, 321*(7268), 1043–1047. doi:10.1136/bmj.321.7268.1043 PMID:11053173

Smith, B. D., & Mogro-Wilson, C. (2007). Multilevel influences on the practice of inter-agency collaboration in child welfare and sustance abuse treatment. *Children and Youth Services Review, 29*(5), 545–556. doi:10.1016/j.childyouth.2006.06.002

Smith, C. (2001). Trust and confidence: Possibilities for social work in "high modernity". *British Journal of Social Work*, *31*(2), 287–305. doi:10.1093/bjsw/31.2.287

Smith, D. (2004). Introduction: Some versions of evidence-based practice. In D. Smith (Ed.), *Social work and evidence-based practice* (pp. 7–27). London: Jessica Kingsley.

Smith, L. T. (1999). *Decolonising methodologies: Research and Indigenous peoples*. London: Zed Books.

Smith, M., & Whyte, B. (2008). Social education and social pedagogy: Reclaiming a Scottish tradition in social work. *European Journal of Social Work*, *11*(1), 15–28. doi:10.1080/13691450701357174

Snarey, J. (1993). *How fathers care for the next generation: A four decade study*. Cambridge, MA: Harvard University Press. doi:10.4159/harvard.9780674365995

Social Work Task Force. (2009). *Building a safe and confident future*. London: Department of Children, Schools and Families. Retrieved from http://www.cscb-new.co.uk/downloads/reports_research/D_Report%20of%20SW%20Task%20Force%202009.pdf

Solomon, P., & Draine, J. (2010). An overview of quantitative research methods. In B. A. Thyer (Ed.), *The Handbook of Social Work Research Methods* (2nd ed., pp. 26–36). Thousand Oaks, CA: SAGE.

Sommer, C. A. (2008). Vicarious traumatisation, trauma-sensitive supervision and counsellor preparation. *Counselor Education and Supervision*, *48*(1), 61–71. doi:10.1002/j.1556-6978.2008.tb00062.x

Stahlschmidt, M. J., Threlfall, J., Seay, K. D., Lewis, E. M., & Kohl, P. L. (2013). Recruiting fathers to parenting programs: Advice from dads and fatherhood program providers. *Children and Youth Services Review*, *35*(10), 1734–1741. doi:10.1016/j.childyouth.2013.07.004 PMID:24791035

Staines, J., & Walters, J. (2007). *Evaluation of a fathers group within a child and family consultation service in East London* [Unpublished report]. Retrieved from groupworksolutions.com.au

Stalker, C. A., Mandell, D., Frensch, K. M., Harvey, C., & Wright, M. (2007). Child welfare workers who are exhausted yet satisfied with their jobs: How do they do it? *Child & Family Social Work*, *12*(2), 182–191. doi:10.1111/j.1365-2206.2006.00472.x

Stanhope, V., & Solomon, P. (2008). Getting to the heart of recovery: Methods for studying recovery and their implications for evidence-based practice. *British Journal of Social Work*, *38*(5), 885–899. doi:10.1093/bjsw/bcl377

Stanistreet, D., Taylor, S., Jeffrey, V., & Gabby, M. (2001). Accident or suicide? Predictors of coroners' decisions in suicide and accident verdicts. *Medicine, Science, and the Law*, *41*, 111–115. doi:10.1177/002580240104100205 PMID:11368390

Stanley, J., Tomison, A. M., & Pocock, J. (2003). *Child abuse and neglect in Indigenous Australian communities*. Melbourne: National Child Protection Clearinghouse, Australian Insitute of Family Studies.

Starnino, V. R. (2009). An integral approach to mental health recovery: Implications for social work. *Journal of Human Behavior in the Social Environment*, *19*(7), 820–842. doi:10.1080/10911350902988019

State of the Field Committee. (2009). *State of the field report: Arts in healthcare 2009*. Washington, DC: Society for the Arts in Healthcare.

Stein, M. (2012). *Young people leaving care: Supporting pathways to adulthood*. London: Jessica Kingsley.

Storey, J., & Billingham, J. (2001). Occupational stress and social work. *Social Work Education*, *20*(6), 659–670. doi:10.1080/02615470120089843a

Storhaug, A. S., & Oien, K. (2012). Fathers' encounters with the child welfare service. *Children and Youth Services Review*, *34*, 296–303. doi:10.1016/j.childyouth.2011.10.031

Strega, S., Fleet, C., Brown, L., Dominelli, L., Callahan, M., & Walmsley, C. (2008). Connecting father absence and mother blame in child welfare policies and practice. *Children and Youth Services Review*, *30*(7), 705–716. doi:10.1016/j.childyouth.2007.11.012

Strug, D., & Wilmore-Schaeffer, R. (2003). Fathers in the social work literature: Policy and practice implications. *Families in Society*, *84*(4), 503–511. doi:10.1606/1044-3894.145

Sundell, K., Soydan, H., Tengvald, K., & Anttila, S. (2010). From opinion-based to evidence-based social work: The Swedish case. *Research on Social Work Practice*, *20*(6), 714–722. doi:10.1177/1049731509347887

Szuchman, L. T., & Thomlison, B. (2011). *Writing with style: APA style for social work* (4th ed.). Australia: Brooks/Cole, Cengage Learning.

Talwar, S. (2007). Accessing traumatic memory through art making: An art therapy trauma protocol (ATTP). *The Arts in Psychotherapy*, *34*(1), 22–35. doi:10.1016/j.aip.2006.09.001

Tamis-LeMonda, C., & Cabrera, C. (Eds.). (2002). *Handbook of father involvement*. Mahway, NJ: Lawrence Erlbaum Associates.

Taylor, J. C., & Simmonds, J. G. (2009). Family stress and coping in the fly-in fly-out workforce. *Australian Community Psychologist*, *21*(2), 23-36. Retrieved from http://www.groups.psychology.org.au.com/publications/

Taylor, B. (2012). Models for professional judgement in social work. *European Journal of Social Work*, *15*(4), 546–562. doi:10.1080/13691457.2012.702310

Taylor, H., Beckett, C., & McKeigue, B. (2008). Judgements of Solomon: Anxieties and defences of social workers involved in care proceedings. *Child & Family Social Work*, *13*, 23–31. doi:10.1111/j.1365-2206.2007.00507.x

Teicher, M. H. (2000). Wounds that time won't heal: The neurobiology of child abuse. *Cerebrum*, *2*(4), 50–67. Retrieved from http://www.dana.org/cerebrum/

The Scottish Government. (2008). *A guide to getting it right for every child*. Edinburgh, UK: Author.

The Scottish Government. (2013). *The Scottish policing performance framework: Annual report 2012-2013*. Edinburgh, UK: Author.

Thoits, P. A. (2010). Stress and health. *Journal of Health and Social Behavior*, *51*(1suppl), S41–S53. doi:10.1177/0022146510383499 PMID:20943582

Thomas, D. R., & Hodges, I. D. (2010). *Designing and managing your research project: Core knowledge for social and health researchers*. Los Angeles, CA: SAGE.

Thomson, A. M., & Perry, J. L. (2006). Collaborative process: Inside the black box. *Public Administration Review*, *66*(s1), 20–32. doi:10.1111/j.1540-6210.2006.00663.x

Thyer, B. A. (2004). What is evidence-based practice? *Brief Treatment and Crisis Intervention*, *4*(2), 167–176. doi:10.1093/brief-treatment/mhh013

Thyer, B. A. (2008). The quest for evidence-based practice?: We are all positivists! *Research on Social Work Practice*, *18*(4), 339–345. doi:10.1177/1049731507313998

Thyer, B. A. (2010). Introductory principles of social work research. In B. A. Thyer (Ed.), *The handbook of social work research methods* (2nd ed., pp. 1–24). Thousand Oaks, CA: SAGE.

Thyer, B. A. (2012). The scientific value of qualitative research for social work. *Qualitative Social Work: Research and Practice*, *11*, 115–125. doi:10.1177/1473325011433928

Thyer, B. A., & Myers, L. L. (2011). The quest for evidence-based practice: A view from the United States. *Journal of Social Work*, *11*(1), 8–25. doi:10.1177/1468017310381812

Thyer, B. A., & Pignotti, M. (2011). Evidence-based practices do not exist. *Clinical Social Work Journal*, *39*(4), 328–333. doi:10.1007/s10615-011-0358-x

Townsend, N. (2002). *The package deal: Marriage, work, and fatherhood in men's lives*. Philadelphia, PA: Temple University Press.

Tracy, S. J. (2004). The construction of correctional officers: Layers of emotionality behind bars. *Qualitative Inquiry*, *10*(4), 509–533. doi:10.1177/1077800403259716

Tracy, S. J., & Scott, C. (2006). Sexuality, masculinity, and taint management among firefighters and correctional officers: Getting down and dirty with "America's heroes" and the "scum of law enforcement". *Management Communication Quarterly*, *20*(1), 6–38. doi:10.1177/0893318906287898

Trinder, L. (2000). A critical appraisal of evidence-based practice. In L. Trinder (with S. Reynolds) (Eds.), *Evidence-based practice: A critical appraisal* (pp. 212-241). Oxford, UK: Blackwell.

Trinder, L. (2000). Evidence-based practice in social work and probation. In L. Trinder (with S. Reynolds) (Eds.), *Evidence-based practice: A critical appraisal* (pp. 138-162). Oxford, UK: Blackwell. doi:10.1002/9780470699003.ch7

Trinder, L. (2000). Introduction: The context of evidence-based practice. In L. Trinder (with S. Reynolds) (Eds.), *Evidence-based practice: A critical appraisal* (pp. 1-16). Oxford, UK: Blackwell.

Tsui, M. S. (1997). Empirical research on social work supervision: The state of the art (1970-1995). *Journal of Social Service Research*, *23*(2), 39–54. doi:10.1300/J079v23n02_03

Turnell, A., & Edwards, S. (1999). *Signs of safety: A safety and solution oriented approach to child protection casework.* New York: Norton.

Turney, D. (2009). *Analysis and critical thinking in assessment.* Devon: Research in Practice.

U.N. Committee on the Rights of the Child, 34th Sess., U.N. Doc. CRC/C/15/Add.215 (Oct. 3, 2003).

U.N. Committee on the Rights of the Child, 40th Sess., U.N. Doc. CRC/C/15/Add.268 (Oct. 20, 2005).

U.N. Committee on the Rights of the Child, 44th Sess., U.N. Doc. CRC/C/GC/10 (April 25, 2007).

Ullman, S. E., & Filipas, H. H. (2005). Gender differences in social reactions to abuse disclosures, post-abuse coping, and PTSD of child sexual abuse survivors. *Child Abuse & Neglect*, *29*(7), 767–782. doi:10.1016/j.chiabu.2005.01.005 PMID:16051351

Ungar, M. (2004). A constructionist discourse on resilience: Multiple contexts, multiple realities among at-risk children and youth. *Youth & Society*, *35*(3), 341–365. doi:10.1177/0044118X03257030

United Nations Department of Economic and Social Affairs. (1981). Definition of youth. Retrieved from http://www.un.org/esa/socdev/documents/youth/fact-sheets/youth-definition.pdf

United Nations High Commissioner for Refugees. (n.d.). Women: Particular challenges and risks. Retrieved from http://www.unhcr.org/pages/49c3646c1d9.html

United Nations High Commissioner for Refugees. (1990). *UNHCR policy on refugee women.* Retrieved from http://www.unhcr.org/3ba6186810.html

United Nations High Commissioner for Refugees. (2001). *Respect our rights: Partnership for equality – Report on the dialogue with refugee women – Geneva, Switzerland 20-22 June 2001.* Retrieved from http://www.unhcr.org/3bb44d908.pdf

United Nations High Commissioner for Refugees. (2011). *Resettlement handbook: Division of international protection.* Retrieved from http://www.unhcr.org/4a2ccf4c6.html

United Nations High Commissioner for Refugees. (2011). *Survivors, protectors, providers: Refugee women speak out.* Retrieved from http://www.unhcr.org/4ec5337d9.html

United Nations High Commissioner for Refugees. (2011). *UNHCR age, gender and diversity policy: Working with people and communities for equality and protection – Women, 1 June.* Retrieved from http://www.unhcr.org/4e7757449.html

United Nations International Children's Emergency Fund. (2013). *The role of social work in juvenile justice.* Retrieved http://www.unicef.org/ceecis/UNICEF_report_on_the_role_of_social_work_in_juvenile_justice.pdf

University of New South Wales Centre for Refugee Research. (n.d.). Welcome to CRR. Retrieved from http://www.crr.unsw.edu.au/

Upshur, R. E. G., & Tracy, C. S. (2004). Legitimacy, authority, and hierarchy: Critical challenges for evidence-based medicine. *Brief Treatment and Crisis Intervention*, *4*(3), 197–204. doi:10.1093/brief-treatment/mhh018

Valtonen, K. (2002). Social work with immigrants and refugees: Developing a participation-based framework for anti-oppressive practice – Part 2. *British Journal of Social Work*, *32*(1), 113–120. doi:10.1093/bjsw/32.1.113

van Breda, A. (2011). Resilient workplaces: An initial conceptualization. *Families in Society*, *92*(1), 33–40. doi:10.1606/1044-3894.4059

van de Luitgaarden, G. M. J. (2009). Evidence-based practice in social work: Lessons from judgment and decision-making theory. *British Journal of Social Work*, *39*(2), 243–260. doi:10.1093/bjsw/bcm117

van der Gaag, M., Smit, F., Bechdolf, A., French, P., Linszen, D. H., & Yung, A. R. et al. (2013). Preventing a first episode of psychosis: Meta-analysis of randomized controlled prevention trials of 12 month and longer-term follow-ups. *Schizophrenia Research*, *149*(1-3), 56–62. doi:10.1016/j.schres.2013.07.004 PMID:23870806

van der Kolk, B. A. (2003). The neurobiology of childhood trauma and abuse. *Child and Adolescent Psychiatric Clinics of North America*, *12*(2), 293–317. doi:10.1016/S1056-4993(03)00003-8 PMID:12725013

van der Kolk, B. A. (2005). Developmental trauma disorder. *Psychiatric Annals*, *35*, 401–408. Retrieved from http://www.healio.com/psychiatry/journals/psycann

van der Kolk, B. A. (2008). Developmental trauma disorder: Towards a rational diagnosis for children with complex trauma histories. In S. Benamer & K. White (Eds.), *Attachment and trauma* (pp. 45–63). London: Karnac.

van der Kolk, B. A., & McFarlane, A. C. (1996). The black hole of trauma. In B. A. van der Kolk, A. C. McFarlane, & L. Weisaeth (Eds.), *Traumatic stress: The effects of overwhelming experience on mind, body, and society* (pp. 5–23). New York: Guilford.

van Santvoort, F., Hosman, C. M., van Doesum, K. T., & Janssens, J. M. (2014). Effectiveness of preventative support groups for children of mentally ill or addicted parents: A randomised controlled trail. *European Child & Adolescent Psychiatry*, *23*(6), 473–484. doi:10.1007/s00787-013-0476-9 PMID:24072523

Van Wormer, K., & Besthorn, F. H. (2010). *Human behaviour and the social environment, macro level: Groups, communities, and organizations* (2nd ed.). New York: Oxford University Press.

Vernberg, E. M., Steinberg, A. M., Jacobs, A. K., Brymer, M. J., Watson, P. J., & Osofsky, J. D., …Ruzek, J. I. (2008). Innovations in disaster mental health: Psychological first aid. *Professional Psychology, Research and Practice*, *39*(4), 381–388. doi:10.1037/a0012663

Videka, L., & Blackburn, J. A. (2010). The intellectual legacy of William J. Reid. In A. E. Fortune, P. McCallion, & K. Briar-Lawson (Eds.), *Social work practice research for the twenty-first century* (pp. 183–194). New York: Columbia University Press.

Visser-Meiley, J. M. A., Rhebergen, M. L., Rinkel, G. J. E., van Zandvoort, M. J., & Post, M. W. M. (2009). Long-term health-related quality of life after aneurysmal subarachnoid haemorrhage: Relationship with psychological symptoms and personality characteristics. *Stroke*, *40*(4), 1526–1529. doi:10.1161/STROKEAHA.108.531277 PMID:19095984

Walmsley, C., Strega, S., Brown, L., Dominelli, L., & Callahan, M. (2009). More than a playmate, less than a co-parent: Fathers in the Canadian BSW curriculum. *Canadian Social Work Review*, *26*, 73–96. Retrieved from http://caswe-acfts.ca/cswr-journal/

Walsh, N. M. (2011). Jean Vanier: An alternative voice for the social work profession. *Journal of Religion & Spirituality in Social Work: Social Thought*, *30*(4), 340–357. doi:10.1080/15426432.2011.619898

Walters, M. (2011). *Working with fathers: From knowledge to therapeutic practice*. UK: Palgrave Macmillan.

Ward, A. (2010). The use of self in relationship-based practice. In G. Ruch, D. Turney, & A. Ward (Eds.), *Relationship-based social work: Getting to the heart of practice* (pp. 46–65). London: Jessica Kingsley.

Ward, T. (2002). Good Lives and the rehabilitation of offenders: Promises and problems. *Aggression and Violent Behavior*, *7*(5), 513–528. doi:10.1016/S1359-1789(01)00076-3

Ward, T., & Gannon, T. A. (2006). Rehabilitation, etiology, and self-regulation: The comprehensive good lives model of treatment for sexual offenders. *Aggression and Violent Behavior*, *11*(1), 77–94. doi:10.1016/j.avb.2005.06.001

Ward, T., & Maruna, S. (2007). *Rehabilitation: Beyond the risk paradigm*. London: Routledge.

Watson, B., & Halford, W. K. (2010). Classes of childhood sexual abuse and women's adult couple relationships. *Violence and Victims*, *25*(4), 518–535. doi:10.1891/0886-6708.25.4.518 PMID:20712149

Weaver, H. N., & Burns, B. J. (2001). "I shout with fear at night": Understanding the traumatic experiences of refugees and asylum seekers. *Journal of Social Work*, *1*(2), 147–164. doi:10.1177/146801730100100203

Webber, M. (2014). From ethnography to randomized controlled trial: An innovative approach to developing complex social interventions. *Journal of Evidence-Based Social Work*, *11*(1-2), 173–182. doi:10.1080/15433714.2013.847265 PMID:24405141

Webb, S. A. (2001). Some considerations on the validity of evidence-based practice in social work. *British Journal of Social Work*, *31*(1), 57–79. doi:10.1093/bjsw/31.1.57

Webb, S. A. (2006). *Social work in a risk society: Social and political perspectives*. London: Palgrave Macmillan.

Wendt, S., Tuckey, M. R., & Prosser, B. (2011). Thriving, not just surviving, in emotionally demanding fields of practice. *Health & Social Care in the Community*, *19*(3), 317–325. doi:10.1111/j.1365-2524.2010.00983.x PMID:21276106

Werner, P. (2004). Reasoned action and planned behavior. In S. J. Peterson & T. S. Bredow (Eds.), *Middle range theories: Application to nursing research* (pp. 125–147). Philadeliphia, PA: Lippincott, Williams & Wilkins.

Wertheimer, A. (2008). *A dented image: Journeys of recovery from a subarachnoid haemorrhage*. London: Routledge.

Wesley-Esquimaux, C. C., & Smolewski, M. (2004). *Historical trauma and Aboriginal healing*. Retrieved from the Aboriginal Healing Foundation website: http://www.ahf.ca/downloads/historic-trauma.pdf

White, M., & Epston, D. (1990). *Narrative means to therapeutic ends*. New York: Norton.

WHO. (2013) *Annual mortality statistics*. Retrieved from http://www.who.int/healthinfo/statistics/mortality/en/

Whyte, B. (2009). *Youth justice in practice: Making a difference*. Bristol, UK: Policy Press.

Wiegand-Grefe, S., Geers, P., Petermann, F., & Plass, A. (2011). Kinder Psychisch Kranker Eltern: Merkmale Elterlicher Psychiatrischer Erkrankung und Gesundheit der Kinder aus Elternsicht[Children of mentally ill parents: The impact of parental psychiatric diagnosis, comorbidity, severity and chronicity on the well-being of children]. *Fortschritte der Neurologie-Psychiatrie*, *79*(01), 32–40. doi:10.1055/s-0029-1245623 PMID:21089005

Wilczynski, A., & Sinclair, K. (1999). Moral tales: Representations of child abuse in the quality and tabloid media. *Australian and New Zealand Journal of Criminology*, *32*(3), 262–283. doi:10.1177/000486589903200305

Wilczynski, N. L., Haynes, R. B., & Hedges, T. (2006). Optimal search strategies for identifying mental health content in MEDLINE: An analytic survey. *Annals of General Psychiatry*, *5*(4). doi:10.1186/1744-859X-5-4 PMID:16556313

Wilkinson, R., & Pickett, K. (2009). *The spirit level: Why equality is better for everyone*. London: Penguin.

Williams, J., Leamy, V., Bird, C., Harding, J., Larsen, C., & LeBoutillier, L. et al. (2012). Measures of the recovery orientation of mental health services: Systematic review. *Social Psychiatry & Epidemiology*, *47*(11), 1827–1835. doi:10.1007/s00127-012-0484-y PMID:22322983

Williams, N. J., & Sherr, M. E. (2013). Oh how I try to use evidence in my social work practice: Efforts, successes, frustrations, and questions. *Journal of Evidence-Based Social Work*, *10*(2), 100–110. doi:10.1080/15433714.2011.597299 PMID:23581804

Williams, R. G., & Pritchard, C. (2006). *Breaking the cycle of educational alienation: A multiprofessional approach*. Maidenhead, England: Open University Press.

Wilson, D. B. (2009). Missing a critical piece of the pie: Simple document search strategies inadequate for systematic reviews. *Journal of Experimental Criminology*, *5*(4), 429–440. doi:10.1007/s11292-009-9085-5

Wilson, R. J., & Yates, P. M. (2009). Effective interventions and the Good Lives Model: Maximising treatment gains for sexual offenders. *Aggression and Violent Behavior, 14*(3), 157–161. doi:10.1016/j.avb.2009.01.007

Winslow, S. (2005). Work-family conflict, gender, and parenthood, 1977-1997. *Journal of Family Issues, 26*(6), 727–755. doi:10.1177/0192513X05277522

Witkin, S. L., & Iversen, R. R. (2012). Contemporary issues in social work. In C. N. Dulmus & K. M. Sowers (Eds.), The profession of social work: Guided by history, led by evidence (pp. 225–259). Academic Press.

Witkin, S. L., & Harrison, W. D. (2001). Editorial: Whose evidence and for what purpose? *Social Work, 46*(4), 293–296. doi:10.1093/sw/46.4.293 PMID:11682970

Women's Refugee Commission. (2010). *UN Security Council Resolution 1325 on women, peace and security: High hopes, unmet expectations.* Retrieved from http://womensrefugeecommission.org/programs/women-peace-and-security/research-and-resources

Women's Refugee Commission. (n.d.). How we work. Retrieved from http://www.womensrefugeecommission.org/about/how-we-work

Wong, Y. R., & Vinsky, J. (2009). Speaking from the margins: A critical reflection on the "spiritual-but-not-religious" discourse in social work. *British Journal of Social Work, 39*(7), 1343–1359. doi:10.1093/bjsw/bcn032

Woodcock, J., & Dixon, J. (2005). Professional ideologies and preferences in social work: A British study in global perspsective. *British Journal of Social Work, 35*(6), 953–997. doi:10.1093/bjsw/bch282

World Health Organisation. (2003). *The mental health context. (The mental health policy and service guidance package).* Retrieved from http://www.who.int/mental_health/resources/en/context.PDF

Wright, M. O. D., Crawford, E., & Sebastian, K. (2007). Positive resolution of childhood sexual abuse experiences: The role of coping, benefit-finding and meaning-making. *Journal of Family Violence, 22*(7), 597–608. doi:10.1007/s10896-007-9111-1

Wright, M. O. D., Fopma-Loy, J., & Fischer, S. (2005). Multidimensional assessment of resilience in mothers who are child sexual abuse survivors. *Child Abuse & Neglect, 29*(10), 1173–1193. doi:10.1016/j.chiabu.2005.04.004 PMID:16315358

Yasmeen, S. (2007). Muslim women as citizens in Australia: Diverse notions and practices. *The Australian Journal of Social Issues, 42*, 41–54. Retrieved from http://www.acoss.org.au/publications/magazines/

Yeo, S. S. (2003). Bonding and attachment of Australian Aboriginal children. *Child Abuse Review, 12*(5), 292–304. doi:10.1002/car.817

Yule, W. (2001). When disaster strikes: The need to be "wise before the event" – Crisis intervention with children and adolescents. *Advances in Mind-Body Medicine, 17*(3), 191–196. doi:10.1054/ambm.2000.0313 PMID:11572847

Yunong, H., & Fengzhi, M. (2009). A reflection on reasons, preconditions, and effects of implementing evidence-based practice in social work. *Social Work, 54*(2), 177–181. doi:10.1093/sw/54.2.177 PMID:19366166

Zala, S. (2012). Complex couples: Multi-theoretical couples counselling with traumatised adults who have a history of child sexual abuse. *The Australian and New Zealand Journal of Family Therapy, 33*(03), 219–231. doi:10.1017/aft.2012.27

Zanoni, L., Warburton, W., Bussey, K., & McMaugh, A. (2013). Fathers as "core business" in child welfare practice and research: An interdisciplinary review. *Children and Youth Services Review, 35*(7), 1055–1070. doi:10.1016/j.childyouth.2013.04.018

Zayas, L. H., Drake, B., & Jonson-Reid, M. (2011). Over-rating or dismissing the value of evidence- based practice: Consequences for clinical practice. *Clinical Social Work Journal, 39*(4), 400–405. doi:10.1007/s10615-010-0306-1

Zelazo, P. D., Carter, A., Reznick, J. S., & Frye, D. (1997). Early development of executive function: A problem-solving framework. *Review of General Psychology, 1*(2), 198–226. doi:10.1037/1089-2680.1.2.198

Zvara, B. J., Schoppe-Sullivan, S. J., & Kamp Dush, C. (2013). Fathers' involvement in child health care: Associations with prenatal involvement, parents' beliefs, and maternal gatekeeping. *Family Relations, 62*(4), 649–661. doi:10.1111/fare.12023

# About the Contributors

**Margaret Pack** is Associate Professor of Social Work and Deputy Head of School, Allied Health Australian Catholic University, Sydney, Australia. Her research interests include trauma and stress, theories of clinician self-care, and social workers' theories for practice. She has worked in a national sexual abuse trauma centre with survivors of sexual abuse trauma as specialist case manager. Her career has included practice as a mental health social worker, where she has developed new services and managed staff as a team leader. Originally from New Zealand where she co-ordinated a national post graduate programme at Victoria University of Wellington, she has since led a team of social work academics at Charles Darwin University, Northern Territory, Australia.

**Justin Cargill** is a Subject Librarian in the Faculty of Humanities and Social Sciences at Victoria University of Wellington, New Zealand. He has served as a reference librarian at Victoria University of Wellington since 1989 and in 2000 became the subject librarian for the University's Graduate School of Nursing, Midwifery and Health. He works closely with staff and students providing teaching, learning, and research support. This includes research consultancy services and training in literature searching and research skills.

\* \* \*

**Carole Adamson** is Senior Lecturer in Counselling, Human Services, and Social Work at the University of Auckland, where her research and teaching focuses on mental health, trauma, resilience, and stress. She is currently an executive member of the Council for Social Work Education Aotearoa New Zealand (CSWEANZ). She has research interests in developing resilient practitioners and in social work curriculum for disaster preparation and response. She has been a mental health social worker and also has experience in community development and residential social work. She became interested in critical incidents and the organisational responsibility for their management during her years in practice and further developed this through doctoral research. She sees a major focal point in her work as the articulation of theoretical perspectives and frameworks for social work practice that can integrate current, contextually-aware best practice and which can effectively be applied in practice settings.

**Ian Dore** is a Senior Lecturer in Social Work at the University of Brighton, England, and qualified Practice Educator. Prior to entering into full-time higher education he was a senior social worker in a front-line child protection team. Since qualifying as a social worker his interests in evidence-based practice and ethics have continued, now incorporating knowing in practice. He also has an interest in practice education, particularly the role of emotion in learning.

**Annette Flaherty** is a Lecturer in Child Protection Studies at the Centre for Remote Health, Alice Springs, Australia, a joint centre of Flinders University and Charles Darwin University. She has worked in Central Australia since 1995, primarily with children and their families in the areas of child protection and maternal and child health. Her research interests include child protection practice, particularly in the area of child neglect and assessment of marginalised and disadvantaged populations.

**Joseph Fleming** works at the School of Health and Social Development, Deakin University. His interest in fathers and the topic of fatherhood began as a newly graduated social worker in the late 1990s while working as a child protection worker. In the period since he has been writing and researching the topic of fatherhood and child welfare and is particularly interested in developing effective practice models for fathers's engagement with services.

**Shiri Hergass** is an art therapist and clinical social worker in Sydney, NSW, and a PhD candidate at Australian Catholic University, Sydney. Her experience has involved children and women in both the public and private sector, in work with Ethiopian mothers and children newly arrived in Israel, in reconciliation efforts between Bedouins, Arabs and Jews, and in other conflict-resolution groups. In New South Wales she ran a group for mothers and their children in Emu Plains Correctional Centre. She also developed groups for parents and children who have experienced trauma, called Free to Be Me. She has served as the country manager at Gunawirra, a not-for-profit organisation, working with 40 Aboriginal preschools throughout New South Wales, and she has a small private practice where she sees women and children from different cultures and supervises therapists and preschool directors.

**Tara Hunt** is a consultant and research assistant with Groupwork Solutions, New South Wales, Australia. She is Treasurer of the Lifeline South Coast (NSW) Board and a doctoral candidate at the University of Wollongong, exploring men's health and suicide counselling.

**Andrew King** is a consultant trainer and programme developer in group work, working with men and strengths based practice at Groupwork Solutions, New South Wales, Australia. He has trained professionals throughout Australia and Canada in "working with men". He is also an experienced practitioner having worked with teenagers who have drug and alcohol problems, young people with mental health issues, parenting education, and families who have children with special needs; he has coordinated a large fathers' centre.

**Fiona McDermott** is an associate professor holding a joint appointment in the departments of social work at Monash University and Monash Health. Her teaching and research is in the areas of multiple and complex needs, health, mental health, and working with groups. She maintains a clinical practice in group work, co-facilitating two long term groups. She has a particular interest in the development, mentoring, and support of practitioner researchers, and in qualitative and action research approaches to research.

**Mary Nash** is an Associate Research Lecturer at Massey University, New Zealand, having recently retired from her position as senior lecturer in Social Work. She is a Life Member of the Aotearoa New Zealand Association of Social Workers. She has researched and published on spirituality and social work, as well as social work with refugees and migrants. She hopes to encourage increasing interest in both these areas of practice.

**Kieran O'Donoghue** is the Head of the School of Health and Social Services, Massey University, New Zealand. His research interests are social work supervision, social work theory and practice, and the social work profession.

**Colin Pritchard** is Research Professor in the School of Health and Social Care at Bournemouth University, a position he has held since 2003. Previously he was a lecturer in the Department of Psychiatry at the University of Leeds and held a Senior Lectureship at the University of Bath from 1976-80 before becoming Professor and Head of Department of Social Work at the University of Southampton from 1980-1987. He then continued in a research and teaching role, and from 1998-2003 he was Research Professor in Psychiatric Social Work in the Department of Psychiatry, School of Medicine, at the University of Southampton where he is now Emeritus and Visiting Professor. He has also been a Visiting Professor at the Universities of Curtin, Flinders, Monash, Queensland, and Sydney. He has served on the Prime Minister's Strategy Group (Education) 2006 to 2008; he has been a member of the Post-Graduate Centre for Medical Education and Research from 2007 to the present; and he was appointed to the Royal College of Surgeons (England) Specialist Recertification Board in 2008. His research interests span neurosurgery, the child protection – psychiatric interface, cancer outcomes, morbidity and mortality and suicide studies.

**Sebastian Rosenberg** is Senior Lecturer in Mental Health Policy, Brain and Mind Research Institute, School of Medical Sciences, Sydney University. After a career as a public servant in both state and federal governments, he was Deputy CEO of the Mental Health Council of Australia from 2005-2009, assisting in the publication of the seminal Not for Service report (2005). In 2011 he worked as expert facilitator to the NSW Taskforce to Establish a Mental Health Commission and was convenor of the first joint meetings of Australian Mental Health Commissions. He was a member of the NHMRC's Prevention and Community Health Committee from 2009-12 and a member of the Board of Social Firms Australia from 2012-2014. He is an Associate at the Menzies School of Health Policy and a member of the Clinical Senate of the ACT. He is a PhD candidate, focusing on mental health and accountability.

**Antoinette Umugwaneza** is a Case Worker at New Zealand Refugee Services in Palmerston North, New Zealand and a tutor at Methodist Social Services. She was born in Rwanda and came to New Zealand as a refugee in 1996 after the Rwandan Genocide and mass killing which took place in 1994.

**Bill Whyte** is Professor of Social Work Studies in Criminal and Youth Justice at the University of Edinburgh. He was also Director of the Criminal Justice Social Work Development Centre for Scotland from 2001-2013. He teaches on youth and criminal justice social work, on practice policy and law, on desistence from crime, and effective intervention for undergraduate, postgraduate and post qualifying programmes. His recent research activities have involved research on routes out of prison, young people under 18 subject to Multi Agency Public Protection Arrangements (MAPPA), young people involved in sexually harmful behaviour, young people connected to organised crime, and restorative practice in serious crime.

**Richard Williams** is a Senior Lecturer in Social Work – Children and Families at Bournemouth University. He is also currently project managing a research project into child protection processes and procedures. His focus is on teaching, writing, and research on outcomes in general and the positive impact of social work in particular.

# Index

## A

Aboriginal 49-50, 187, 189, 191, 202, 261-262, 267-270, 272-273, 275-280, 287, 344
accreditation standards 85, 325, 337
Acoustic Neuroma (AN) 220, 234
adult survivors 187-188, 191-192, 199-200, 211
advocacy 101, 121, 327
art therapy 261-262, 270-280, 287, 344
assimilation 133, 140, 202, 344
attachment theory 196, 244-245, 268
Australian Association of Social Workers 86, 238, 324, 338
Australian National Committee on Refugee Women 101

## B

Better Access Program 114, 119
Boolean operators 46-47, 63
brain development 245, 262-264, 268, 275
burnout 70, 193, 292

## C

cancer mortality rates 221
child abuse related deaths (CARD) 166-167, 185
childhood sexual abuse (CSA) 211
child mortality rates (CMR) 185
child protection 66, 75, 82, 86-87, 121, 130-143, 148, 151, 156-157, 167-168, 170, 173, 176, 178, 188, 235, 238-239, 250, 303, 306, 347-348
child protection workers 130-139, 141-142, 148
child welfare 11, 40, 133, 142, 151, 156, 235, 237, 239, 260, 266, 293, 348
client satisfaction 291
clinical supervision 83, 87, 143, 193, 196-197, 203, 289-291, 293-294, 301, 305, 314, 329, 345

cognitive development 267
cognitive impairment 212
cognitive processes 65
collaborative mental healthcare 114, 119, 121, 129
collaborative practice 118, 122, 135
community development 106-107, 326, 330, 344
community mental health 114, 117, 120-121, 123, 129, 196-197
continuing professional development 325, 328, 338
controlled vocabulary 43-44, 63-64
criminal responsibility 151-152, 155, 165
critical appraisal 38, 58-59, 68, 307
critical incident 302-310, 312-317, 323, 346
critical incident stress 302-304, 306, 308-309, 315, 323, 346
critical incident stress debriefing (CISD) 302-303, 323
critical incident stress management (CISM) 302, 304, 323
critical reflection 1, 22, 24, 37, 73, 87, 348
critical-reflective practice 95, 350
critical thinking 12, 69, 75-76, 81
cultural sensitivity 103, 105, 295

## D

database 36-44, 46-48, 50-51, 63-64, 67, 150, 186, 188, 292, 306, 313, 341
decision-making 6-8, 11-13, 19, 21-23, 41, 65-72, 75-76, 81, 86-88, 90, 120, 122, 136, 140, 142, 290, 295, 342, 345
decolonising methodologies 95, 344, 350
Delinquent Act 165
descriptors 44, 63
dirty work 130-133, 135-137, 140-143, 148, 342
disclosure 187-189, 191-195, 197-200, 202, 311
displacement 99, 107, 268, 272

## E

early childhood 191, 241, 261-263, 267, 277, 279, 287
emotional development 262-263
emotional intelligence 294-295, 297, 301
emotional support 242, 292-293, 295-297, 309, 323, 327
empathy 89-90, 177-178, 291, 295, 297
empirical 1-5, 8-10, 12, 14, 18-19, 21, 23-24, 35, 37-38, 68, 70-71, 76, 81, 84, 89, 151, 159-160, 194-195, 199, 201-202, 223, 292, 329, 339, 343, 346-348
Employee Assistance Programme (EAP) 323
empowerment 6, 88, 99, 105, 115-116, 129, 154, 262, 273, 277, 305, 325
evidence-based practice 1-2, 5-8, 14, 16, 18, 22-24, 35, 59, 66-67, 82, 86, 88, 116, 170, 235, 250, 290, 295, 301, 312, 329, 339, 341-342, 344, 346, 350
evidence-informed practice 23-24, 84-85, 289, 301, 329, 340-342
expressive arts 261, 270-272, 274

## F

fatherhood 238-240, 246, 250-251, 260
free text 43-46, 48-50, 63-64

## G

generativity 246-247, 249-250, 260
Good Lives model 90

## H

health funding 119
heuristics 67, 71, 76, 81
homicide 166, 175
humanitarian assistance 100
human rights 86, 98-100, 107, 129, 133, 152, 154-155, 166, 187, 260, 305, 313, 325, 333, 348

## I

interagency collaboration 130-131, 134-136, 141, 143, 148
interdisciplinary teams 117-118, 121
International Association of Schools of Social Work 150
interpersonal skills 143, 297
interpretivist 67, 122
intuition 3, 65, 67, 71, 76, 81, 271, 341, 350

## J

job performance 292
job stress 292
judgement 3, 12, 15-16, 19, 24, 37, 65-68, 70-74, 76, 81, 86, 214, 347, 350
juvenile delinquency 39, 152-153, 165
knowledge-aware practice 81, 350

## L

liminal spaces 95, 340, 346
lived experience 84, 116
longitudinal study 185, 200
looked after children (LAC) 185

## M

masculinity 235-236, 238, 250
mental healthcare 113-116, 119-121, 124, 129
mental health policy 115-117, 121, 124
mental illness 88, 114-117, 120-121, 124, 129, 175-178, 185, 225, 268
methodological filters 36, 46
Mitchell model 309, 311

## N

National Disability Insurance Scheme 114
neglect 66, 74, 132, 137-141, 143, 148, 157, 167, 177, 189, 195, 268, 270, 287, 303
neurobiology 263, 270-271, 287
neurosurgery 212-214, 217-221, 343, 347

## O

occupational identity 131-132
organisational culture 69, 76, 293, 314
organisational planning 315

## P

peer support 114, 117-118, 124, 129
perception 4, 65-67, 71-74, 81, 148, 172, 243, 272, 313
person-in-environment 65, 71, 85, 113, 116, 122, 167, 187, 304-305, 338, 341, 348, 350
positivism 19-22
post-traumatic stress disorder (PTSD) 190, 213, 234, 265
practice guidelines 6, 10, 12, 18-19, 35, 41, 84, 86, 90, 305, 307, 315-316, 342, 346
practice paradigm 150, 155, 157-159, 165

probation 89, 157-158, 160, 170
professional identity 131, 136, 139-140, 324
professional judgement 12, 16, 19, 67, 73, 86, 350
professional obligation 12
professional standards 18, 82, 298
professional supervision 289-291, 294, 301, 314
protective factors 189-190, 193-195, 199, 201, 211, 280
psychiatry 5, 39, 170, 226
psychological debriefing 302, 306, 308-309, 311, 323
psychological first aid 306, 310, 313-314, 317, 323

## Q

qualitative studies 14-16, 20, 37, 46, 56-58, 86, 294
quantitative studies 57

## R

randomised controlled trial (RCT) 35
rationality 71, 86, 339
recovery 48, 85, 87-90, 95, 113-118, 120-124, 129, 187, 189, 192-196, 199-200, 211, 215-217, 219-220, 238, 264, 273, 275-277, 280, 312-313, 323, 344-347, 350
recovery movement 88, 195, 211
recovery paradigm 88, 90, 95, 116, 346-347, 350
reflective practice 22, 35, 87, 307, 314, 328
refugee 97-107, 111-112, 188, 333, 342
refugee resettlement 97-100, 112
rehabilitation 48-49, 90, 118, 120, 166, 212, 217-218
religion 98, 111, 326-327, 329, 333, 338
resilience 17, 98-104, 107, 112, 187, 189-191, 193-194, 196, 199-203, 211, 280, 302, 305-306, 308-309, 312-315, 317, 346
risk factors 185, 193, 195, 201, 211, 275, 309

## S

search engines 36-37, 39, 306
search strategy 36, 42-43, 46-47, 51, 64, 114, 137, 150, 186, 188, 239, 292, 297, 303, 325
self-esteem 89, 131, 140, 193, 199, 262, 328
self-perception 271
sensemaking 67-69, 72-73, 81
service-users 65, 68, 70, 87-91, 95, 116, 123, 129, 292, 303, 305, 324-325, 327, 329, 333, 342, 344-348
social pedagogy 165
social policy 40
social stigma 88, 148

specialist neurovascular nurse (SNVN) 212, 217, 234
spiritual genogram 329-330
spirituality 20, 192, 275, 280, 324-331, 333, 338, 345
staff support 302, 304, 313-314
stolen generations 133, 139-140, 267, 269
sub-arachnoid haemorrhage (SAH) 212-213, 234
subject headings 39, 43-46, 48-51, 63-64
suicide 84, 123, 174, 176-177, 212, 223, 225-226, 266-267, 303, 328
supervisory relationship 291-292, 295, 345
systematic reviews 10, 14, 16, 37-38, 50, 55, 58, 84, 86, 90, 290, 341

## T

thesaurus 44, 63-64
transgenerational trauma 261-262, 267-269, 276, 278, 280, 287
trauma 95, 101, 187, 189-191, 195-196, 198-200, 202, 211, 261-273, 275-280, 287, 302-303, 305-310, 315, 317, 344-346, 350
traumatic event 199, 234, 265-266, 273, 303, 306, 323

## U

United Nations Convention on the Rights of the Child 149
United Nations High Commissioner for Refugees 97-98

## V

values 5-8, 10-16, 21-24, 35, 37, 68-69, 74-75, 82, 85-88, 90, 102-103, 105-106, 115, 130, 133-134, 139-140, 142-143, 150-151, 158, 165, 187, 192, 197, 268-269, 279, 305, 326-327, 330, 338-339, 345, 347-348, 350
vicarious traumatisation 192, 303
virtue ethics 81

## W

working relationships 130, 142, 324

## Y

youth 47-48, 54, 89-90, 115, 149-162, 165, 226, 271, 297, 347-348
youth justice 89-90, 149-155, 157-162, 165, 347-348